An Uneasy Victorian

Ann Monsarrat

An Uneasy Victorian

THACKERAY THE MAN
1811–1863

DODD, MEAD & COMPANY

NEW YORK

1   2   3   4   5   6   7   8   9   10

Library of Congress Cataloging in Publication Data
Monsarrat, Ann.
An uneasy Victorian.

Includes bibliographical references and index.
1. Thackeray, William Makepeace, 1811-1863 —
Biography. 2. Novelists, English — 19th century —
Biography. I. Title
PR5631.M66   1980   823'.8 [B]   80-20640
ISBN 0-396-07866-4

To Nicholas

CONTENTS

ILLUSTRATIONS

Mrs Jane Brookfield in later years (*Sir Charles Elton Bt*)
Sally Baxter of New York (*Ann Fripp-Hampton*)
Back view of the ageing Thackeray (*Mrs Edward Norman-Butler*)
Thackeray, shortly before his death (*Mrs Edward Norman-Butler*)
His Palace Green library and office (from *The Bookman, 1911*)
A Thackeray joke (*Charterhouse, City of London*)
The author at the end of his story (*National Portrait Gallery*)
The Lord's Prayer on a threepenny piece (*Charterhouse, City of London*)

All the chapterhead sketches were made by Thackeray himself, except those for Chapter 20, by Eyre Crowe, and Chapter 27, by Frederick Walker.

ACKNOWLEDGEMENTS

I should like to thank the many individuals, institutions and libraries which have helped so generously in the preparation of this book, in particular Mrs Belinda Norman-Butler, Thackeray's great-granddaughter, guardian of his memory and of many family treasures, whose assistance, encouragement and enthusiasm has been invaluable; also the Philip H. and A. S. W. Rosenbach Foundation, of Philadelphia, which has allowed me to quote extensively from its collection of Thackeray's manuscript letters to Mrs Brookfield, Kate Perry and Jane Elliot; the Abbot of Downside, for permission to quote from the Brookfield family papers, and the Deputy Headmaster of Downside School, Dom Philip Jebb, for his kind welcome and assistance; Dr A. I. G. McLaughlin, for his generous medical diagnoses; and the Harvard University Press for permission to quote from *The Letters and Private Papers of William Makepeace Thackeray*, edited by Gordon N. Ray, in four volumes, Cambridge, Mass.: Harvard University Press, Copyright © 1945, 1946 by Hester Thackeray Ritchie Fuller and the President and Fellows of Harvard College; renewed 1973, 1974 by Belinda Norman-Butler and Gordon N. Ray; and the Oxford University Press, who published the *Letters and Private Papers* in Britain.

Any student of Thackeray owes a very great debt to Dr Gordon N. Ray for his wise and scholarly editorship, his two-volume biography, and other published works. I also wish to thank him for allowing me to quote from Lady Ritchie's manuscript reminiscences.

Lady Elton has given me many new insights into Jane Brookfield's family, and Sir Charles Elton, Bt., has kindly given permission for the use of a portrait and photograph of Mrs Brookfield. Mrs Elizabeth Atthill, a great-granddaughter of Mrs Brookfield and a granddaughter of one of Thackeray's cousins, has also provided most welcome aid, as have Mrs Sadie Gentry, Mr Claude Prance, the British Museum, the University of Malta Library, and its librarian, Dr Paul Xuereb, the Gozo Public Library, the British Council, Malta, the National Library of Scotland, and the New York Public Library.

The Master and Fellows of Trinity College, Cambridge, have allowed me to quote from their Houghton and Cullum collections, and the Pierpont Morgan Library, New York, from Thackeray's letters to John Blackwood. I should also like to thank *Punch* for allowing me to quote from the typescript of Henry Silver's diary.

A.M.

AUTHOR'S NOTE

In his private correspondence, Thackeray delighted in the waggish misspelling and the occasional misuse of words, and had an individual way with punctuation, particularly apostrophes. In the following pages, wherever he is quoted, these idiosyncrasies have been faithfully reproduced.

Carlyle on Thackeray

'. . . he is a big fellow, soul and body . . .
A *big*, fierce, weeping, hungry man'

Pendennis

'. . . could we know the man's feelings
as well as the author's thoughts
—how interesting most books would be!'

1

The Pedigree

Three generations to make a gentleman

In his lifetime no one was argued about more passionately than Thackeray. He was a Victorian, living in an age which put the greatest value on appearances, and he committed the unforgivable sin of showing what went on behind the immaculate façade. Ruskin complained that he settled like a meat fly on what you were going to have for dinner and made you sick of it. *The Times* described his characters as 'flayed anatomies'. And the man himself was abused just as roundly.

Now his books are accepted classics, but the life and character of their author is far less well known than that of his rival contemporary, Charles Dickens. Many a reader who has thrilled to *Henry Esmond* and gained the most intimate acquaintance with Becky Sharp, of the scheming green eyes and 'famous frontal development', has no idea what kind of man created them. And yet Thackeray, of all writers, has the ingredients in his life-story not just for one novel, but for a whole set of them, all in three volumes in the grand old manner and all, as the man himself would have said, 'hot with . . .'

Much of it he used in his own books. His pampered childhood, wretched schooldays, a misspent year at Cambridge, and the gambling away of his patrimony appear several times. The early struggle as magazine contributor and political correspondent make splendidly funny chapters in *Pendennis* and the much later *Adventures of Philip on His Way Through the World*. But there were other passages too tender to work over in this way—like the insanity of his wife after four years of marriage, a 'living sorrow' which was to outlive him by thirty years; and his love for his best friend's wife, a beauty who lured and then rejected him.

In the very peak of Thackeray's achievement there were strands of melancholy and sadness, and at a time when he should have been most miserable—as a young man suddenly without the fortune he had been brought up to expect—he was most carefree and content, living in Paris on as little as £5 a month, and managing to buy a new waistcoat out of his exchequer.

When he introduced this mixture of good and bad in all things into his books it brought cascades of trouble on his head. He is said to have been the first novelist to hold a mirror up to life, and inevitably many a reader was made uncomfortable by the images he displayed. It was considered acceptable for Dickens to leaven his novels with agreeable low-life rogues and hideous villains: his readers did not know such characters and were well content to be amused or disgusted by them. But Thackeray chose to dissect the middle and upper classes—the people who read and reviewed his books—and to turn their morality inside out. 'You, dear reader, have faults and petty vanities,' was his theme, 'and I know them well, for have I not those same frailties myself?'

Behind the sweetest countenance he found a quantity of selfishness, weakness, or even downright folly, and, equally unforgivable, some of his greatest rascals were given very redeeming features indeed. Even that wicked old showground, Vanity Fair, was an exceedingly pleasant place at times, and one which most people would not have refused to enter had the invitation come from a stallholder of sufficiently substantial wealth or rank.

It was too confusing, said his critics. It was not moral. And besides, the writer was so cynical! So satirical! You couldn't tell when the fellow was being serious and when he was making a fool of you.

This was something which worried his acquaintances, too. To his intimates, he was 'that dear, good Thackeray', loved as much for his silliness, his terrible puns, and his mad animal spirits, as for his wisdom and the generosity of his great bruised heart. To them he was both sage and clown.

Others, who shared neither his humour nor his trust, found him 'cold and uninviting,' with a biting wit, a pride easily touched, 'egotistical, greedy of flattery and sensitive to criticism to a ridiculous extent.'[1] To them his very height (6ft. 3in.), and the fact that he had the audacity to walk upright, seemed intentionally provocative. In this respect, if in no other, they had to look up to him, and looking up is an exercise some men find beyond them.

Even that great granite pillar of Victorian letters, Thomas Carlyle, lost some of his awful certainty in the company of Thackeray. He admired the man's works and thought him the supreme stylist of his day. But the man himself? Carlyle told Emerson:

'. . . he is a big fellow, soul and body; of many gifts and qualities (particularly of the Hogarth line, with a dash of Sterne superadded), of enormous *appetite* withal, and very uncertain and chaotic in all points except his *outer breeding*, which is fixed enough and *perfect* according to the modern English style. I rather dread explosions in his history. A *big*, fierce, weeping, hungry man; not a strong one.'[2]

The outer breeding was the one thing on which friend and foe agreed. In appearance and manner Thackeray was always the perfect English gentleman, which was what he had been reared to be. He wrote like a gentleman, and much of his work was propaganda for a new gentlemanly code, rule one of which was to proclaim that a man should be judged by his behaviour, not his birth. His own undoubted gentlemanliness caused considerable confusion in his early days as an impoverished journalist (not at that time a gentlemanly occupation); then, like *Philip*, 'theoretically a Radical, and almost a Republican,' he could be exceedingly aristocratic in his behaviour and 'had a contempt and hatred for mean people, for base people, for servile people, and especially for too familiar people, which was not a little amusing sometimes, which was provoking often, but which he never was at the least pains of disguising.'

He came by this unconscious superiority in the traditional British manner: six years at a brutal public school, followed by a spell at Cambridge University where he qualified in the art of running up debts and living beyond his means. It was also the fulfilment of one of the chief British breeding precepts: that it takes three generations to make a gentleman.

Family was something which meant a great deal to Thackeray, not so much for its snobbish aspects—though he was glad to have come from good old stock—but for the wider ones of continuity and growth. Just as he liked to endow his characters with pedigrees, he was interested in his own.

Family papers showed that there were men of his name (though of individual spelling) in the West Riding of Yorkshire in the fourteenth century, when one William de Thackwra, followed by an assortment of Thackras and Thacquaryes, leased land and houses from the monastery of St Mary of Fountains. They were, it was said, tall men, like their descendant, and good and handsome too.

The first of the line to spell his name as we know it today was one Walter Thackeray, of the little village of Hampsthwaite, on the banks of the river Nidd, in the shadow of the great forest of

Knaresborough. There he tilled his fields and tended his crops until his death in 1618, after which the land, the husbandry and the Elizabethan farmhouse were passed from son to son, from Walter to Thomas, down to the last Hampsthwaite Thomas of all who died, childless, in 1804, seven years before the birth of the most famous of the clan.

In the last year of his life Thackeray made pious pilgrimage to this small West Riding community, inspecting the records of his fore-bears in the village church, crossing the ancient three-arched bridge over the Nidd which they had crossed; and in his Cockney heart, he no doubt saluted his great-grandfather, one of the many Thomases of the line, who, inspired by a pioneering uncle, turned his back on yeomanry at the beginning of the eighteenth century, ventured south, and founded a new race of Thackerays.

The pioneering uncle, Uncle Elias, left the north in 1682 to inaugurate the family's connection with Cambridge University, a union which was to blossom in bewildering profusion during the author's own student days. Established at Christ's College, he imported young Thomas, sending him first to Eton, and then also to Cambridge, where, in due course, he was elected a Fellow of King's. Like Elias, Thomas entered the church, but while the uncle was con-tent to return to the north and live out his bachelor days in a country rectory, nephew Thomas went back to Eton as an assistant master, progressed to much praised headmastership of Harrow, was made Archdeacon of Surrey, and appointed Chaplain to His Royal Highness Frederick Prince of Wales, son of George II.

In 1729, this 'man of very graceful and portly stature' married the daughter of a Sub-Prosser of Eton, and became over the next twenty years the father of sixteen children. The Benjamin of the brood, born in 1749, was named William Makepeace, after a family martyr (said to have suffered in the time of Bloody Mary), whose stripes, perhaps, his parents by this time felt they shared.

This William Makepeace was articled at fourteen to the East India Company, and eighteen months later set sail for India, the Bengal Civil Service, and one of the greatest gambles of the age: his for-tune—or his death. In those early days the odds were not favourable. Of the eleven companions who sailed out with him, only one was still alive thirty-six years later, plus Thackeray himself. The salary of-fered to these young men was small, but their licence was large: they were expected to make their fortunes by private trade—a practice which led to recognized corruption and deceit, an idea which young Master Thackeray appears to have embraced with some enthusiasm.

Under the tutelage of the prime rogue of the British Raj, Richard Barwell (later 'Nabob Barwell', with a palace at Stansted and a mansion in St James's Square), he farmed land in his own interest which he should have let out to natives for the Company, took to himself the monopoly of supplying salt in his district, and finally overstepped the mark by selling sixty-six decrepit elephants to his employers, only sixteen of which reached their destination alive.

Eleven years after his arrival in India, he was on his way home again with £20,000 and a tarnished reputation. In the eyes of his descendant and namesake, however, this first William Makepeace made good all errors by marrying a Webb. It was with the Webbs that the wits came into the family, his author grandson used to say; the Saxon Thackerays having been simple, serious people.

The Webbs were Normans. They could trace their lineage back to the Conquest, and it was one of these ancestors, General John Richmond Webb, whose exploits Thackeray celebrated in *The History of Henry Esmond*, where he wrote:

'He came of a very ancient Wiltshire family, which he respected above all families in the world: he could prove a lineal descent from King Edward the First, and his first ancestor, Roaldus de Richmond, rode by William the Conquerer's side on Hastings field.'

Thackeray chose to use the Webb coat of arms, and if he had had a son he would have called him Richmond, his father's name, and the one to which the Webbs were most faithful.

William Makepeace the first married his Amelia Webb, daughter of Lieutenant-Colonel Richmond Webb, at Calcutta the year before he quit India. On their return to England, they bought a low, white house on the rim of Hadley Green, in Hertfordshire, where they were soon surrounded by a colony of other Anglo-Indians, and Grandfather Thackeray spent the rest of his life taking care of the affairs of friends left behind in the East, supervising the education of their children in England, and, with the aid of his otherwise in- dolent wife, in producing seven sons and four daughters of his own. It was the second of these sons, Richmond Makepeace, who was to be the father of the author.

Like four of his brothers, Richmond, immediately on leaving Eton, sailed for India, where for his generation the way to speedy riches lay in the high salaries paid by a chastened East India Company and investment in the Indian banks with their dazzlingly high rates of interest. By the time he was twenty, this most diligent young man was earning £1,200 a year—plenty for saving and for spending too.

He bought a house in Chowringhee, Calcutta's European village of gleaming white mansions and palaces, sent home for two of his sisters to launch on the local marriage market, and was soon living in some state with twenty or more servants, coaches, carriages and riding horses, a saloon organ in the music room, a well-stocked library, dinner parties for thirty or forty guests, balls in the cold season, and nightly sunset carriage parades when everyone met everyone on Calcutta's Esplanade.

'It is known,' Thackeray was to write many years later in *The Newcomes*, 'that there is no part of the world where ladies are more fascinating than in British India.' Hearts which beat quite coolly in their native land, kindled quickly under this fierce foreign sun. And so it proved with Emily Thackeray: within nine months she was married to John Talbot Shakespear, a 'writer', as clerks of the East India Company were called. It was not a great match—at nineteen the bridegroom was three years younger than his bride, and still had his way to make in the Company—but it was to be a good one for India, producing in the next generation a public servant of rare wisdom and devotion.

Richmond also busied himself in a romantic way during these years, as the inscription on a small monument next to his own grave at Calcutta shows:

In memory of
Mrs. Sarah Blechynden
lady of the late
James Blechynden Esq.
and only daughter of the late
Richmond Thackeray, Esq., B.C.S.
Died 15th May 1841, aged 35 Years.

In a society deplorably short of white women, native mistresses were a recognized solace, and Mrs Sarah Blechynden was Thackeray's daughter by his Indian or Eurasian mistress, Charlotte Sophia Rudd, Radfield or Redfield. More reliable records than the tombstone show that she was born in 1804, and sixteen years later married the child of a similar union, James Blechynden, son of an English architect.

Marrying Indians or half-castes was against Company rules for all British employees, except for private soldiers, but concubinage received official blessing and no stigma was attached to it by either side. In these days of interesting moral values, the ladies involved considered European 'protection' as socially acceptable as marriage to a compatriot. They were provided for in the wills of their protectors, as Richmond Thackeray provided for 'the Mother of my illegitimate Child', and the illegitimate child herself, in his. It was all considered very natural and only caused comment—and that amused rather than disapproving—when taken to excess.

By 1807, Richmond had risen to the important position of

Secretary to the Calcutta Board of Revenue. He was twenty-six, handsome, in the darkly serious Thackeray way, and eminently eligible. But with his remaining unmarried sister, Augusta, to act as hostess and keep house for him, and Mrs Rudd, Radfield or Redfield to minister to his other needs, he was not tempted into matrimony himself until the winter of 1809 when he fell in love with a ravishing new arrival, Anne Becher, seventeen years old, dispatched from England to mend a broken heart. Richmond went wooing her on a prancing white horse, carried off the belle of the season, and married her in St John's Church, Calcutta, on 13 October 1810.

Anne Becher's story was a curious one. Her grandfather had been a captain in the Royal Navy, but another branch of the family had even more links with India than the Thackerays and her father, John Harman Becher, opted for an Eastern career rather than a naval one. At fifteen he was sent out to Bengal on the nomination of a relative who had previously escaped by a hair that terrifying episode known to every British schoolchild as the 'Black Hole of Calcutta'. There he slowly plodded his way up the promotion ladder, married a girl called Harriet Cowper (who, by Thackeray family tradition, had some Indian ancestry), and produced four children, all of whom were shipped back to the quiet naval community of Fareham, near Portsmouth, to be raised by their commanding, Bible-quoting grandmother.

In 1793, Becher succeeded to one of the plum jobs in the Bengal service, then quickly and mysteriously fell into bankruptcy and ill-health. Out of employment altogether eighteen years after arriving in India, he made a sad little will, hoping his creditors would allow him to leave a few mementoes to his family: a Bible, one or two volumes of Shakespeare, and some plain gold rings inscribed 'This from poor Jack'.

His wife, who had left him some time before, was not mentioned, but two years later she appeared in the will of Charles Christie, an army captain much loved by his native troops, and much mourned by 'Mrs Christie', as Harriet Cowper Becher was then called, though there appears to be no record of a marriage. Four years after this, she joined hands, with well-documented propriety, with another military man, Captain Edward William Butler, of the Bengal Artillery, and in 1807 she and the Captain sailed for England, Mrs Butler to see her now teenage daughters, and Captain Butler to be reunited with a child by one of his Indian mistresses, who was also in England being educated.

Anne, the second of Mrs Butler's daughters by her first husband, was fifteen the year her mother arrived home, and just about to be launched into society by her grandmother. In the winter of 1807–8 she was taken to Bath, where her sparkling dark beauty was greatly admired, particularly by a young army officer, Lieutenant Henry Carmichael-Smyth, on medical leave after ten years of courageous service in India.

The daring lieutenant came of excellent family (his father, a successful London doctor and Physician Extraordinary to George III, was a member of the distinguished Scottish clan of Carmichael and related to the Earls of Hyndford), but he himself was only a second son, he had no money, and though his tales of valour and brave battles with exotic names—Laswari, Aligarh, Rampura and Bhurtpore—won the heart of young Anne Becher, her pious, God-fearing grandmother had more worldly ambitions for her charge. Anne was taken back to Fareham; Henry Carmichael-Smyth followed her; and there they met secretly, Anne waiting on a terrace at the bottom of her grandmother's garden for Henry to come punting up the river which conveniently skirted it. When their meetings were discovered, they carried on the liaison by letter, with Anne's maid as postman.

Then one day, Grandmama Becher came tap-tapping into her granddaughter's room, leaning on her stick, and looking particularly serious. Anne, she said, must prepare herself for a great blow: Lieutenant Carmichael-Smyth had died of a sudden fever, sending her messages of undying love from his death-bed.

The girl went into such a severe decline that a family conference was called. A complete change of scene and the company of other, suitable, young men was thought to be the only remedy. So when Captain and Mrs Butler returned to Calcutta in April 1809, Anne and her elder sister, Harriet, went with them.

Four months after their arrival, Harriet married Captain Allan Graham, of Captain Butler's regiment; but Anne took a year, mending her broken heart and enjoying her reign as 'Queen of Calcutta', before she put aside the memory of the young lieutenant and accepted Richmond Thackeray, a man already well on his way to the highest rewards of the Indian service.

Less than a year later, on 18 July 1811, a son was born to them— William Makepeace—a seven-months' child, which, said the doctors, was lucky for the mother: had it been a normal pregnancy she would almost certainly have died. Even so, she was told she could have no more children.

Anne Thackeray was a long time recovering from this difficult birth, which had come at the hottest and most debilitating season in India, but by the following year the Thackerays were taking their part in the social round once more, and when Richmond met a particularly 'delightful and interesting officer' at his Club one day, a man who had only just arrived and knew no one, he was able to offer immediate relief by asking him to join their dinner-party that night.

A few hours later, with the other guests already assembled in the Thackerays' Chowringhee drawing-room, the newcomer arrived, and the servant at the door announced in clear, ringing tones: 'Captain Carmichael-Smyth'. It was Anne's first love, the dashing young lieutenant of Bath, still very much alive.

They had no chance to talk before dinner and Anne spent an hour and more of agony, sitting at the head of her long table, playing the hostess, and wondering not only how her former lover could suddenly have appeared again so miraculously, but why he seemed so little pleased to see her. When the gentlemen rejoined the ladies near the end of that interminable evening, she explained to the Captain how her grandmother had told her he had died of a fever and how she had believed him to be dead for more than three years. And the Captain explained how the same determined old manipulator had told him that her granddaughter no longer cared for him. As proof, all his letters had been returned unopened and when, in despair, he had pleaded again and again for one more meeting, he had received no word nor sign of any kind. For more than three years he had believed that he'd been jilted.

The situation now became impossible. In a community as tightly knit as theirs, no secret could be kept for long. Richmond Thackeray had to be told. When he was, it is said that 'he listened gravely, said little, but was never the same to Anne again.'[3]

And so things remained for another three years, until the rainy season of 1815, when Richmond Thackeray became ill of a lingering fever. He was taken aboard one of the hospital ships anchored out in the fresher air of the Ganges, and Anne and Augusta took turns in nightmare months of nursing. But there was to be no cure, and in September Richmond Thackeray's name was added to the list of honest men who served India—and the East India Company—with devotion and died too young. He was thirty-three.

During the last years of his life Richmond Thackeray had been earning well over £4000 a year, and saving £300 a month. When he made his will, he estimated that he was worth around £15,000 and left annuities of £450 to his wife (half to go to their son if she remarried), and of £100 each to his son William, his sister Augusta, and his illegitimate daughter Sarah. Much smaller annuities went to Sarah's mother, and the widow of an old servant killed by a horse in Thackeray's service.[4] In fact, Richmond was worth £2000 more than he had thought, and young William's share was doubled. As the other beneficiaries died, their shares were also to fall to him, and any money not spent in maintaining and educating him each year was to be accumulated until his twenty-first birthday. It was not great riches, but in 1815 it promised a most handsome competence.

Anne Thackeray, her little 'Billy-boy', and her sister-in-law stayed together for the year of mourning. Then Augusta married a fifty-year-old judge with eight illegitimate children, and Anne prepared herself for a parting which had to be borne by all English families living in India. William, at five and a half, had already stayed longer than was wise in that punishing climate.

Since Anne herself was to stay behind and marry the faithful Henry Carmichael-Smyth, William and a four-year-old cousin, Richmond Shakespear, were put in charge of a friend going back to England on furlough. It was a traumatic parting for Thackeray. He was a sensitive child even at this early age, and to the end of his life could picture the awful morning he left India: 'A ghaut, or river-stair, at Calcutta; and a day when, down those steps, to a boat which was in waiting, came two children, whose mothers remained on shore.'[5] In later life he could never see or hear of children being parted from their parents without his 'spectacles getting very dim'.

Even at five and a half, Master Thackeray travelled in some style, attended by his own servant, an inquisitive Indian, who, when their ship put into St Helena, took his young charge on a long walk, scrambling over rocks and hills, until they reached a garden and saw a man walking there.

'That is he,' cried the servant, 'that is Bonaparte! He eats three sheep every day, and all the little children he can lay hands on!'[6]

The two small boys were escorted first to London, to the home of their Aunt Ritchie (another of Richmond Thackeray's sisters) in Southampton Row, a home and a family which were to bring solace to Thackeray for very many years. 'I think that Southampton Row was the only part of my youth that was decently cheerful,' he wrote in gratitude to his aunt many years later; 'all the rest strikes me to have been glum as an English Sunday.'[7]

He eased his homesickness by drawing pictures of the house at Calcutta, with his pet monkey looking out of a window, and his favourite 'Black Betty' on the roof, drying her towels. He pointed out the large room in which his last birthday party had been held, and told, with pride, of the many people who had gathered for it.

It was his Aunt Ritchie who one day found her young nephew playing with her husband's hat and discovered with alarm that it fitted him perfectly. Suspecting water on the brain and all other kinds of madness, she rushed him off to the doctor, only to be told, according to family legend: 'Don't be afraid, he has a large head; but there's a good deal in it.'[8]

It was this large head that had given so much trouble at his birth, and there is little doubt that his mother made him fully aware of the agony she had suffered in bringing him into the world. Throughout his life, on his birthday, it was Thackeray who wrote to her in celebration of the event, rather than she to him.

Soon after his arrival in London, Thackeray appears to have been given a brief taste of school life at the Chiswick Mall establishment of a great-uncle, the Reverend Dr John Turner, a man whose rendering of the Ten Commandments each Sunday was so powerful that his family and admirers said it reminded them of Mount Sinai itself. In his very first letter (illustrated with a spirited drawing of a gentleman on horseback), young Master Thackeray piously told his mother: 'I like Chiswick there are so many good boys to play with.' He also confided that he thought St James's Park 'a very fine place' and that he had found St Paul's Cathedral a very much 'finer place' than expected. Exchanging laborious pen and ink for pencil, he finished with a message for his new stepfather: 'I hope Captain Smyth is well. give my love to him and tell him he must bring you home to your affectionate little Son William Thackeray.'[9]

For the following autumn and summer terms, however, both Thackeray and Richmond Shakespear joined Richmond's elder brother at an appalling boarding-school at Southampton. Word had circulated in India that this was an excellent academy and the Thackerays and the Shakespears, like many another deluded parent, had believed it. But over forty years later, Thackeray was still bitterly protesting that he had been starved and caned there by the wretched tyrant in command, an 'odious little blackguard' called Mr Arthur, and driven to praying as he knelt beside his bed each night that he might dream of his mother.[10]

At Southampton, even such blessed escape as sleep could not always be relied on. One night the young inmates were woken up, made to troop, one by one, down a dark garden path to an old shed, and told to thrust their hands into a sack. Unknown to most of them there had been a theft at the school. The sack was full of soot, and it was thought by some twisted mind that the boy who came back·from this nocturnal voyage with a white hand instead of a black one would be the culprit they were looking for.

In his strictly rationed letters home, six-year-old Thackeray complained of chilblains, told of learning Latin, geography and 'ciphering', and on one unusually glorious occasion was able to report: 'Mrs Arthur took some of the young Gentlemen and me to the Play and I was much entertained with it.'[11] It was the beginning of a lifelong love affair.

While the unfortunate Masters Shakespear remained at school for the holidays, Thackeray was whisked away to the house of his great-grandmother at nearby Fareham. This formidable woman was eighty when he first saw her, an astonishing and beautiful relic of another age, leaning still on her long tortoiseshell cane, her hair puffed and powdered, her feet encased in exquisite black velvet slippers with delicate high heels.

She lived with an unmarried daughter, whom she always called Miss Becher, in the pretty, old-fashioned house, fronting on to Fareham High Street and backing on to the river, in which Thackeray's mother had also spent her childhood. The little town appeared to be inhabited solely by the wives, widows and daughters of naval officers, and life there was so like one of Jane Austen's novels that Thackeray came to wonder if she had been born or bred there. But, no, he decided, 'we should have known and the good old ladies would have pronounced her to be a little idle thing, occupied with her silly books and neglecting her housekeeping.'[12]

Though there were few men to be seen in Fareham there were constant reminders of their exploits in the prints of sailing ships and sea skirmishes which decorated all the houses, and Thackeray, taking his cue from these spirited designs, also launched into battle: against being sent back to the Arthurs at Southampton. With that neat victory achieved, he then felt able to give himself up to all the delights of an English summer, as he told his mother in June 1818, in a splendid mixture of courtly language and nursery enthusiasms:

My dearest of all dear Mamas

I have much pleasure in writing to you again from Fareham to tell how happy I am. I went to Roche Court to see M^r and Mrs Thresher. I saw a birds nest with young ones in it in a beautiful Honeysuckle bush, and a Robbins in another place. This has been Neptune day with me I call it so because I go into the water & am like Neptune Your old acquaintances are very kind to me & give me a great many Cakes, & a great many Kisses but I do not let Charles Becher kiss me I only take those from the Ladies. I don't have many from Grandmama . . . Aunt Becher bought me a Caliduscope, it is a very nice one . . . I am grown a great Boy I am three feet 11 inches and a quarter high I have got a nice boat. I learn some poems which you was very fond of such as the Ode on Music &c. I shall go on Monday to Chiswick to see my Aunt Turner & heare the Boys speak. I intend to be one of those heroes in time. I am very glad I am not to go to Mrs Arthurs. I have lost my Cough and am quite well, strong, saucy, & hearty; & can eat Granmammas Goosberry pyes famously after which I drink yours & my Papa's Good health & a speedy return.

believe me my dear Mama   Your dutiful Son   W. Thackeray[13]

After all this, and the celebration of his seventh birthday, the dutiful son resumed his schooling at Chiswick Mall (a setting he used many years later for Miss Pinkerton's academy for young ladies in *Vanity Fair*), where he stayed for the next three years in tolerable discontent—and where he was joined by one of the half-Indian sons of Captain Butler, husband of Thackeray's roving grandmother. Once again, he had to undergo that terrible first night at a new school: 'hard bed, hard words, strange boys bullying, and laughing, and jarring you with their hateful merriment.' '. . . we most of us remember what *that* is,' he was to write when such ordeals were long past. 'And the first is not the *worst*, my boys, there's the rub.'[14]

He had one try at running away, when an unfavourable likeness of one of the ushers was found amongst his papers and referred to the sonorous Dr Turner. He got as far as the Hammersmith Road, but confused by the traffic, at a loss as to where to make for next, he trotted back to school again to face the music.

The contrast between these bleak institutions and the cosseted life of India, with his pets, his old black Betty, and his beautiful, indulgent mother, seemed like a terrible, undeserved punishment to the child. Even the glum English weather and the inevitable chilblains could be seen as personal persecutions. In this suddenly stern world, Thackeray's heart, like young Henry Esmond's, ached for someone to love. And, as with Esmond, these years of bewildering loneliness taught him for ever after 'to be gentle and long-suffering with little children.'

Manfully he soldiered on, quickly conquering anything which interested him, cultivating indolence whenever he could get away with it, drawing caricatures to delight his young friends, and rejoicing above all in the holidays, when, armed now with a peashooter for a little target practice *en route*, he boarded the coach for Fareham and blessed release from the barbarities of school.

It was after another of these blissful interludes that he wrote to his mother of seeing the Prince Regent's yacht in Southampton Waters, '& the bed in w^h his R^l Highness breaths his *royal snore*.'[15] And it was now, in the garden of his great-grandmother's house, that Thackeray commenced 'the noble study of novels.'

He started off with Miss Porter's *Scottish Chiefs*, in five volumes, but never quite managed to read it through. Having sneaked an alarmed look at the last pages, he couldn't get to the end for crying. 'Good heavens! It was sad,' he wrote long after, 'as sad as going back to school.'[16] It made such a deep impression that over forty years later, he could not only remember the story with accuracy and affection, but quote much of the dialogue, too.

Then, in July 1820 came the day young William had yearned for.

His mother, with her new husband, returned to England. The Turners wouldn't let him go to Chatham to meet her ship—they wanted his parents to see him 'in full bloom', fresh from their exemplary care—so he had to wait in an agony of excitement until the following day, when one of his guardians, Robert Langslow (husband of Richmond Thackeray's youngest sister), collected him from Chiswick and escorted him across London to the home of his new step-grandfather, Dr Carmichael-Smyth. There, the nine-year-old boy saw his mother for the first time in three and a half years. He couldn't speak, but kissed her and kissed her, and gazed at her as though he could never gaze his fill.

2
Charterhouse
Lulled into indolence, bullied to despair

Captain and Mrs Carmichael-Smyth had intended their stay in England to be no more than a long leave from India, but while they were still visiting relatives and touring the country neither had seen for many years, changing circumstances changed their minds. Less than a year after their return old Dr Carmichael-Smyth died, leaving his second but favourite son handsomely provided for, and the following month the Captain was promoted to Major, with a consequent advance in pay. Suddenly, there was no urgent financial need for them to go back to the East, and much to young William's delight his parents decided to remain in England, though by this time they had many reservations about their native land.

They found the British at home sadly selfish and censorious compared with the close communities of India, where under the burden of a gruelling climate and in constant acquaintance with death, they helped each other and took a more generous view of human failings and peccadilloes. In India, hard work and long service brought guaranteed success, and the life-style of a minor prince for £1,000 a year, while in Britain an impossible £3,000 was needed for similar comforts. What was more, they now saw the rigid British class system (and honest John Bull's delight in truckling to a Lord) with fresh eyes, and pronounced it intolerable. Even so, they decided to stay, and, as Radicals, to fight for the liberal cause: politics they were to pass on to their son.

This decision made, they were able to offer a home to a small orphaned niece, five-year-old Mary—or Polly—Graham, daughter of Mrs Carmichael-Smyth's sister, Harriet, who had died in England shortly before the Carmichael-Smyths' return. Like Laura Bell in *Pendennis*, little Polly Graham was to grow up with Thackeray. Four years his junior, she was a loving, even adoring, companion in their youth, and later came to his financial rescue in time of desperate need—also like Laura. But there the similarity ended. Far from marrying each other and living happily ever after in peculiarly cloying domestic bliss, Polly was to shock Thackeray profoundly in later life by turning from 'a simple generous creature', into a cold, complacent coquette—Becky Sharp, he thought, was 'a trifle to her.'[1]

After Dr Carmichael-Smyth's death, the new Major and his wife, plus little Polly Graham, left the family house at Charlton, on the outskirts of London, and rented a house at Shanklin on the Isle of Wight, where they were well settled in time for the Christmas holiday of 1821. William, released from Dr Turner's Chiswick Mall school in mid-December, travelled down with Henry Carmichael-Smyth's younger brother, Charles (also an Indian Army officer), and Charles's natural (almost inevitably half-Indian) son, Charley, ready to enjoy all the delights of home, family and festivity with a particular relish: in the new year he had once more to endure another awful first night at a new school. He was to go to Charterhouse, where the Major had also learned his Latin and Greek.

The Duke of Wellington described Charterhouse at this time as 'the best school of them all', which can only be seen as a terrible indictment on the others. The headmaster, Dr Russell, was a vigorous, hectoring man, who, by Charterhouse tradition, gave ten-year-old Thackeray the kind of welcome guaranteed to kill ambition. When he arrived for his first day, Russell called out to the porter: 'Take that boy and his box . . . make my regards to Mr Smiler, and tell him the boy knows nothing and will just do for the "lowest form."'[2]

Thackeray proved him wrong by leaping two classes in his first four months and another two the following year: an advance which can have owed little to Dr Russell's methods of instruction. To economize on masters, the junior boys were taught by seniors from the top two forms. These older students, or *praepositi* as they were called, could rarely keep order even if they had enough knowledge themselves to inform a parcel of unwilling young rascals, and Thackeray later amused a Founder's Day audience with an account of the kind of chaos that reigned all too frequently in his day.

One morning, he said, Dr Russell had stormed into a particularly noisy classroom, and seeing no one in charge of the uproar, cried out: 'Where is your *praepositus*?'

'Please, sir, here he is,' had come the answer. And they had pulled the very small boy who had been set to rule over them from under a desk where they had placed him to be out of the way.

What masters there were compensated for the frailty of the *praepositi* system with savage strength of tongue and forearm. Thackeray, if he learned little else at Charterhouse, continued his noble study of the novel, often in class with one of the Waverley romances or other current favourites propped up behind the great Latin and Greek books he should have been using. But it was a dangerous business, as he and other Old Carthusians were to testify. If caught, the engrossed boy was almost certain to be brought smartly back to duty as the master, in mortar board and swirling black gown, came up behind him like a dervish with a book in each hand between which he smashed the culprit's head.

Wounding with words was equally popular—particularly with Dr Russell himself. To the end of his life, Thackeray could remember 'the tingling cheeks, burning ears, bursting heart, and passion of desperate tears', with which he looked up after having made a blunder, while the Doctor held him up to public scorn before the class, and cracked his great clumsy jokes upon him.

Don't use the weapon of ridicule against a child, he later pleaded. Point out the fault, lay bare the dire consequences of it, but don't 'laugh at him writhing, and cause all the other boys in the school to laugh.' Better by far 'the block itself, and the lictors, with their fasces of birch-twigs, than the maddening torture of those jokes!'[3]

It was a comparison he could make from intimate knowledge of both evils. Even his Greek grammar began with 'τύπτω: I thrash', and it wasn't from humour alone that he gave his fictional schoolmasters such names as Swishtail, Wackerbart, Birch and Buckle. Charterhouse itself became 'Grey Friars' in *Pendennis*, *The Newcomes* and *Philip*, but in earlier works, when the bitterness was still fresh, it was the 'Slaughter House'—a doubly apt title since in those days the school was in London, close to Smithfields meat market.

Living conditions were as rugged as those of the classroom. For the first two years, Thackeray boarded in the house of the Reverend Mr Penny, which was situated, appropriately enough, in Wilderness Row. There, fifty-six boys of assorted ages were cramped together with no peace or privacy. They washed in a large lead trough, glazed with ice in winter, the water congealed with great lumps of fat yellow soap, slept in beds jammed one against the other in open dormitories, and shared one recreation room, called the 'long-room', where the older boys had desks and the juniors only a small locker each for their personal belongings.

Like schoolboys everywhere, in every age, they grumbled about the food, had repulsive names for the regular dishes (boiled beef was 'boiled child'), and once or twice ganged together to try to eat the housemaster out of house and home. In delicious contrast were the wares of the pastrycooks' shops, where most of their money was spent. Thackeray later admitted to having invested half-a-crown in one memorable session—his chief weakness being for open raspberry tarts and three-cornered puffs—but even then didn't care to mention the real figure, for fear of perverting another generation of boys by such a 'monstrous confession'. Such indulgence naturally took its toll in other ways, and then, said Thackeray:

'The school apothecary was sent for: a couple of small globules at night, a trifling preparation of senna in the morning, and we had not to go to school, so that the draught was an actual pleasure.'[4]

In the summer there was the delight of sharing with a privileged friend a bottle of specially brewed liquorice-water, as lethal-sounding as anything the school apothecary could produce: a halfpenny-worth of liquorice, mixed with the same amount of brown sugar, topped up with water in a small flask, and set to mature in a warm trouser pocket. Before being offered, the potion was shaken till a froth appeared on the top, and the host marked with a firm finger exactly how far down the bottle his guest might drink.

In other traditional playground enterprises, Thackeray did not distinguish himself. He had no interest at all in sport, didn't relish the hard gravel or paved surfaces he was supposed to play on, and was so short-sighted he couldn't see the balls he was expected to field at cricket. In his case, however, this was no bar to popularity. He was 'wonderfully social' for a non-playing boy, a contemporary remembered, 'full of vivacity and enjoyment of life . . . Never was any lad at once so jovial, so healthy, and so sedentary.'[5]

Only on one occasion was he provoked into action, and that during his first year at the school, when he found himself involved in the most manly of all the sports: fisticuffs. Fights between the boys provided one of their greatest entertainments, brawn rather than brain being highly valued. The 'cock' of the school was the boy who could lick all the rest with his fists, whatever Dr Russell might do to instil a regard for the classics. They had their own rules and code of honour for such encounters which owed something to the days of duelling and more to the heroics of the great pugilists of their own time, as Thackeray was to make clear in his short story, *Mr. and Mrs. Frank Berry*, with its account of a 'Slaughter House' marathon of a hundred and two rounds.

The reason for eleven-year-old Thackeray's début in the ring was a difference of opinion with fellow student George Stovin Venables—

at twelve the veteran of the bout. The cause of the quarrel has not survived, but since Venables was later to describe his adversary, during his early schooldays, as 'a pretty, gentle, and rather timid boy', it may have had something to do with an earlier expression of this opinion. Whatever the trouble, the only honourable way out was a fight. A 'second' was dispatched to the monitors for permission to stage the contest, and since it was a wet half-holiday and the seniors were bored, the young gladiators were invited into the long-room for an immediate settlement.

Some rounds later Thackeray felt a sickening crunch to his nose, and 'the claret began to spirt.' Venables was proclaimed the winner; his opponent was left with a permanently flattened bridge. They shook hands afterwards, as all boys should, and became friends for life: 'my brave old Venables', Thackeray was to call him many years later, 'one of the finest scholars in England'—'my old schoolfellow you know who spoiled my profile.'[6]

The following year there was a more protracted dispute with a classmate, one which left less obvious scars, but the wounds went deep for all that. The possession everyone craved during the summer term was a silver pencil-case with a movable calendar on the end. One boy, 'an immense screw' destined in later life for Millionaires' Row or shady bankruptcy, had such a case for sale, and Thackeray coveted it. A deal was arranged: the purchaser was to pay the inflated price of three shillings and sixpence when he had the funds, which of course he hadn't, nor anything like it, when the bargain was struck. But Thackeray was sure, absolutely sure he would get the money pretty soon. In the meantime, he enjoyed the pencil-case enormously, twiddling the movable calendar, and ostentatiously taking it out and studying the date before envious non-owners.

But no money arrived. Relatives came to see him and unaccountably did not tip him. The pleasure began to wear off. Hawker, as he called his creditor, was a large and violent boy.

On half-holidays, Thackeray went to visit uncles and aunts in nervous anticipation. They were very kind; they fed him generously; but they gave him no money. Hawker began to taunt him with the meanness of his connections. His scowling eyes and coarse reminders were to be met with everywhere in school and playground. Then, suddenly, relief seemed certain: Thackeray was sent for to say good-bye to a relative leaving to take up a lucrative position in India. This must mean money. As much as five pounds, even. Eagerly, he ran off to tell Hawker all would be well just as soon as he returned.

The voyaging relative asked his young visitor how he liked Charterhouse, heard him construe a passage of Eutropius, said 'God bless you', and sent him back to school empty-handed. And there was Hawker waiting. When he saw Thackeray's scared face, his own 'turned livid with rage. He muttered curses, terrible from the lips of so young a boy'.

The agony continued until the very end of term, by which time the pencil-case was a guilty torment and in urgent need of repair. After two months of sharing a trouser pocket with a top and string, a penknife, cobbler's wax, several bullets, a bottle of liquorice-water, a 'Little Warbler', marbles, hardbake toffee, bull's-eyes, and a brass-barrelled pocket pistol which could, and did, shoot buttons off fellow-students' jackets, the once proud possession no longer worked.

Salvation came only at the beginning of August when Thackeray prepared to join his parents at Tunbridge Wells for the Bartlemytide holidays. His housemaster's servants booked his coach and paid the fare, but his housemaster handed over five shillings in actual cash for his expenses on the journey and an extra twenty-five shillings for Major Carmichael-Smyth, a refund on an overpaid account. Thackeray discharged his debt. The relief was tremendous.

But next morning, he was in agony again. After sharing a hackney carriage to the Fleet Street coaching inn and tipping the porter to put his luggage on board, he had run through all his own money and had only his stepfather's twenty-five shillings left. There was an hour to wait until the coach departed. His friend, 'Rasherwell', dived into the inn coffee-room for a nourishing breakfast. Thackeray resisted. He set out on a brisk walk and immediately succumbed to a placard in a window round the corner: '*Coffee, Twopence, Round of buttered toast, Twopence.*' Fourpence in debt to his stepfather, he was back in purgatory. All the joy of going home for the holidays vanished. The thought of seeing his dear mother's face became a misery instead of the longed-for joy. For thirty-seven miles the round of buttered toast choked him and the coffee was poison on his tongue.

At Tunbridge Wells, his parents were waiting; out spilled the story from silver pencil-case to toast and coffee, before a greeting could be exchanged.

'But why didn't you have a proper breakfast?' asked the Major.

'He must be starved,' said his mother.

The rest of the holiday Thackeray spent with a gloriously light conscience, scaring himself silly reading *Thaddeus of Warsaw* and *Manfroni, or the One-Handed Monk*.

Novels, 'sweet and delicious as the raspberry open-tarts of budding boyhood',[7] were still Thackeray's greatest passion and escape. The glorious Scott cycle of romances, which he first read at twelve or thirteen, were his favourites, especially *Ivanhoe* and *Quentin Durward*—the ones with happy endings. How well he remembered in later years lingering at his school locker after prayers to read one little half-page more—and how well he remembered the monitor's dictionary coming down upon his head.

'Rebecca, daughter of Isaac of York,' he sighed, looking back on this dangerous addiction, 'I have loved thee faithfully for forty years! Thou wert twenty years old (say) and I but twelve, when I knew thee. At sixty odd, love, most of the ladies of thy Orient race have lost the bloom of youth, and bulged beyond the line of beauty; but to me thou art ever young and fair, and I will do battle with any felon Templar who assails thy fair name.'[8]

Next to Scott, and sometimes racing neck-and-neck with him in Thackeray's young admiration, were James Fenimore Cooper's Leather-Stocking tales, and even when age had spread his own waistline, he was to rank Leather-Stocking himself alongside Sir Roger de Coverley and Falstaff as one of the great heroic creations of fiction. *The Arabian Nights* must have been another prime favourite, judging by the images it continued to evoke throughout his life, and the story of *Bluebeard*, which was to be forever surfacing in his thoughts, and which he was to rewrite several times.

Miss Edgeworth's *Frank*, though it belonged 'to a fellow's sisters, generally', and was therefore publicly dismissed as 'stuff for girls!' was also avidly read, and compulsively cried over; while Smollett's *Peregrine Pickle* met with exactly the reverse reaction. Knowingly praised in the playground, since liberal-minded fathers ('the sly old boys') admired it and recommended it as 'capital fun', it caused much puzzlement in private, and quite bewildered Thackeray.[9]

Much more to his taste were the revels of *Corinthian Tom, Jeremiah Hawthorn, and their friend Bob Logic*, whose escapades he was later to think no more suitable for impressionable young minds than *Peregrine Pickle*. But the adventures of Tom and Jerry were illustrated, with pictures that were the schoolboy's delight and the rage of half London. They had elevated George Cruikshank to the pinnacle of fame, and launched Thackeray on a lifelong admiration of the artist. They also inspired his own pen when other ardent young readers called on him to illustrate their own favourite stories, with a cry of: 'I say, old boy, draw us Vivaldi tortured in the Inquisition,' or 'Draw us Don Quixote and the windmills, you know.'

Ah, thought Thackeray, looking back on these sweet fictional pleasures: 'It may be that the tart was good; but how fresh the appetite was!'[10]

*

For his last three and a half years at school, Thackeray became a day boy, leaving the Reverend Mr Penny's sordid quarters in Wilderness Row, and moving into an independent boarding-house at 9 Charterhouse Square, which took in young gentlemen from his own academy and the nearby Merchant Taylors'. He didn't always see eye to eye with his landlady, Mrs Benjamin Boyes—if they survived a whole term without 'a single tiff', it was something to write home about—but her son, Merchant Taylors' boy, John Frederick (Freddy) Boyes, became a valuable friend both to Thackeray and future biographers.

Boyes described his mother's lodger as rosy-faced, with dark curling hair, and a quick, intelligent eye, always twinkling with humour, and *good* humour at that. He was stout, broad-set— 'gustative, never greedy'—and showed no signs of the great height to which he later rose. That happened at the very end of his schooldays, during a three-months' illness which also involved the temporary loss of his curling hair and the use of a wig. Like Barry Lyndon, his later anti-hero, Thackeray emerged from his sick-bed 'prodigiously increased in stature', having shot up from 5ft. 6in. to his definitive altitude of 6ft. 3in.

'People must have looked astonished at you,' gasped an impressionable young cousin on hearing of this remarkable achievement.

'Oh, I don't know,' Thackeray told him. 'My *coats* looked astonished.'

It wasn't a development which he himself found particularly impressive. '. . . after six feet,' he said, 'it all runs to seed.'[11]

Boyes never saw Thackeray really angry, and though he had enviable powers of sarcasm even at this age, he rarely used them unkindly. He never tried to get his own back for the miserable years of fagging and beatings, either.

'He was eminently good-tempered to all, especially the younger boys,' said Boyes, 'and nothing of a tyrant or bully. Instead of a blow or a threat, I can just hear him saying to one of them. "Hooky . . . go up and fetch me a volume of *Ivanhoe* out of my drawer, that's a good fellow; in the same drawer you will, perhaps find a penny, which you may take for yourself." The penny was, indeed, rather problematical, but still realized sufficiently often to produce excitement in the mind of the youth thus addressed, and to make the service a willing one. When disappointed, it was more than probable that the victim would call Thackeray a "great snob" for misleading him, a title for which the only vengeance would be a humorous and benignant smile.'[12]

Thackeray was particularly lucky in his fellow boarders at

Charterhouse Square—his 'ripeners', as Boyes called them. Besides the discerning Boyes himself, there was William Withers Ewbank, a scholar in the best sense, as well acquainted with Shakespeare and Milton as with Aeschylus and Tacitus. He helped the lazy Thackeray with his homework, as a rhyme in Thackeray's hand on the back of a sheet of mixed drawings and Latin translations testified:

> These verses were written by William Ewbank,
> And him for his kindness I very much thank.

Then there was Joseph Carne, who could recite Pope's *Homer*, Walter Scott and Southey *ad infinitum*: a great debater. And William Wellwood Stoddart, quiet, well-read, two years older than Thackeray but with 'an infinite relish' for the younger boy's humour. He was, said Boyes, the most faithful of friends and Thackeray's greatest favourite among them all. 'Noble-hearted' Stoddart had several calls on their affection: his aunt had been married to William Hazlitt, and his father, a lawyer and journalist, knighted for his achievements, actually knew many of their other heroes—Scott, Coleridge, Wordsworth, Lamb—whose books they read, and whose articles they devoured in the great periodicals, *Blackwood's*, the *New Monthly*, the *London Magazine* and the *Literary Gazette*. They clubbed together to buy these marvellous feasts of wit, lapped up their treasures, laughed at them till they cried, debated them—and imbibed the idea that here was a form of literary production they might even attempt themselves.

There was some talk of starting a Charterhouse magazine, *The Carthusian*, which came to nothing, but not before Thackeray had prepared his first contribution, a parody of a sentimental little ditty on *Violets* ('deep blue violets!') by the then popular poetess L.E.L. Thackeray's robust burlesque was entitled *Cabbages* ('bright green cabbages!'). By private circulation, it brought him as great a reputation as his drawings, and was thought to be very witty indeed by his contemporaries.

Humorous prints were another passion with the young gentlemen of Charterhouse Square. On half-holidays they roamed Fleet Street, Ludgate Hill and Sweeting's Alley, making the most of the free exhibitions provided by the windows of the best print shops, mingling with another great band of connoisseurs, the crowds of genial workmen, as one or two spelt out the songs and captions for their less literate brothers, and all received the points of humour with great roars of appreciation. By forming their own 'joint-stock company' they were able to buy whole sets of Cruikshank's incomparable offerings, drawing lots for them later and taking their choice of the individual gems in strict rotation.

They started a select speaking club, too, in which Thackeray joined more from good nature than pleasure in the sport. He loved the idea of debate, had glorious visions, then and later, of swaying an audience with the power of his words, astonishing with the brilliance of his wit, but when it came to the actual performance, the dream became a nightmare. He always felt he had made a fool of himself. Acting, however, was different; that he did well, and with boundless enthusiasm for anything to do with the stage, prised his friends from the polemics they preferred, and made them take part in proper plays, both at Mrs Boyes's house and at his Aunt Ritchie's in Southampton Row. It was the only organized amusement Boyes ever knew him to join in '*con amore*'.

From his first sight of the stage Thackeray had been a theatre fanatic. Whenever he had the money, he would dive into the pit of one of the professional theatres ranged on his London doorstep for instant discovery and delight. At sixteen, he went to see a play called *Paris and London: Or, a Trip across the Herring Pond*, starring Mrs Elizabeth Yates, and wrote to his mother in ecstasy:

> 'I went to the Adelphi on Saturday night, and fell in love with Mrs Yates. I have thought of nothing but Mrs Yates, since then— Mrs Yates. Mrs Yates. Mrs Yates! She is so pretty, and so fascinating and so ladylike and so—I need not go on with her good qualities—'[13]

Over the years, the names changed, but the enthusiasm remained undiminished.

At Charterhouse, as befitted an ancient senior who thought he had 'THE GOUT', Thackeray kept an avuncular eye on another member of the family, little Charley Smyth (the Indian-born son of Major Carmichael-Smyth's brother), helping him none too successfully with his Ovid, and making sure he had enough money.

'Shall I give Charley any tip,' he asked his mother soon after the boy's arrival at school. 'I think half a crown would be acceptable to him & it would be no loss to me.'

A few months later, young Charley, having invested in some fishing tackle and run through his allowance in a fortnight, was taking matters calmly into his own hands, and demanding five shillings.

During his last three years, Thackeray also watched over another junior—'brought him up', he was later to claim. This was John Leech, six years younger than his protector, and first spotted as a small tremulous figure in a little blue, closely buttoned suit, set up on a bench and made to sing 'Home Sweet Home' for the other boys crowding round him. Years later, when Leech had grown into a tall, distinguished and eminently successful cartoonist, they mulled over the corruption rife in their shared academy for the edification of colleagues at *Punch*'s weekly dinners, recalling the pornographic literature which had found its way into their hallowed cloisters, and the fresh innocent voices of their contemporaries singing bawdy songs which few of them understood:

> 'Are your apples ripe, are they fit for plucking?
> How's your daughter Jane—Is she fit for—?'[14]

Sydney Smith's observation that the only way public schools prevented boys being corrupted by the world was by corrupting them before they got out into it, was borne out by another story Thackeray told at *Punch*. One of the first orders he had received from a senior boy at Charterhouse, he said, was 'Come & frig me.'[15]

Though the years and increasing seniority removed Thackeray from the bullying of older boys, they brought him into the direct fire of another tormentor: Dr Russell and his withering sarcasm. Like any outraged schoolboy who can't get his masters to see his genius, Thackeray wrote complaining letters home, with a heart full to bursting:

'I really think I am becoming terribly industrious, though I cant get Dr Russell to think so, or at least to say so . . . Every day he begins at me. Thackeray Thackeray! you are an idle profligate shuffling boy . . . Doctor Russell is treating me every day with such manifest unkindness and injustice, that I really can scarcely bear it: It is so hard when you endeavour to work hard, to find your attempts nipped in the bud—if I ever get a respectable place in my form, he is sure to bring me down again; today was such a flagrant instance of it, that it was the general talk of the school . . .'[16]

The wounds are familiar, but a contemporary was to bear witness that Russell was rough with Thackeray. Not more so than with many others, but when he saw Thackeray's spirit and humour rising it gave added edge to his already cutting tongue.[17]

Since he was manifestly not progressing under the Doctor's system, Major and Mrs Carmichael-Smyth decided to take him away from school shortly before his seventeenth birthday, to leave time for private coaching before he went up to Cambridge. The thought of freedom was intoxicating:

'I feel everyday, as if one link were taken from my chain,' Thackeray wrote home. Even Dr Russell's increased fury could now be borne—just:

'On every possible occasion he shouts out reproaches against me for leaving his precious school forsooth! He has lost a hundred boys within two years, and is of course very angry about it—There are but 370 in the school, I wish there were only 369.'[18]

He was full of tremendous plans for his home studies. He would rise at five o'clock every morning, he said, put in four hours' 'sweat' before breakfast, then there would be only two more hours to do and the whole day would be his. Over the next few years, his mother received many such communications.

Freddy Boyes summed up his friend in Charterhouse days as a fellow with plenty of pride and ambition but 'no school industry'. His exercises were constantly left till the last minute while he busied himself with a burlesque drawing of the subject he was supposed to be tackling seriously, or in extra-curricular study of Shakespeare, Addison, Goldsmith, or indeed of any book, other than a school book, that came to hand. He had 'small confidence in his own powers, and was naturally inclined to rate himself below his mark.'

Thackeray's verdict on Charterhouse, written with all the authority of ten months' absence and a few weeks at Cambridge, was not one Dr Russell would have cared to put in his prospectus: 'I cannot think that school to be a good one, when as a child, I was lulled into indolence & when I grew older & could think for myself was abused into sulkiness and bullied into despair.'[19]

2.

Thackeray's early holidays from Charterhouse were mostly spent at Addiscombe, near Croydon, where for two years his stepfather was Governor of the East India Company's military academy. Their quarters were in a noble old mansion (built by diarist John Evelyn's son-in-law, William Draper), stupendously decorated with mythological paintings which swept up the walls of the grand staircase, round the great salon and over all the ceilings. The main fireplace was adorned with an allegory of Britain (stout Britannia) presenting Justice (a fair goddess) to her Eastern empire (an elephant), but elsewhere there were enough good pictures to stimulate his interest and educate his taste, and, together with the mellow old buildings and traditions of Charterhouse, to awaken a potent sense of history in him.

When the Major's reign at Addiscombe came to an end in the spring of 1824, the Carmichael-Smyths moved down to Devon, leasing some land and an attractive white house a mile or so outside Ottery St Mary from a fellow Anglo-Indian, Sir John Kennaway. It was to this house, Larkbeare, that Thackeray repaired when his days at Charterhouse were mercifully done with. And it was this part of the country that he was to immortalize in *Pendennis*.

Though Thackeray was and always would be a city man, he enjoyed short bursts of rural life, and like that young snob Pendennis rather favoured the idea of a country seat, with its stables and barns, walled kitchen garden and livestock; the mare and her foal in the paddock, Prince and Blücher at the plough or pulling the gig, and his stepfather's gun-dogs in the kennels.

Attempts to turn young Bill into a shooting man were not successful since he couldn't even hit the life-sized figure of a man chalked on the garden wall for target practice, but it was not a failure likely to have caused him much heartache. Except for a brief flirtation with fencing at Cambridge, the only forms of exercise he ever enjoyed were riding and walking, and there is little doubt that he spent most of his time at Larkbeare as indolent young Pendennis spent his at Fairoaks: lazing on a sofa reading novels, or galloping the twelve miles to Exeter, or the shorter distance to Sidmouth on the coast, 'spouting his own poems', seeing himself as Byron, and casting breathlessly about for a first love on whom to bestow the 'inestimable treasure of a heart which he was longing to give away.'

In *Pendennis*, Exeter and Sidmouth were to be called Chatteris and Baymouth; Ottery St Mary, Clavering St Mary; and the real river Otter, which ran past the Carmichael-Smyths' Larkbeare, became the fictional Brawl, on whose banks young Pen had many an amatory meeting with the dangerous flirt, Blanche Amory.

Exeter's greatest attraction was the theatre, and if Thackeray did not bestow his eager heart on at least one of the actresses there it would have been very out of character. If he became as entangled with any of them as did Pendennis with the belle Fotheringay, he never told, but the looks and style of that splendidly stolid charmer had a suspiciously long run in his affections—the much earlier *Ravenswing*, with her glistening black hair and 'eyes as big as billiard balls', being her twin in many ways.

He certainly mirrored Pendennis's literary career by now appearing in print for the first time in a local paper. Thackeray's début was made with a humorous poem on an Irish political incident,[1] but, like his fictional hero, he also dashed off verses of 'the most gloomy, thrilling and passionate cast,' and began a classical drama, *Ariadne in Naxos*, which he was later to think would do very well for *Punch*, if only he could find it.

His models were Byron and Moore. He had their works by heart and became so inflamed with their exotic themes that, imagining himself 'sworn fire-eater and Corsair', he took a wide-eyed young Polly Graham by the hand and confided to her in tragic tones, 'Zuleika, I am not thy brother.'[2]

*

There were not many mornings when Thackeray rose at five o'clock and put in four hours of study before breakfast, but as soon as he had recovered from the unnamed illness (possibly a complicated attack of erysipelas[3]) which began his stay in Devon, he had to buckle down to a certain amount of cramming for Cambridge, an uncongenial business in which he was encouraged by a local schoolmaster, Dr Sidney Cornish. This jovial young clergyman lent Thackeray his copy of *The Birds*, by 'the charming wicked' Aristophanes, and had it returned to him with three funny water-colour illustrations in the margins. Whatever the schoolmaster thought of this at the time, he was later to regard it as a considerable treasure.

In an effort to free his stepson's studies from such artistic diversions, Major Carmichael-Smyth personally coached him in his weakest and least-loved subject, mathematics, and was pleasantly astonished at the ease with which he sped through the first books of Euclid, a display of cerebral application and agility which came to an abrupt halt when they turned to the more abstract science of algebra.

Thackeray's feelings for this trim little military man with kind blue eyes, who had so persistently wooed his mother and now watched over her with proud and jealous deference, were often in turmoil. Inevitably, man and boy were in competition for Mrs Carmichael-Smyth's affection, and there were many times when Thackeray saw his stepfather as an intruder, and felt disgusted at the thought of him snoring in his mother's bed. It was a problem exacerbated by the two men's differences in temperament, interests and humour.

Like many a small, quiet man who follows his wife's lead in most things, the Major held very definite views on some topics, notably politics, and clung to them with John Bullish tenacity. In his later Paris exile he christened an insultingly small dog 'Waterloo', so that he could call it constantly to heel and show his contempt for Napoleonic nonsense.

Often oddly dressed, in a cape which he called his 'poncho', a fur hat on his balding head in winter and a straw one in summer, he had what his step-granddaughter was fondly to call 'an ingenious turn of mind'[4]—a doubtful blessing which manifested itself in a speculative interest in other people's inventions, with which he was always confident the family's fortune would be made. For months, the elaborately carved hoof and a diagram of the cast-iron insides of a mechanical wooden horse decorated the Carmichael-Smyths' drawing-room, giving rise to a family tradition that the Major had anticipated the motor-car.

In other fields he had little imagination, and there were times throughout his life when Thackeray was to exclaim impatiently at 'that stupid old Governor of mine'. But when he put him into a book and called him Colonel Newcome, it was the Major's shining virtue—his intrinsic goodness—that he made to stand out way beyond his frailties. With his courtly code of honour, his kindness and integrity, he provided Thackeray with a model he was long to use as a yardstick for the world, just as Mrs Carmichael-Smyth was to present him with a pattern for feminine loveliness and purity.

Thackeray's traumatic parting in India and the long intervals of separation during his schooldays helped him to keep an unquestioning, childhood adoration for his mother for many years. He saw her as a gentle angel interposed between himself and misery. But inevitably, cruelly, she could not retain such blind love for ever, and during this time in Devon he began to discover that, adore her though he always would, she was a difficult lady to live with.

Imperial in manner, beautiful, with clear grey eyes and abundant black hair, Mrs Carmichael-Smyth was a woman of passionate temperament: tender, loving, humourless, possessive. A fervent champion of cults, causes, strange medical practices and troublesome human flotsam, she demanded equal fervour from others, and total agreement at all times.

In these days of comparative affluence, when she went to the theatre in her beauty and diamonds, she cried so profusely she embarrassed her family. In later poverty, she wrapped herself in a worn crimson cloak with a lining of fur, like a retired empress wearing out her robes. Politically, she was a crusading radical, bent on social upheaval; in religion, a fundamentalist, believing every vengeful word of the Old Testament, eternally threatening those she loved best with the wrath of God and a constant flow of grim evangelical literature. Her son, in loving despair, was to call her a dear old gospel-mother, who always had chapter and verse to prove everything.

Since William was her only child, since she had known from his birth that he would remain so, she focused on him the full force of her maternal possessiveness. When he was away at school, 'Bill' was referred to constantly, in connection with every conceivable topic. When he was home, such attention could be suffocating. Through marriage, fatherhood and until his death, she treated him as a child.

For some years after this Devon interlude between Charterhouse and Cambridge, Thackeray was to sense rather than understand his own changed feelings, but there was to come a day when he would write: 'When I was a boy at Larkbeare, I thought her an Angel and worshipped her. I see a woman now, O so tender so loving so cruel.'[5]

3
Cambridge
A sparkling draught of pleasure

After nearly a year under such watchful parental eyes, Thackeray's joy at going up to Cambridge was immense. He had been delayed a term by his long, post-Charterhouse illness, but now, at last, the leading-strings were to be cut. He was fully primed to savour 'all the novel delights and dignities of freedom', as he was to call the benefits of this transition in *Pendennis*; poised to dash at the cup which held the heady draught of pleasure and drain it to its last delightful drop.

Escorted by the Major, also a Cambridge man, he headed first for London where he presented his tailor with an order for 'a buckish Coat of blue-black with a velwet collar',[1] and paid a diplomatic call on his Uncle Francis Thackeray, rector of Belgrave Chapel, and another member of the family with literary inclinations: Uncle Frank had not only had a book published—*A History of William Pitt*—but had been accorded the honour of a review by Macaulay. Together with Uncle Robert Langslow, he administered a part of Thackeray's fortune, a task in which his Christian understanding was soon to be sorely tried.

At last, on a cold, dark February's day, Thackeray entered Trinity College as a 'pensioner', one notch on the university's social scale above the reduced-fee sizars, and one below the glorious noblemen and fellow-commoners who wore gold tassels to their caps. His College Master was Dr Christopher Wordsworth, younger brother of the poet, a recluse well insulated from contact with his students. William Whewell, Trinity Tutor, was almost as remote—probably a happy circumstance, considering his character. The brilliant son of a Lancaster joiner, 'Mr. UL.' was a large and forceful man with a red face, a loud voice, and a reputation for arrogance. 'Science,' said Sydney Smith, 'is his forte and omniscience his foible.'

The actual job of teaching was done by privately engaged graduates, and Thackeray was soon kitted out with one of these, too: Henry Edward Fawcett, who looked, thought his new pupil, with no great enthusiasm, 'a decided reading character.'

He was allotted most coveted rooms in Great Court, opposite the Master's Lodge, and just beneath those Sir Isaac Newton had occupied in his days at Cambridge. 'Men will say someday, that Newton & Thackeray kept near one another!' Thackeray wrote to his mother in a typical piece of undergraduate bravado.[2] In his case, the boast came true, Cambridge men and guide-books being happy to point out that Newton, Thackeray—and Lord Macaulay, too—all had rooms on the same staircase.

As soon as Major Carmichael-Smyth left him, Thackeray conquered an attack of unexpected depression by settling into his new quarters, hanging up pictures and arranging his possessions. But before many days had passed he decided that, to be entirely comfortable, a thorough renovation job would be necessary. His bedroom, his 'keeping room', the little hall, and the pantry for his gyp were all to be wall-papered, painted, bookcased and cupboarded, by 'much the cheapest man in Cambridge', of course, at a cost of £13 plus £5 for the fittings.

He had chosen a genteel drab-coloured paper, he informed Larkbeare, and perfectly agreed with his mother that all rooms should be painted to resemble oak; then couldn't resist one of the awful puns of which she did not approve—his rooms, he said, would be more than oak, 'I shall have them oaker!!!' When the final touch was added in mid-April, and the newly dyed curtains hung on handsome brass rods, the place looked so 'stilish', so grand, he could scarcely keep his eyes off it. Now, he could begin to think of inviting friends in to share the 'pekooliarly good' Sauterne he'd received from Devon.[3]

But life was not all household decoration and wine parties, as he took care to impress upon his parents. He was working hard at his algebra, his geometry and his Greek plays, getting on 'like a little bean, like a brick, & like a house on fire'—all the newest Cambridge terms—even though constant reading by himself was proving a hard, hard matter which went very much against the grain.

The good intentions of getting up at five each morning were renewed, and unhappily thwarted by the failure of his alarm clock and the bad faith of a College porter tipped to call him. He benefited more from seeing his tutor before breakfast than after dinner, he explained, since the Cambridge ale was such a 'fascinating beverage' and the plum pudding so 'amiable', that he was more inclined to fall asleep after such fare than concentrate. He naturally intended to commence, almost immediately, a systematic course of reading and planned always to keep his door firmly closed (to 'sport the oak') while he was so engaged.

But he could never keep such dedicated talk going for long in his daily journal-letters home. News of his latest pranks would burst through. His old 'crony' Carne, from Charterhouse Square days, was already well established at Cambridge when Thackeray went up, and the two of them soon got into all sorts of mischief.

'Carne has got a pretty washer-woman I gave her a kiss this morning!—She said she was never so insulted in her life!' Thackeray told his parents after two weeks at Trinity.[4]

Later, on a night-time stroll back to College from the Union, they were passed by a fire engine and watched startled, night-capped heads pop out of all the windows along the street. When one of the heads asked them what the trouble was, Thackeray shouted that there was a fire at the back of the inquirer's own house. The head shot back in alarm, but not before the two suddenly chastened gownsmen had recognized it as belonging to the university's Senior Esquire Bedell.

'I shall call tomorrow & apologize for my beayvier,' Thackeray promised.[5]

However, when his mother asked if he were wise to see so much of Carne, who did not appear to be taking Cambridge as seriously as he might, Thackeray was astonished.

'I do not find any harm from Carne's idleness, rather good,' he told her, 'for I am always rebuking him, & consider I ought to act up to the principles I profess.'[6]

'I am so steady & sober that I am quite a pattern, the imitation of all the youths in the University,' he added, most improbably, a few weeks later.[7]

Carne was the kind of young man who does very well in the eyes of his contemporaries. His first time in Hall, like every other freshman, like Thackeray himself, he had his brand new, much-prized mortar-board, or 'cap', swapped for a battered, greasy veteran. But unlike most freshmen, he spotted the thief taking it, walked up to him and said:

'Sir, you have got my cap I believe.'

'Have I? I'm sure I knew it not,' said the culprit.

'I wonder how you could mistake them,' said Carne, holding up the miserable replacement.

'Why I change my cap almost every day—'
'And generally for the better I presume,' cut in Carne.[8]

'This is so characteristic of the man,' Thackeray told Boyes, when relaying the saga. With such keen wits, Carne shone in Union debates, and became one of the leading speakers of his time. Thackeray hungered for similar acclaim. He joined the Union within days of entering the university. On 17 March, having already followed a couple of debates closely, he told his mother he thought he might give the gathering 'a little jaw' at the next one, which was on a favourite subject: Napoleon and whether he had advanced the interests and merited the thanks of the French nation. But, oh dear, five days later, such shame and humiliation:

'I have made a fool of myself!—I have rendered myself a public character, I have exposed myself—how? I spouted at the Union. I do not know what evil star reigns to day or what malignant daemon could prompt me to such an act of folly—but however up I got, & blustered & blundered, & retracted, & stuttered upon the character of Napoleon. Carne had just been speaking before me and went on in a fluent & easy manner but it was all flam—as for me I got up & stuck in the mud at the first footstep then in endeavoring to extract myself from my dilemma, I went deeper and deeper still . . .'[9]

Two months later, his courage was sufficiently repaired for him to boast of planning to 'tip them a little eloquence' in a debate on Shelley, but only if he felt perfectly confident of making a respectable show. When the time came, he didn't. He decided to *write* his thoughts for a university magazine instead—Shelley and his dangerously seductive morality then being very much in favour with undergraduates—and never again risked looking foolish in that august assembly.

Within days of arriving at Cambridge, Thackeray became acquainted with an astonishing assortment of relatives, most of them based on King's, the college of which his first southbound ancestor, Thomas Thackeray, had been a Fellow more than a hundred years before. Both the Provost and the Vice-Provost were Thackeray cousins; Joseph Thackeray, another cousin, was a Fellow of King's when Thackeray first arrived, and Joseph's younger brother, George, became one later the same year. Professor George Pryme, 'very scientific & wondrously ugly', whose lectures on Parliamentary economy Thackeray attended, was married to a Thackeray; and practising in the town as a consulting surgeon was Dr Frederic Thackeray, a brother of the Vice-Provost. He asked

Thackeray searching questions about his troublesome eyesight: 'Now can you see that tree, Now can you see that Kings College Chapel . . .' Ninety-one-year-old Mrs Thomas Thackeray, mother of the surgeon and the Vice-Provost, was also in residence. She 'talked of nothing but fevers and deaths, though she said she loved the name of Thackeray'—which, in the circumstances, could only have been fortunate. [10]

The whole clan generously made the newcomer welcome in their homes and pressed invitations on him for all manner of entertainments, but Thackeray soon found the dons' parties desperately stupid, and deserted them for undergraduate activities. He told his mother that the wine parties given by his friends were stupid, too, but with less conviction since he was always going to them. Years later, he looked back on these gatherings 'with a sort of wonder':

'Thirty lads round a table covered with bad sweetmeats, drinking bad wines, telling bad stories, singing bad songs over and over again. Milk punch—smoking—ghastly headache—frightful spectacle of dessert-table next morning, and smell of tobacco—your guardian, the clergyman, dropping in, in the midst of this—expecting to find you deep in Algebra, and discovering the Gyp administering soda-water.' [11]

Reading men (that is good swots) always gave the largest wine parties, he told his mother, in one of those unlikely statements the young fondly expect their parents to swallow. It was the same when he described a dinner-party for ten, given in his newly decorated rooms: 'Soup, Smelts, Sole, Boiled Turkey, Saddle-Mutton, wild ducks, cream Jellies &c'. He wasn't the host, he said, that was 'Hailstone . . . a very hard reading man.' [12]

To keep in shape for such excesses, he rode hired hacks, took ten-mile walks, and fenced, lunging about with a button on his foil while imagining himself a desperate eighteenth-century rake fighting for his life or his lady's honour. As a truly desperate measure, for one meal only, he put himself on a diet of mutton broth and boiled chicken.

Very early in his undergraduate career, Thackeray began studying the magazines and planning what to write for them, and quickly decided that *The Snob* (which billed itself as 'A Literary and Scientific Journal. Not conducted by members of the University') was the one to be honoured with his contributions. It was an odd production: six pages of pink, green and yellow paper issued each week for twopence-halfpenny. In Cambridge parlance, 'a snob' was anyone who was not at the university—a Townsman as opposed to a Gownsman. Outside, the term was used loosely to describe the stingy, the vulgar or the objectionable. It was Thackeray himself, twenty years later, who was to grapple with the word and make it mean what it does today.

He made his début with a mock Prize Poem, a form of competition taken very seriously in some quarters, on the subject chosen for that year: Timbuctoo. (The prize was eventually carried off by an undergraduate called Alfred Tennyson, with a suitably adapted version of some verses he had happened to have in hand on the Battle of Armageddon.)

Thackeray dressed up his offering with all the scholarly footnotes, some of them in Greek, appropriate to such a work. ('Line 13. "Pop goes the musketoons." A learned friend suggested "Bang," as a stronger expression; but, as African gunpowder is notoriously bad, the Author thought "Pop" the better word.') The poem itself he began with a general description in spanking rhyming couplets:

> In Africa (a quarter of the world)
> Men's skins are black, their hair is crisp and curl'd

then with a change of pace and style—which 'the Author' pointed out and congratulated himself upon in the footnotes—turned to prophecy:

> The day shall come when Albion's self shall feel
> Stern Afric's wrath, and writhe 'neath Afric's steel.
> I see her tribes the hill of glory mount,
> And sell their sugars on their own account;
> While round her throne the prostrate nations come,
> Sue for her rice, and barter for her rum. [13]

It was a great success. 'Timbuctoo received much Laud,' he told his mother. 'I could not help finding out that I was very fond of this same praise—The men Knew not the Author, but praised the Poem, how eagerly did I suck it in! "All is vanity"—' [14]

The editor noted that *The Snob* would be glad to hear again from 'T', and Thackeray was swift to act upon the hint, sending in some tortured effusions from a Mrs Dorothea Julia Ramsbottom, a lady 'on terms of the greatest contumacy' with many an 'extinguished' person, and mother of a Cambridge undergraduate whose tutor had assured her the lad would be 'a tripod'—a forerunner of his later murderer of the English language, Mr Charles James Yellowplush, the gentleman's gentleman whose 'buth' was wrapped up in a 'mistry'.

Once an idea appealed to Thackeray he was remarkably loyal to it. Snobs, that reference to 'all is vanity', the mangling of the language he was to learn to use so marvellously—they were all with him in his first term at Cambridge, and were to remain with him, to be worked over in a hundred different ways, in all his future books.

The editor of *The Snob* was one William Williams, of Corpus Christi, seven years older than Thackeray and, at first, not particularly congenial to him. But they were soon working side by side on the weekly issues, and laughing so much that after one all-night editorial session Thackeray was ill for three days with an upset stomach and cracking headache. After self-administered calomel and 'Salts' had failed to cure him, Dr Frederic Thackeray was called in to apply leeches to the 'head'-quarters of the trouble. When Thackeray offered to pay, his kinsman held up his hands in horror. 'What, do you think me a cannibal?' he asked.

This infirmity, which lost Thackeray ten whole days of study, would naturally seriously affect his performance in the coming examinations, he told his parents. He had hoped at least for mediocrity, but now even that was gone. In fact, when the results came out, he had not done too badly for a man who had gone up a term later than most of his contemporaries: his name appeared in the Fourth Class, one higher than he had dared to hope for—a class where 'clever "non-reading men" were put, as in a limbo'.[15]

2.

Thackeray had spent his first vacation in College, studying; but now for the long summer break he set off for Paris, with Williams of *The Snob* as chaperon and tutor in mathematics. He had been brought up to think of himself as a gentleman of some fortune, and Cambridge had already shown him many ways of living up to such a reputation. At the end of his first term, he had admitted, with a fine show of surprise, to having spent £157 (and whoever confessed to *all* their debts? he was later to ask many a time in his novels). Even this sum, he informed his parents, was considered moderate by his peers.

Now, at nearly eighteen, he was to travel; to enjoy the role of the young Englishman abroad. It was all quite new, from his first stomach-churning crossing of the Channel to the bustle of Calais and the curious ways of the French. In figured-silk waistcoat, a monocle dashingly screwed into his right eye, his undershot jaw quivering with pleasure, Thackeray was on his way to see the world.

Soon he was writing to Larkbeare, describing his splendid adventures—and his letters were enough to turn the head of any fond parent stark white with terror. He and Williams quickly left the quarters that had been selected for them in the rue de Rivoli, and moved into a boarding house 'close to the Boulevards'. There they found a mixed society—'Medes Parthians & Elamites'—who dressed in stunning finery for the nightly dinners and weekly soirées provided by their hostess, a lady of suspect rank known to her boarders as Madame la Baronne de Vaude. They were all 'inordinate card players' and the stakes were 'rather high'. Among them was a fascinating Mrs Twigg, who had been brutally treated by her husband from whom she was now mercifully separated. Thackeray was 'very thick' with 'the charming Twigg', and Williams was 'if possible thicker.'

When Mrs Carmichael-Smyth screamed across the Channel to leave Mrs Twigg alone, Thackeray was very hurt. The unfortunate lady was the soul of propriety, he declared. She never entertained them without her sister being present, and had only once invited them to her own private salon: 'I receive from her plenty of good advice, w^h as it comes from a very pretty mouth is the more pleasant, & yet luckless I—I am to cut her!'[1]

He had discussed his mother's heartlessness, he reported, with another new friend, a young Irish gentleman, and *he* had said he would be proud to have a sister like Mrs Twigg. (For good measure, Thackeray told his evangelical mother that he had long theological discussions with this new Catholic acquaintance.)

But before Mrs Carmichael-Smyth received this rebuke, Williams and his charge had decided that the Medes, Parthians and Elamites were all English after all and that, in consequence, their French was not progressing. They had therefore left the 'idle dissipated écarté-playing boarding house' and moved into lodgings at 54 rue Neuve St Augustin, where they could hire their own cook and enjoy proper English food again. Thackeray admired French wine, he told them at Larkbeare, but not the local cuisine. The first verdict was to remain unchanged throughout his life; the second he revised.

In fact, he was a perfect John Bull on this first visit abroad. Surveying French paintings, he was disgusted to find that the 'odious French style' predominated; while the people he thought far too like their own furniture: 'plenty of varnish with but little *bottom*'.[2] Only the theatre escaped his censure, and this he greatly admired. He went often and wrote home in raptures:

'Mademoiselle Mars is most glorious, and Leontine Fay at the Theatre de Madame the most delightful little creature I ever set eyes on; she has a pair of such lips! out of w^h the French comes trilling out with a modulation & a beauty of w^h I did not think it capable.' And as for Taglioni—she had 'the most superb pair of pins, & maketh the most superb use of them that ever I saw dancer do before.'[3]

His mother wrote again. And received another hurt reply. 'I wonder at your objecting to the Theatre-going,' sighed her much misunderstood son, 'for it gives me the best French lesson possible, and I am quite enough used to it not to feel the effects of it in the morning.'[4]

The news wasn't all bad, however: the prodigal had engaged a French teacher (who had served under Napoleon 'as—Sergeant Major!'); he was applying himself to algebra; had joined a circulating drawing library which provided items for artists to copy; he was taking dancing lessons—and dancing was an accomplishment which certainly became all young gentlemen. His master was the great Coulon, and a fine sight master and pupil must have made, reflected in the mirrored walls of an Opéra practice room— Thackeray at 6ft. 3in., and little Coulon 'four feet high with a pigtail.'

In *Fitz-Boodle's Confessions*, Thackeray was to tell how this partnership came to an inglorious end: the mirrored difference in altitude struck him one day as so supremely ridiculous that he burst into a yell of laughter; the diminutive M. Coulon drew himself up to his full four feet, walked abruptly away and begged M. Thackeray not to repeat his visits in the future.

Items of mixed merit also relayed back to Devon were the news that Williams was composing a Euclid in verse, while Thackeray was finally at work on his Shelley dissertation, had had his hair cut in the 'derniere mode' (very George IV), and was reading novels. Bulwer-Lytton's *Devereux* he thought not as good as its predecessor, *The Disowned,* even though it was set in the time of Swift and Bolingbroke (and Henry Esmond), a period he already considered his own territory. He could write just as good a story himself, he thought.

His taste for old books and prints was increasing wonderfully. Could he borrow £10 to buy items which would cost £20 in England?

Throughout his letters there were references to card-playing, especially écarté, for money, but the real thunderbolt came less than half-way through his stay. Thackeray had been to Frascati's, the elegant gaming rooms on the rue de Richelieu. And not only had he been, and watched, but—he had played. And even that was not all:

'. . . had I stopped at one time I should have come away a winner of 200 Francs as it was I neither one or lost . . . The interest in the game Rouge et Noir is so powerful that I could not tear myself away until I lost my last piece—I dreamed of it all night—& thought of nothing else for several days, but thank God I did not *return*. The excitement has passed away now, but I hope I shall never be thrown in the way of the thing again, for I fear I could not resist . . . I am told that there were some of the men of the table watching us the whole time, evidently expecting to make something by our party. There is however a game w^h they say is infallible, it requires a capital of 75000 Francs w^h I have not about me just now . . .'[5]

Mrs Carmichael-Smyth's reply to this intelligence must have fairly sizzled through the post. Even Thackeray was stunned; then deeply wounded. He did not believe he deserved to be called avaricious and mean, he coldly retorted, and prayed God might grant that his mother would never again call her son such terrible names when he was merely curious, simply taking an opportunity to see another chapter in the book of life. And, showing that he too could use the Bible to point a moral, he quoted the parable of the proud Pharisee and the humble Publican, to show what a blessing the whole incident had been: but for that chance encounter with the tables, he said, he would never have known his own weakness or realized that he must guard against it. By the end of his defence, he had worked himself into a magnificently aloof mood of injured innocence, and no doubt saw his postscript as a killing thrust of icy obedience:

'I said in my last letter I think, that I should go into one of the low gaming houses—this of course unless I receive permission from you—I shall not now do.'[6]

Mrs Carmichael-Smyth's letters must have become progressively chilly, too, for at the end of September, Thackeray proposed going straight to Cambridge from Paris instead of spending the last two weeks of his vacation at Larkbeare as originally planned. Williams would give him more tuition in College, he said.

Family tensions were not allowed to interfere too greatly with his pleasure, however, and he was 'much delighted' with the début of Miss Fanny Kemble, as Juliet, which he caught on his way through London at the beginning of October. Soon the actress's charming picture was gracing his walls, as it did most other undergraduate rooms at Cambridge, and through her brother John, a fellow student, Thackeray was to find himself in time a friend of the whole teeming race of Kemble.

Except for an occasional madness, like playing the heroine in amateur theatricals (dressed in a white gown borrowed from his College bedmaker, and embellished with his own needle and thread), Thackeray now settled down to what appeared to a contemporary to be 'a somewhat lazy but pleasant and "gentlemanlike" life' at the university.[7] He contributed to *The Snob*'s successor, *The Gownsman*—'A Literary and Scientific Journal, now conducted by Members of the University', and dedicated to all Proctors, 'whose virtues it is our duty to imitate, and whose presence it is our interest to avoid'—and through Williams met a circle of clever literary men, many of whom were to remain good friends for life: Edward FitzGerald, future translator of Omar Khayyám; James Spedding, erudite editor of Francis Bacon; bony, awkward John Allen, who became an Archdeacon and the model for Dobbin in *Vanity Fair*; Richard Monckton Milnes, later first Lord Houghton, MP, poet, the most brilliant host in London, and owner of the best library of erotica; the poet, Tennyson; and William Brookfield, a young man with such style, such wit, and such a reputation for brilliance, it was an honour to be seen walking with him, even though he was only the son of a Sheffield solicitor.

Of them all, Edward FitzGerald, a quiet Irishman of shy and fitful genius, was Thackeray's favourite. They shared the same idiotic sense of humour and made marvellous fun of James Spedding's vast and luminous forehead, seeing it in all things. Thackeray thought it particularly apparent in a milestone, and drew pictures of it rising over Mont Blanc, its spacious dome reflected in lake Geneva. They were still laughing at it ten years later. 'No wonder that no hair can grow at such an altitude,' wrote FitzGerald then.[8]

Thackeray was going through a rupture in faith, and John Allen, the Archdeacon to be, took great pains with his theological gropings, affecting him sometimes to tears with his honest simple devotion, instilling in him the determination to lead a new life ('tomorrow'), and going away afterwards to pray for him, for FitzGerald and himself, with tears pouring down his own good face.

With Allen, Thackeray joined a small literary/debating society, which one of the seven members suggested should be called The Covey, since they made such a noise when they got up—to speak. But such a formal, serious group could not be to his taste for long. The other members, he told his mother, were 'very nice fellows only they smell a little of the shop.'[9] He preferred more relaxed gatherings in friends' rooms, drinking, smoking, discussing metaphysics and morality late into the night; lauding the English novelists, especially Henry Fielding who was then, and was to remain, his hero and his model. But even on these occasions Thackeray was more of an observer than a talker and, as at Charterhouse, his contemporaries failed to see in him 'even the germ of those literary powers' which were to bring him fame.[10]

At Christmas time, Thackeray warned his mother that he might have to eat his turkey in College if he hoped to take anything like a respectable degree. At Easter he told the University and his parents a lie. He was going off to join another College man in Huntingdonshire, he said, then nipped smartly across the Channel to join FitzGerald in Paris. It was a trip which made him feel guilty for the next thirty years.

This time it wasn't gambling, or an innocent enthusiasm for actresses' lips or pins which would have sent the shock waves rippling through Larkbeare had they known there what Master Bill was up to. On this occasion, Thackeray's book of life had fallen open at a very basic chapter. Eleven years later, he told pretty well the whole story for readers of the *Britannia* magazine (and for desperately needed money).[11]

His adventures began on Shrove Tuesday, when he and a group of other 'great raw English lads', went to one of the vast public masked Carnival balls that preceded Lent. It was noisy, dirty and disgusting, and Thackeray was about to slink away in disappointed misery, when he was tapped lightly on the shoulder and greeted by name. He didn't recognize the 'lady' who then folded her arm through his and walked him up and down the room, but it is unlikely that he objected too much: an eighteen-year-old's reputation among his contemporaries is made up of just such pieces of good fortune. His companion was dressed like a man, in dirty white trousers, dirty white shirt, an oilskin hat decorated with a great quantity of multicoloured ribbons, and a greasy wig of Louis XVth antiquity. She appeared to be about thirty-five and, though not pretty, like Becky Sharp had a certain *je ne sais quoi*. She told Thackeray she had pawned her dress to hire her costume for the masquerade.

'Don't you know me?' she asked.

Thackeray confessed his forgetfulness.

So she told him who she was; and then he did remember her.

He had last seen her as the governess ('selected especially because she was a *Protestant*') in an extremely sober English family. She had been a good governess and, when her charges no longer needed her, their father had been prepared to give her an excellent reference. As Thackeray pointed out, she could have spent the rest of her life among all the delights and refinements of English family life: a hot joint every day with the children in the nursery at one, a healthy walk in the park each afternoon; delicious evenings in the drawing-room, listening to or playing the piano, and making tea for the gentlemen when they came upstairs after their wine.

But Mademoiselle Pauline, as Thackeray called her, had decided she had had enough of such excitements. She had been a Parisian *grisette* before becoming a governess; she would return to being a *grisette*.

Thackeray next sought out this 'jovial devil-may-care patroness of the masked ball' in the dubious alleys of the rue du Bac, where he found her eating garlic soup in a porter's lodge. She left the garlic to conduct him—'with the air and politeness of a duchess'—up a damp and mouldy staircase to her own apartment on the seventh floor.

There they discussed the half-dozen shirts he thought she might care to make for him, her interesting history—and who knows how many other things?

After this incident, Thackeray's step on the great slide to disaster never faltered. On his return to Cambridge he took as his model Henry Matthew, son of a parson, President of the Union, four years his senior, and an appalling example. Matthew had already been sent down from Oxford and only survived a year at Trinity before sidling off to little Sidney Sussex College to take his degree at last. FitzGerald warned Thackeray that he was 'a bad one and a sham', but for the next six months Thackeray worshipped him, saw him as his idol of youth, found him the 'most fascinating accomplished witty and delightful of men' [12]—mistook the dross for pure gold.

Harry Matthew sired many a seedy fictional rascal in Thackeray's later works and, as an undergraduate, is enshrined for ever as Bloundell Bloundell, the bounder who had already been to Camford, before turning up at Oxbridge (Thackeray's own amalgamations) to lead impressionable young Pendennis astray with his 'flashy grace, and rakish airs of fashion'.

Matthew most probably encouraged Thackeray to gamble again, just as Bloundell set Pendennis on that ruinous path—he certainly cost the younger man money one way or another. Perhaps Thackeray needed no such persuasion. But however it came about, gamble he did, and he was soon so obvious a target for the sharpers that two professionals set up shop opposite the College gates with the intention of relieving him of his patrimony.

It was all done in the most gentlemanly fashion. Thackeray was invited to a little supper of champagne and *pâté de foie gras*; then, 'having eaten, the young man was devoured in his turn'.[13] The chosen game was écarté. At first he was allowed to win, and, as Thackeray had noticed on his fateful initiation at Frascati's, it was winning not losing that inflamed the mind. Many years later he was to give all the symptoms of gambler's frenzy to a most unlikely character: Lady Kicklebury, the conceited, snobbish, bullying little mother-in-law of *The Kickleburys on the Rhine*. One taste of the tables and she was a woman possessed. Thackeray knew the sensation only too intimately. Soon he began to lose and went on losing until a morning came when one of the sharpers escorted him in his cabriolet to the Thackeray family brokers in London and arranged for a transfer of £1500.

Towards the end of his life, when Thackeray had tamed his lust for play, he saw this old adversary again at a Rouge et Noir table at Spa in Belgium, and pointed him out to his companion, Sir Theodore Martin. The man was tall, with a certain distinction of manner and a seedy brown frock coat—a gentleman fallen on hard times.

'That was the original of my Deuceace,' Thackeray told his friend. 'Poor devil! My money doesn't seem to have thriven with him!'[14]

For the many plump and willing young 'Mr. Pigeons' that Deuceace and his like plucked so easily in the pages of Thackeray's stories, the author had a model much closer to hand.

4
Weimar

Days of youth most kindly and delightful

Shattered by his losses at cards, uncertain of gaining his degree (and doubting its value to him even if he did), Thackeray left Cambridge at the end of the disastrous Easter term, sixteen months after first taking up residence. Ten years later, when he wrote *A Shabby Genteel Story*, he was still bitter at what Charterhouse and Cambridge had taught him and wondered how many others had been ruined 'by that accursed system which is called in England "the education of a gentleman."'

It undoubtedly gave a man 'a pretty knack of Latin hexameters and a decent smattering of Greek plays,' he wrote then, but it also taught him to despise the less fortunate and to compete with associates far more wealthy than himself; to disregard money and to stress honour—the honour of dining and consorting with his betters.

By the time he came to write the Oxbridge chapters of *Pendennis*, however, the perspective had cleared, and he could see, with some humour, that it was not the system which was at fault so much as the eagerness with which some young men fell into temptation.

Thackeray now persuaded his parents to let him continue his studies in his own way. It was agreed that he should go to Dresden, stay with a good German family, and learn the language. A few days before his nineteenth birthday he set out from Devon, engaged a temporary German master in London, collected letters of introduction from family and friends, and tried to make travel arrangements in a city loyally shuttered and black-draped for the funeral of George IV. Even the theatres were closed! He managed to delay his departure long enough to see Kean in his farewell performance, then started for Holland and the long sail up the Rhine.

Rotterdam he thought impressive, Cologne hot and 'beastly', and the sights in between almost non-existent. At night, escaping the squalid cabin with passengers draped over stools and sofas, on tables and under them, he slept 'snugly' on a pile of coals on the open deck. But then the 'beauties of the journey began', and Thackeray felt able to give the Rhine an Englishman's supreme accolade. It was, he wrote home, 'almost equal to the Thames.'

There were beauties to be found on board, too, he discovered, and as the boat approached the romantic 'castled crag of Drachenfels', and the ladies brought out their copies of *Childe Harold*, Thackeray indulged in a little man-of-the-world, nineteen-year-old flirtation with the prettiest girl on board, talking 'the most delicious sentiment', quoting 'Shelley and Moore to her great edification & delight.'

'I really did feel rather sentimental,' he told his mother, '& intended to have made some pathetic verses on her & the Rhine but she came from a boarding school at Boulogne, & that staggered my sentiment; & dinner was ordered & that entirely destroyed it.'[1]

At Frankfurt he continued his career of falling in with charming rogues when he met one Franz Anton Schulte, described loosely, for Mrs Carmichael-Smyth's peace of mind, as 'a Cambridge acquaintance' which might have been true, but, according to university records, did not mean he had studied there. Herr Schulte was, however, travelling with two *bona fide* Oxford men, and Thackeray was invited to join them.

Putting the thing in its best possible light, he told his parents that Schulte would give him an hour's reading in German a day and, after a month living in most reasonable lodgings in Godesberg—'a village in the neighbourhood of the most beautiful part of the "Father of Rivers"'—would take him to spend another month at the Schulte family home in Westphalia.

As this seemed the cheapest and pleasantest plan he could pursue, Thackeray reported that he had decided to adopt it instead of making straight for Dresden.

The fortnightly 'gems epistolary poetical & graphical' which now reached Larkbeare contained dutiful references to German grammar, a noble regard for economy, and tremendous descriptions of student life at Bonn University, where, as in most other places, the invaluable Schulte had friends. The duels, the pipe-smoking, the songs and the toasts were watched and entered into with spirit. When it was Thackeray's turn to provide a song, he 'piously & patriotically chanted out God save the King', and, as he reported in genial detail:

'On breaking up I found myself the only strictly sober man in the party although during the evening I had positively imbibed no less than six bottles of the wine—My potations cost me a dollar. 3 shillings—It was after the Port wine and Punch of Cambridge like so much milk and water or vinegar & water for it had an unpleasant effect on my internals; in fact the wine and the dinner have kept me &c &c'. [2]

He was pursued everywhere by fleas, which throughout his life appear to have attacked him with especial venom, and, judging by his tale of Miss Löwe, daughter of the Jewish banker and forger of Bonn, it seems he was also pursued by human vermin.

He wrote this story twelve years later as one of Fitz-Boodle's confessions for *Fraser's Magazine*, but withheld it when the others were published in book form. Fear of libel appears to be the only reasonable explanation for the omission, and it is certainly the easiest thing in the world to imagine Thackeray, like the young Fitz-Boodle, so enraptured by a pair of exquisite blue eyes that he failed to notice that their owner and the rest of her horrible family (including an unpublicized *fiancé*) were systematically bleeding him dry; to see him surrounded by cases of undrinkable wine, boxes of unsmokable tobacco, bales of unwearable shirts, all supplied to him as a particular favour, at outrageously inflated prices, by the best-known rogues in town.

Schulte kept his word in helping Thackeray with his German, but as they drew near his family home his other promises crumbled. His sister had broken her leg, he said; his mother was too unwell to receive visitors. By this time a certain amount of money had changed hands, which Thackeray was still trying to recover long after he returned to England.

The two men parted company, and Thackeray, wandering miserably on alone towards his original goal of a parent-approved family in Dresden, found himself in Weimar, the little city-state that had fostered Goethe and Schiller; a gentle pocket of Saxony whose hey-day was twenty years in the past.

Here he discovered a genuine old Cambridge friend, William Garrow Lettsom, a colleague from *Snob* days, now preparing to be a diplomat. Thackeray moved in with him and wrote to his parents asking for permission to stay. He could find in Weimar, he told them, the three things they had wished for him in Germany: good society, a first-class German master, and a respectable family to live with. Additional attractions were a capital library, and an excellent theatre where drama and opera could be enjoyed for the modest sum of one shilling a night.

He had already fallen in love with a Princess of the ruling house ('I must get over this unfortunate passion w^h will otherwise I fear bring me to an untimely end'[3]), met Goethe's daughter-in-law, and sampled most of the other benefits of the little place. In order to become a complete courtier, he had taken a master 'in the arts of Waltzing & Gallopading' ('my natural grace & symmetry of person greatly contributes to my advancement in that Science'); and made his first bow at the court of the Grand Duke, 'airing' his legs in 'a pair of trowsers cut into breeches.'[4]

His complete court costume of black coat, black waistcoat, black breeches and cocked-hat, made him look something like a cross between a footman and a Methodist parson, he told his parents, and to save him from such sombre attire in the future he somewhat bashfully asked 'a very absurd favour': would they persuade their neighbour and landlord, Sir John Kennaway, to give him a cornetcy in his yeomanry, so that he could wear the uniform at court? It was true he *could* do without it, but most of the men wore something of the sort, and if he went to other courts in Germany it would indeed be essential. Of course, if it was *expensive* he would instantly give up the idea.

His indulgent parents indulged him once again, and within a month Thackeray was gallopading round the Grand Duke's palace in dazzling fashion; the pink rosettes on his leather breeches, and touches of sky-blue here and there, were the only things about the new ensemble which did not entirely delight him.

Years later when, under the pseudonym of the Hon. George Savage Fitz-Boodle, he wrote of Weimar ('Kalbsbraten-Pumpernickel', he called it), he brought the brief glory of Fitz-Boodle's dancing days to an undignified end in a mid-floor collision of embarrassing magnitude. If such a disaster actually happened to Thackeray he did not write home about it, but the fear was obviously deeply embedded in his mind, and long after Fitz-Boodle's spectacular fall, dandy Pendennis was to have his pride punctured by a similar humiliation.

Most of Fitz-Boodle's other confessions are reflected in the letters to Larkbeare, and show how much fact Thackeray wove into his fiction—and what a remarkable memory he had, not only for the deeds and disappointments of youth, but for the yearnings and rash folly of it, too. Fitz-Boodle called the ladies who stirred his passion *Dorothea* and *Ottilia*; Thackeray knew their originals as Melanie von Spiegel, daughter of the Hof-Marschall of Weimar and maid of honour to the Grand Duchess, and Jenny von Pappenheim, 'love-child' of Napoleon's brother, Jerome, one-time King of Westphalia. Both in their turn inspired in him a ferment of desire.

He fell in love with Melanie, the prettiest woman he had seen in all his nineteen years, within the first two days of setting eyes on her, and hoped the sensation would continue since he found it so 'novel & pleasing'. There were even hints of making her Mrs Thackeray. But that was in October. In November, he had a different story for his mother:

'The last time I wrote, I was if you remember violently in love; I am still violently in love but it is with another person: Tho' as there are only two young ladies at the Court of Weimar with whom one can fall in love, I don't know what I shall do at the end of another fortnight, about which time I expect to be free.'[5]

This second love was shattered by the arrival of an ex-Guards officer, heir to ten thousand a year, who had several waistcoats of the most magnificent pattern, and made love speeches to admiration. Miss Pappenheim's wandering eyes, which Thackeray had previously tolerated since he thought they wandered more often in his direction than any other, wandered away for good.

'Flirting is a word much in vogue—' he complained bitterly, 'but I think jilting is the proper term'.[6]

The young Englishmen had a great advantage in Weimar since the girls all spoke excellent English and their mothers none at all. The opportunities for a *tête-à-tête* were thus unlimited. But it took the edge off any desire to learn German, and since most of the older generation chose to speak French, the language he had come to learn proved elusive. In these circumstances a good teacher was essential, and Thackeray, like many another young compatriot, was particularly lucky to come under the wing of Dr Friedrich Weissenborn, a gentle eccentric, who guided his young men's studies, took a fatherly interest in their lives, and was ready with financial aid in moments of desperate need—moments which Thackeray still regularly experienced, despite chastened, filial references to economic reform, and the limited temptations of simple Weimar.

Eighteen months and more after leaving the little state, he was still refunding the Doctor's loan, but that Weissenborn was in no hurry, and had marked well, and liked, the character of 'little Thackeray', is evident from a letter he wrote to another former pupil who had asked for Thackeray's address.

'If he have the organ of adhesiveness sufficiently developed for the occasion to keep him in the same house in the same city till now,' replied Weissenborn, 'he is still drawing both breath and caricatures at the Hotel Lille, Rue Richelieu . . . If you should write to him, remember me kindly to this old friend of ours.'[7]

Under Weissenborn's guidance, the German language 'opened' for Thackeray and he found it a pleasant thing to be able 'to roam (chained as yet to a dictionary it is true)' through German literature. He read *Faust*, and though fascinated was a good deal more shocked and not quite as delighted as he had expected to be.

It was the romantic Schiller who proved to be his hero, who, next to Shakespeare, he was to consider 'The Poet', and it was with enormous pride that he wrote to tell his mother that he was in possession of a sample of Schiller's handwriting and 'his veritable court-sword'.[8] This last item he added to his own startling court uniform, and later carried back to England where it hung on his study wall until the last years of his life.

As a melancholy lover, jilted by the two beauties of Weimar, he translated Schiller's tragic love poems:

> This world is empty
> This heart is dead
> It's hopes & its wishes
> For ever are fled[9]

and, on reading Shakespeare in German, thought how proud he would be to confer a similar benefit on his own country by giving it a complete translation of the German poet's works.

He began putting Mannert's history of Germany into English (an endeavour which would gain him the pious double advantage of learning the history while he improved his German), and thought of writing a travel book: one based more on the people of the country than the sights—a policy he was to follow when he actually did write travel books later in life. With a friend, he began a play in English on the life of William Tell, but 'in a moment of sobriety', they burnt it.

Many of his evenings were spent, with the other young Englishmen at Weimar, round the tea-table of Madame von Goethe, wife of the great man's reprobate and absent son, an eager Anglophile and student of letters. There they passed many hours, night after night, with talk and music, reading novels and poems in French, German and English. Thackeray, in turn, entertained his hostess's children with sketches and caricatures, some of which he was proud to be told had been looked at by Goethe himself—a massive presence constantly felt, though rarely seen.

At eighty-one, still writing as hard and drinking as copiously as he had done twenty years before, Goethe lived almost entirely in his own apartments, but his mind still ranged abroad, demanding information and taking a keen interest in all strangers. His daughter-in-law's coterie of young Englishmen sent him their newspapers and magazines from home, and hoped, with mixed fear and excitement, for the privilege of an audience with this giant whose shadow enveloped little Weimar and touched the farthest corners of the world. Thackeray was given nearly a month in which to anticipate this honour, and when the summons finally came his trepidation was suitably intense.

He found the 'Patriarch', a rosy-cheeked old man with a red ribbon in his buttonhole, standing in a small antechamber surrounded by antique casts and bas-reliefs, and, with *Faust* so freshly digested, immediately thought he recognized in his piercing, brilliant eyes the look of an individual who had 'made a bargain with a Certain Person, and at an extreme old age retained these eyes in all their awful splendour'[10]—an idea which did little to steady his already uncertain composure.

For half an hour, in French, which connoisseur Thackeray was at first astonished, then rather relieved, to find the great man spoke with 'not a good accent', Goethe asked his visitor questions about himself, and the awed nineteen-year-old stumbled through his replies as best he could, until they were interrupted by the arrival of the Grand Duke of Weimar, 'as silly a piece of Royalty as a man may meet.'[11]

Thackeray was inclined to think he had been treated very kindly and in a rather more 'distingué manner' than Goethe used for the other young Englishmen he saw, but when he was asked many years later if the meeting had not in fact been an awful experience, he answered: 'Yes, like a visit to the dentist.'[12]

'If Goethe is a god, I'm sure I'd rather go to the other place,' was to be his mature judgement on both the man and his works, and even before leaving Weimar, he had reluctantly come to the conclusion that, though a noble poet, he was in fact little better than an old rogue and libertine, and to regret that a man of such extraordinary genius should not be exempt from 'little mean money-getting propensities.'[13]

If Thackeray thought little of the reigning Duke of Weimar, he felt very differently about the Grand Duchess. She was a great favourite with all the young expatriates. She lent them her books, borrowed their own, and talked to them of their literary tastes and pursuits. Twice a week, they felt proud to pay her court as, in their splendid uniforms, they chartered sedan chairs and jogged to her palace.

To begin with Thackeray had thought it all absurdly ceremonious—a good way to rub off some of the 'rust' which school and university had given him, nothing more. But he was soon to become very fond of Weimar, and to look back on his time there as 'days of youth the most kindly and delightful.' When G. H. Lewes asked him to recall it twenty-five years later, for his life of Goethe, he did so with happy nostalgia. In the intervening years—spent in England, America and Europe—he had never, he said, seen a society more simple, charitable, courteous and gentlemanlike.[14]

Nevertheless, as Christmas drew near, Thackeray began to feel homesick and lonely. There was not a soul, he thought, in the whole of the dukedom who cared twopence if he stayed or went. He had already fallen in love with the only two possible candidates for his affection, and outworn the early interest of eager mamas who had seen in him, as they saw in all Englishmen, a wealthy contender for their daughters' hands. Slow to suspect the mercenary nature of the original welcome tendered by these 'respectable dowagers', Thackeray was deeply shocked when the truth dawned. Partly to see if such a scandalous suspicion could be true, partly to kindle again a little warmth at this season of goodwill, he hinted that he was heir to £15,000 a year.

'. . . the respect I received was wonderful,' he wrote home, 'but I have undeceived the natives, & am treated sans respect & ceremony.'[15]

It had, on the whole, proved a bitter experiment.

In restless discontent, he began to mull over his failures at school and Cambridge, and lashed out at his parents for their dissatisfaction with his endeavours, for the charges of idleness, irresolution and extravagance that seemed always to be levelled against him. Then, having deeply hurt them, he owned in contrition that the attack had been no more than an absurd and unkind attempt to put off the sense of his own unworthiness, and lay it at their door.

'I have been idle extravagant & ungrateful,' he groaned, 'thwarting as it were by a regular system, all the plans your superior affection & experience had formed for me.'[16]

But, as he added, he was young as yet, and there was time still for him to earn for himself a name, and for them satisfaction and confidence. Most of his wretchedness stemmed from this very problem of 'making a name'—of choosing a profession in which to make it: the terrible prospect of settling down.

The idea of becoming a diplomat, like Lettsom, had appealed for a time, but not for reasons guaranteed to stir his parents' hearts. Most of the diplomats he had met, he said, had been rich and idle; what could not a man with the incentive to get on achieve? Despite his claims of self-knowledge and reform, the Carmichael-Smyths would hardly have been human had they not doubted that incentive, and wondered if idleness and a competence might not prove the greater attraction.

The army was another possibility, but since there was no likelihood of war, Thackeray could see no prospect of advancement.

A clergyman he could not be, nor a physician. So it had to be the law. He knew it was the only career which suited him at all, but it would be such a long haul to get to the top. His youth would be spent poor and miserable; by the time he reached the pinnacle, his eyes would be too dim to see the prospect. The more he thought of it, the more his spirits quailed.

Encouraging letters from home eventually stiffened his resolve, and with something like determination he pronounced his own life sentence: he would read for the Bar; he would think of it not with despondency, but with gladness, and if he could only count on feeling the next day as he did on that, he would go to with a will and achieve a certain glory.

'I have been long eager to acquire this fame,' he told his mother, 'and my method has been an original one, lying on my sofa, reading novels, & dreaming of it—but there is yet time and may God grant me the means of properly employing it!'[17]

He was ready to put behind him the toys of childhood, and bend his thought towards home.

5

Journalism *v.* the Law

The heir manqué

In a state of suspense

Thackeray was admitted to the Middle Temple in the early summer of 1831, took chambers at 5 Essex Court, and began his law studies under Mr William Taprell, a special pleader with gloomy quarters at 1 Hare Court. From midday to five or six in the evening, he could be found sitting on a high stool, a 'wonderful Monster', perched high above ordinary-sized mortals, drawing up declarations with a thick volume of Chitty at his elbow; unenthusiastic still about his reluctantly chosen profession; proud to have the freedom of the ancient Inns of Court.

As he wandered the crooked passageways and tiny sunlit squares between Fleet Street and the Thames, his beloved eighteenth century strolled before him, and, as with Pendennis, it was peopled not with legal but with literary characters, fact and fiction merging into one. For him Dr Johnson rolled through the fog, 'with the Scotch gentleman at his heels', on his way once more to Nol Goldsmith's chambers in Brick Court; in Temple Garden, Sir Roger de Coverley and Mr Spectator surveyed the beauties in their hoops and patches as they sauntered over the grass; and Harry Fielding, hero supreme, sat in his rooms with ink-stained ruffles and a wet towel round his head, dashing off articles at midnight for the *Covent Garden Journal* while a printer's boy slept outside his door.

Even the law proved not quite so dry a study as feared when he was put onto an early case of debauchery, but such excitements were all too rare, and he soon came to the conclusion that a lawyer's preparatory education was 'one of the most cold blooded prejudiced pieces of invention that ever man was slave to . . . for a fellow sh^d properly do & think of nothing else than L.A.W.'[1]

Such singleness of purpose was beyond him and within weeks of making his first appearance at Mr Taprell's tall desk his old Cambridge friend, Edward FitzGerald, was staying at Essex Court with him, helping to dispel even the modest display of duty he had managed until then.

These two young men, both reticent in their relationships with most of their contemporaries, entered into a passionate friendship greater than either had known before. It came at a time, as Thackeray was to write many years later, before he had learned to love a woman, and appears to have been a heady meeting of thought and humour rather than the physical passion their abandoned expressions of devotion would indicate to later generations grown wary of expressing love for their own sex.

They continued their debates on Christianity, shared a deep delight in music, literature and art, and spent long hours imbibing 'fat chocolate', fragrant cigars, and the latest magazines in London's coffee houses and smoking divans. And, joy of all joys, they went to the theatre three nights a week.

The fervour stayed with them throughout the long summer vacation when, separated by half England, they spilled out their thoughts in long autobiographical letters. 'How happy you make me by telling me that you love me,' wrote Thackeray;[2] while FitzGerald, after his evening glass of port, the scudding Norfolk winds rattling his windows, the cockles of his heart warmed by thinking of his friend, set out his feelings in verse:

> I cared not for life: for true friend I had none
> I had heard 'twas a blessing not under the sun:
> Some figures called friends, hollow, proud, or cold-hearted
> Came to me like shadows—like shadows departed:
> But a day came that turned all my sorrows to glee
> When first I saw Willy, and Willy saw me! . . .[3]

It was long remembered by both of them as 'that immortal summer of foolscap', but with his Ned, his Yedward, his Teddibus there only in his heart and in his thoughts, young Willy soon surrounded himself with less worthy heroes from the past. After a brief visit to Larkbeare, where he tried to puzzle out why his mother aggravated him, and why he felt superior to her, when she could write much better letters and just as good poetry as himself, he escaped to Somerset to continue translating the German history he had begun in Weimar—'German my object bold resolve my guide.' There he found Schulte, who was soon to add to his undischarged debts by ordering clothes on credit from Thackeray's tailor, and the prime rascal of his Cambridge acquaintances, Henry Matthew, whose father was rector of the nearby village of Kilve.

Matthew had encountered some sad and trying experiences since their last meeting and come through them 'honourably'; 'he is improved in mind, & appearance for he does not look the rake he used', Thackeray told FitzGerald.[4] And so he went to stay with him, and celebrated his twentieth birthday in a fit of gloom, surrounded by unsavoury reminders of misspent youth; determined only in one thing—never to practise law.

In a belated thank-you to Madame von Goethe for her many kindnesses in Weimar, he set out the goal he really longed for. The theatre was still his 'rage', he told her, and he still aimed to write for it. But whether it would be a farce, a tragedy or a comedy, that he could not say; perhaps all three. In the meantime, he sent her some verses for her multi-lingual magazine, *Das Chaos*.

In December, his disapproving uncles had to sell stock so that he could pay off a 100-guinea gambling debt, and by the following spring his diary, begun to shame him into industry and thrift, contained very little law and much remorse. He was gambling regularly now; in his chambers with friends sometimes, more often in the gaming hells which flourished around Piccadilly and Regent Street. Number 60 Regent's Quadrant was a favourite haunt, and 'to 60 *for the last time, so help me God*' was a typical diary entry—as, inevitably, was the one which followed it:

'Took a lesson in dancing, & dined in chambers with Caldwell played ecartè [*sic*] till four o'clock in the morning & lost eight pound 7 shillings—before I knew where I was, so much for reform.'[5]

The day after that when he sent to Lubbocks, his bank, for more funds, he received his cheque back again. Major Carmichael-Smyth came to his rescue with £30, to last three months, and he promptly went out and bought himself a pair of boots. 'Segars' and theatre tickets were soon eating into the rest.

Before long he was noting down his gambling losses in German, just as Pepys had recorded his lecheries in honourable Latin. Some of his indiscretions will never be known, for busy fingers (most probably those of his eldest daughter) later snipped phrases and tore whole pages from his diaries.

In mid-April, Thackeray recorded that he hadn't been to Taprell's and hadn't read a word of law for three days: 'I must mend, or else I shall be poor idle & wicked most likely in a couple more years.'[6]

The following day he was negotiating backing for a bill: he was in the hands of the money-lenders and bill discounters, trapped in that mysterious labyrinth where bills were passed from hand to hand, making originally small debts high as a king's ransom; a disreputable maze which figures in so many Victorian novels, Thackeray's among them. Within a year, he had decided to join the vultures and was trading in bills himself, allying himself to a discounting firm in Birchin Lane and filling his account book with all the unsavoury details of usury.

He doesn't appear to have been ashamed of the connection, even writing to tell his mother that his 'Birchin Lane business' was in 'good condition'; and when his later rascal-hero, Barry Lyndon, was lured to his just reward, it was by being tempted with the prospect of a loan from a 'respectable firm in the city' with a 'counting-house in Birchin Lane.'

He knew that for him the only chance of resisting temptation was to stay well away from it, a policy he found easier to apply to anything—even love—than cards: when he began neglecting his law books to write poems for Charlotte Shakespear, sister of his small companion on the voyage home from India, even Thackeray recognized the danger signs. Asked to join a family trip to Paris, he told himself: 'it won't do—I sh^d fall in love with Charlotte before I got back', and, with considerable resolution, declined the invitation.

Desperately grasping for some permanent alternative to the law, he tried turning his poetry to profit, but could find no one willing to publish it. With his drawings he was more fortunate: a printseller in Great Newport Street agreed to take any number and split the proceeds. At last there was an outlet for the sketches which had over-spilled every drawer he had ever owned. A scene, a face at the theatre, a joke caught his imagination, he sketched it off, took it round to the printer, and there was his work in the window to be laughed at and admired by passers-by, just as he had laughed and lingered over the works of Cruikshank as a schoolboy.

No doubt one of the operatic *prima donnas* of the day met with this kind of celebrity, for when Thackeray heard her in *The Barber of Seville* he noted in his diary: 'Miss Inverarity sang charmingly but has a mouth big enough to sing two songs at once.' It was a thought which blossomed later in *The Ravenswing*:

'Larkins sing!' says the mother of one soprano of her daughter's rival. 'I'm sure she ought; her mouth is big enough to sing a duet.'

Thackeray's passion for the theatre never dimmed. If he were out of London for more than a few days he was wretched for the sight of a green baize curtain. 'O the delight of seeing the baize slowly ascending—' he wrote to FitzGerald, 'the spangled shoes w^h first appear then as it gradually Draws up legs stomachs heads'.[7] Christmastime, even when he was twenty, drew from him the trumpet cry: 'in a few days come the Pantomimes huzza.' The show didn't have to be good. It just had to be the theatre. In later life he asked a friend if he didn't also love 'the play'.

'Ye-es—I like a good play,' came the cautious reply.

'Oh! get out,' said Thackeray, 'I said *the* play; you don't even understand what I mean.'[8]

It was an addiction he had every opportunity to indulge. He already knew the actor Charles Kemble's scholarly eldest son, John, from Cambridge days; now he met John's younger brother, Henry, a nineteen-year-old Lothario, devastatingly handsome, deplorably extravagant, with the priceless additional asset of an entrée backstage.

Together, this pair of young bucks laughed at the eternal actors' scandals and squabbles, appraised the painted actresses from the proximity of the wings, and sauntered through costume departments, where reprobate Henry was dunned for waistcoats he'd had made and never paid for.

Thackeray's social life during these early years in London was split into three layers. Through his family he was welcome at a wide circle of prosperous Anglo-Indian houses. Major Carmichael-Smyth's sister and brother-in-law Colonel and Mrs Forrest, were especially kind, while his Uncle Frank Thackeray overdid the hospitality by asking him to dinner three times a week. And then there were the Ritchies, the Shakespears, the Pattles (with a series of ravishing daughters); and Dr Turner, of the Chiswick Mall school, who provided a constant supply of grandchildren for him to entertain with pantomime tricks.

Mrs Forrest became a particular favourite. He thought her good and kind, qualities he began to discover in most women as soon as he knew them well. 'I hope my ideas are all true,' he jotted in his diary. He didn't explain what these ideas were, but they were probably founded on the noble theory he expounded in *Pendennis* and *Philip*, that women were the purifiers of men, the givers of grace.

Like St Augustine, however, he was not ready to be purified quite yet, and spent much of his time with a very different set: gambling friends, like his neighbour in chambers, Caldwell, who introduced him to 'sporting men' of the style of Dick Blewitt in *The Amours of Mr. Deuceace*: hearty, swearing, singing, back-slapping fellows, ready to bet on anything and to relieve anyone of the money to keep them afloat.

Sandwiched between the middle-aged worthies and fast young men were a handful of more admirable contemporaries, men with brains as well as high spirits. They were to become the equivalent of his 'ripeners' at Charterhouse. Many of them he had known at

Cambridge, like Alfred Tennyson, now a struggling poet, also living in the Temple, and Arthur Hallam, the golden youth of the day, clever as he was beautiful. 'He was as near perfection as mortal man could be,' Tennyson mourned in later years, when Hallam's tragically early death had inspired his great poem, *In Memoriam*. Together, these three strode the streets of London, Tennyson, wild-haired and bony-faced, bursting with his latest creations, shouting out his favourite lines as they went.

'And see the great Achilles, whom we knew,' he roared, again and again, when he was wrestling with *Ulysses*.

Gangling Thackeray, at his side, delighted in the absurdity of the situation—in the implication that they had indeed made the acquaintance of that ancient gentleman, and were so proud of the fact they had to shout it to the world.[9]

Alexander Kinglake, another Cambridge friend, a neat little fellow shortly to tour the East and write *Eōthen*, was another of the coterie, as was Venables, his early nose-breaking adversary, who had already blighted his own life with a rashly unsuitable marriage—a tragedy Thackeray was to pass on to young Pen's mentor, George Warrington. Another Old Carthusian, Robert Curzon, later 14th Baron Zouche, a member of Parliament at twenty-one, was also re-encountered at this time, and got Thackeray into the House of Commons for the reading of the Reform Bill. Most important of all, he came to know the Bullers, Charles and Arthur, bright, clever, amusing, who could boast of having had Carlyle for a tutor.

Like Thackeray, many of them were reading law; all were eager to write or were already doing so; most were fascinated by politics.

With Arthur Buller and Kinglake, Thackeray dined one night at the Bedford in Covent Garden and then sallied forth to canvass for a most improbable cause: 'Percy & reform.' The Reform Bill was then threatening to bring Parliament, King William, and country top-pling to the ground, and 'Percy' was Hugh Percy, Duke of Nor-thumberland, a Tory landowner who epitomized resistance to reform of any kind.

'It was a silly prank,' Thackeray wrote in his diary, 'but has shown me how easy it is to talk men over.'[10]

Thackeray found the whole Buller family congenial. Charles, the eldest son, was already in Parliament, a brilliant speaker tipped for high office. He was also making money by writing for the magazines, an achievement Thackeray was determined to add to the other similarities between them: for Charles also had a broken nose, was 6ft. 3in. tall, and specialized in the same style of mocking humour.

His mother, a woman of great beauty, charm and wit who in her Calcutta youth had been wooed by Thackeray's father, fought dissatisfaction with her domestic role by being unconventional, in things both trivial and great. At one of her dinner parties Thackeray and Charles Buller were seated on either side of her, like two large, broken-nosed sentinels, while further down the table, her husband and the writer, Harriet Martineau, formed another pair—both were deaf and, since they were flanked by an unfilled seat and the softly-spoken John Stuart Mill, they were left to wield their ear-trumpets only at each other.

In a more dramatic stand against convention, she received Charles's mistress in her own home and adopted Arthur's illegitimate daughter, Theresa Reviss, a monstrous young woman. Though she was only in her early teens when Thackeray was writing *Vanity Fair*, many thought they saw traces of Theresa Reviss in Becky Sharp, and Pendennis's Blanche Amory, with her wiles and her *larmes*, was considered an even closer copy.

In April 1832, Thackeray added a fourth dimension to his social life: Fleet Street and the tavern revels of the gentlemen of the press. Since he could find no one to print his attempts at writing and reviewing, the young heir, still several months short of twenty-one, up to his broken nose in gambling debts, decided to buy a paper of his own. Negotiations were put in hand with a money man called Goldshede or Goldsched, and a shadowy Mr Gunnell.

After several days of feverish activity, the deal fell through and Gunnell disappeared, most probably with some of the purchasing money in his pocket since Thackeray spent several days scouring London for him. Before he went to ground, however, Gunnell had set up a meeting between Thackeray and the legendary Dr William Maginn, LL.D., Irish ex-schoolmaster, writer, roisterer, and editor of *Fraser's*, the magazine he had helped to found two years earlier, and to which Thackeray had already, unsuccessfully, submitted some poems.

'The Doctor', volatile and unprincipled, well advanced on a drunken path to squalid death in a debtors' jail, was notorious for his versatility. He would, it was said, write a leader for the respectable Tory *Standard* one evening, answer it in the liberal *True Sun* next morning, and abuse both pieces in pugnacious *John Bull* the following Sunday. He was a Grub-street writer in all but his considerable scholarship, and Thackeray fell for him immediately. '. . . hearty, witty Maginn,' he called him in his diary, '. . . a very loveable man I think.'

They matured their friendship over many a bottle of wine, while the Doctor initiated his eager disciple into the mysteries of the press and writing for it. He introduced him to the editor of the *Standard*, who showed him how a newspaper was put together, and to the artist Daniel Maclise, a young Irishman of dazzling charm, just making his own reputation with a series of sketches of literary men for *Fraser's*. He sketched Thackeray, too—though not for immediate publication—and the result showed a full-faced, thoughtful young man, pince-nez deployed like a monocle with one lens screwed negligently into his right eye, a pad on one knee, a pencil in his hand—the budding writer personified, and the fact that the pad was unused was not altogether untypical.

Other introductions were not so successful. James Fraser, proprietor of the much-admired magazine which, by coincidence, bore his name, turned out to be 'neither clever or good', and a night on the town with Maginn and his colleagues was another disillusionment: 'a dull party of low literary men.'

Maginn retained Thackeray's affection through countless disappointments and seamy revelations, and so did his raffish friend, Francis Sylvester Mahony, the unfrocked Jesuit priest who wrote under the name of 'Father Prout' and described himself as 'an Irish potato seasoned with Attic salt'—another son of Cork with a scholarly wit and a thirst for wine. But the rest of Maginn's tipsy Irish train were not to Thackeray's taste; and what these and other low-lifers of the press thought of a strapping amateur enthusiast, with public school manners and an aura of wealth, is not hard to imagine.

'When I first came up to London, as innocent as Monsieur Gil Blas,' Thackeray was to reminisce late in life, 'I also fell in with some pretty acquaintances, found my way into several caverns, and delivered my purse to more than one gallant gentleman of the road.'[11]

Maginn, for one, was soon to relieve him of £500, in between inspiring him with an enduring love of Homer, and leading him into a lair so sordid that even Thackeray had not ventured there before: a common brothel, where the chief attractions revealed themselves to be an old bawd and a repulsive young whore, both pregnant. Thackeray bolted, disgusted that Maginn should so disgrace himself, but still ready to excuse him with the thought that his financial pressures had made him reckless.

'Thank God that idle & vicious as I am, I have no taste for scenes such as that', Thackeray wrote in his diary.

Two days later, he fled the capital and threw up all pretence of studying law. Charles Buller was fighting an election in the family's seat of Liskeard, and Thackeray dashed down to Cornwall with brother Arthur to help him win. The month he spent there, at the Bullers' home at Polvellan, was balm to his soul: a month of sunshine and innocent indulgence, surrounded by the glory of Cornwall, and spiced with the thrill of electioneering.

He was still there on 18 July, his twenty-first birthday: the day for which, as he wrote in his diary, he had been panting so long. Gloomily introspective as always on these anniversaries which notched the unsatisfactory progress of his life, he found that this one, like the last, did not bring with it 'any sensations particularly pleasant'. But he was a man now, he decided, and must deal with men.

As a man, he drew on his bankers for £25, left 'dear little Polvellan & all the kind friends there', and crossed to the Isle of Wight for a few days with his mother and young cousin, Mary Graham, before boarding the packet for Le Havre and a long dreamed of voyage of adventure: to France, certainly; to Italy and Spain, perhaps—master of himself and a handsome fortune, all Europe at his command.

2.

Thackeray had plotted this first voyage of manhood during the 'immortal summer of foolscap.' FitzGerald was to have been his companion, and together they had planned to tramp the Continent with an old *calèche*, a horse or two, and an aged country servant. Thackeray had pictured them carrying their own bedding to foil the fleas, '3 brace of pistols each & a trusty Toledo to repel the attacks of brigands, likewise a pair of seven-league boots to run away if necessary.'[1] Recollect, he now told FitzGerald, reviving the old dream, 'I shall have money enough for us both of my own.'

But FitzGerald did not join him; the fleas flushed the solitary, bedless traveller from the romantic byways of Normandy into Paris; and he was followed from August to November by 'rowing' letters from his bank and bleak financial news from his mother. As soon as the young heir came into his money, the money evaporated.

For four months, while the financial clouds darkened, Thackeray played, determined that nothing should rob him of the life he had anticipated as master of his own property. The best of restaurants, the best of wine, the best and worst of theatres—and Frascati's—all had his custom. His winnings from the tables were soon burning like touch-paper in his pockets once more, and being chanced and lost before the flames could be subdued.

His usual *spielte*, meaning played or gambled, was now joined by another German word in his diary—*fegelte*. And *fegelte*, properly spelt *fögelte*, translates as a crisp little English word, also beginning with 'f' which can most politely be described as 'having sexual intercourse'. '. . . spielte und fegelte. . . . a very active day', he recorded not long after, groaning that he did not feel inclined to mention even in these private pages 'the expences and occurances' of his life in Paris.

In his quieter times, he devoured French literature with critical relish, sifting the themes and attitudes he would later use himself, and by chance met the great poet of Napoleon's day, Pierre Baour-Lormian, blind and old now, who called Thackeray 'le gros drôle d'Anglais', until he peered at the young man's caricatures of him, after which he refused to speak of him at all.

When he could squeeze money out of his bankers, he spent and lent it to friends—and remembered old debtors, like Dr Weissenborn of Weimar. When he had none, he took to calling hungrily on polite, well-victualled society. He lived as he had planned to live when he became a man; but he still felt guilty, a sensation he had hoped to escape once in control of his own affairs.

Indications that all was not well with his inheritance had come at the beginning of 1832, six months before that much panted-for twenty-first birthday. In a letter from India, Richmond Thackeray's sister, Augusta, had accused her nephew of failing to pay the annuity to his Eurasian half-sister, Mrs Blechynden, as he was bound to do under the terms of his father's will, and did so in a manner that caused as much anger as alarm in the Carmichael-Smyth household.

Thackeray, deciding to do nothing until he heard from Mrs Blechynden herself, took himself off to his favourite hostelry for the temporary solace of turtle soup and cold beef, and then wished the meal had choked him. '. . . there is poor Mrs Blechynden starving in India,' he wrote in his diary, 'whilst I am gorging in this unconscionable way here.'[2]

Like Colonel Newcome, he was a victim of the collapse of the great Indian banking houses. How much he lost is uncertain, but a wry joke in a letter to his mother probably supplies the figure. He was going to see pretty Theodosia Pattle, he said, and if only she had '£ 11325 in the 3 per cts' he would not hesitate above two minutes in popping the question which was to decide the happiness of his future life.

This oddly precise figure was almost certainly the missing patrimony—or part of it, for Thackeray was also to discover bungling and chicanery closer to home.

Just as he made use of his Indian misfortunes in *The Newcomes*, he told the more domestic particulars of his ruin in *The Adventures of Philip*. Philip Firmin, the hero of that story, is brought up to believe himself heir to his dead mother's fortune, but when he arrives at his majority the money is gone: one of the trustees has

carelessly signed a document, leaving Philip's swindling father free
to make use of the loot.

In Thackeray's own true-life story, the bungling trustee was the
Reverend Francis Thackeray—hospitable Uncle Frank—and Uncle
Robert Langslow, conveniently out of reach dispensing justice as
Attorney-General in Malta, was the wicked absconder. The two
uncles only administered a small portion of their nephew's money,
probably that amount not spent out of his income each year during
his minority, but on his twenty-first birthday Thackeray had been
expecting the acceptable sum of £4000, and in 'money & not stock as
we had supposed', as he told his mother. When he set off for France,
he had believed it needed only a power of attorney from Uncle
Langslow to release the cash into his waiting hands.

But two years later at least £700 of the £4000 was still unpaid, and
it was discovered that Mr Langslow had also made use of funds put
into his and Francis Thackeray's care for the two Shakespear boys.
Uncle Frank gamely offered to take in pupils and pay his nephew at
the rate of £150 a year, even though, as he made clear to his young
creditor, it would be with the greatest unwillingness, since neither he
nor his wife was fit enough to shoulder the extra burden.

Thackeray, however disappointed or close to destitution, was not
the man to agree to such a sacrifice. Even Langslow he could pity
rather than blame, and thirteen years later when this injudicious
gentleman was in public disgrace, suspended from office as Judge of
Colombo, Thackeray wrote to every influential man he knew in the
cause of his 'unfortunate relative'.

Eventually, he managed to salvage enough of his inheritance to
pay his mother and Mrs Blechynden their annuities and keep a little
for himself, a meagre portion which finally stabilized at £25 a
quarter. Both then and later, however, he was inclined to look upon
the disaster as a blessing. A few wretched hundreds of pounds a year
could numb a man's whole existence, he was to write in *Philip*. With
that modest competence, he saddled himself with home, family and
servants, lived up to the very edge of his income, had creditors upon
his estate as insatiable as any usurer, as hard as any bailiff: he was a
slave not a man.

Thackeray, like Philip, preferred independence and shabby boots
to such crimped respectability, and, with a year's experience of both,
wrote to his mother:

'I believe that I ought to thank heaven for making me poor, as it
has made me much happier than I should have been with the
money.'[3]

The truth was that by the time he came into his inheritance
Thackeray's tastes had outstripped even the substantial income he

would have had from the whole of his father's fortune. Most of his friends were rich or spendthrift; his interests lay in an expensive collector's delight in literature and art, and in a desire to burst upon the world as a fully wrought genius in one or the other. He could never curb his gambling while there was hope of paying his debts, no matter how guilty he felt. This, allied with a social conscience, which told him that a man in his fortunate position was expected to, and should want to, do something with his life, often made him a sadly melancholy young man, beset by 'blue devils', frustrated by his own lack of purpose.

With his inheritance, Thackeray might never have had the determination to defy social convention and enter permanently the disreputable world of the arts. The money gone, he experienced a blessed sense of freedom, and his family helped him to realize a dream they would only have fought before. With a gift from his grandmother, Mrs Butler of the chequered past, and backing from his stepfather, Thackeray set out once more to buy a newspaper, and this time succeeded. It was a modest publication, with a substantial title which embodied all his most cherished interests: *The National Standard of Literature, Science, Music, Theatricals, and the Fine Arts.*

The *National Standard* had been in existence only a few months when Thackeray took it over, and had got off to an inauspicious start in the hands of F.W.N. ('Alphabet') Bayley, a particularly low literary type. There were few in all Grub-street who waded in dirtier gutters than this former chief scavenger of scandal for *John Bull*, a man who modelled himself entirely on Dr Maginn, but came near to matching his master only in his capacity for drink.

Once again, Thackeray had stumbled on a pretty gallery of rogues, if his description, in *Lovel the Widower*, of Mr Batchelor's acquisition of a newspaper is based on his own experience. '. . . had I been Moses Primrose purchasing green spectacles, I could scarcely have been more taken in', he wrote in that story, and depicted Batchelor as the kind of dupe no self-respecting crook could be expected to resist.

Such knowledge, however, did not come immediately, and Thackeray set about relaunching the *National Standard* with confident enthusiasm. For his first number he composed a rallying address, announcing that though the paper still retained 'a host of literary talent', F. W. N. Bayley was no longer a part of it. 'We have got free of the Old Bailey, and changed the Governor.' Readers, he promised, would soon discover that 'the sort of Paper we shall give them for twopence is not to be despised.'[4]

The bulk of that 'host of literary talent' was supplied by

Thackeray himself, aided by a sub-editor, James Hume, and with advice available from Dr Maginn for the price of a loan and a bottle or two of claret. Thackeray, the novice editor, vastly enjoyed his new status. He spent his days at St Paul's Churchyard, where the *National Standard* was printed, and in the evening took his pleasure as befitted a literary man at the newly founded Garrick Club, among 'a pleasant enough society—of artistes of all kinds, & gentlemen who drop their absurd aristocratical notions.'[5]

One of his first acts as a clubman was to join the lobby for a smoking-room, a refuge which was to prove one of the greatest comforts of his life. Like his creation, Fitz-Boodle, Thackeray had a passion for cigars and many a time, after dining at a house with a taboo on that 'gentle stimulant', the 'kindly weed', he was to flee the cruel embargo as soon as decently possible to end his night in contented indulgence in that smoke-filled haven of the 'dear, little G'.

On one occasion, during his famous years, he had already set his escape in motion, standing up as soon as dinner was done, murmuring his apologies—the importance of 'a particular engagement'—when his host's brother, disappointed at losing such an entertaining guest so early in the evening, asked, what, wouldn't he even stay for a cigar?

'A cigar?' said Thackeray, immediately brightening. 'Oh, they smoke here, do they? Well, to tell you the truth, that *was* my engagement.'[6]

All through 1833 Thackeray was involved with his Birchin Lane bill-discounting firm, and continued to add to his purse by dashing off caricatures for the printsellers, but for the first two months of newspaper ownership, the *National Standard* was the great focus of his life. He wrote, drew, drummed up business, and did a fine scissors-and-paste job in the interests of the new concern, peppering his letters with phrases such as 'les affaires!' and finding himself wanting to end every sentence, even in private correspondence, with a 'pert critical point.'

All in all, he behaved very much as did Mr Batchelor with his new toy:

'I daresay I gave myself airs as editor of that confounded *Museum*, and proposed to educate the public taste, to diffuse morality and sound literature throughout the nation, and to pocket a liberal salary in return for my services. I daresay I printed my own sonnets, my own tragedy, my own verses (to a Being who shall be nameless, but whose conduct has caused a faithful heart to bleed not a little). I daresay I wrote satirical articles, in which I piqued myself upon the fineness of my wit, and criticisms, got up for the nonce, out of encyclopaedias and biographical dictionaries; so that I would be actually astounded at my own knowledge. I daresay I made a gaby of myself to the world.'[7]

It was all most valuable experience. Thackeray never was, nor ever could be, a good editor. Constitutionally, he had none of the tough, businesslike qualities necessary for the job, but the *National Standard* gave him practice in the craft he would one day excel in above all others—the simple, fluid use of the English language. The newspaper was there, it had to be filled each week: there was no time now for leisurely labouring over high-style literature which might never see the light of day. Like Pendennis, he became a reasonably reliable hack, 'naturally fast in pace, and brilliant in action'. And like Pendennis he discovered that the trick, once acquired, quickly lost its invigorating glamour.

Within a very short time of installing himself in his London office, the editor of the *National Standard* needed new stimulus. He took off for France, optimistically planning to gather enough material in a few weeks to furnish a column for ten months. It looked well, he told his proprietors—the Major and Mrs Carmichael-Smyth—to have 'a Parisian correspondent.'

More ominously he confided that he was seriously thinking of turning artist. Since he could draw better than he could do anything else, and liked it better than any other occupation, why shouldn't he? he asked. To be sure it would mean a three-year apprenticeship, which would not be agreeable, but after that the way would be clear and enjoyable—doubly so for an independent man who was not obliged to look to his brush for his livelihood. There was still just money enough left in the family kitty for him to be tempted into ease and pleasure.

Thackeray returned to London, but not for long. It was grey, miserable and destitute of female companionship, he complained—a dismal verdict which may have had something to do with the recent marriage of his pretty young cousin, Charlotte Shakespear. By the end of October he appeared to be reconciled to journalistic work again, sending his mother an unusually rosy report on the paper's progress and its likelihood of providing a pleasant occupation and income, but he was reporting from an artist's *atelier* in Paris, surrounded by wild, impoverished painters—the happiest fellows in the world.

A few weeks later he was back in a choking London fog trying to recover a £100 loan from an old gambling friend thought to be on his deathbed, and stayed on to administer the last rites to his ailing paper.

The *National Standard of Literature, Science, Music, Theatricals and the Fine Arts* had never really been a feasible proposition, but for the next three months Thackeray worked hard to keep it alive. In the new year he shortened its name to the *Literary Standard*, increased the price to threepence, and supplied a particularly rich bill of fare, most of it written and drawn by himself while sub-editor Hume went off to the country for Christmas. In the previous two months he had gained only twenty new readers, and was forced to admit that if the face-lift failed, it would be better to cut his losses of around £200 and close down. Which was what, at the end of January, he did.

Most of Thackeray's contributions were ephemeral, day-to-day journalism, but some of his stories, mostly free translations from the French, have lived on, and one of them in particular—an amusingly cynical piece called *The Devil's Wager*—shows strong indications of the unique talent which was to blossom in adversity.

The paper's greatest benefit was that it provided him with a literary apprenticeship recognized by the people who would be in a position to give him employment a few years later when work was no longer a matter of choice. Before the last issue appeared, Maginn's friend, the editor of the more weighty daily *Standard*, asked him to become his Madrid correspondent with a salary of £300 a year, and though Thackeray turned down the job, it was to give him confidence when he finally sorted out his twin ambitions and settled permanently for writing.

6
Isabella Shawe
Portrait of an artist in love

Thackeray, newspaper editor, now turned his hat round and became Thackeray, student artist. When Colonel Newcome allowed his son, Clive, to take up the same extraordinary calling, that old stickler for the proprieties, Major Pendennis, summed up respectable feeling with a fine bellow: 'I don't know what the dooce the world is coming to. An Artist! By gad, in my time a fellow would as soon have thought of making his son a hair-dresser, or a pastry cook, by gad!'

From Thackeray's description of young Clive's introduction to student life at Mr Gandish's Soho academy, it seems that he too began his serious studies in London, under Henry Sass of Charlotte Street, an excellent teacher with Millais and Frith to his later credit, but, like Gandish, unsuccessful with his own paintings and noisily despairing of a world which refused to acknowledge the genius of his massive historical canvases—to give patronage to ''igh art', as Gandish would have put it.

For Thackeray, painting was always the supreme accomplishment. The 'happy mixture of hand and head work' appealed to him immensely, and since he had been born with considerable natural talent, he embarked on the course towards professional perfection with easy confidence—and a pair of splendid artistical moustachios which, in due course, as perfection eluded him, appeared in many a melancholy self-portrait, one of which was to bear the sombre caption: 'Portrait of that eminent Artist drawn by himself an hour before his suicide.—& dedicated to his inconsolable creditors.'

Other painters, however, he unfailingly described as the merriest and most sanguine of fellows, and during this period in London he made friendships among them that were to remain for life. But even now he wasn't entirely satisfied. Paris, to his mind, was the only place to study art properly, and he could marshal a great many arguments to prove the point, from the superior social position of the artist in France, to the low cost of tuition (£10 a year), and the incomparable benefit of being allowed to copy great masterpieces in the Louvre, a privilege granted only reluctantly and with miserly restrictions by London's new National Gallery.

The Parisian art student, he was later to write, might sleep in a garret and dine in a cellar, but what a drawing-room he had!—the great gallery of a palace such as all the money of all the Rothschilds could not buy; a room half a mile long, its walls decorated by 'Paul Veronese, or a hundred yards of Rubens.'[1]

Thackeray got his wish, though not in quite the manner he had envisaged. In the autumn of 1834, his roving grandmother, a widow once more, decided to sample life in the French capital, and her grandson was invited to accompany her—as courier and factotum, leg-man and whipping boy . . . and, way down the list, as student of art. Mrs Butler paid him a small stipend, and treated him as abominably as she used her wretched female companion, 'Arriet' Langford, a lady Thackeray described as 'a snob of the first water', who 'puts rouge on her cheeks, & sports little bits of sticking plaster on her countenance not to cover her pimples but to haggravate her beauty.'[2]

This oddly assorted trio settled into a boarding house in the rue Louis le Grand, where Thackeray writhed so under the stripes of his grandmother's sarcasm and the public expression of her wrath that it became a positive pleasure to launch himself on his studies and escape to a crowded studio or that luxurious living-room at the Louvre—to copy Titian, de Hoog and Leonardo.

Several years later, in *The Paris Sketch Book*, he was to describe the typical Parisian *atelier* as cloudy with tobacco-smoke and resounding with a din of puns, choice French slang and a roar of bawdy choruses—'the easiest, merriest, dirtiest existence possible.' It is a fine, man-of-the-world account, recollected through the tolerant haze of time. And it contrasts very nicely with a diary entry written immediately after his first life class at the studio of yet another painter of heroic, historical subjects, the sixty-year-old Charles Nicolas Rafael Lafond:

'The conduct of the model, a pretty little woman, the men & the master of the establishment was about as disgusting as possible—The girl w^d not pose but instead sung songs & cut capers; the men from sixty to sixteen seemed to be in habits of perfect familiarity with the model; and Lafond himself a venerable man with a riband of honour maintained a complete superiority by the extreme bathos of his blackguardism . . . It is no wonder that the French are such poor painters with all this—'[3]

At twenty-three, Thackeray could still be shocked—and homesick for the more phlegmatically merry companions he had left behind in England, as he discovered when a great batch of letters arrived from them the following Easter, warm-hearted messages written under the influence of whisky-and-water in a tavern at Lord's.

Maclise, son of a Cork shoemaker, sounded exactly as he remembered him: mad, Irish, a little tipsy, but infinitely kind. George Cattermole, the water-colourist who had been exhibiting at the Royal Academy since the age of nineteen, lived up to his reputation as illustrator of the Waverley novels and wrote as he spoke, full of unconscious 'Walter Scottisms'. While Frank Stone's short, hearty note, written in a round, clerk-like hand, was as bluff as the honest, down-to-earth son of a Manchester cotton-spinner himself.

It did him good to think that he could count on the affection of such friends, none of them with the advantages he had had, yet all making their way in the world already. Of Frank Stone, he jotted in his diary: 'I am sure this man would serve me in a pinch, though I know him the least of the 3', and it was to solid Frank Stone that he unburdened his heart:

'God bless all the boys and watch over the liquors they drink and the pictures they draw. As for myself—I am in a state of despair—I have got enough torn-up pictures to roast an ox by—the sun riseth upon my efforts and goeth down on my failures, and I have become latterly so disgusted with myself and art and everything belonging to it, that for a month past I have been lying on sofas reading novels, and never touching a pencil.

'In these six months, I had not done a thing worth looking at. O God, when will Thy light enable my fingers to work, and my colours to shine? . . . I wish you would tell me how you used to make that nice *grain*. I have tried all ways in vain . . .'[4]

Thackeray had another reason for sombre reflection—a shadow which came suddenly out of the past and as swiftly departed, leaving him to think: there but for the grace of God . . . The substance of the shadow was a fellow Carthusian, a swaggering blackguard as a schoolboy, now a blackguard down on his luck. Thackeray described their Paris encounter and what followed in a stark moral tale called *A Gambler's Death*.

His old schoolfellow—Jack Attwood he called him—dirty, shabby, his circumstances obvious for all to read in the elbows jutting out of a once-smart frock-coat, accosted him one evening in a café noted for its Holland gin. Under the influence of that beverage, Thackeray gave up a vital £5 note for a dubious I.O.U., and woke next morning to anguished despair when he discovered the chit in his pocket. He was still wondering how he would survive the next two months when in burst Attwood, strangely flushed, with handfuls and pocketfuls of gold, silver and greasy banknotes: £500 won at the gaming tables with Thackeray's money for the stake.

'. . . the passion of envy entered my soul,' wrote Thackeray. 'I felt far more anxious now than before, although starvation was then staring me in the face; I hated Attwood for *cheating* me out of all this wealth.'

For some time Attwood's luck held. He spent, gambled, and won enough to spend and gamble again. He spread his good fortune among his friends and lived like a gentleman once more—albeit like a gentleman of the Macheath school. But, inevitably, there came a day when the last napoleon was gone, and Attwood, rather than face renewed poverty, shot himself.

His friends found him, in a garret of the house in which in his affluence he had rented the most handsome apartments, clothed in his only possession—a fine lawn shirt, held back from the pawn-brokers to serve as a shroud.

Attwood's three fellow English revellers, who had benefited from his last success, kept a drunken wake for their friend before seeing him nailed into a paltry coffin and buried at the expense of the *arrondissement*—a raffish band so reeking of cigars and brandy that they scared the unfortunate parson.

In Thackeray's story, the mourners finished the funeral day 'royally at Frascati's', but his own gambling it seems had ended. He kept a brief, spasmodic diary during these months in Paris, and there is not one entry which refers to his old obsession.

His days of vacillating over a career, however, were not yet past. Embarked as he was on the study of art, and finding instant fame as far beyond his grasp as ever, his thoughts returned to writing, and when, through Eyre Evans Crowe, Paris correspondent of the London *Morning Chronicle*, he learned that the paper was planning to send a man to Constantinople, he made strenuous efforts to get the job. The East was becoming fashionable, and quite apart from enjoying the *Chronicle*'s generous salary, he could visualize filling his sketchbook and publishing a 'Picturesque Annual' on his return; 'it would be a grand piece of good luck', he told FitzGerald; but, like his 'ten thousand other hopes', this too turned out to be 'humbug'.

Money was now becoming a serious preoccupation. Having endured the 'wonderful eloquence and ingenuity' of his grandmother's complaining tongue for a year he had finally rebelled, thrown up her allowance, and taken himself off to humble, bachelor quarters in the ironically named rue des Beaux Arts. He had made the break as gently as he could, he told his mother, and he and his grandmother were the better friends for it. ('She comes to see me very often—and I walk stoutly up three times a week to be scolded.'[5]) But doctors' bills after a mild bout of fever and a mad accident—falling off a donkey on an excursion with Anthony Trollope's brother, Tom—turned it into a precarious time financially, and he was soon fearing that his modest remnant of capital would not be long in joining the rest of his inheritance.

Tantalizingly, he had had a good offer of work from a French publisher, but it was for views of cities, a subject so far removed from his natural talent for caricature that he tackled it with something near despair:

'I have made five drawings of one place here in Paris,' he wrote home, 'and cut them up one after another for they were too bad to show him, these repeated disappointments make me ready to hang myself. in fact I am as thoroughly disheartened as a man need be—for I can do nothing—and yet I know I have got the stuff to make as good a painter as the very best of them.'[6]

As always when the course of duty proved too daunting, he lost himself in books, devouring a rich mixture of history, novels and politics, French and English, and in the theatres, haunting them now with an ex-Cambridge friend, John Bowes Bowes, who was even wilder for the stage than himself.

The illegitimate son of the tenth Earl of Strathmore, Bowes was an exceptionally wealthy young man, already a Member of Parliament, and consumed by two great passions: horse racing, which in 1835 brought him the first of four Derby wins and the title 'the luckiest man on the turf'; and the theatre, which was soon to lead him into managing a dingy Parisian house of varieties. As a child, he had been the centre of a great legal *cause célèbre*, his father, on his deathbed, having tried to make him legitimate under Scottish law by marrying the by then nine-year-old boy's mother, a belated tidying-up of affairs hotly contested by other members of the Strathmore family, and eventually disallowed by the courts. Bowes was granted only his father's Durham and Yorkshire properties, Streatlam Castle and Gibside Park, but even this fragment of the estate amounted to forty thousand acres and brought in an annual income of some £20,000.

He was a generous friend to Thackeray, feeding him in his Paris penury, paying for him to have his first book printed, and talking, talking, talking with him about the theatre, even when the two of them didn't actually attend the show.

Despite his artistic disappointments, Thackeray in later years looked back on this time as one of the happiest of his life, and invariably referred to the lotus-eating land of Bohemia as the pleasantest in the world. Like Philip Firmin, he learned to eat his dinners in seventeen-sous cafés, and to make merry over small beer and *caporal* tobacco while friends, such as August Stevens, an artful English dentist pulling teeth in Paris, greeted the dawn with a thunderous chorus of the German student song, *King Death*. But he seems to have made few lasting friends among his fellow art students—those wondrously bearded, outlandishly dressed, swaggering young men he was to describe so affectionately in the *Paris Sketch Book*—and he never completely relinquished his passport to the respectable world beyond Bohemia's borders.

Probably through Bowes, he had the *entrée* to at least one elegant Parisian literary salon, where he was later remembered for his height and his drollery, and was a regular visitor to such polite entertainments as the weekly musical *soirées* of Mrs Crowe, wife of the *Morning Chronicle* correspondent. It was most probably round the piano in Mrs Crowe's drawing-room that he first met Isabella Shawe, daughter of an Indian army colonel, and the 'gal of his art'.

2.

For several years Thackeray had been ripe for marriage. During his twenty-first birthday trip to France, he had found himself 'growing loving on every pleasant married woman' he met, and, after discussing 'debauchery & it's consequences' with some other young scapegraces, sighed for the salvation of a good wife and a happy home. Then, as his inheritance slipped away, he began, like Pendennis, to flirt with the idea of marrying for money, a scheme that seemed doubly sensible when he saw some of his 'ancient flames', and wondered how he could ever have been smitten by them.

'Now this would be an awkward circumstance in marrying a wife,' he suggested to his mother, 'it will be better I think not to be in love with her at all—only to have a kind of respect & esteem for the sharer of one's couch, & the payer of the baker's bills.'[1]

But as with many another cool theoretician, when Thackeray fell in love and determined on matrimony, it was his heart and not his head which ruled the business.

Isabella Shawe, the object of his desire, was small and shy. She had unfashionably red hair, no money, and a Gorgon of a mother.

Henry Reeve, an English friend ·who saw a good deal of Thackeray—'that excellent and facetious being'—in Paris at this time, described her as 'a nice, simple, girlish girl.'[2] She had a well-trained, sweet and true singing voice, and a small, carefully rehearsed repertoire of operatic arias, which delighted Thackeray and provided welcome relief from the great mass of drawing-room entertainment.

But apart from that, Thackeray's must have been an infatuation which had most of his friends shaking their heads and asking what he could see in the girl. And those who had the honour of an introduction to the loved one's mama no doubt echoed Philip Firmin's well-wishers when they cried: ye powers! what a mother-in-law the poor fellow was laying up for his future days.

For Mrs Shawe was a long-faced, long-nosed lady, soured by circumstance. Her husband, an officer of conspicuous gallantry, had died in the East, blessedly discharged after twelve years of marriage, leaving his widow with five children, a life interest in his small estate, and a pension of £80 a year. Having enjoyed a prosperous Irish childhood, and the rank of Lieutenant-Colonel's lady, Mrs Shawe was now reduced to envious, penny-pinching gentility in a Paris boarding house, one of hundreds of ex-officers' widows eking out an existence in the French capital. She was Irish: not generous, gregarious Irish; but bigoted, boastful, and vindictive. 'A singular old deevil', who 'talks as big as Sr Paul's', Thackeray called her, and wreaked vengeance on her a thousand-fold in a whole catalogue of horrifying fictional mothers-in-law.

Isabella, the second child and older daughter of this horror, had mercifully inherited neither her mother's looks nor her disposition, but even she had faults which Thackeray, having fallen quite besottedly in love, set out to rectify.

She was lazy, he told her, stayed in bed too long of a morning, never wrote letters and was cold and undemonstrative. Though she prattled away to her sister, she was stilted with him. He asked her repeatedly if she loved him, and she answered yes only one time in ten. She was thin and unwell when he wanted her fat and happy. From a few indelicate references in his letters to her, it seems she was constipated and wouldn't take his advice on appropriate treatment. Above all, having chosen a timid, over-protected eighteen-year-old, he told her he wanted 'not a thoughtless, frivolous girl, but a wise & affectionate woman'.

Two of Thackeray's stories, one written early and the other later in his life—each with an Isabella-type for heroine—give the key to this equivocal obsession. In the later one, *Lovel the Widower*, he describes the young, wistful Elizabeth Prior as 'a thin, freckled girl of fifteen, with a lean frock, and hair of reddish hue .. . . a tawny-haired filly of a girl, with great eyes.' The one good character in an odious, bullying family, there is a look of desperation in those large eyes, which shakes the love-crossed Mr Batchelor out of his own morbid preoccupations and into protective action.

Caroline, in the *Shabby Genteel Story*, arouses the same masculine instincts:

'But look, I pray you, at an innocent, bashful girl of sixteen: if she be but good, she must be pretty. She is a woman now, but a girl still. How delightful all her ways are! How exquisite her instinctive grace! All the arts of all the Cleopatras are not so captivating as her nature. Who can resist her confiding simplicity, or fail to be touched and conquered by her gentle appeal to protection?'

Both heroines were extremely young, uneducated and with no material advantages. Isabella Shawe, though older in years, was child-like in manner; she was also rather better educated. But all three offered a champion the combined excitements of Pygmalion and the traditional knight in shining armour riding to rescue a pure young virgin and waken her with a kiss to passionate devotion and happiness ever after. In his own case, Thackeray had even found himself a dragon to slaughter first.

He was later to understand this big-strong-man/small-frail-woman attraction very well indeed, and to smile at his own preference for ladies of a 'milk-&-water' disposition, with 'just enough sense to be agreeable.' Most men are Turks, as he wrote often in his books, and like a little subjugation. But at twenty-four, all Thackeray knew was that he was madly, crazily, dizzily in love.

In a letter to his Aunt Ritchie's eldest son, William, ostensibly written to give the young man advice for his first term at Cambridge, he poured out his plight:

'I am arrived at such a pitch of sentimentality (for a girl without a penny in the world) that my whole seyn, etre, or being, is bouleversé or capsized—I sleep not neither do I eat, only smoke a little and build castles in the clouds; thinking all day of the propriety of a sixième, boiled beef and soup for dinner, and possession of the gal of my art.'

He did manage to warn: 'My dear fellow, in the name of the Saints, of your mother, of your amiable family, and the unfortunate cousin who writes this—keep yrself out of DEBT'—but it was his own fascinating condition that interested him most.

'God knows how it will end, I will, if I can, bolt before I have committed myself for better for worser', he sighed. 'But I don't think that I shall have the power . . . like the foolish fascinated moth I flickers round the candle of my love.'[3]

He haunted Isabella's boarding house, endured her mother's Indian garrison stories and mean, self-righteous monologues, courted and bribed her young brothers, turned down the banquets of visiting swells—and cast prudish eyes at their dubious female companions—all for the love of this pure, good maid, and the chance of a *tête-à-tête* in a crowded salon.

Looking back, with the amused clear-sightedness of age, he saw himself as brash and overbearing in his rapture: wreathed in cigar-smoke, shabby as to shoes and dress; gentle to those he liked, swaggering and disrespectful to those he did not; loud in his laughter, revelling in his poverty. A youth at ease with himself, and insufferable to much of the world.

When Mrs Carmichael-Smyth arrived on the scene towards the end of the summer, it was to find her son already far gone in this infatuation. She met Isabella (and, no doubt, her formidable parent), gave the love-sick moth a few francs to stay away from the flame for at least a day, and planned a tour of distraction. But not all the bribes, nor all the travels in the world could cool this ardour, and when it became clear that in his love, as in nothing else in his life, Thackeray was determined to succeed, both she and the Major set about finding him a job which would enable him to marry.

In despair over his slow progress in art, Thackeray had turned again to writing, and while he earned a little money in Paris editing an obscure English-language paper in optimistic rivalry to *Galignani's Messenger*, the Major seized the chance of helping to found a new militantly radical newspaper in London, largely to secure one of the foreign correspondents' jobs for his stepson. A company was formed, with the Major as chief proprietor and chairman, a dying newspaper bought and rechristened, and in the spring of 1836 Thackeray prepared to cross the Channel to assist in the launching of the enterprise: *The Constitutional*—and the idea of a daily *Constitutional* sounds remarkably like one of Thackeray's own terrible puns.

He left Paris confident that his love was returned. Isabella had agreed to marry him as soon as he had money enough to support them: indeed, after their 'second quarrel', they had decided they were already 'bound together & married before God'.[4] Mrs Shawe allowed him to spend his last days in France with her and her family at Chaillot, and either sanctioned the engagement or indicated that the lovers might hope for this grim blessing when the livelihood materialized.

If she withheld complete approval, her caution was understandable. A novice writer or artist—or even both combined into one large package—could never have been seen as an ideal suitor, and now even Thackeray's parents were hazarding the remnants of their fortune in a risky newspaper venture. The Major, with money in the last of the Indian banking houses to fail, had stayed doggedly loyal, like Colonel Newcome, even after his stepson's losses, and had almost certainly been caught in the disaster. Larkbeare was given up, and when Thackeray joined his family for stirring days of newspaper activity it was at 18 Albion Street, a newly mortgaged terrace house, not quite on the rim of London's Hyde Park—nouveau Tyburnia.

The returning prodigal was fussed over by Mrs Carmichael-Smyth, graciously received by Mrs Butler, and fêted by Mary Graham, who, in the belief that 'all the world' would want to see him, dispatched fifty invitations to 'a grand tea party and hop'. When he ventured outside this pampered feminine cocoon, the welcome was almost as balmy.

Even people whom he had imagined didn't care a straw for him had met him with the greatest cordiality and kindness, he told Isabella, his 'Puss', his 'dear Trot', in long, journal letters to this 'dearest little Wife', whose 'little red-polled ghost' pursued him everywhere, the phantom of whose songs was for ever in his ears.

In return for these outpourings of the soul, Thackeray received from Paris a bleak little half-page once a week which told him scarcely anything at all.

By return of post he complained and cajoled, but at the same time publicly blazoned abroad the virtues of his loved one and the news of his impending marriage, aided by 'the greatest scandal monger in Europe', Francis ('Father Prout') Mahoney, the unfrocked Jesuit priest. As a prelude to the coming alliance, Isabella's uncle, Colonel Merrick Shawe, was entertained to dinner at Albion Street, and proved a welcome contrast to his half-brother's widow.

A bachelor club-man, Merrick Shawe had earned a comfortable niche for himself amongst the highest in the land. In his youth he had been a polished, prudent and resourceful officer on the Duke of York's staff. Later, he had progressed from aide-de-camp to secretary to confidential friend to the Marquis Wellesley during his rule both in India and Ireland, and still performed discreet services for that septuagenarian philanderer and his brother, the Duke of Wellington. There is little doubt that a decade later he provided much of the inspiration for Pendennis's 'selfish old Mentor', Major Pendennis,[5] but at twenty-five Thackeray saw this sixty-year-old worldling as 'a dear old gentleman . . . so good so honest', and so fond of his niece, Isabella, that he completely won her suitor's heart.

And, 'of course as you may suppose,' Thackeray told Miss Shawe, 'I was very kind to him.'

To indulge in more talk of his dear Puss, he haunted the Knightsbridge home of Irish journalist Edward Sterling and his family, great friends of the Shawes and already known to Thackeray through his Cambridge contemporary, John Sterling, a son of the house. Kindly Mrs Sterling had already been busy among their acquaintances, describing Isabella in the most affectionate terms.

'Why don't you write to her, Pussy?' Thackeray asked. 'It is a great blessing to have such good friends, and a great folly to lose them for the sake of a little indolence.'[6]

Thackeray himself had never been so energetic. Albion Street vibrated with newspaper bustle: the Major, bursting out as an orator, privately bombarded his family with political pyrotechnics, and publicly addressed rousing words to shareholders' meetings and dinners; Mrs Carmichael-Smyth raised funds with radical fervour; and Thackeray, spurred by thoughts of matrimony, whirled into action at any opportunity to further the paper's prospects—or his own.

He had arrived in London just in time to see his first publication off the presses, and to turn his hand to publicizing it. Financed by John Bowes Bowes, and appropriately reflecting his and Thackeray's passion for the theatre, it was a slim folio of satirical ballet sketches showing the public and private life of *Flore et Zéphyr*—Flore, a sadly overblown blossom, and Zéphyr a very windy old practitioner indeed. 'Théophile Wagstaff' was given credit for the designs, and while M. Wagstaff, alias W. M. Thackeray, felt obliged to remain modestly silent as to their merits, he saw no reason why his friends should be so reticent. His smiling little rogue of a publisher was stirred into sending copies to every old acquaintance with influence over the review columns, and Thackeray made sure that each was accompanied by a personally tailored 'puff-provoker'.

His artistic ambitions also flared again when he heard that the illustrator of *The Pickwick Papers* had committed suicide with his work only just begun. Thackeray had never met Dickens, but fortified by the success of his *Flore et Zéphyr* campaign, he bearded him at Furnival's Inn and asked to be allowed to finish the job. Dickens, six months his junior and already enviably famous, looked at a sample of his sketches and was not sufficiently impressed.

George Cruikshank, Thackeray's great boyhood hero, a friend since *National Standard* days, and that rare being, a jovial militant teetotaller, was to diagnose the chief cause of Thackeray's failure to excel as an artist as lack of patience.

'I used to tell him,' Cruikshank liked to recall in later years, 'that to be an artist was to burrow along like a mole, heaving up a little mound here and there for a long distance.'

To which Thackeray had inevitably replied that he thought he would presently break out into quite a different element and stay there.[7]

That other element, in the form of the *Constitutional*, was also demanding patience. After the first surge of enthusiasm, capital was proving elusive. However, the list of 'nominal subscribers' flourished; the leading radicals in Parliament promised their active support; and one of them, Sir William Molesworth, a rich young baronet whose 'infidel and radical opinions' had caused several outraged fathers to refuse their daughters to him in marriage, had actually taken shares. Even Lord Melbourne's Whig government was to give timely encouragement by lifting the oppressive taxes on newspapers and granting them free passage through the mails.

Versatile Laman Blanchard was signed on as editor; Douglas Jerrold, who was later to have many an argument with Thackeray across the *Punch* table, was to be drama critic; Charles Buller agreed to write the leaders; and Thackeray—Thackeray was appointed Paris correspondent with a salary of £450 a year, a most handsome sum, due in part to the Major's generosity in forfeiting his own £200-a-year director's fee.

Marriage was now a certainty, thought Thackeray, as he wrote to warn Isabella to make ready her little shifts and pretty nightcaps. But Mrs Shawe was of a different opinion. Almost immediately word came back across the Channel that she proposed moving forthwith from Paris to Brussels—with both her daughters.

'I grieve, but can say nothing,' Thackeray told his Puss, 'only some fine morning I must come & fetch you to a snug apartment in Paris with a spare bedroom, w^h please God your Mother will occupy often & long.'[8]

The judiciously pious desire to entertain Mrs Shawe was the result of grim experience, gained when Thackeray had attempted to instruct Isabella in the course of wifely duty. He was worried that she appeared to have given no thought to the change in condition and sentiments that matrimony would demand of her. While there was no chance of an early marriage, he agreed that she had probably been wise not to do so, but as soon as his job with the paper was assured he urged her, in a tender, wise and loving letter, to prepare her mind as well as her wedding clothes.

Was she ready to give up her home, her sisterly bedfellow, and her mother, he asked, 'to share the fate of a sulky grey headed old fellow with a small income, & a broken nose?'

That Mrs Shawe was outraged by these suggestions was clear from Isabella's reply, and Thackeray's next letter found him asking:

'What in God's name have I been saying to hurt you (for I see you are hurt) and your Mother?'

Accustomed to speaking freely all his life, he then spelt out with undiplomatic clarity exactly what he had meant, in terms which Mrs Shawe would have found no difficulty in labelling coarse and vulgar.

'The separation to w^h I alluded,' Thackeray enunciated with care, 'did not go farther than the bedroom—If I recollect rightly this was the chief object of my thoughts at the moment, and I opined that you would be unwilling to quit your bedfellow, and your present comfortable home for another with me. If you are my wife you must sleep in my bed and live in my house—voila tout—I have no latent plans—no desire for excluding you from those whom I sh^d think very meanly of you, were you to neglect.'[9]

Seriously underrating Mrs Shawe, Thackeray was soon restored to buoyant good humour and enthusiastic wedding plans. But he wanted Isabella plump and happy first. Blandly, he informed Paris that he had been telling his mother of her ills and thinness, and Mrs Carmichael-Smyth, a recent passionate convert to homœopathy, had earnestly advised consulting a Parisian homœopath. Thackeray pressed Isabella, '*as an especial favour*', to do so.

At this there was an ominous silence, not even a half-sheet of paper the following week, which Thackeray, unconscious of the implied criticism of both daughter and mother, put down to his loved one's laziness.

This indolence—or her mother's outraged embargo—had already thwarted one cherished dream. Thackeray had asked his 'little Wife' to pack up the various oddments he had left in his Chaillot room and had devised a romantic reward for her. Before leaving, he had taken a chain from around his neck and draped it over a mirror. Sentimental youth that he was, he had pictured her discovering it and slipping it round her own slim neck to comfort her while they were so far apart, and, oh, how he had envied it that position! But Isabella did not pack his things. And didn't find the chain.

When Mrs Shawe eventually wrote to inform Thackeray that her daughter was perfectly well and entirely content, he either failed once again to read the danger signals, or purposely defied them.

'I don't know what conjurations you have used, dear Pussy,' he wrote, 'but I can't live without you that's flat—and I have grown to such a pitch of jealousy, that I was actually quite angry at your Mother's telling me that you were so well & happy—I was in a rage that you were not miserable like myself—'[10]

Despite the threat of instant departure, when Thackeray returned to Paris in the early summer he found the family still in residence, at their boarding house off the rue Faubourg St Honoré. But the doors were no longer freely opened to him. He and Mrs Shawe were at war over Isabella's heart and little red-polled body, a battle he described in still raw detail in his last completed book, *The Adventures of Philip.*

Like Mrs General Baynes in that story, Mrs Shawe was a possessive mother, showing love through jealous guardianship rather than warmth, demanding total loyalty to herself. Having allowed Isabella to fall in love, having been gratified to see her courted in preference to other people's daughters, she now refused to let her go, and to keep her daughter's sole regard set about undermining the timid young girl's confidence in the man of her choice.

Thackeray, like Philip Firmin, was stretched on an infernal rack of torture by this envious, malicious tyrant and no doubt he too learned to tremble before her and take 'her boxes on the ear with much meakness', for, like Philip, he knew that his loved one was a hostage in her mother's hands and liable to be made to suffer for his crimes.

In *Philip*, Mrs Baynes invents 'a hundred culumnies' against her daughter's lover; tells the miserable young girl that Philip is a drunkard, that he has never loved her, 'that he had loose principles, and was forever haunting theatres and bad company'. From Thackeray's defence of himself it is clear that Mrs Shawe used the same tactics, making Isabella believe that his love was not 'pure', even though, as he vowed to her, he had prayed to God to give him aid in quelling any 'improper desires' which might create disgust in her or lessen him in her esteem.

Moving to the attack, Thackeray asked: 'if I have hurt you by my warmth, have you never wounded me by y^r coldness?—And w^h was the most praiseworthy sentiment of the two? mine when I gave up to you everything—soul & body—or yours when you remembered that there was one thing stronger than love in the world & that— Decorum?'[11]

He was sure, though he thought Isabella herself was not aware of it, that her heart had never been allowed fair play: 'where your words are questioned rudely, and your feelings scarcely permitted to shew themselves, there is no wonder that a certain habit of coldness & indecision should have sprung up.'

He urged her to cure 'these evils' by putting her whole trust in him, and by writing to him every day: 'you must love me with the most awful affection, confide in me all your hopes and your wishes your thoughts and your feelings.'[12]

It was asking too much of a girl brought up under such chilly domination. But Thackeray was as determined in his generous passion as was Mrs Shawe in her version of that emotion. He accepted the severe rationing of his meetings with Isabella, hoping that the ever-present Mrs Shawe would grow fonder of him if she saw him less; but an official embargo on correspondence he would not comply with, even if it meant undignified dealings with servants to get his messages through.

'I must and will write to you and hear from you every day,' he told his 'dearest Wife', in a letter dispatched by lodging-house porter, 'and will let no squeamishness as to servants prevent me. If you were a decided little woman you w^d make a point of giving your letters to me to Augustine to put in the post, and let her & the porteresses tell what stories they may.'[13]

But Isabella was not a decided little woman and though Thackeray did his best to bolster her resolve, he could only write from exile, or talk, on the rare occasions when he was allowed that privilege, with her mother and sister in the room. Mrs Shawe had no such disadvantages, and the only reply Thackeray received was a letter breaking off the engagement.

For three terrible days he tried to accept his banishment, to leave Isabella and her apparent heartlessness. But he knew whose decision it really was, and fought back to win. Isabella had already committed herself in the eyes of the world, he told her; she had written to all her relations and declared to them that she had no doubt of her feelings for him. If his conduct since then had been such as to change her love, she was in honour bound to tell him how he had offended. She owed him justice if nothing more. He demanded to be told in person, by Isabella herself, that she would not marry him. He couldn't say outright what he believed: that it was Mrs Shawe who was preventing her from doing what she herself really wished, but he did the next best thing.

'Should anything occur to your Mother, w^h God forbid, where will you & your sister live?' he asked her, '—with your Aunt Mary?—Or will you return to the man who loves you still, better than you deserve, Isabella.'[14]

In *Philip*, the struggle ends with the heroine in a dangerous state of hysterical collapse, and the hero rushing in from his hollow-eyed pacing of the street outside her boarding house to claim her, backed in his bid by her mother's disgusted fellow-inmates. There is evidence that Isabella, too, was made seriously ill by the battle for her love and loyalty. And Thackeray certainly won her. On 20 August 1836 they were married at the British Embassy at Paris, by the Chaplain, Bishop Luscombe, with Mrs I. G. Shawe, of the parish of Donerail in the County of Cork, as a witness.

Many years later, Thackeray admitted that a mother might

genuinely believe she had a duty to protect her daughter from marriage with a pauper, no matter how much love was there. He was also to wonder at the rash daring of a young man who embarked cheerfully on matrimony with as little, and as precarious a livelihood, as he had had. But he could never forgive Mrs Shawe the foul means she had used to separate him from Isabella, or believe her motives to have been fair.

In the course of his courtship, Thackeray had given Isabella a ring, a diamond set between two opals, which he had shown in triumph to a friend.

'But, William, see what you have done,' cried the confidant, gazing at the black enamel round the stones, 'this is a mourning ring, not an engagement ring.'[15]

It was to prove an ominously appropriate token.

3.

The honeymoon was spent at Versailles, where Mrs Shawe duly appeared after a few days on 'a visit of condolence', and then with the laughing, loving, romantic Aunt Ritchie, another member of the family making a shrunken income spin further in Paris. Accepting his aunt's invitation, Thackeray wrote full of newly married pride:

'WE, (does it not sound very magnificent?) shall be delighted to come and occupy your pretty little rooms, and stay with you for a few or a great many days—, for this place has a certain dulness, in spite of my peculiar situation . . .'[1]

In September, he and the 'diminutive individual' who now bore his name, returned to town, to the not too arduous labour of writing for the finally launched *Constitutional* and the heady joys of keeping house in a small apartment in the rue Neuve St Augustin, a few doors away from the rooms he had taken with Williams of *The Snob* on his first visit to Paris seven years before.

Thackeray sank into matrimony with a sigh of huge contentment. His dear Puss was the 'best little wife in the world', he told his mother. 'I never knew a purer mind or a warmer heart (for me & mine).' To generous FitzGerald, who had sent the best of all wedding presents, he extolled the virtues of the wedded state:

'As for the little wife it does not change one in the least it is only a new quality that one discovers in ones'self, a new happiness if you will, for my dear old friend, any thing so happy, so quiet, so calm you can't fancy; at this moment I am smoking a segar (w^h my little woman has got for me) in the very drawing room—the state apartment of the race of Tackeray! I intend with your money to buy chairs and tables, to decorate this chamber, for as yet I have only hired them; and I have got your portrait and further more as the comble of sentiment I shall make Mrs Tack write to you on this very sheet of paper.'[2]

He was happy. He had Isabella, his own establishment, and, after the years of struggle and indecision, a regular job bringing him £8 a week. Even Mrs Shawe promised to contribute to their purse by paying Isabella's portion of £50 a year, a promise which lasted just long enough to cover the first two quarterly instalments, and which, if executed with the same self-righteous abuse that Mrs Baynes employed in handing over her daughter's small sums—in contemptuous mounds of five-franc pieces—was not a pleasant experience even when the money materialized. But even this monstrous mother-in-law and her broken contracts could not dent Thackeray's euphoria for long. In the rue de la Paix he would no doubt have felt poor, but in the rue Neuve St Augustin he was a man of substance. For the first six months he even managed to save.

In his snug little study, grandly called 'Le Cabinet de Monsieur', he smoked with abandon, distilled the Paris papers with killing perspicacity, then, majestically pacing the room, dictated to a clerk the wickedly satirical dispatches of correspondent 'T.T.' which were to enlighten the mighty readership of the *Constitutional*.

'I am sorry to say that I like the newspaper-work very much,' he confessed to FitzGerald, who, like most men of fine feeling in those days, had no great respect for journalism. He fancied he did it pretty well too, and though both he and dear old Fitz had long since agreed that sarcasm had no place in literature, enjoyed employing that weapon against politics, 'where all are rogues to deal with (y^r hble Servt among them)', and where it was thus impossible to 'sneer and scorn too much, and bring the profession into disrepute'.

But even among politicians there were different shades of roguery, and as the weeks and months went by, Thackeray made the uncomfortable discovery that the greatest rascals were on his side. In the turbulent affairs of post-Napoleonic France he found his sympathies warming to the royalists, or at least to liberal Thiers and his followers, and angrily confided to his mother what he could never write in his newsletters: 'the Republican party is the most despicable I ever knew: They are bigoted and despotic.'

As with many a good man, when it came to politics Thackeray's head and heart were in uneasy conflict. Reason told him that the radicals were right: there had to be social reform, the class system was objectionable and should be abolished. But his senses murmured that there was a great deal to be said for gracious living, for art and civilization, the refining influence of inherited wealth—for 'dandyism', as his mother called it.

One of the greater benefits he was to bestow on Victorian England in his mature writing was a compassionate plea for a mingling of the best of the old order with that of the new. But at twenty-five, with the presses calling him to join the new crusade, with £450 a year to be earned, he took another glass of absinthe to make the ink run and impart a fine eloquence to his style, and set about belabouring the poor French 'citizen king', Louis Philippe.

Isabella had blossomed with marriage into just the kind of charming companion Thackeray had envisaged, but even here small clouds emerged to trouble an otherwise delightful horizon. Her laziness had not been cured by matrimony, and her inability to get up in the morning soon proved contagious. In a mood of self-disgust, Thackeray told his mother:

'I am sorry to tell you we are the laziest people in all Paris, my wife has fairly beaten me, and we never breakfast before eleven o'clock. I am ashamed and angry every morning of my life, but do what I will scold or laugh she won't get up, & I am only too glad of an excuse to lie in bed—the consequence is I am grown so fat that you will hardly know me when you see me again, and what is worse my whole day is over in five hours; I tell you this to unburden my mind for it makes me disgusted with myself, to think I waste my time so dreadfully.'[3]

Isabella's boarding-house upbringing, and consequent lack of domestic skills, also presented problems, like the one Thackeray used many years later in *Philip*:

'Philip,' he wrote, 'had a joke about his wife's housekeeping which perhaps may apply to other young women who are kept by over-watchful mothers too much *in statu pupillari*. When they were married, or about to be married, Philip asked Charlotte what she would order for dinner? She promptly said she would order leg of mutton. "And after leg of mutton?" "leg of beef, to be sure!" says Mrs. Charlotte, looking very pleased, and knowing.'

But if Isabella was not to shake off her indolence, news of prompt fatherhood galvanized her husband. New papers were risky enterprises and the *Constitutional*'s circulation was already proving disappointingly sluggish. Thackeray set about consolidating his own position in case of disaster, writing letters—'entirely about my own pocket and interest . . . as all letters from married men should be'—to every old friend in London who might rally to his cause.

Jack Kemble, another recruit to matrimony, now editing the *British and Foreign Review*, was asked to put in a good word for him with the proprietors of a new evening paper he had heard was to be started in London. It would be another radical publication, but setting aside his political qualms, Thackeray offered himself as Paris correspondent:

'I suppose you know how I exercise the same office for a Radical morning paper, the "Constitutional"—who in fact has not heard of T.T.? But I have plenty of time for another similar duty and plenty of employment for the additional weekly-guineas it might bring— My dear fellow, do your best for me for our friendship is old, our life is short, and our fortune uncertain: also as you know, I am a married man (and you can understand my situation), and have an alarming prospect before me of many additions to the race of Roaldus de Richmond. You also are probably in a similar state— wife, children coming, and nothing in three per cents.'[4]

He offered his services to Kemble for his own *Review*, too. A little 'lightness' was what was needed there, he suggested, a proposition not guaranteed to endear him to his dedicatedly serious friend.

In the early days of marriage he had told FitzGerald that his 'poor picture-painting' had been quite neglected in his literary pursuits— 'and for this neglect I can give you no better illustration, than to tell you that it seems like quitting a beautiful innocent wife (like Mrs T. for instance) to take up with a tawdry brazen whore'—but now art, too, was put back into harness.

He sent off a batch of paintings to Frank Stone and George Cattermole, asking them to place them in a friendly fashion before the hanging committee of the Water Colour Society. He had doubts about the quality of the workmanship, he told Stone, but suggested that 'the waggish line' he had adopted might make them acceptable for variety's sake.

It was a long shot, and he was philosophical about the outcome, but the thought he had given to his approach—the selection of paintings which might be accepted for their subject if not for their skill—showed a new determination to succeed in ambitions which had previously been vague yearnings.

With the new year of 1837 came indications that his concerted siege on London was beginning to pay off. Harrison Ainsworth, then at the peak of popularity with his historical romances, praised him so highly to his publisher, John Macrone, that Thackeray, was considered as illustrator for Ainsworth's new novel, *Crichton*. It was exactly the kind of work he had hungered for, and might well have swung his precariously balanced scales away from literature for ever.

He sent a gleeful, bawdy, rhyming letter to Ainsworth, together with a preliminary sketch, and despite delays in getting the text to work from and the lack of any response to his letters from either Ainsworth or Macrone, pushed ahead with the project, sending progress reports to London through the ubiquitous 'Father Prout'.

But it was a fatally rushed job. He appears to have been given only two weeks to complete the commission, and when, to save time, he tried engraving the plates himself, the results were disastrous. Two months later the book was published without any illustrations at all.

Eager to make the most of any opening, he tried to interest Macrone in a book of his own; 'in 2 Wollums. with 20 drawings, entitled Rambles & Sketches in old and new Paris by ₩ '. Naturally, he hadn't written a word of it, he told the pub- lisher, which was why he was offering it so cheaply—£20 down and another £30 on publication—but he wanted 'to be made to write', to bind himself 'by contract or fine.'

Macrone was not overwhelmed by the offer, even at a discount, and Thackeray was probably not too sad when he was called back to London in February to help shore up the tottering *Constitutional* from its Fleet Street headquarters. At least, if the paper failed, he would be in the right place to bargain for other work in person.

His last newsletter from Paris appeared in the *Constitutional* in mid-February 1837, and by early March he and Isabella were in London, sharing the Albion Street house with the Carmichael-Smyths. Soon afterwards the paper's managing director resigned, and Thackeray was temporarily appointed to the post. For some time the Major had been bearing most of the costs himself, and in April Thackeray wrote a stern and most businesslike letter to the other directors, urging them to raise at least £1,000 between them to save the venture. Without it all was lost, but with such a sum he confidently predicted that the paper would break even within three months, and yield 'a very large dividend' in a year. He himself, he said, was prepared to make a loan of £100.

'The paper would long since have stopped,' he wrote, had not the day-to-day expenses 'been met as they occurred by one of the Directors the only one who has remained at his post, & whose extraordinary exertions & sacrifices, have maintained the Con-stitutional hitherto—Major Smyth—It would be folly on the part of that gentleman, to continue to meet alone, the risk & cost of an establishment in which you are as much interested as he—'[5]

He was banking on the clubs and coffee-houses taking the paper, as he explained in a private covering note to his Uncle Ritchie, asking him to support the appeal—and incidentally reminding him that a £10 instalment was still outstanding on his original stake in the company. A thousand coffee-shop men had 'sworn' to take copies, he said. This in itself would have put the paper's finances in the black, but the clubs and coffee-houses didn't rally, and when Thackeray's first child was born on 9 June she arrived into a household deep in public and private disorder: facing financial ruin, and enduring the profound miseries of domestic uproar.

The baby was named Anne Isabella, in tribute to her two grand-mothers who were both present for the birth; and the discomforts of an establishment containing both Mrs Carmichael-Smyth and Mrs Shawe are reflected in a paragraph Thackeray wrote in *A Shabby Genteel Story* three years later:

'A house with a wife is often warm enough; a house with a wife and her mother is rather warmer than any spot on the known globe; a house with two mothers-in-law is so excessively hot, that it can be likened to no place on earth at all, but one must go lower for a simile.'

When Isabella became feverish, and the baby seriously ill, Mrs Carmichael-Smyth insisted on calling in a homœopath, and then the heat must have become well-nigh intolerable. Thackeray, fleeing the furnace as often as possible to attend to his other ailing concern in Fleet Street, knew nothing of the danger the child was in, or the steps his mother had taken, until it was almost too late. Just in time, he brought in a regular physician. The baby's life was saved and Isabella recovered, though she was unable to feed her first child, and was a long time convalescing.

In July, less than a year after the appearance of the first issue, the *Constitutional* folded. The Major stayed to salvage what he could, then retreated to Paris to escape the threat of debtor's jail. Thackeray, with a wife, a baby, and no money, launched himself on a decade of desperate freelance journalism, a life and death struggle which was to culminate in *Vanity Fair*, and the eventual repayment of all his stepfather's debts.

7
Magazinery
Writing for his life

Within weeks of the failure of the *Constitutional*, Thackeray was able to report that he was in full employment once more, but it was a precarious existence, writing and drawing for any journal which would print his work: much labour for small returns.

Dapper Sir William Molesworth, who had also lost money on the *Constitutional*, set him reviewing books for his more prosperous concern, the *London and Westminster Review* (starting with Dickens's *Sketches by Boz*); Jack Kemble, with less grace, found occasional space for him in the *British and Foreign Review*; even an old Charterhouse friend helped in a small way by commissioning illustrations for his own literary effusions, lovingly printed at the author's own expense; and, for wider circulation, he did twelve full-page plates for *Men of Character*, by Douglas Jerrold, the *Constitutional*'s former theatre critic, a venture which earned him sharp abuse from the *Athenaeum*:

'According to the prevailing fashion the work is illustrated by etchings *after* Cruikshank, which are only remarkable for the badness of the drawing, and the total absence of humour.'[1]

In September 1837, Dickens, in his first job as magazine editor, published Thackeray's first story to appear in a journal over which he himself had no control. The journal was *Bentley's Miscellany*, and the story, *The Professor*, a charming fantasy woven around an actual man—Dando, an oyster addict none too squeamish as to how he came by his supplies. Undeterred by the *Athenaeum*'s view of his drawings, Bentley's also commissioned him to illustrate one of their books—at the slave-labour rate of £20 for eighteen colour plates.

For the next few years, however, the bulk of Thackeray's bread and small scraping of butter came from two main sources: *The Times* and *Fraser's Magazine*. Through Uncle Merrick Shawe's great friend, *Times* writer Edward Sterling, Thackeray was introduced to editor Thomas Barnes, the man who turned *The Times* into 'the Thunderer', and walked away from the interview with his first reviewing assignment, Carlyle's *French Revolution*.

This book was itself revolutionary, as Thackeray quickly appreciated, even if he couldn't resist remarking on its peculiarities of style: 'It is stiff, short, and rugged, it abounds with Germanisms and Latinisms, strange epithets, and choking double words, astonishing to the admirers of simple Addisonian English.'

He lauded it highly for its fairness and the vividness with which it brought history to life, and assured readers they would soon discover 'the real beauty which lurks among all these odd words and twisted sentences, living, as it were, in spite of the weeds.' Most of all, he approved this 'extraordinary work' because it had 'no CANT', the cardinal sin he was to fight in all his literary criticism.

Carlyle himself was not sure what to make of such a tribute.

'The writer is one Thackeray,' he told his sister, 'a half-monstrous Cornish giant, kind of painter, Cambridge man, and Paris newspaper correspondent, who is now writing for his life in London. I have seen him at the Bullers' and at Sterling's. His article is rather like him, and I suppose calculated to do the book good.'[2]

Some three years earlier, Thackeray, wearing a monocle, carefully curled hair and a worried expression, had appeared with Carlyle in Daniel Maclise's famous sketch of the *Fraserians*: twenty-six of the finest writers of the day, gathered round a table listening to Maginn making an after-dinner speech—'God knows what about.' He had been included then, among such other luminaries as Coleridge, Southey, Walter Scott's son-in-law and biographer, Lockhart, the exquisite Count d'Orsay and the equally beautiful Harrison Ainsworth, solely as friend (and banker) to Maginn and the recording artist. Now, in his days of dire need, the group genuinely opened its ranks to him as a writer.

Maginn by this time was fading out, leaving control to publisher James Fraser, a shrewd businessman not highly regarded for his taste or intellect, and Thackeray appears to have behaved towards him on occasion with much the same kind of swaggering superiority George Warrington inflicted on Mr Bacon in *Pendennis*—putting his hat *on* to talk to the man and addressing him from an insolent perch on a table-top—in the belief that such people enjoyed being 'treated with rudeness by a gentleman.'

When he chanced on a ridiculous etiquette book and had the idea of reviewing it in the guise of a footman, Thackeray offered the result to Fraser in a curt, take-it-or-leave-it letter which gave no indication of his desperate need for work. Fraser took it, and in 'Fashnable Fax and Polite Annygoats', a review of *My Book; or, The Anatomy of Conduct*, by John Henry Skelton (or Skeleton, as the footman/critic insisted on interpreting the name), a magnificent new comic character was born: Charles James Yellowplush, a linguistic eccentric, named after a pair of coachman's 'inexpressibles', and a firm believer in the 'three W.'s . . . plenty of work, plenty of wittles, and plenty of wages.'

Having dissected that 'slap-up heppycure' Mr Skelton and his *Anatomy* with a deservedly sharp scalpel, the garrulous young Yellowplush was encouraged to write his memoirs, and Thackeray had the relief of a long-running series to ease the murderous piecemeal gamble of freelance work, a series so successful that he soon felt confident enough to hazard it by threatening to strike for higher pay.

Bad as he was, Mr Yellowplush was the most popular contributor to the magazine, he told Fraser, and should be paid accordingly, whereas he had discovered he was getting less than other writers, including 'the monthly nurse'. He would produce no more except at the rate of 12 guineas a sheet (sixteen magazine pages), plus another £2 for each illustration.

'Pray do not be angry,' he commanded; 'it is simply a bargain, which it is my duty to make . . . I dare say you will be very indignant, and swear I am the most mercenary of individuals. Not so. But I am a better workman than most of your crew and deserve a better price.'[3]

This time it was not entirely bravado. He had another series attracting attention in the rival *New Monthly Magazine*, and Fraser wisely paid to keep Yellowplush in his own livery. Having gained his point, Thackeray quickly lost his bluster and stayed demurely clear of Fraser's offices. 'The fact is after bullying you about money matters,' he explained, 'I am rather ashamed to show my face.'

The hero Thackeray had invented for the *New Monthly* was the tremendous Major Goliah O'Grady Gahagan, whose outrageous exploits in India (illustrated in best military history style with diagrams of baffling simplicity), were his revenge for the Anglo-Indian stories of high endeavour and elaborate detail he had had to endure from early childhood. The pseudo-Indian words, and Irish hyperbole, rolled from his pen with wicked invention, and his tales of love for the ravishing daughter of Colonel Julius Jowler of the Bengal Cavalry, and his 'rhubarb-coloured wife (I believe that her skin gave the first idea of our regimental breeches),' combined with daring deeds at Laswaree, Dum-Dum, Furrackabad, Futtyghur, Bhurtpore, Hurrygurrybang and Boggleywollah, had thousands of other victims laughing with him.

The following summer, for the first of his annual reviews of the major art exhibitions, he took yet another pseudonym—that of Michael Angelo Titmarsh; and Mr Titmarsh was to become his *alter ego*, most famous of all his many disguises, far better known than Thackeray himself, until he launched *Vanity Fair* under his own colours nine years later.

The 'Titmarsh' part of the name may have come from a seventeenth-century tract printed for one Samuel Tidmarsh which was listed as part of Thackeray's library when he died. It had just the degree of absurdity which appealed to him, and he used the full name a few years later for his *History of Samuel Titmarsh and the Great Hoggarty Diamond*; but for his 'Strictures on Pictures', as he called his first art reviews for *Fraser's*, he went appropriately artistic and prefaced it with the name of another broken-nosed man of genius, Michelangelo.

Each year the exhibitions put Thackeray into an agony of rapture and remorse. As he viewed the Royal Academy's wares at the newly built National Gallery (which he always referred to as a wretched 'little gin-shop of a building'), and strolled across Trafalgar Square to Pall Mall, where the water-colour societies held their shows, he was consumed with a fever of excitement which ultimately set him buying paintboxes and groaning that he had missed his vocation.

Michael Angelo Titmarsh, it was made plain, had also had his disappointments in this line, notably the rejection of his great painting *Heliogabalus*, which were said to account for a certain bitterness on his part towards more fortunate exponents of the vast historical canvas. This, together with the frenzy of joy he experienced in *some* of the other exhibits, resulted in a rash of grand madness and absurdity every May.

Despite the clowning which distinguished his reviews, however, Thackeray's great love of the subject shone brightly and infectiously. He knew all the technicalities, but wrote in easy, layman's terms, letting his thoughts spill over into all kinds of byways, which was what he believed art should make thoughts do. As in literature, what he looked for was 'heart'. If there were exquisite craftsmanship too, so much the better; but craftsmanship alone, however good, was not enough. A painting, he said, like an early Mozart symphony, should set the soul soaring—for reasons not wholly comprehensible and by means impossible to teach or describe.

His writings still stand as a guide to early Victorian art, and convey the greatest benefit any critic can bestow: they make the reader want to see the works for himself, with newly awakened eyes.

His old friends Stone, Cattermole and Maclise were generously treated each year, though they didn't always escape the great Titmarsh's censure, and William Etty, who revelled in the nubile female form, was a perennial source of wonder and sly humour. His flesh tints were superb, thought critic Thackeray, 'as luscious as Rubens, as rich almost as Titian', and how his figures were drawn!—'a deuced deal *too much* drawn'.

In the early years of Queen Victoria's reign, when Etty and several fellow artists were chosen to paint frescoes on the walls of a Buckingham Palace garden house, the royal patronage was welcomed by the art world, Thackeray included. But when Etty's naked nymphs were chipped out again, in blushing confusion, and news of how little the artists had been paid for their labours made known, 'republican' Thackeray rushed to their defence. He was furious that 'humble men who could not refuse' should have been paid ten times below their value by such august patronage. And to have the work of 'such a great man as Etty . . . hacked out of the palace wall—that was a slap in the face to every artist in England'.

Reviewing the following year's exhibitions, he was delighted to note: 'Quite unabashed by the squeamishness exhibited in the highest quarter (as the newspapers call it), Mr. Etty goes on rejoicing in his old fashion. Perhaps, this year, his ladies and Cupids are a little *hasardés*; his Venuses expand more than ever in the line of Hottentot beauty; his drawing and colouring are still more audacious than they were . . . If you look at the pictures closely (and, considering all things, it requires some courage to do so) . . . It must be confessed that some . . . would *not* be suitable to hang up everywhere . . .'

As for Joseph Mallord Turner, that rising, controversial genius, and his 'incendiary' paintings, they amazed and mesmerized Thackeray, as they have amazed and enthralled a later century of viewers, but he had the wit to appreciate their brilliance, as did few of his contemporaries. In 1839, when the *Fighting Téméraire* was exhibited for the first time, Thackeray's description of it was almost equal to the canvas itself:

'The old "Téméraire" is dragged to her last home by a little, spiteful, diabolical steamer. A mighty red sun, amidst a host of flaring clouds, sinks to rest on one side of the picture, and illumines a river that seems interminable, and a countless navy that fades away into such a wonderful distance as never was painted before. The little demon of a steamer is belching out a volume (why do I say volume?

not a hundred volumes could express it) of foul, lurid, red-hot malignant smoke, paddling furiously, and lashing up the water round about it; while behind it (a cold grey moon looking down on it), slow, sad, and majestic, follows the brave old ship, with death, as it were, written on her.'

As 'grand a painting as ever figured on the walls of any Academy, or came from the easel of any painter', he called it. To the last, Turner remained a great and awful mystery to him, with his 'dabs of dirty putty *slapped* on to the canvas with a trowel', the sunshine fairly scintillating out of his thick smeary lumps of chrome yellow—a magician, whose spell Thackeray did not care to contemplate too deeply.

'What a marvellous power is this of the painter's!' he wrote; 'how each great man can excite us at his will!' And so, flying from the turbulent effects of Turner and Etty ('and full time too'), he escaped to the gentle calm of the Water Colour Society, where there were more pleasures than just the paintings to delight the eye. There was nothing more cheerful or sparkling than the first impression made by this little gallery, he confided:

'In the first place, you never can enter it without finding four or five pretty women, that's a fact; pretty women with pretty pink bonnets peeping at pretty pictures, and with sweet whispers vowing that Mrs. Seyffarth is a dear delicious painter, and that her style is so "soft".'

It was, he maintained, a fact which deserved to be more generally known, and was alone worth the price of his article.

Many of the painters were none too pleased with this kind of foolery year after year, but there was a wealth of serious comment mixed with it, and Thackeray was certainly in earnest in his long crusade to make other papers give proper attention to art, a neglected field when he began his own reviews.

His first short novel, which appeared in instalments in *Fraser's* during 1839–40, was written as part of another crusade, this time against the vogue for 'Newgate literature', which made heroes of murderers, highwaymen and burglars. Bulwer-Lytton had begun the fashion with his *Paul Clifford* and *Eugene Aram*, the last of which beatified an eighteenth-century murderer; Harrison Ainsworth swiftly followed with *Rookwood*, in which Dick Turpin once more made his glorious ride to York; then Dickens joined in with Bill Sikes, Fagin and the winning Miss Nancy; and early in 1839 came the most popular crook of all, Ainsworth's *Jack Sheppard*. By the end of the year four London theatres were showing versions of Ainsworth's story, and 'Sheppard-bags', complete with a handy selection of burglar's tools, were being touted for sale in their lobbies.

'. . . one or two young gentlemen have already confessed how much they were indebted to Jack Sheppard who gave them ideas of pocket-picking and thieving w^h they never would have had but for the play,' wrote Thackeray. 'Such facts must greatly delight an author who aims at popularity.'[4]

Thackeray himself decided to try for a different kind of fame: he would give the public such a villain, in such un-rosy terms, that it would be put off sham romanticism for good. Like Bulwer-Lytton and Ainsworth, he turned to the *Newgate Calendar, or the Malefactors' Bloody Register* for a suitably nasty subject, and selected Catherine Hayes, burned at Tyburn in 1726 for the deliberate murder of her husband in particularly revolting circumstances. His ' "Catherine" cathartic', he called it. Its narrator, 'Ikey Solomons, Esq., Junior' (who had acquired his education in Birchin Lane), was presumably meant to be the son of Ikey Solomons senior, a notorious receiver·of stolen goods.

During the course of the story Thackeray indulged in the sport of parodying Bulwer's absurdly highflown prose, and pointed out to his readers what a splendid assortment of characters he had assembled for them: how 'agreeably low' they were, how 'delightfully disgusting', and at the same time how 'eminently pleasing and pathetic.'

Before long his terms of reference were lying in disorder all about him. As his supporting rogues took shape, they did indeed become delightfully disgusting, from the rascally rake Count Gustavus Adolphus Maximilian von Galgenstein, down to the doomed Ensign Macshane, forerunner of Captain Costigan and other comic Irishmen. For the first time, Thackeray was dealing with his adored eighteenth century, and as *Catherine* unfolded in his beautiful, leisurely prose, so casually prodigal of original phrases and humorous insights, the atmosphere of that former age rose and lived again, never laboured or force-fed with data, but saturating the whole work with a deceptive ease and an attractiveness totally at odds with his original purpose. When he found himself taking a liking to his purposely vile heroine, and insinuating a redeeming feature here and there, the game was lost and neither the author nor his readers were very happy to see poor Mistress Cat burn at the stake at the end of it all.

Carlyle praised the story when it was done, and in his last chapter Thackeray professed himself pleased with the experiment and the newspapers' abuse of it 'as one of the dullest, most vulgar, and immoral works extant.' The *Catherine* cathartic, he wrote, had acted most efficaciously. But, in fact, apart from the dreadful details of Catherine's fiery end, quoted verbatim from the *Newgate Calendar*, he had made the dose immensely easy to swallow—too easy, as he admitted privately.

Catherine was followed early the next year by *The Bedford Row Conspiracy* for the *New Monthly Magazine*, a shorter, more tightly written tale, 'stolen' from the French. Mrs Carmichael-Smyth, that ardent radical, told him she didn't 'care a fig' for the 'ordinary people' he had taken to writing about; but ordinary people, as she called them, were those with whom her son now mainly came into contact, and he studied them with the attention he gave to every man, woman and child who ever came his way, capturing them on paper with a truth and humour which will forever make his readers laugh—or blush—when the thrusts strike home.

George Cruikshank also gave him work during these difficult years, and for two consecutive Christmases he produced stories for his old hero to illustrate in his *Comic Almanack*. But it was time-consuming labour for only £20 each year, suiting his story to Cruikshank's ideas, while he was juggling with his book reviews and as much other work as he could find buyers for.

Cruickshank never brought him great financial gain. Thackeray's long poem, *The King of Brentford's Testament,* which Cruikshank also commissioned, earned him exactly £1, and when he wrote a lengthy appreciation of the caricaturist and his work for the *Westminster Review* in the June of 1840, he was paid very poorly— '$\frac{1}{2}$ price', he claimed—and received nothing at all, despite his loud complaints, when it was published in book-form the following year.

The tradition of anonymous journalism made it difficult for any writer to win the kind of reputation which commands superior pay, and Thackeray exacerbated the problem. During his journalistic career, he invented at least forty pseudonyms for himself, most of which took on quite distinct personalities of their own. His fame thus grew disjointedly, but grow it did, and after only two years it had already spread across the Atlantic.

In the summer of 1839, when that curious American phenomenon, Nathaniel Parker Willis, descended on London, he claimed that one of the first things he set out to do was discover the authors of *Yellowplush* and *Major Gahagan*, 'the two best periodical series of papers that have appeared for twenty years', and was delighted to discover that the same man had written both.[5]

Being admired by Willis was, however, a dubious honour. With Dr T. O. Porter, he ran a New York magazine which specialized in pirating pieces printed elsewhere. With bland honesty they called it the *Corsair* and on the few occasions when they paid for contributions it was usually a pittance which tended to evaporate entirely after the first few instalments.

Thackeray, eager even for shillings, and doubtless won by the American's genuine and spirited admiration, as usual took up with the rogue, and Willis joyously informed his partner that he had signed him on for a series of newsletters: 'for a guinea a *close column* of the *Corsair*—cheaper than I ever did anything in my life. I will see that he is paid for a while to see how you like him. For myself, I think him the very best periodical writer alive. He is a royal, daring, fine creature, too.'[6]

Thackeray sent off eight 'Letters from London, Paris, Pekin, Petersburgh, &c.' and still hadn't been paid for them all when the *Corsair*, in its more usual swashbuckling way, began commandeering his *Fraser's* articles. It was the kind of experience he became an expert at turning to his own advantage. Many years later he used the memory of these early impecuniary dealings to excellent effect in *Philip*, and he didn't let N. P. Willis go to waste, either. Long before that last book, the deficiency in his coffers was made good with the proceeds of several articles on the curiously naïve and shrewd American who had caused such a stir in London society by accepting its hospitality and then dissecting its prize ornaments in print, much as an anthropologist might anatomize a newly discovered species of Man.

In 1845, his review of Willis's *Dashes at Life* got him into that most prestigious of British journals, the *Edinburgh Review*, for the first time, and earned him £20, a handsome sum made less attractive by the editorial butchering inflicted on his favourite jokes and most cherished phrases.

'From your liberal payment,' Thackeray told the earnest men of Edinburgh, 'I can't but conclude that you reward me not only for labouring but for being mutilated in your service.'[7]

He never gave them another opportunity to use their blue pencils on him.

For one brought up to think of himself as a gentleman of independent means, there was much indignity involved in Thackeray's chosen profession. To beg for work was not pleasant, and to be rejected, as he was, by *Blackwood's* and several other publications, was both galling and financially disastrous. Socially, it could also be embarrassing. Carlyle, during his period of bondage, said even street-sweeping was regarded as a more respectable trade, and certainly, for a while, Thackeray became savagely embittered by the slights he received as a poor dog who had to earn his living by his pen, a savagery reflected in much of his early work with its dark emphasis on wickedness, rogues and class toadies.

From time to time he considered improving his position by devoting himself to the slightly more respectable field of political journalism. Revolution, he thought, would come to Britain as it had to France, and he was eager to play a part not only in shaping the new Utopia, but in choosing the means by which it came to pass. Not for him the Chartists and the riots with which they were terrorizing half the country: he could see as much evil in their extremes as in the most unyielding Tory rule.

'We are living in wonderful times, Madam,' he told his mother, 'and who knows may see great things done: but no physical force— the bigotry of that & of the present Chartist leaders is greater than the bigotry we suffer under.'[8]

He was a republican, he vowed, who wanted to see all men equal and the 'bloated aristocracy blasted to the wings of all the winds', but not by the present fomenters of trouble. It was men like these who had broken up the fair commencement of the republic in France, and brought about the necessity for the tyrant Napoleon. What was needed, he thought, was for a few enlightened moderates to speak out honestly—to 'dare to do and say the truth.'

There were days when he could see himself as such a man. He proposed to Jack Kemble writing an article on Socialist and Chartist publications for the *British and Foreign Review*: 'With this I will make a grand row if you will let me: shouting for household suffrage & a citizen-guard as our only safeguard.'

But Jack Kemble did not let him, and though he and his 'humbug' of a wife were awfully good about taking Isabella to the opera, Jack Kemble now assumed such superior airs that Thackeray decided to trouble him and his magazine no further. More to his taste was the elegant Albany Fonblanque, editor of the *Examiner*, the recognized voice of the Philosophical Radicals, and when Fonblanque offered him a job, Thackeray was very tempted to accept it, despite the poor pay which went with it. If he could but keep to it for three years, he reckoned he would have a good smattering of politics and might hope to maintain himself 'in a comfortable dishonesty' for the rest of his days: a sentiment which showed what he basically thought of all political parties, whatever their colour.

He did do some drawings for Richard Cobden's *Anti-Corn Law Circular*, and wrote occasionally for the Whig evening paper, the *Globe*, for which Charles Buller was a leader writer. But he failed when he tried to work his way into the liberal *Morning Chronicle* with an article on the Bedchamber Crisis: the young Queen, he considered, had acted in 'the most disgustingly unconstitutional insolent and arbitrary' manner in that episode. (When Mrs Carmichael-Smyth took Queen Victoria's part, Thackeray rounded on her too: 'Don't talk about the spirit of a woman—the Queen has no business to be a woman.')

Ironically, two concerns, *The Times* and *Fraser's* which were prepared to give him decently paid work were both solidly Tory, a burr that caused him constant irritation. And while the 'abominable old Times' was at least respectable, even this could not always be said of *Fraser's*, which still kept up the slashing attacks on individuals and institutions begun by Dr Maginn.

2.

Despite the occasional disappointment, there was no lack of work for Thackeray: the 'juice' of it was the wear and tear of it, and the wear and tear of life in London. For days it seemed that every five minutes the door-bell rang or the knocker knocked, and between times in tripped Isabella, with little Annie slung across her back and the prettiest excuses in the world.

A few months after the collapse of the *Constitutional* and the departure of the Carmichael-Smyths for Paris, Thackeray had sublet the Albion Street house and taken a smaller one at 13 Great Coram Street, Bloomsbury, an area which should have been fashionable, as he wrote in *The Bedford Row Conspiracy*, since only people with their own carriages could get to it with any kind of convenience. It was near the Foundling Hospital (the 'Fondling', as good Caroline called it in *Philip*), where Isabella went to hear the music, and just across the road from John Allen, the Cambridge friend whose goodness and ungainliness were to live forever in Dobbin.

Even in Bloomsbury the Thackerays retained the dignity of a manservant, in the ancient shape of John Goldworthy, who had been with the family at Larkbeare and still wore the yellowplush breeches Mrs Carmichael-Smyth had ordered for him in palmier days. A sad coward in pain, old John was more often than not stretched on his bed with lumbago, from whence he could be heard all over the house groaning and shouting down blessings and instructions to the two maids who saw to his coal scuttles and answered the ever-ringing door-bell for him.

'The poor are very good to the poor,' mused the master of this disorder, as he longed for 'a lodge in some vast wilderness', where he could write in peace.

Even when all hands were up and working the house was still not properly cared for, and with the warm weather the bugs began to bite, giving Thackeray nights of agony and unrest. Then, and only then, out came the camphor and turpentine and the beds and floors were doused. There was, however, a constant and more successful battle to keep Mrs Shawe at bay. Even Mrs Butler was thought to be preferable to that lady, and vague plans for taking in a paying lodger were regularly, and not too reluctantly, put aside each time she indicated she might join them. There or not, she helped to pay for the servants, while Mrs Shawe reneged on Isabella's dowry.

FitzGerald, as ever, was a noble friend in need, sending back Thackeray's repayments of loans with a 'What the devil do you mean?' and for an ingenious man there were many ways of stretching the budget. When the stair-carpet was reduced to 'an elegant state of raggery', Thackeray made a bargain with the carpet man: a new one, in exchange for a poem praising the supplier.

Most of their troubles, said Thackeray, could have been cured by a little 'order and early rising . . . (d— the bell there it is again) (My wife has been in twice)', but as it was he wrote, sold his ideas and wares, made up his accounts for articles used, reminded reluctant publishers to pay, and juggled with the proceeds surrounded by bedlam.

Money was spent as soon as it entered the house, or was promised before it was made, and though he assured his mother 'we get on very comfortably with none', it was a continuous knife-edge struggle. He had made over the small remaining income from his inheritance to the Major when his parents moved to Paris, and even that enterprising gentleman was a safer repository for it than the young Thackerays. When Charles Buller was in line for a Cabinet post and the consequent dispensing of patronage, Isabella suggested that the Major, rather than her husband, should be given preference if they were offered anything.

'. . . when we are in a straight Pa has always something to pull out of his purse, but I fear it would not be so if the tables were turned though I assure you,' she told her mother-in-law, 'I keep my account very right and W complains how little he is allowed to spend and how Mrs T. will ask how!'[1]

But the fact was that Isabella was still not a good manager. She had, said her husband, 'a noble want of the organ of number', and when she and little Annie were pulling a cart round his room, yelling 'Taytoes' and remarking on the high price of that commodity, it occurred to him that young Miss T. knew as much of the matter as her mother.

Thackeray was no laggard when it came to spending, either. If he had a few pounds in his purse he could think of a dozen ways to squander them, and was soon to write of literary men as 'those doomed poor fellows of this world whose pockets Fate has ordained shall be perpetually empty.' If their darlings showed literary tastes, he warned fond mothers, they should make up their minds to the fact that they would be 'idle at school, and useless at college; if they have a profession, they will be sure to neglect it; if they have a fortune, they will be sure to spend it.'[2]

The battle to survive had the same chancy element as the gaming tables, and in the main he relished it. It made the adrenalin flow, and stirred his naturally lazy talents to work. 'O this London is a grand place for scheming, and rare fun for a man with broad shoulders who can push through the crowd,' he cried, and then off he would whisk Isabella, away to Greenwich for a whitebait dinner when he had only a sovereign in the world and the cost of the treat was seventeen shillings.

It was a way of nerving himself up and exciting him to write, which he understood full well. And so was the male company he continued to keep at the Garrick Club, the Reform (which he joined when his funds were so low he had to borrow to pay the subscription), at little literary, drinking, talking and singing clubs, and at the dinner-tables of his bachelor friends.

'W. gets up early works hard all day and then I let him gad of an eveng', Isabella wrote with matronly magnanimity to her sister, Jane. But, in fact, her permission had little to do with it, and his gadding was resisted and resented, especially when it extended to long weekends in the country while she was left to fend alone in town.

'I am half cross with Fitz and his tail (Mr Morton forms part of it)', she told Mrs Carmichael-Smyth. 'They seem as if they could not breathe without William, and thats all very well but they forget they have 300 or 400 a year to take life easy upon, and though we may have *double* that yet it must be earned.'[3]

She owned that FitzGerald would give Thackeray his last shilling and was always thinking of ways to oblige her, but her concern was not ill-founded. When FitzGerald was in London, Thackeray always had thrown work to the winds; and 'Mr Morton'—Mr Saville Morton—was the kind of companion to worry any young wife. A laughing, sparkling blue-eyed charmer, trained in architecture and medicine, a devotee of the fine arts and an accomplished practitioner in most of them, he was also a confirmed rake, with the notorious Lola Montez among his future conquests.

Thackeray, who was to try to make many a besotted woman see sense as far as Morton was concerned, admitted that he was constantly 'in some feminine mischief' and had 'a genius for scrapes such as no man out of Ireland' could ever hope for. Ten years later, he mourned but was not surprised when this busy Don Juan met a sordid end at the head of a Paris staircase: killed with a carving knife by a cuckold whose hysterical wife had announced that her newly born fifth child was Morton's not her husband's.

Knowing all his faults, Thackeray still cherished the memory of his virtues and used him in part as a model for his hero Philip, writing nostalgically when that book was done of the ringing laughter and the bold, generous, reckless, tender-hearted spirit of the man. It was friends such as Morton who quickened his imagination and sent him back to his desk ready to concoct more nonsense for the magazines. And it was another, newer friend, of a very different type, John Forster, who was to help to get that nonsense recognized as the work of a rising star.

Two years younger than Thackeray and Dickens, to whom he acted as lifelong henchman and adviser, Forster was already a power in the literary world. As chief critic of the magazine he was later to edit, the *Examiner*, he helped to make—and break—many a reputation, and began to host the celebrated dinners and breakfasts at his chambers in Lincoln's Inn Fields, where the wit flew fast and brilliant for a quarter of a century.

The son of a Newcastle cattle-dealer, he was a stout, loud young man, irascible and opinionated, quick to do a good turn, and just as quick to take offence; generous to men on their way up, often brutal when they had arrived. His 'great patron king manner' and ponderous size made him a favourite target for sly humour. Many years later, Dickens, in a description of an earthquake, wrote: 'I was awakened by a violent swaying of my bedstead from side to side, accompanied by a singular heaving motion. It was exactly as if some great beast had been crouching asleep under the bed, and was now shaking itself and trying to rise.'

'Forster!' cried the wits.[4]

As a caricaturist, Thackeray found him irresistible, but he never ceased to admire the brilliance of the man, even while he laughed at him. 'Forster is the greatest man I know,' he wrote to a mutual friend. 'Great and Benificent like a Superior Power . . . Whenever anybody is in a scrape we all fly to him for refuge. He is omniscient and works miracles . . . His bath is a miracle too—he gets into it every morning he so stout and the bath not much bigger than a Biddy.'[5]

Despite these masculine diversions, Thackeray felt himself becoming a decidedly domestic character, deeply in love with his wife, and if, after some such spree as a visit to a boxing bout, he arrived home at dinner time with his cohort still behind him, he did so with a disarming apology: 'I gave them no encouragement, my dear, but they *would* come.'

During the first lengthy separation after their marriage, when he went to Boulogne to try to squeeze some of his long loaned money out of the debt-exiled Dr Maginn, and gather material for Yellowplush's *Foring Parts*, he wrote to Isabella:

'I feel as if I had left one of my legs in Coram Street, and get on very lamely without it—all this serves to show one how closely a wife gets about the heart, and how ill one can do without her . . . Here have we been nearly 2 years married & not a single unhappy day.'[6]

The parting was almost a blessing, he said, since it had allowed him to appreciate his good fortune to the full: 'This kind of happiness is like a fine picture—you only see a little bit of it, when you are close to the canvass,—go a little distance and then you see how beautiful it is.'

He gave himself the opportunity of appreciating the view even better, by moving on to his parents at Paris and extending his visit from a few days to a month.

Isabella now responded to his loving messages with good long news-sheets of her own, and kept the Carmichael-Smyths up-to-date on family affairs in letters full of good sense, endearingly seasoned with her husband's mannerisms and absorbed opinions, and warm in his praise ('that article on Lord Brougham was William's It was very much talked of at the Reform Club').

The baby, young Annie, was another considerable factor in Thackeray's burgeoning domesticity. She was a noble little girl, he said, whose voice drove all cares out of his head. She was dubbed Pussy and Missy, and compared with other children of her age.

'Kemble's child can sing twelve tunes but is as ugly as sin in revenge,' Thackeray told his mother. 'However we must n't brag: for every body who comes into the house remarks Missy's squint that strange to say has grown quite imperceptible to me.'

He watched her tantrums which turned suddenly to laughter, and marvelled at the mysteries of her young brain. When she went to the zoo and decided the rhinoceros's skin must be tied on, since it was not smooth like her own, this clever observation was passed swiftly on to Paris. And when John Allen made her a present of grim Bible pictures, and she cried and screamed when she came to the one of Abraham sacrificing Isaac, saying 'No, he should not kill poor little boy,' as she tried to pull him off the altar, her father commended her sagacity to his stern Old Testament mother with a reference to the wisdom that came out of the mouths of babes and sucklings.

Thirteen months after Annie's birth, another daughter was born into the loving chaos of Coram Street: Jane, named for Isabella's sister. And this time the affair was managed a great deal better than the first, with only Mary Graham and Sir Charles Herbert, 'the very pink of accoucheurs', in attendance.

Isabella produced children 'with a remarkable facility', Thackeray told his mother-in-law, in announcing the safe arrival. 'She is as happy and as comfortable as any woman can be . . . We have been [none] the worse I assure you for being alone: the last time there were too many cooks to our broth, all excellent ones: but I make a vow that for the 15 next confinements there shall not be more than *one.*'[7]

Of course the baby was hideous, he added. And Miss Thackeray 'on seeing her new sister wanted to poke one of her eyes out and said teedle deedle, w^h is considered very clever.'

This carefully organized good fortune was not, however, to last. Within weeks of the birth of her sister, Annie became dangerously ill, and her father thought up jolly ideas for the Christmas magazines and badgered publishers to pay up promptly to meet the doctors' bills, in the constant fear that she was dying.

When Annie recovered, it was the baby's turn to sicken, and for Jane there was to be no reprieve. On 14 March 1839, aged eight months and five days, she died. It was a date Thackeray marked in his diary many a year until the end of his own life, and the moving episode of a baby's death and its parents' grief in the *Great Hoggarty Diamond* was written a few years later from a still tormented heart. Even as late as *The Virginians*, the pain still came back fresh and sharp when he wrote of a similar tragedy.

Three months after the funeral he and Isabella let the melancholy Coram Street house and, with toddler Annie, set off for France. All through these two years of frantic hack writing, he had been working on a book—a collection of articles and stories connected with Paris. If successful, it would add to his status and increase his fees. At last he had a publisher for it—Hugh Cunningham, who had taken over the firm of the now dead John Macrone, to whom Thackeray had first offered the idea—and an advance which might just see him through to completion.

Throughout the summer and autumn months of 1839 he wrote in the relative peace of the Carmichael-Smyths' apartment off the Champs Elysée, and when finally he returned to the thick yellow fogs of a London winter he felt he could look forward to the new decade with optimism. The next ten years, he told his mother, would be luckier for them than the previous ten: 'though God knows I have had luck enough for my latter share: and you have only a right to complain because it is the fashion to say that people are unfortunate who have lost their money. Dearest Mammy we know better than that . . .'[8]

8

Public Triumph, Private Grief

A wife deranged

Before 1840 was much advanced, Isabella's 'arrondissement' was discovered to be increasing daily. She was pregnant for the third time in three years, and despite his professed contentment with poverty, her husband's concern, as he contemplated this addition to his family, was security and the fate of his growing band of dependants should he, the only breadwinner, die. He had no insurance, nothing saved, parents in debt, and a mother-in-law with little to spare and less on offer.

No company would insure Thackeray at a reasonable premium because of an old medical problem which over the years he was to refer to by many a euphemism. To doctors it was known as a stricture of the urethra, a legacy which, in the days before penicillin, many a young man bore for the rest of his life after an early bout of gonorrhoea—venereal disease. Though the infection had long since been cured and there was no danger of contagion, the damage caused was often painful and sometimes embarrassing. It was possible to have an operation to cut the contracted tissues, but since primitive antiseptics and no chloroform made most cures more hazardous than the complaint, Thackeray learned to live with the miseries of his misfortune, and to joke about them in all-male company.

'WMT talks of Miss Peawell', a young *Punch* colleague was to write in his diary, '& of his being inclined to say to her—My dear Miss Peawell—I wish I could.'[1]

With age the 'hydraulic' uncertainty, the risk of kidney infection, and the discomfort which made him sit with his long body so curiously entwined that innocent onlookers were surprised to see him most at ease when they would have thought him most uncomfortable, grew wretchedly worse, and so did the need for relief from painful probing instruments.

At this time, however, he was remarkably untroubled by the old irritant, and set himself to secure his own future with tremendous zeal and a patently precarious venture: a weekly broadsheet of humour, to be drawn, written and launched solely by himself, with all the profits accruing to the same quarter. It was to be called the *Foolscap Library*, and to begin with the pictorial adventures of Dr Dionysius Diddler, a character based on Dr Dionysius Lardner, scientist, writer and editor of *The Cabinet Cyclopaedia*, a celebrity Thackeray had already treated quite mercilessly, along with Bulwer-Lytton, in *Mr Yellowplush's Ajew*, for *Fraser's*.

The idea was a fortune, he told his mother, 'but wants ab^r £30 to start it: however I have some, and shan't want yet. 1000 gives us 8£ profit Why shouldn't I sell 5000, 10000 copies? they will pay me 40 or 80 a week: 80 a week is 4000 a year of w^h I would put by 3 at the very least &c &c: see Alnaschar in the Arabian Nights.'[2]

Isabella, cautiously suggesting he should halve the risks by taking a partner, even if it did mean halving the profits too, was called a coward for her pains, but contented herself with the conviction that their temperaments were 'properly balanced'. To Mrs Carmichael-Smyth she excused the enterprise by explaining: 'It is a kind of pastime for W. for you know it gives him no trouble to *sketch*'; and when the glorious dreams crumbled, loyally insisted that the engraver had spoiled his designs in 'the most *cruel* manner.'

By May, this 'properly balanced' pair discovered they had spent £200 in four months, despite ominous harassment from the Major's old creditors. Mrs Carmichael-Smyth's directives that they should cut down on staff and move to cheaper quarters were smoothly parried by her son. When the lease on the Coram Street 'mansion' was up, they would certainly move, but to exchange Brodie, the fine new nannie they had just taken on, for a cheaper, untrained country girl, he could see only as a false economy. Within months, Brodie was to prove his estimate of her value a thousandfold.

Isabella thrived during her third pregnancy. She was fat, rosy, healthy, never better than when she was in that condition, said her husband, and she even got up before eight in the mornings. When she was six months' pregnant, the two of them took a walk in the countryside round London looking for a house for Mrs Shawe. The birds of the air had nests, and foxes had holes, whereas she had no place to lay her head, that lady had ominously written to her daughter, in figurative language that needed little translation.

Too broke to hire a carriage, Isabella and Thackeray walked to the 'pretty little village' of Watford, where they sat on a sunny bench eating a penny roll for their lunch, before returning via Harrow, always managing to be either too late or too early for the train. From Watford to Harrow is seven miles, and from Harrow back to London, twelve. They took the whole day over it, didn't find a house, and quite convinced themselves that living in the country would not do for *them*.

As the time drew nearer for the 'parturient Mrs Thackeray' to be 'stretched on the straw', Mrs Shawe still posed a threat, and urgent pleas were sent to Paris for either Mrs Butler or Mrs Carmichael-Smyth to occupy their spare room, otherwise they would be in for 'storms, whirlwinds, cataracts, tornadoes.' In the meantime, they filled it with Isabella's brother, Arthur, an idle young rogue delaying as long as possible his departure for India and the army.

After two months of Arthur's breezy company, Thackeray told Mrs Carmichael-Smyth: 'He is a lazy good-humoured ignorant youth perfectly at ease with himself as perhaps you may have remarked young gentlemen of his age are, and a great hand with the ladies.'[3]

Mrs Carmichael-Smyth was not amused. Suspicious of any contact between her son and his in-laws, she made determined, long-range efforts to winkle this one out of Coram Street, but Thackeray refused to be bullied. The poor lad didn't cost him more than ten shillings a week, he said; they hadn't drunk wine since his first appearance, and a bottle of gin lasted them nearly a week. What he didn't say, but what was probably equally important to him, was that Arthur took Isabella off his hands and conscience, leaving him with peace to work and freedom to seek his own amusements.

Since their stay in Paris, Mrs Carmichael-Smyth had taken to more obtrusive meddling in her son's affairs, and Thackeray was soon accusing her of being rather hard on Isabella and her housekeeping. As for his own conduct, he protested that he could never bear to think of showing any neglect towards a wife so good and uncomplaining, not any 'positive neglect', anyway. As for his 'jollifying after a day's work', that he couldn't help, and would be good for nothing without it.

When Arthur left, however, he sought more frequent refuge at the Garrick Club or the Reform, where he ate three o'clock dinners, and worked solidly through afternoons and long evenings in more peace than he could find at home, juggling his time half distractedly between the long overdue Paris book, his annual art reviews, the beginning of *A Shabby Genteel Story*, and sundry smaller items. A few days later he too left town in a concerted bid at least to finish the book and gain money enough to meet the bills of the confinement, though he could never quite rid himself of the fear that the baby might be born while he was away.

When he returned, in plenty of time for the birth of his third daughter, he did so with all but the last page of his manuscript ready for the printer. It took him more than three days in his own study to finish those last few sentences, and the prospect of the £50 due to him, as he thought, on delivery of the completed work was the only beam of light in the melancholy which was always to settle on him at the end of such a project. Even this was to fade.

When he presented himself to his publisher, with his last seven shillings and sixpence in his pocket, he discovered that the £50 was due not on delivery, but on publication—an unfixed date which might be months away. As usual, he groaned, dug his fists into his near-empty pockets and contemplated pawning his watch, before remembering that *Fraser's* owed him £20, and deciding that 'a dreadful scuffle of work' would be better for him than the idleness which would surely have come with a full purse.

In the event, he had little more than a month to wait before *The Paris Sketch Book*, by M. A. Titmarsh, appeared in the bookshops, and only a few weeks after that he was rejoicing in the sale of four hundred copies; 'Enough to pay all the expenses of authorship printing &c. and to leave 500£ profit to the publisher if the rest are sold.'[4]

He had had eight or nine good 'puffs' in the newspapers and magazines. Forster had 'tried' to praise him in the *Examiner*, but obviously wasn't too keen, particularly on the drawings. *The Times* had been very kind, but in small print, 'a great difference in the Publisher's view'. *Fraser's* had refused to mention him at all, since he had failed to acknowledge that some of the pieces had first been published by them.

The twin births of a baby and book were also marked by a handsome consignment of wine and cakes from two most sensitive barometers of talent, Bryan Procter and his wife, an intriguingly contrasted couple, who for half a century presided over London's most enduring literary salon.

Though he too was a writer of some acclaim, Procter's true genius lay in spotting that commodity in others, and in encouraging it with the substantial fees he earned as a conveyancing lawyer. Carlyle dismissed him as a decidedly pretty little fellow, both in body and spirit, but most of his contemporaries admired Procter for the remarkable sweetness of his nature, and regarded him as the most likeable man of his time.

His wife, Anne, on the other hand, was famous for her wit, which was acerbic enough for any man's dyspepsia: 'our Lady of Bitterness', Kinglake called her. The mother of six children and no great beauty, she was twelve years older than Thackeray, but he relished both her friendship and her conversation, which he analysed as jocose, sneering, good-humoured, scandalous and sentimental. She made, he told her, the best jokes and the best tea in the world.

In thanking this bitter-sweet pair for their praise and their presents, Thackeray proudly mentioned the great critic Chorley's four-column review in the *Athenaeum*. It was a capital notice, he said, and he was determined to take even its sly reproach for ungentility as a compliment.

There were many good things in *The Paris Sketch Book*, some old, much new, some borrowed from the French themselves. The most memorable were accounts of scenes Thackeray himself had witnessed and described with freshness and humour: pieces written 'under the *excitement of travelling*', as Isabella morosely admitted, when her husband wanted to go jaunting off by himself again. Even the dedication was a charming oddity: to Monsieur Aretz, a Paris tailor, who had waived payment for a certain number of coats and pantaloons and courteously offered a thousand-franc note to a customer in temporary financial embarrassment.

Among its generally unappreciated illustrations it also contained one of Thackeray's most famous sketches: 'An Historical Study— Rex, Ludovicus, Ludovicus Rex'—a cynical view of monarchy. On the left of the drawing hang the king's clothes: the vast wig, the mighty velvet mantle with its ermine trimming, the gold chains and jewelled stars, the slashed satin breeches, fine silk hose, and princely high-heeled shoes. In the middle is the king: bald, spindly-legged and paunchy in his underclothes—a sad bundle of sagging flesh and brittle bones. On the right stand the two combined: imperious majesty, impressive to behold.

As far as Thackeray was concerned, the best thing about the book was the interest it sparked in other, better, publishing houses. Chapman and Hall, Carlyle's and Dickens's publishers, and the great Longman both showed readiness to negotiate with him. 'Titmarsh in Ireland', he fancied as his next endeavour, and estimated that it would take him only three months to tour the country and write it up. For that he would expect £150 in advance, £150 on completion. Thus, he would have £150 in hand to begin another book—for which he would be paid £400. After that, another, for a similarly enlarged stake. 'Fancy having 500,' he crowed, 'ye Gods what a treasure!'

It was, as yet, only another Alnaschar vision, as he readily admitted, but the prospects at last looked rosy enough to justify such dreams.

For Thackeray the family man, the forecast was not set so fair. His third daughter had been born on 27 May 1840, and at first both 'patients' appeared to prosper. The child was christened Harriet Marian so that she could be called Polly and Harry, but in fact graduated from 'baby' to Harriet, and then on to Marian before becoming Minnie, which she remained for the rest of her life. She was thought to be very like the little one they had lost, 'strangely like in voice'.

Mrs Carmichael-Smyth, immobilized by a sprained ankle, had sent a Paris friend to deputize at the birth, one Mrs Parker, a hearty, talkative creature who amused Thackeray with her tales of his mother's Parisian court of English exiles, and gossiped to Isabella as she sat up in bed in becoming nightcaps made by the excellent Brodie. Then, shortly after the baby's appearance, Mrs Butler, plus maid, arrived at last, and settled into the back drawing-room-cum-bedroom so recently vacated by Arthur Shawe.

In this household full of women, Thackeray found great solace in three-year-old Annie. She visited him in his makeshift bed next to the nursery in the mornings; trotted in to tell him when his meals were ready; delighted him by chuckling 'What a funny fellow you are Papa.'

After a month or so, Thackeray was reporting to Paris that during her entire stay, Mrs Butler had neither heard nor used a rough word and, what was more, was to stand him two bottles of champagne on his twenty-ninth birthday. Saville Morton and an Irish journalist, O'Donnell, helped him to drink it, but by that time Thackeray was in little mood for celebration.

Domestically, the clouds were beginning to gather. Isabella, so well and cheerful to begin with, had started to ail. It was nothing to worry about, said the elderly accoucheur. But Thackeray did worry, especially when she remained strangely lethargic after the trouble was said to be cured.

He had also given himself a prime dose of the blue devils by going to a public hanging with Richard Monckton Milnes, leader of the anti-hanging faction in the House of Commons. The bestiality of the act, coupled with the festive mood of the massive, gloating crowd had left him with an extraordinary feeling of terror and shame to add to his confirmed belief that the principle of an eye for an eye was not only barbarous and evil, but useless as a deterrent. He cursed himself for the curiosity which had taken him to such a brutal sight, and the face of the poor hanged wretch swam constantly before his eyes as he tried to write it out of his system for *Fraser's*.[5]

'. . . the scene mixes itself up with all my occupations', he told Mrs Procter. 'Notes, however small, are not even exempt from it: and I expect to be very agreeable and lively tomorrow with long full particular descriptions of it.'[6]

Eventually, the joys of successful authorship chased off the grim phantom. Plans, visions, opportunities for scaling still more dazzling heights hovered in the exciting air. He finished off his old work and searched out the best terms for the new in a flattering bustle of celebrity; he was talked of in the clubs and literary circles, written about in the right places.

Then he would return to Great Coram Street, to find his grandmother in command of the drawing-room, puzzling over Dickens's strange new magazine, *Master Humphrey's Clock*, with Isabella curiously still and silent on the sofa at her side. At the end of July he escaped for three days to the Bullers' at Leatherhead, and returned stimulated and recharged with plans for a longer trip to Antwerp. He wanted to see the paintings, he told Isabella. He would write it all up for *Blackwood's*, which would pay his costs and more—Titmarsh in Belgium was bound to be a success, just as Titmarsh in Paris had been. When she argued, he told her it was necessary for his own health that he should get away.

As his long legs strode the deck of the Belgian steamer, and he felt in his pocket for a friendly cigar, the strain and struggle of three years fell away with the creaming wake. For the first time, he could see his way clear to success and freedom from the desperate gamble of freelancing, which he reckoned would kill any writer in six years, and which he was to remember bitterly to the end of his days.

'Heartless! insatiable! bloody! destroying monster!' he cried shortly before his death, pointing an accusing finger at the relentlessly turning presses of *The Times*. 'What brains you have ground to pulp! What hopes you have crushed, what anxiety you have inflicted on us all!'[7]

For a space he was his own man, a truant from work and family, his immediate financial cares solved by a surprise gift from Mrs Butler who, 'like a trump', had handed over £25—enough for his journey and for Isabella, too. For two blessed weeks, it was pleasure and sunshine all the way. Under the innocent blue skies of Antwerp and Bruges, it seemed a sin not to be happy. He feasted his eyes on walls of voluptuous Rubens and his cooler Flemish rivals, and his stomach on good Belgian dinners. He slept away whole afternoons on shade-dappled benches, and kept his conscience clear with copious travel notes.

When he had closed the door on 13 Great Coram Street at the start of this balm-giving expedition, he had heard Isabella begin to laugh. At the time, he had not thought it strange.

2.

A few days after her husband's departure, Isabella wrote a sad, strained letter to her mother-in-law. She had been ill, she said, her body had been unhealthy and '*consequently*' her spirits low. But she was quite a different person now, and had 'a kind of wish that every body should feel happy.' She told of the success of the Paris book, of the admirable sobriety of Annie at her sister's christening, and left unfinished an uneasy comparison between the new baby and the one that had died, before going on:

'I confess to you I feel myself excited my strength is not great and my head flies away with me as if it were a balloon. This is *mere* weakness and a walk will set me right but in case there should be incoherences in my letter you will know what to attribute it to.'

She had tried to persuade Thackeray not to go to Belgium, she said: 'but it seems as if I was always to damp him, and that I am to go a round of old saws such as "It is the tortoise and not the hare wins the race" mais enfin il ne m'écoute pas and I must e'en let him make his fortune his own way. I do mind my own business as much as possible but one cannot but be interested . . . I try to think my fears imaginary and exaggerated and that I am a coward by nature, but when people do not raise their expectations to too high a pitch they cannot be disappointed.'[1]

The reference to raised expectations was as applicable to Mrs Carmichael-Smyth as to Thackeray and his eagerness for success. Isabella felt too much was expected of her by her husband and his family, and if that particular hint was not meant as a gentle reproach to her mother-in-law, the last paragraph of her letter certainly was. Mrs Parker, the Parisian envoy, was, she said, '*une femme sans tête*'; she made the 'most injudicious repetitions. Let us be frank but let us not say things that hurt the feelings of others.'

As Thackeray was soon to discover, hearty Mrs Parker, whose revelations had been so amusing in the drawing-room, had spread nothing but poison upstairs. Well primed by Mrs Carmichael-Smyth and Mary Graham as to Isabella's faults and failures in wifely duty, she had taken the expectant mother to task for them immediately before the baby was born. In the depression which followed the birth, Isabella worked up the charges until she imagined herself the most miserable of sinners, 'a perfect demon of wickedness—God abandoned.'

And this was what greeted Thackeray when he stepped over his

George Chinnery's painting of Thackeray and his parents in India, with the future author prophetically seated on a pile of books.

The youthful Thackeray painted by himself and friends.

(*Left*) The embryo writer, by Daniel Maclise, 1832.

(*Above*) With the mass of dark hair that astonished his daughters, by Frank Stone.

(*Below*) And his self-portrait with artistical moustache and beard.

Maguinn

Thackeray
Churchill   Southey   Irv.ng

Ains-
worth   D'Orsay

Coleriage   Theo. Hook

Dunlop   Fraser   Lockhart
THACKERAY AMONG THE "FRASERIANS."
Drawn by Daniel Maclise, 1835.

Maclise's sketch of Dr Maginn addressing a dinner for contributors to *Fraser's Magazine*. Thackeray at twenty-four was included more for his financial contributions to the libatious Maginn than his literary achievements.

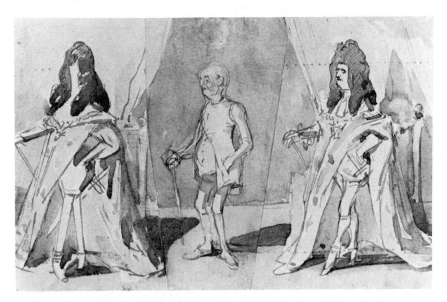

Rex, Ludovicus, Ludovicus Rex. Thackeray's original drawing of his cynical view of majesty, which appeared in the *Paris Sketch Book*.

Isabella. Thackeray's portrait of his adored young wife.

Thackeray's 'mater dolorosa' in old age, with her second husband, Major Carmichael-Smyth, the inspiration for Colonel Newcome.

Reverend William Brookfield, painted by Samuel Laurence, and his wife Jane — Thackeray's perfection of womanhood — painted by Ludovici.

Thirteen Young Street, Kensington:
the house in which Thackeray wrote
Vanity Fair and returned to some
semblance of family life after his wife
became mad.

Annie, Thackeray's eldest daughter, painted by himself
– his 'fat lump of pure gold'.

A Thackeray sketch of Queen Victoria as a young bride, complete with a spare
waving hand and admiring Prince Albert.

A page from one of Thackeray's early sketchbooks.

The title page from Thackeray's first published work, *Flore et Zephyr*, a pictorial parody of the ballet as performed in his youth.

Thackeray at the time of *Vanity Fair*, sketched in convivial mood by Count D'Orsay, one of the splendid dandies in whom he took great delight.

Old Gentleman: "I AM SORRY TO SEE YOU OCCUPIED, MY DEAR MISS WIGGETS, WITH THAT TRIVIAL PAPER 'PUNCH.' A RAILWAY IS NOT A PLACE, IN MY OPINION, FOR JOKES. I NEVER JOKE—NEVER."

Miss W: "SO I SHOULD THINK, SIR."

Old Gentleman: "AND BESIDES, ARE YOU AWARE WHO ARE THE CONDUCTORS OF THAT PAPER, AND THAT THEY ARE CHARTISTS, DEISTS, ATHEISTS, ANARCHISTS, AND SOCIALISTS, TO A MAN? I HAVE IT FROM THE BEST AUTHORITY, THAT THEY MEET TOGETHER ONCE A WEEK IN A TAVERN IN SAINT GILE'S, WHERE THEY CONCOCT THEIR INFAMOUS PRINT. THE CHIEF PART OF THEIR INCOME IS DERIVED FROM THREATENING LETTERS WHICH THEY SEND TO THE NOBILITY AND GENTRY. THE PRINCIPAL WRITER IS A RETURNED CONVICT. TWO HAVE BEEN TRIED AT THE OLD BAILEY; AND THEIR ARTIST—AS FOR THEIR ARTIST. . ."

Guard: "SWIN-DUN! STA-TION!"

(*Exeunt two Authors*)

The most famous of Thackeray's *Punch* series, 'Author's Miseries' (1848), showing himself and Douglas Jerrold discomfited on a train.

own threshold once more, refreshed, invigorated, the material for another book in his pocket.

His grandmother and his wife were coldly at odds with each other. Mrs Butler, 'a pestering old body' for all her generosity, had taken it into her head that Isabella didn't like her. She wouldn't answer when spoken to, which Mrs Butler attributed to sulkiness. Isabella herself was in such an extraordinary state of languor and depression that Thackeray once more rushed in the doctor, who prescribed a trip to the sea. No need to call in another physician, he assured the anxious husband; there was nothing the matter that a change of air couldn't cure. The cause of the trouble was the stomach—indigestion, thought Thackeray—and Isabella's constitutional 'indolence and apathy' with regard to medicine. Though he used tears, prayers and threats, she could never be made to take it for long. It was the same story as in the days when he was wooing her: that old unromantic constipation, aggravated now by childbirth, for which she refused all remedies.

He reassured himself that she couldn't be very ill since she still had plenty of milk for the baby; and the baby, a 'dear little fat flourishing podge of flesh', was always at her mother for more—a cycle which was bound to pull her down.

He stayed in London just long enough to sell his Belgian notes to Chapman and Hall and begin negotiations with them for Titmarsh in Ireland, and then, on the fourth anniversary of his wedding day, packed Isabella, Brodie and the children onto a steamer for Margate. That night, the only one awake in their lodging-house, Thackeray sat in the small, odd sitting-room with a glass door leading straight out onto the street, listening to the soothing ripple of the water, watching the gas-lamps thrusting reflections like flaming swords into the sea, and unburdened a softened heart in a letter to his mother.

He had had a sad battle to fight since his return to England, he told her, but even the short sea trip, the fresh air, sunshine and small excitement of travel appeared to have done Isabella good. She had gone to bed weary but happy. They had eaten their anniversary dinner alone at the neighbouring inn, and returned to find Annie, more than half asleep, lying on her tummy, eyelids drooping, but determined to wait up for them.

'I have come a long long way,' she had told Brodie, 'but I wish to kiss Papa & Mama before I go to bed.'

'God bless her,' Thackeray wrote to Mrs Carmichael-Smyth. 'Your big heart would have thumped to see her toddling about the deck, embracing in her fine innocent warmth every little child about her. I find myself growing much more sentimental as I grow older.

This world is not near such a bad one as some of your orthodox pretend. We are not desperately wicked but good & loving many of us: our arms reach up to heaven, though the Devil to be sure is tugging at our heels.'[2]

The proposed few days at Margate stretched to a fortnight and then three weeks. Some days Isabella seemed better; on others she was frighteningly worse. In the mornings, especially, her spirits were often so low and her mind so absent that he daren't leave her alone. He couldn't work with her pitiful looks always fixed upon him, and was with her so much he felt in danger of catching the infection himself. Without any outlet for his usual high spirits, his favourite talk of books and art, he felt useless—except, perhaps, as a nurse to Isabella for a while, and he prayed many times a day to be kept stiff to that purpose.

But the two duties of tending his wife and earning enough money to keep them alive were hard ones to combine. Work he had to do, or they would all perish. He solved the problem by leaving his family in Brodie's care for parts of the day, while he walked two miles off to the deserted tea-garden of a quiet inn, where in a sunny arbour he finished the *Shabby Genteel Story*, with its gentle little red-headed heroine, for *Fraser's*, and wrote a great critical study of Henry Fielding and his works for *The Times*.

Finding the article on his old hero eight years later, Thackeray thought ruefully how his apology for that full-blooded, hard-living, eighteenth-century male supreme sounded like a plea for someone else too—someone closer to home.

Twelve days after it was published, Isabella tried to kill herself. Unknown to Thackeray, she had already attempted to drown Annie, but had recovered her reason just in time to pull the child out of the sea again.

When they returned to Great Coram Street, with £32 drained from their meagre store, she seemed quieter, but three days later was as bad as she had ever been, and Thackeray knew that if he were alone with her much longer he too would sink into morbid melancholia.

He thought of taking her to Boulogne and asking his mother to join them there, but the Carmichael-Smyths were away on a long-planned and cherished holiday. He couldn't bring himself to wreck it for them; and, after Mrs Parker's disclosures, it might, anyway, have done more harm than good.

The obvious solution was Mrs Shawe, who had settled once more in Ireland, the country Thackeray needed to visit for his new book. To be beholden in any degree to his mother-in-law was not an attractive proposition, but Thackeray consoled himself with the thought that returning her to her mother and sister might provide the best cure for his wife. Whatever he did, he would need money for it, a fact which struck grimly home as, with the children crying in one room and Isabella raving in another, Brodie asked for essential household expenses and he gave her his last £5.

Turning to the two mainstays of his income for the past three years, the journals to which he had given of his best, he was rebuffed by *Fraser's*, who owing him £13 10 shillings refused to make it up to a round £15; while *The Times* wouldn't give him a penny more than five guineas for the Fielding article, the fruit of an entire week's work.

Only Chapman and Hall came to his aid. They had already paid £70 for his Belgian notes and received no finished manuscript, but they immediately drew up a contract for the Irish book and offered a liberal advance of £120. All they asked was for someone to guarantee the sum in case he failed to deliver.

Mrs Butler, approached for this favour, refused in a fright, thinking he was trying to squeeze more money out of her. Mary Graham, the only other capitalist left in the family, readily agreed, but before her letter arrived from Paris, Thackeray had come to a simpler arrangement: he had lodged his plate-chest with the publishers, 'as a kind of genteel pawn.'

Old John Goldworthy was left to garrison the Coram Street house, which Thackeray made a half-hearted attempt to let; the cook was paid off; Brodie and the children were to go with him.

'O Titmarsh Titmarsh why did you marry?' Thackeray asked as he made his miserable preparations; and answered himself: 'why for better or for worse'.

For a long time there was to be no better, and few things could have been more terrible than the sea voyage on board the steamship *Jupiter* from London to Cork. For Thackeray it was three days and four nights of hell, during which Isabella's melancholy 'augmented to absolute insanity.' For three of the nights he was constantly on the alert while she made repeated attempts to destroy herself. On the second day out he thought she had succeeded when she flung herself from a water-closet into the sea, where she remained for twenty minutes before the ship's boat found her, floating calmly on her back, paddling with her hands.

By the time they arrived at Cork she was perfectly demented, and for the first week in Ireland there was still no peace for her husband. At night he had to tie a ribbon round their waists so that her slightest movement woke him, otherwise as soon as he slept she tried to steal out of bed.

Brodie now also became ill, with a fever. She had been sick every

quarter of an hour on board the *Jupiter*, but was up again immediately, staggering after the children, feeding one and comforting
the other. The knowledge that she too was suffering was an added
anguish.

As he had watched this staunch Scots nurse tending his children,
Thackeray had thought that of all God's creations a woman's heart
was the most beautiful. But he was soon made to realize that for all
His bounty, there was one woman sadly deprived of this gem, and
this was the one he now relied on for any small drop of comfort, any
slight easing of his burden: Mrs Shawe.

Isabella's mother said that she too had been ill, which Thackeray
could see was true, and though she had a spare room in her cottage
refused to have her daughter there. It would be too much for her
nerves, she said; too much of a responsibility; too much for her
darling Jane.

They were forced to lodge next door in a filthy, crumbling
tenement, no more than forty years old but already a mad ruin. The
windows had no pulleys and the doors no locks: a broken chair kept
the former propped open and the latter closed. Cracks in the
woodwork let in whistling draughts and the gleam of prying eyes.
The unpapered walls were hung with pictures which set Thackeray's
artist eyes on edge; there was no poker to the hearth—and the coals
were brought upstairs in a fine china bowl. But in the midst of this
chaos, there were souls so kind and hands so loving that Thackeray
wrote of them with deepest gratitude, when he was able to write
about them at all.

Here, the baby was bounced and fondled and jealously fought for,
while Annie found a pack of plump, rosy-cheeked, grubby
playmates, and a raft of new 'relations'.

'Who's your friend?' Thackeray asked, when he met his elder
daughter in the street one day, deep in confidential conversation
with an old man in a great coat.

'Don't you know him?—THAT'S UNCLE JAMES!' Annie
crowed in purest Munster brogue.

And so it was. It was the tall old gentleman with huge pockets to
his coat—pockets guaranteed to contain an apple for any hungry
young stomach, even an English one—whom Thackeray heard
entering the house every afternoon, bawling for the maid and the
'materials' for his reviving punch; a man Thackeray suspected of
sleeping in an upright piano, since that was the only stick of furniture in the room to which he retired each night.

Mrs Shawe's hospitality provided grim contrast. She had been
denied Isabella in health, she said, only to have her forced upon her
in sickness. She pumped the convalescent Brodie to find out if

Thackeray had been ill-treating her daughter; she never gave her son-in-law a meal but she added an insult for him to swallow with it; she bragged, bustled, bothered, and prated incessantly of her own superior merits and sacrifices. She was, groaned Thackeray, 'really & truly demented', and should not be judged too hardly.

The only comfort she offered was cold comfort indeed. She too, she said, had been affected with melancholy when she nursed her children. More heartening was the local doctor who told of five hundred similar cases he had cured, and who, after his fifth fee, suggested calling every other time 'as a friend'.

After a week of this 'skillful and tender' man's attentions, Thackeray could see extraordinary progress in the patient. He listened with a thankful heart as Jane, devotedly nursing her sister, read verses from the psalms, and Isabella, in the sweet voice that never failed to touch her husband, repeated them with perfect good sense, a feat way beyond her powers only three days earlier. As relief washed over him, he longed for someone to fling his arms around, someone with whom he could share his happiness; but within all the bounds of Ireland he had only Brodie to call a friend.

Even Jane held herself aloof. She was cordially jealous of Thackeray and the Carmichael-Smyths, and took her mother's part in all disputes, a loyalty her brother-in-law could look upon, even in the midst of all these miseries, with understanding approval. She had her own problems too, poor girl. Like Isabella, she had also been allowed a lover who had been encouraged enough to propose, before the mother's possessive storms and whirlwinds blasted the romance. The man, an Irish country parson, a most suitable suitor, had braved the fury eight times before giving up the fight, leaving Jane wretched that he had finally accepted her refusal. It was a pattern, with the actors in it brutally described, which Thackeray was to use in his grim tale of *Dennis Haggarty's Wife*.

When he grasped the full magnitude of Isabella's illness, a curious calm settled on Thackeray. He could see then that it had been brewing for many months, only he had obstinately closed his eyes to it. Now he could work towards the cure, and try to snatch some benefit from the ashes. Neither of them had fully shouldered their responsibilities, he said. If his wife had failed, he had been no less to blame. He must learn to be more humble, less selfish—to do his duty by the fireside as well as in his writing room.

And so he sat by his wife's bedside. She no longer tried to kill herself, but was silent and apathetic, caring neither for him nor her children, though troubled if he left her. He sat on, and started to write—a comedy in five acts which the manager of Covent Garden had promised to read with particular attention. From heaven knows what resources of imagination he managed to find 'some good lively stuff' to put into it.

How he would jump, he said, if the play were accepted, 'but that is too much luck'. And so it proved. After a six months' silence, he discovered his attentive friend had never even looked at it. When Jane or Mrs Shawe relieved him at Isabella's side, he turned to his daughters, compensating for their mother's lack of interest.

Isabella progressed from apathy to fits of rambling gloom, wallowing in a '*moral* melancholy', deploring her own un-worthiness, thinking she had entailed all manner of misery on her husband, that she never had been fit to be a wife. And, alas, thought an exhausted Thackeray, it was indeed partly the truth. But at least she was talking: for the first time in three months her tongue was growing fluent again.

By the end of September, she was recovered enough to be taken for short drives, and to be touched by natural beauty, a commodity with which the neighbourhood was blessed in astonishing measure. As they jogged down Grattan's Hill and along the country lanes, Thackeray longed to stop and sketch, but daren't relax his vigilance. He longed to go into Cork too, on the day Daniel O'Connell—the great 'Liberator'—made a state entry there. It would have been good material for the Irish book, if ever that book were written. But he would be away for three hours—too long to leave his 'rogue of a wife.' As Isabella's health improved, life only became more dif-ficult.

'My wife won't sit still, wont employ herself, wont do anything that she is asked & vice versâ,' he told his mother. 'Mong Jew what a time of it, from four o'clock till nine this morning—as soon as ever I was asleep my lady woke me. She had had a decent slumber herself from eight until four, & when awake herself will give me no rest. Never mind as Anny says when she breaks the tumblers, the discipline is good for one's disposition if not very improving to the mind.'[3]

It was impossible to write at all now. Chapman and Hall's precious advance was flowing away in a great torrent with nothing to show for it. He could only hold his head in his hands and think that this had been the time of his fortune. But for Isabella's illness he had been a made man.

And in the middle of it all, Mrs Shawe proved marvellously true to form: 'We have just had a scene—' wrote Thackeray; 'fancy that—in the midst of all this trouble she can't keep her monstrous tongue quiet.'[4]

He had been holding himself back for weeks, taking all her insults in silence, knowing that if he quarrelled she would revenge herself on

Isabella by withdrawing herself and Jane from her completely. When his own mother wrote offering every aid, he replied:

'I knew very well that you would sell your smock if need were to help me in my want, yet it is pleasant to have the testimony of it, & I have been half tempted to fling it in Mrs Shawe's face, and say there Madam you who prate about self-sacrifices, you bragging old humbug see the way in w^h my mother welcomes your daughter, & think how you have received her yourself.'[5]

He had kept Mrs Carmichael-Smyth away till now, but as he lay in bed, awake for four hours in the dark dawn of a mid-October morning, with Isabella worse than she had been for weeks, and Annie howling in the distant gloom, he decided, with an astonishing burst of relief, to leave Ireland and head for Paris. With the doctor's blessing, he set the packing in progress and said not a word to Mrs Shawe until an hour before the boat was due to sail—just as she was advising him to put Isabella into a madhouse.

On the voyage to Bristol, the shortest sea route he could take, Thackeray wrote a nine-page 'very free' letter to his mother-in-law, but decided instead to send only a curt, cold one, suggesting that since she had at last lodged some of Isabella's money with her London agents, she should, knowing her daughter's condition, make it payable to him. And, knowing as she did how he himself was situated, asking that she might use her best endeavours to see that the arrears were also made up.

He had spent one month and £58 in Cork. After settling his London debts, he had less than £20 left—and Brodie was soon to leave him, to marry. He could bear the strain no longer. 'Do come dearest Mother,' he wrote; 'give me some money—somehow or the other.'

But Thackeray had to endure one more sojourn in hell before he could find a bosom on which to lay his own weary head. In this season of sickness, Mrs Carmichael-Smyth was not well enough to travel, and Thackeray was left to shepherd his family to France alone, except for Brodie, who was to give up her marriage rather than desert him. Since there was no money for a private coach, he packed wife, children and nurse into a creaking public diligence for the all-night journey to Paris, a night of such misery that three-year-old Annie could still recall every detail of it to the end of her life.

'I wanted to get out and walk,' she remembered, 'and they wouldn't let me, and I cried on and on. There was a man in a cap I didn't like, with his nose against the window. He frowned at me when I looked at him. My father was in the corner of the diligence opposite to me and the nurse and baby, and he struck a match, and lit up a little lantern, which he held up to amuse me. But I only cried the louder. Then he said gravely, "If you go on crying, you will wake the baby, and I shall put out the candle;" so I went on crying, and I woke the baby, who began to cry too; then the man in the corner scolded again, and my father blew out the lantern, and suddenly all was dark. I could not believe it, never before had I been so severely punished. "Light it, light it," I screamed. "No," said my father's voice in the dark, "I told you I should put the light out if you cried." All the time the man in the corner kept on moaning and complaining, and the diligence jogged on, and I suppose I went to sleep on my father's knee at last. I remember hearing him long afterwards speak of that dreadful night, and of the angry Frenchman, who kept saying, "J'ai la fièvre, mon Dieu. J'ai la fièvre.'"[6]

The next thing Annie remembered was arriving quite cheerful at Paris early next morning, to see her grandmother and grandfather running down their curling staircase, opening their arms to them all.

9

The Restless Years

A time of great affliction

The five years which followed his night flight to Paris were bitter, restless ones for Thackeray. He was doomed to remain a bachelor in all but name, the father of two children without home or wife; destined to struggle on as a magazine hack, when he had tasted the promise of greater things. He willed himself to believe that Isabella would recover. Every cure was tried, including more long months of his own spirit-breaking attention. At first all appeared to have miraculous effect; within days, weeks, or months, all were shown to have failed.

At the end of 1840, violent and feverish, she had been admitted to the famous Esquirol's *Maison de Santé*, at Ivry, outside Paris. When Thackeray was allowed to see her six weeks later, she had returned to a silent state of melancholy.

'She knows everybody and recollects things but in a stunned confused sort of way,' Thackeray told FitzGerald. 'She kissed me at first very warmly and with tears in her eyes, then she went away from me, as if she felt she was unworthy of having such a God of a husband. God help her.'[1]

The charges were £20 a month—a bill FitzGerald paid on at least one occasion—but Thackeray was assured that his wife '*doit guérir*'—should get better. While waiting, he and his children stayed with his parents, his grandmother, and Mary Graham at their apartment in an old courtyarded mansion on the Avenue Sainte Marie, a broad, tree-lined street leading to the Arc de Triomphe, and there, in a small room overlooking a cheerless, snow-covered garden, with the sound of nuns at their devotions floating across from a neighbouring convent, he wrote once more for his life.

In December of 1840, he had witnessed the last triumphant entry into Paris of Napoleon, when the body of the Emperor, nearly twenty years dead, had been brought back from St Helena to rest at last on French soil at Les Invalides. The occasion, thought Thackeray, was humbug and French braggadocio from the tinsel trappings and fake marble statues which lined the route, to the emotions of the onlookers and organizers of the incredible occasion.

Vanitas vanitatum, he cried, as he wrote it up in three long letters to an imaginary young English friend, Miss Smith. It took him four days, and he added as an afterthought the epic anti-war ballad, *The Chronicle of the Drum*, which Saintsbury was to praise as 'one of the very greatest things in serio-comic verse-literature.' [2]

Hugh Cunningham, who had published *The Paris Sketch Book*, brought out prose and poem together as a slim volume called *The Second Funeral of Napoleon*—price 2s.6d., author's royalty, 7½d. Thackeray did his usual wildly optimistic accounting in a letter to Mrs Procter, a confidante as intimate now as Mrs Carmichael-Smyth. His own share from the ten thousand copies already printed (plus another improbable ninety thousand), he told her, would work out like this:

100 copies.	=	750 pence	=	£3: 2:6
1000 copies	=	7500 ,,	=	£31: 5:0
10000 copies	=	75000 ,,	=	£312:10:0
100000 copies	=	750000 ,,	=	£3125: : [3]

By then, the beginning of January, precisely one hundred copies had been sold, and the public could never be persuaded to buy more than three thousand. But the book was praised by the critics, and Thackeray once more consoled himself with the thought that it would be good for his reputation if not for his purse.

For the first time, in this work, he produced the gently ironic, contemplative writing that was to become the hallmark of his style. It was a reflection of his own state of mind. At the beginning of 1841 he confided to FitzGerald: 'This blow that has come upon me has played the deuce with me that is the fact.' At twenty-nine, his hair already heavily streaked with silver, he felt himself to be an old man, with the good things of life behind him.

'Ah, my dear!' he sighs to the imaginary Miss Smith, 'you are young now and enthusiastic; and your Titmarsh is old, very old, sad, and grey-headed.'

It was to be the underlying tone of all but a very few of his future works. His narrators from this time were mostly to be spectators rather than actors in the pageant of life; men who, however amusing they might be for the moment, carried with them a wealth of experience, a melancholy knowledge of the world, and in that moving phrase from *The Virginians*, some bankruptcy of the heart.

Richard Monckton Milnes, like an exuberant, dimpled, worldly little Cupid, materialized in Paris at just the right moment to take this battered Thackeray in hand, and introduce him to the solace he needed: a pretty young woman to soothe him with her sympathy and undemanding prattle. Milnes's candidate was Lady Cullum, Irish, like Isabella, the second wife of a genial bore of a Suffolk squire, who, in his mid-sixties, was haunted still by nightmares of being flogged at Charterhouse. Thackeray was to spend many an hour at the Cullums' Paris tea-table—hours which he knew might well have been spent in far less reputable company.

In Bohemia, he found similar comforts at the home of the artist Collignon, who gave him tips on painting, a restless urge to change professions yet again, and a generous share of his admirable *soupe maigre*. Collignon also had a charming, artless, smiling young wife. That 'blasé dog', as Thackeray called himself, that silly, sentimental soul, was launched on a long career of falling in love with other men's wives—a career, except in one notable instance, always generous, innocent, and uncovetous.

With such kindly friends to turn to after his labours, he braced himself for work, and soon found himself 'flaring up' with a novel—a three-volume saga set in the time of Henry V, which he hoped would do for romanticized medieval fiction what *Catherine* had done for Newgate literature: explode the pretty myth and show life as it had really been in those dark ages. It was a vast undertaking, involving enormous research, and all the time the need to make quick money with magazine articles fatally hampered its progress. He struggled with it through the winter and spring, writing often in a club, surrounded by unknown, chattering, smoking, billiard-playing Frenchmen, but was never to finish more than the first seven chapters.

Somehow he did manage to complete a shorter story in a very different vein: *The History of Samuel Titmarsh and the Great Hoggarty Diamond*. Written, as he was to say many years later, at a time of great affliction, when his heart was very soft and humble, this developed into one of the most charming of all his early works, and one of his own favourites. He put a great deal of his married happiness and trials into it, a great deal of humour too, but the publisher Bentley sat on the manuscript so long he had angrily to demand it back again, and once more it appeared in the faithful *Fraser's*.

He had higher hopes of quick profit from a collection of some of his early pieces, mainly Yellowplush and Gahagan, which Cunningham had promised to bring out as *Comic Tales and Sketches*, and in preparing new illustrations for this production, he met yet another young couple whose shoe-string happiness touched his heart. But this time the dedication of the husband, the engraver, Louis Marvy, and the sweet voice of his wife as she sang about her work, moved Thackeray not to pleasure, nor to self-pity, as it might well have done, but to self-reproach.

He wrote a touching account of Marvy and his household for *Britannia*,[4] a magazine then taking almost as much of his work as *Fraser's*, and in a letter to his mother drew some uncomfortable comparisons:

'. . . what noble characters does one light on in little nooks of this great world!—I can't tell you how this man's virtue and simplicity affects me. Bon Dieu to think of one's own beastly gormandizing egotism after this—I am trying however to correct some and yesterday walked to Ivry from the Barrier & back, and there with Isabella, & then from the Louvre, all to save 3 francs—There's virtue, my god, & think of Marvy toiling for 365 [days] 5090 hours . . . in a year, never grumbling, never exceeding, and always having a 5 franc piece—for a brother-artist in distress.

'Another instance of virtue, I wouldn't drink any brandy & water yesterday.'[5]

On a golden day of the Paris spring, with his parents and Mary Graham away in Italy, Thackeray tried a different kind of alcoholic experiment. He went again to Ivry, and having walked Isabella across the fields to a small riverside restaurant, plied her with champagne. Two glasses brought a sparkle to her eyes, and for the first time in six months, she flung herself into his arms and kissed him—at which moment the door to their private room burst open and in walked the waiter.

Instead of disaster, greater success followed. Isabella laughed—a peal of genuine delight—also the first for six months. She begged to be taken to the theatre. And after the theatre, she asked to go home with her husband.

Comparing some of the other women, wild and fierce, that he had seen at Esquirol's, with Isabella's gentle, childish ramblings, Thackeray determined not to send her back. He would continue the treatment, so excellently begun, at home.

'Only let her get well and I shall be the happiest man in the world,' he prayed. 'Ye Gods how I will venerate champagne—I always did.'[6]

The measure of how little he had come to expect from his marriage can be found in his description of Isabella at this time: she was recovering, he wrote, 'and perfectly quiet, and every now & then affectionate.'

To be with her again, to witness that occasional return of feeling, made him happier than he had been for months, and he fought every parental doubt and argument that came through the mails from Italy to keep her with him. For six weeks he was virtually her sole companion, and once again he almost broke under the slavery of it, and the torment of living with a wife he dearly loved but no longer dared make love to.

'Oh Lord God—there is not one of the sorrows or disappointments of my life, that as I fancy I cannot trace to some error or weakness of my disposition,' he wrote in his diary. 'Strengthen me then with your help, to maintain my good resolutions—not to yield to lust or sloth that beset me: or at least to combat with them & overcome them sometimes. . . O God, O God give me strength to do my duty.'[7]

But such duty as this was no job for a man, he at last confided wearily to Mrs Procter. After a while, no matter how dear the patient, a man became indifferent, *ennuyé*. He hired a woman to do the chores which had nearly broken him, and watched, with renewed wonder at the female sex, as she tackled them cheerfully for ten francs a week.

Released from bondage, he fled to England to restore his own health and sanity in the intelligent company and stately homes of Milnes and John Bowes Bowes, squaring his conscience with the dictum that no man could afford to be miserable for nine months together. When he thought of another writer, Charles Lamb, who had devoted a lifetime to his mad sister, he could only call him 'Saint Charles', and say that role was not for him.

At Streatlam Castle, Durham, he helped Bowes campaign for Parliament, and later turned the experience into a rattling N. P. Willis burlesque for *Fraser's*: *Notes on the North What-D'Ye-Callem Election*, by Napoleon Putnam Wiggins, of Passimaquoddy, writing to his aunt in Babylon, Kentucky, to whom he is 'under considerable pecuniary obligations, which he wishes naturally to increase'.

On his return to Paris, he threw all former prayers and good intentions to the wind, and caroused on the town three nights in a row with Stevens, the dentist, and the journalist O'Donnell. But even as he sported, the yoke of duty was being prepared for him once more.

The Carmichael-Smyths, still on their European travels, had learned of a new cure for Isabella—hydrosudopathy. The Major was particularly keen to test it, but then, as Thackeray pointed out, over the previous twenty years, his stepfather had been successively a convert to Abernethy's blue pills, which he had swallowed by the pound, to Morison's tablets, which he had flung down by the spoonful, to Sir John Long, to whom he had paid £100 for rubbing a vast sore on his back, and then off again, to homœopathy, which had put the nose of all the other systems out of joint, and now to the latest miracle of medicine, hydrosudopathy. Nevertheless, he sought out the treatment in Paris and when it seemed that it might achieve results, journeyed with Isabella to the main shrine of the cure, the Convent of Marienburg, near Boppard on the Rhine.

For nearly two months, Isabella was set to sweat in blankets at five each morning, had buckets of water poured over her at eight, was hosed down for five minutes at midday, and at five in the afternoon began again with the blankets and ice-cold water. For the first few days, she wouldn't stand still for the great sluicing of the hosepipes, and Thackeray had to undergo the ordeal with her.

'It would have made a fine picture,' he wrote to FitzGerald. 'Mrs Thack in the condition of our first parins, before they took to eating apples, and the great Titmarsh with nothing on but a petticoat lent him by his mother, and far too scanty to cover that immense posterior protuberance with w^h nature has furnished him. I'm the contrary of a cherubim that's the fact.'[8]

In the interests of science, the Major forswore all wine and undertook the same punishing routine.

After the first month, hydrosudopathy seemed to be the great remedy for which they had been searching. Isabella was virtually recovered—not quite like other people, but laughing, talking, happy. It was exactly a year since she had thrown herself from the steamship *Jupiter*, and for the first time in those long months Thackeray began, cautiously, to plan for the future.

Miraculously, his financial burdens appeared to have lightened. Mrs Blechynden had died in India, releasing the £500 from which her annuity had been paid, and Mary Graham, like Laura Bell in *Pendennis*, had lent him another £500. Relieved of immediate strain, confident of Isabella's full recovery, Thackeray began to write another play—a blank-verse tragedy, which he hoped to get into the hands and repertoire of the magnificent Macready, the greatest Macbeth of his day.

Then came the usual reversal. Isabella once again became excessively violent, which the doctors said was a good sign, but which Thackeray couldn't stand. He was packed off to Munich to look at modern German paintings, which he knew he would loathe and planned to 'expose' in an article. But he hadn't the heart even for a crusade such as that. At Heidelberg, miserable as the deuce, he turned towards Boppard once more, and retraced his steps full of deep forebodings about the winter ahead. He knew he couldn't face another with his family.

As he had watched his mother shoulder his problems and comfort his children, he had come to admire her again almost to the point of veneration, but her life and the court she had built around herself in Paris, could never be his. It was a society Annie was to describe as *'Cranford en Voyage'*,[9] peopled by brisk little English ex-patriots in bonnets, who complained of their *bonnes* and the prices at the *fruitière*, who matched the majestic Mrs Carmichael-Smyth neither in intelligence nor beauty, who agreed with her opinions as readily as they accepted the Major's globules and assistance with their pension papers.

The prospects on returning to London were equally bleak. Thackeray still had the Coram Street house, but he had lent it to Mary Graham, who had been at Boppard on her wedding tour. Not having seen the Major's younger brother, Colonel Charles Carmichael-Smyth, since the long-ago Christmas the family had spent together on the Isle of Wight, when she was six, Mary had nevertheless fallen in love with him by letter, and after a parting of two decades, the fifty-year-old warrior had returned from India to claim her as his bride.

Both Mary and her doting new husband believed that there was no other woman so clever, so charming, so stylish and so ravishingly beautiful as herself, a view which was to be increasingly stressed as Mrs Carmichael-Smyth tried to take over the management of the newly-weds' lives, and to insist that it was her son, Thackeray, who was the divinest creature in the world, a being so exquisite that neither of them was fit to tie his shoe-strings.

When Thackeray did eventually join his cousin in Great Coram Street, after more long winter months devoted to Isabella in Paris lodgings, jealousy and financial stress corroded their already delicate relationship. More Indian banks were failing, threatening the Colonel's savings of thirty years, and Mary, with an envious eye to the fortune of their shared grandmother, embarked on unsavoury inquisitions into how much relief Thackeray had already drawn from that source of indeterminate abundance.

Presently a son was born into the household, and born with two cataracts, which added constant medical visits to the gloom. The housekeeping, Thackeray was quick to point out to his mother, was even worse than in Isabella's time—'such dirt & cobwebs on the walls, suffered so calmly!'—while the Colonel, as unimaginative and uxorious a husband as his brother in Paris, provided a less satisfying contrast. A good, honest, kindly man not cursed by sentiment and genius made the best partner for a woman, Thackeray concluded; a man with love for weekdays as well as Sundays.

With Isabella, again acknowledged to be beyond his own management, placed in a less severe asylum in Paris, and with his chief hope of fame and wealth in London, he was to spend the next four years in an uneasy state of divided loyalty. To Annie he seemed to appear and disappear with equal abruptness. A few days of wandering by his side in the country lanes of Montmorency or Chaudefontaine, where the Carmichael-Smyths spent their summers; a few days in Paris, where he saw her off to school in her tartan dress and black pantalettes; and then she would wake one morning to find him there no more.

For Thackeray there were endless Channel crossings, desolate pacings of the deck at night, his daughters' last tributes in his pockets; in London or Paris, the constant, irreconcilable desire to be where he was not; a nagging belief that he was losing so much of the best kind of happiness by missing the childhood of his daughters, coupled with the occasional bleak admission that children without a mother lost some of their attraction.

Throughout it all, he worked.

2.

At the beginning of 1843, Chapman and Hall had taken over the *Foreign Quarterly Review*, and Thackeray was soon to find ready acceptance there for the long, learned articles, at £40 a time, that his old friend Jack Kemble had been so reluctant to take from him. Eager for the prestige it would bring him, he also made a bid to become editor, but despite the uncharacteristically serious survey of *The Last Fifteen Years of the Bourbons* which accompanied his application, he was passed over in favour of John Forster.

For Harrison Ainsworth's magazine he revived the tremendous Major Goliah Gahagan, and covered the art exhibitions, but it was still *Fraser's* which was the prime repository for his works, and in the autumn, under the new editorship of George Nickisson, he scored an immediate success there with an original and delightful persona—George Savage Fitz-Boodle.

Fitz-Boodle was a clubman, a bachelor, a 'heavy man', a martyr to the passion for cigars, a fool over pretty women, and, on his own testimony, the third-best whist-player in Europe. It was this last accomplishment which had brought him to the distasteful necessity of earning money by writing for the periodicals, a visiting Frenchman, by a strange turn of luck ('for I cannot admit the idea of his superiority'), having left him financially embarrassed.

As well as telling many of Thackeray's Weimar adventures, Fitz-Boodle invented three ingenious new professions for younger sons of the nobility: auctioneer-de-luxe (to preserve the effects of the aristocracy from contact with vulgar hands); the professional foreigner (on the lines of N. P. Willis); and, most brilliant of the trio, the dinner-master, a dedicated *gourmand*, to assist the benighted middle classes in the noble art of giving great dinners.

The previous year, Thackeray had also begun his famous connection with the newly launched *Punch*, but having achieved modest success with some early offerings, he failed to please with his first series, *Miss Tickletoby's Lectures on English History*. Miss Tickletoby (from 'toby' meaning buttocks, and 'tickle', the effect of a cane thereon), was a silly old bird, and her discourses came to an abrupt end with Edward III and the Burghers of Calais. At the rate he had been going with his eleven published instalments, Thackeray had enough history left to last into his dotage—and, as he told *Punch*'s publishers, he had taken just as much trouble for them as he would have done for 'any more dignified periodical'. Having delivered that thrust, he philosophically pocketed their £25 compensation fee, and promised to try again later.

By the time he received the notification of Miss Tickletoby's early demise Thackeray was in Ireland, preparing to fulfil at last the £120 contract with Chapman and Hall which had hung over him for two years. He had sailed from England at precisely the same time that Dickens had returned to it—to a rapturous welcome—after his first tour of America.

'Boz & Titmarsh reached Liverpool the same day,' wrote Thackeray: 'but the journals have not taken notice of the arrival of the latter. Gross jealousy!'[1]

FitzGerald was to have gone with him, but pulled out at the last moment, horrified at the extent of the trip. Anything over two days, he said, and he got 'dull as dirt'. But he gave Thackeray many an introduction to his Irish relatives, whose bursting homes and 'elastic hospitality' were to inspire some of the pleasantest episodes in the book.

Though he was often to find the loneliness almost unbearable, Thackeray recognized that it was just as well for 'a lazy man' to have no distractions and temptations, and for the reader the benefit is obvious in every page. He interested himself in everything: workhouses, theatres, law courts, slums, agriculture, pretty girls with their red petticoats and redder legs, the races, and, inevitably, politics and religion. He looked into the past, and visualized the future—when tourists would fly in from England in 'an aërial machine'. He took a terrifying sea-trip to view the Devil's Causeway, and gazed at the spot where Sir Walter Raleigh planted the first potato.

Though the Irish Question raged then, as ever, Thackeray's business was not with finding solutions, which seemed to him more impossible and bewildering the more he knew, but with the people and the essence of the land. His book was to be one man's view of an island quite as magnificent and strange as any foreign country. Above all, it was to be a Londoner's view: *The Cockney in Ireland* he wanted to call it, but Chapman and Hall pulled such pathetic faces he let them have their way with *The Irish Sketch Book.*

The very consistency of Irish inconsistency amused and infuriated him. Everywhere there were unfinished houses, mills and churches ('in a sort of bastard or Vauxhall Gothic'), begun on far too magnificent a scale, and when they failed the fault was laid 'upon that tyrant of a sister kingdom'. Even the shop signs started off with huge letters and dwindled down to cramped, pygmy characters as the space ran out. The whole country was full of such 'swaggering beginnings that could not be carried through,' he wrote, 'grand enterprises begun dashingly, and ending in shabby compromises or downright ruin.'

And yet the Irish, he thought, had a far superior basic intelligence to the rest of the British. He had never seen such bright-eyed, wild, clever, eager faces, and was delighted to overhear two young boys as, dressed almost in rags, they lolled over a harbour wall and talked brilliantly about one of the ancient Egyptian Ptolemys.

Though he had been predisposed towards the Catholics—in some part as a reaction to his mother's violent prejudice in the opposite direction—he was saddened by the sombre priestly seminaries and a Church which appeared to condone squalor and poverty. As he was shown round a convent in the south by the youngest and prettiest nun, he fumed at such wastage of God's precious gifts. The British, he wrote, had as much right to permit Sutteeism in India as to allow women in the United Kingdom to take such 'wicked vows'. Be Magdalens first, he urged. Surely a young girl served God to better purpose with a husband by her side and a child on her knee.

The Protestants, with their fashionable extemporary preachers delivering dazzling hour-and-twenty-minute sermons, pleased him no better.

He made a private, sad pilgrimage to the house he had lived in with Isabella near Cork, and wrote of some of the happier recollections of that time. And, at last, he was able to sketch, as he had longed to do when he travelled the country lanes with his sick wife—but still not without distractions. No sooner did he settle to the task than he was surrounded by curious, jovial, idle crowds, blocking the view, assessing his talent, and calling out descriptions for those too far back to see for themselves.

It was, however, with his pen, not his pencil, that he captured the true beauty of the country.

During two longish stays in Dublin, Thackeray was befriended by Charles Lever, one-time doctor, full-time *bon vivant*, editor of the Dublin *University Magazine*, and famous on both sides of the Irish Sea as 'Harry Lorrequer', popular author of rollicking tales of Irish army life; and it was through Lever that he met one Major Dwyer, who was to turn the tables on the Cockney traveller and leave a splendidly baffled portrait of the observer observed:[2] a tall, guarded Englishman who at first showed no 'external manifestation of his supposed humouristic proclivities', but seemed rather to be something of an *agent provocateur*, eager to betray the Irish into boastful talk.

From Dwyer's subsequent account, it would seem that not too much provocation was needed, and that Lever and his friends were more willing to accept a dash of foreign blarney than to proffer their own home brew. Towards the end of a dinner-party, when Lever showed himself ready to accept compliments on his recent fictional treatment of the Battle of Waterloo, Thackeray caused some hostility with his hesitant confession that it had been rather too imaginative and high-flown for his taste. His murmured mental note that something might well be made of Waterloo added to the injury. But he quickly gained favour again with a massive dollop of praise for one of Lever's verses, and won applause for a lively demonstration of the absurdities of French drama, acted out with a pirouette, a majestic handwave, and, thought Major Dwyer, rather too much fondness for showing off his French pronunciation.

At no time was the Major more buffaloed than when he escorted Lever's guest to a military review at Phoenix Park, a duty he performed with the utmost seriousness, believing he should make quite clear the general object and nature of each charge and manoeuvre. For a time Thackeray listened with polite attention, then saying really it was very kind, but he felt he would never understand, he affected a fine alarm at the ferocity of the Irish cavalry, and headed briskly for that part of the ground where the prettiest ladies were gathered.

It was all very curious, thought the Major, though not nearly so surprising as the mastery of military detail his unwilling pupil displayed when he eventually 'made something' of Waterloo. The battle chapters in *Vanity Fair*, the Major was convinced, owed everything, somehow, to Thackeray's knowledge of the regimental mess at Newry.

Thackeray also managed to baffle Lever, by offering the far more successful writer both money and introductions if he moved to London, where he would find men of his own calibre to sharpen his wits on. It was, said the Irishman, like someone struggling to keep his head above water offering to teach a friend to swim.

When the *Irish Sketch Book* was finished, Thackeray dedicated it to this generous Dublin host, and Lever courageously repaid the compliment with a handsome review in the *Dublin University Magazine*. Most Irishmen were not so appreciative. Having intercepted a fierce glance from Daniel O'Connell at the Reform Club soon after publication, Thackeray felt he had managed to offend every party in Ireland, and suspected he would be massacred if ever he returned there. In England, however, the book brought him excellent reviews in the right places, a letter of praise from Dickens, and a second edition within months.

In other respects, 1843 was less cheering. As Thackeray left Paris on New Year's Day, Mrs Butler pressed a sovereign into his hand for old John Goldworthy: a genteel way of revoking her agreement to pay his annual £12 wages. The papers releasing the first small portion of his Indian capital, held up by a drunken Thackeray uncle who wanted him to continue supporting his half-sister's family, went to the bottom of the Red Sea with the ship carrying them; and the most persistent of the *Constitutional* creditors, who had long been making rumbling noises, erupted with a writ.

Having failed to stir the Major into settling the debt for so much in the pound, Thackeray, as the only accessible member of the family, now faced the prospect of having to find £400 or go bankrupt. For a while he was in real fear of being forcibly escorted to the Fleet prison.

As he dealt with solicitors and tried once more to prod the Major into action, his 'old complaint', the stricture, flared up again, into an abcess which took six weeks to cure; and since the Coram Street lease was due to expire, and the Colonel and Mary had returned to India to repair their shattered fortunes, he spent much of his time tramping the streets looking for somewhere else to live, hankering after impossibly large houses with gardens in which he could picture Annie and Minnie at play.

To add to all these miseries, in the spring an attack was made on him in the press—in *Fraser's* of all journals—by a man he had long regarded as a friend. Only two weeks earlier, David Deady Keane, barrister, journalist and Cambridge contemporary, had shaken him cordially by the hand, yet when Thackeray opened his copy of *Fraser's* April edition, he found Keane's vicious description of him as 'Bill Crackaway', writer, bill-discounter, and member of the 'Grubwell' club, a character who was said to have not only a broken nose, but a sinister sneer, an inhuman squint, and to be incapable of the candour of an honest laugh.

Thackeray had done more than his share of satirizing the works of other writers in the past, and was to continue to do so in the future, but he had only ever made sport of the personal features of two of them—Bulwer-Lytton and Dr Lardner[3]—men he did not know at the time, and he had come to regret even those youthful exuberances. Keane's assault, and the fact that it had appeared in *Fraser's*, hurt him deeply. It went, he felt, way outside the rules of the game. With great restraint, aided by the fact that no one else appeared to have noticed or recognized the portrait, he wrote to editor Nickisson, informing him that should Mr Deady Keane continue to write for the magazine, he, Thackeray, would feel bound to stop his own contributions.

In August of this unfortunate year, he made a trip to Holland and Belgium with the intention of writing yet another travel book, but the blight persisted. At the outset he had his pocket-book and £20 stolen, and his travelling companion, the ebullient dentist, Augustus Stevens, made writing, and even sightseeing, impossible.

Thackeray described this old friend in the finest of all his poems, *The Ballad of Bouillabaisse*, as 'brave AUGUSTUS' who 'drives his carriage', and if Stevens could now afford his own transport it was due less to tooth-pulling than to a sideline in restored paintings for which, as Thackeray observed, he was so clever at finding pedigrees. For him, the sole purpose of the excursion was to buy more canvases, a hunt in which he demanded Thackeray's exclusive participation.

With the 'usual supercilious airs w^h make Englishmen so much beloved on the continent',[4] he refused to speak to strangers, and made sure his companion had no chance to do so either. Even their meals he ordered to be served in the safe seclusion of their own rooms, and since Thackeray had little money left to pay the bills, he was in no position to argue. When he did manage to escape for a few hours at The Hague and rushed off to view some genuine old masterpieces, Stevens' artistic enterprises continued to haunt him: in the royal collection he discovered four paintings that he had last seen being varnished in the dentist's Paris workshop, and thought to himself that the poor Dutch King had been greatly humbugged.

The more he saw of the 'illustrious Stevens', the more Thackeray longed for the companionship of FitzGerald or Saville Morton, though he was honest enough to admit that he liked his own way too much to be fit to live with any man for long. Miserable, unable to work, he at last prised a loan out of the dentist and slipped back towards Paris on a roundabout route of his own, getting as far as Lille before his funds ran out once more.

There he put up at an inn, ashamed to look his host in the face, sent off a desperate S.O.S. to the long-suffering, long-pursed Mrs Butler, and, while he waited for relief, composed the most charming memento of the tour: *Titmarsh's Carmen Lilliense*, which tells in verse the story of his embarrassing predicament. Back in Paris eventually, he was bailed out for the third and last time by the Carmichael-Smyths' cook, who paid off his threatening coachman at the door.

At Dr Puzin's Chaillot asylum, he found Isabella so well that he couldn't understand why she wasn't completely well, and at last he began to doubt that she ever would be.

10
A Bachelor Old and Grey

Care, like a dun,
Lurks at the gate:
Let the dog wait;
Happy we'll be!

The Mahogany Tree

Taking on bachelor lodgings in both Paris and London, Thackeray now began to straddle the Channel with greater ease. He was soon to describe his life as eating all night, scribing all day, and as far as work was concerned he was ready to take on anything to keep his family afloat.

For more than a year he was art critic and literary reviewer for the *Pictorial Times*, younger rival of the *Illustrated London News*. He sent monthly newsletters to India where his old *National Standard* leg-man, Hume, had started the *Calcutta Star*. He flirted cautiously with another American entrepreneur of the N. P. Willis school, Henry Wickoff, of the New York *Republic*. He read widely for a small volume on Talleyrand; began translating a French novel—and stopped when the publishers failed to pay; contributed to *Ainsworth's Magazine*, and the *New Monthly*; continued his work for *Fraser's*; made a great hit with *Punch*; wrote *Barry Lyndon*, an Eastern travel book, and a long short story, the delightful *Legend of the Rhine*. He started a Christmas book; began 'A Novel without a Hero'; and at last achieved his aim of joining a respectable, liberal daily paper.

Having broken with the 'abominable old *Times*' in 1840, he had had to wait four years before his old Paris friend, Eyre Evans Crowe, finally got him onto the more congenial *Morning Chronicle* as principal book reviewer, occasional leader-writer, and tyro political commentator. He made around £20 a month from the connection and it was his own fault, he said, that he didn't earn more: 'the fact is I cant write the politics and the literary part is badly paid.'[1]

For a man passionately interested in the turbulent affairs of his time it was a galling admission to have to make, but the blow was the less bitter since he had another outlet for political comment of a more rumbustious nature in *Punch*.

When the idea of launching the satirical magazine as a co-operative venture had first been raised by a group of fellow hacks as impecunious and improvident as himself, Thackeray, cautious at last, had taken legal advice—wrong legal advice, as it turned out—and scuppered the plan with the scare that they would all be liable for each other's personal debts as well as those of the paper.

In 1841, when the group tried again, and *Punch* finally staggered into the world with very little more financial backing, neither Thackeray nor his lawyer was consulted. The leading lights then were Henry Mayhew, a lazy, irresponsible young writer who was to earn lasting fame with his *exposé* of life at the bottom, *London Labour and the London Poor*, and his joint editor, Mark Lemon, a shrewd Jew of splendid girth, who had been clerk at a brewery and manager of a London tavern before turning to writing, mainly for the stage.

Mayhew's acerbic, bitterly radical father-in-law, Douglas Jerrold (late of the *Constitutional*), was the magazine's chief writer, and 'Alphabet' Bayley, the Grub-street journalist from whom Thackeray had bought the *National Standard*, contributed to the first numbers. Dr Maginn, dying in the Fleet, was said to have given advice in prison, just as Finucane was to do before the launching of the *Pall Mall Gazette* in Pendennis.

Also on the staff, as *Punch's* first cartoonist, was John Leech, the little fellow in the buttoned-up jacket, singing 'Home, Sweet Home', that Thackeray had taken under his wing at Charterhouse. Now tall, handsome and superbly elegant, with a dry wit, a core of deep melancholy, a reverence for good wine, and an unlikely passion for riding to hounds, Leech added a much needed touch of class, though not enough in FitzGerald's view. He cautioned Thackeray to wait before joining such a motley crew, but by the middle of 1842 Thackeray was already an occasional contributor.

That he was writing for this disreputable newcomer was a secret, he told his mother. It was 'a very low paper . . . only its good pay, and a great opportunity for unrestrained laughing sneering kicking and gambadoing.'[2]

Soon afterwards the original owners were bought out by the publishers Bradbury and Evans, who put the hard-headed Mark Lemon in sole editorial control, raised the pay and the paper's general tone, and Thackeray, after his *Miss Tickletoby* fiasco, finally hit his stride and became one of its brightest stars. By the spring of 1844, he was calling it his 'great card', and for nearly ten years was to pour into its pages the brightest fruit of all his magazinery, a cornucopia of burlesques, parodies, political squibs, travel notes, stories, pungent topical comment, chronicles of the French, cartoons, illustrations, serious social discussion, hilarious absurdities: papers and drawings wise and witty, mad and moving.

One week he was *Punch*'s 'Fat Contributor', turning a plethoric London eye on Brighton or the pyramids; the next Mr Jeames of Buckley Square, noble heir to Yellowplush; or Mr Spec, or Dr Solomon Pacifico; the dreaded discoverer of snobs, or the gentle Mr Brown, who wrote such wise letters to his nephew, a young man about town.

Many of Thackeray's finest poems first appeared in *Punch*, and he had the distinction of contributing a cartoon so obscure that a rival journal offered £500 and a free pardon to anyone who could explain it. The prize was never claimed, and it wasn't until many years after Thackeray's death that Annie provided the answer. The sketch showed the scene which had greeted her father when he returned home one day: Annie, dressed up as a queen, sentencing Minnie to instant execution. He had captioned it 'Horrid Tragedy in Private Life'.

His union with *Punch* was to become a celebrated match, but for a while Thackeray still lobbied for something more statesmanlike, and yearned for the power and prestige of editorship. Why didn't *Punch*'s new publishers bring out a more brilliant, aristocratic, sixpenny, literary paper, with a 'decided air of white kid gloves', he asked them, and put him at the head of it?—a magazine which aimed at a select, gentlemanly circulation, with signed articles by good men. He pictured himself taking over the fine arts, light literature, drama, and the weekly editorial dinners—all except for paying the bill at the end.

But it was not to be. The nearest he came to an editor's chair in these years was by accepting for a few months Albany Fonblanque's renewed offer of a mixed bag of writing and sub-editing for the *Examiner*, a niggling job which took up too much of his time but brought him a regular four guineas a week and provided valuable early information for his *Punch* 'pleasantries' and Indian newsletters.

Another ambition which was not yet to be fulfilled was the making of his name as a novelist, a title for which he aimed with *The Memoirs of Barry Lyndon* (or *The Luck of Barry Lyndon*, as it was first called), a savage tale of knaves and fools.

By the time he began writing it he had had the story simmering in his brain for two years, since his electioneering visit to John Bowes Bowes at Streatlam Castle. One of Bowes's ancestors, Andrew Robinson Bowes, an eighteenth-century Irish adventurer who had made his way in the world by gambling, roguery and the marrying and maltreatment of heiresses, provided the spark for the story, though Thackeray was to add much new material of his own.

Once again, the love of the century he was writing about made the work a masterpiece of historical reconstruction, and the use of his anti-hero as narrator turned it into a *tour de force*. A totally amoral charmer, Lyndon describes his appalling exploits with tremendous zest, seeing in them nothing but glory and fair game, while all but the most dim-witted recognize them as something very different.

It reads as though it were written at one inspired, impassioned sitting, but it gave Thackeray more trouble than any of his early works. For a full year he was to do battle with it, with a great deal of unwillingness and labour, as he struggled to produce it in monthly instalments for *Fraser's*, and had it lying like a nightmare on his mind whenever he broke off to tackle other work.

Towards the end, there were so many complaints from morally outraged dullards that he had to add footnotes to explain the irony of Lyndon's shameless revelations. At last, as tired of the public as of his hero, he cut the story short, bitterly disappointed that no publisher had come forward to turn it into the handsome, saleable volume he had envisaged.

If he treated the Irish with more savagery in this book than in any of his other works (with the exception of *Dennis Haggarty's Wife*), he had fresh reason for venting his spleen. Shortly after he began writing it, the journalist, O'Donnell, played him a particularly scurvy trick.

Thackeray knew that the Irishman was noisy, uncouth and no gentleman (having been badgered by the man into giving him a letter of introduction to Mrs Procter, he was immediately appalled by what he'd done and followed it with a swift note of apology to the lady), but, even so, he regarded the rogue as the staunchest of friends, and had been keeping him alive for a year with regular, hard-earned handouts. At last O'Donnell had come to him with a different kind of financial proposition:

'I say, Thack, you're a writer for the magazines. Now, I've got a paper that I think would suit a magazine, and I wish you'd get it into one of them for me . . . a few guineas would come in handy.'

Thackeray got it into a magazine—*Fraser's*—and kept back one of his own pieces to do so. Two weeks later a gloomy George Nickisson silently handed him an earlier journal containing the same article. When confronted with the evidence of his plagiarism, O'Donnell laughed in Thackeray's face.

'That's how my Irish friend served me,' Thackeray exclaimed when he told the story nearly twenty years later; 'but oh! he was the nicest friend, the dearest most delightful fellow, I ever knew in the world.'[3]

Despite this incident, and the rising importance of *Punch*, Thackeray stayed on good terms with Nickisson, still writing his literary and art reviews for him—and ruffling sensitive feathers in both departments.

Of course, *he* didn't mind Thackeray's forays into the art world on his *own* account, the phlegmatic Frank Stone told FitzGerald, as he grabbed him by a button on a London street; he dearly loved old Thackeray, but these yearly outpourings were sorely trying for his friends. And one day, the infuriated artist finally hissed through his teeth, old Thackeray would get himself horsewhipped.

On the literary front, the bad feeling was even less expected, and longer lasting. In the February of 1844, old Thackeray approached a round-up of recent novels in unusually mellow mood. In the critical line, Titmarsh, he admitted, had freely wielded the tomahawk and had a scalp or two drying in his lodge, but now was the time to leave such youthful sports and savage pastimes and turn to the benevolent philosophy of mature age. In this spirit, he reviewed an assortment of works, ranging from Lever's *Tom Burke of Ours* to Dickens's *A Christmas Carol*.

Though he didn't enjoy Lever's army frolics himself, he reviewed *Tom Burke* for those who did, stressing the pleasure 'Harry Lorrequer' gave to thousands of readers round the world, awarding him much praise, a great deal of space, and far more weighty, philosophical comment than Lever usually earned. But writers are sensitive creatures: if a four-page panegyric contains an 'if' or a 'but', it is the 'if' or the 'but' they remember. Nothing short of eulogy will do, and this Thackeray reserved for Dickens.

Dickens, naturally delighted, wrote to say how the notice had touched him to the quick, encouraged him and done him good; while Lever, who had praised the *Irish Sketch Book* so bravely, terminated their short friendship with cries of base treachery. They were hard people to deal with, these literary men, sighed Thackeray, massaging his own tender feelings.

In Lever's case, Thackeray loved the man though he couldn't like his works. With Dickens, he revered the genius of Boz, already author of eight magnificent successes, but found Boz himself not quite a gentleman.

'Did I write to you about Mrs Procter's grand ball,' Thackeray asked Isabella at this time, 'and how splendid Mrs Dickens was in pink satin and Mr Dickens in geranium & ringlets?'[4]

In contrast with his outward flamboyance, Dickens dwelt with morbid solemnity on many a subject Thackeray could not treat seriously at all. The boy who had endured resentful months in a blacking factory, while Thackeray was at Charterhouse—loathing it, but learning to be an undisputed, unconscious 'gentleman'—was to remain raw for the rest of his life to every real and imagined slight; to be bitter at what he considered to be Society's low view of literary men, and yet to spurn Society's overtures when his brilliance brought him fame. Expecting to be treated as an entertainer, rather than an equal, Dickens refused to entertain.

'The Dignity of Literature' was a topic on which he and Thackeray were to have many an argument, futile tussles which ended only when Thackeray, unwilling to pursue the chimera any longer, stamped about the room, laughing and twisting his hands in his hair in mock rage and frustration.

At this time, with Thackeray still several paces away from success, the two men were as good friends as they were ever to be, but for Thackeray a far more congenial writer in the crusading field proved to be Matthew James Higgins, a wealthy, urbane, much-travelled Irishman, with a splendid talent for fighting injustice and bureaucratic abuses under the pen-name of 'Jacob Omnium'.

Admiring each other's contributions to the *New Monthly Magazine*, both Thackeray and Higgins asked the editor for an introduction to the other, so beginning a twenty-year friendship, and one of the most curious sights in London—for Higgins, known as the 'gentle giant', topped Thackeray's height by another five inches. This superior growth caused some distress to another Higgins living in Rome, where, after a visit of the 6ft. 8in. 'gentle giant', his namesake, a mere 6ft. 4in. tall, found himself referred to as 'little Higgins'; but Thackeray revelled in such proportions, and both he and 'big Higgins' showed a keen interest in others similarly endowed.

On a joint excursion to view a show giant at a fair, Thackeray, indicating his elegant companion, whispered to the door-keeper that they too were in the profession. They were ushered in free, though, unwilling permanently to deprive another large fellow of his fees, handed over their shillings on the way out.

One of the stories Thackeray most liked to tell involved another show giant—a dead one—and the day he came across the deceased exhibit's showman, sitting by the roadside deep in grief, more for the giant himself, as he was anxious to make clear, than for the money he had brought him. Thackeray offered himself as a replacement, but after weighing up carefully both the candidate and his proposal, the showman turned him down. 'Well, you're nigh tall enough,' he said, 'but I'm afraid you're too hugly.'[5]

Known as Gog and Magog by the wits, Thackeray and Higgins were to fight together in at least one crusading cause: for the abolition of the archaic Palace Court, Whitehall, where Higgins was charged with refusing to pay for the stabling of a horse stolen from him and left to run up the bill by the thief. Thackeray's chief contribution—one which was doubtless considered frivolous by Dickens—was *Jacob Homnium's Hoss*, one of his 'Ballads of Pleaceman X' for *Punch*, in which he urges Higgins to ply his 'iron pen', and shut up that 'sty for fattening lawyers in, On the bones of honest men.' Between them, they got the court put down.

As a bachelor, living in cheerless rooms up many a pair of stairs, under the eaves of a narrow Jermyn Street lodging-house, Thackeray now lived his social life in London at as punishing a pace as his professional one. During the Season, he said, all he needed was to keep a brougham to be quite the man of the world. He was rather proud of receiving eleven invitations to dinner when he had to spend Christmas Day in town, and of another from Lord Melbourne, though this came to him under a slight misapprehension, since Lord M. insisted on confusing him with his parson uncle, Frank. He regularly attended the famous breakfasts of Richard Monckton Milnes, who collected about him such a rich and unusual blend of talents that Carlyle was to say: 'If Christ was again on earth Milnes would ask him to breakfast, and the Clubs would all be talking of the good things that Christ had said.'[6]

Yet still he took much of his pleasure in the smoke-filled haunts of Bohemia such as Evans's Late Supper Rooms, in Covent Garden, the Cyder Cellars, or any number of the other odd London dives that he was to re-create in his books as the Back Kitchen and the Haunt—noisy, convivial clubs in the tap-rooms and back parlours of taverns, frequented by writers, lawyers, doctors and artists. The racket suited him better than a peaceful life, he told his mother, and FitzGerald, in some astonishment, agreed:

'Old Thackeray,' FitzGerald reported, 'goes on in his own way, writing hard for half a dozen Reviews and Newspapers all the morning; dining, drinking, and talking of a night; managing to preserve a fresh colour and perpetual flow of spirits under a wear-and-tear of thinking and feeding that would have knocked up any other man I know two years ago, at least.'[7]

The feeding was now becoming as important as the drinking—as Thackeray's waistline showed—and a modern psychiatrist would no doubt find plenty to say about a young man, deprived of his wife, who threw himself into this other sensory pleasure.

With the Reform Club's famous chef, Alexis Soyer, he conspired to invent new dishes, unusually sauced. He reviewed cookery books with profound artistic fervour, and devoted an article in the *New Monthly*[8] to the ritual combination of Greenwich and the whitebait season—Greenwich with its mingling of nations and classes, its peaceful sweep of river with ships under sail gliding silently by, and its magnificent temptations for the palate, from humble flounder-souchy ('as fresh as the recollections of childhood') to the greatest attraction of all, the bait.

On a summer's evening at the Trafalgar or the Old Ship, he wrote, there were Ministers of the Crown, holding their 'annual Ministerial Saturnalia', office parties, private banquets, lawyers' dinners, the gentlemen of *Punch*, young sporting types, with cutaway coats and riding whips ('which must be very useful on the water'), 'honest pudding-faced Germans', voluble little Frenchmen in stays, and gentlemen with their wives, drinking tea with their whitebait. 'I don't wish to quarrel with the enjoyments of any man,' said Thackeray, 'but fellows who take tea and whitebait should not be allowed to damp the festive feelings of persons better engaged.'

Good dinners, he proclaimed, had proved to be the greatest vehicles of benevolence since man first began to eat, and a taste for good living, in moderation, was as praiseworthy as all his other qualities and endowments. The only difficulty was moderation. Feverish symptoms regularly followed Thackeray's dinner-party excesses, and there is a definite whiff of the wine fumes about some of the stories told of him at this time, particularly one by the painter, William Powell Frith.

Frith, at twenty-six, a rather prissy young man, a little too con-scious of his precocious elevation to the status of an Associate of the Royal Academy, had long admired the writings of Titmarsh, especially the appreciative references to his own works, and at last arranged with a mutual friend to beard him in one of his favourite lairs to effect a cherished introduction.

They chose 'The Deanery', a small club close to St Paul's Cathedral, named for its founder and principal light, Richard Harris Barham, author of the *Ingoldsby Legends* and Dean of St Paul's. Like the Haunt in *The Newcomes*, it was a smoky den in the back parlour of a tavern where a hard core of boon companions gathered to talk, sing, and to 'chaff' interlopers until they either went away or became boon companions themselves.

'Father Prout', the unfrocked priest, was in mid-song, with Thackeray sitting by his side, when Frith and his friend first entered, but at the end of Mahoney's performance the young painter achieved his introduction and a handshake, and then sat in awestruck silence listening to the talk which seemed to him quite terrifyingly brilliant.

Thackeray was also called upon to sing—*Little Billee*, his famous tale of gorging Jack and guzzling Jimmy. When the applause died down, he turned on the wide-eyed newcomer.

'Now then, Frith,' he growled, 'you damned saturnine young Academician, sing us a song!'

Frith, literally struck dumb, retreated into mute misery which was only to be increased later in the evening when Thackeray returned to the attack.

'I'll tell you what it is, Frith, you had better go home,' he suggested; 'your aunt is sitting up for you with a big muffin.'

Still tongue-tied, Frith took his tormentor's advice, and left the boon companions to their wit, their songs, and their brandy-and-water.[9]

No doubt Thackeray regretted his rudeness next morning, just as he was to do on another occasion when he brusquely cut short one of Alfred Tennyson's dissertations on poetry, though Tennyson, with his great bony yellow face, growling voice, and boa-constrictor's capacity for swallowing and digesting knowledge, was a very different target from the bewildered Frith.

'Manliness and simplicity of manner go a great way with me,' Thackeray had told Mrs Procter, when enlisting her interest in the future Poet Laureate, but sometimes, late at night, even they did not go far enough, and towards the end of one convivial evening, when Tennyson began to quote examples to demonstrate the perfection of Catullus, Thackeray broke in with his own dismissive opinion: 'I do not rate him highly, I could do better myself.'[10]

Mortified next day, he wrote to apologize. He had woken at two o'clock in a sort of terror, he told his friend:

'When I have dined, sometimes I believe myself to be equal to the greatest painters and poets. That delusion goes off; and then I know what a small fiddle mine is and what small tunes I play upon it. It was very generous of you to give me an opportunity of recalling a silly speech: but at the time I thought I was making a perfectly simple and satisfactory observation.'[11]

Thackeray was to provide many a tavern dinner for the struggling poet, entertainments to which that glittering Cambridge contemporary, William Brookfield, was also often summoned with a typically absurd note:

If you like two or three
Of your cronies to see
There's a swarry
To-morry
At Mitre court B. [12]

With his flow of stories and genius for mimicry, Brookfield, now a hard-working parson and dramatic preacher with the brooding dark looks of a city Heathcliffe, slotted into Bohemian society with genial ease—or, as it seemed to his beautiful young wife, with dangerous imprudence.

Thackeray had fallen in love with the statuesque Jane Brookfield at their first meeting, but she, with an eye to a bishop's mitre, had not returned his approbation.

'You seem very hand in glove with Thackeray,' she was soon warning her husband; 'don't become a second Father Prout.' To another letter, she added a stinging postscript, suggesting that Brookfield might care to send her 'Mr. Thackeray's Cookery Book', so that she could copy out some recipes for the making of 'Refreshing Drinks.' [13]

To Thackeray himself she showed none of this caustic wariness, and he was soon singing her praises round the town, infiltrating the parson and his lady into all suitable society, and taking a schoolboy glee in Mrs Procter's fury that the lions at her tea-parties should so obviously prefer Mrs Brookfield's beauty to their hostess's wit.

The Brookfields' house in Great Pulteney Street was soon a happy meeting ground for all the old Cambridge comrades, and an irresistible one for Thackeray.

Mrs Carmichael-Smyth had long brooded on the vulnerability of her thirty-year-old son alone among the temptations of London, her fears fuelled by cousin Mary's tales of his late hours and soda-water breakfasts, and with the advent of Jane Brookfield, her letters from Paris became more urgent. Strong pressure was put on Thackeray to leave grimy, expensive London and make his home permanently in Paris. Even young Annie was pressured into coaxing him back by Mrs Carmichael-Smyth's busy, bonneted friends, and made perfectly miserable by this attempt to divide her loyalty.

When he remained adamant, the services of Mrs Butler were pressed upon him, as guardian and housekeeper, but if he couldn't have Isabella and his children, he certainly wasn't going to have his grandmother. A great deal unhappier without his wife than he had thought it in his nature to be, Thackeray wrote to Isabella constantly, simple, kindly letters, as to a child, and puzzled over her rambling, desperately stupid replies until some gleam of sense emerged to comfort him.

He was a great palpitating mass of love and emotion, but if he confirmed Mrs Carmichael-Smyth's worst fears and took a mistress for consolation, he left no record of the fact. Born in the licentious Regency and drawn, with a mixture of sympathy and disgust, to the greater frankness and freedom of the previous century, Thackeray lived his adult life as an uneasy Victorian. He could understand and forgive the lusts and lecheries of his hero, Henry Fielding, and translate Béranger's poem, *The Garret*, with a sensuality reminiscent of the even earlier Herrick:

> And see my little Jessy, first of all;
>> She comes with pouting lips and sparkling eyes:
> Behold, how roguishly she pins her shawl
>> Across the narrow casement, curtain-wise;
> Now by the bed her petticoat glides down,
>> And when did woman look the worse in none?
> I have heard since who paid for many a gown,
>> In the brave days when I was twenty-one.

But his heart was a very tender mechanism. He had what many of his friends described as an almost feminine sensitivity of feeling. Had he set up 'another establishment', as he was often to hear gossip claim to be the case, he would have been aware, to an unusual and intolerable degree, of the position of the woman and her children.

He was also hampered by his taste for gentle feminine innocence. 'Men serve women kneeling—when they get on their feet, they go away,' he wrote in *Pendennis*. A strong-minded rebel against convention, such as George Eliot, who lived openly with G. H. Lewes (whom Thackeray knew well), would have scared him to his feet and away in no time at all.

If he sought no permanent solace, however, it is unlikely that he went without any. At a *Punch* dinner, when Percival 'The Professor' Leigh, a former surgeon, insisted, against much barracking, that it was man's duty to subdue the flesh and cultivate better things, Thackeray led the chorus that shouted him down: 'But we don't want better things.'[14] He was also to surprise a sheltered young cousin, Richard Bedingfield, grandson of the Dr Turner whose sonorous rendering of the Ten Commandments had formed such a feature of Thackeray's Chiswick Mall schooldays, by the number of social outlaws of both sexes that he shook by the hand on his walks around London, and even more by his assertion that many a whore was a very good woman.

2.

In the summer of 1844, Thackeray escaped his lonely lodgings, and his mother's nagging pen, by making a voyage as sudden and astonishing as an Arabian night's dream. On the evening of 19 August, he attended a farewell dinner for James Emerson Tennent, MP for Belfast, Secretary to the India Board, and passenger-to-be on a cruise-ship bound for the Mediterranean—Spain, Gibraltar, Malta, Rhodes, Athens, Smyrna, Constantinople, Jerusalem, Cairo, Alexandria and home.

Thackeray's mind was so obviously inflamed by this glittering new odyssey that Tennent invited him to join his family party. He had only thirty-six hours to get ready; he had engagements in London and had promised to visit his parents and children in Belgium; he couldn't afford it. But, with every glass of claret his enthusiasm mounted, and the difficulties began to fade, the most awkward of all vanishing miraculously when Tennent assured him that his friends, the directors of P & O, would doubtless be delighted to make Mr Titmarsh a present of a berth for the voyage.

His acceptance of this free passage was to cause a flurry of ill-feeling, of the kind spawned all too easily in incestuous literary circles, when he eventually published a book on his Mediterranean experiences. It was a cruel blow to the dignity of literary men, said Carlyle and *Tait's Edinburgh Magazine*, two thrifty Scottish concerns, who both chose to describe him, one dyspeptically to his face and the other in print, as being no better than the blind fiddlers who plied the Scottish ferry-boats fiddling for halfpennies.[1]

As always, Thackeray was to be deeply wounded by the criticism, but such stings were way in the future when he tore around London for a day and a half, gathering up sovereigns from his various publishers, finishing his work for *Fraser's*, arranging to swap his proposed book on Talleyrand for one of foreign travels, topping up with eighteen shirts and a sea stock of cotton trousers, sending letters to his family to say he couldn't see them as expected since he would be in Jerusalem that day. On the coach to Southampton he feverishly wrote an article for *Punch*. Three days later he set foot on foreign soil for the first time of the trip, at Vigo in Spain. After that the sights came so fast and dazzling he despaired of ever shaking down the brilliant kaleidoscope into a readable book.

He was seasick for much of the time, and everywhere pursued by bed-lice and mosquitoes. The Eastern flea, he was to discover, bit more bitterly than the most savage bug in Christendom. Was Alcibiades persecuted by these monsters, he wondered, and 'did the brutes crawl all over him as he lay in the rosy arms of Phryne?'

In his cabin, he thwarted the fleas by sleeping on a table. Ashore, he experimented with every anti-insect device, from mosquito-netting to laying about him with a towel, until at a Greek convent caravanserai at Ramleh, he experienced a human horror which made the insects seem infinitely preferable—a greasy, grinning monk, who fell upon him and began tickling just as he was drifting into his only vermin-free slumber of the voyage.

As with the *Irish Sketch Book*, Thackeray's aim was to give a personal 'Cockney' account of the wondrous lands he saw, the view of a man at a street-corner café, absorbing the sights and sounds with a long, cool glass in his hand, and when reluctantly he moved he gave almost as much space to his many means of transport as to the visions they allowed him to see.

In Spain, he went ashore in the provision boat, foraging for Vigo's famed oysters, and fresh milk for his tea (to replace the slimy inter-port substitute of whipped egg yolks), and for the last few yards to the beach found himself being carried on the shoulder of a bare-legged, ragged Spaniard who rushed into the water to perform the service.

'The approved method seems to be,' he instructed future travellers, 'to sit upon one shoulder only, holding on by the porter's whiskers; and though some of our party were of the tallest and fattest men whereof our race is comprised, and their living sedans exceedingly meagre and small, yet all were landed without accident upon the juicy sand, and forthwith surrounded by a host of mendicants, screaming, "I say, sir! penny, sir! I say, English! tam your ays! penny!"'

In Alexandria, he followed local custom and rode around on a donkey, descending onto the unfortunate beast, rather than mounting it, and wondering if, out of compassion, he shouldn't have one for himself and another for his legs.

For the trip to Jerusalem, his party was equipped in more magnificent style. Guarded by 'mahogany-coloured infidels' and noble, turbaned Arabs with sabres curling round their military thighs, with the ladies in a litter, the French *femme-de-chambre* caracoling manfully on a frisky grey mare, with a dozen or so other domestics, flunkies, guides, grooms, pack-mules and outriders, Thackeray and the rest of the gentlemen rode astride horses with towering Turkish saddles, fire-shovel stirrups ('deucedly short'), worsted reins, red padded saddle-cloths, and an array of tags, fringes, glass beads and ends of rope for purely decorative purposes. How they would have stared in the Strand, he thought, as he wedged an umbrella across his mountain of a saddle for additional support.

His stay in the Holy City seemed like ten days passed in a fever.

'Titmarsh at Jerusalem will certainly be an era in Christianity,' FitzGerald had written on learning of the pilgrimage, and Titmarsh's chapter on Jerusalem might well have brought tribulation to its author had not Mrs Carmichael-Smyth persuaded him to tone down his heterodoxy. As it was it cost him more pain in the writing than anything else in the book, and is raw with his horror at the murder and crime of the Old Testament, and the vile jostling commercialism of the latter-day exploiters of the holy places.

Greece was also to anger him at first. It was too great a concept altogether, he said, too tainted by memories of schooldays, and Athens itself was too filthy, beggarly, rackety, buggy, too full of dogs, donkeys and human sharks, its mouldy ruins too reminiscent of rotten Stilton cheese.

After inspecting the Parthenon, however, Titmarsh had to admit that walking among the nests of the eagles, and seeing the prodigious eggs they had laid, brought a certain feeling of discomfiture to such small birds as himself. It stretched the mind painfully, he wrote, to try to comprehend even part of the beauty of a single column, a broken shaft lying beneath an astonishingly blue sky, amidst unrivalled scenery. He left feeling that at last he had achieved a feeble glimpse of the ancient Greek spirit that had peopled that peerless landscape with sublime races of heroes and gods, a glimmer he had never been able to find in any school-book—even though the master had flung it at his head.

In Egypt, set upon two miles before he reached the pyramids by a pack of jostling beggars and guides, and thereafter unable to shake or kick them off, his bulk was pushed, pulled and bullied to the top. At the very summit, he told his *Punch* readers, he pasted *Punch* posters. The 'Fat Contributor' had found a glorious cause: 'I had to introduce PUNCH to Cheops—I had vowed to leave his card at the gates of History'. In a private letter to the *Pictorial Times*, he threatened to post them up in the same place—as defaulters. Why didn't they pay the money they owed him? he asked.

But of all the resting-places of this odyssey, Constantinople was to be the one which provided him with the experience he was to turn into the most glorious passage in all his eventual *Notes of a Journey from Cornhill to Grand Cairo*—the delights and terrors of a Turkish bath.

Staggering on wooden pattens, dressed in three small cotton napkins and a turban, thinking of Pall Mall with a sort of despair, he had sunk, he reported, into a not unpleasant reverie in the steam room (where the sensation was that of a 'soft boiling simmer, which, no doubt, potatoes feel when they are steaming'), when he was jolted to attention by a terrifying apparition: a great brown, half-naked, grinning, gleaming-eyed monster with shaven head, protruding ears, a horsehair glove and demonic designs on his victim's body.

Having had his brutal way with the horsehair, the grinning brown ogre made another attack with a basin of lather containing an object Thackeray described as 'something like Miss MacWhirter's flaxen wig that she is so proud of, and that we have all laughed at.' Remonstrance brought no relief: 'the thing like a wig is dashed into your face and eyes, covered with soap, and for five minutes you are drowned in lather: you can't see, the suds are frothing over your eyeballs; you can't hear, the soap is whizzing into your ears; you can't gasp for breath, Miss MacWhirter's wig is down your throat with half a pailful of suds in an instant . . .'

Back in the cooling room, however, gently reposing on a bed, with his cotton draperies mercifully restored, the torture seemed eminently worthwhile: 'somebody brings a narghilé, which tastes as tobacco must taste in Mahomet's Paradise; a cool sweet dreamy languor takes possession of the purified frame; and half an hour of such delicious laziness is spent over the pipe as is unknown in Europe, where vulgar prejudice has most shamefully maligned indolence.'

Unwilling to risk the Bay of Biscay in November, tempted by the alternative of a leisurely homeward route through Italy, Thackeray left the ship at Malta, where he surrendered to the compulsory quarantine for travellers arriving from the East. The *Iberia* had visited this golden rock of an island outward bound, when, none of the party speaking Maltese or Italian, and being unable to make themselves understood in English, Thackeray had stepped into the breach with operatic arias: '*Un biglietto! Eccolo quà!*' he had sung out to the ticket collectors; then, '*Là ci darem la mano*', gallantly, though even less usefully, as he handed Mrs Tennent down the gangway.

It was just the kind of place he liked, a sunlit bustle of life and commerce, where the poor appeared to live in handsome stone palaces and the narrow streets were thronged with a chattering mixture of nations. But now all this was lost to him as he was immured in the Lazaretto.

Throughout the voyage, he had kept up a tremendous flow of writing and drawing: 'Fat Contributor' dispatches, full of the most absurd aspects of his travels, for *Punch*; that tyrant *Barry Lyndon*, even more difficult away from his reference books; and the travel book itself, which he had done his best to keep up-to-date as he voyaged between ports.

During his first week in quarantine he at last finished *Barry*

Lyndon, 'after great throes late at night.' The next day he wrote three papers for *Punch*. The following day, yet another. After that, he planned the characters for a Christmas book—*Mrs. Perkins's Ball*.

Between times, he had the company of a young Egyptian colonel, who instructed him in the skill of his countrywomen at *double entendre* and their eagerness to vary the carnal pleasures of their lords. For public Victorian consumption, Thackeray claimed that he had found the conversation anything but edifying.

After sixteen days—and an output of work which would have satisfied the most energetic of men—he was released. He was, he wrote in his diary, glad to be free of 'an imprisonment w^h I had hoped to put to much greater profit.'[2]

By way of Naples, Herculaneum, Rome and Florence, he moved slowly towards Paris, his pleasure in at last visiting the country he had longed to see above all others diminished by another chronic shortage of money, of Lille proportions and longer duration. Established at Franz's Hotel, in the via Condotti, Rome, he soon found his way to the garrets and entertainments of the 'Artist banditti', and having distributed discreet largess among his poorer companions in the knowledge that there was more to come from England, suddenly found his own pockets bare. For thirty-five days he called at the 'dd dd-dd-ddd-ddd' post office, looking for letters of credit from Chapman and Hall. For thirty-five days all knowledge of such letters was denied. On the thirty-sixth, they were relinquished to him. They had been there all the time, awaiting a Mr Jackeray.

In the meantime, he had written to *Punch*, asking them to help bail out 'a man alone, unhappy, in the hotbed of Popery and in pawn.'[3] If anyone was going to try converting Thackeray to Rome, quipped Douglas Jerrold, they should start with his nose.

11
Punch

The flood-tide of success

In 1845, the year of Thackeray's return from his Eastern and Italian travels, he made more money than in any previous twelve months of his working life, yet he still managed to end it as he had begun, with the coffers bare and debts to be paid. Like many another speculator in this 'abominable railroad mania year', he had gambled on what had seemed an absolute certainty, and lost £500.

He put the experience to humorous use in *The Diary of C. Jeames de la Pluche, Esq.*, for *Punch*, the immensely popular chronicle of a footman whose paper speculations swept him up to the dizziest social heights, within ambitious marital grasp of the daughter of his impoverished old employer, Lord Bareacres, and brought him crashing down again. But privately Thackeray's own stock dealings were a wretched embarrassment. Since he had borrowed most of the money to finance them, he had the dismal task of paying it back long after the euphoric bubble had burst.

He owed his mother £200, and in four years had repaid only £50 of his cousin Mary's loan. For a long time yet he was to be 'always earning always paying never having', and while some of his trouble stemmed from unwise investments and self-indulgence, a good deal was also due to his generosity to those in even greater need.

For two months he supported Coventry Patmore, whose father had been far harder hit by 'the sanguinary railroads', and got him into *Fraser's* by prophesying that the young poet would one day be a genius, and by promising Nickisson one of his own increasingly rare contributions in return for the favour.

He tried to help Saville Morton in the same way when Morton, having run through his fortune, took off on a series of foreign correspondent jobs. But this time none of his contacts would co-operate, and Thackeray was soon telling FitzGerald that the two of them would have to put their hands in their pockets for 'poor honest Elizabeth', one of Morton's many deserted ladies. He couldn't afford much, he said, since he had so many other pensioners and expenses, but was good for £3 or so a month.

In the end Milnes saved him this sum, Thackeray having passed on to him a message from Morton: '*Milnes owes me 10£ for a sketch w^h I haven't done*'—an expression Thackeray described as 'beyond measure felicitous'.[1]

Though he still intended to write his postponed book on Talleyrand, he helped one of his mother's Paris friends, Madame Colmache, widow of the statesman-Prince's secretary and a prime rival in the field, to place her articles with English magazines, and even this noble deed was topped by his offer of aid to yet another Irish rogue and charmer of whom he was soon to write that the world did not contain a greater villain.

Like Thackeray's 'dear old Fitz', the Irishman was called Edward FitzGerald—Edward Marlborough FitzGerald. He was well known in London literary circles as a boaster of formidable ingenuity, and, to Thackeray at any rate, as a libertine who had neglected and ill-treated his wife, taken home his mistress, tried to abduct his children, and sunk the family so deep in debt that even the servants and small traders could not be paid (a crime Thackeray was to condemn in *Vanity Fair* as crueller by far than many a legally greater one). He had even, at some time, tried his philandering charms on poor little Isabella.

When Thackeray caught up with this last treachery, he forbade the knave to call on him, but he was still prepared, for the sake of Marlborough FitzGerald's wife and children, and perhaps in remembrance of shared follies, to offer him a lifeline: £5 to get him to some cheap place abroad, £5 for the unpaid washerwoman, and £1 a week for six months while he wrote articles which Thackeray promised to dispose of in London, the proceeds from which would keep him and his family alive for another six months.

'Go away in God's name & work & humble yourself and amend . . .' Thackeray told him. 'God knows I don't write in any proud spirit. May Heaven pardon the sins of both of us.'[2]

Marlborough FitzGerald did go away, but he didn't amend. Later in the year, Alfred Tennyson's brother, Frederick, writing to Thackeray from Leghorn, asked if he knew a most amusing Irishman who was enchanting them all: a friend of Canning, George

IV, Bulwer-Lytton and the Duke of Wellington, a man who had mixed in the highest social and political circles for the past twenty years and who claimed to be a nephew of Lord FitzGerald.

'Who can this be?' Thackeray dryly asked a mutual friend.

In marked contrast with Dickens's hard bargaining in financial matters, and his breaking of publishing contracts he considered outstripped by his fame, Thackeray under-valued all but his magazine work, worried if he thought he was being overpaid, and sought his rightful share of the profits most courteously in the few instances of disagreement.

'I was always a bad hand at accounts, and put myself honestly into your hands as men of business to deal fairly with me,' he told Edward Chapman, when Chapman and Hall showed reluctance to pay royalties on a second edition of *Cornhill to Grand Cairo*, after the first had notched up more sales in a month than the *Paris Sketch Book* had achieved in three years.[3]

Any confidence he had had in his ability as a novelist had been seriously dented by the failure of *Barry Lyndon*, and was to be diminished even further when the first chapters of his 'Novel without a Hero'—*Vanity Fair*—which he had begun writing early in 1845, were rejected by several publishers and nearly lost for ever to one of them: Henry (Bacon or Bungay) Colburn.

Thackeray had submitted them to Colburn, along with another shorter story which Colburn had partially paid for but not used by the time he sold his *New Monthly Magazine* to Harrison Ainsworth. In a most unethical manoeuvre, since he was the one reneging on the agreement, Colburn then refused to return either manuscript until he got his money back. It took several progressively angry letters to both old and new owners before Harrison Ainsworth finally organized their release, by which time Thackeray had written a satirical blast for *Punch* on a snobbish advertisement for the magazine under new management, promising contributors 'not only of talent but of rank.'

'I always must think it a very objectionable advertisement—but shouldn't have lifted my hand to smite my friend; had explanation come earlier,' he apologized to Ainsworth. 'So that now *you* must be called upon to play the part of forgiver in w^h I'm sure you will shine.'[4]

After this unpropitious start, Thackeray leaped at the first sum mentioned when *Punch*'s Bradbury and Evans offered to buy the book for publication in separate monthly instalments, a relatively modest £50 a month, illustrations included. On reflection, he said he was deuced sorry he hadn't asked for another tenner since he was sure they would have given it, but his beaming face, as he burst in on friends to cry the good news of the sale, showed no serious regret— and in the end he got his extra £10, too.

He was pinning his hopes of fame on this novel, but it was with yet another anonymously written series for *Punch* that the flood-tide began to break. Three weeks after the fall of Jeames the railway speculator he began *The Snobs of England*, fifty-three weekly papers laying bare the anatomy of British society. They caused the same kind of furore that U and Non-U was to generate a hundred years later, and sent the sales of *Punch* soaring.

When he began, the word snob was loosely used to describe anyone low or vulgar. Thackeray brought it closer to the meaning it has today, and astonished, amused, or outraged his fellow Victorians by suggesting that snobbishness was not confined to the lower classes only.

'An immense per-centage of Snobs, I believe, is to be found in every rank of this mortal life,' he wrote in his first paper. 'You must not judge hastily or vulgarly of Snobs: to do so shows that you are yourself a Snob. I myself have been taken for one.'

It was this personal involvement, the aspect of the fallible insider seeing the faults and foibles of his peers, that made the exercise so appealing. As G. K. Chesterton pointed out, Dickens, Douglas Jerrold, or many another writer might have planned a book of snobs, but it was Thackeray, and Thackeray alone, who wrote the great subtitle, 'By One of Themselves'.[5]

Beneath the levity, as he surveyed week by week the follies and vanities of social and institutional Britain, there was a deeper moral, one to which all his future works were to point. He no longer wished to blast the aristocracy to the four winds, but to stop the middle class (his own class) being so abominably servile to them—as in Ainsworth's advertisement—and from wreaking their vengeance in turn on those they considered inferior to themselves. He wanted not to banish the old courtly code, but to make everyone a gentleman, a course which would be brought about, he now believed, by love, simplicity, and natural kindness, rather than destructive radicalism.

It was, said Chesterton, 'his special contribution to that chaos of morality which the nineteenth century muddled through: he stood for the remains of Christian humility, as Dickens stood for the remains of Christian charity.'[6]

It was also a philosophy which was to cause feathers to fly round the *Punch* table, and change for good the course of the magazine. Influenced by William Brookfield, a flawed but compassionate clergyman, Thackeray championed the Church, one of *Punch*'s prime targets, in his first paper on Clerical Snobs, and murmured the suspicion that those who cried out loudest against parsons had seldom gained their knowledge of the Church by going there very often.

Douglas Jerrold, that 'savage little Robespierre' as Thackeray was later to call him, took this as a personal assault, and there is little doubt that it was intended as such. It was an extension of many an argument at *Punch*'s weekly dinners, when Jerrold, with his great head and flowing mane of hair, his stunted, rheumatism-racked body, and a mind embittered by a childhood which made Dickens's seem a most comfortable apprenticeship, took on the rest of the table in his bid to keep *Punch* true to its hard-hitting, radical course. Throwing his peas down his throat with a knife, a practice Thackeray found as hard to stomach as his adversary's anarchical politics, Jerrold argued, almost alone, for a continuance of the slashing attacks on Church, State and personalities that had marked *Punch*'s early years.

Editor Mark Lemon, shrewd and inscrutable, listened to both sides. He was never entirely at his ease 'with Thackeray. He always seemed 'so infernally wise', he explained in later years. 'He was genial: but whatever you talked about, you felt he would have the wisest views upon the subject. He seemed too great for ordinary conversation.'[7] Nevertheless, in the Jerrold–Thackeray battle, Lemon eventually came down on the side of the infernally wise Thackeray, and set *Punch* on the road to middle-class respectability.

Though Thackeray attended the magazine's weekly dinners until the end of his life, he too could not feel completely at home with some of his colleagues. He admired their talents, joined in the discussions, contributed his jokes, and, when the argument grew too hot, his song too, but his private view of socializing with *Punch* is clear from a diary description of one of its summer outings, afloat on the river, in August 1846, when 'many instances of Bacchic fury occurred.'

Even Percival 'The Professor' Leigh was utterly stupid and speechless with drink several hours before the party broke up, so much so that Thackeray had to escort him home. Young Bradbury, eldest son of the superbly distinguished-looking publisher, was rolling around on the box of the fly being sick, with his father's partner, Evans, a Pickwickian gnome of a man, merely cheerfully drunk at his side.

Earlier, the ladies had vied with each other in the musical field, Mrs Robert Chambers sweetly singing Scottish airs, which the gentle Gilbert à Beckett's wife had tried to *écraser* with a shrieked performance of 'Charlie, Charlie'. John Forster, in magnificent, bantering form, confounded all who would listen with the power and splendour of his oratory; Jerrold 'chirped and laughed & made laugh with all his might'; and little Evans, before getting drunk had his hat knocked off. Thackeray amused himself by telling Mrs à Beckett what a charming voice Mrs Chambers had. It was not his kind of party.

But, if he couldn't find all of them congenial companions all of the time, he kept his feelings to himself about all except Jerrold, for whose political beliefs he did little to disguise his contempt. Jerrold, for his part, liked to dismiss Thackeray as simply a large, crotchety fellow with a broken nose, but had to admit there was something there he didn't understand. He had known him for eighteen years, he used to say, and didn't know him yet.

As winner of the *Punch* battle, Thackeray extended if not the hand of friendship at least a flag of truce—'What is the use of quarrelling with a man if you have to meet him every Wednesday at dinner?' he shrugged[8]—and took care to instruct Mark Lemon that the final words of the *Snob* papers, written almost a year after the Parson–Snob controversy, were not aimed at his old antagonist.

Increasing fame and more frequent contact with his growing daughters had completed Thackeray's metamorphosis from bitter young satirist to mature philosopher, and it was in this role that he added his last 'benedictory paragraph' to the great *Snob* saga. Having listed the follies and social injustices exposed in the course of the series, he concluded:

'To laugh at such is *Mr. Punch*'s business. May he laugh honestly, hit no foul blow, and tell the truth when at his very broadest grin— never forgetting that if Fun is good, Truth is still better, and Love best of all.'

What he had written, he told Lemon, applied as much to himself as to anyone else who aimed at being a 'Satirical-Moralist':

'A few years ago I should have sneered at the idea of setting up as a teacher at all, and perhaps at this pompous way of talking about a few papers of jokes in Punch—but I have got to believe in the business, and in many other things since then. And our profession seems to me to be as serious as the Parson's own.'[9]

It was in this mood of gentle preacher that late the following year Thackeray wrote what Dickens was to regard as the best of all his *Punch* contributions—*The Curate's Walk*—a remarkable tribute to the lives of proud, neat poverty that existed in the cramped courts and crooked lanes behind Victorian London's fashionable thoroughfares. Based on his parish visits with Brookfield (thinly disguised as the Revd. Frank Whitestock), he introduced the reader to three old, old children, aged from five to ten, minuscule daughters of a charwoman, who in their mother's absence tended the family's spotless 'second floor front', and did the honours of that bare little apartment.

It is a miraculously moving document, rooted in very Dickensian territory, but Thackeray made his impact in quite a different way from Dickens. Writing with all the wonder of a stranger coming suddenly upon an unexpected world, he described his discovery with a respectful awe. The words he had used to praise *A Christmas Carol* could equally well be applied to this small gem, for it too is 'a national benefit, and to every man or woman who reads it a personal kindness.'[10]

2.

Between the *Snob* papers and *The Curate's Walk*, Thackeray wrote another much talked-of series for *Punch—Punch's Prize Novelists*, or *Novels by Eminent Hands*, as it was later called—a collection of good-natured parodies of the most popular writers of the day. It was, said Thackeray, sparring with the gloves on, 'friendly and meek in spirit', and though he included Sir Edward George Lytton Bulwer-Lytton in his list ('George de Barnwell. By Sir E.L. B.L. B.B.L.L. B.B.B.L.L.L., Bart.') the tone was well in keeping with his proclaimed belief in kindness, love and painless fun.

Bulwer-Lytton ('In the Morning of Life the Truthful wooed the Beautiful, and their offspring was Love'), was followed by Disraeli ('Codlingsby, by D. Shrewsberry, Esq.'); Charles Lever ('Phil Fogarty. A tale of the Fighting Onety-Oneth, by Harry Rollicker'); Mrs Gore ('Lords and Liveries, by the Authoress of "Dukes and Déjeûners," "Hearts and Diamonds," "Marchionesses and Milliners," etc. etc.'); James Fenimore Cooper ('The Stars and Stripes, by the Author of "The Last of the Mulligans"'); G. P. R. James, then enormously successful with his tales of chivalric romance; and 'Crinoline by Je-mes Pl-sh, Esq.', an exercise in self-immolation.

Dickens, who was also to have featured in the series, let it be known through Forster that such sport 'did no honor to literature or literary men, and should be left to very inferior and miserable hands'. He was then 'strongly impressed by the absurdity and injustice' of being left out, as he had the good grace to tell Thackeray himself.[1]

To be chosen as a *Prize Novelist* was a tribute to an author's renown, since the whole point of the exercise depended on immediate recognition from the reader, but in dwelling on this aspect and the kindly nature of his imitations, Thackeray failed to consider that few men enjoy seeing their life's blood made sport of in public, however sympathetically. He did warn Albany Fonblanque, who was eager to play Cupid between Bulwer-Lytton and his former tormentor, that with the series soon to start it was not the best of times to bring them together at the same dinner-table, but he was totally unprepared for the reactions of some of his other victims.

Only Mrs Gore and the American, James Fenimore Cooper, carried on unperturbed after having their writing styles crystallized in this way. Bulwer-Lytton, whose use of long words and 'premeditated fine writing' made Thackeray furious no matter how hard he tried to appreciate the man, had only just published a defence of his works in response to a damning notice in *The Times*, a review he was so sure had been written by Thackeray that he had dramatically asked Forster if he shouldn't call him out.[2]

'George de Barnwell', however, drove him to take yet another look at *Eugene Aram*, the work on which the *Punch* parody was largely based, and for a new edition two years later to revise it drastically. In future, he did his best to chasten his rococo imagination.

G. P. R. James, who regularly turned out two novels a year, apologized for starting them all in exactly the same way, and invented alternatives for his long-cherished two cavaliers, or the solitary horseman who had ridden into view on the first page of all his previous works.

After the all too brilliant 'Codlingsby', Disraeli publicly cut the man who had dared to parody him, and got his own back (though not until both authors were dead) with his portrayal of Thackeray as St Barbe, 'the vainest, the most envious, the most amusing of men', in his posthumously published novel, *Endymion*.

Charles Lever moved more swiftly. In *Roland Cashel*, his first novel after 'Harry Rollicker's' outrageous frolics, a work very different in style and story-line from anything he had attempted before, he drew a vicious portrait of Thackeray as the travelling Cockney, 'Mr. Elias Howle . . . a publisher's man-of-all-work, ready for everything, from statistics to satire, and equally prepared to expound prophecy, or write squibs for "Punch".'

As the author of '"Snooks in the Holy Land,"—the wittiest thing of the day,' Howle had gone to Ireland, wrote Lever, 'not to counsel nor console, not to lament over nor bewail our varied mass of errors and misfortunes, but to laugh at us . . . His mission was to make "Punch" out of Ireland, and none more capable than he for the office.'

Mr Howle in the flesh was then described:

'He was large and heavily built, but neither muscular nor athletic;

his frame and all his gestures indicated weakness and uncertainty. His head was capacious, but not remarkable for what phrenologists call moral development, while the sinister expression of his eyes— half submissive, half satirical—suggested doubts of his sincerity. There was nothing honest about him but his mouth; this was large, full, thick-lipped, and sensual; the mouth of one who loved to dine well, and yet felt that his agreeability was an ample receipt in full for the best entertainment'.[3]

Thackeray tried hard to prove that he at any rate could take a joke. It was rather good, he said, coming just two days after the *Morning Chronicle* had described him as a satirist without an enemy, but that he was deeply wounded is evident from the letter he wrote to his and Lever's mutual publisher, Edward Chapman. Once again, it was the remarks about himself, rather than his writings, which he claimed to find most distasteful. They wouldn't hurt him professionally, he told Chapman:

'I have pushed the caricaturing of myself almost to affectation— but it won't profit Lever to gibbet a rival in that way . . . Somebody should tell him that such behaviour will hurt him without in the least injuring me . . . Make fun of my books, my style, my public works—but of me a gentleman—O for shame.'[4]

Many years later, when he was at the height of his fame, and Lever almost forgotten, Thackeray forgave this man he liked so well, but whose books he couldn't praise, and took the first steps towards renewed friendship. In *Pendennis* he tossed in the name of Elias Howle, along with a string of other strange authors, and within weeks of Lever's onslaught appearing in print, he salved his wounds by using the attack as the basis for an 'Author's Misery' sketch for *Punch*.

This process of the hurt writer turning pain to profit was one Thackeray was to view with increasing appreciation. A few years later, when he made Pendennis think of publishing his early love poems, he had Warrington scoff:

'That's the way of poets . . . They fall in love, jilt, or are jilted; they suffer and they cry out that they suffer more than any other mortals: and when they have experienced feelings enough they note them down in a book, and take the book to market. All poets are humbugs, all literary men are humbugs; directly a man begins to sell his feelings for money he's a humbug. If a poet gets a pain in his side from too good a dinner, he bellows Ai, Ai, louder than Prometheus.'[5]

But at the end of his life, in an imaginary conversation with Laurence Sterne, he paid due tribute to this literary alchemy.

'You are ashamed of that quality by which you earn your subsistence, and such reputation as you have?' mocks Sterne. 'Your sensibility is your livelihood, my worthy friend.'[6]

There are many reflections of Thackeray's sensibility, many personal pangs of pain and pleasure, old and freshly won, to be found in the pages of *Vanity Fair*, the novel that was just a few numbers old when he began the *Punch* series of parodies, and which, as much as the parodies themselves, was to make so many of his then more famous contemporaries change their writing-styles for something nearer his own.

As this work progressed, Thackeray found it a more congenial vehicle for his philosophy, his joys and his hurts, than the neat parcels of humour demanded by *Punch*. As he juggled his time, breaking off work on the novel to fulfil his commitments to the magazine, he was often to grumble that being funny to order was an arduous and dreary business, and to find that *Punch* itself was getting perfectly odious to him.

'O brother wearers of motley! Are there not moments when one grows sick of grinning and tumbling, and the jingling of cap and bells?' he asks in *Vanity Fair*. But he still relied on *Punch* for a large portion of his income, and remained a regular contributor until 1851, many of his papers taking on a decidedly domestic flavour as he became once more a paterfamilias.

12

Young Street

A family without a wife

In the autumn of 1845, Thackeray had brought Isabella back to
England. He had spent months advertising for and interviewing
families willing to look after her. He had visited an appalling British
asylum, the best in the country according to Bryan Procter, a newly
appointed Lunacy Commissioner (a job thought appropriate to
literary men). And at last he had put her into the care of a Mrs
Bakewell and her daughter, Mrs Gloyne, at Camberwell.

For a while Isabella had seemed so sprightly and showed such
pleasure in seeing her husband again that he dined with her many
nights a week, took private boxes for her at the theatre, and paid for
carriages to take her calling on her friends. In gratitude and hope he
became a regular visitor to the Bakewell household.

'You should have seen the three Camberwell ladies the other day,'
he told his mother, 'my wife Mrs Gloyne and Mrs Bakewell—one
mending the right hand breeches pocket another the left the third a
hole in my coat-tail! Such a Paris among these three Venuses.'[1]

But the improvement was again short-lived. The trips to Camberwell became increasingly poor holiday-making after a day's work
and were continued only through a sense of duty. On Isabella's good
days, Thackeray could still cherish the hope that when the children
were older she would be able to return to him. In more clear-sighted
moments, he could see that she was getting no better, and was
playing 'the nastiest pranks' more frequently than ever.

He too had moved into more cheerful lodgings, at 88 St James's
Street, next door to the coffee house where Swift had once written

his letters to 'Stella', and, on the death of old John Goldworthy, had found a brisker, younger man to run his errands and look to his comfort. But more than ever he longed for a proper home. After a visit from his mother and children, when he had packed all the juvenile pleasures of the town into a few brief days, he wrote to Paris that he wished they had never been. Until then, he said, he had fancied himself perfectly happy.

With the dual success of his Eastern travel book and the *Snob* papers, he was soon house-hunting again—'like a maniac'. If his bankers, with a more realistic appreciation of his earnings and commitments, had not refused to answer for his respectability—a most wounding incident—he would have moved into a choice property in Belgravia. When that fell through, he tried to tempt his parents back to England with a seven-acre farm three miles out of town. If he had a steady home to go to, he told the Major, he reckoned he could make £1200 that year, and pay off all their debts in three. But the Major refused to move. London was the only battlefield from which this gallant old soldier had had to lead his troops in defeat, and he still had creditors there, though no longer pressing ones.

When Thackeray at last took a house (at the rational rent of £65 a year) in Young Street, Kensington, his stepfather still remained adamant, and Thackeray was faced with another dilemma: he couldn't bring himself to part his mother from the grandchildren she had cared for for almost six years, and yet he was uneasy about leaving Annie in her sole charge any longer. For some time there had been complaints of the child's refusal to obey the simplest instructions, her wilfulness and tantrums, and now Thackeray wrote to Jane Shawe:

'I am afraid very much she is going to be a man of genius. I would far sooner have had her an amiable & affectionate woman—but little Minny will be that, please God.—and the Sisters love each other admirably. As for me I am child-sick, and when I see in Kensington Gardens or my friends' houses a pair of little girls at all resembling my own, I become quite maudlin over them.'[2]

Part of Annie's trouble can be guessed at from the awesome impression Mrs Carmichael-Smyth made on another young girl, Henriette Corkran, daughter of one of Thackeray's Paris correspondent friends. Left one day in the austere presence of Mrs Smyth, Henriette endured with a bad grace a reading from the Bible, and the stern catechism on her favourite Scriptural heroes which followed. Having named some acceptable, if unconventional, candidates, this small rebel then added that she would have liked to have seen the serpent talking to Eve.

During the furious lecture which ensued, Henriette burst into tears and was defiantly shouting through her sobs that she hated religious people, they were so severe and dull, when she was rescued by the Major, an unlikely-looking knight errant, wearing turned-up-at-the-toe boots, an old coat slung over his shoulders with the sleeves swinging loose, and a red scarf wound round his hat for warmth.

Certainly, after Annie returned to her father, there was no more talk of her waywardness. To Thackeray, his plump, plain, clever eldest child was soon revealed as 'a fat lump of pure gold.'

The house at 13 Young Street, double bow-fronted like a miniature fortress breached with an unexpected array of large and cheerful windows, was set in London's ancient Royal Borough, midway between Kensington Palace and Kensington Square, both of which Thackeray was to people afresh with eighteenth-century characters for his *History of Henry Esmond*. Quite as obstinate as his stepfather, he apportioned rooms to every member of the family, and with the same kind of relish he had shown in making his Cambridge rooms so 'stilish' seventeen years before, set about buying old lots of furniture and opening up musty family trunks, which disgorged everything from his own childish shirts of Indian vintage to Mrs Butler's finest table linen.

Sometimes lonely, occasionally suffering bouts of cold feet— afraid that once he had the longed-for home and family he would neglect them ('It is the nature of the beau to be dissatisfied')—he ploughed on with hiring servants, and was soon taking cover from regiments of would-be governesses.

'For God's sake stop Mme. Bölte,' he wrote to Mrs Carlyle. 'I have governidges calling at all hours with High Dutch accents and reams of testimonials. One today, one yesterday and a letter the day before, and on going to dine at Punch, by Heavens! there was a letter from a German lady on my plate. And I don't want a Ger-woman'.[3]

The whole governess problem was an extremely tricky one, for, as he unwisely explained to his mother: 'Unless I liked a Governess I couldn't live with her and if I did—O fie. The flesh is very weak, le coeur sent toujours le besoin d'aimer. What a mercy it is that I have kept clear hitherto.'[4]

For a while in the half-furnished house he had the company of his brother-in-law, Arthur Shawe, married now to a sickly, neglected wife, and obviously hoping for a financial hand-out. But this was one direction in which Thackeray was not prepared to see his money flow away, and he countered such hints with the suggestion that Arthur's mother should show a little recognition of Isabella's family claims by paying her monthly bills occasionally. Over the years, he was to meet many Shawe relations who instructed him in his mother-in-law's version of his conduct towards her daughter, and, though he had compiled a dossier of her letters to refute such slanders, he learned to shrug them aside. If anyone left him £10,000 a year, he knew the whole brood would soon find him virtuous enough.

There were to be four months of impatient waiting before he had the company he really wanted, before Mrs Carmichael-Smyth, insisting that it was for no more than another brief holiday, brought his daughters to London. Once there, Thackeray persuaded her that the children should stay, and with tears and many a desperate look of recrimination, his mother returned alone to Paris.

It was a dark, wintry evening when Annie and Minnie, now aged nine and six, first saw the house that was to be their home for the next eight years, and Thackeray, not expecting them so early, was not there to greet them. But the fires were lit, and Eliza, the new maid, showed them round. '. . . there was a feeling of London,' wrote Annie later, '—London smelt of tobacco, we thought.'[5]

In their own rooms they found pictures already decorating the walls, chosen for them by their father: Thorvaldsen prints, Hunt's sleepy boy yawning at them from over the chimneypiece, and a drawing of Thackeray himself as a child, which Eliza told them he had put up with his own hands. Once more, after his first happy married years, Thackeray had a home and a family, if, as Annie said, two young children, a maid, a manservant, a cook, and a small black cat could be called a family.

With their arrival, Young Street sprang to life. The school-room windowsills, high at the top of the house, were soon cluttered with Minnie's menagerie of snails and flies, half-drowned invalids rescued from milk jugs and set to convalesce on rose leaves. The ragged garden, with its medlar tree and Spanish jessamines, its rosy clumps of London Pride, rang with their young voices and the more raucous cries of stray cats, lured with a row of saucers placed beneath Thackeray's study window, and christened by Minnie after her favourite fictional characters: Nicholas Nickleby, Martin Chuzzlewit, and half-starved Barnaby Rudge.

Thackeray's woodblocks, sketches and notebooks found their way into every corner of the house, printer's boys swung their legs in the hall, waiting for perennially overdue copy, and, as *Vanity Fair* got under way, an engraver called once a week to 'bite in' the plates for the illustrations, in the dining-room.

Eugenie Crowe, daughter of Eyre Evans Crowe, one of a series of young beauties in whom Thackeray was to take an equivocal interest—avuncular, if only because it could be nothing else—was called on to sit for Amelia and the Osborne ladies in turn; Annie and Minnie proudly held their poses as squabbling children on the floor; pieces of furniture were commandeered as stand-ins for the long-suffering Dobbin and the multitude of other characters who seemed as much a part of Annie's and Minnie's daily lives as any breathing creature.

There was a bustle and variety in splendid contrast with the sombre, orderly existence of the Avenue Sainte Marie. Though their father was busy, and often away from home, Annie later paid him the tribute of saying 'we seemed to live with him.' Birthdays were celebrated with carefully planned excursions and feasts, but all through the year there were impromptu visits, mainly to artists, whose great books of sketches and marvellous new paintings provided entertainment for the girls while their father talked.

Mrs Procter also took them under her wing, as she had done their father, and even childless Jane Carlyle, despite a certain coolness between their menfolk after Carlyle's 'blind fiddler' remarks, entertained them with a warmth and sensitivity they were never to forget.

On their first visit to Cheyne Row, after a winter walk through the snow-covered country lanes which then lay between Kensington and Chelsea, Annie and Minnie found cups of hot chocolate waiting for them, kept warm before a blazing dining-room fire with saucers placed on top to seal in the heat.

'I thought ye would be frozen,' said their hostess, and turned the thoughtful feast into an eagerly anticipated tradition.

Slim, bird-bright, and handsomely gowned, Mrs Carlyle seemed to Annie quite as impressive as many of the noble ladies her father later took her to visit, and the conversation in her dim, still, panelled room, with its accumulation of little tables covered with silver and mother-of-pearl knick-knacks, took on a flatteringly grown-up tone, as Mrs Carlyle discoursed with untiring vigour of 'Carlyle', his genius, his dyspepsia and his sayings.

'If ye wish for a quiet life,' she told them, 'never ye marry a dyspeptic man of genius.' And all the time, the presence overhead in his study of the dyspeptic man of genius himself distinctly added to the pleasure—so long as he remained upstairs. [6]

Visits to the Dickens household were more formal affairs, usually for a children's party, events which stood out like blazing landmarks in Annie's and Minnie's childish lives. They went to other parties, and found them very pleasant, but a party organized by Dickens was a shining, magical evening of enchantment, which nothing could spoil, not even the consciousness that their bronze shoes and gaudy plaids (a much-resented tribute from one of their father's Scottish admirers) formed a terrible contrast with the white sashes and satin slippers of the graceful Dickens girls.

During one evening more memorable even than all the others at Tavistock Square, Annie watched as Charles Dickens junior gathered the young boys of the party into great ranks on either side of the staircase and led them in three roaring cheers as Thackeray, coming to fetch his daughters, ascended between them.

'That is for you!' said Dickens, stepping quickly forward to greet him, while Thackeray, surprised, pleased and touched, settled his spectacles on his nose and nodded gravely to his miniature guard of honour.[7]

For everyday pleasure there were other young friends on their Kensington doorstep: eight Irvine cousins at Little Holland House, overshadowed by the magnificence of great Holland House, but still a country mansion with its own splendid grounds; and Laetitia, Henrietta and Mary Cole, daughters of Thackeray's influential friend, Henry Cole, who, under the name of 'Felix Summerly', wrote children's books which delighted them almost as much as Dickens's.

Despite the presence of his daughters, the Young Street house was never quite to lose its air of being a bachelor establishment, its customs, like its equipment, varying from elegance to rough simplicity. The plainest dessert of dried figs and dry biscuits was eaten off fine Derby china; the breakfast table, set with cracked cups and saucers of catholic pattern and size, was graced by a silver Flaxman teapot, which left much of its contents on the cloth.

Sometimes even the teapot was outshone by the chance guests the girls found already installed when they ran downstairs in the morning: Trelawny, the dashing adventurer who had plucked Shelley's heart from the funeral pyre, caught surveying himself in the dining-room mirror; or Count d'Orsay, 6ft. 3in. of gleaming studs, boots and curls, draped on a chair, a cracked cup of tea before him, filling their bow window with the radiance of an Apollo. Her father, thought Annie, had a certain weakness for dandies, 'those knights of the broadcloth and shining fronts.'[8]

Towards evening, the drawing-room with its circular table bearing an ever-changing dial of the best, the popular, the most talked-of books of the day, also saw its share of celebrities. Though Annie and Minnie seized on the bound volumes of *Punch* and the red silk *Annuals* and *Keepsakes*, with their pretty poems and drawings of languid beauties, and admired Ruskin's *Seven Lamps of Architecture* solely on account of its binding—which seemed to them deliciously reminiscent of moulded slabs of chocolate—they were also able to study the authors of the other works which took their turn in that constantly refreshed circle. Many of them were the golden youths of Thackeray's Cambridge days come now to their middle years and a state of inner melancholy which served to enhance, rather than diminish, their appreciation of the humorous and the absurd.

Alfred Tennyson, in that curious poet's sing-song chant, read his own verses in the Young Street drawing-room, and once more had his conversation interrupted by a Thackeray, this time by an unimpressed Minnie, who, looking up from a well-thumbed copy of her favourite story, asked suddenly: 'Papa, why do you not write books like *Nicholas Nickleby*?'[9]

During his years with his young daughters, Thackeray was to become accustomed to many such blows to his vanity.

'Papa, they've been to fetch that sketch that Count d'Orsay made of you,' Annie greeted him one day. 'I think it's uglier than you are.'

Thackeray reported this welcome in several of his letters, and turned it into a sketch in which Minnie, with her soothing 'I don't think you're ugly at all,' was replaced by an odious little boy saying 'O no it isn't.'

He saw the girls through chickenpox and other childish ailments and disasters, his concern doubled at such times by the knowledge that his mother was brooding alone in Paris, convinced that they were being poisoned by conventional medicine and deprived of all other proper care. Though France was undergoing yet another revolution, with street fighting and barricades, the merest hint of Chartist troubles in England brought anguished pleas for the children to be sent to her for safety. It was, thought Thackeray, the greatest thing to come out of the setting up of France's Second Republic.

2.

The arrival of the children had been quickly followed by that of Mrs Butler, a frail old lady wrapped in Indian shawls, who was to spend most of the remaining year of her life at Young Street, reading devotional works and her grandson's novel, annoying the servants and ringing bells with infuriating abandon. And hard on her heels had come Bess Hamerton, one of two unmarried sisters who formed part of Mrs Carmichael-Smyth's Paris circle, and who had been good friends to Thackeray in the months he had coped alone in Paris lodgings with Isabella.

For five progressively unhappy months, Bess Hamerton, a capable Irishwoman, managed Thackeray's household, and to begin with he was loud in her praise. She was, he said, the best and briskest of housekeepers, kept his children in excellent order, and if she had a fault it lay only in giving him too good dinners. But soon the ladies of the establishment were at battle stations. Bess Hamerton and Mrs Butler were locked in endless disputes, Annie was wretched, and Thackeray himself was driven to ordering his breakfast in his room and then, once more, to fleeing his own home in utter despair.

'She's not an English lady—that's the fact,' he told his mother. 'I sit entirely dumb & stupified before her . . . The commonplaces in that enormous brogue kill me: and she falls to worrying Nanny as soon as I go out.'[1]

Miss Hamerton was dispatched with a kindly letter, but weeks later Thackeray was still fuming when he remembered her coarseness and rebukes to the children. 'She tell my little princesses they were vulgar!' he cried in paternal wrath when Mrs Carmichael-Smyth tried to persuade him to change his mind.

It was the beginning of a furious, long-distance battle between mother and son that was to culminate in the greatest argument they were ever to have. Mrs Carmichael-Smyth viewed the series of governesses that took Bess Hamerton's place with jealous, meddlesome suspicion, and contributed to the sacking of at least one of them. Her assault was begun immediately, with accusations against Mrs Gloyne, Isabella's part-protector, who had become a favourite of Mrs Butler and a regular visitor to the Young Street house. Mrs Carmichael-Smyth demanded she be refused entry.

Thackeray would not comply—though he agreed that she was an awkward customer to have around the home, 'being neither a servant nor a lady. Poor woman.' On his Camberwell visits, he had obviously not been averse to the company of the troublesome Gloyne himself, but he fought this particular skirmish on the grounds that his grandmother, lonely, feeble, with probably not long to live, should see whomever she wanted to see, and it cost him a week's work to do so.

Then came Miss Drury, a Staffordshire clergyman's daughter, twenty-seven, ladylike, shy, kind and unaffected, though not quite the paragon he had been led to expect. '. . . not ill-looking, but of such a countenance & complexion as don't render her dangerous,' Thackeray was careful to tell the guardian of his morals.[2]

His chief problem with Miss Drury, as with her successors, was that she was not intelligent enough for Annie. He had almost as great a veneration for his eldest daughter's brains as his mother had for her prodigy of a son. 'My dear old girl,' he called her shortly before her eleventh birthday. 'She is as wise as an old man. In 3 years she will be a charming companion to me: and fill up a part of a great vacuum w[h] exists inside me.'[3]

He was often to wonder if he should send his daughters to school for a better education, or keep them at home with a kindly, sensible woman who would, to some degree, mother them as well as teach them their lessons. Minnie, sweet, willing and still uncomplicated, gave him little cause for concern. But in Annie, Thackeray detected much of the anguish he himself had felt as a child, some of the yearning he was to ascribe to the solitary young Henry Esmond. A governess would at least give her companionship and a focus for affection, and as for her studies, with her brains and discernment, he was content that she would learn more for herself than most people could teach her, at home or at school.

'I am obliged to snub her continually,' he told his mother, 'with, delight at what she says all the time. They are noble children. Thank God.'[4]

As he coped with his first Christmas alone with the girls, he described himself as mighty happy in his paternal character, presiding over legs of mutton most comfortably, going to church early in the morning and liking it, paying his rates and taxes like the most sober of respectable citizens. And, as he sat at midnight in the sleeping house, with 'a quiet cigar and the weakest gin-and-water in the world', ruminating over a children's ball from which he had just returned, he could think with the satisfaction of duty done: 'Law! what a comfort it was over!'

During the Season he was to become as involved in his daughters' social lives as his own. In the first flush of his role as Social Secretary, he wrote to Mrs Procter:

'The little girls are glad and free, to wait upon the Misses P. You ask my children as I see, to come to dinner and to tea, but why the deuce you don't ask me, that is a point I cannot see.'[5]

Three Seasons later, however, the more arduous position of chaperon was beginning to take its toll, as he grumbled in a delightful piece on *Child's Parties* for *Punch*. All that weak negus, he groaned, and that tired old conjurer who appeared at house after house, season after season, so that one hardly dared to look either the man or his tricks in the face any more; and as for the cost, what with hairdresser's fees at eighteen pence *par tête*, and the bills for silk stockings, sashes and white frocks, he hadn't been able to pay his own tailor for years.

Bored though he undoubtedly was after his first amused interest in the airs and conceits of the miniature coquettes and dandies who took part in this juvenile social whirl, he remained as alert to the beatings of their small hearts as to the passions raging in many a more battered breast. No poor, plain wallflower-in-the-making ever needed to despair for long if he were there to put a friendly hand on the shoulder of a likely partner and encourage him with a 'Go and dance with her, my boy.'

No child that ever came within his compass ever left it without a shining memory of the occasion. He rarely saw a boy without giving him a bright new sixpence, or in later, richer years, a sovereign, but it was for far more than these timely tips that they loved him. In many ways a child still himself, he delighted them with glorious rhymes, stories and buffoonery, and found as much pleasure in escorting them to that magnificent new invention, the Zoo, as he did in taking them to the theatre.

'If I have cares in my mind,' he said, 'I come to the Zoo, and fancy they don't pass the gate.'[6] With Annie and Minnie, he played the game of finding ludicrous likenesses to friends and enemies in the beasts behind bars, and sent the young Cole children home chanting a poem which was to go down in family lore:

> First I saw the white bear, then I saw the black,
> Then I saw the camel with a hump upon his back.
> Then I saw the camel with a HUMP upon his back!
> Then I saw the grey wolf, with mutton in his maw;
> Then I saw the wombat waddle in the straw;
> Then I saw the elephant with his waving trunk,
> Then I saw the monkeys—mercy,
>   how unpleasantly they—smelt!

Carving chickens at a children's party, he told his waiting customers:

> Any little child that wants a little fowl
> Must raise its little hand and give a little howl!

And when he struck a tough bird, he dramatically mopped his brow and said he was 'heaving a thigh'.

Henriette Corkran, astonished that this splendidly genial giant should be a son of the austere, religious Mrs Carmichael-Smyth, was charmed by the way he endowed her dolls, whose names he infallibly remembered, with individual pedigrees and family histories, and even more by his sympathetic understanding of a greedy child's interest in cake-shops.

'Oh, give her a tart,' she heard him call out to her absent-minded father, when he came across her in Paris, nose pressed to a tempting shop window. Then, having given her the freedom of the establishment himself, he commended her capacity with rueful nostalgia, doffed his hat, bowed and addressed the mouth-watering display: 'Dear old plum-cakes! how they remind me of my schooldays.'

Thackeray was to champion all the young Corkrans in a

longstanding battle with their *bonne* over some dreadful soup, and, having tactfully negotiated a victory for his side, to scoop all five of them into his carriage for a celebration gorge at yet another pastrycook's. On the way, he told them the story of a giant who had a bed made of chocolate, which he licked continually, pillows made of sponge-cakes, blankets of jellies, and chairs of delectable bonbons. On the way home, they asked for the end of the tale.

'Ah, poor giant!' cried Thackeray, wiping his spectacles as though in tears, 'after he had licked up the whole of his chocolate bedstead, eaten his sponge-cake pillows, and the blankets (made of jellies), he roared with pain, he had such a fearful indigestion; but'—and here he opened a paper parcel—'he had a dose of this medicine, a bottle of fluid magnesia. I bought this at the chemist in case you have eaten too many tarts like the poor giant.'[7]

He was often to worry that he didn't give enough of this kind of attention to his own children, that in his own home he was too preoccupied with work. It was the old, unresolvable problem he had had with Isabella, but this time he was determined to strike a better balance. Constant thought for his daughters, he told his mother, chased he didn't know how many wickednesses from his mind.

'Their society makes many of my old amusements seem trivial & shameful. What bounties are there of Providence in the very instincts w^h God gives us.'[8]

Though he had fought so hard to gather the whole family together at Young Street, he soon realized that the Major's obstinacy was in fact a blessing. There couldn't be two heads to a household, and he knew that had his mother been there too, they would either have been at odds and secretly jealous of each other, or he would have resigned the parental place to her entirely and remained a bachelor still.

13

Vanity Fair

A phoenix of a year

The year which had begun with the success of *Cornhill to Grand Cairo* and the *Snob* papers, and had seen him established once more in the longed-for home with his daughters, ended with another minor triumph for Thackeray: the publication of his first Christmas book, *Mrs Perkins's Ball*, a light-hearted little work in which illustrations and letterpress played almost equal part. It never threatened to eclipse Dickens's seasonal offering, *The Battle of Life*, but fifteen hundred of the first edition of two thousand copies were sold before Christmas Eve, and Thackeray regarded it as his greatest success so far.

Then, on New Year's Day of 1847, delayed eight months by his *Punch* work and domestic upheavals, came the first monthly number of *Vanity Fair—Pen and Pencil Sketches of English Society*, 'A Novel without a Hero', price one shilling, bound in bright yellow covers, by, as the advertisements announced, 'W. M. THACKERAY (Titmarsh)'. His real name was about to be made at last.

Acting as his own public relations man, as he had to act as his own agent, secretary and accountant, he wrote to friends asking for 'puffs'—big puffs in the kind of magazines that had previously ignored him. If he could make a push now, if his friends would shout 'Titmarsh for ever! hurrah', he told William Edmonstoune Aytoun, he felt he might well go up with a rush to a pretty fair place in his trade and be recognized as one of the first fiddles.

An article in *Blackwood's* would be a very good thing, he hinted. Until then he believed he had never had any real ambition, or cared what people thought of his writings. But now the truth had forced itself upon him: if the world would take to admiring Titmarsh, all his guineas would be multiplied by ten. And guineas were good. He had children, only perhaps another ten years to the fore, and if he managed to make some money this time, he vowed by the Lord to try and keep it.

Thackeray knew in his heart that *Vanity Fair* was '*not* small beer', but he was uncertain of its reception, particularly in London. The only thing he was sure of was the title, which had come to him in a flash of inspiration in the middle of the night, after months of brain-racking, and sent him leaping out of bed and running round his room, crying out those two God-given words as he went.

For a year and a half he now had three or four chapters to produce each month, plus two plates, initial letters and several wood blocks, while continuing his work for *Punch* and the *Morning Chronicle*, and writing and illustrating another Christmas book. Inevitably, he delayed getting down to his quota until the last two available weeks, and it was a rare month if the printer's boy or one of his publishers wasn't waiting in his hall, dunning him for overdue copy.

As delivery day drew near he grew so nervous he scarcely spoke, and on at least one occasion the pressure became so great that he gave up all hope of sleep, went down to his study, and worked in his 'night-shimee'—'but that don't happen often,' he told his worrying old mother.

As the months went by the reviews became ecstatic. 'Everything is simple, natural and unaffected. Common sense sits smiling on the top of every page,' said the partisan *Morning Chronicle*. But even they were beaten by the independent *Sun*: 'If Mr. Thackeray should die to-morrow, his name would be transmitted down to posterity by his "Vanity Fair." He is the Fielding of the nineteenth century.' No tribute could have been sweeter than that.

It is difficult to imagine now the first impact of *Vanity Fair*. It was a totally new development of the novel, based less on deeds than the growth of character, dwelling more on the vicissitudes of marriage than the trials of courtship. It showed how a man like Rawdon Crawley, a stupid, selfish, heavy dragoon, could, through love for a woman, however misguided, and devotion to his son, win a kind of grace and perhaps redemption; it showed how a woman like Becky Sharp, though she knew she was witnessing the ruin of herself and her ambition, could stand back and admire her husband as he thrashed Lord Steyne.

'Well,' said Thackeray, when complimented on that particular stroke, 'when I wrote that sentence, I slapped my fist on the table, and said "*that* is a touch of genius!"'[1]

It could even put forward the startling idea that Becky might well have been a good woman had she been blessed with £5000 a year.

Month by month, *Vanity Fair*, 'brilliantly illuminated with the Author's own candles', set British drawing-rooms aflame. Phrases like Becky's 'I'm no angel' and young Fred Bullock's 'them's my sentiments', became part of the English language, as controversy raged over this astonishing work and its assault on Victorian morality and humbug.

'There are things we do and know perfectly well in Vanity Fair, though we never speak of them,' Thackeray wrote. '. . . and a polite public will no more bear to read an authentic description of vice than a truly-refined English or American female will permit the word breeches to be pronounced in her chaste hearing. And yet, Madam, both are walking the world before our faces every day, without much shocking us. If you were to blush every time they went by, what complexions you would have!'[2]

Though he claimed in one of the many asides that were to become a hallmark of his style (endearing him to, or infuriating his readers) that he had submitted to the fashion of the day and touched on such matters only in a light, easy and agreeable manner, so that nobody's fine feelings might be offended, he was to show up folly and wickedness on every page, stripping naked as he went the hollow household gods of middle-class respectability and aristocratic superiority.

When friends and reviewers later took him to task for crying out breeches to the exclusion of almost everything else, he defended himself with strong conviction. The world *was* a desperately foolish and wicked place, he told them, and though he no longer wished to attack it with the savagery he had used in *Barry Lyndon* and the Yellowplush/Deuceace stories, he still felt a mission to expose its sins to the ignorant, the complacent and the wilfully blind.

Though he glossed over the seamier episodes, such as Becky's activities during her fall, there were many readers with over-bright complexions as they read on, and some with disturbed, discomforted consciences. But whatever the view of Thackeray's moral teachings, there was no doubt about the beauty of his prose.

For much of its life in monthly numbers, the yellow covers of *Vanity Fair* were competing with the green ones of Dickens's *Dombey and Son*, and while Thackeray could burst into Mark Lemon's office, slap down the latest number of *Dombey* on his desk, and cry out: 'There's no writing against such power as this—one has no chance! Read that chapter describing young Paul's death: it is unsurpassed—it is stupendous!'[3] few of his more intelligent readers would have agreed with him.

They quickly discovered, as have succeeding generations, that the more knowledge a reader brings to Thackeray's writings, the greater the wealth he finds there. His simple, deceptively easy style is rich with images from Shakespeare, the great rolling phrases of Ecclesiastes, and a use of the classics which no doubt astonished the 'vulgar bullies' of Charterhouse who had tried to beat them into his head.

Nowhere can a Latin tag have been employed more splendidly than in his description of the ball at Government House, Calcutta: the vast, kindly campaigner, Peggy O'Dowd, lady now of Colonel Sir Michael O'Dowd, having performed a jig in which she danced down two aides-de-camp, a Major of the Madras cavalry, and two gentlemen of the Civil Service, is persuaded by Major Dobbin to retire to the supper room, and *'lassata nondum satiata recessit'*—she withdrew, exhausted but not satiated—the words used in Juvenal's *Satires* to describe the reluctant departure of the Empress Messalina after her night in the brothels of Rome.

Before the last chapters were published, Thackeray was toasted at the Royal Literary Fund's annual dinner as one of the most distinguished novelists of the day—and plunged wildly through an astonished reply. True to form, the *Quarterly Review*, which he had always accused of praising no one but dandy lords and men of already made reputation, suddenly discovered evidence of brilliance in his earlier works, which they had previously failed to note. *Fraser's*, in an article on Charterhouse, placed him alongside John Wesley as an 'ornament' of that establishment; and, prodded by Mrs Procter, who marked up the quotes and suggested the approach, lawyer, reviewer and author, Abraham Hayward, produced a vast critique of all his writings for the *Edinburgh Review,* a journal which three years earlier had been cautiously ignorant of his existence.

The editor, Macvey Napier, had then written to Hayward, a London contributor of proven rectitude:

'Will you tell me—confidently, of course, whether you know anything of a Mr. Thackeray . . . One requires to be very much on one's guard in engaging with mere strangers. In a Journal like the *Edinbro'*, it is always of importance to keep up in respect of names.'[4]

It was on the strength of Hayward's reply that Napier had taken—and mutilated—Thackeray's solitary contribution to the august *Review*. Now, they devoted twenty pages to him.

In fact, the monthly numbers of *Vanity Fair* did everything but sell. For a time, Bradbury and Evans even feared they might have to stop publication altogether, and Thackeray was so worried when he came across his daughters and the nursemaid delivering free copies to one of Mrs Butler's friends on the other side of the park that he nearly sent them home again, mission uncompleted. In the midst of unprecedented praise, he kept this depressing aspect constantly in mind and felt bound to make a clean breast of it to anyone who congratulated him. The morning after the Literary Fund dinner, he told the man who had showered him with public compliments the night before that his publishers were several hundred pounds out of pocket on the book, and that he used the knowledge to keep down any undue pride or elation.

The reputation of *Vanity Fair* was always to outweigh its profits, though Bradbury and Evans certainly didn't end with a deficit. Thackeray, besides earning £60 for each of his eighteen instalments, was to notch up another £1000 over the next fifteen years from the various bound editions—more than he made on any of his earlier works, but still modest pay for a masterpiece. As the serial went into its second year, however, and he won yet more acclaim for his second Christmas book, *Our Street*, he told his mother that there was no use denying the matter or blinking at it: 'I am become a sort of great man in my way—all but at the top of the tree: indeed there if the truth were known and having a great fight up there with Dickens.'

He was never to match Dickens's sales of 30,000 or 35,000 a number, or the wide range of his appeal, but what his readership lacked in quantity it made up in quality. As the fame of *Vanity Fair* spread through the country, the doors of some very great houses indeed were thrown open and its author beckoned inside. It was an acceptance as extraordinary as the welcome received by Beaumarchais at the death-dancing court of Marie Antoinette, as the Dowager Lady Stanley of Alderley, a veritable old Lady Kew, made clear to her daughter-in-law:

'How can you tolerate Thackeray for shewing you all up in the manner he does,' she wanted to know. '. . . Really he should be banished from the society he has so wonderfully found his way into only to hold it up to ridicule . . . I *have* read Vanity Fair & how anybody can like to associate with the author astonishes me—tho' I daresay his conversation may not be like his book exactly but I should so dislike the man who could give such a work to the publick. Where do you meet him?'[5]

The answer to the last question could only be in her daughter-in-law's own home, at the Duke of Devonshire's, Lord Lansdowne's, Holland House, and many another elegant address. As Major Pendennis was to remark, times had changed since his young days, when poetry and genius were considered devilish disreputable. Now, there was 'a run upon literature' in high society: 'clever fellows get into the best houses in town, begad!'[6]

To begin with, bruised and prejudiced by his years in the wilderness, Thackeray walked these glittering corridors with a supercilious mistrust, seeking out and finding evidence of Vanity Fair toadying and hypocrisy at every turn. It was always going on, he said, and he was just as great a humbug as his neighbours. To exercise away some of the excesses of rich living he bought himself a horse, a handsome brown cob, and when he emerged into the fashionable arena of Hyde Park, saw many another sight from its 'punchy' back to add to his growing knowledge of the world.

'The great people I know would make your eyes wink,' he told Arthur Shawe, but when he wrote to his still fiercely radical parents in Paris, he was ashamed to go into the details of his social progress. What was the good of telling them what he had for dinner? he asked. It was always the same. He guttled down a quantity of claret, wallowed in turtle, swam in champagne, and laughed a great deal, but he hadn't the face to put down such transactions on paper. It made him blush to think of them.

For a while he justified his presence in the society which had provided him with so much good sneering material by taking the role of devil's advocate. Having dined with the prominent ⋅London hostess, Mrs George Fox, he wrote in his diary:

'I tried in vain to convince the fine folks . . . that revolution was upon us: that we were wicked in our scorn of the people. They all thought there was poverty & discomfort to be sure, but that they were pretty good in themselves; that powder & liveries were very decent & proper though certainly absurd—the footmen themselves would not give them up . . . Why, the gladiators at Rome were proud of their profession, & their masters saw nothing wicked in it.'[7]

But he also recorded one of Mrs Fox's dry little tales about the lady of a newly-minted baronet who had been surrounded in her spanking new carriage by a Chartist mob and cursed for an aristocrat. 'Lady Hogg,' Mrs Fox had reported, 'was never so much pleased in her life.'

Thackeray enjoyed the brittle gossip that went on around these candle-lit, well-ordered tables, and his own acceptance there. It was too congenial a world, with too kindly a welcome for him to struggle for long. After a hard battle, and many trials, he had come home, back to the cocoon of elegance and ease from which he had been torn at the age of five, when he was sent off alone from India. Wealth, he was to rediscover, led to simplicity and soothing order. The air was 'freer' in great drawing-rooms than small ones, and the dinners of the great were not only better but shorter.

He was never to give up the fight against injustice, great or petty, but to understand afresh that a rich woman could be as good and as caring as a poor one, a wealthy aristocrat as clever and benevolent as a poor struggling devil who had to give most of his attention to staying alive, and to have confirmed what he had always known, that good food and good wines were preferable to bad ones.

There were fools, rogues and vulgarity in polite society as in every other corner of the globe, as he was to point out in *Vanity Fair* and his writings for *Punch*, but on the whole it was polite, and it contained the men, many of them dedicated, hard-working and intellectually brilliant, who held the destiny of Britain and much of the world in their hands. It was, after all, very pleasant to be sought out and praised by Sir Robert Peel, Lord Palmerston or Lord Lansdowne, not for snobbish reasons (though they added a certain relish), but because the experience, intelligence and the competition for the attention of such men, gave added value to their notice and opinions.

Warmed by the dual suns of literary and social acclaim, the bitterness within him began to melt away. People had been so kind to him, he told Lady Blessington: 'whilst my back was turned too— that is the rarity of it—no it isn't. The world is a much kinder and better world than some bilious-covered satirists have painted it—I must give up the yellow cover I think and come out in a fresher tone—'[8]

Writing of class jealousy in the *Second Funeral of Napoleon* six years earlier, Thackeray had said that being a potato himself, he couldn't help seeing that the tulip was given the choicest place in the garden, the most sunshine and the best tending, and not liking him over well. But once admitted to the tulip-bed, he found himself very much at case among his bright companions and was not a little tart when Abraham Hayward, who had laboured assiduously for a small niche in the same sunny corner, condescendingly pronounced that he was a success there—'his manners are brusque but they like him.'[9]

Hayward, and perhaps the great people too, said Thackeray, seemed surprised that he was a gentleman. Little did they know who his parents were, and that there were two old people living in Paris on £200 a year, as grand as they had ever been. 'I have never seen finer gentlefolks than you two—' he told his mother, 'or prouder.'

As the Bohemian George Augustus Sala was to point out, Thackeray was and always had been 'a swell', only for some years he had been a swell in difficulties.[10] He entered the circles of rank, riches and influence as the latest diversion, expecting, as did most other students of the social scene, that his reign as a fashionable literary man would be as brief as most similar entertainments, but, except for a short exile when his own public statements outlawed him, he stayed for the rest of his life.

There were times when he felt he was being patronized, as he was to indicate in *The Newcomes*, but when he came to know many of the people he had once considered insolent and air-giving, he realized that the fault lay more with his own prickly sensitivity than in any intentional slight from them. 'It's we who make the haughtiness of the grandees—not they,' he was to say. 'They're never thinking of it at least my experience goes so far.'[11]

It was fellow commoners, like Abraham Hayward, who did most to remind him that he was a naturalized, rather than a birth-right, citizen of the highest spheres of the *beau monde*, as he discovered after one of his first evenings at Holland House. Strolling home from that magnificent red-brick palace with another guest, Thackeray enthused on Lord and Lady Holland's admirable custom of choosing their company for agreeability rather than rank and quarterings.

'Oh, yes,' replied his new acquaintance, one Mr Rumbold, 'I hear they *even* receive Mr Thackeray of *Punch* celebrity.'[12]

His old friends, naturally, resented his elevation and were constantly on the alert for an alteration in his attitude towards themselves: a burr which, together with the problems of surviving prosperity, was to become yet another thread in all his future writings. Mrs Procter taunted that he wouldn't dine with her 'because, we haven't got a Lord', and even FitzGerald was ready to lend an ear to Carlyle's rumblings that Thackeray was too grand now to bother with his old comrades. At *Punch* the atmosphere was liable to become particularly awkward, as it did on the evening Bradbury and Evans held their weekly dinner in the back parlour of a grimy little steak-house in the City. Thackeray, amused by the dandified West End airs they all gave themselves for this slumming expedition, had his good humour sorely tried when the party moved on to watch a French equestrian entertainment at Drury Lane.

Sitting in the pit with *Punch*, he was spotted and beckoned into a stage box by three genuine, noble dandies and a fashionable homœopathic surgeon—Count d'Orsay, the Lords Chesterfield and Granville, and Dr Quin—and, joining them for a while, was as diverted by the frankly childish enthusiasm with which these four bucks were cheering on the pretty Parisian riders as he had been by the bogus attitudes he and the other literary gents had thought fit to adopt in the City. He was still smiling at the stage box antics when he returned to his original seat, and a decidedly frosty welcome. Even

Leech was sulky, neatly picking off two of his new friends with the well-turned opinion that Dr Quin bore as little resemblance to a regular physician as d'Orsay did to a regular gentleman.

'I wonder what he and Lemon were talking about: when I left the pit and went into the genteel box?' Thackeray wrote in his diary that night. '"That d—— lickspittle Thackeray" &c—it was all evident: and yet I didn't kiss anybody's tails at all.'[13]

There was no end to such quarrels in this wicked Vanity Fair, he said, and his feet were perpetually in hot water. A wild, dare-devil Irish adventurer and politician, reputedly the survivor of thirteen duels, had taken it into his head that Thackeray's appalling Mulligan of Ballymulligan in *Mrs Perkins's Ball* was a libellous portrait of himself, and threatened to kill and eat the author whenever they met. There were four other Mulligans in London, sighed Thackeray, though not so warlike.

He was still being taken to task by Bess Hamerton's friends for dispensing with that lady's services, and his brother writers were proving anything but fraternal:

'Jerrold hates me, Ainsworth hates me, Dickens mistrusts me, Forster says I am false as hell,' he reported to Paris, 'and Bulwer curses me—he is the only one who has any reason—yes the others have a good one too as times go. I was the most popular man in the craft until within ab' 12 months—and behold I've begun to succeed. It makes me very sad at heart though, this envy and meanness—in the great sages & teachers of the world. Am I envious and mean too I wonder? These fellows think so I know . . . I scarcely understand any motive for any action of my own or anybody else's—'[14]

Stout John Forster, Dickens's close friend and adviser and, as editor now of the *Examiner*, an even more impressive literary force, was at the root of this depression with his 'false as hell' charge. He had used the words to Tom Taylor of *Punch*, who repeated them to Thackeray as an excellent example of Forster's explosive personality and extravagance of phrase, without stopping to consider that Thackeray, as the object of this particular outburst, might not find them as amusing as other examples he could have chosen, and without mentioning the cause of Forster's anger.

Sensitive as ever, Thackeray mulled over the charge, took it to be a reflection on his personal honour, and refused to shake hands with Forster when next they met at the Procters'. It was the off-signal for the start of A Great Literary Row. Seconds were chosen, curt, almost legally cautious notes exchanged, and tale-telling Tom Taylor was called upon to explain his part in the affair.

Half-way through, when it became clear that Forster's abuse had nothing to do with honour, but had been wrung from him by one of

Thackeray's caricatures of his extraordinary shape, Thackeray immediately forgave. Forster, after all, he said had only been 'roasting' him, as he had previously roasted Forster. He offered an immediate apology, and summed up the rumpus in a few simple phrases:

'Forster ought not to have used the words: Taylor ought not to have told them: and I ought not to have taken them up. And I for my part am sorry I did.'[15]

But the ball, once set in motion, could not be stopped so easily. Forster, with plenty to resent in the sketches that flowed from Thackeray's pen, had called in Dickens to act for him and Thackeray was also forced to call upon the services of a friend, Sir Alexander Duff-Gordon. The two seconds went through the delicate minuet of upholding the dignity of their principals with all the gravity that had formerly gone into arranging a meeting at dawn and the death of the guilty party.

It was the kind of affray which made Thackeray thoroughly miserable, and Duff-Gordon took the sane man's view that it was a pity if friendships should be put at risk simply because Thackeray for once in his life had taken something too seriously. But Dickens was in his element. He was never too busy to tackle such manly affairs as this. He knew exactly what everyone should have done, what they should not have done, how the matter should be settled, and, when all the proper forms had been gone through to his satisfaction, was delighted to host a conciliation dinner, and stage-manage a dramatic handclasp of forgiveness.

In this case, he decided that Thackeray was to blame, and that such altercations 'arose in his jesting much too lightly between what was true and what was false, and what he owed to both, and not being sufficiently steady to the former.' And since Thackeray's mediator didn't argue, but concentrated on healing the breach, Dickens pronounced him an excellent fellow: 'Nothing could possibly be more frank, sensible, or gentlemanly in the best sense, than Gordon's behaviour through the whole affair', he told Forster. 'There did not appear to be the smallest difference of opinion between himself and me.'[16]

2.

With regard to Thackeray, Dickens could never be so glowing in his praise, and though they remained on cordial terms for many years— until the next time Dickens acted as second in one of Thackeray's more serious disputes—he was always to doubt his rival's sincerity, and like many another friend and acquaintance, to think he had sold his soul to the aristocracy. But there is plenty of evidence to show that Thackeray was not the tufthunter he was labelled. He chose his new friends as he had done the old, because he liked them; and the sad, the troubled and the young continued to find in him a sympathetic listener and ready benefactor, whatever their station.

James Hannay, a young midshipman turned writer, who worked for a while as Thackeray's secretary and was 'loaded with benefits' by his employer, was later to write:

'There was nothing more charming about Thackeray than the kindly footing on which he stood with the younger generation. He was not a man to have a little senate; he held sycophants, and all who encouraged them, in contempt; his friends and acquaintances were of all varieties of class and character, and differed from him in their ways of thinking about everything. But he made it a duty to befriend and cherish anybody in whose merit and sincerity he believed, however casual the accident which had brought them under his notice.'[1]

Sometimes the accident was casual in the extreme. One day his friends found him on their doorsteps, a cab bulging with drawing-room mirrors at the kerb, urging them to make a selection and take as many as they liked. This Aladdin's treasure trove was the entire stock of a looking-glass maker, too ill to work, whose children Thackeray had found crying for bread in a back street of Soho. In Paris, he prepared equally unconventional aid for one of Mrs Carmichael-Smyth's lamer ducks: a pillbox full of napoleons. '*To be taken occasionally when required*', he wrote on the lid. '*Signed* Dr. W.M.T.'

But more important than these fleeting acts of charity were the long hauls of friendship, assisted sometimes by timely hand-outs, more often by sympathy and thoughtfulness. A man without a job could count on his purse and contacts; a girl without a suitor gave him almost as much pain. Though the beautiful Eugenie Crowe made his own heart beat faster, Thackeray rounded up young men for her and arranged match-making dinners. When her father fell on hard times, he took one of Eugenie's brothers into his employ, and later a younger sister into his home, and saw her married from it to a Thackeray cousin. And as Hannay discovered, to no one was he kinder than to young men interested in his own profession.

Frederick Goldsmith, a family acquaintance, who had first known Thackeray in his *National Standard* period, when he himself was a schoolboy, and Thackeray, some eight years his senior, had seemed a good genius whose presence shed added lustre over half-terms and holidays, met him again in this first flush of success and was overwhelmed by his consideration. Having committed the indiscretion of publishing a tragedy in five acts, Goldsmith had been sent off to India by his parents, and was by this time a subaltern home on sick-leave from his Madras regiment. After a chance meeting, he was thrilled to receive a note inviting him to dinner at Young Street, giving full directions for getting there, signed 'Your affte. Aunt', and offering the services of a maid with a lantern to walk him home at the end of the evening.

Thackeray also took the younger man on some of his night-time rambles for his *Punch* pieces on London, and, when Goldsmith was posted to the East India Company's Military College at Addiscombe, accepted his invitation to revisit the scenes of his own early holidays from Charterhouse.

It proved a most moving pilgrimage. As he wandered through the old familiar rooms of the Governor's mansion, and gazed, with an emotion that startled his guide, upon the bed his mother had slept in, recollections of his youth flooded back—'dark and sad and painful,' he wrote in his diary, 'with my dear good mother as a gentle angel interposing between me and misery.'

It was a mood he was to re-create a few years later for Henry Esmond's sad boyhood, and to deepen with the haunting cry of rooks, which cawed at Esmond's Castlewood, as they had done at Addiscombe during Thackeray's youth, and again on this later visit.

Goldsmith was delighted to see the knowing looks of the cadets as he accompanied his supposedly incognito guest to chapel that evening, and remained delighted by the simplicity and kindness of Thackeray, who, even at this time of early fame, could be so generous to a young man with no claim to his interest, and by the care with which, when he was invited to one of Thackeray's grander parties, his host introduced him to the most exalted and the prettiest of the other guests. It all went quite splendidly to the heart and head of a young army officer with literary inclinations.[2]

Thackeray, launched upon the world, was now having to return its hospitality and, as host and hostess, the performance caused him agonies of disruption and organization. In his 'Mr Brown' papers for *Punch*, he made a plea for simplicity in such affairs. Most men, he wrote, normally lived on plain fare and liked it, so why should they flare up in such a magnificent manner when they entertained? But he admitted that he was quite as bad as his neighbours, and his letters and the delightful short story, *A Little Dinner at Timmins's*, show an intimate knowledge of the trepidations and discomforts of trying to dine too many people in too small an establishment, with too few plates and hired servants.

'The house is turned upside down—' he wrote to William Ritchie some years later. 'Frantic knife-cleaning goes on—sham footmen prowl the premises—My rest is destroyed . . . I wish we might do it au hotel—My mind trembles with fear and fluster even now a week off!'[3]

Mrs Dickens and her sister, Georgina Hogarth, had prodded him into giving his first gala dinner, a few weeks before the last number of *Vanity Fair*, and it put him into 'a great funk', financially, as well as domestically. By then the money was pouring in, but it was also gushing out again, with frightening velocity.

'I have a leg of mutton and live at the rate of a coach and six,' he told Mrs Procter, groaning over a pile of bills he described as perfectly ludicrous. And now, with growing fame and reputed wealth, the bills were accompanied by begging letters, and family demands. For a while he had his 'black niece' to stay with him, Mrs Blechynden's daughter, who wrote to Mrs Carmichael-Smyth as 'dear Grandmamma', a form of address Thackeray imagined would cause some astonishment in Paris.

His own grandmother contributed very little during her year-long residence at Young Street, and when she died on a visit to Paris in the November of 1847, it was found that her fortune had been greatly overrated by her hopeful heirs. The Major had no money to bury her, her London bank refused an advance, and Thackeray had to send £50 in a hurry. But with judicious juggling of Mrs Butler's small legacy, his own earnings, and some wrangling for terms with the Major's old creditors, he was at last able to free the family of all embarrassments.

On 18 July 1848, his thirty-seventh birthday and the day on which the bound volumes of *Vanity Fair* first appeared, he took an advance from Chapman and Hall on another Christmas book, settled the last of the Major's debts, and acknowledged that he himself was all of a sudden a great man.

He was half ashamed of it, he said, but couldn't help seeing it, and being elated: 'In spite of himself a man gets worldly and ambitious in this great place: with every body courting & flattering. I am frightened at it and my own infernal pride and arrogance'.[4]

How anxious Isabella's timid little soul would have been, he thought. She had always been afraid of people flattering him, and now he had a great deal of that 'meat'. It was almost eight years since the nightmare voyage to Cork, by which he measured the end of his marriage, and for him she had been dead or worse ever since.

'Good God what a year of pain and hope that first one was and bitter bitter tears . . .' he wrote, looking back on the struggle for her sanity. 'Love, hope, infernal pain and disappointment.'[5]

The pain, though dulled, remained. He still hungered for the dear, sweet girl, whose artless honesty had so enraptured him. But hope at last was gone. Wanting to see neither husband nor daughters, his wife had sunk irretrievably into contented apathy, not caring '2^d for anything but her dinner and her glass of porter'.

Softened rather than embittered by the tragedy, Thackeray dwelt increasingly on the brief months of shoe-string happiness they had been allowed together, seeing them as the chief blessing of his life. Despite his own experience, he was still to claim that there was no wife so good as a daughter of Erin, and to encourage other penurious young couples intent on treading the same precarious path.

'Though my marriage was a wreck, as you know,' he told the young diplomat William Webb Follett Synge, 'I would do it once again, for behold, Love is the crown and completion of all earthly good. A man who is afraid of his fortune never deserved one. The very best and pleasantest house I ever knew in my life had but £300 a year to keep it.'[6]

He had undergone disaster and grief, he told another imprudent bridegroom, but had also found immense joys and consolations.

Of the latter, Annie and Minnie were the most enduring. They acted on him after his forays into the world like soda-water, he said; and the world itself, and fame, provided further solace.

He was soon claiming to care not a straw for the great people he knew, except that knowing them made him more impatient with the airs of the 'small great', but even so when the Hon. Mrs Caroline Norton indicated that the Duke of Devonshire, that immensely wealthy patron of literature—'the kindest-hearted of the great'—wished to meet him, he sent his regrets to his favourite Lady Castlereagh and accompanied the beautiful poetess to Devonshire House. And when the Duke showed an interest in the further histories of the characters in *Vanity Fair*, he spared time in a week of hectic endeavour to write a delightful, private sequel to his story:

My Lord Duke,—Mrs. Rawdon Crawley, whom I saw last week, and whom I informed of your Grace's desire to have her portrait, was good enough to permit me to copy a little drawing made of her 'in happier days,' she said with a sigh, by Smee, the Royal Academician.

Mrs Crawley now lives in a small but very pretty little house in Belgravia, and is conspicuous for her numerous charities, which always get into the newspapers, and her unaffected piety. Many of the most exalted and spotless of her own sex visit her, and are of the opinion that she is a *most injured woman*. There is no *sort of truth* in the stories regarding Mrs. Crawley and the late Lord

Steyne. The licentious character of that nobleman alone gave rise to reports from which, alas! the most spotless life and reputation cannot always defend themselves. The present Sir Rawdon Cràwley (who succeeded his late uncle, Sir Pitt, 1832; Sir Pitt died on the passing of the Reform Bill) does not see his mother, and his undutifulness is a cause of the deepest grief to that admirable lady. 'If it were not for *higher things*,' she says, how could she have borne up against the world's culumny, a wicked husband's cruelty and falseness, and the thanklessness (sharper than a serpent's tooth) of an adored child? But she had been preserved, mercifully preserved, to bear all these griefs, and awaits her reward *elsewhere*. The italics are Mrs. Crawley's own.

She took the style and title of Lady Crawley for some time after Sir Pitt's death in 1832; but it turned out that Colonel Crawley, Governor of Coventry Island, had died of fever three months before his brother, whereupon Mrs. Rawdon was obliged to lay down the title which she had prematurely assumed.

The late Jos. Sedley, Esq., of the Bengal Civil Service, left her two lakhs of rupees, on the interest of which the widow lives in the practices of piety and benevolence before mentioned. She has lost what little good looks she once possessed, and wears false hair and teeth (the latter give her rather a ghastly look when she smiles), and—for a pious woman—is the best-crinolined lady in Knightsbridge district.

Colonel and Mrs W. Dobbin live in Hampshire, near Sir R. Crawley; Lady Jane was godmother to their little girl, and the ladies are exceedingly attached to each other. The Colonel's *History of the Punjaub* is looked for with much anxiety in some circles.

Captain and Lt.-Colonel G. Sedley-Osborne (he wishes, he says, to be distinguished from some other branches of the Osborne family, and is descended by the mother's side from Sir Charles Sedley) is, I need not say, well, for I saw him in a most richly embroidered cambric pink shirt with diamond studs, bowing to your Grace at the last party at Devonshire House. He is in Parliament; but the property left him by his Grandfather has, I hear, been a good deal overrated.

He was very sweet upon Miss Crawley, Sir Pitt's daughter, who married her cousin, the present Baronet, and a good deal cut up when he was refused. He is not, however, a man to be permanently cast down by sentimental disappointments. His chief cause of annoyance at the present moment is that he is growing bald, but his whiskers are still without a grey hair and the finest in London.

I think these are the latest particulars relating to a number of persons about whom your Grace was good enough to express some interest. I am very glad to be enabled to give this information, and am—

Your Grace's very much obliged servant,

W. M. Thackeray.

P.S.—Lady O'Dowd is at O'Dowdstown arming. She has just sent in a letter of adhesion to the Lord-Lieutenant, which has been acknowledged by his Excellency's private secretary, Mr. Corry Connellan. Miss Glorvina O'Dowd is thinking of coming up to the Castle to marry that last-named gentleman.

P.S.2—The India mail just arrived announces the utter ruin of the Union Bank of Calcutta, in which all Mrs. Crawley's money was. Will Fate never cease to persecute that suffering saint? [7]

14

Mr and Mrs Brookfield

The ogre and his wife

Among the many changes the success of *Vanity Fair* brought to Thackeray's life was a shift in emphasis in his relationship with the Brookfields. As his star rose, so theirs declined, and Mrs Brookfield was soon prepared to look upon the famous, fashionable author with a far more welcoming gleam in her entrancing grey-blue eyes than she had formerly turned upon her husband's not entirely suitable companion.

The youngest of eight daughters and three surviving sons of Charles Elton, scholar, writer and future sixth baronet, Jane Octavia Brookfield was a chestnut-haired beauty ten years younger than Thackeray, twelve years younger than her husband. She had been born in 1821, on 25 March—Lady Day—which, together with her stately manner, led Thackeray to think of and write to her as his 'dear Lady'.

She had been brought up at Clifton, near Bristol, within a few miles of the Elton family seat, Clevedon Court, a medieval manor house of great distinction and beauty, home of her grandfather, the Revd Sir Abraham Elton, and of four Sir Abrahams before him. But, for most of her childhood, she saw little of this ancient splendour, her eccentric grandfather, notorious for his wild crusade against Methodists, having banished her father from the family portals when he ran off with the daughter of a Bristol merchant known to have leanings towards that loathed persuasion.

The bride for whom Charles Elton gave up so much was, according to the sycophantic family history written by Mrs Brookfield's son and daughter-in-law,[1] 'one of the beautiful Miss Smiths', ladies so admired for their complexions and their grace that admiring crowds clambered onto chairs and tables to view them whenever they appeared in the pump-room at Bath.

This exquisite paragon died when Jane was ten, and for the next six years her life was dominated by governesses as concerned with her posture as with her accomplishments. A 'spider'—a web of iron covered with chamois leather—encased her from neck to waist, a sprig of holly was pinned to her collars to thwart a drooping chin, and her lessons were taken in a reclining position, on a hard board with a hollow for her head.

When she escaped this discipline, however, she was the undoubted darling of a close-knit, loving family. While still a child, her charm was so great that her sisters vowed no one could resist it, not even the servants. Her elders, it was said, took care to write her their very best letters, and her own, from her earliest years, were received by the whole family with rapturous applause.

In a household devoted to literature, where Lamb, Southey, Coleridge and Landor were personal friends, this was heady stuff. Though not in the same league as his great contemporaries, Jane's indulgent, cigar-smoking father had some success himself with his contributions to the magazines, his tragic verses on the drowning of his two eldest sons, and his translation of Hesiod, but he would have been hard pressed to raise his large brood on the proceeds of his pen had he not been blessed with a wealthy and generous brother-in-law, the historian Henry Hallam, father of the golden youth whose untimely death was to inspire Tennyson's *In Memoriam.*

A handsome, hand-rubbing, nervously energetic man, so disputatious that the wags claimed he leaped out of his sickbed to argue the precise time and state of the weather whenever the night-watchman passed his window, Hallam subsidized Elton until he came into his inheritance, and took a particular interest in his youngest niece.

When Jane was sixteen the Eltons moved to Southampton, and it was there that she met the Revd William Henry Brookfield. By this time she was 5ft. 9in. tall and burdened with the Swiftian nickname of 'Glumdalclitch', neither of which hindered her popularity. She was soon proclaimed the belle of the town and besieged by admirers, among them Brookfield, a local curate. Though only the son of an obscure Sheffield solicitor with the kind of religious views guaranteed to excite her grandfather's most aggressive eccentricities, worldly, witty Brookfield, at twenty-seven, was by far the most exotic of this galaxy of courtiers, and Jane was soon in love with him.

After Cambridge, where he had glittered so brightly, Brookfield, undecided about a profession, had gone for a brief spell as tutor to the eldest son of Lord Lyttelton, and found a welcome there which had encouraged him to believe that all his life would be one of easy acceptance and advancement. At the Lytteltons' Worcestershire estate, Hagley, and at Lady Lyttelton's family homes of Althorp and Spencer House in London, he heard much gossip of the affairs of state and the doings of great men, and quickly learned to hold his own in after-dinner wit with the highest in the land.

'Why do they not sometimes, by way of doing a man great honour, bury him *alive* at Westminster Abbey?' he contributed to the general mirth one evening,[2] a *bon mot* which, like a great many more he made and heard through life, was recorded in his diary, along with audience reaction (always stupendous).

Influenced by Lady Lyttelton and one of her sailor nephews, he at last decided to take Holy Orders and see the world as a naval chaplain. The best he could say of the Church at this time was that he had no repugnance for it, but he had no great enthusiasm, either, and to enter it was perhaps the greatest mistake of his life. Immediately after his ordination, he found himself not at sea, as he had hoped, but back in the north of England, as curate in the tiny West Riding village of Maltby.

'Nothing changes in this most lithic spot,' he was soon writing to young Lyttelton. 'The inventive spirit of a *Times* reporter would fall into lethargy in five minutes from the dearth and drought of notabilia . . . my wits lie all five huddled and stifled in a leathern elephantiasis of sloth—incapable and inaccessible. Oh, for one term of Cam. Oh, for one week at Trin. Oh, for one hour with that bumptious but capital duo-decimo, the Apostle . . .'[3]

Cambridge had indeed been Brookfield's 'dawn-golden time', as Tennyson was to call it,[4] and the very talents which had caused such aristocratic wits as the Apostles, the most select of Cambridge groups, to take him up, and which might have brought him glory on the stage or at the Bar, were to cripple his clerical career. The man who had had roomfuls of grave and learned dons rolling on the floor, roaring with agonized laughter at the brilliance of his inventive wit and mimicry, was never prepared to tailor his personality to suit the cloth he wore.

Though he was later to claim that he despised the High Church, the Low Church, and the Church in between, in the pulpit he managed to restrain some of his flamboyance. Outside it he continued to dazzle, and later in life to let off dramatic steam by giving several public Shakespeare readings each year (audience reaction— 'Tremendous applause'—once more noted in his diary).

In Maltby, where he remained for two years, there was no one to impress. In Southampton he did better, soon gaining a reputation with his sermons, the love and admiration of his parishioners, and an entrée to the Elton household, where he was liked for his cleverness and humour and laughed at for his affectations of speech.

When Jane said she wanted to marry him she was encouraged only by one lone relative who said 'Oh dear, yes! Mr. Brookfield's sure to get on, sure to get on.' Her father was less confident, but Jane was not to be denied and a few months after her seventeenth birthday an engagement was allowed, on the understanding that the marriage must wait until Mr Brookfield had indeed got on.

For two years Brookfield's progress existed in nothing more remarkable than moving from one Southampton parish to another, but he wrote Jane beautiful poems—which he asked her to show to her father for his professional opinion.

'In the veranda,' the curate wrote in his comedian's joke-book of a diary, 'Jane told me, "Papa likes the verses and says they are like Coleridge's. *I* think them a great deal better."' [5]

Then, at the end of 1840, he achieved what appeared to be the first step up to greater things: a London curacy, at St James's, Piccadilly. The salary of £190 a year was, however, still far from enough to marry on. His Southampton parishioners, reluctant to let him go, said farewell with meetings and speeches, a silver teapot, one hundred guineas, and a set of academic robes, precisely the assortment of trophies Thackeray was to give the Revd Charles Honeyman, his 'sweet and popular preacher . . . always gallant in behaviour and flowery in expression', in *The Newcomes*.

In London, Brookfield was immediately swept into an active and fashionable life, leaving Jane, a beauty engaged but bereft of a lover, to taunt him from afar on his extra-clerical activities.

'What do you mean, you ugly slut,' the Revd Mr Brookfield asked her, "You seem to be a very grand Person . . ."' [6]

The letters they wrote to each other throughout their engagement and for several years after their marriage are curious documents. Brookfield, brought up in a stern, dissenting family, disliked any mention of love or sentiment and was psychologically incapable of expressing it. Instead, he insisted on neatness, brilliance and an economical regard for the maximum number of words transmitted for the amount of postage paid, which, given Jane's bold handwriting and the high cost of excess postage, was understandable, if not particularly romantic.

With remarkable complacency, they told each other all the nice things that had been said about themselves or the other, and vied to cap each other's wit, apologizing when they considered their current letter unworthy of the one just received. They picked out phrases to admire, not so much for what was said, but for how it was said, and he pounced on any mistakes she made, devoting a page to ridiculing the slip when she once wrote 'where' for 'were'.

The kind of stories that usually ended up in his diary were now sent to Southampton, like the one about the newly consecrated bishop.

'The new Bishop of New Zealand,' Brookfield told Jane, 'in a farewell and pathetic interview with his mother, after his appointment, was thus addressed by her in such sequence as sobs and tears would permit.

'"I suppose they will eat you my dear—I try to think otherwise, but I suppose they will. Well! We must leave it in the hands of Providence. But if they do—mind, my dear, and disagree with them.'"[7]

If Jane failed to shine in turn, her efforts were called sluttish or blackguardly. If she succeeded she was rewarded with fulsome praise:

'I received your twopenny at the happy hour of breakfast this morning—most charming and brilliant—and will form a very eclipsing contrast to this present writing which will not—I foresee—emit one single scintillation.'[8]

Since marriage would put an end to her letter-writing, he said he was seriously considering whether that project should be gone ahead with.

Enjoying the freedom of London, surrounded once more by his Cambridge friends, Brookfield, indeed, showed little sign of wishing to hasten that event, and when his income was boosted by an additional appointment to the preachership of Tenison's, a fashionable London chapel, Jane had to hint that her relatives were now writing to congratulate her on what they felt sure must be the coming nuptials.

But Brookfield, with unusual caution, having set an income of £800 as the minimum on which they should marry, returned to his tales of breakfasts, luncheons and dinners, leaving Jane to threaten that when next they met she would sing to him at length: '"They tell me thou'rt the favoured guest of every fair and brilliant throng. No wit like thine to wake the jest, no voice like thine to breathe the song. And none could guess, so gay thou art, That thou and I, are far apart" . . .'[9]

She would try not to think about marriage, she told him wistfully, if he said it was impossible, but would prefer life with him, even in the greatest poverty, to the wretchedness of living apart.

In the autumn of 1841, having broken the news to her formidable grandfather, gained his blessing and the promise of a portion, Jane finally achieved her aim. She and Brookfield were married quietly at Clifton, in the absence of certain close relatives who prophesied that she was going to be starved. Brookfield characteristically referred to the occasion as the burying, but in the weeks immediately preceding it, he sent his fiancée of three years touching letters of praise and confidence, together with a tortured declaration in which he attempted to refute her charges of coldness and repression and explain his inability to express his deepest feelings of love.

As a rule Brookfield's neat writing flowed easily over the page, admirably filling the available space. But in this letter the script is minute, cramped into one and a half sides of a four-sided, folded sheet, and the words are so obscure that had he not mentioned the length of time he'd known her, it would be impossible to guess what traumatic occasion had wrenched them from him. In the end, apologizing for his failure, he told her she would have to continue to interpret and excuse him by herself supplying the meaning for what he said and did, as was already her long-tried habit.

2.

Thackeray first met Brookfield's bride shortly after the honeymoon. He was alone in London (Isabella, after the failure of the Boppard cure, was at Chaillot), and Brookfield, meeting him unexpectedly, asked him back to his lodgings for dinner. Jane, the brand-new wife, faced with a surprise guest and a sparse menu, surreptitiously sent her maid to the nearest confectioner's for a dish of pastries, and when these commercial additions appeared on the table towards the end of the meal offered them timidly.

Thackeray, bursting through polite convention, showed with a beaming smile, and his decision to take 'a two-penny one', that he knew the precise history of those hastily bought tarts. It broke the constraint that had, until then, hung over the occasion. Jane lost her shyness, and Thackeray forever cherished the memory of that first meeting as 'the dear old two-penny tart dinner.'

Jane Brookfield had a great deal more in her head than the 'just enough sense to be agreeable' which Thackeray had once said was as much as he liked in a woman, but she also had the beauty and soothing sympathy of a Madonna, and that indefinable charm that felled almost every man who ever met her. Those who knew her well also discovered a lively sense of humour and a dryly malicious wit, especially for her rivals, a feminine trait Thackeray enjoyed immensely. Captivated from the start, he soon decided that Mrs Brookfield spoke, acted and thought exactly as a woman should.

In 1846, when he had been enamoured for four years—'though not so as to endanger peace or appetite'—he recorded in his diary a story Bryan Procter had told him about Hazlitt when he was in love with Sarah Walker, inspiration of his frantic *Liber Amoris*:

'He was quite wild about her and talked of his passion to everybody. One day he met Basil Montagu's son: seized upon him and in a walk of many miles told the story to him. Montagu left him near Haydon's. Haydon [the artist] was not at home: but his man & model was. Hazlitt unbosomed himself to the model. By God Sir says he I couldn't help it so I told him. He then went to look for lodgings; and the woman of the house remarking his care-worn appearance asked the cause of it—by God Sir he said she seemed a kind soul so I told *her*!'[1]

Thackeray was the same. He admired and told the world. Everyone was invited to view the lady. To all, her praises were sung. Dickens, meeting Jane for the first time, didn't take long to recognize her as Thackeray's great favourite, the 'little woman' he had tried to persuade him and Forster to go and drink tea with.

For several years Brookfield, a confident rather than a complaisant husband, made no objection to what Thackeray called his uncouth raptures. His ego boosted by holding a prize so many other men would have liked to have taken, he enjoyed boasting of Jane's legion of admirers—her 'seven hundred and ninety-nine lovers.' As Thackeray was to exclaim in later misery, a part of the parson's pride of possession was that other men should admire his wife and envy him.

Jane, too, accepted their attentions with a very easy grace. She was foolishly, blindly fond of being liked and admired, she told her husband after four years of marriage, and if she had not some restraint of conscience and the even greater one of a deep affection for him, she believed she would still be on the look-out for conquest.

In old age she confessed to having been a coquette and to having broken many a heart. Effie Millais, suffering Victorian ostracism for the indelicate exposure of Ruskin's marital inadequacies, considered her so dangerous that she begged her second husband not to accept when the Brookfields asked him to dinner, and at least one other woman, Dickens's daughter, Kate, thought of her as a siren.

But if Mrs Brookfield enjoyed playing with fire, there was never the least suggestion that she would do anything to staunch the flames. Enslaving many, she encouraged only those who understood the rules of the game, and had no charity for less fortunate sisters who lost their spotless reputations.

When asked to join a party which included Mrs Caroline Norton, Mrs Brookfield declined. The divorce action ten years earlier, in which the notoriously bestial Mr Norton had cited Lord Melbourne, outlawed her. The fact that she had been found innocent was not relevant. Lord Melbourne lived on unscathed to become Queen Victoria's favourite Prime Minister, but the beautiful Mrs Norton, with her Sheridan blood, wit and lack of respect for convention, was tried and found wanting by many of the Queen's female subjects, Jane among them. Though Brookfield pleaded that surely it was unfair to punish people simply because they had been *accused*, Jane, quite rightly, given the social climate, saw only danger in such a contact.

In their early months together, Brookfield had told his wife that it was a great gain having a wench such as her to jest with, but as the unprosperous years crept by, the laughter withered and the differences in their characters and upbringing became more obvious. The danger signals had all been there in their engagement letters: Brookfield's tortured inhibition and his admired 'strong mindedness', which, in marriage, revealed itself as an uncomfortable insistence on the divine right of male domination; Jane's confidence that her beauty, charm and a little playful wheedling or remonstrance would win her most things that a briskly working brain could devise.

Before long the parson's lady was turning to amusing, freethinking women friends for the kind of companionship her husband could not give her, and Brookfield, seeing their influence as subversive, did his best to freeze them out. Having such a constitutional detestation of sentiment and feelings himself, he told her, he could hardly be expected to sympathize when she indulged in such twaddle with others, and he would be obliged if she would remember that reserve was the great law for women.

Jane, docile in appearance, was not so in spirit. Two years later she was still putting her side of that particular argument, telling him that if she had not so much sentiment for others, she would not have so much for him: 'It is my nature to love, & I cannot help it, & you must let me talk to you *"sentimentally"* about my friends sometimes, or I shall shrivel up & feel a buckram barrier lies between us.'[2]

A part of her trouble was that she had too much time for talk and brooding, and no desire to occupy herself with the usual chores of a poor curate's wife—another area of contention. Had Brookfield 'got on', as they had both expected, their troubles would have been minimized, but, despite their influential friends, his career floundered.

He turned down his only real chance of advancement, the

Bishopric of Barbados, which came within a year of his marriage, expecting, as did Jane and her family, that it would be followed by a more acceptable prize. But nothing comparable was ever offered, and the following year he was glad enough to take a very small step up the ladder, to become Minister of St Luke's, Berwick Street, Soho, a dependency of his old church in Piccadilly.

Though it often meant giving three sermons on a Sunday, he swelled his purse and satisfied his need for attention by keeping on his preachership at Tenison's, the kind of chapel where the fashionable congregation arrived with a quantity of fine cambric in the expectation of a fine religious weep, and was gratified when Mrs Carlyle told him he had a real influence on many young men of rank and position who would not listen to other preachers.

Kinglake offered a more waggish comment on his popularity after Brookfield, looking very yellow, had been taken ill at the Procters': 'You'll have jaundice if you don't mind. Now do attend to it, my dear fellow. *You owe it to your congregation* to preserve your complexion.'[3]

But from Tenison's, as from St Luke's, the income was still meagre, and Brookfield became corrodingly conscious that by his marriage he had placed his wife in a position very inferior to that of all her sisters. He was also aware that he had done nothing to lessen the early, unfavourable impression which he believed he had made on the menfolk of her family, and admitted that for someone as vain as he still was, and as petted as he once had been, it was not easy to recover from so bad a beginning. This galling sense of failure had been accentuated when Charles Elton inherited the baronetcy and Clevedon Court. Brookfield, having wandered alone for the first time round this ancient home, with its wide terraces and sweeping grounds, had written to Jane:

'I placed you there pacing along in perfect harmony with all about, and thought how much more natural, more everything-in-it's-right-place it would be that you should be shedding calm lustre on some such home than that you should be sequestered in Duke Street, St. James's, tied to a half begotten, quarter conceived, one-eighth born, one-sixteenth brought up, one thirty-second fortunate, one sixty-fourth deserving, one one-hundred-and-twenty-eighth part of a curate, who at best is only the one two-hundred-and-fifty-sixth part of a man,—who is only the one five-hundredth-and-twelfth part of what he might be—and only the one-thousand-and-twenty-fourth part of what he thinks he is—'[4]

Awareness of his own insignificance led him into impatience and petulance, which, in turn, he tried to cover with a brash self-assertiveness. At home with Jane, his only chattel, he became a tyrant. In his church, he displayed the flamboyant side of his provocative personality.

For a while he appeared to preach in 'Romish collars' and a surplice, a rash affectation in the days when anything more elaborate than an academic gown and discreet neck-bands was regarded as a step towards Catholicism. He encouraged the singing of chants, another precarious move on the incense trail, and turned the baptizing of adults into a feature of St Luke's.

Outside the church, he wrapped himself in a flowing cloak, which he called his great mark of identity, and made up for his lack of preferment by cultivating popularity with a dedication which had Jane fearing that the god she had so recently worshipped would degenerate into the kind of clergyman Thackeray was to describe in *The Virginians*, Castlewood's obsequious Mr Sampson, with his old jokes, stale puns, and tarnished anecdotes, slopped with the wine of a hundred dinner-tables.

This troubled pair had one other great disappointment: they had no children, a lack which Brookfield blamed partly on cruel fate and, after a miscarriage while Jane was holidaying with one of her sisters in Devon, partly on the recklessness of his wife. Jane, three years married, spent several months in bed after the loss of the baby, and for several years after that took refuge in ill-health, becoming a semi-invalid, a beautiful lady draped on a sofa, a martyr to daily headaches.

She never expected to be really well again, she told her husband. Relief from violent pain she might hope for, but actual ease of body she did not suppose would ever be hers. Her complaints were those familiar to unhappy women: recurring back pains, languor and depression. If anything particularly pleased or interested her, it seemed that she could be as energetic as other people for a time, she explained, but suffered for it afterwards. In winter she was pulled down by colds, in summer by the debilitating heat.

As with many another interesting invalid, Mrs Brookfield's social life suffered very little; she travelled a good deal, though it naturally exhausted her; and she lived to a ripe and sturdy old age.

3.

With Jane so often away experimenting with hot air treatments, sulphur baths and plain country pleasures, Brookfield turned to Thackeray, another footloose male, for the stimulation of a smoke, a drink, and the easy exchange of sense and nonsense after his parochial duties, and Thackeray, seeing more of him than anyone else for a space of two years, learned to respect the parson as much as he delighted in the gifted, story-telling entertainer.

Though he was often to write in his books of the curious friendship it is possible to feel for the relatives of those we love, if that friendship allows us to see or hear of the object of our desire, there is little doubt that a genuine and rare affection developed between the parson and the author at this time, the kind of comradeship which over the centuries has made men fight each other's battles and take on each other's burdens. Thackeray and Brookfield, in a small way, did both these things: when Thackeray was hit by railway debts, Brookfield scraped together £100 to see him through the crisis, and when Brookfield's character was questioned, Thackeray leaped into the breach to defend it.

At the beginning of 1847, abandoning hope of promotion within the Church proper, Brookfield had applied to become an inspector of Church schools, a relatively well-paid job then attracting many clergymen. His application had gone to John Allen, the gangling, God-fearing innocent, who had wept tears of compassion over Thackeray's and FitzGerald's religious doubts at Cambridge, and Allen, remembering Brookfield's undergraduate levity and looseness of talk, turned him down.

Thackeray's first reaction was to tell Brookfield that he thought Allen was right and that it wasn't the job for him, but when he saw how humbly Brookfield absorbed the blow, he wrote to Allen himself, suggesting a reappraisal of the hard-working parson of thirty-six, doubly anxious to have the damaging judgement reversed since he suspected the clergyman's association with such a reprobate as himself had helped to form it.

Even in a matter such as this, Thackeray couldn't leave his admiration for Jane out of the argument. She was a sort of angel in his eyes, he informed Allen. But Allen refused to be weaned away from his Cambridge memories, and Thackeray, angry with this other old friend, who was even then unconsciously making his debut in *Vanity Fair* as the guileless, clumsy, good-hearted Dobbin, went over his head to Henry Reeve, then in the Privy Council Office, asking him to explain to his superiors the difference in temperament between the two men.

Clergymen didn't win the kind of esteem and affection from their flock that Brookfield had for nothing, he told Reeve, the kind of love he had witnessed in Southampton, where Brookfield's old parishioners turned his visits into fête days and had him walking through the town blessing them like Sir Roger de Coverley. Geniality and humour could often awaken good in others which perfectly spotless people would never know how to create, a fact he could answer for in his own case. For while he had known and loved Allen for years, he had had no religious effect on him, whereas Brookfield had, and on *Punch*, too.

It was a just assessment. When Brookfield became an inspector, his unconventional approach led him to challenge many weaknesses in the educational system overlooked by others, and his devastatingly readable reports gained his disclosures wide circulation. But he didn't get his inspectorship for another year—with the more weighty assistance of the Duff-Gordons and Lord Lansdowne, and the elevation of Allen to an archdeaconry—and in the meantime had to suffer further humiliation, for now it was his turn to be embarrassed by railway speculation, and in order to pay his debts his modest Pulteney Street rooms had to be given up.

Jane, pale and thin, reluctantly embarked on a round of country visits which she knew was no ordinary excursion, but an open-ended charity tour. The difference between staying with family and friends by choice, as an invited guest, and being forced to descend on them to be 'taken in gratis', was one she felt keenly, and her mortification was not lessened when one of her sisters handed her £5 for pocket-money.

In these circumstances even the company she had once sought seemed a penalty she was now being made to endure, and, hurt and ashamed, she did not spare her husband the details of her discomfiture (since their funds were so low, he was even offered a share of the offensive £5), though he himself was suffering far greater indignities.

Brookfield had taken to the only piece of real estate in London to which he had a claim—the vaults beneath his church—and while he joked and called it 'my subterranean Palace', 'the Kattercome', or, in Thackeray's words, 'L'horrible Bouge', and wrote to friends as 'Unburied Ones', it was a public admission of failure his vanity found hard to bear. For a long time he dealt sympathetically with the steady trickle of salt Jane poured into the open wounds of his pride, but when he finally called a halt he left no doubt that he intended to be obeyed.

'If I refrain from showing any irritation at your *renewed* expostulations (—the pretext being shifted to *my* discomforts makes very little difference—they are still expostulations)—pray do not take it as any encouragement to reiterate them', he warned. 'These are exceedingly unacceptable to me & answer no good purpose. I should think it impossible that four months of embarrassment & straightened means could by an ingenuity *have been broken up into more tolerable payments*—& you talk as if you had been exiled as many years in a Fisherman's hut in the Shetlands . . . It is an entire fortnight since I left you at a place which agrees with you—with a

doctor when you seemed to need one—among people you like—I
have written daily—I proposed coming to you in a week—and yet
you seem to think yours an unprecedentedly cruel destiny . . . It is
true this hole is not so comfortable as Forest Lodge,—but I trust I
shall for some years retain energy enough to avoid making an
unhappiness of such outward things.'[1]

Jane, by now, was at Southampton, dividing her time between the
homes of the medical Bullar family and that of her greatest friend,
Mrs Fanshawe, another lady of charm married to a clergyman who
had not lived up to her expectations. 'M^{rs} f.', or 'Pincushion', as she
was called, because of her small stature, had dangerous thoughts
brewing in her attractive little head, and Brookfield had long before
warned Jane to remember that though she was very engaging, she
detested her husband, loved another, and in the hands of a clever
villain would soon be in a questionable position.

The thought of the statuesque Jane talking 'sentiment' and
feminine rebellion with this pocket Amazon as they gossiped over
their teacups or brushed each other's hair at night, did not greatly
appeal to him now, though Mrs Fanshawe's extraordinary jumbles
of religious texts and feminist observations had often amused him in
the past. With humour, rather than the icy voice of command,
Brookfield told Jane: 'I commission you, to give her either a blank
stupid stare of unapprehension or a box on the ear as may seem most
expedient, from me, every time she utters an incoherent abstraction
against the male persuasion.'[2]

Under Mrs Fanshawe's lively influence Jane thought up several
schemes for seeing more of her husband and repairing their finances.
One was romantic: to live incognito, like a mistress, in some cheap
lodgings near London, where Brookfield could make surreptitious
visits to see her. Another was more businesslike: to take in pupils,
preferably the children of friends, such as Thackeray's daughters.

Jane had been quick to recognize the potential of *Vanity Fair* and,
though still not entirely approving of its author, was not at all averse
to transferring some of his earnings to the Brookfields' yawning
coffers. Her 'plan for Governessing', as she called it, had, as far as
she was concerned, two great advantages: it would pay the
household expenses and do her good. She wanted to contribute, to
feel that she was no longer a mere cumberer of the earth, and to have
some stimulating occupation which would take her mind off her
minor ailments and the deadening limitations of poverty.

It was a worthy idea and she was full of enthusiasm, but the
details of the scheme as expounded to Brookfield in further letters
were not encouraging, for although she calmly proposed turning

Thackeray out of 13 Young Street, which he had just made ready to receive his family, and putting him back into lodgings, while she took his children into her own as yet non-existent home, she did not plan to take on the burden alone.

She would need, she thought, a nursery governess to walk out with the children and keep them in order when she wasn't there, and several masters to assist her, since she herself could teach little beyond a code of morality. Such a service, she reckoned, could be provided for between £300 and £400 a year, and she was rather amused to think how horrified Mr Thackeray would be at the purely financial way in which she was contemplating taking over his daughters.

She had not then met Mrs Carmichael-Smyth, or she would have realized that if anyone was going to appropriate Mr Thackeray's children, it would not be the lovely clergyman's lady already too well admired by Mrs Carmichael-Smyth's son.

Brookfield mentioned the plan to Thackeray, who talked about it rather 'wildly', but the idea of letting his wife become a governess, no matter how supervisory, in order to meet the household bills, was not one to repair his pride, and it was largely this understandable but tactless harping on their straitened means, and the implication that Brookfield could not get them out of the mess alone, which caused him to write his glacial rebuke for her 'expostulations'.

No matter how stern her husband became, however, Jane refused to be cowed. 'I hope to continue my course as "Clay in the hands of the Potter,"' she told him demurely, '—you being the Potter—but I think you expect too much from *sentient* Clay in excluding liberty of speech.'[3]

She could get through repugnant things better if persuaded into them, rather than ordered, she said, and having once been allowed to express her feelings, could the more easily hold her peace afterwards. With cajoling good humour, she called Brookfield 'Crustiferous', or 'My dear Curmudgeon', but refused to accept as gospel the thoughts of a man who had left her without a home of her own, and whose dream of glory was still the university triumph of his youth.

Early in their enforced separation, Brookfield had again escaped into this golden world. He had gone to Cambridge for the installation of the Prince Consort as Chancellor, but attended none of the celebrations. Instead, introduced by Jane's undergraduate cousin, Harry Hallam (an only slightly less glittering version of his dead elder brother, Arthur) into the student world he loved, he spent his days and nights in Shakespeare readings and buffoonery, and at the age of thirty-eight revelled once more in the adulation of eighteen-year-olds.

'La, sir, I knew you again first moment you came into the Court,' an old gyp told him. 'Many a time I have laughed out when you have been at table! No doubt you are a good deal altered from what you was.'

'Not at all, Pleasance,' Brookfield assured the man; 'there was nothing in me to alter.'

'Oh, no, sir—I only mean you are little *dried down* from what you was.'[4]

But Brookfield was not *'dried down'*, and his letters to Jane were so full of joyful nostalgia that she tried to apply a little dehydration of her own. However harmless an occasional burst of such company might be, she suggested, Man was not intended to go through life looking at all things with a humorous eye. The realities he had to struggle through were, in the end, more wholesome, and though she could understand that he might wish to alter things as they were in the present, that did not mean he had to go back to what they had been in the past.

It was with this same kind of wisdom that she wrote to her husband a few months later, on their sixth wedding anniversary, the ·first they had spent apart. Brookfield had told her that the mildly eccentric Sir Alexander Duff-Gordon and his unconventional wife—the writer, who sported men's shirts and jackets and made a showy feature of their precarious income—had asked them to share their London house as lodgers. Brookfield was tempted. They were people he had always had rather a weakness for, he told Jane. But Jane, having drunk her husband's anniversary health in her morning glass of medicine, sat down to compose a careful reply, which showed her personal distaste for the scheme and a cautious regard for both their reputations. As always, she ended with a flurry of apologies for having spoken her mind, but the message itself was a most decided document:

'I think it exceedingly kind of course—*but* that it w^d be extremely imprudent on many a/c's to accept the offer—I quite felt with you, at first, how convenient & easy it w^d be to step in to comfortable lodgings all ready for one, & either use them for a month or so while seeking *permanency*, or stay for good if all suited—& the house is oldfashioned & quite to y^r taste I know—so that I had the feeling very strongly of disliking to say to you that I do not think it w^d answer because I am afraid you will be disappointed, but when we consider *you* as a Clergyman & me as a quiet sort of person whom few have much real acquaintance with, so as to know exactly what I may really be—would not it be a.most incongruous liaison for you & me to be *taken up*, & (as it w^d probably turn out) introduced & *vouched for* by Lady Buff with her g^t goodnature desiring to give one *a lift* in Society,—which *lift* I should think very undesirable in our circumstances—I think you have been thrown as it is, quite as much as is in any way prudent for a Clergyman into that *literary set* from wh: I do not think a wholesome influence proceeds, however pleasant & kind they are,—I say so much with regard to you because I think the case w^d be very different if you were not a Priest, but being one, & being of a social temperament & likely, as it is, to startle weak minds by some of y^r free ways, which have no shadow of wrong in them, but which pilling people might easily take umbrage at, w^d not it be very rash to put your head into the very Lion's den . . . and with regard to me, would it be well for me to be in the same house & so (however unjustly) *taking caste* as it were from a person of such *notoriously* equivocal *manners*, however free from a shadow of actual blame her conduct is?—*I could never be intimate* with Lady Buff because she appears to have neither a woman's *delicacy*, nor *reverence* . . .'[5]

And so the letter went on—and on, and on—sensible, well-intentioned, infuriating, the writing crossed at the end in a bewildering, paper-saving maze. Clichés of the 'weak brother' and 'birds of a feather' variety sprawled across the pages; Thackeray and Mrs Norton appeared as examples of the undesirable company likely to be encountered at the Duff-Gordons' cosy little Sunday dinners; that particular area of London was contrasted unfavourably, and in detail, with a whole raft of other districts. It was a production virtually tailor-made to set Brookfield grinding his teeth and issuing the kind of chilly rebuke that so astonished his wife.

Thackeray, unaware of Jane's opinion of him, had also offered temporary shelter. He told his mother that it had been Brookfield's idea, and that he had wisely parried it—'loving her as I do—mong Dieu what a temptation it was!'—but a letter to Brookfield tells a different story. In that Thackeray begs, implores and entreats his 'dear old Reverence' to take three of his Young Street rooms, and promises to pop preserved apricots from Fortnum & Mason under Jane's pillow each night.

Even Brookfield thought this would hardly do, and Jane did not return to London until he had taken independent rooms in Ebury Street. Soon afterwards he was at last made an Inspector of Schools, and the new year of 1848 found the clergyman and his lady celebrating their modest return to good fortune as guests of Lord

John Manners at Belvoir Castle, from which elegant address Brookfield jested that Jane, asked to sing by their friend's father, the Duke of Rutland, played the tune of the *New Tabernacle* and warbled with exquisite tact and promptitude:

> As pants the hart for cooling streams
>   When heated in the chase,
> So long'd so long my soul to sit
>   At table with your grace.[6]

In the spring, financially aided by Henry Hallam, now a widower, and yet another admirer of his delightful niece, the Brookfields found a permanent home: a comfortable house at 15 Portman Street, with a staff of three to look after it, and so began a new chapter in their marriage and their relationship with Thackeray.

15

Liaison Dangereuse

The stormy region of longing passions unfulfilled

Had Thackeray not always been so ready to help his friends, his eagerness to assist Brookfield to his new job could have been seen as the kind of shady manoeuvre for which Mrs Carmichael-Smyth would have readily supplied chapter and verse from her favourite Book: II Samuel, xi, 1–27. Thackeray was not made for such guile, but the result was the same: Uriah Brookfield, soldier of Christ, was away for six days most weeks, travelling the southern counties on a second-class railway ticket, inspecting and reporting. His wife, Jane/Bathsheba, remained at home, beautiful, twenty-seven, disappointed in her husband, reclining on her Portman Street sofa, quietly witty and unwell. King Thackeray, a lonely man without a wife, nearing the end of his triumphant monthly numbers of *Vanity Fair*, saw his opportunity and seized it.

His sturdy brown cob could carry him through Kensington Gardens and Hyde Park to Portman Street in no time at all, and in Jane's new drawing-room he found an increasingly warm welcome—though he was still by no means alone in his desire to entertain its engaging mistress.

In the early summer, Brookfield, apologizing for leaving his wife without a companion in the house, wrote to her: 'but . . . you have plenty of consolations in M^r this and M^r that & M^r tother. How often has Aubrey—has Makepiece—has Spring—has—nay call them Gad—a troop cometh—been I should like to know.'[1]

Aubrey de Vere sent Mrs Brookfield pretty volumes of his poems, for which she thanked him in timid, overwhelmed little letters.

Stephen Spring Rice, eldest son of the first Lord Monteagle, also maintained an attentive regard for the parson's lady. As deputy chairman of the Board of Customs, he had a revenue cutter at his disposal each summer, on which he took Brookfield for an annual cruise, but neither his friendship for the husband, nor his own marriage, dimmed his ardour for Jane.

'Will you throw away a jewel because a snail has left its slime upon it?' he asked, when Jane threatened to abandon her monogram because a man she didn't like had addressed her as Mrs JOB. 'Your initials are so dear to so many of us you ought to think twice or three times before you give them up.'[2]

How gallant! said Jane, handing over the entire exchange to Thackeray.

But when Spring Rice began angling for invitations to dine with her when Brookfield was away, the Inspector's lady gently turned him down. If she received him, she asked, how could she refuse those others of her husband's friends who might also wish to 'compassionate' her solitary dinners?

Soon she was to have a resident courtier in her young cousin, the Cambridge graduate and fledgeling barrister, Harry Hallam. Despite all this competition, however, Thackeray gradually gained the ascendancy, and having been awarded the convenient title of honorary brother to both the Brookfields saw no harm in visiting his 'dear sister' every day. Brookfield appears to have allowed the growing intimacy out of generosity to a friend whose own domestic life was in shreds, and in the misguided belief that women do not fall in love with overweight buffoons of no obvious physical attraction.

Thackeray, believing what he wished to believe, proclaimed his feelings for Jane to be pure and fraternal, and was morally outraged when young Harry Hallam caused 'a *breeze*'—as Jane called the temporary unpleasantness—by questioning the propriety of his constant presence in the house. He had Brookfield's permission, Jane's, and that of his own heart and conscience for seeing her whenever he wished, Thackeray insisted, and if none of those three objected, who else had the right to deny him his great happiness?

He had arrived at this privileged position through half a year of sympathetic attendance beside her couch. He knew the reason for her illness—her hypochondria, as he bluntly called it—and showed that he cared with a patience and sensitivity rare in a full-blooded man. But then, as he told his dear lady: 'you know it has been agreed that at one time of my existence I must have been a woman— darling duck, what a beauty I must have been!'[3]

To Mrs Carmichael-Smyth, who looked upon his attachment with her customary jealous unease, Thackeray explained Jane's troubles:

'I am afraid my dear Mrs Brookfield will die. She sinks and sinks and gets gradually worse. She lies on a sofa now and the Doctor says she must confine herself to a floor of the house. She will go to bed presently, and then—Amen. It will be better for her—She never says a word but I know the cause of a great part of her malady well enough—a husband whom she has loved with the most fanatical fondness and who—and who is my friend too—a good fellow upright generous kind to all the world except her.'[4]

With Jane herself, he was not so fatalistic. If she didn't speak of her problems, she listened to his advice on them, and Thackeray urged her to think for herself rather than blindly follow the whirling dictates of her favourite Dr Packman, who told her one day to lie flat on the peril of her life, and the next to run around drinking porter at midday and quinine all the afternoon.

There were a great many other ladies, and gentlemen too, living as she was, he told her, in smart papered rooms with rats gnawing behind the wainscot. She must learn to have a poker ready, and if the rats came out, bang, beat them on the head.

He helped to keep the rats at bay himself by taking her daily batches of manuscript and choice samples from his mailbag; he wrote her silly notes signed 'Author of "The Death Shriek" "Passion flowers" and other poems', 'Octaviophilus', 'Clarence Bulbul', and similar absurdities. Seats for the theatre and opera which had been offered to him were turned over to her, and occasionally he had the exquisite pleasure of accompanying her himself, when like some towering pasha he escorted his harem to the show—Annie and the governess, the lovely young Eugenie Crowe, his own dear lady—and squeezed his long legs into the back of the box behind them all.

And when Jane was too ill to leave the house, he arranged for the stupendous Adelaide Sartoris, Charles Kemble's youngest, opera-singing daughter, to give a private, sofa-side concert for the invalid.

On his travels he wrote her long, loving, brilliant letters, chattering away with his pen as he did beside her sofa, sparking off ideas for *Punch* articles as he described all he had seen and done and thought. He turned incidents she witnessed at the hairdresser's into other funny publishable items, and, thinking of her always, told her she was partly his model for Amelia in *Vanity Fair*. He even called Amelia's maid Payne after one of her attendants, and then, when the name was already in print, worked himself into a great tremor, fearing the wrath of both mistress and servant.

Jane, though flattered at inspiring a fictional heroine, was not over-pleased with either Amelia or Lady Jane Sheepshanks, whom she took to be another likeness.

'I wish he had made Amelia more exciting,' she told Harry Hallam half-way through the story. '. . . on the plan of 2 negatives making one affirmative, I suppose I may take the 2 dull ones of the book to make one Mrs. B. You know he told William that though Amelia was not a copy of me he should not have conceived the character if he had not known me—and though she has the right amount of antiphlegm and affectionateness she is really an uncommonly dull and selfish character, and very apathetic to the only person who cares for her, the quaint Capt. Dobbin.'[5]

Brookfield, who all too often encountered the steely side of her nature, told Thackeray that Jane was far more like Fielding's resilient Amelia than his, but Thackeray continued to see her as in his youth he had seen his mother. She was his kind sweet gentle lady, his *chère soeur si douce et si bonne*, made of the same soft stuff as himself, and Jane took care in his presence to reflect the angelic image he held up for her.

While there had been much talk in the Brookfield household of Jane herself writing a book, one which, in Brookfield's words, would make Lady Duff-Gordon swallow poison with envy, and Tennyson, Thackeray, Spring Rice, Captain Codrington, Edward Dean, James Spedding, Venables, Kinglake and the Bullers drown themselves for distracted love, to Thackeray she gave no hint of such ambition.

Her letters to him contain a strain of timid awe, a self-doubt and uncertainty not at all apparent in those to her husband, and when Thackeray occasionally grumbled at receiving the kind of note 'w[h] apologizes for everything, and whereof the tremulous author ceaselessly doubts & misgives', she merely produced more apologies. She could not express herself in writing, as he did, she said: very commonplace things occurred, and she could only describe them in a very commonplace way. And when he pictured himself sinking into rambling, incoherent old age, she told him how much better suited she would be to him then, when he was brought down a little more to her own level.

She listened to his hopes, his triumphs, his woes and his ambitions with kind sympathy shining from her beautiful eyes; she gave him a taste of domestic peace in an orderly home—and a handsome little silver and mother-of-pearl paperknife, which sharp-eyed Annie immediately recalled having seen at Portman Street. She fussed over him when he worked too hard; teased him when he bragged of social success or moaned about the petty trials of fame; she told him, with sincerity, how happy he must be to be able to do so much good with his writing; and showed admirable surprise that even with his generosity of nature he should for one moment see Dickens as a rival. She stirred his blood, fired his imagination, sent him to his desk determined to shake the world—used him, his love and admiration to make good the deficit within her marriage.

There were times, before passion blinded him completely, when Thackeray could see Jane's charm working, chameleon-like, to entrap others besides himself, and suspected that she and Brookfield laughed together at his extravagant devotion.

'How many people are you?' he asked her. 'You are Mr Packmans M^{rs} B and Mr Jackson's M^{rs} B and ah you are my M^{rs} B (You know you are, now) and quite different to us all, and you are your sisters M^{rs} B and Miss Wynne's—and you make gentle fun of us all round to your own private B, and offer us up to make him sport You see I am making you out to be an Ogre's wife and poor William the Ogre to whom you serve us up cooked for dinner—Well stick a knife into me, here is my busam. I wont cry out—you poor Ogre's wife—I know you are good natured and soft hearted au fond.'[6]

He was right, Jane and Brookfield did laugh together at his transparent manoeuvrings to be with her, his demands to have his strength of character praised if he wrote only every other day, or for once resisted the temptation to call. But the joke ended for both of them when Jane, her morale boosted by Thackeray's pep-talks and flattering attentions, strengthened her resistance to her husband's domination. Then it was the clergyman's turn to question the wisdom of so free a friendship, to doubt Jane's loyalty and discretion, if not her sexual morality. There are, after all, more ways of alienating a man's wife than by tempting her into an extra-marital bed, and Thackeray, while professing love for both the Brookfields, deepened the rift between them.

Jane, apparently oblivious to the increase in warmth, shared jokes and barely suppressed longing in Thackeray's letters passed them on to Brookfield with sharp instructions to take care of them since she intended to keep them. In her replies she addressed Thackeray informally as 'My dear friend' and when Brookfield, in an attempt to lower the temperature, objected, bared her teeth prettily in a saucy show of rebellion:

'I had a long letter from M^{rrrr} Thackeray this morning M^{rr} Brookfield,' she informed him. 'Perhaps I may enclose it for y^r perusal but mind you let me have it back again as it may be intended for ultimate publication for anything we know.'[7]

Brookfield did peruse the vast document, with its brilliant prattle of travels abroad, its loving, euphoric references to a certain clergyman's lady left behind in London, and wrote back tersely: 'Thank you for the Thackeray note. I think him a very much overrated person.'[8]

Jane took no heed of such rumblings, reserving her artillery for outright complaints, and when Brookfield next remonstrated against the growing warmth with which she ended her letters, she was ready with a volley of mixed shot. She could not believe that 'Yours aff*ly*' was so unusual a signature as he seemed to think, but then he was hardly intimate enough with ladies' ways to know, she told this hard-pressed son of a Sheffield solicitor. She beat him down with detailed examples, scoured him for unworthy thoughts, and insisted that surely a woman of near thirty might judge for herself how much friendship to show.

'. . . it is not as if M' Thack. were some young Adonis in the Guards,' she told her handsome husband; '. . . he is far too *wide awake* not to understand the sisterly feeling I have for him wh: could not ever by any force of circumstances *clash* with any other affection. It is a totally different thing.'[9]

It all sounded reasonable enough, but only a few weeks earlier Jane had found Thackeray carrying that innocuous 'Yours aff*ly* J.O.B.' as a talisman in his purse, where it had been discovered by another of his favourites, Mrs Sarah Prinsep, one of the many Pattle sisters he had known from his youth.

'Oh, it's a bit of a note from a man named James O'Brien, a friend of mine,' Thackeray had blustered, before whisking round to Portman Street with schoolboyish glee to report the incident to Jane.[10]

Brookfield and his wife were now completely at odds, unable or unwilling to understand each other, and at last Jane turned openly from her husband's disagreeable lecturing to Thackeray's soothing adoration, calling him to her side late one night at romantic Clevedon Court and spilling out her woes in a way which sent the blood pounding through his veins in joyful madness.

It is unlikely that she did more than confide her marital miseries and disappointments, and promise always to look to him—as to a brother—for comfort and strength in the future, but it was an emotion-charged interview which sent Thackeray into ecstasies of excitement. He left Clevedon in turmoil, and spent the next few days at Oxford in such delirious preoccupation that he later felt bound to apologize to his university host, Charles Neate, for his erratic behaviour.

Since Neate, a Fellow of Oriel, was, among many other things, a French scholar, and since French was the language of love, Thackeray told his friend of the '*horribles peines de coeur qui sans cesse me poursuivent*'.[11] Suffer and say nothing, he added with unlikely fortitude—'*Du courage Spartiate!*' All the time he had been at Oxford, his thoughts had been with someone else: *'Elle ne m'aime pas. Elle me plaint'*, he admitted, but even to be pitied by that dear creature was rapture. Jane's voice, the sweetest he had ever heard, speaking to him out of the Clevedon night, surprising him in his loneliness, at once consoled and inflamed him. He vowed to love for ever the house where he had heard it, where he had known days happier than any that had gone before.

'Clevedon in '48' was emblazoned on his heart and mind like a seal of rare vintage, signalling a new phase in his emotional life.

His sofa-side conversations and letters now pulsed with the kind of sentiment for which Brookfield had such an inbuilt psychological fear. He thought of Jane on waking and sleeping. Her beautiful eyes followed him everywhere. He pleaded with her: *'Benis moi O Madame, O mon ange—Il me semble que j'ai quelque chose du Ciel, quand j'ai un regard ou une pensée de vous.'* [12]

'I must tell someone that I love you', he cried: 'Why not? to you, to William, to whoever will listen to me. One must speak when one has a heart so full. and why should I be ashamed of the love I have for you. It is very tender, and very pure. I am proud of it—and you, dear Lady, trust in it . . . we will love each other while we may here and afterwards . . . If I were to lose you I should despair and go wrong.' [13]

The well-publicized purity of Thackeray's love was more than a social gloss applied in order to make his friendship possible. His thoughts were honourable, in the sense that he had no intention of putting the impure ones into practice, but beneath his immaculate adoration there raged a strong physical desire, and another unexpectedly tender meeting with Jane set him writing poetry through the night in an agony of frustration:

> In the midst of all the joy as I behold it,
> When I seek the recollections of long years,
> When I labor & endeavour to behold it
> Giving way to the infirmity of tears.

> O my grey hairs
> What a fool I seem
> What a fitful dream
> Which thy life declares.
> How I wake all night
> When the moon shines bright
> With a ghastly light
> On my grey hairs.

Though we may not say it
And the secret rests
In 2 sad breasts
In silence folded
Yet we both obey it
And it throbs and smarts
And tears our hearts
But we never told it.

Though my lips are mute
And its signal flies
In a flash from my eyes
When your own behold it,
And reply unto it
With a glance of light
O beaming bright
Yet we never told it. [14]

Like a boy, he let Jane know when he had written such poems, promised to send them to her, then hesitated until she begged to see them. She must have known what loving anguish they would contain, yet having read them, having lured him on, her acknowledgement was stiff with formal caution. She would keep them 'as a curiosity', she told him, and leave them, together with his letters, to Annie, for her eventually to work into his memoir—according to her discretion.

'Do you know,' she added, 'that if you do not write in more commonplace style to me I shall be quite unable to answer you at all.' [15]

Alternately, she wooed him and held him off. Six weeks after Clevedon, when she and Brookfield made their annual Christmas visit to Southampton, she told Thackeray she felt a hypocrite playing the happy wife still before her kind, honest friends there. Then, a few days later, having touched his heart with the sadness of her predicament, and having received from her husband another lecture on the warmth of her correspondence, she reintroduced Brookfield as a fully paid-up member of the trio:

'I can't help adding from a sudden impulse how very kind W^m has been to me all the time we have been here—& he is now I think much fonder of you than of anyone and would not ever wish you less intimate with us both . . . but I think he sometimes wishes less said:—only you are a poetical kind of writer.' [16]

She signed herself: 'Good-bye dear friend, Ever Yours Jane', a considerable advance on 'Yours aff^{ly}, J.O.B.'

There had been a time, many months before, when Brookfield had challenged Thackeray about his increasingly personal praises of his wife, and had been appeased by the declaration that they were not in the least dangerous, stemming as they did from a sort of 'artistical delight—a spiritual sensuality', such as he found in nature, music, harmonies of colour, and young Annie and Minnie above all. Jane's innocence, looks, angelical sweetness and kindness all ravished him to the highest degree, but it was absolutely nothing to worry about.

Now, with Jane also behaving so oddly, Brookfield's pride would not let him tackle directly the great cuckoo that had invaded his nest. He gave Thackeray the impression that he condoned, with certain reservations, his brotherly relationship with them both, an impression Thackeray was very ready to receive, and did his best to awaken Jane to the perils of the game she and his best friend were determined to play, laying down some ground rules and putting the onus on her for seeing that they were obeyed: Thackeray and she could meet and write, though not so often, and no matter what Thackeray said, Jane must keep to the commonplace.

But what was 'commonplace', Jane now asked, passing on Brookfield's directives in their mildest form. Thackeray reassured her that he had everything clear in his mind. Since Brookfield had been so generous to him, and didn't like too much writing, he would reply only when she wrote to him, 'dignified and quite proper'.

But of course he couldn't keep to such discipline, and Jane didn't wish him to. When she returned to Portman Street at the beginning of 1849, in stronger health than for many months, he was once again called to her side, and though she told her husband that there would be comparatively few opportunities for seeing him now that she was no longer confined to her sofa, the scope widened rather than diminished.

Brookfield, away on his 'gin-horse circuit', as he called his inspectoral duties, must soon have been aware of the delicious new element that had been added to their relationship, as he read his wife's daily bulletins and noticed how often Thackeray's name appeared among those she had met at the dinners, luncheons and evening tea-parties, which, she implied, she had not really wanted to attend, but people were so kind, calling expressly to ask her, how could she refuse?

In *The Newcomes*, Thackeray wrote of the convenient coincidence which allows two people to appear so frequently on the same guest lists, and describes the zest given to social gatherings by the secret interplay of love: the eyes that light up when a certain person enters the room; the thrill that charges the most ordinary occasion. There were two frames of mind under which London society was bearable to a man, he said: to be an actor in one of those sentimental performances, or to be a spectator.

Thackeray, the observer of mankind, continuously practised the latter role, but he found more excitement in participation. As well as his visits to Portman Street, and Jane's family meals with Annie and Minnie, who he was determined should love her as much as he did himself, there were now several houses in which he could indulge this blood-tingling sport, and in none did he find a more sympathetic welcome than at the Chesham Place home of another Jane and her Colonial Office husband, Thomas Frederick Elliot, a nephew of the first Earl of Minto, a connection to which Thackeray dryly attributed his fondness for the family.

In later years, he came to rely on the quiet sympathy of Mrs Elliot, but he was first attracted to Chesham Place, a haunt of many of the old Cambridge set, by the unmarried sister who lived with her, Kate Perry, a bright young beauty, with abundant wreaths of crisp, waving auburn hair and graceful manners. He had first met her and one of her brothers at Brighton, at the start of *Vanity Fair*, and within no time at all was reading his daily quota of work to her, calling her 'Mademoiselle', and telling her the story of his life.

In London he quickly became as welcome in the Elliots' drawing-room as he was at Portman Street, and often visited the rough schoolroom where the two sisters gathered together three hundred waifs to feed, clothe and teach, leaving behind as evidence of his presence a sovereign tucked into the subscription list for their country outings, or a sketch of children clamouring for their daily meal in the middle of Kate Perry's soup-kitchen accounts.

Only the singing of the ragged little 'Arabs' was too much for him, and wandering into the bare room as they rocked the rafters with 'O Paradise! O Paradise! Who doth not crave for rest? Who would not see the happy land, Where they that love are blest?' he quickly marched out again, muttering 'I can't stand this any longer—my spectacles are getting very dim.'[17]

It was in Miss Perry's autograph book that Thackeray first wrote one of the most touching of his poems, *The Pen and the Album*, which the 'speaking' pen ends with words of gratitude:

> Dear, friendly eyes, with constant kindness lit,
> However rude my verse, or poor my wit,
> Or sad or gay my mood, you welcome it.

> Kind lady! till my last of lines is penn'd,
> My master's love, grief, laughter, at an end,
> Whene'er I write your name, may I write friend!

Not all are so that were so in past years;
Voices, familiar once, no more he hears;
Names, often writ, are blotted out in tears.

So be it:—joys will end and tears will dry—
Album! my master bids me wish good-by,
He'll send you to your mistress presently . . .

The name most often writ, but by then blotted out in tears, was, of course, that of Jane Brookfield, and of all the people to whom Thackeray poured out his love and longings, no one heard more of them than Kate Perry, loving confidante of the lover and the loved. She had found out his secret—if the affairs of Thackeray's heart could ever have been considered so—very early on. It was clear to her, she told him, that he was always thinking of something else: 'your soul's not in your work; you go about to parties but don't take any heed of 'em—your hearts in the Highlands your heart is not here.'[18]

To her Thackeray gushed out the anguish he was not allowed to write to Jane. His passion, he groaned, was like the genie in the *Arabian Nights*, who would have puffed himself up as big as the world had not the seal of God been on the bottle that contained him.

'*Je l'aime Je l'aime Je l'aime . . .*' he cried. '*Je tremble d'amour quelque fois devant elle—que de flammes ont passé par mes lunettes!*'—how many flames had shot through his spectacles![19] He loved her so much, he said, it was as though he did not love her at all. He desired nothing, only to adore her, only to see her now and then.

And she? Did she love him? What agonies he went through over that, until he found the comforting formula that yes, she did, but as angels love—with a sweet compassion, with saintly tenderness, with maidenly modesty.

And so, with the purest emotions in the world and the greatest respect for her angelic affection, he tried to persuade her to accompany him to Lord and Lady Ashburton's Hampshire estate, The Grange, where all the romantic opportunities of country-house visiting would be open to them—whispered conversations in the shrubberies, sham-chance meetings in the library . . . He had written two replies to Lady Ashburton's invitation, he told Jane, and sent them both to her: she was to choose which one should go, and to burn the other. Jane, in this instance, chose angelic discretion.

2.

Reading the letters between all three parties in this unhappy triangle, it is easy to see that what Jane really wanted was the love of Brookfield—or, rather, the love of the man she had imagined him to be when she was still a girl and viewed him through romantic, untutored eyes. If she could not have that, she was determined to retain the flattering attentions of the kindest friend, the most amusing companion a lonely woman was ever likely to know—no matter what it did to her husband, or to Thackeray himself. Even during the first wild months after 'Clevedon in '48', it would have been so easy for her to release her lover from the tortures of 'longing passion unfulfilled'.[1] One chill word, and Thackeray caught an ague, lost all confidence in her affection, and prepared to depart. Jane always called him back.

'I am so glad that you will come in to-morrow at dinner,' she told him early in 1849, fresh from a new battle with her husband over the extravagance of Thackeray's communications. 'I thought you *talked* before just as if you were going your way & intended to leave me to mine, as any other acquaintance. You do not know I am sure how very much pain the idea of lessened friendship w^d cause me—it has made so great a part of my happiness ever since I felt that you really were so exceedingly kind as to care about me—that I have a sort of superstitious dread of its coming to an end some day.'

What could she do to convince him of her affection, she asked, when she was permitted to feel as much as she liked, but not to express it? Why could he not believe what she *said*, and not think her cold because she did not write more openly?: 'you can do as you please for yourself & you know that I should have a hard struggle to feel easy in receiving a stiff cool letter from you, altho' I have a morbid dread of your doing the reverse merely out of kindness.'[2]

With almost brutal honesty, she continued to show his letters to Brookfield, and to be angry if he disapproved.

'I feel provoked with myself for having written. or sent you what has evidently only annoyed you', she told her husband at this time. 'I have always tried to be entirely open with you ever since I first knew you, and I don't think you have *ever encouraged* me in it. I believe very few people under so much difficulty thrown in the way of it by yourself, w^d continue *to force* free speaking upon you where it only leads to annoyance and misunderstanding . . . Still I feel that you have a perfect right to make what rules you choose—if you wish me never to see anyone but yourself again, I will agree—only in that case you must *give me yourself* & allow me always to be with you—if this were possible I should never lament for others—but if I am left so much alone, it seems hard to scoff at my ''abundant friendships"—and to raise up bugbears w^h would never cross my mind . . . I can only say in entire simplicity that I should be ready to proclaim through a speaking trumpet under the Trafalgar Square Fountains if you like, that I feel quite as fond of "the party" in question as if he were my brother, & that I am very grateful to him for caring for me as he would for a sister, & it is entirely untrue to say that I sh^d be "confounded" if all his letters were proclaimed on Charing Cross tomorrow . . . I only hope that you will always be as open to me, as I have been to you, and then if we don't agree, we can at least understand each other as of all things I dislike a cold in-different silence when I see that I am not pleasing you, & yet cannot tell how to do so. I hope I may really succeed at last.'[3]

Forty years later, after the deaths of both Brookfield and Thackeray, when Jane did proclaim the offending letters to the world, she had less difficulty in deciding what was proper and what was not. Her editor's pen butchered them, scoring through phrases and sentiments to which her husband objected, obliterating some completely. Others she changed more subtly, making it appear that Brookfield was also included in the endearments. Enough longing passion remained, however, for another of Thackeray's old friends, Lady Stanley, to cry out in revulsion at such a coining into filthy lucre of the heart's blood of a man who had offered her the treasure of his innermost thoughts and love.

It may be that Mrs Brookfield never did realize what a unique gift she had been given when Thackeray made her a present of his great, soft, loving heart, or understand what fevers of desire she roused in him. For all her charm she was above all a survivor, with a shaft of iron in her nature, a steely core unconsciously revealed when she gave Thackeray her verdict on *Werther*, a tragedy which in so many ways mirrored their own.

'It evidently was not only from his unfortunate attachment that he blew his brains out,' she wrote, 'as he was unfit for the world altogether, and was most horribly selfish and cruel in putting his suicide upon his love for Charlotte, and actually allowing her to lend him the Pistols, on some other pretext, so that he might have the satisfaction of knowing how doubly comfortable she would feel when she heard he was dead. But it is curiously like a real story and interested me a good deal, 'tho I did not cry over it, as most people seem to have done—except I think when Charlotte has to ask him not to come again till the Fete day, and tried to suggest it in an easy enpassant manner.'[4]

It was Charlotte, not poor desperate Werther, that Jane felt sorry for, and it was herself she pitied when the strain of trying to meet the demands of both husband and admirer became too much for her.

She had lost all confidence in her own judgement, she told Thackeray in a mood of tearful, muddled misery, and felt she did justice neither to her own character nor to that which had been grafted onto it—'& between the two I take refuge in a stolid silence which is only a type of the useless blank of all my life—& yet I cannot find anything *to do* that w^d take me out of such a painful state of sensitiveness that it seems as if it w^d come to a *crash* & end in insanity some day . . .'[5]

Thackeray, with the awful example of Isabella before him, with remembered remorse at his own neglect, rushed to the rescue. But it is clear that he did not fully understand either Mrs Brookfield's message, or her husband's bitterness, since a few days later, having overstepped the bounds of propriety, he took off at speed for France, ironically begging Jane to try to conserve the same regard for him that her husband had. 'As I get older,' he promised, 'I will grow so polite calm and elegant in my behaviour that I will never at least offend you by too much abandon.'[6]

He called his flight a great and decisive step, and no doubt had in mind the good advice he was to give in *The Newcomes* when Clive was breaking his heart over Ethel—that there are some perils from which it is wise for even the bravest to run away.

But Thackeray's retreat was of very short duration. Two weeks and at least two long, loving letters later, he was back at Portman Street, reinforcing Jane's self-confidence so successfully that Brookfield complained of the levity with which she treated his sternest remonstrances. He blew the whistle, read out the rules, and demanded a penalty. Jane reluctantly obliged. On her husband's insistence, she wrote a most formal letter to Thackeray, and Thackeray, the astonishing innocent, complained to her husband.

'Thackeray stamps & growls at your having written a very chill letter to him—& I tell him I think you are quite right,' Brookfield wrote to his wife. 'I don't like the hypocrisy of concealing that I have anything to do with it—but plainly it would not do for me to say that your goodnature would lead you to more cordiality of language if I did not check it. I am also very sorry for any disagreeable feelings which you may have had in writing less frantically than desired—but whether I am right or wrong in my prudery there is no doubt you were right in doing what I wished—& I am much obliged to you—& hereby give you a   [*a blob of sealing wax*]'[7]

Jane, ignoring his sarcasm, replied: 'I w^d throw snowballs if I have a kiss from you,—& not only in sealing wax. You do not know how happy I feel if you are pleased with me . . . I have a great yearning to be with you again.'[8]

Thackeray, who could penetrate the innermost secrets of a

stranger, failed to see the wretchedness he was inflicting on a man he'd known for twenty years. 'How blind love is,' as Brookfield had sneered to Jane one day when Thackeray had patently misjudged her emotions, too.

The parson's hints were too mild and infrequent to curb his ardour for long; his show of friendship too constant. Shortly before the letter that had made him stamp and growl, the two men had returned to Cambridge together, where Brookfield had basked in the reflected glory of the author of *Vanity Fair*, revelling in the whispered recognition of gyps and undergraduates, which Thackeray vowed he'd not noticed, and together they had drunk Jane's health in college beer and soda water. Later in the spring, with Jane away at Clevedon, they returned to their bachelor habits of Hampstead walks and clubland dinners.

Slowly, with a perspicacity and delicacy of thought he was rather proud of, it dawned on Thackeray that Brookfield might occasionally like to spend some time with Jane without his own 'abominable mug' appearing on the scene, and with much-flaunted virtue and self-denial rationed himself out in smaller doses; but the evenings he did spend at Portman Street, with young Harry Hallam laughing at his jokes, Brookfield looking up from his favourite study of murder trials to survey them over the top of his newspaper, a bottle of port on the table, were remembered by him in later years as pleasure pure and simple, free from all undercurrents of deception and mistrust.

Profusely, Thackeray thanked his old friend for his generosity and confidence. And just as ardently he championed his old friend's wife against him, both in private and in print. If Brookfield complained about Jane's housekeeping, Thackeray consoled her. After all what was she called upon to do? he asked. It was all very well for some women to scold servants and make pickles and puddings, but he hoped she wouldn't become too much involved in such affairs. If she knew a great deal about meat and poultry, he assured her, she wouldn't know so much about other things.

Publicly, as 'Mr. Brown' in *Punch*, he proclaimed that if he died for it, he had to own that women did not get fair play in life:

'In the bargain we make with them I don't think they get their rights. And as a labourer notoriously does more by the piece than he does by the day, and a free man works harder than a slave, so I doubt whether we get the most out of our women by enslaving them as we do by law and custom. There are some folks who would limit the range of women's duties to little more than a kitchen range— others who like them to administer to our delectations in a ballroom, and permit them to display dimpled shoulders and flowing ringlets—just as you have one horse for a mill, and another for the Park. But in whatever way we like them, it is for our use somehow that we have women brought up; to work for us, or to shine for us . . . It would not have been thought shame of our fathers fifty years ago, that they could not make a custard or a pie, but our mothers would have been rebuked had they been ignorant on these matters. Why should not you and I be ashamed now because we cannot make our own shoes, or cut out our own breeches? We know better: we can get cobblers and tailors to do that—and it was we who made the laws for women, who, we are in the habit of saying, are not so clever as we are.'[9]

So Brookfield was not only a domestic tyrant, Thackeray implied, but fifty years out of date, too. Yet on the one occasion when he came close to sharing domestic bliss with Jane, he too was so irritated by her household management and bad time-keeping that he had to go out for a walk to get himself into a good mood again.

'I see I must be a very loose hand if I get hints at my laxity in management from a casual joiner in,' Jane told Brookfield then, '& I must come & ask my crusty old husband to be tolerant with me & not to be angry tho' I am provoking . . .'[10]

More overtly, Jane appeared in *Punch* as the charming 'Mrs. J', whom 'Mr Brown' recommends to his nephew as a refining influence. She might have been a countess blazing with diamonds, had fate so willed it, wrote Thackeray, and the higher her station the more she would have adorned it. Yet there she sat, for young Master Bob's edification, sewing buttons on her humble husband's waistcoat, and hiding her work behind a cushion when chance visitors called—a piece of domestic confusion in which Thackeray had surprised Jane, only in reality it had been Brookfield's 'chest of drawers' Jane had been mending, not his waistcoat.[11]

With knowledge of this mature and complicated lady, Thackeray fell out of love with the childish simplicity he had worshipped in Isabella and deified in Amelia Sedley, a character he lost patience with and consigned at last to Dobbin as a very dubious reward for his years of devotion. To the last word of *Vanity Fair* he believed he had been drawing on Mrs Brookfield, and his mother too, for Amelia's character, and it was not until some months later, while rereading the *Great Hoggarty Diamond*, that he recognized Isabella as the inspiration of all his heroines till then—a pattern with which he consciously broke for his next book, *Pendennis*.

Laura Bell is still too much of a legless Victorian virgin for many a modern taste, but she is an advance on the 'whimpering little goddess' Amelia,[12] and genuinely shares many of Mrs Brookfield's characteristics—bad as well as good. Laura's rejection of Fanny Bolton, the girl from a porter's lodge, who loved and nursed young Arthur Pendennis, is precisely the kind of cruel thrust Mrs Brookfield would have delivered.

'I . . . cannot help being sorry you dignify the F.B. fancy with the name of "love"—' Jane wrote after reading the chapters which told of Pen's raging passion, 'it seems degrading the word to apply it to the "dear little girl who drops her H's." ' [13]

In fiction, Thackeray understood well the prudery of such women. In real life he was bewildered by their disciplined emotions. Wanting Jane's whole heart, not mere friendship or sisterly affection, he bounced from euphoria to despair as her kindness raised his hopes, and decorum bruised his shins. Constantly he miscalculated the sum she owed him, as he told her with hurt pride when she refused him the emotive token of a lock of hair. But he never doubted he was right in his own great passion: he was proud, he said, to rank himself among the 'spoonies'. Like Warrington, he admired a man who showed he could have a great unreasonable attachment for a woman, and agreed with the sentiments he gave to Miss Crawley in *Vanity Fair*: 'That was the most beautiful part of dear Lord Nelson's character, he went to the deuce for a woman. There *must* be good in a man who will do that.' [14]

No matter how many times he was rebuffed, Thackeray, his heart bleeding on his sleeve, went back for more, until in the summer of 1849 his foolish paradise was shattered by a most unlikely thunderbolt: after nearly eight years of marriage, Mrs Brookfield was again pregnant.

Jane's tales of separate bedrooms, of Brookfield walking out of houses where he found he was not to have a dressing-room to himself, had doubtless led Thackeray to believe that their sexual relations were in as great a disarray as the rest of their union. He was stunned when Brookfield told him the news in strictest confidence, and then infuriated his repressed old friend by immediately blurting it out to Harry Hallam.

Consumed with intense rage and jealousy, he paraphrased the lines he had written about another beauty, Peg of Limavaddy, in *The Irish Sketch Book*—'Children if she bear blest will be their daddy'—and tortured himself by thinking of the lucky man who had the right to perform the part of husband to so sweet a creature.

He tried to write and keep his social engagements, but he was a miserable villain, he told Kate Perry and her sister, flogged night and day by a cruel tyrant: 'and at my age too—' he wrote round a drawing of a fiendish cupid swishing a bunch of birch twigs—'to be whopped so by a boy!' [15]

He fled from Young Street, from his visiting mother's oppressive concern, and made for Brighton, always his favourite escape-hatch, and discovered that Mrs Brookfield was staying with her brother at Ryde, on the Isle of Wight, two tantalizing hours away. He wrote to her, long, yearning letters. He was pursued, he said, by thoughts of her, Brookfield and the baby, but he claimed to be tranquil at last, pleased even that she and William should have their happiness—and 'a happy marriage'. He angled for an invitation to visit her, told her with what difficulty he had resisted the temptation to jump on a special excursion train that would have taken him and two thousand other Cockneys to her door, and groaned and moaned at the thought of young Harry Hallam joining her a few days later, admitted with the easy passport of cousinship.

As his thirty-eighth birthday approached, he faced it in a mood as restless and dissatisfied as he had met any in his youth. He didn't see that living was such a benefit, he told Jane when she wrote of the illness of a friend, and could find it in his own heart pretty readily to have an end of it all. Sketching Jane's face on the paper which should have borne the next chapters of *Pendennis*, he scored out the unsatisfactory likeness and added some verses comparing all existence to this small artistic failure:

>   . . . What's life but this?—a cancelled sheet
>   A laugh disguising a defeat,
>   Let's tear and laugh and own it so—[16]

But even now Jane tightened her hold on him, telling him at last what he had waited so long to hear: that she loved him.

Shortly afterwards, he was summoned to her side, and settled into the Elton circle with a feeling of fitness Brookfield could never share. They were more like relations than friends, he wrote wistfully to Jane, when, with grim misery, he returned to London and his labours. The Young Street house, empty now, his parents and children gone holidaying to Wales, was no more tempting nor conducive to work than when full of family bustle, and soon he was on his travels once more, this time to Paris, where one of his aunts was dying.

There he learned that he himself had been thought to be dead by his Paris relatives, *Gallignani's Messenger* having reported the demise of another W. M. Thackeray. In fact, two W. Thackerays had died within the previous month, he told Jane: 'There's a glum sort of humour in all this . . . and I grin like a skull'.[17]

The taint of sadness ran through most of his visit. His Aunt Ritchie had been widowed since he had seen her last, and when he went to call upon the once glittering Count d'Orsay, he found him faded and unhappy, living with Lady Blessington's nieces at Chambourcy, thrown on the charity of his sister.

Earlier in the year, Thackeray had attended the sale of Gore House, where d'Orsay and Lady Blessington, that woman of generous heart and equivocal reputation, had gathered in elegant splendour the cream of masculine wit and achievement. Thackeray had contributed to those gatherings, as he had contributed to the velvet-bound *Keepsake* albums Lady Blessington had edited to keep the bailiffs at bay, and the sight of her house crowded with the vulgar, the curious and the feeders on disaster, filled him with dismal fury.

'Brutes keeping their hats on in the kind old drawing-rooms—' he had written. 'I longed to knock some of 'em off: and say Sir be civil in a lady's room'.[18]

Finding one old retainer still at his post, watching over the dismemberment of past glories, undid him, and he slipped the man a pound, an act which earned him a grateful mention when the servant wrote to his former mistress. Thackeray, he said, had had tears in his eyes as he viewed the sale: '*C'est peut etre le seule personne que j'ai vu réellement affecté en votre départ.*'[19]

Now Lady Blessington was dead, her nieces near destitute, and d'Orsay on the verge of madness. But there was to be one pleasant reminder of Gore House for Thackeray on this visit: Prince Louis Napoleon, whom he had met there in its hey-day—and described as looking 'like a courier'—had at last come into his inheritance. As President of France, he graciously invited the famous English author to dine with him at Fontainebleau, a public honour which went some way towards assuaging Thackeray's private grief. Mrs Brookfield, the baronet's daughter, soon to become mother to a humble school inspector's child, was informed of the distinction.

She was also told, with obvious, wicked delight, the serial story of Thackeray's meetings with a French actress. An old friend from art student days, Roger de Beauvoir, an ex-dandy and man of letters, had taken him backstage after the play, introduced him to the green-room, and then, O goodness gracious, into the leading lady's dressing-room. The luscious occupant, her revealing black satin peignoir, the glittering complexion which emerged from beneath her make-up, were described with teasing relish. He had pitched in with a great many compliments of the large and heavy English kind, Thackeray told Jane, and mon Dieu had received an invitation to visit the glorious thespian at her home. Would he go? Mrs Brookfield must wait for the next letter to find out.

And the next letter said yes, he had gone, and in the lady's drawing-room had fired off even stronger compliments, but having elicited from the beauty that she had only one fault in the world, that of having '*trop bon coeur*', he had decided he was, after all, past the age when Fotheringays inflame, and claimed, to Mrs Brookfield at any rate, that the only use he intended to make of the actress, her yellow satin boudoir, and her '*trop bon coeur*' was to put them into a book some day.

He was in equally skittish mood when he met the roly-poly French writer Jules Janin, who delighted and intrigued him by claiming to be always happy, with no knowledge whatever of his own torments—blue devils, repentance, and satiety. Thackeray fed the jolly little man with absurd information about Britain, a joke he continued some years later when Janin visited London. Hoping that the Frenchman was planning to write about the curious English and their ways, he told him then that all the statues in London represented the Duke of Wellington: 'That on the arch opposite Apsley House? the Duke in a cloak, and cocked-hat, on horseback. That behind Apsley House in an airy fig-leaf costume? the Duke again . . .' With the utmost gravity, he showed him a whole army of iron Dukes.[20]

He tried to involve Macaulay, another summer visitor to Paris, in a similar deception. Since they had both been invited to a dinner-party at which they were told there would be an American lady 'whose great desire in life was to meet the Author of Wanaty Fair and Author of the Lays of A. Rome', Thackeray suggested that the popular novelist and the great historian should exchange names and roles for the evening to confuse their joint admirer. But Macaulay would have nothing to do with the plan. He did not, he said solemnly, approve of practical jokes.

The picture of the jester with a melancholy face behind the grinning mask, which Thackeray was to use so often in his books, was drawn from intimate knowledge, and never was it more appropriate than on this trip to France. Restless, sore at heart, he cracked his jokes and won a pleasant sense of self-denial and duty done by his attentions to sad relatives. He even climbed a hundred stairs to Bess Hamerton's apartment, to make his peace with the garrulous Irishwoman who had so disrupted Young Street, but the grin on the mask itself became a ghastly shadow when he went to see that prosperous puller of teeth and disposer of dubious artistical gems, Augustus Stevens.

The dentist had married—an attractive, adoring little wife, who reminded Thackeray of Isabella; and they had just had a baby, which made him think of someone else. '. . . the tones of a mother's voice speaking to an infant play the deuce with me somehow—' he wrote to Mrs Brookfield; 'that charming nonsense and tenderness work upon me, until I feel like a woman or a great big baby myself fiddledydee—'[21]

His old friend's happiness was a painful reminder of all he had lost, and was unlikely ever to regain.

A cholera epidemic was sweeping the French capital while Thackeray was there, and as soon as he returned to London he was struck by a severe bilious fever. With the Carmichael-Smyths and his daughters still deep in inaccessible Wales, he took to his bed, and, used as he was to internal troubles, waited for this one to subside. But worn down with anguish over Jane's coming maternity, suffering morbid presentiments following the sudden, tragically early death of Charles Buller, he was in poor shape for the contest. Within a week the illness became critical, and for seventeen days, nourished only by an occasional glass of *eau sucrée*, he rallied and relapsed, was bled and blistered, while the doctors fighting for his life feared that even if he survived the fever his old complaint, the stricture, might flare up again and put an end to the struggle.

Young Harry Hallam, his youthful anger at Thackeray's attentions to Jane long forgotten, was the first to come to his aid. Only a few months earlier, he had amused Thackeray by the artful ploy of saying nice things about him to the Elliots, knowing perfectly well that those ladies would pass them on. Now, the gentle young lawyer organized the Young Street household, lending a Hallam servant to augment Thackeray's own, and alerted Bradbury and Evans to the likelihood of a delay in the monthly numbers of *Pendennis*.

Brookfield also took a turn in the sick-room when his inspectoral duties allowed, and the two Janes, Brookfield and Elliot, hovered over the patient, their kind, worried faces to be long remembered as they appeared to him in his semi-consciousness. But of all people it was John Forster who probably saved his life. This fiery friend-and-foe, alarmed at Thackeray's condition, insisted on bringing in his own medical man, and Thackeray, in dedicating *Pendennis* to Dr John Elliotson, attributed his recovery to this genial philanthropist's constant watchfulness and skill—and to the friend who had brought him to his bedside.

In future years, whenever Forster was ill, Thackeray remembered this debt, and, though he knew they would feud again as soon as the irascible Northcountryman was back on his feet, did his best to repay it. There is a nice glimpse in one of Thackeray's letters of Elliotson grinning knowingly from his carriage as the two men crossed paths outside Forster's Lincoln's Inn chambers—the doctor just leaving his rheumaticky patient, Thackeray sheepishly on his way to cheer him up. On another occasion, a few months after his own illness, seeing Elliotson thundering through Hyde Park, drawn by his great horses, Thackeray caught up with him on his gallant little cob, and shook hands and chatted through the doctor's carriage window—all at a capital pace.

Even if Thackeray had not sometimes called Elliotson 'Dr Goodenough', it would be easy to see that here was the real-life counterpart of the understanding practitioner on hearts as well as bodies, who made his début in *Pendennis* when Thackeray was well enough to write again. The generous-hearted fictional doctor, who laughed at the idea of taking a fee from a literary man, just as Elliotson refused money for saving Thackeray's life, is an even handsomer tribute than the dedication at the front of the book.

On Thackeray's instructions, Mrs Brookfield had not immediately summoned Mrs Carmichael-Smyth at the onset of the fever. She was a fidget in a sick-room, he said. But as soon as she was informed, she bundled the Major and her granddaughters into a coach and set off for London in desperate fear for her only child.

At Monmouth, as they rode through the town, the bells were tolling and a black-clad population streamed into the churches for a day of solemn prayer for deliverance from the cholera, which was now spreading through Britain too, and that night, unable to bear the slow pace of a family party any longer, the distracted matron took off alone by swifter transport. Her arrival at Young Street can be imagined from the description of Mrs Pendennis's appearance at her delirious child's London chambers: the haggard-eyed mother, sweeping in, Bible in hand, to take possession of her son.

'Oh how like Granny is to Mrs Pendennis, Papa,' said Annie, when that book was eventually finished.

'Yes,' replied her father, 'and Granny is mighty angry that I should think no better of her than that.'[22]

Despite Thackeray's assurances that it was only Mrs Carmichael-Smyth's figure-head which was awful—'her guns are never shotted'[23]—Mrs Brookfield had long been frightened of this Mater Dolorosa, with a heart bleeding with love, as Thackeray thought of both Mrs Pendennis and her model; and Mrs Carmichael-Smyth had her own reasons for fearing Jane. She let Mrs Brookfield take Annie and Minnie to Portman Street until the risk of infection was over, but even so the confrontation of the two women over the wasted, wan-eyed body of son and would-be lover cannot have been pleasant to witness, and the presence now at Thackeray's bedside of such an intense, humourless, possessive guardian did not promise a comfortable convalescence.

There was a complaint, he wrote a few months later, which when exhibited in women, neither poppy, nor mandragora, nor all the drowsy syrups of the East could allay—neither homœopathy, nor hydropathy, nor mesmerism cure. And so, within a week of his jealous mother's arrival, Thackeray took to his stick-like legs and absconded to Brighton, leaving Mrs Carmichael-Smyth to contract a passion for that last-named medical wonder from Dr Elliotson and to bombard him and his friends with pamphlets on the subject.

The precise nature of Thackeray's illness is still not certain. 'If it has been Cholera, he has no idea of it himself, but calls it a liver attack,' Brookfield wrote to Harry Hallam in one of the deceptive lulls at the beginning of the fever,[24] and Thackeray himself looked back on it, with that almost mystical Victorian aversion to naming the enemy, as the time when he was 'all but gone.' But whatever it was, it left him weak enough to need a bathchair, and convalescence proved a long, glum business.

Even his cheerful, untiring manservant, John, who had watched night after night by his master's bedside, began to fall to pieces when the crisis was over. There were days when his step was unsure, his voice a little thick, his laugh a trifle queer, and, as he prepared to administer Dr Elliotson's prescribed quinine, his hand so unsteady that instead of placing the glass to the patient's mouth, he struck him sharply in the eye with it.

'Drinking?' Thackeray would suggest, as his assailant retreated from the room, clinging to the back of a chair.

And there were other days when he stirred a convalescent wrath by demanding payment for seventeen pounds of sugar which he swore Thackeray had consumed at the height of his fever.

Nevertheless, not-quite-honest John was always there to push his master's bathchair on his morning outings, and canny enough to anchor it alongside the prettiest female convalescent on the chain-pier. And with the gentle stimulant of these invalid *tête-à-têtes*, fresh sea breezes and restorative sea-water baths, 'Dr Brighton' presently worked his cure.

When Harry Hallam arrived at the end of October, he found the patient tackling mutton chops with renewed gusto and ready for a strong young arm to lean on as he rose from his chair to take his first walk. After that it was only a matter of hours before the sight of a blank sheet of paper set him thinking it would be good to write again.

16

Pendennis

Out of the shadow of death

Many friends, knowing Thackeray's income was spent as soon as it was made, pressed money on him so that he could delay his labours, the immense Higgins offering to support him for a year if he cared to lie fallow that long. Thackeray declined them all. Having so recently fought his way out of the worst of his debts he had no wish to return to that particular treadmill. He also knew that for him work was the best remedy of all—the only way to temper his urge to hanker after vain desires. So, draped like Mrs Brookfield on a sofa, instructed by Dr Elliotson on no account to put pen to paper, he set to work on a Christmas book.

His three previous seasonal offerings had been little more than collections of character sketches, equally balanced between text and illustrations, bound together by the presence of Mr Michael Angelo Titmarsh, a short-legged version of Thackeray himself. Mr Titmarsh, like his creator, surveyed the world through a pair of absurdly small spectacles which were nevertheless peculiarly clear-sighted. He pointed out both good and bad with gently satirical humour, fell hopelessly and unsuitably in love, and was constantly having to bind up his poor old wounded heart as he watched the sweet young creatures it beat for swept off by hulking great blond-whiskered military bucks or dapper little dandies in varnished boots. Like Thackeray, Mr Titmarsh found as much to laugh at in himself as in others.

But even in these small books, with their innocent white bindings, the social comment was sharp as well as humorous—the Member of

Parliament, Jolly Newboy, Esq., in *Our Street*, was compared, perhaps a little rashly, with Machiavelli by *Douglas Jerrold's Weekly*—and there were also some characteristically unseasonal touches.

Mrs Stafford Molyneux, 'the lady whom nobody knows', another, fleeting, inhabitant of *Our Street*, gained Thackeray unexpected praise from *The Times*, though her luxurious lifestyle, painted beauty and masculine company, brought squeals of horror from many of his feminine readers.

The following year, in *Dr Birch and his Young Friends*, the sad shadow was cast by a poor idiot nephew of Becky Sharp's wicked old Marquis of Steyne, the gentle Plantagenet Gaunt Gaunt, and by its final wise and melancholy poem which mourns the sudden death of Charles Buller, verses written after Thackeray returned as an honoured guest to his own brutal old school's Founder's Day and heard himself elaborately praised in the speech of one of the governors, Sir Robert Peel.

For Christmas 1849, this episodic pattern was broken. Not strong enough to tackle both story and illustrations, Thackeray signed up young Dicky Doyle of *Punch* for the artwork and turned to an idea he had had in mind for twenty-five years, ever since he had first fallen in love, at the age of thirteen, with Sir Walter Scott's Rebecca, the dark-eyed daughter of Isaac of York. He would write a sequel to *Ivanhoe*, a middle-aged novel, in which *his* heroine, beautiful, tender and heroic, would be righted at last and win Ivanhoe from that frigid piece of propriety, that infuriatingly faultless, icily prim, 'niminy-piminy' Rowena. He had the bones of the tale already to hand in an article he had written for *Fraser's* three years earlier, and on this he built a delightful fantasy.

He couldn't deny that Sir Wilfred of Ivanhoe had married Rowena, but with the story now in his own hands, Thackeray made sure that there was to be no living happily ever after about the union. His Rowena was a most uncomfortable mate, a jealous, pious humbug, forever rolling her china-blue eyes towards heaven and harping on Sir Wilfred's having been *'locked up with the Jewess in the tower'*, or, adopting saccarine sweet sarcasm, exclaiming: 'Ivanhoe my dear, more persecution for the Jews! Hadn't you better interfere, my love? . . . the Jews were *always such favourites of yours.'*

Robin Hood fared little better. Now the eminently respectable Earl of Huntingdon, Thackeray made him so fat he needed a horse as strong as an elephant to mount him, and a magistrate so conscientious that local poachers trembled at his name. As in his earlier *Legend of the Rhine,* there was plenty of fun and a great deal of good-natured debunking of the conventions of historical romance, but *Rebecca and Rowena* also contains darker undercurrents of convalescent sadness.

'I have ridden in a caïque upon the waters of the Bospherus,' he wrote, 'and looked upon the capital of the Soldan of Turkey. As seen from those blue waters, with palace and pinnacle, with gilded dome and towering cypress, it seemeth a very Paradise of Mahound: but, enter the city, and it is but a beggarly labyrinth of rickety huts and dirty alleys, where the ways are steep and the smells are foul, tenanted by mangy dogs and ragged beggars—a dismal illusion! Life is such, ah, well-a-day! It is only hope which is real, and reality is a bitterness and a deceit.'[1]

Thackeray himself said he had walked in the Valley of the Shadow of Death, and one wonders if he had strayed even further, into those golden halls which we are now told are seen by the almost dead, and tasted the peace of paradise. It seems that perhaps he had, for when his ageing Ivanhoe (the 'Knight of the Spectacles') is nursed back to life, he is not greatly pleased with the miracle, and just as he had not been made content by his first marriage, so Thackeray did not think he would be very boisterously happy when he finally won Rebecca. 'Of some sort of happiness,' he wrote, 'melancholy is a characteristic.'

There was one more delayed job to finish before he could give his whole-hearted attention once more to *Pendennis*, an enterprise he had started to help Louis Marvy, the gifted engraver whose bread, cheese and threadbare domestic happiness he had so often shared in Paris in the grim days when Isabella first went to Esquirol's *Maison de Santé*. As a refugee from the political unheavals that had put Prince Louis Napoleon into power, Marvy had found a ready welcome at Young Street. When he first arrived, Thackeray had insisted he should stay with him through the winter, put the plates for *Dr Birch* into his care, and set about finding a project which would not only keep the industrious Frenchman occupied and alive, but give a boost to his superior process of engraving.

In the months before his illness, he had persuaded several leading artists and collectors to let Marvy copy their works for a volume of *Sketches after English Landscape Painters*, and a printseller, scenting a *coup*, had agreed to publish it if Thackeray supplied a text. This was the job, detailed, time-consuming, with his own share of the profits uncertain, that awaited him in convalescence, and to help him get through it he put another insolvent young friend on his pay-roll: Eyre Crowe, eldest son of his *Morning Chronicle* mentor, a trained painter without customers.

Thackeray set young Crowe researching and as soon as he

returned from Brighton called him to his Young Street bedside with plates and notes for early morning sessions to polish off the 'dem bugbear'. Propped up on pillows, 'whiffing', as Crowe called it, his first cigar of the day, Thackeray dictated. His contribution, however, was destined to help not Marvy, who died in Paris, at the age of thirty-five, a few months later, but Marvy's young widow, who became yet another of Thackeray's pensioners. As Trollope was to write, he was a man who liked to broaden his back for the support of others.

Pendennis, the book Annie said was more like hearing her father talk than any of his other works, had reached roughly the half-way stage when Thackeray's own near-fatal illness struck, and since, as usual, he had been scrambling to meet each deadline, no yellow-covered instalments appeared during the last three months of 1849.

Delving back into his childhood and youth for this loosely autobiographical novel, he regarded Arthur Pendennis as a fond self-portrait, so true to his own image of himself that some years later, leafing through a copy in a New York drawing-room, he was to smile and exclaim how like it was.

'Like whom, Mr Thackeray?' he was asked.

'Oh, like me, to be sure; Pendennis is very like me.'

'Surely not, Pendennis was so weak!'

'Ah well, Mrs Baxter,' said Thackeray, with a shrug of his great shoulders and a comical look, 'your humble servant is not very strong.'[2]

Many other friends failed to see a resemblance between the author they knew and the pert, dandified young goose he endowed with a few additional talents and almost the same capacity for falling into temptation. Like the imperious Lady Rockminster, they preferred Pendennis' older, wiser and more battered friend, George Warrington, and imagined that here was the revelation of Thackeray in middle age. But while he was writing, Thackeray himself had other candidates in mind for Warrington's original.

Like most novelists, he created his characters from a wide range of well-digested observations and stored knowledge—scraps, heel-taps and odds and ends, he called them—and was often to be astonished by the independence they showed once he had formed them: 'The personage does or says something, and I ask, how the dickens did he come to think of that?'[3]

Occasionally, having invented such a figment, he later met the composite man, living, breathing, exact in every important detail, as he and Brookfield met Captain Costigan in a tavern parlour, long after the tipsy Irishman had appeared in print, and as, in New York, he was to come upon Beatrix Esmond. When he thought he was describing a specific person, however, Thackeray was unusually keen to acknowledge his indebtedness.

He told George Morland Crawford, like Warrington a barrister and journalist, that he had contributed to the character, and admitted that Venables' true life-story had supplied him with the details for Warrington's confession of the early folly that had blighted his life: the marriage into which he had been lured at eighteen by a cunning labouring family, leaving him inextricably bound to an illiterate woman older than himself, and the knowledge that if ever he made a name in the world, she and his children would come out of the past to claim a share of his fame and riches, just as surely as they had been bribed with his patrimony to stay in obscurity. And from Lady Ashburton's description of Venables entering every drawing-room as though he were Prometheus preparing to defy the vulture, it is clear this was not all Thackeray borrowed from his old Charterhouse sparring partner.

There were other faces in *Pendennis* Thackeray expected his intimates to recognize, too, most notably that of Andrew Arcadeckne, a tubby little man about town, 'a genuine low-comedian off the stage',[4] who appeared, in part, as the 'downy' young Harry Foker. Arcadeckne himself laid proud claim to the connection, though he also felt he 'owed Thackeray one' for having used him in this way, and delighted in settling the score by tormenting him at the Garrick Club.

'Hallo! Thack my boy! gettin' inspiration, eh?' Arcadeckne would grate in his nasal voice, as Thackeray stood before the smoking-room fire, his mind engrossed in solving some problem in the manuscript tucked into the pockets he was warming. Having ruined his concentration, Arcadeckne would then dart out of the room before Thackeray had time to retaliate.

At other times, he waited until Thackeray had sunk into an armchair with a contemplative cigar, his head thrown back, one leg crossed over the other, the sole of his boot well exposed, a sole on which Arcadeckne, as though obeying some irrepressible impulse, would strike a match to light his own cigar, before limping off again as fast as his gout would let him.

'Awfully good chap was old Thack,' said Arcadeckne when his victim was no longer there to tease. 'Lor' bless you, he didn't mind me a bit. But I *did* take it out of him now and again. Never gave him time for a repartee.'[5]

Giving his books to the public in monthly instalments, Thackeray was subjected to this kind of cheerful abuse all the time he was writing, and to much advice, too, on how the story should continue.

There were ladies who pleaded that Warrington should be allowed to marry Laura, but on the other hand made it clear they did not think Pendennis quite bad enough to deserve Blanche Amory. There were other ladies who cried out and refused to read another word when he described Pen's passion for Fanny Bolton, even though he fought it with unlikely resolution.

'Since the author of Tom Jones was buried, no writer of fiction among us has been permitted to depict to his utmost power a man,' Thackeray wrote in the preface to the bound edition. 'We must drape him, and give him a certain conventional simper. Society will not tolerate the Natural in our Art. Many ladies have remonstrated and subscribers left me, because in the course of the story, I described a young man resisting and affected by temptation. My object was to say, that he had the passions to feel, and the manliness and generosity to overcome them. You will not hear—it is best to know it—what moves in the real world, that passes in society, in the clubs, colleges and mess-rooms,—what is the life and talk of your sons.'

It was this last element, his audience's personal identification with his stories and characters, which was the main cause of Thackeray's trouble. Victorian readers were not averse to the truth, so long as it didn't hit home. In the also autobiographical *David Copperfield*, which began to appear six months after the first number of *Pendennis*, Dickens made Steerforth behave far worse than poor Pen, but, as a reviewer in the *Scotsman* pointed out, he got away with it by enveloping that seducer's career in 'a cloud of sentiment, fancy, and fine writing.' (And, since Steerforth was only a subsidiary character, he could also be punished with the obligatory nasty end.) It was Thackeray's very excellence as a delineator of modern life and manners, said the *Scotsman*, which imposed on him special limitations.[6]

In his own family, and from his very youngest critic, Thackeray met with the same problem. When he killed off Mrs Pendennis, ten-year-old Minnie pleaded: 'O! papa, do make her well again; she can have a regular doctor and be almost dead, and then will come a homœopathic physician who will make her well you know.'[7]

Now that he was famous, every word he wrote was scrutinized, and deeply sinister meanings were discovered by those who wished to find them. The Irish, still raw from his early assaults on their glorious land, were particularly assiduous in seeking out gibes which had not been intended, as they did in the same controversial number that introduced Fanny Bolton.

In a casual reference to criminals and tyrants, later deleted, Thackeray mentioned Catherine Hayes, the *Newgate Calendar* murderess who had featured in his early crusading story for *Fraser's*, forgetting or unaware that there was another quite uncriminal lady of the same name then living, an Irish soprano who, unhappily, was appearing in London when the number was published.

The Irish press leapt to the defence of their countrywoman, Dublin's *Freeman's Journal* leading the way with an article satirically entitled *The Age of Chivalry—Mr. Thackeray!!!* in which they called him 'Big Blubber man . . . the hugest humbug ever thrust on the public', and saw a malicious plot to ruin the singer's career in this latest example of 'those rank exhalations which rise up betimes from the fetid lamp of Mr. Thackeray's genius'.[8]

A question was asked in Parliament, and threats were made to Thackeray's personal safety. One Mr Briggs, also of Dublin, informed him that a company of young Irishmen, determined to chastise him for this and other insults of an equally serious nature, planned to come over to London one by one until they had completed the job. Mr Briggs himself, forerunner of this army, had already taken lodgings opposite Thackeray's home and awaited a meeting.

The following day a cheerful, stout detective, in an alarming mustard-coloured coat, established himself in the bow-window of 13 Young Street, to protect the premises and their owner. By lunchtime, however, when the policeman descended to the lower regions for his dinner, Thackeray decided he could stand the ridiculous situation no longer. He had invited a Scottish artist and young Eyre Crowe to eat with him, and leaving them on guard, he armed himself with a light rattan stick for use in the direst emergency, and strode across the road for a confrontation.

The Scot, Alexander Christie, usually peaceable headmaster of the Edinburgh School of Design, peeled off his coat, rolled up his shirt-sleeves, and flexed what Eyre Crowe was relieved to note were a fine pair of biceps. Crowe, with less relish, followed his example. Annie held her breath. For twenty minutes they waited, then Thackeray returned, with the matter amicably settled—and a Chippendale chair, assessed during the course of his conversation and bought from the Irishman's landlady.

The English papers and literary journals kept a generally more benign eye on the progress of *Pendennis*, but they too were always ready to pounce, and Thackeray, still convalescent, found himself embroiled in yet another 'dignity-of-literature' skirmish just as he was trying to start up again in a particularly brilliant manner to recapture his audience and compete with Dickens, who had not only had the market to himself for so long but also, thought Thackeray, greatly improved his style, along the lines of a certain rival.

The *Morning Chronicle* and the *Examiner*, engaged in a verbal battle over the propriety of literary men being awarded public honours, used parts of *Pendennis* to illustrate their opposing views, neither of them kindly. Both were angry at his description of the snobbish, banal literary dinner-party, Pen's first introduction to such delights, and Warrington's question after it: 'And now that you have seen the men of letters, tell me was I far wrong in saying that there are thousands of people in this town, who don't write books, who are, to the full, as clever and intellectual as people who do?'[9]

This heresy, together with Thackeray's assertion in a later chapter, that writing was a trade like any other and that men of letters, 'and what is called genius', should be no more exempt from the ordinary duties of daily life than their neighbours, had Forster accusing him in the *Examiner* of 'fostering a baneful prejudice' against literary men, and 'condescending to caricature (as is too often his habit) his literary fellow-labourers in order to pay court to the non-literary class'.[10]

Thackeray had spiced his dinner-party scene with several recognizable portraits—notably Theodore Hook and John Wilson Croker as Wagg and Wenham, and Dr Maginn as the brilliant, tipsy Captain Shandon—but to say that he had done so to flatter non-writers was patently absurd. However, if Forster still smarted at the thought of Thackeray's more personal caricatures, Thackeray was as ready as ever to rise when he thought his honour was under attack. Gobbling bait, hook and line, he defended himself in a long, long letter to the *Morning Chronicle*, agreeing with Forster on the initial issue, that pensions, ribbons and titles were as good for writers as for anyone else and should be readily accepted whenever offered, and then tackling at length the subsidiary charges.

If he stooped to flatter anybody's prejudice for some interested motives of his own, he pointed out, he was no less than a rogue and a cheat—and a fool too, since he had never found that 'that considerable body of our countrymen described by the Examiner "as the non-literary class" has the least gratification in witnessing the degradation or disparagement of literary men.'

It would be best, he suggested, for men of letters silently to assume that they were as good as any other gentlemen, and to be less ready to see insults where none were intended. But that did not mean they were all saints, who could not be discussed or joked about like the members of other professions.

'I never heard the Bar felt itself aggrieved because *Punch* chose to describe Mr. Dunup's notorious state of insolvency, or that the picture of Stiggins in "Pickwick" was intended as an insult to all Dissenters . . .' he wrote, 'are we to be passed over because we are faultless, or because we cannot afford to be laughed at?'[11]

Having made this detailed defence of himself, Thackeray characteristically came round to his critics' point of view, and a few days later told Abraham Hayward that Warrington's words were 'untenable be hanged to them: but they were meant to apply to a particular class of literary men, *my* class who are the most ignorant men under the Sun, myself included.'[12] And in his next number he made a curious act of contrition, laughing at *Pendennis* under the guise of Pen's autobiographical *opus*, and having Warrington tell him he was a humbug for selling his feelings for money.

The affair was still in his mind nearly a year later when he wrote the preface and spoke there of the very nature of serial writing encouraging honesty in an author. The monthly instalments were, he wrote, like a confidential talk between writer and reader, in which he was forced into frankness of expression, and to speaking out his own mind and feelings as they urged him.

Thackeray became famous—or infamous—for this quality of direct communication. '. . . perhaps of all the novel-spinners now extant,' he admitted late in life, 'the present speaker is the most addicted to preaching. Does he not stop perpetually in his story and begin to preach to you? When he ought to be engaged with business, is he not forever taking the Muse by the sleeve, and plaguing her with some of his cynical sermons?'[13]

Most of Thackeray's own views, passions and doubts are clearly set out in his books for all who know something of his life to recognize. The classic Chapter Sixty-One of *Pendennis*, with its great debate on the human predicament, reflects the scourges he had been using on himself for several years, and though he was careful to put the words into Arthur Pendennis's mouth, not in a preaching aside, his religious scepticism, tirade against dogma, and support of both Newman brothers—John, who had just turned to Rome and was to become a cardinal, and Francis, who advocated intellectual pantheism—was a dangerous display of free-thinking in a land which had recently seen rioting against the re-establishment of Catholic bishops, the first in Britain for three hundred years, and where an Anglican churchman could lose all hope of promotion by questioning a word of the Bible—as Brookfield did.

Six years later, when Brookfield said from the pulpit that it was not absolutely necessary to salvation to believe that Christ was tempted by the conventional physical Devil, Lord Shaftesbury rose from his pew and left the church.

'We can't make Brookfield a Bishop,' he warned Lord Palmerston. 'It's impossible, *the man's a Freethinker.*'[14]

Mrs Brookfield, staying with the Ashburtons at The Grange,

urged her husband to join her immediately: 'Lady A. says the cart
for heretics shall meet you any time you like . . . and she hopes you
won't risk your Inspectorship in the vain attempt to drive common
sense into fashionable heads.'[15]

Thackeray also debated whether he should risk his livelihood in
such a cause, and decided that his 'lazy epicurean nature' was not
made for martyrdom. *Pendennis* was to be the last book in which he
discussed his doubts at any length.

2.

Thackeray's love for Mrs Brookfield is built into the very fabric of
Pendennis, as he discovered himself when he reread the first thirty
chapters or so, after his illness, to remind himself what it was all
about.

'I remembered allusions w^h called back recollections of particular
states of mind,' he told Jane. 'The first part of that book was written
after Clevedon in '48—que de souffrances!'[1]

It was in those early chapters that he wrote 'It is best to love
wisely, no doubt; but to love foolishly is better than not to be able to
love at all,' thus beating Tennyson to ''Tis better to have loved and
lost than never to have loved at all,' a sentiment Mrs Brookfield
pointed out to him in *In Memoriam*, though she had not commented
on his own version.

A year later, while he was reliving his post-Clevedon sufferings in
the Fanny Bolton episode, he claimed to Jane that his emotions were
under control: 'I am an extinct crater and my volcano is poked
out.'[2] It was not true. The flames still kindled and flared uncomfortably hot at times, but the lassitude and minor disorders
which followed his illness, and the birth of Jane's child in February
1850, tempered the terrible torment of unfulfilled desire, forcing
him to review the relationship.

Throughout the heart-searching, miserable or happy, ill or well,
near Jane or missing her, he continued to write, often at a punishing
pace, and *Pendennis* reflects the progress from the first ebullient
springtime of their understanding, to the resigned acceptance of
autumn's fading bounty.

Pausing one day in his work, his hand weary with the latest
chapter, his head boiling up with some nonsense that had to be
written for *Punch* after dinner, Annie and Minnie waiting to be
taken for a walk, he asked Jane: 'Isn't it strange that, in the midst of
all the selfishnesses, that one, of doing one's business, is the
strongest of all? What funny songs Ive written when fit to hang
myself! To day I read a bit w^h was done when I thought you were

lying in—early one grey morning, but that's solemn & pretty. You said it was,—about "the child to be born into the world & take it's part . . . in the suffering and struggling, the tears and laughter, the crime, remorse, love, folly, sorrow, rest . . ."'[3]

On the day Mrs Brookfield did give birth to that first child, Thackeray was at Portman Street a quarter of an hour before the event. It was a daughter—Magdalene, as the clergyman called her, with typical disregard for convention—and Thackeray received the news later in the day in a brief note from her father: 'It's a wench & came at 12.30 P.M. this day. Both seem well.'

Thackeray sent equally crisp congratulations, and a tender letter to Miss Brookfield, telling her that he would like her always to remember that he was very fond of her dear mother, and that he and her Papa were very good friends, helping each other as occasion served through life.

Two days later, he had a brief audience with Brookfield and Mrs Fanshawe, who had come up from Southampton to run the household. He would have liked to have seen the baby, but it was not produced, and though he listened for cries from the nursery, Magdalene did not oblige. After that, the door closed on him. Brookfield, morbidly afraid of showing his feelings, intent, perhaps, on a new start to his marriage, wanted no visitors. Thackeray and his faithful brown cob haunted the area for a week, then 'sick of waiting outside a certain door in P-rtm-n St,' as he told Kate Perry and her sister, he took off in a huff for Paris, trying to get his wounds healed, being 'tolerably gay and very unhappy.'[4]

As he couldn't see her and wasn't allowed to visit little 'Pincushion' Fanshawe, he might as well not be in London, he grumbled to Jane: 'but don't fancy that I am come here to forget you, quite the reverse—the chain pulls tighter the farther I am away from you. and I don't want to break it, or to be other than my dear sisters most faithful Makepeace to command.'[5]

Jane also clung to that chain. Sitting up in bed a few days after Magdalene's birth, she once more threw herself upon his pity:

'I long so much to see you again—' she wrote, '& feel idiotic whenever I deliberately get into a train of thought about you, now that I am so weak it always makes me cry to think over all your goodness to me, & I have to make a vigorous effort to be quiet again.'[6]

But he should not have said that her husband had shut the door on him, she chided, as though the Portman Street ban applied to no one else: 'you hardly know yet, how W^m dislikes to betray any real feeling, whether painful or otherwise—he is naturally so reserved that it w^d be peculiarly trying to him to be *seen*, if he was feeling at all excited or anxious . . . I believe in a few days time he w^d have taken it quite as a matter of course that you sh^d be here—tho' not to be admitted *upstairs*, so that *I* am not the loser by your being at Paris now.'[7]

Three weeks later, however, when Thackeray returned and Jane had descended to the drawing-room, the door was still barred to him. Mrs Carmichael-Smyth was admitted, but not her eager son. Once more he haunted the area, and wrote notes in every style he knew—hurt, humorous, pleading—but his hints brought no reprieve. He was not invited to the christening, and as soon as Mrs Brookfield was well enough to travel, she and the baby moved to Clevedon for many weeks.

'Ah I should like to be with you for an hour or two,' Thackeray told her, 'and see if you're changed and oldened in this immense time that you have been away. But business and pleasure (likewise expediency & the not being asked) keep me here nailed.'[8]

From Clevedon she drifted to Southampton, to her trusted Dr Bullar, and even during the few weeks she was in town in the spring and summer, Thackeray saw little of her. Having howled and moped and tried to reassert his brotherly claims, he at last took warning from the prolonged exile, and, when the embargo was eventually lifted, did his best to honour the clergyman's marital and parental position. His letters, though still loving, were less emotional. Duty, and cheerfulness, not passion, were what he now urged on Jane.

But Jane was no healthier nor happier after achieving her 'nine years' dream' of motherhood than she had been before, and Brookfield was no more companionable. The merry jester at a thousand feasts, the black-coated consoler, who for so many soothed away all fear of dying, could not compassionate his wife, and she, it seems, no longer expected him to.

It was to Thackeray she wrote of her weakness and fears. To her husband her letters were brisk, cheerful, matronly, as though Brookfield had been relegated to the nursery along with little Magdalene—someone else's child who had to be considered and who occasionally gave pleasure. Even when she recalled the devotion she had once given him, the love that was still his if only he knew how to cherish it, she did so in a manner that smacked of a rap on the knuckles rather than the desperation of a breaking heart:

'I have been spending part of today with the Fanshawes', she told him in the summer of 1850, '& reading "In Memoriam" and applying some of it to you, my boy—

> These two—they dwelt with eye on eye
> Their hearts of old have beat in tune
> &c—

Their love has never past away
The days she never can forget
Are earnest that he loves her yet

Her life is lone: he sits apart
    He loves her yet, she will not weep
Tho' wrapt in matters dark & deep
    He seems to slight her simple heart.

He seems so near, & yet so far
He looks so cold, she thinks him kind. . . .
Her faith is fix'd & cannot move
She darkly feels him great & wise

She dwells on him with faithful eyes
I cannot understand: I love—

'Are they not very beautiful?' she asked, and then almost immediately, with no tremor in transition, ran on: 'I heard from M^r
Thackeray proposing that the children & their Governess should join
in taking lodgings & keeping house here, as they would be all better
for change of air, & he w^d like me to know them better—but I have
said in answer that nothing is yet decided, & I fancy you w^d feel
rather bored by the Governess however much she might stick to her
Schoolroom—& I daresay he will be flown off to Scotland, or Russia
or Switzerland before *we* have had time to discuss whether it w^d do
or not.'[9]

The scheme, nevertheless, was put into effect. Mrs Brookfield
took a house at Carlton Crescent, Southampton, large enough for
both families. Brookfield went off on his summer cruise, and
Thackeray flew nowhere but to Jane's side. Having accompanied
Annie, Minnie and the latest governess to see them settled, he
established himself in the nearby Dolphin Inn, where he stayed, and
stayed, and stayed. For what else did he care in all the world, he
cried, let it be known from China to Peru, but his children and his
dear lady.

'Contrary to what might be expected,' Jane wrote to Brookfield
two weeks later, 'Mr Thackeray is still at the Dolphin having got into
his new number & working hard at it.'[10]

Despite his disapproval of Mrs Brookfield's unpunctuality and
less than perfect housekeeping, it was an idyll Thackeray was never
to forget.

'I wonder whether ever again I shall have such a happy peaceful
fortnight as that last?' he asked Jane when he returned to London.
'How sunshiny the landscape remains in my mind, I hope for
always, and the smiles of dear children and the aspect of the kindest

and tenderest face in the world to me. God bless you God bless you my sister. I know what you'll do when you read this—well, so am I. I can hardly see as I write for the eye-water. But its not with grief: but for the natural pathos of the thing. How happy your dear regard makes me! How it takes off the solitude and eases it. May it continue pray God till your head is as white as mine, and our children have children of their own. O Love and Duty—I hope you'll never leave us quite . . .'[11]

On the train back to town, he had found the tarnished young beauty Cecilia Gore, daughter of the society authoress, who informed him that she was Blanche Amory. '. . . and I think she is Blanche Amory,' Thackeray told Mrs Brookfield, 'amiable (at times) amusing, clever and depraved.'[12]

They had talked and 'persifflated' all the way to London, and the meeting, he said, would help him to a good chapter, in which Pen and Blanche would play at being in love—a wicked, false, humbugging love such as two *blasés* Londoners might indulge in and deceive themselves they were in earnest. It would complete the cycle of Pendennis's worldly experiences, and after that he would try to make a good man of him.

Thackeray did exactly that, and rewarded young Pen with Laura, but the puppet-master himself was becoming resigned to the belief that fate had no such gift in store for him. Southampton, that taste of life as it might have been, was followed by further attempts at honourable restraint, and more melancholy letters from Jane, and though he comforted her and shared her woe—'what can we do better than our best either of us?'—it was in a mood of partial surrender that he finished *Pendennis*.

If he could not have Jane himself, he wished to think of her content. And so, writing in bed early one November morning as the sun walked into his room, he ended the final chapter with an idealized version of his tripartite agreement with the clergyman and his lady.

Pendennis (in this instance standing for Brookfield), was to be happy in his marriage with Laura who, seeing his faults and wayward moods, owning that there were better men in the world, would nevertheless love him with constant affection. Whilst George Warrington, who had also yearned for her, would remain their friend, go through the part of godpapa perfectly, and live alone, entirely heart-whole, since the malady of love had never yet proved fatal to a sound organ.

'I think [it] means', he told Jane, 'a benediction upon W^m and your child and my dear lady.'[13]

17

The Lecturer

And a scandal: Thackeray and Charlotte Brontë

As soon as Thackeray gained success as a novelist, he began to wonder how long it would last, and to look around for a secondary job with a more reliable income to fall back on when he ran out of readers, stories or stamina, a search which became more determined after his *Pendennis* illness.

He was often to be criticized for not showing enough respect either to his work or his readers, for the slipshod habits which led in later years to curious phenomena, such as the strategic death of Lord Farintosh's mother in one chapter of *The Newcomes* and her miraculous reappearance some pages later. Even Trollope, knowing, loving, and admiring him, believing his books to excel most written precepts, chided him for not putting his best foot foremost, for shirking the 'elbow-grease of the mind'[1]—for not being like himself, a disciplined, sturdy, two-thousand-five-hundred-words-before-breakfast man.

Thackeray himself admitted most of the charges. Though his brain was physically vast he had no illusions about his intellectual capacity, claiming rather that he had no head at all above his eyes. Detailed plotting was beyond him and he wrote with envy and wonder of Alexandre Dumas who lay silent for days on the deck of his Mediterranean yacht, planning unalterably the course of his novels before ever he put pen to paper.

His own Pegasus, he said, wouldn't fly so as to give him such a good view of the landscape: 'He has no wings, he is blind of one eye certainly, he is restive, stubborn, slow; crops a hedge when he ought to be galloping, or gallops when he ought to be quiet. He never will show off when I want him. Sometimes he goes at a pace which surprises me. Sometimes, when I wish him to make the running, the brute turns restive, and I am obliged to let him take his own time.'[2]

He still needed a deadline before he put the animal into harness at all, and many a night, after dining at one house and drinking tea at another, was to be found at the Garrick, settling down to work at eleven-thirty, filling small sheets of paper with his 'mean literary man's fist', the clear, upright script he had trained himself to use in place of his original, larger, slanting hand, and which he could form with such minute dexterity, and mischievous vanity, that baffled friends had to reach for their magnifying glasses to read what he had written with no stronger aid than his own small spectacles.

In his own fashion he gave just as much thought to his books as Trollope, who was, after all, to be called 'the lesser Thackeray', and at the end of the course, after one and a half or two years of producing with knife-edge, monthly tension, woodblocks, plates, initial letters and fifteen thousand words, exactly tailored to cover thirty-two printed pages, he collapsed in exhaustion. As the adrenalin ceased to flow, as he said a reluctant farewell to the characters who had haunted him, plagued him, pinned him to his task for so long, the post-partem blues took over, and he felt, he told his mother, as he imagined she would, if the backbone of her stays were out.

By contrast, regular eleven-to-five employment with a reliable salary often seemed immensely tempting: not a sinecure (he would have been wounded to the quick by that suggestion), but some kind of public place which he could fill with honour both to himself and his country, and yet which would free him financially to write a book as an entity at a less punishing pace.

With this kind of occupation in mind he had kept his nameplate on display at Tom Taylor's Temple chambers, and shortly before finishing *Vanity Fair*, seventeen years after he had first mounted Mr Taprell's high stool and with very little more knowledge of the law than he had had then, he was called to the Bar. Henry Fielding, a far greater reprobate, had been a Justice of the Peace, and Thackeray could see no reason why he should not perform the role of London magistrate with equal credit—until he discovered that only barristers of seven years standing were eligible to apply.

Leaving his nameplate where it was, he told Milnes, who had offered to use his influence in the matter, that he thought he might just manage to last that long as a writer. The books wouldn't be as good as if he had been able to rest for a while, but he doubted if the public would find him out for a few years.

Even this modicum of belief in himself and his readers' lack of discernment was not always easy to maintain, however, and he was soon crying his availability around the town and letting it be known that the vacant position of Assistant-Secretary at the Post Office was just the kind of thing he was after.

'What a place for a man of letters!' he joked, as he urged friends to press his cause with the Postmaster-General.

Anthony Trollope, a hard-working, unappreciated Post Office employee, was justly furious at the concept of placing a novice over the heads of men who had slaved in the department for most of their working lives, and was still ready to boil up with indignation when he thought of it fifteen years after Thackeray's death. As he rightly said, the job would have become so wearisome to Thackeray after the first month or so, he would have found it impossible to do properly, and then would have been tormented by the knowledge that he was taking the pay without earning it.

In his heart Thackeray also knew this to be true, but he had children, a sick wife, an insecure profession, uncertain health, and had seen too many hats passed round for the dependants of improvident literary men to wish to subject his own family to that kind of charity. He had to find some quicker, less taxing way than novel-writing to build up a legacy, and at last he decided to do so with his own resources, by turning lecturer.

Considering his deplorable record as a speaker, it was a decision brave almost to the point of lunacy, but the rewards, especially for a man who took his wares to America, were well worthy of the attempt. Having finished *Pendennis*, and his fifth Christmas book, *The Kickleburys on the Rhine*, he chose his subject—the English humorists of the eighteenth century—and left for Paris with Annie and Minnie, a bag full of research material, and the noble aim of leaving Jane Brookfield free to devote her tender sympathies to a man who needed them even more than he did.

Their relationship had only just settled again into some kind of tolerable pattern, sadder, without hope of improvement, but equally necessary to them both, when family tragedy had shattered it. Harry Hallam, at twenty-six, had died as suddenly and inexplicably as his elder brother, leaving his widowed father with one daughter as the sole survivor of a golden brood of eight. In his wretchedness, Hallam senior turned to his favourite niece, for whom his love was probably rather more than avuncular, and Thackeray urged a reluctant Jane to forget her own grief, ill-health and need for sleeping potions, in order to comfort him.

Duty, *cheerful* duty, was the thing, he told her when she complained at being left to cope alone. She would be freer without him pestering her with his needs, and wherever he was, she would always be with him.

'I know you think that I drop you when I'm away from you', he wrote: 'whereas. whereas—the manner in w^h a man manages to accommodate 2 thoughts into his mind is curious. You're never away from me from waking to night-cap time. Will you always be there my dear and let your name and my young ones go together in that last small prayer?'[3]

To cheer her in her misery, he covered his earnestness with a jester's grin, telling her: 'though my nose is a broken pitcher yet lowandbyold there's a well gushing over with kindness in my ♡ where my lady may come and drink.'[4]

As he settled in Paris, he prepared to write her long letters of sympathy and sentiment, but once installed in her uncle's London home, Jane's replies became few and fleeting.

'My dear Sir I have only 3 minutes to save the post & say &c . . . But I am interrupted by Dr Locock', Thackeray parodied. '. . . If some folks' letters were published as some folks dread after my & some folks' death—I think Posterity would smile rather. I would if I were Posterity . . .'[5]

Even so, he still daydreamed of letting Young Street to some of the thousands of visitors packing into London for the Great Exhibition and lodging himself in the house Jane was soon to move into in elegant Cadogan Place, Belgravia, and when he returned home it was not long before she was by his side again, more deeply involved in his life than she had ever been.

He had left himself only three months in which to prepare six hour-long lectures, and Mrs Brookfield (with her husband away in Sheffield, sitting beside his father's death-bed) turned amanuensis, taking down his words in her great, bold handwriting, as he paced the room, smoking, thinking, talking in short fluent bursts, helping him to prepare the great *coup* that was at last to bring him money enough to save.

Once again, Thackeray was living in an emotional fool's paradise. That his relationship with Brookfield had deteriorated is clear from his reply when the clergyman finally wrote to say that his stern, revered father had died. The mood was one of sadness for more than death, the phrases curiously formal and stilted for such old friends as these.

'Thank you for thinking that I'm interested in what concerns you, and sympathize in what gives you pleasure or grief . . .' Thackeray wrote. 'We've lived as much in 40 as your good old father in his fourscore years, don't you think so—and how awfully tired and lonely we are?'[6]

Brookfield, trapped in a job he did well, but which brought him few earthly rewards and little glory, his wife involved in Thackeray's more glamorous ventures, was the more wretched of the two, and as Thackeray and Jane drew closer, building afresh a companionship that gave zest and solace to their lives, he withdrew from them physically and mentally. Like Jane, so long before, he immersed his misery in a preoccupation with ill-health, turning his attention to his cough, an affliction which had caused concern throughout his married life.

Several years earlier Thackeray had urged him to go to a German spa famed for its treatment of 'tubercles in the lungs', but now, when Brookfield at last began to take his symptoms seriously, Thackeray was less concerned, uncertain even of their existence. 'Is W^m really unwell?' he asked Jane, when, shortly before the first lecture, Brookfield went to consult the Bullars at Southampton.

Jane also showed little sympathy. As Thackeray's début approached and excitement mounted, her letters became spirited and gay, scribbled on the wing, with breezy apologies for signs of haste. Lecture gossip, technical details, Young Street traumas and triumphs spilled over from page to page. Brookfield, in his replies, ignored them all. From Southampton he moved to Dieppe, from Dieppe to Jersey, describing his daily routine of rest and treatments as desperately dull and yet somehow not utterly intolerable. His letters were deeply moving: loving and sad, stamped with the numb acceptance of loneliness.

In Victorian—or Albertian—England, where learning was fashionable and entertainment limited, lecture-going was a popular pastime. Lecture-giving, on the other hand, with its affinity to acting, was not highly regarded. Carlyle, who had tried it, considered it a mountebank's career, and Forster managed to restrain Dickens from putting his show on the road for another seven years.

There were noble lecturers, like the literary-minded George William Frederick Howard, seventh Earl of Carlisle, who had once raised the sensitive hackles of a posse of writers—Thackeray's among them—by asking them to dinner like a literary ghetto: all wits and no distinguished audience to perform to. But a man without a suitably impressive entry in the new Victorian household bibles, *Debrett* and *Burke's Peerage* (even if he did claim descent from Roaldus de Richmond, 1066) had to be either very sure of, or indifferent to, his social position before making a public show of himself for money. Thackeray was neither, and, with a trail of shattered speeches behind him, was not even confident that he could last an hour without breaking down.

In *Philip* he was describing his own sufferings when he made Pendennis confess that he was in a state of tremor and absence of mind before making a speech, in a condition of imbecility during the business, and sure of a headache and indigestion next morning; and James T. Fields, the American publisher, told what all that nervous uproar looked like to an observer.

Fields had accompanied Thackeray to Manchester for the opening of the Free Library Institution there, a glittering occasion for which tickets had been snapped up at unheard of prices. Dickens, Bulwer-Lytton, and Sir John Stephen, three guaranteed spellbinders, were to head the bill. Thackeray, despite previous experience, was determined to outshine them all. As the train carried them north he expounded on the effects he intended to produce on the local dignitaries, none of whom were to escape the subtlety of his persuasion, the insidious phrasing of his appeals to each individual pocket, and Fields, he insisted, must sit directly in front of him, in order to receive the full force of this magic eloquence.

The crowd, three thousand strong, welcomed him with tremendous applause, and as he rose to speak, Thackeray gave his American friend a confidential half-wink from beneath his spectacles. 'Now for it,' he seemed to say. 'The others have done very well, but I will show 'em a grace beyond the reach of their art.'

He began with clarity and charm, and remained in that eloquent vein for about three minutes. Then, in the middle of a most earnest and elaborate sentence, he stopped suddenly, gave a look of comic despair at the ceiling, crammed both hands into his trouser pockets, and deliberately sat down. There were no signs of surprise or discontent from the audience. Everyone seemed to understand that it was just another of his unfinished speeches, and he continued to sit on the platform looking perfectly composed.

'My boy, you have my profoundest sympathy,' he told Fields when the meeting ended; 'this day you have accidentally missed hearing one of the finest speeches ever composed for delivery by a great British orator.'[7]

To Fields, Thackeray never mentioned the fiasco again, but he was not as unconcerned as he appeared. To John Bright, the radical statesman and genuine British orator, to whom he had ceremoniously doffed his hat at the Reform Club for being the most consistent politician he knew, he was more open.

'Who will ever come and hear me lecture,' he asked, 'if I break down like this before such a number of people?'

'You come along with me this evening,' ordered Bright, forthright son of a Rochdale cotton-spinner. 'I'm going to another meeting; I'm not going to speak to fine fal-lal folks, but to a set of good, honest working men, and you must try again.'⁸

Thackeray did have another go, and Bright later reported that he had never heard a better speech in his life; everyone had been delighted with him.

It was simply a matter of practice, Thackeray wrote to Minnie a few days later. But, for his first lectures, practice was precisely what he did not have. He had tried out one or two of the talks, to a group of staunch friends in Mrs Brookfield's new drawing-room, and tested his voice by reciting multiplication tables to an obliging waiter in the hall where he was to deliver them, but now, as a novice, he had to go before the finest fal-lal and knowledgeable audience he was ever likely to speak to. He was risking a great deal to provide his daughters with an inheritance, and was still nervously contemplating catastrophe when, on the morning of 22 May 1851, advertisements appeared in the newspapers announcing the start of his ordeal.

The day before, in sending Dicky Doyle a complimentary card of admittance, Thackeray had enclosed a list of instructions for the ideal listener:

'You and your friend will please to sit in distant parts of the room.

'When you see me put my hand to my watch-chain, you will say, "God bless my soul, how beautiful!"

'When I touch my neck-cloth, clap with all your might.

'When I use my pocket-handkerchief, burst into tears.

'When I pause say Brav-ah-ah-vo, through the pause.

'You had best bring with you a very noisy umbrella: to be used at proper intervals: and if you can't cry at the pathetic parts, please blow your nose very hard . . .

'God save the Queen. No money returned. Babies in arms NOT admitted.'⁹

To the Carlyles, he signed himself 'Equilibrist and Tightrope dancer in ordinary to the nobility & the Literati'.

He was still making strained jokes when his carriage rolled up to the front door to carry him off for the first performance. Annie, Minnie and Mrs Carmichael-Smyth smiled loyally as they packed into the unlikely vehicle—a commercial fly which Thackeray had hired for many an excursion and finally bought impulsively one day, in a job lot with bony horse and grizzled coachman. But their grins became increasingly ghastly as they endured a half-hour wait in Willis's Rooms, St James's, the gilded salons founded in the century of which Thackeray was to speak, scene of those most select of gatherings, the Almack balls.

'Oh, Lord, I'm sick at my stomach with fright!' Thackeray groaned to Fanny Kemble, when she appeared among the first arrivals and found him standing like a disconsolate giant amid the blue damask sofas that served as benches in that elegant arena.

Miss Kemble was a good deal too strong-willed and dramatic for Thackeray's taste as a rule, but she was an experienced lecturer, and as she turned to find a seat he clung to her like a child, begging her not to leave him.

'But, Thackeray,' she told him, 'you mustn't stand here. Your audience are beginning to come in.'

Half his size, she led him into the retiring-room beside the rostrum, and as he began pacing the small cubicle, nervously wringing his hands, asked what she should do next: 'Shall I stay with you till you begin, or shall I go, and leave you to collect yourself?'

'Oh,' groaned Thackeray again, looking towards his lecture notes already set out on the platform, 'if I could only get at that confounded thing, to have a last look at it!'

'Well,' said Miss Kemble, 'if you don't like to go in and get it, I'll fetch it for you.'

She gave her own Shakespeare readings seated at a low table close to the retiring-room door, and only noticed the size of the desk at which Thackeray had elected to stand when she darted back on to the platform, hoping to grab the notes unseen. The monster towered before her, with Thackeray's apparently bound manuscript resting on it almost out of reach. Disconcerted, but determined, she made a half-jump and a clutch at the book—and every page inside it scattered and fluttered down around her. Scarcely knowing what she did, she scrambled on all fours gathering the fallen leaves, and finally held out the wreckage in an agony of dismay, crying: 'Oh, look what a dreadful thing I have done!'

'My dear soul,' Thackeray told her, 'you couldn't have done better for me. I have just a quarter of an hour to wait here, and it will take me about that to page this again, and it's the best thing in the world that could have happened.'[10]

Her kind shake of the hand, he called it, when he wrote to her a few days later.

To Annie, her father's voice sounded strained for an instant as he began to read to the packed hall, then almost immediately it softened and settled into his usual tenor range. After that nothing registered until she heard the applause at the end and saw from the proud glow on her grandmother's face that it had been a success.

He had done it. And done it so well that his ease and composure were the most marked features of his delivery. There was no flamboyance, no gestures or theatricality. He relied on his carefully honed prose to enthral, and it did. At his first attempt he caused a two-month eclipse of the Great Exhibition as the talking-point of the 1851 London season.

Not since Sydney Smith had lectured nearly half a century before had so long a line of carriages been seen outside a lecture hall, said Forster, as he niggled away in the *Examiner* at Thackeray's treatment of Swift, and pointedly quoted Smith's assessment of that earlier triumph: 'the most successful literary imposture of the season.'

It was not until the talks were published two years later that Forster made it clear that Thackeray's carriage-owning audience was also 'a great, intelligent, admiring crowd, stirred and agitated in every part with genial emotions and sympathy.'

Thackeray's aim was not the deep literary discussion Forster and some other critics would have wished on him, but the re-creation of a forgotten era and the men who had adorned it. Like the subjects he had chosen, he wished to be 'the week-day preacher', speaking of the ordinary actions and passions of life, using the word humorist to cover not only the makers of mirth, but the arousers of all the humours he himself most admired: love, pity, kindness, scorn for untruth, pretension, imposture, tenderness for the weak, the poor, the oppressed, the unhappy.

It was an intensely personal view in which he blended wisdom, prejudice, research and intuition with laughter and the insight of a current master into the minds and hearts of those who had gone before. 'Would we have liked to have lived with him?' he asked as he turned to each of his chosen twelve, a question which set Carlyle growling to Venables: 'I wish I could persuade Thackeray that the test of greatness in a man is not whether he would like to meet him at a tea-party.'[11] But greatness was not what interested him, and his more domestic approach made an instant appeal to the majority of his listeners, who were as curious about the lecturer and his opinions as about the personalities he discussed.

When he professed to admire the serene Addison above all others, and then gave that 'sad loose fish' Richard Steele, who 'sinned and repented, and loved and suffered', a vastly more entertaining and sympathetic lecture to himself; when he laughed at the exquisite Congreve and the idle epicurean Gay, championed sensitive, sickly, hunchbacked Pope, berated impure Sterne, scorned Dean Swift for a cringing bully, and revelled with gentle Nol Goldsmith, he said as much about himself as any of those long-dead heroes, and when he had done there were many listeners ready to apply to him the words he had used to describe Henry Fielding: 'He has an admirable natural love of truth, the keenest instinctive antipathy to hypocrisy . . . His wit is wonderfully wise and detective; it flashes upon a rogue and lightens up a rascal like a policeman's lantern.'

The serious historians, turning out in force to inspect the amateur, applied different standards and were less enthusiastic. In public, Macaulay, the most well disposed of the mighty, presented a double-edged compliment to his humour and imagination. In the privacy of his journal, superficial was the word he used. Thackeray, he wrote, 'knew little of those times, & his audience less.'[12]

Henry Hallam said nothing but was betrayed by his daughter, who told Mrs Norton she could tell from his face that he had been trying not to say 'Pooh! Pooh!' all the time, a remark Mrs Norton wickedly carried round to Thackeray, and which he referred to obliquely in his next lecture, when commenting on Addison's cool praises of the young wits of his time. '. . . how can I ask my superior to say that I am a wonder when he knows better than I?' he asked. '. . . How was he [Addison] who was so tall to look up to any but the loftiest genius? He must have stooped to put himself on a level with most men.'

It was extravagantly generous when applied to Hallam, but Mrs Brookfield assured her uncle that it had been meant for him and his 'Pooh! Pooh!' Mrs Norton would be punished, threatened Hallam. In future he would believe all the stories told against her.

Andrew Arcadeckne, as usual, lowered the tone even further. 'Ah! Thack my boy!' he said, sidling out of the door at the Garrick, 'you ought to ha' 'ad a pianner.'[13]

But the view of Charlotte Brontë was that shared by most of Thackeray's listeners. After attending the second lecture, on Congreve and Addison, she told her father:

'The audience was composed of the *élite* of London society. Duchesses were there by the score, and amongst them the great and beautiful Duchess of Sutherland, the Queen's Mistress of the Robes. Amidst all this Thackeray just got up and spoke with as much simplicity and ease as if he had been speaking to a few friends by his own fireside. The lecture was truly good: he had taken pains with the composition. It was finished without being the least studied; a quiet humour and graphic force enlivened it throughout.'[14]

Miss Brontë, whose humility bristled as readily as her pride, had prepared herself for being ignored by 'the great lecturer' in this rarefied assembly, but, on the contrary, she was able to report home, he had seen her the moment she entered the room, had welcomed her kindly, and presented her to his mother, a fine, handsome, young-looking old lady. What she did not say was that he had introduced her as 'Jane Eyre'—blasting her cherished anonymity and causing half the room to turn and stare at the notorious, mysterious 'Currer Bell'. The next day, George Smith, her publisher and host, returned home to find Thackeray standing miserably on his hearthrug, Miss Brontë before him, her head thrown back, her face white with anger.

'No, Sir!' she was hurling up at him. 'If *you* had come to our part of the country in Yorkshire, what would you have thought of me if I had introduced you to my father, before a mixed company of strangers, as "Mr. Warrington"?'

'No, you mean Arthur Pendennis!' Thackeray countered desperately.

'No, I *don't* mean Arthur Pendennis!' retorted Miss Brontë, looking twice as fierce and strong as her prey. 'I mean Mr. Warrington, and Mr. Warrington would not have behaved as you behaved to me yesterday.'[15]

It was one of a series of disputes she was to have with the man whose *Vanity Fair* had roused in her a ferment of admiration, and who, when at last she met him, refused to behave as she thought he ought. She complained that his lecture on Fielding was immoral, and, with brother Branwell's disastrous course in mind, liable to corrupt. She upbraided him for postponing his reading for the second week of June to oblige the 'duchesses and marchionesses' who were to go to Ascot with the Queen and court that day. Miss Brontë could see only toadying subservience in such a decision. For Thackeray—though he was always happy to accommodate a duchess, or even a marchioness—it was also a choice between a full hall and an empty one.

He even managed to anger her by stepping down from the platform at the end of a lecture and immediately asking her opinion of what she had heard. It showed an 'absence of what I considered desirable self-control', she wrote when she described a similar incident in her next book, *Villette*. 'He should not have cared just then to ask what I thought, or what anybody thought; but he *did* care, and he was too natural to conceal, too impulsive to repress his wish. Well! if I blamed his over-eagerness, I liked his naïveté.'[16]

They were, her friend and future biographer, Mrs Gaskell, noticed, almost exactly the same words, including the last, rather rich piece of condescension, that Miss Brontë had used to her, to explain her own annoyance and awkwardness. With praise in her heart, Charlotte Brontë had been silent; had her verdict been less pleasant, she would have felt it her duty to speak out, as Thackeray by this time had good cause to know.

His had not been the vain or idle question she imagined, either. Still uncertain of his powers as a lecturer, he needed an honest answer, and when the fearless little prophetess of truth failed him he turned to a reporter who had given him a less than glowing review— and succeeded in annoying that prickly young gentleman, too.

Charles Cooper, invited to Young Street to elaborate on his criticism, considered that he was received with only perfunctory courtesy, and was hurt beyond redemption when his host explained what he wanted: an opinion *ex oribus parvulorum*—out of the mouths of babes.

2.

Thackeray had first met Charlotte Brontë when she was thirty-three, and he was still weak from his *Pendennis* illness. And they put the fear of God into each other. She, in her wild northern fastness, had conceived the most extraordinary picture of the man she believed to be 'the first of modern masters . . . the legitimate high priest of Truth',[1] and when George Smith accepted *Jane Eyre*, she found a confidant in his reader, W. S. Williams, deluging his mailbag with throbbing screeds on this towering giant to whom she thrilled with a mixture of reverence and indignation, and whom she felt only she truly understood.

'Critics,' she told the mild, stooping Williams, '. . . do not know what an intellectual boa-constrictor he is. They call him "humorous," "brilliant"—his is a most scalping humour, a most deadly brilliancy: he does not play with his prey, he coils round it and crushes it in his rings. He seems terribly in earnest in his war against the falsehood and follies of "the world." '[2]

Such a man, she suspected, would distrust anything good in human nature, would have a galling suspicion of bad motives lurking behind good actions. 'Are these his failings?' she wanted to know. But she also sensed a deep vein of truer feeling beneath his seeming sternness, and imagined him burdened by his inherent genius, the greatness which had made him, she did not doubt, different as a child from other children, caused him unusual griefs and struggles, and made him a writer unlike any other writer.

In words that would have astonished her subject, she pictured him standing alone—'alone in his sagacity, alone in his truth, alone in his feelings . . . alone in his simplicity, alone in his self-control. Thackeray is a Titan, so strong that he can afford to perform with calm the most herculean feats . . . *he* borrows nothing from fever, his is never the energy of delirium—his energy is sane energy, deliberate energy, thoughtful energy . . . Thackeray is never borne away by his own ardour—he has it under control. His genius obeys him—it is his servant . . . Thackeray is unique.'[3]

As 'Currer Bell', she asked Williams to send him an early copy of *Jane Eyre*, and when Thackeray's praise was relayed to Haworth it meant a great deal more to her, she said, than Smith's generous cheque which had followed hard on its heels.

This tale of passion, as *Jane Eyre* was advertised, had fascinated and moved Thackeray for many reasons. He spent a whole day reading it when he had printers waiting for his own copy, and some of the love passages made him cry, to the astonishment of his manservant who blundered in with coals for the fire. Like everyone else, he wondered who this new talent could be, scarcely doubting that it was someone in his own London circle: Kinglake, perhaps, until he decided that it must be a woman, though a woman who knew her language better than most ladies did, and had the un-feminine knack of carrying a metaphor logically through to its conclusion.

The plot was one with which he was familiar, he told Williams, a statement Charlotte Brontë took to heart, as a reflection on her originality. He did not explain that he had been referring to his own history—the mad wife and the tempest of unfulfilled passions—until, with *Vanity Fair* still only two-thirds of the way through its monthly appearances, 'Currer Bell' included a fresh stream of her torrid praises in a preface to the second edition of her own runaway success, and dedicated it to him.

Flattered, flustered, 'upset', Thackeray regarded it as the greatest compliment he had ever received, but out of that tremendous dedication, in which he was described as a new son of Imlah coming before the modern equivalents of the throned Kings of Judah and Israel with a truth as deep, a power as prophet-like, a mien as dauntless and as daring as the original, grew rumours that were to haunt him for the rest of his life.

Still only Charlotte Brontë's publishers and family knew the identity of this powerful new author and the question of her sex almost overshadowed that of her genius. If *Jane Eyre* were the work of a man it should be praised, but if it were that of a woman it was odious, proclaimed the *Economist*, while another journal decided that if the author were indeed a woman, she must be a woman unsexed.

Soon after Thackeray had dedicated *Vanity Fair* to Bryan Procter, he heard gossip at the Athenaeum that Procter and his wife had written this rival sensation between them. 'It is just possible', he told Brookfield, 'and then what a singular circumstance is the x fire of the two dedications'.[4]

The most popular theory, however, ignoring the fact that 'Currer Bell' had claimed to be a total stranger to the new son of Imlah, made Jane Eyre an ex-governess, and not only a governess, in Thackeray's household, who had portrayed him as Mr Rochester, in retaliation for his portrait of her as Becky Sharp. The scandal was inflamed by an article in the *Quarterly Review*, living up to its nickname of the 'hang, draw and quarterly', which maliciously linked *Vanity Fair, Jane Eyre*, and the *Report for 1847 of the Governesses' Benevolent Institution* in one titillating package.

The writer, Elizabeth Rigby (soon to marry Sir Charles Eastlake, a painter Thackeray had not treated particularly kindly in his Titmarsh reviews), did not believe that 'Currer Bell' was a woman: 'no woman attires another in such fancy dresses as Jane's ladies assume', she assured John Lockhart, editor of the *Quarterly*.[5] And neither did Lockhart.

'I know nothing of the writers,' he had replied a month before the article appeared, 'but the common rumour is that they are brothers of the weaving order in some Lancashire town. At first it was generally said Currer was a lady, and Mayfair circumstantialized by making her the *chère amie* of Mr. Thackeray. But your skill in "dress" settles the question of sex.'[6]

Even so, Miss Rigby wrote, and Walter Scott's son-in-law published, a salacious resumé of the 'rumours, more or less romantic', and declared that if they were true, then 'it is evident that the author of "Vanity Fair," whose own pencil makes him grey-haired, has had the best of it, though his children may have had the worst, having, at all events, succeeded in hitting that vulnerable point in the Becky bosom, which it is our firm belief no man born of woman, from her Soho to her Ostend days, had ever so much as grazed.'

If the author of *Jane Eyre* were indeed a woman, Miss Rigby added, it was clear from her writing that she was one 'who had forfeited the society of her sex'—the most offensive charge one Victorian female could hurl at another.

The slur took hold. 'Currer Bell', safe in anonymity and a remote Yorkshire parsonage, could afford to ignore it. When Thackeray at last told her that her dedication had seemed to confirm gossip which his own circumstances made plausible, she was '*very very* sorry', the more so since he made no reproaches, but still refused to tell her name and clear the air.

'Should Mr. Thackeray again ask after Currer Bell,' she instructed Williams, 'say the secret is and will be well kept because it is not worth disclosure.'[7]

For Thackeray, already a household name and living in the metropolis of gossip, as Elizabeth Rigby called London, there was no escape. Nearly three years after the glowing dedication, he told Mrs Brookfield that he was staying on at The Grange to confront the Bishop of Winchester and some of his clergy, who had been spreading calumny, or at least giving credence to it. 'Do you remember my telling you,' he asked her, 'how my friend Gale at a dinner of Winchester big wigs had heard that I was a wretch with

whom nobody should associate, that I had seduced a Governess by
the name of Jane Eyre by whom I had ever so many &c?'[8]

More than ten years later the gossip was still going the rounds on
both sides of the Atlantic.

'Tell me, Mr. Thackeray, is it true, the dreadful story about you
and Currer Bell?' asked an arch American at a London dinner-party.

'Alas, Madam,' Thackeray replied, 'it is all too true. And the
fruits of that unhallowed intimacy were six children. I slew them all
with my own hand.'[9]

He built an amusing *Roundabout Paper* around this and similar
insults: 'That is sufficient,' he quoted a self-righteous matron as
admonishing a maid when she saw Thackeray's name on her
references. 'You may go. I will never take a servant out of *that*
house.'[10] But the thrusts hurt and the wounds never healed.

In 1856, when he championed Pierce Butler in his matrimonial
troubles with his wife, Fanny Kemble, he spoke out so strongly on
Butler's hint that he had been charged with being over-fond of his
children's governess that he could see he had hurt Fanny's loyal
sister, Adelaide Sartoris. Writing to apologize, he explained that his
parents' attitude and public gossip had made him totally biased on
the subject:

'My relations some 7 or 8 years ago accused me too', he told her,
'(no didn't accuse, only insinuated) that I had cast unlawful eyes on
a Governess—the story of Jane Eyre, seduction, surreptitious family
in Regent's Park, &c., which you may or mayn't have heard, all
grew out of this confounded tradition . . . and as the calumny has
been the cause of a never-quite-mended quarrel and of the cruellest
torture and annoyance to me, whenever I hear of poor gentlemen
and poor governesses accused of this easy charge, I become wild and
speak more no doubt from a sense of my own wrongs than their's.'[11]

Despite having stirred up such a reeking brew, when Charlotte
Brontë made her first visit alone to London in 1849, Thackeray was
the only man she really wanted to meet—but, as she informed
George Smith, it had to be on her own terms. Thackeray was not to
know who she was.

Smith, at twenty-five, three years at the helm of the banking and
publishing firm his father had founded, the healthy, handsome Dr
John of *Villette*, had himself never met Thackeray at this time, but,
having admired him from boyhood, when his first discovery of
Titmarsh had so carried him away that he failed to perform a
publishing mission for his father, he was very ready to use Miss
Brontë as a means of introduction.

Indulging in a little masculine collusion, he invited Thackeray to a
small family dinner-party, at which there was to be no one but his

mother and sisters, and the Scottish physician and writer, Sir John Forbes—and 'Currer Bell', who wished to remain strictly incognita. It was important, he begged, that Thackeray should not say a word or do anything to indicate that he knew her secret.

'I see!' Thackeray agreed, in what Smith called 'his large way.' 'It will be all right: you are speaking to a man of the world.'

But, inevitably, it was not all right. Having heard that Thackeray was miserable if he didn't have a cigar after dinner, Smith broke the habit of his house and provided them, causing his own downfall. As soon as they rejoined the ladies, he heard Thackeray, benign and refreshed, quoting a much criticized passage from *Jane Eyre*, in which Charlotte Brontë had described the warning fragrance that signalled the approach of Mr Rochester:

'Sweetbriar and southern wood, jasmine, pink and rose, had long been yielding their evening sacrifice of incense. This new scent was neither of shrub nor flower. It was—I knew it well—it was Mr. Rochester's cigar!'

Miss Brontë killed the quotation with a chill word, and shot Smith through with an accusing glance that made him squirm. Thackeray, however, showed no sense either of awkwardness or guilt. From Smith's house he went straight on to the Garrick Club, where he announced as he walked through the smoking-room door: 'Boys! I have been dining with "Jane Eyre"!'[12]

Charlotte Brontë summed up that evening in one triumphant cry to her old friend Ellen Nussey: 'I have seen Thackeray.' To her father, she described him and, with less than total frankness, their meeting:

'He is a very tall man—above six feet high, with a peculiar face—not handsome, very ugly indeed, generally somewhat stern and satirical in expression, but capable also of a kind look. He was not told who I was, he was not introduced to me, but I soon saw him looking at me through his spectacles; and when we all rose to go down to dinner he just stepped quietly up and said, "Shake hands"; so I shook hands. He spoke very few words to me, but when he went away he shook hands again in a very kind way. It is better, I should think, to have him for a friend than an enemy, for he is a most formidable-looking personage. I listened to him as he conversed with the other gentlemen. All he says is most simple, but often cynical, harsh, and contradictory.'[13]

Only to Mrs Gaskell and Williams did she rail at her awkwardness and confess a sense of failure. '. . . woe to him that thinks of himself in the presence of intellectual greatness!' she wrote, to explain her lack of self-possession when at last, as in a dream, she had looked up at his tall figure and listened to his voice. With everyone else she had met in her three weeks in London, she had been sufficiently at her ease. With Thackeray she knew she had been painfully stupid. Even the mighty Forster she felt superior enough to patronize: 'I by no means dislike Mr. Forster--quite the contrary,' she assured Williams, 'but the distance from his loud swagger to Thackeray's simple port is as the distance from Shakespeare's writing to Macready's acting.'[14]

Miss Brontë was not an easy guest: quickly tired; made 'savage work of' by any routine which was not Haworth's; scurrying into dining-rooms and sitting resolutely beside her hostess, whatever the table plan; generously, but ostentatiously, seeking out the governess of the house and giving her the kind of attention she had never received in that despised position. Speechless when asked for an opinion, she could be vociferous on uncomfortable topics. Her views on the artificial acting of Macready, and the wordy, obscure poetry of Elizabeth Barrett Browning, were not always appreciated by audiences made up largely of those artists' friends.

'I was, indeed, obliged to dissent on many occasions,' she told her former headmistress, 'and to offend in dissenting . . . London people strike a provincial as being very much taken up with little matters about which no one out of particular town-circles cares much'.[15]

Only Thackeray was she prepared to worship blindly, and Thackeray, when she got him to herself, with only George Smith as a witness, proved an unwilling idol. Even in the most robust health, this passionate little woman, with her trembling frame, great honest eyes, and impetuous desire for truth, would have daunted him. Still convalescent and surprised to be alive, he was in no shape to deal with her at all, and the more intense she became, the more mundane were his responses.

'He declined to pose on a pedestal for her admiration,' wrote Smith, 'and with characteristic contrariety of nature he seemed to be tempted to say the very things that set Charlotte Brontë's teeth, so to speak, on edge, and affronted all her ideals. He insisted on discussing his books very much as a clerk in a bank would discuss the ledgers he had to keep for a salary. But all this was, on Thackeray's part, an affectation: an affectation into which he was provoked by what he considered Charlotte Brontë's high falutin'. Miss Brontë wanted to persuade him that he was a great man with a "mission"; and Thackeray, with many wicked jests, declined to recognise the "mission."'[16]

Unambivalent herself, Charlotte Brontë could understand neither Thackeray's attitude to society, which he enjoyed and needed, even as he satirized it, nor to his work, which, though he used it to crusade and put forward profound convictions, he saw primarily as a means of keeping himself and his many dependants alive. She returned to Haworth bewildered and disappointed, convinced that Thackeray's conversation was very peculiar, far too perverse to be pleasant, and his feelings such as could not be gauged by ordinary calculation: 'variable weather is what I should ever expect from that quarter,' she told Ellen Nussey, 'yet in correspondence as in verbal intercourse, this would torment me.'

Unable to tell when he was joking or in earnest, she studied every word for ulterior meanings, and, crediting him with thinking about her a great deal more than he did, suspected him of maliciously devising mean little tricks expressly to provoke her. When he went to commiserate with her on a particularly brutal attack on *Shirley* in *The Times*, she decided that he had called out of base curiosity, simply to see how she had borne the abuse. She had cried when she first read the review, but with steely determination refused to let him see she knew anything about it, priding herself on forcing him to mention it first, which, of course, since he lacked desirable self-control, he did.

Her lavish praise diminished, and when she wrote to the great 'social regenerator' after her return to Haworth, it was with more of her customary lecturing frankness and less of the ardour she had poured into her first 'Currer Bell' communication a year or so before—a document, Thackeray had told Lady Blessington, which would have made him blush, if anything could. When Thackeray replied, she was disappointed that he instructed her to show his letters to no one, but it was a perceptive embargo on his part: Miss Brontë was a great sharer of her postbag, even letting friends read the tormented letters of curate and future husband, Arthur Bell Nicholls, when her father banished him from the parsonage.

By the time she returned to London again, the following summer, she had lost much of her awe and regained her composure, and this time when Thackeray went to pay her a morning call he had to sit through a very different two-hour ordeal. Once again George Smith was their only chaperon.

'He described it afterwards as a queer scene,' Miss Brontë wrote; 'and I suppose it was. The giant sat before me—I was moved to speak to him of some of his shortcomings (literary of course) one by one the faults came into my mind and one by one I brought them out and sought some explanation or defence—He did defend himself like a great Turk and heathen—that is to say, the excuses were often worse than the crime itself. The matter ended in decent amity—if all be well I am to dine at his house this evening.'[17]

All was well, in the sense that Miss Brontë dined at Young Street, but in other respects all was painfully wrong. Only Annie, just two days past her thirteenth birthday, and ten-year-old Minnie enjoyed the occasion. They had stolen *Jane Eyre* whenever they could spirit it away and had thrilled to an unheard of, largely unintelligible, whirlwind of emotions. For them, the arrival of its author was quite the greatest event they had ever known.

It was a warm June evening, and the drawing-room windows were thrown wide open onto Young Street, as the household waited for George Smith to bring the guest of honour—the governess, Annie and Minnie, an expectant trio on the sofa, Thackeray, who usually found other things to do at such moments, waiting with them, listening for the rattle of the carriage wheels before going down into the hall.

Then, at last, the drawing-room door opened, and the trim form of Miss Brontë appeared, wearing prim mittens and a demure dress with a vague pattern of faint green moss: a serious little lady, so tiny that she barely reached Thackeray's elbow.

Annie sensed a certain sternness in her manner, especially towards young girls who wished to chatter, a suspicion George Smith confirmed when he told her that she had later remarked on Thackeray's wonderful forbearance and gentleness with his daughters' uncalled-for intrusions into the conversation.

At their father, however, she gazed with rapt attention, her eyes kindling with added interest every now and then as she answered him, or leant forward over the table, not eating but listening to him talk as he carved the dish before him.

After dinner came the carefully chosen tea-party guests, mainly women since Miss Brontë could be particularly unforthcoming with what she called the coarser sex: Mrs Brookfield, Mr and Mrs Carlyle, Mrs Procter and her poet daughter, Adelaide (future writer of *The Lost Chord*), Mrs Crowe, Mrs Elliot and Kate Perry. Richard Monckton Milnes, asked at the last moment, did not appear.

Only Annie and Minnie, roaming the house excitedly, sparkled. For them an extra dish of biscuits was still enough to mark out an evening as special: now tea was spread in the dining-room, elegant ladies decorated the drawing-room—and gloom hung everywhere as everyone waited for the brilliant conversation which was never to begin.

Miss Brontë, retiring to a sofa in Thackeray's study, murmured a low word now and then to the governess. The room looked dark, the lamp began to smoke, conversation died, and Thackeray, overcome by the uneasy silence, felt the power to cope oozing from him.

Since wit was obviously not to be the order of the evening, Jane Brookfield leant forward with a polite banality:

'Do you like London, Miss Brontë?'

There was a long pause. 'Yes . . . and . . . no,' Miss Brontë finally answered gravely.

With literary ambitions of her own, Mrs Brookfield surveyed the timid little woman with the firm mouth who had achieved so much, and noted with a certain relish that since she did not have enough hair of her own to form a fashionable wreath of plaits, she had resorted to a false crown, a very false crown, of brown silk. It was a small point, but comforting.

When Thackeray, with some relief, escorted Miss Brontë downstairs again that night, he addressed her as 'Currer Bell', at which the Muse of Haworth tossed up her head and said she believed there were books being published by a person of that name, but the person Thackeray was talking to was Miss Brontë, and she saw no connection between the two.

It was all finally much too much for him and when Annie wandered out on to the landing soon after the lions had left, she was surprised to see her father, with his hat on, opening the front door. Putting a warning finger to his lips, he disappeared into the night. As Mrs Procter winkled out of him later, unable to face the remaining ladies, he had made a run for his club.

A year later, during his lectures, Thackeray several times offered to introduce Charlotte Brontë to the society he so enjoyed himself, but, considering that such company and its adulation of his readings had spoiled him, she declined the opportunity of exposing her own character to its influence. He also, rashly, tried another dinner in her honour: this time lifting the intellectual tone by gathering together a clutch of fellow authoresses. But it was no more successful than the first. '. . . such a comedy it turned out,' Kate Perry remembered. '. . . there was no one present but these advanced ladies, about six or seven of them, and by accident, Carlyle, who had not been asked.'[18]

After this, Thackeray and Miss Brontë went their separate ways. Smith, who secured Thackeray's next book, *Henry Esmond*, sent it to her in manuscript, volume by volume, and her comments, though deeply considered and fair, were not exuberant. 'As usual, he is unjust to women, quite unjust,' she wrote. 'There is hardly any punishment he does not deserve for making Lady Castlewood peep through a keyhole, listen at a door, and be jealous of a boy and a milkmaid. Many other things I noticed that, for my part, grieved and exasperated me as I read; but then, again, came passages so true, so deeply thought, so tenderly felt, one could not help forgiving and admiring.'[19]

'Alas! Thackeray. I wish your strong wings would lift you oftener above the smoke of cities into the pure region nearer heaven!' was her cry.[20] The George Warrington of her dreams had, after all, turned out to be Arthur Pendennis: a mere indolent intellectual Hercules.

Thackeray was not sad to be relinquished, but he too found that knowledge of the author diminished his pleasure in her work. When *Villette* followed *Esmond* as the literary success of the day, he thought it very clever, but rather vulgar. 'I don't make my *good* women ready to fall in love with two men at once,' he told Mrs Carmichael-Smyth, 'and Miss Bronte would be the first to be angry and cry fie on me if I did.'

To Lucy Baxter of New York, a pretty young girl on the threshold of her seventeenth birthday, he went into greater detail, linking the romantic eagerness of Miss Brontë's heroine with Miss Brontë's own desires.

'The poor little woman of genius! the fiery little eager brave tremulous homely-faced creature!' he wrote. 'I can read a great deal of her life as I fancy in her book, and see that rather than have fame, rather than any other earthly good or mayhap heavenly one she wants some Tomkins or other to love and be in love with. But you see she is a little bit of a creature without a penny worth of good looks, thirty years old I should think, buried in the country, and eating up her own heart there, and no Tomkins will come. You girls with pretty faces and red boots (and what not) will get dozens of young fellows fluttering about you—whereas here is one a genuius, a noble heart longing to mate itself and destined to wither away into old maidenhood with no chance to fulfil the burning desire. Not that I should say burning—les demoiselles ne brulent pas—'[21]

Charlotte Brontë did burn, as Thackeray suspected, and little more than a year after he wrote that letter she found herself a 'Tomkins' in one of the curates she had always professed to despise. Nine months later, she died, pregnant, leaving unfinished another novel, *Emma*, which Thackeray later published in the *Cornhill Magazine*.

Introducing it in a *Roundabout Paper*, he praised the author's noble English and passionate love of truth, and told of their first meeting, when she had marched on London like 'an austere little Joan of Arc . . . rebuking our easy lives, our easy morals.' Recalling some of the things said about himself in Mrs Gaskell's biography of her, he added: 'She formed conclusions that might be wrong, and built up whole theories of character upon them . . . She was angry with her favourites if their conduct or conversation fell below her ideal. Often she seemed to be judging the London folk prematurely: but perhaps the city is rather angry at being judged.'

Mrs Procter, reading *Villette*, came upon a passage which made her think that Miss Brontë had perhaps judged more soundly than Thackeray imagined, and quoted to him the heroine's description of Paul Emanuel's heart: 'in its core was a place tender beyond a man's tenderness: a place that humbled him to little children, that bound him to girls and women, to whom rebel as he would, he could not disown his affinity nor quite deny that, on the whole, he was better with them than with his own sex.'[22]

It could have been written, as could a great deal about M. Paul Emanuel, with Thackeray in mind—Thackeray, perverse, elusive, emotional, grafted onto M. Héger, the inspired Brussels teacher, the great, tragic love of Charlotte Brontë's life. But Thackeray only responded to a matching tenderness, and clever women appealed to him only when they gartered their blue stockings with a dash of eighteenth-century wickedness. Miss Brontë was altogether too intense.

'. . . there's a fire and fury raging in that little woman a rage scorching her heart w^h doesn't suit me', he wrote. And though his all-seeing eye told him that she too had suffered a great grief, her manner of dealing with it drove away sympathy and pushed him to rebellion.

'Currer Bell is right', he wrote defiantly. '. . . I don't care a straw for a "triumph" Pooh!—for for my art enough. It seems to me indecent and despicable to be doing the novelist business of "On a lovely evening in January 2 cavaliers &c—and then the description of the cavaliers, their coats, horses the landscape &c—Shall one take pride out of this folly?'[23]

Like most dramatic statements, it was not wholly true. But he did believe there were more important things in the world than writers and their works, and Miss Brontë failed to persuade him otherwise.

18

Home and Abroad
The faithful fool

WITHOUT HIS HAT.   IN HIS COMIC HAT.

One sleety summer morning, within a week of his last London
lecture, Thackeray and his daughters drove to St Katharine's Wharf
on the Thames, on the first stage of a six-week journey that was to
take them in a two-thousand-mile loop through Europe. The Rhine,
the Lakes, Venice, Prague and Weimar were all on their itinerary,
everything but scaling peaks: 'Y should we go up a dimd mountain',
asked Thackeray, 'to see a dimd map under our feet?'

Hats were the great travelling item that year. Thackeray walked
the decks in a new grey wide-awake; Annie and Minnie were confident that whatever the other deficiencies of their wardrobes, their
carefully packed new bonnets would see them triumphantly through
any crisis; and Charles Kingsley—'the socialist parson'—and his
brother, who joined their boat at Antwerp, did so in poetical brown
felts with high pointed crowns and great broad brims.

Only the grey wide-awake escaped indignity. When the Kingsleys
stepped ashore at Cologne, the German police, surveying their acres
of brown felt and suspicious-looking fishing tackle, threw them into
prison as Italian revolutionaries. Annie and Minnie suffered only
slightly less humiliation. At their first hotel, when they bonneted up
and presented themselves for their first day's land-based sightseeing,
one adorned with bright pink streamers, the other with vivid blue,
both wreathed around with nodding acacia blossoms, Thackeray,
who had never consciously spoken an unkind word to a child in his
life, sent them back to change.

'My dear children, go back and put those bonnets away in your box, and don't ever wear them any more!' he told them in alarm. 'Why, you would be mobbed in these places if you walked out alone with such ribbons!' [1]

With his own childhood misery ever fresh in his mind, he was a sensibly indulgent parent. In his books he preached that too many rules led to, at best, indifference and subterfuge, at worst, contempt and open rebellion, and he practised what he wrote. He taught the girls manners and tolerance, explaining the reasons for both; he encouraged their interests and a feeling for history, art and nature ('the more you indulge this pleasure (that's the beauty of it) the better you are'); [2] he suffered their laziness, their piano practice, their weaknesses, and if he had to find fault, it put him in a flutter for days.

From their earliest years with him he treated them as young adults, confided in them, trusted them, loved them, and felt guilty that all he did was not enough. Had he been consistent, Minnie would have been his favourite, but in his affection for his daughters he was more clear-sighted than in some other affairs of the heart.

'Minny keeps all her claws for poor Nan,' he wrote to Mrs Brookfield, having heard some of his younger daughter's tantrums and sarcasms through thin cabin partitions. 'It's all smiles & good humour for me. The little hypocrite! the little vixen! the little woman! She has little Beckyfied ways and arts. It's almost disloyal the way in w^h I find myself observing her; and rather pleased if my speculation regarding her subsequent conduct comes right.' [3]

When Mrs Carmichael-Smyth was present, the eleven-year-old coquette dropped her father and treated her grandmother to her prettiest wiles, a wounding switch in allegiance actively encouraged by that passionate, possessive Mater Dolorosa. Immediately after the lectures, Mrs Smyth had made one of her many attempts to take Minnie back to Paris with her, and there had been tears and tantrums when Thackeray refused—an embarrassing scene witnessed by Jane Brookfield, who was penalized for being present with a fine show of haughtiness from Mrs Carmichael-Smyth once she had dried her eyes and reflected on the indignity of losing her self-control. But no matter what scenes he had to endure, Thackeray was determined that his daughters should not be parted.

He himself played absolutely fair, showing no favouritism, telling both girls what a blessing it was they 'suited' him, but it is clear from what he wrote about them that it was staunch, brave Annie, muddling through life with conscientious tenacity, who suited him best. As he watched her being ostentatiously busy on the Antwerp steamer, he imagined her reasoning to herself that since she was plain and clumsy, she must try to make herself useful and liked by helping people.

She wasn't good for show, Thackeray told pretty Lady Cullum, 'having none of her fathers exquisite personal attractions.'[4] In fact, she took after him in features as in character, and though she had to share in many a joke at the expense of her own looks and his broken-nosed charms, she was neither so plain, nor so plump, as Thackeray described her. From babyhood, she had suffered with a humble heart his nicknames for her of 'Fat' or 'Fatty', and in later years learned to endure some flat-footed parental attempts to bolster her confidence and tone down Minnie's pertness and desire to shine.

The best of all qualities in the world, Thackeray told them, was not wit, but good nature, and when he was seated at a dinner-party between a lovely but intolerably stupid young rattle, and a very nice, natural, ugly girl, it was the nice, natural, ugly girl he recommended as a model. Annie understood well her father's little homilies, and if she couldn't please him by being a beauty, she made him happy in other ways.

'Anny,' Thackeray told Mrs Brookfield from Switzerland, 'is a fat lump of pure gold—the kindest dearest creature as well as a wag of the first order . . . we were looking at a beautiful smiling in-nocent view at Berne on Saturday, and she said "It's like Baby Brookfield"—there's for you: and so it was like innocence and brightness . . . O may she never fall in love absurdly and marry an ass! Luckily as she has no money nor no beauty people won't be tempted: and if she will but make her father her confidant, I think the donkey wont long keep his ground in her heart.'[5]

Mrs Brookfield, womanly, good and 'humble-minded', was another example he held up for his children to copy, and so was their mother, of whom he talked with love and remembered happiness as the castles of the Rhine slipped by and the sun came out at last to bless their expedition.

Travelling as paterfamilias, 'with a daughter in each hand', was a very different business, Thackeray found, to his usual lazy bachelor jaunts. 'You don't see things so well à trois as you do alone,' he wrote. 'You are an English gentleman: you are shy of queer looking or queer-speaking people, you are in the coupé, you are an Earl, confound your impudence.'[6] Wicked gambling spas and racy European society were fled from 'like the juice', and at the end of the day, when he might have indulged in his own pursuits, his multiple role of tour-manager, guide, companion and nursemaid left him too tired for anything but a cigar and exhausted sleep.

At Baden, taking his first blessedly solitary walk after five days of undiluted attendance on his children, he was tempted to linger in the adult world by a chance-met London beauty who invited him to join her in a little tea and society, but when he returned to his hotel and found Annie cradling Minnie in her arms, telling her stories to while away her boredom, he pulled out their bags, set about the packing, and shook the dust of that tempting resort off his boots next morning.

Had he been alone, he knew he would have dropped anchor at the first pleasant watering-place he had come to and yawned away a couple of weeks in ladies' drawing-rooms and at the no longer inflammatory gaming tables. As it was, his caravan pressed on into territory he had never seen before, and, as the Swiss countryside unrolled before him, London, its labours, its entertainments, and its intrigues shrank in importance with every turn of his carriage wheels. There was only one good thing in that smoky city, he thought, as he breathed in the clean mountain air, and he wished she could be there with him, living *en famille*, travelling *en prince* at a cost of £1 per head a day.

He had left behind him the most serious argument he had had so far in his literary life. That contentious old bone, the dignity of literature, was once again to blame, and Forster and Dickens were the chief protagonists. While Thackeray had been proving every Thursday afternoon at Willis's Rooms, and almost every night in equally gilded salons, that writers and their works were anything but despised, Dickens and his henchman had been deploying the chips on their shoulders like martial epaulettes in a new battle for the glory of their profession. With Bulwer-Lytton, they were preparing to establish a Guild of Literature and Art, to elevate the status of all writers. The good, the bad, the profligate and the drunken were all to be equally honoured, and succoured in time of need, for all were brothers in the most noble of callings.

Outside Dickens's own circle, this blanket idolatory was not popular. Even Carlyle, who had proposed such a society a decade earlier, had learned that poverty was no bad school for a genuine writer; that merit generally won through and was rewarded. Thackeray's experience had taught him the same lesson. He saw the guild as special pleading for a profession that was no worse off than any other, and he particularly disliked Dickens's proposed method of fund-raising: amateur theatricals, with Dickens himself at the head of a band of literary and artistic strolling players. That, to his mind, was embarrassingly undignified.

Having simmered in private for several months, he had spoken out publicly against the scheme and the 'certain persons' who insisted on representing writers as despised and degraded, as still the miserable old literary hacks of the time of George II, at a Royal Literary Fund dinner, shortly before the start of his lectures. The forum he had chosen was well suited to the subject; his speech, spurred by anger, was unusually coherent; but his timing could scarcely have been more unfortunate.

He had let go his broadside on the very night Dickens had bounced onto the stage at Devonshire House in the first gala benefit performance of Bulwer-Lytton's *Not So Bad as We Seem*. It left him wide open to charges of treachery, and though he had said nothing he had not written as a young man before his fame, and expanded in the *Pendennis* furore the previous year, the charges were, inevitably, made.

A week later it was Thackeray's turn to cry 'Sneak!', when Forster damned his first lecture with qualified praise and niggling criticism.

'Suppose Dickens or Bulwer had written and read that Swift-paper, fancy F's article about them!' he wrote to Mrs Procter, having seen her wince at the prospect of yet another storm among her tea-cups. 'And it's I, that these fellows accuse of being artful and false.'[7]

The three lions stayed out of clawing distance of each other, but Forster, having invited Thackeray into his den for a reconciliation, gave and received a mauling. Blunt always to the point of rudeness, Forster countered accusations of partisanship by swearing that he had genuinely found not one word of wit or humour in the lecture in question and imagined its sole aim had been to please the women and toady to the bishops.

Thackeray, stung afresh by the imputation of dishonourable motives, threatened to mention Forster's biography of Goldsmith in a later reading, and say there was not one word of wit or humour in that—nor any of Goldsmith's nature or grace. And with that silly outburst, his fury subsided, to disappear completely when he noticed the solitary invitation to a great house among the pasteboard decorating Forster's chimney-glass. Poor Forster, whose caddish behaviour had nearly got him thrown out of even the Garrick Club— a 'spewrious' gentleman, one wit had called him, after he had been drunkenly sick in a fellow-member's pocket—of course he would suspect toadying and kowtowing in any man who succeeded where he had tried so hard and failed, especially in one he had taken into his patronage as an obscure magazine writer.

But as Forster's carping *Examiner* reviews continued, Thackeray lost his Olympian vision. The desire to find fault was altogether too apparent—so determined that the great literary pundit tripped over his own plump little feet in his eagerness to find flaws. What a pity, Forster regretted portentously, that Thackeray in his unfair appraisal of Congreve had failed to mention his famous tribute to Lady Elizabeth Hastings, that 'to love her is a liberal education'. A week later, after Thackeray had correctly attributed the saying to Steele, he published a graceless apology.

In a rage at such needle-pricks, the culmination, as he saw it, of two years of treason, envy and foul play, Thackeray returned to his belief in a cabal, and fuming at the constant scheming and suspicions of 'little folk', ended by metaphorically slapping Forster's face with a furious letter in which he threatened to bring out a rival paper.

At the end of his lectures, in an effort to make his own feelings perfectly plain and above board, he had again publicly given his reasons for objecting both to the proposed guild and to the would-be martyrs who were painting their faces and begging for money in the name of literature.

Jogging through the German countryside to Heidelberg, Thackeray looked back with astonishment at the exasperation he had felt during those weeks of petty dispute, and when, towards the end of his great sweep round Europe, he once more trod the streets of friendly little Weimar, the trials and minor irritations of decades gave way entirely to sweet memories of youth most kindly and delightful. There was the house he had lived in with his Cambridge friend, Lettsom, he told his daughters; and this was the palace in which he had danced in his magnificent uniform, Schiller's sword at his side, the greatest beauty in Saxony on his arm; and here was the inn, where the waiters still knew him, and welcomed him, and brought the intervening years crashing back when they presented him with a bill suitably inflated to match his changed status.

Even his old tutor, Dr Weissenborn, was still there, a tall thin figure in a broad-brimmed straw hat, a white Pomeranian running before him, who came stalking down the street, exactly on cue, just as Thackeray was wondering if he were still alive. Only the dog had changed—a new but identical model.

'I am Thackeray, my name is Thackeray,' Annie heard her father saying, eagerly, shyly, to the old man, who stared hard at the grey-haired stranger. Then came the friendly light of recognition, the exclamations and handshakes, the little dog leaping and yapping. The doctor had followed his former pupil's career with interest, he said, had heard of him from this man and that, had read one of his books—not all of them. 'You must bring your misses and all come and breakfast at my lodging,' he told them.[8]

From there he carried them off to Madame von Goethe, where there was another great welcome: recollections, news of twenty years, talk of Thackeray's still-preserved sketches, an invitation to tea in the famous summer-house in the park, where Goethe had written.

There was only one disappointment. Melanie von Spiegel, the Hof-Marschall's daughter, who had so inflamed his young heart, the 'Dorothea' of his Fitz-Boodle papers, the oft-talked of beauty whom Annie and Minnie were longing to see, was away from home. She was now, they learned, Frau von Seckendorf, with several children, and she was on holiday.

It was another two years before Thackeray saw again the girl he had once dreamed of making Mrs Thackeray, and it was not in Weimar, but Venice, where he was staying once more with his daughters. Annie and Minnie, down first to breakfast for a change, had been watching a stout, silent lady, dressed in a considerable yardage of light green silk, as, with a pale fat little boy at her side, she solemnly transferred from one seat to another in the great marble *sala*, shunning the shafts of early sunlight that slanted through the palms and orange trees. She was applying herself, with equal deliberation, to a breakfast egg, when Thackeray strode into the room in high excitement. Looking through the hotel guest book, he had seen the name of Frau von Seckendorf geboren von Spiegel. It must be Melanie!

'She must be *here*—in the hotel,' he told them, as he beckoned a waiter to confirm his hopes.

'I believe that is Madame von Seckendorf,' said the man, indicating the stout lady in green.

Frau von Seckendorf looked up for a moment, then returned to the steady demolition of her egg.

'*That* Melanie! That cannot be Melanie,' Thackeray breathed, in a low, overwhelmed voice.

'Aren't you going to speak to her? Oh, please do go and speak to her! Do make sure if it is Melanie,' chorused Annie and Minnie, surprised at his sudden change of mood.

But Thackeray shook his head. 'I can't,' he told them. 'I had rather not.'[9]

Dreams were preferable to such certainty as that, and he clung to his memories. A year or two later, walking onto a platform in Scotland to deliver one of his lectures, he noticed another of Weissenborn's old pupils, Dr Norman Macleod, sitting among the dignitaries. Without missing a stride, Thackeray leant towards him as he passed, and murmured gravely in his ear, '*Ich liebe Melanie doch*', then moved smoothly on to his reading-desk and a discussion of one of the *Four Georges*.

2.

At every main halting-place on his tour, Thackeray headed for the post office, hoping to find letters from Mrs Brookfield. At all he was disappointed. His fortieth birthday came and went unmarked. Six weeks passed without any return for his tender flood of love, thoughts, longings and travel notes. Towards the end of August, when he led his daughters back to Young Street, the reason became clear. Within days of his quitting London, Brookfield had returned, determined to re-establish his mastery over his own household. Jane had resisted, and then, at last, succumbed.

The storms, the misery and the emptiness of Cadogan Place haunt one of the first letters Thackeray wrote as he tackled his backlog of mail. Frederick Gale, an old legal friend, had sent him news of his own forthcoming marriage, and after the briefest of blessings, Thackeray launched into a lecture on matrimonial etiquette which must have formed a strange contrast with Gale's other notes of congratulation.

'Always treat her as if she was the finest lady in England. Never be rude to your wife: that's the advice I give you', Thackeray instructed. Then, having held up his stepfather's courtly deference to his mother as the ideal: 'I could shew you quite a different story and a ménage that promised every happiness, (where the man was a good fellow, & the woman a mere angel,) rendered miserable by the man forgetting he was a gentleman, and a lady's husband.'[1]

Brookfield had been far from gentlemanly. Among other more reasonable complaints, he had taunted Jane with being too much of a lady, both for his requirements and his taste. Jane, submitting to his will, had agreed to return to her duty as wife and mother; to act out, if she could no longer feel, conjugal devotion. Thackeray's counters in the loaded game they had all been playing were placed firmly back on square one; he could write occasionally, but only in the most commonplace of terms, and only in reply to letters from Jane. After the years of intimacy, the almost domestic closeness of the weeks in which they had prepared his lectures together, the rules were more impossible than ever, but he did his best to acquiesce.

'It pleases God to afflict the good and gentle like you', he wrote to her: 'having determined on your line, I say Amen—and watch you with a sad heart . . . We've before talked of these "lies" pardonnez moi le mot—they are called virtues in women—they are part of the duty w^h my dear has set herself, and in w^h I say God speed her—The fact of your position makes it impossible to write almost—I am not to show that I feel you are miserable. I am not to show that I think your husband is wicked and cruel to you. I am not to show that I think you know you are unhappy, and are treated with the most cruel tyranny—nobody is to know anything of your misery—we are to go on grinning as if we were happy, because W^{ms} cough is certainly very bad, and he should not be disturbed in exercising his temper. Why dont you speak to your brother Arthur? Psha—you see I get back to the forbidden subject; what have I but that?'[2]

When he saw blue eyes and round faces, he looked wistfully after them; when he saw tall women in black he felt queer; when he went to bed, he lay awake long hours thinking of her. And when he had finished his letter, he didn't send it, because he knew it would only bring more tears to her eyes.

The tension dragged on through most of September, lowering like the threat of a summer tempest. Jane, under Brookfield's tuition, became so cold and cruel that Thackeray at last wished he had never met her, had never known what it was to love her. In pain, as in his joy following the Clevedon understanding three years earlier, he turned to Kate Perry and Jane Elliot, pouring out the agony of the next few weeks, the ache of the ensuing years, in a small, sad parcel of letters that charted the course of his wretchedness.

'*I* have been played with by a woman, and flung over at a beck from the lord & master—' he wrote, 'that's what I feel—I treat her tenderly and like a gentleman: I will fetch, carry, write, stop . . . do what she wishes in decency and moderation—It's death I tell you between us. I was packing away yesterday the letters of years—*these* didn't make me cry. They made me laugh, as I knew they would. It was for this that I gave my heart away. It is "When are you coming dear Mr Thackeray", and "William will be so happy" and "I thought after you had gone away how I had forgot to &c"—and at a word from Brookfield afterwards it is—"I reverence & admire him and love him with not merely a dutiful but a genuine love"'.[3]

The belief that he had been made a fool of was the most bitter of all. 'I dont see how any woman should not love a man who had loved her as I did J.', he told the sympathetic sisters of Chesham Place. But he knew it was a false premise, as he showed in *Esmond*, the book he began in the midst of this emotional turmoil.

'You were ever too much of a slave to win my heart,' Beatrix tells the hero of that story, and Esmond wonders if others, reading of his life, will also have known what it is to have 'knelt to a woman, who has listened to them, and played with them, and laughed with them—who beckoning them with lures and caresses, and with Yes smiling from her eyes, has tricked them on to their knees and turned her back and left them?'[4]

'What is it? Where lies it? the secret which makes one little hand the dearest of all? Whoever can unriddle that mystery?' Harry

Esmond asks. Thackeray could find no answer. Like his fictional hero, burning with the fever of balked desire, he determined on retreat only to go crawling back, still hopeful, still kneeling, with his heart in his hand for Jane to take, humiliating himself before both her and her husband, striving to cling to that wretched sop of a three-party agreement.

Finally the storm broke. In an angry confrontation, Thackeray told his old friend what he thought of his treatment of his wife, in terms he swiftly realized were quite unjustifiable, and Brookfield hit back 'like a man'.

Just as Becky Sharp had done when Rawdon attacked Lord Steyne, Thackeray stood back and admired even as his dreams came crashing round him. Mr Inspector of Schools fighting openly for his own was at last an object he could respect, and though he later tried to salvage something from all the years of friendship, he knew then, in his heart, that the rupture was complete. Brookfield would behave better after the crisis, he decided, and must be given a chance to mend his shattered marriage.

A few days later, when Jane sent him messages through little Mrs Fanshawe, that other lady who had been disappointed in her husband, he surprised himself by holding to his decision. Brookfield, he told both go-between and principal, was acting nobly and gently and must be nobly and gently used. Until he authorized a correspondence, there must be none.

He knew he should have broken away long before, and swore he would have done had he not felt safe—protected from the ultimate transgression by the presence of his own children and Jane's: 'I'm sure that one or the other on their side were wrong in not dismissing me', he told his own confidantes, '. . . and of all this weakness goodness love generosity vanity, *playing with edged tools*, we are all paying the penalty. I don't see how it can be averted for any of us. I see nothing, but time to heal this wound of amputation w^h it is: we must all suffer and limp for the rest of our lives . . . I grieve that we are all wretched'.[5]

'I have loved his wife too much, to be able to bear to see her belong even to her husband any more—thats the truth', he admitted. 'There's a decency after the past w^h says go you must stay here no more!'[6]

He headed for the lonely Derbyshire Dales, where at last he was rescued by the Duke of Devonshire, who, hearing that he was at the local inn, sent over Joseph Paxton, his gardener extraordinary, to transport him and his bags to Chatsworth. But neither travel, nor ducal kindness, nor ancestral splendour could shake off this particular devil, and as Thackeray wandered the galleries and state rooms of Bess of Hardwick's provincial palace, was shown the paintings and the treasures of the library, his dark companion continued to gnaw at his heart. 'Show me the Bluebeard Closet where the dead wives and the murdered secrets are,' he longed to ask: 'You must have a Bluebeard closet—everybody has one. Let me go & sit in that—it's that I like best!'[7]

He tried to write and the results were satanic; he 'raged about with a dreadful gaiety'; he forgot his own pain only in pitying Jane's. Long before Kate Perry and Jane Elliot wrote to say that Mrs Brookfield was not the cruel traitress he had thought, he had forgiven her and sought to ease her suffering.

'. . . if she's in torment take a drop of water will you from another soul in purgatory?' he wrote from Chatsworth. 'I know it will soothe her to think that I'm unhappy—or rather that she w^d be more unhappy if she thought I didn't feel at parting with her—O me—the only thing is Duty Duty Duty. Her husband *is* a good fellow and does love her: and I think of his constant fondness for me & kindness and how cruelly I've stabbed him and outraged him with my words—Well, I'd do it again—though I wish that it could have been any other dagger than mine to strike the blow—The sword must have fallen someday or the other. I am glad that she did her duty and threw me over for him—and though in my moments of pique & rage I dont forgive her, I do at better times & say God bless her. But we must bear our fates. We shant and cant and mustnt meet again as heretofore—it was for that I stabbed the husband express to put her up as high as I could and to make the zusammenkunft impossible. Poor old boy, I forget that he has ever been cruel, and think of 500 jolly meetings and kind greetings I have had from him. Who would have divined that all that friendship, that such a good fellow, should end in treason?—for a treason it is say what I will.'[8]

Even now Brookfield was incapable of making a clean break. Though he rejected Thackeray's request for a meeting, to cover their scars with decent amity, he continued to correspond.

'I daresay it relieves the poor fellow to write as it does me to see a letter that has come from out of her house. I think in a state of grief he would depict it by wearing long hair. He is full of queer ceremonies, punctilios unheard of amongst men of a franker sort— He clings to the fancy that nobody knows anything about his interior: and I shall of course hold my too wagging tongue and speak of his affairs as little as possible', Thackeray wagged with his pen.[9]

'Tomkins,' he now called the parson, dismissively, but he was not wholly unfair, and without letting go of one point which Brookfield would have been happy to forget—that he had been cruel, ungrateful and neglectful of his wife in the past—he answered the clergyman's letters as magnanimously as he could.

Thackeray too found it hard to believe that the relationship was over for ever, and turning again to his clandestine message-bearers, asked them: '. . . will it soothe my dear to know that I'm always here, and that I admire her bless her love her? I'll keep that light burning though she mayn't be there to see it: and who knows but some day she may come again & knock at the door.'[10]

He returned to London resigned to wait, gloomily bracing himself with the knowledge that he would, in all probability, suffer the least of the three. He had his work, better health than for many years, and even without Brookfield's 'treachery' he knew he would have seen little of Jane for many months as he took his lectures round Britain and on to America.

Such peace as he had found was shattered, however, when he heard by chance that Brookfield was taking his cough, his wife and child to Madeira for the winter. The thought of Jane, deprived of all help and consolation, alone with a man beset by dark spirits, 'not fit to be the mate of such an angelical creature', was almost insupportable. 'What hasn't she given up to that man?' he cried out again, in pain and anger; '—youth and happiness and now her dearest friend—what a friend—and to what a man.'[11]

It tormented him to think that after all the years of friendship they should part with the quarrel still raw between them, as they would have done had not Lady Ashburton taken the affair in hand at the eleventh hour.

This commanding daughter of the Earl of Sandwich, allied in marriage to the wealth of the Barings, was one of the most prominent women of her time. A great and astringent wit, she liked to have other wits about her, at The Grange, near Winchester, and at Bath House, Piccadilly, where she channelled her many talents into the only fields then open to such women, good works and brilliant entertaining. Lady Jersey, with the kind of insolence that had made Dickens determined to start his Guild, referred to her many literary guests as 'Lady A.'s Printers'. Carlyle, one of those 'Printers', and after the death of Charles Buller her chief 'philosopher in chains', said she had the soul of a princess and a captainess, and rocked his marriage by his servitude.

Thackeray, oddly, found it more difficult to bend his neck. At the time of his self-conscious entry into society, her sharp jests at his expense had so pierced his tender pride that for a while he had refused all her invitations. When finally he was won round, he indicated his submission by returning her card with a sketch on the back showing himself kneeling at her feet, his hair in flames from the hot coals she was pouring on his head.

Even when he had become more confident, and learned what a generous heart beat beneath her formidable exterior, he still resented the general instinctive urge to act the humble parasite in her presence. It was this quality that he now relied on, however, to effect what he called 'not a reconciliation but a conciliation' between himself and Brookfield.

The popular parson dearly loved a title, and held their owners in proper awe, an attitude in which he felt Thackeray, with his unduly flippant manner to the great, was often sadly deficient, and through Thackeray's introduction, he had already stayed at The Grange on his inspectoral rounds. Now Lady Ashburton set out to whisk him and Jane back there for a peace-making.

Explaining, not with complete honesty, his unexpected presence at that house, Brookfield wrote to his mother:

'We came here Saturday, the Ashburtons, upon receiving a note of "good bye" from me, having driven in to Southampton to hunt us up.'[12]

He did not mention Thackeray, and neither did his son and daughter-in-law when they published the letter in *Mrs. Brookfield and Her Circle*, a book which contains no hint of the Brookfield/Thackeray breach, no reason for Lady Ashburton's flattering concern. But Thackeray was there, and he later described that October weekend with a wry attempt at humour as 'better than the Bloomer Ball'. Having spent the morning in 'parleys', the two men at last shook hands, Thackeray thankful that Jane's heart should be made tranquil at least on the score of their enmity.

'Friends of course we're not,' he told Kate Perry: 'but bear each other: and in 6 months things may be better. I think it is not he who is ill it is she God bless her. It gave me a pang to take her hand so lean it has grown. But thank God I've shaken it, and now Heaven speed her.'[13]

When the *History of Henry Esmond* was finished, Thackeray added, in eighteenth-century style, appropriate to the period of his story, a 'Dedication to the Patron'. He chose for that tribute 'The Right Honourable William Bingham, Lord Ashburton . . . for the sake of the great kindness and friendship which I owe to you and yours.' He guessed it would bring cries of 'O the sneak! he has dedicated his book to a grand seigneur', and when a French friend and critic proved him right, he explained: 'I am indebted to Lord and Lady Ashburton for the very greatest kindness at a period of the deepest grief and calamity. They knew very well the meaning of that dedication. I have said somewhere it is the unwritten part of books that would be the most interesting.'[14]

*

'The Brookfields,' in the words of the family historians, 'had a pleasant sojourn in Madeira on the whole; as usual they knew all there was to be known of interesting and cultured people there.' Jane's spare, lifeless journal tells a different story: of a man and a woman living together and thinking apart, enduring day by day the Funchal routine, closing their minds to the past, not caring to contemplate the future. Thackeray, hearing that the Inspector had given a Shakespeare reading on the island, remarked that he seemed to have got immensely better, but the Funchal doctor did not agree. At the emotional, tearful ebb of misery, as much as physically ill, Brookfield was warned that he would have to stay at least a month longer than planned, and maybe for another winter. Jane's refusal to leave without him brought praise from her Uncle Hallam, who told her:

'You are behaving like a human angel. God knows how much I have thought of you, sympathized with you, admired you; and Jane, strong words notwithstanding, given you a certain degree of blame, but which is so interwoven with what I do admire, that I might love you less were you more perfect.'[15]

Hallam, who had largely financed the Cadogan Place house and the Madeira expedition, remained friendly with Thackeray, dining at Young Street a few weeks after his niece's departure; and the rest of the Elton clan, said Thackeray, sided with him rather than Brookfield. But outside the family circle, the clergyman's charm still won him many admirers and several fond financial donations from departed parishioners. Hearing, towards the end of the year, that Brookfield had been left yet another considerable legacy, this time by a Southampton spinster who had thought him the most loving of mankind, a perfect partner in a model marriage, Thackeray wrote: 'O, no satire is as satirical as the world is—no humbug in books like those out of 'em.'[16]

But such bitterness was of relatively short duration, dead long before he recovered from the gnawing malady of thwarted love. 'The truth is I've had an awful time of it,' he told Mrs Carmichael-Smyth, a fortnight after the parting at The Grange; 'and don't know how miserable I was until I look back at such & such days.'[17]

The fiercest pain was over, but a week later, he continued: 'As a man's leg hurts just as much after it's off they say: so you suffer after certain amputations; & though I go about and grin from party to party & dinner to dinner, and work a good deal and put a tolerably good face upon things I have a natural hang dog melancholy within—Very likely it's *a* woman I want more than any particular one: and some day may be investing a trull in the street with that priceless jewel my heart—It is written that a man should have a mate above all things The want of this natural outlet plays the deuce with me. Why can't I fancy some honest woman to be a titular Mrs Tomkins? I think that's my grievance: and could I be suited I should get happy and easy presently'.[18]

But he knew it was not that simple. '. . . say I got my desire,' he admitted, 'I should despise a woman; and the very day of the sacrifice would be the end of the attachment.'[19]

This was one area in which he could not confide in his children, though he imagined they saw all and understood much, and even with Mrs Carmichael-Smyth, recipient of so many astonishing confessions, he now felt unable to unburden all the griefs of his elderly heart. But spill out his woes he had to, and when a girl he could scarcely recall from Larkbeare days wrote to ask for help in getting work as a governess, he went and poured them out to her in a letter which she honourably burned at his request. When he actually saw her again, in her maturity, with red hair and red nose, as scarlet almost as the woman of Babylon, that source of solace also died.

At last, *Esmond* became the repository for his wounds and rages, a charting of his own passions, a text-book of desire. And every book that followed bore traces not only of his own scars, but pity for all women locked by convention within the prison of a loveless marriage.

19

Esmond

Dark months of grief and rage

'If its out of mere spite I'll do something Big yet', Thackeray told the ladies of Chesham Place,[1] as he thrashed around in the agony of losing Jane. That something was *The History of Henry Esmond, Esq., Colonel in the Service of Her Majesty Queen Anne. Written by Himself*, a brilliant piece of historical reconstruction which he had had 'biling up in his interior' for nearly a year when the Brookfield disaster struck. Clevedon Court, Jane's ancient family home, had provided him with the inspiration for its setting, and dispensing with knaves and fools, he planned to people it only with characters lofty and generous.

The charges of cynicism and misanthropy which had determined him on this last noble aim had been borne in on him afresh at a gathering at the Elliots, where one of the guests, the essayist Arthur Helps—'a man of the *deadly-serious* sort, moral to the finger-ends', according to Mrs Carlyle[2]—had taken advantage of his late arrival to probe his personality.

'Is he an *amiable* man? I want to know for his books don't give me the impression that he *is*,' Helps was asking tetchily, when the door was thrown open, and Thackeray, adopting one of Brookfield's favourite party tricks had himself announced not in his own name, but in that of the most notorious criminal of the day—Mr Sloane, a man then on trial for beating a servant girl with calculated savagery.

The timing was impeccable. Helps looked agreeably guilty, and Thackeray, when the full impact of the joke was explained to him, took the essayist's words to heart. Perhaps he was a cynic, as his critics insisted, but, as he was to write in *Philip*: 'Ah, my worthy friends, you little know what soft-hearted people those cynics are! If you could have come on Diogenes by surprise, I daresay you might have found him reading sentimental novels and whimpering in his tub.'[3]

With *Esmond* he planned to confound not only Helps, but all his detractors. After researching for his lectures, he felt as at home in the century he was to write about as his own, and subsidized by their fees he could at last produce at leisure a meticulous masterpiece in three finished volumes.

George Smith, who had published *The Kickleburys on the Rhine* and had long been ambitious to capture one of Thackeray's major works, bid for the book as soon as he heard of it: £1200 for a first edition of two and a half thousand copies, £600 down on account, and half profits thereafter.

Jubilant, Thackeray had set to work. Then had come the Brookfield upheaval, and as the promised delivery date approached in January 1852, his conscience began to gnaw. Only volume one was finished. He still had Smith's cheque for £600 in his drawer, never having trusted it to his whirling bank account. There seemed to be only one honourable course open to him, and Smith returned home one day to find the cheque waiting for him with Thackeray's apologies. Shaken by such scrupulous attention to the terms of a contract on the part of an author, Smith, who prided himself on being the most liberal of publishers, took the perambulating cheque back to Young Street and, with a great deal of difficulty, persuaded Thackeray to keep it.

Four months later he was rewarded with the finished manuscript. In the midst of lecture tours and deepest personal anguish, *Esmond*, the most complex of all his works, into which he felt he had poured enough care and antiquarianism for a dozen volumes, had taken Thackeray just ten months to write.

Half-way through, to speed up the work, he had begun dictating large slices of it, sometimes to fourteen-year-old Annie, more often to Eyre Crowe, whom he had taken into his employ again as secretary/researcher and incidental professor of drawing to young ladies.

When he was in London, Thackeray packed in extra research in the excellent library and insidiously comfortable armchairs of the Athenaeum, the most distinguished of all his clubs, and the one from which, at his first attempt to join, he had been embarrassingly blackballed, by one gentleman of the committee determined not to offer himself up as a model for the popular satirist.

At Montague House, first home of the British Museum, he also

worked in privileged, though not so luxurious, quarters: one of the
cramped closets high in the book-lined galleries above the reading-
room. There, behind a door disguised with the filleted spines of old
bindings, he spread out the great *Gazettes* and mottled volumes of
Queen Anne's reign, and dictated to Crowe his scorching attack on
the Duke of Marlborough, his vindication of his own collateral
ancestor, General John Richmond Webb, the bravest, handsomest,
vainest man in Queen Anne's army.

The story he told was one of high adventure: of Harry Esmond
growing up in the political and religious turmoil of the late seventeenth century, taking part in the great Marlborough wars, and
finally plotting to prolong the doomed dynasty of the Stuarts. The
period, its heroes and its villains (for he found he couldn't, after all,
dispense entirely with rogues) are brilliantly evoked, and the royalist
conspiracy, though oddly confusing at the end, is stirring stuff.

Yet for all its drama and historical perfection, it is the timeless
aspects of the book that haunt the mind, the seething passions and
domestic tragedies that linger and disturb: Castlewood Hall, the
noble, battle-scarred house, briefly awakened to love and laughter,
then chilled again by marital despair; the guilty love of Lady
Castlewood for Esmond, her husband's young kinsman; the
yearning of Henry for Lady Castlewood's daughter, Beatrix, the
exquisite young temptress born for the destruction of mankind, one
of the great creations of literature.

Esmond, Thackeray told his mother, was something like
Warrington—'a handsome likeness of an ugly son of yours'—and his
history was pervaded with a 'cutthroat melancholy' suitable to the
author's own state of mind as he wrote it. He had nothing to tell,
Thackeray said, that shouldn't be written on black-edged paper and
sealed with a hatchment.

To Lord and Lady Castlewood, he gave the sad story of the
Brookfields' marriage: the early delight and happiness while the
young bride was a-worshipping her lord; the years of wretchedness,
when neglect and the cruel thrusts of her husband's baffled pride
crushed her idolatry.

'Much of the quarrels and hatred which arise between married
people come in my mind from the husband's rage and revolt at
discovering that his slave and bedfellow, who is to minister to all his
wishes, and is church-sworn to honour and obey him—is his
superior . . .' Thackeray has Esmond write; 'and in these con-
troversies, I think, lay the cause of my Lord's anger against his lady.
When he left her, she began to think for herself, and her thoughts
were not in his favour. After the illumination, when the love-lamp is

put out . . . and by the common daylight we look at the picture, what a daub it looks! what a clumsy effigy! How many men and wives come to this knowledge, think you? And if it be painful to a woman to find herself mated for life to a boor, and ordered to love and honour a dullard; it is worse still for the man himself perhaps, whenever in his dim comprehension the idea dawns that his slave and drudge yonder is, in truth, his superior; that the woman who does his bidding, and submits to his humour, should be his lord; that she can think a thousand things beyond the power of his muddled brains; and that in yonder head, on the pillow opposite to him, lie a thousand feelings, mysteries of thought, latent scorns and rebellions, whereof he only dimly perceives the existence as they look out furtively from her eyes: treasures of love doomed to perish without a hand to gather them; sweet fancies and images of beauty that would grow and unfold themselves into flower; bright wit that would shine like diamonds could it be brought into the sun; and the tyrant in possession crushes the outbreak of all these, drives them back likes slaves into the dungeon and darkness, and chafes without that his prisoner is rebellious, and his sworn subject undutiful and refractory. So the lamp was out in Castlewood Hall, and the lord and lady there saw each other as they were.'[4]

Bluff, womanizing Castlewood, though not Brookfield in character, was Brookfield in his treatment of his wife, bringing impotent tears to his lady's eyes with his taunts and sarcasms, just as Brookfield made Jane wince and weep by spitefully mimicking her in front of others. And Lady Castlewood, though not a complete portrait of Jane, was Jane as Thackeray chose to enshrine her in his memory—the angel of constancy and compassion.

A year or so later, when he wrote of her to Kate Perry, he said: 'I remember a passage of a novel called Esmond w[h] says when M[r] E thought of the splendor & purity of his dear mistress's love, the thought of it smote him on to his knees &c. I behold that beautiful constancy with wonder & thanks to God—with such a feeling as one looks at the Alps or the Stars in Heaven. I admire human nature in thinking of her.'[5]

When Lady Castlewood visits Esmond in prison, and assuages her remorse for loving him in a brutal burst of fury, it is easy to imagine that her words were an echo of the accusations Jane had used to stab Thackeray during the days he considered her a traitress.

'Why did you come among us?' Lady Castlewood asks. 'You have only brought us grief and sorrow; and repentance, bitter, bitter repentance, as a return for our love and kindness . . . And you pretended to love us, and we believed you—and you made our house wretched, and my husband's heart went from me: and I lost him through you—I lost him—the husband of my youth, I say. I worshipped him: you know I worshipped him—and he was changed to me . . . He loved me before he saw you; and I loved him. Oh, God is my witness how I loved him! Why did he not send you from among us? 'Twas only his kindness, that could refuse me nothing then.'[6]

Yet in the superb staircase scene at Walcote, when Esmond first sees Beatrix grown to burgeoning womanhood, it is the young girl, uncommon tall, with a mouth and chin too generous for classical perfection, who is the physical counterpart of Jane, and it is this lustrous and melting beauty who sends the blood coursing through Esmond's veins and brings upon him the gnawing fever of desire.

It was of Beatrix that he wrote, in the mock *Spectator* letter: 'this fair creature was but a heartless worldly jilt, playing with affections that she never meant to return, and, indeed, incapable of returning them. 'Tis admiration such women want, not love that touches them'—a cry, surely, from the past, when he too had felt he was playing the Faithful Fool, touching only Jane's vanity, not her heart.

Rochefoucauld's maxim, quoted by Thackeray in a later book,[7] that in every love affair there is one who loves and one who allows himself to be loved, is at the emotional centre of *Esmond*. Lady Castlewood, the other lover in the piece, also receives a lesser return for the outlay of her devotion—gratitude and adoration, rather than the fire that inflames both soul and flesh. As a child, Esmond worships her as a mother, as a *Dea certe*; as he grows older, he learns to smart from the lashings of her jealous nature, the progression Thackeray had experienced with his own mother.

Though he may well have seen Jane Brookfield as he wrote of the mistress of Castlewood Hall, Mrs Carmichael-Smyth, pious and humourless, envious of every woman he had cared for since the day she returned from India and found him adoring his laughing Aunt Ritchie, who, when Jane Brookfield was no longer a threat, nagged him into a sleepless night with her strictures on Jane Elliot, seems to have contributed more to the character.

While he was working on *Esmond*, Thackeray wrote that it gave her the keenest tortures of jealousy and disappointment that she could not be all in all to him—'mother sister wife everything'.[8] She twisted the cords that bound them till he felt strangled by guilt—guilt that he could love her only as a son.

When Thackeray began to write *Esmond*, it was this relationship, already treated in *Pendennis*, that he intended to give his hero and Lady Castlewood. Then, with the Brookfield crisis, he changed his plans, playing out his own dreams and hurts in the altered patterns of desire, and though he went back and reworked the beginning of the story to suit his new themes, his original intention still lurks in those early chapters, giving the book the lowering air of near-incest that so shocked Victorians, and which still nags uncomfortably at the mind today.

When a devoted reader put the question many wished to ask— why, oh why, had he made Esmond marry that old woman, the widowed Lady Castlewood?—Thackeray returned an author's easy answer: 'My dear lady, it was not I who married them. They married themselves.'[9]

He himself may not have known the complete reason. As he said in the guise of his hero, the heart is often a secret even to the one who has it in his own breast, and a man can have a thousand thoughts lying within him that he knows nothing about until he takes up his pen to write.

In uniting Esmond and Lady Castlewood, he returned his hero to an uncomplicated, childhood acceptance of love, where there was peace for a bruised and bankrupt heart, a truce to the conflict between duty and desire. Beatrix, the exquisite young temptress, was consigned to moral damnation. Even so, it was Harry Esmond's passion for her that spurred him to plot and fight for glory. And it was desire for Jane Brookfield, not adoration of an angel, that set Thackeray writing the most profound and disturbing of all his novels.

The electric web of emotions in *Esmond* sent a shock wave through Victorian sensibilities, challenging their most sacred taboos. Thackeray himself felt there was something not quite decent in the remarriage of middle-aged women with children, and never completely reconciled himself to his stepfather, yet here he was marrying off a widow to a man she had once treated as a son.

Many of the reviewers were horrified. Lady Castlewood, said *Blackwood's* critic, was 'as pure as an angel, and as severe in her judgment of the back-sliding as a pure woman may be—a wife,— and, still more, a mother defended by the spotless love of little children,'[10] yet she was made to cherish for years a secret attachment to a boy to whom she had given the protection of her roof—and to marry him at the end of the third volume. It was an intolerable idea.

Fraser's reviewer was so upset he lost all sense of fact and fiction. By that second marriage, he said, Lady Castlewood had shown from whence sprang the evils that leapt in the blood of her daughter.

If the morality outraged, however, the writing, research and brilliance of *Esmond* delighted, winning Thackeray laurels greener than any he had worn before. Only Forster, among the early reviewers, struck a wholly discordant note, and his hostility was not entirely undeserved.

Thackeray had put him into the book (in a scene deleted from later editions) as 'Tom Boxer of the *Observator*', and quite plainly accused him of scurvy partisanship:

'Mr. Boxer and my husband were friends once,' Captain Richard Steele's wife confides to Mr St John, 'and when the captain was ill with the fever no man could be kinder than Mr. Boxer, who used to come to his bedside every day, and actually brought Dr. Arbuthnot who cured him . . . But when the Captain's last comedy came out, Mr. Boxer took no notice of it,—you know he is Mr. Congreve's man, and won't ever give a word to the other house,—and this made my husband angry.'[11]

In the *Examiner*, Forster took his revenge. Then, at the end of the year, lagging way behind the other papers, came a review in *The Times*—a malicious 'slasher' which Thackeray was convinced killed future sales, and for which he never forgave the reviewer.

Thackeray had had his own doubts about *Esmond* as he read the proofs in their stately Queen Anne type. He had written it in a period of grief so severe he scarcely liked to think back on it, and felt that the misery of the author showed all too plainly in the finished work.

'How you will yawn over it when you read it!' he told Mrs Gore, '. . . you will remark Bon Dieu (you know you often speak French)—in what a state of mind this man must have been when he wrote these thousand dismal pages!'[12]

But he need not have feared. The first edition sold out within two weeks, and Mudie's, the great London circulating library, finding that four hundred copies were not enough, ordered an extra hundred. Even the slashing *Times* could cause little more than a tremor in its enduring reputation, and Thackeray, feeling that the laughter-springs within him had dried for ever, was grateful to his public for accepting this grave history, so different from anything he had written before.

Despite its sad associations, it was the work he had laboured over with the greatest care, the one of which he was most proud. A few weeks after it was published, brandishing a copy to James Fields on a snow-covered Boston street, he called out: 'Here is the *very* best I can do . . . I stand by this book, and am willing to leave it, when I go, as my card.'[13]

2.

Much of *Esmond* was written in hotel rooms, provincial lodgings, and the homes of far-flung friends, as Thackeray 'barked' his way round Britain with his lectures. The distraction of travel suited him. Just as Harry Esmond was to smother his abject sighs and impotent longing by riding off to plot and fight for the languishing Stuarts, so Thackeray threw his misery into a valise and set out for financial conquest.

Young Street was becoming objectionable to him, and household responsibilities intolerable: 'a very little domestic rose-leaf rumpled', he said, and he was put off work for the rest of the day.[1] He was better amid the bustle of strangers, surveying the impersonal aspect of a rented room, or with friends who gave him peace to write, comfort and stimulation when his daily shift was over.

Within days of the Brookfields' departure for Madeira, he was dividing his weeks between the two great university cities—Mondays and Tuesdays at Oxford, Fridays and Saturdays at Cambridge—spreading his readings over three weeks, taking £100 to £150 away with him from each establishment.

He enjoyed the praise, and liked the profits—'How are the receipts?' he asked the money-man at the end of each performance—but never lost his pre-lecture panic nor the belief that he was engaged in a not quite gentlemanly occupation. Having decided on it, however, and being determined to invest every penny for his daughters, he set his mind to extracting high returns with as little indignity as possible.

He pumped friends on the most propitious season for a 'mountebank' to peddle his wares in their part of the country, demanding details of the most suitable halls and lively organizers. With brazen resolution, he drove hard bargains over seat prices and his percentage of them, and, finally, needing an agent to send ahead to tie up the loose ends, he found just the man in an unlikely quarter—his butler-cum-valet, Samuel James, the best servant he ever had.

Small, youngish, with a look of Holbein's portrait of Sir Thomas More, and an imperial grip on his own domain below stairs, James had been absorbed into the Young Street household in the midst of Thackeray's misery soon after the birth of Magdalene Brookfield. He was, said Thackeray on first inspection, 'a capital man an attentive alert silent plate-cleaning intelligent fellow.'[2] Two months later, he dubbed him his 'Vice-regent upon earth', and eventually used him as the basis for the literary butlers, John Howell and Dick Bedford, in *The Wolves and the Lamb* and *Lovel the Widower*. The man's ingenuity constantly surprised and charmed him.

'The garden has been raked the weeds pulled out and the lawn mown,' he told Annie and Minnie during James' first summer. 'Who do you think did it? James the Viceregent: and with what? He mowed it with a dessert knife!'[3]

The admirable James also contributed letters to the newspapers, signing himself in the name of Thackeray's *Punch* footman, 'Jeames de la Pluche, 13 Young Street'.

'Like to see my last, miss?' he would ask Annie, setting down a paper on the schoolroom table.

Having attended to his employer's neglected garden, he turned his enterprising mind to the establishment's chipped and mismatched breakfast china. In due course a hamper arrived, with a fine china bowl for 'the Governor', decorated with his initials, in gold, set among a trellis-work of roses; cups for the young ladies, handsome gilt milk jugs, and in place of a note an anonymous verse pasted together with printed letters cut from *The Times*:

> Of esteem as a token,—
> Fate preserve it unbroken—
> A friend sends this tea-dish of porcelain rare.
> And with truth and sincerity
> Wishes health and prosperity
> To the famed M. A. Titmarsh of *Vanity Fair*.[4]

The identity of their poetical fairy-godfather exercised their minds at many a breakfast-time, but neither Thackeray nor his daughters came near to the truth, and it wasn't until James left that he reproached them in a fine, farewell epistle: 'I sent you the breakfast things; you guessed a great many people, but you never guessed they came from me.'

Annie and Minnie were brought close to tears by the fear that this paragon would replace them in their father's affections. He seemed to have an occult line to his master's thoughts, always knowing beforehand what he would need or like, so much better than they did themselves.

One wet, chill evening, as they stepped out of a theatre, Thackeray, feeling unwell, shivered and said it had turned cold.

'Coat, sir?' said James, appearing suddenly beside them. 'Brought it down.'

Thanking him for coming all the way from Kensington in the rain, Thackeray mechanically felt his pocket for a possible cigar-case.

'Cigar? Here,' said the invaluable de la Pluche, popping one into his mouth and producing a lit match.[5]

At Edinburgh, Thackeray's next stop on the lecture circuit, James was there before him, sending back front-line reports of healthy subscription lists and rosy prospects, which Thackeray received with caution. Believing Sassenach myths, and viewing the broad deserted streets on the night of his arrival, he prepared himself for more praise than pounds in that handsome city. James, however, was proved right. The crowds turned out and paid too—£300.

He took that cultivated new Athens by storm, and left it with its noses deep in the works of the eighteenth-century writers he had celebrated. In between, he was dined, luncheoned and suppered by a wealth of new acquaintances, none of whom gave him more pleasure than Dr John Brown, medical man and gentle essayist, originator of Thackeray's first public tribute—a silver Mr Punch inkstand sent to him by eighty Edinburgh admirers at the time of *Vanity Fair*.

Brown, scholarly and humorous, a venerator of fine wine and fine writing, became his 'adviser and backer, guide philosopher & friend,'[6] and though Thackeray had elected to stay at a hotel, in order to write, he was soon haunting the home of the doctor, his sympathetic wife and their two young children, unburdening his heart and binding up his wounds at their welcoming fireside.

'. . . he comes and sits for hours,' Brown wrote, 'and lays that great nature out before us, with its depths and bitternesses, its tenderness and desperate truth. It is so sad to see him so shut out from all cheer and hope.'[7]

With such a friend Thackeray could set aside the jester's mask and bare his soul, sharing not only his griefs, but his profoundest thoughts and half-formed ambitions, and Brown, so long an ardent admirer of the author, became even more devoted to the man himself.

'I wish you had been here . . . to have seen, heard, and known Thackeray,' he told another kindred spirit, '. . . a strong-headed, sound-hearted, judicious fellow . . . much better and greater than his works . . . He is 6 feet 3 in height, with a broad kindly face and an immense skull . . . He makes no figure in company, except as very good-humoured, and by saying now and then a quietly strong thing . . . He is as much bigger than Dickens as a three-decker of 120 guns is bigger than a small steamer with *one* long-range swivel-gun . . . He has a great turn for politics, right notions, and keen desires, and from his kind of head would make a good public man. He has much in him which cannot find issue in mere authorship.'[8]

Back in London, it was this last interest—politics—that immediately occupied Thackeray. It had been evident for some time that Lord John Russell's Whig government, with which he more or less aligned himself, was tottering, and could not long survive the uproar caused by Lord Palmerston's Foreign Office approval of Louis Napoleon's bloody *coup d'état* in France. Eyre Evans Crowe had already proved an early casualty of the coming upheaval: manoeuvred from his post as editor of the *Daily News*, penalized for his pro-Palmerston stance as soon as Palmerston's own resignation seemed assured. His journalist son, Joseph, had also lost his job with the paper, thus bringing the family from prosperity to penury at a single blow.

'Good God what are they to do?' Thackeray had written to Mrs Carmichael-Smyth shortly before taking off for the north. 'I see 50£ out of somebodys pocket before long . . . I am on my knees to Stanley and Palmerston to get something for Crowe, who has been the best servant Lord P has ever had—but one stands aghast before the fate of these poor people, and cowardly self-love cries Save Save Save—or you may starve too.'⁹

Self-love, however, flew to the four winds when he saw how *Punch* was handling the political crisis. Knowing more of both Palmerston and Louis Napoleon than any other man around the *Punch* table, he considered the magazine's assaults on the one grossly unfair, on the other unwise, and in a heated exchange with Mark Lemon told him so. Before leaving for Edinburgh he had received a promise of better behaviour in the future, but, three weeks later, when he walked into Young Street again and opened the latest edition he found the famous cartoon of the President of France as 'A Beggar on Horseback; Or, the Brummagem Bonaparte out for a Ride'—Louis Napoleon galloping to hell brandishing a sword reeking with blood. It was too much. He could pull no longer, he said, in a boat with such a crew and such a steersman, and handed in his resignation.

He had been at odds with Lemon and his boys for a year or more, briefly flaring up and resigning once before over one of Jerrold's articles, and then, in the 'general scorn and sadness' of his break with the Brookfields, withdrawing more amicably, leaving the permanent staff, but still contributing the occasional article.

Despite its misdemeanours, he still had a great affection and loyalty for the magazine, attributing the whole of his success to his connection with it. But he could no longer produce at will the kind of light-hearted banter needed for its pages. 'The fun goes out of a man at 40,' he had told James Spedding a year or so earlier, after trying for three days to whip up the humour, 'and not canning.'¹⁰

After his Palmerston/Napoleon resignation, he wrote nothing more for Lemon for two and a half years, and then, offended by the lower rates of pay he was given, stopped completely. Once his fury was spent, however, the weekly dinners continued to draw him for the rest of his life.

Participation in politics was more attractive to him now than the sideline sneer, and he watched with interest as Lord Stanley followed his patron, Lord Palmerston, by resigning his post of Under Secretary at the Foreign Office. '*The* Party', Thackeray told Lady

Stanley, was still to be formed in Britain. Were she and her husband of it? Could he do anything for Stanley, by writing or any other means, to get it going? Or: 'Is it preposterous in a mere light littérateur talking in this way?'[11]

Lady Stanley passed on the offer to her husband, and mindful of the mischievously malicious tongue which had given rise to his nickname—Ben, after Sir Benjamin Backbite—asked him not to snub the author if he thought it of little use.

The urge to enter Parliament himself and work on it from the inside was already taking hold of Thackeray, but first he had his daughters' futures to secure, and in the spring he set the Titmarsh Lecturing Van rolling again, back to Scotland, to take Glasgow and Greenock in tandem, doing some gentle research en route and marvelling at the ease of railway travel—four hundred miles in twelve hours, reading and note-taking as he went. Clattering through Carlisle, his thoughts flew back over fifteen years, to the first months of his marriage, when he had been offered the editorship of the *Carlisle Patriot* and refused it because the paper was too Tory for his taste.

'What queer speculations the "might have beens" are!' he wrote to Mrs Carmichael-Smyth. 'I might have gone down there, and my wife might have remained well, & we might have had ten children.'[12]

In all his years of lecturing he rarely took Annie and Minnie with him, not caring, as a protective papa, to expose them to the life. When he did, one glint in a waiter's eye was enough to convince him that they had been taken for part of the performance and would be expected to turn out in trousers and spangles and sing a comic song. Even on his own he had awkward moments. At Glasgow, already a little subdued by a less doting reception than Edinburgh had given him, he had a particularly nasty experience for a Victorian gentleman used to consorting with the great. Presenting a letter of introduction from the distinguished Stirling of Keir to a wealthy local merchant—who, for all his liberal views, Thackeray could not quite see as an equal—he was waved away and told to call the following afternoon.

'He thinks I'm a sort of actor, and he's quite right too,' Thackeray told Dr Brown. 'I shall go, I think, and be very respectful and humble. It'll be good fun.'[13]

But it was obvious that he thought it pretty grim fun, and was glad when the portly old merchant, having learned a little more of the stranger at his gate, came genially puffing up his stairs next morning, pressing hospitality upon him.

On the whole, Thackeray enjoyed these odd encounters and the entertainments they led to: the visits to mills, factories and docks;

the insights into different people and their ways. The rich merchant, he was amused to find, had just as many toadies at his table, vying for his patronage, as any noble lord. He was touched by the number of families who took him into their homes and made him so welcome there that there was 'quite a little heart-pang at parting'; by the old friends who appeared suddenly out of the past, like the officer who had kept an eye on him on the voyage home from India and had seen him safely into the care of his Aunt Ritchie. Thirty-five years later this 'kind old affectionate gentleman with the curiousest love of children, and faithful memory of old times,' took charge of him once more, putting him up at his Manchester home while he lectured in the city. [14]

What he could not get used to was the general familiarity with which he—'the great and illustrious Titmarsh'—was treated as a public entertainer: the provincial dowagers and blue-stockings, the 'aspiring damsels', who pressed round him at the end of the readings, striving to enrapture him with their brains or their beauty, wanting, at the very least, a few words in their albums. One young man, thinking to tempt him into rather more than his customary signature, flashed a galaxy of contributions from musicians and singers under his nose. See what excellent company he would be joining, he said.

'What!' cried Thackeray, 'amongst all these fiddlers!'

What on earth did they want the signatures of musicians for? he wondered. And why should he sign his name under that of 'Signor Twankeydillo'? [15]

'Now your address,' said the young man.

But that was too much. Only for friends, or friends of friends would he take the album back to his hotel and compose a poem or sketch.

At Oxford, he had had an even more chastening experience when he went to ask for formal permission to lecture within the University. Dr Plumptre, Vice Chancellor and Master of University College, had led him through a catechism that was doubtless not as absurd as Thackeray reported it to be, but still wounding enough.

'Pray what can I do to serve you, Sir,' Plumptre had asked.

'My name is Thackeray.'

'So I see by this card.'

'I seek permission to lecture within the precincts.'

'Ah! you are a lecturer; what subjects do you undertake—religious or political?'

'Neither; I am a literary man.'

'Have you written anything?'

'Yes, I am the author of *Vanity Fair*.'

'I presume a Dissenter—has that any connexion with John Bunyan's book?'

'Not exactly; I have also written *Pendennis*.'

'Never heard of these works, but no doubt they are proper books.'

'I have also contributed to *Punch*.'

'*Punch*! I have heard of that; is it not a ribald publication?'

Thackeray claimed he was required to augment his unsatisfactory replies with a character reference, and clinched his admittance only by giving the name of a particularly useful friend, Samuel Wilberforce, Bishop of the diocese.[16]

It was not a proud position, certainly, Thackeray sighed, to lecture from town to town—but the money? but the children? If by 'a little posture making' he could fill their purses, he would fix his grin and carry on—to Manchester, to Liverpool, to America.

20

America

Steward! Bring me a basin!

Towards the end of May 1852 the Brookfields returned from Madeira, bearing with them cigars which Thackeray was immediately invited to sample. Pleading prior engagements, he refused, but the temptation was terrible. It spurred him to finish the last few pages of *Esmond*, and before many days of June had passed he was away, out of danger, across the Channel at the start of a long-promised Continental tour with his parents and children.

He had planned a leisurely farewell family holiday before returning alone to prepare for his American adventure, but in the event one week of sightseeing *à cinq* proved more than enough. His mother was more dolorous than ever, having scared herself into a panic of nerves by buying him a life-belt for the Atlantic crossing, and the inevitable parting with his daughters acted as another shroud on all pleasure. At Frankfurt, suddenly, without warning, he whisked down a side street, whispering to the Major: 'I don't intend to come back. Tell them I am gone.'[1] And there, as he later wrote in relief, was the tooth actually out without the dentist and the awful chair.

But if the tooth were gone, the pain still nagged. He travelled from Frankfurt, 'one of 6 miserable Jonases in the stomach of a grumbling diligence,'[2] and for nearly two months carried on alone through Germany and Austria, looking at paintings, and feeling again the old yearning to turn artist; visiting the battlefield of Blenheim, which he had described sight-unseen in *Esmond* and found a satisfactory match for his imagination; fleeing from a

London he couldn't bear to contemplate: a London which contained Jane Brookfield, but a Jane he couldn't visit.

In Munich he sat in a beer garden for an hour watching a soldier and his girl drinking beer out of the same mug. 'I drink my beer alone God help me,' he groaned. 'What right have I to envy another man's liquor?'[3]

Discontent dogged him, followed him home, and sat on his shoulder as he put his affairs in order for the coming ordeal. He did not expect to like America or the Americans, and his thoughts of the two-week voyage were grimly shadowed by the drowning of his friend and fellow writer, Eliot Warburton, earlier that year, and by Dickens's horrendous description of his first Atlantic crossing, when the flames and sparks belching from the ship's gaping funnel had threatened to consume sails and passengers, if the raging seas did not get them first. Having petitioned for State pensions for others in the past, he now asked friends to do the same for Isabella should his ship also founder, and made FitzGerald his literary executor and honorary guardian to his daughters.

'Old Fitz', burdened with a mighty portion of the melancholy that marked so many of his most intimate friends, doubted Thackeray's continuing affection as he doubted his own worth. At forty-three, his poetic powers were just bursting into flower; he was soon to begin the study of Persian that was to result in his translation of the Rubáiyát; yet he saw his life as a total failure and mess and his only ambition as an epicurean desire 'to keep on the windy side of bother & pain.'[4] He believed neither Thackeray's grateful tribute that he felt young again when they met, nor the genuine friendship that set him bouncing into his rooms, looking grey, grand, and good-humoured on FitzGerald's rare visits to town.

'Thackeray is in such a great world that I am afraid of him; he gets tired of me: and we are content to regard each other at a distance,' he told Frederick Tennyson, in a letter which mourned his increasing shyness with even his oldest friends, and gave the lie to such talk of Thackeray's rejection.

With thirty years still to live, secure in his Suffolk stronghold, FitzGerald was also sorting his papers and making a will. To Annie and Minnie, he left £1000, but to future Thackeray lovers he was less kind, burning the letters of twenty years in a great holocaust of self-mortification.

'I had two reasons—' he told the old friend of his youth: 'first I am rather *ashamed* (and nothing else) of your repeated, and magnanimously blind over-estimate of myself; and secondly I thought that if I were to die before setting my house in order those letters might fall into unwise hands, and perhaps (now you are become famous) get published according to the vile fashion of the day.'⁵

Thackeray's mood was equally morbid. Keyed up to move, he was pinned to England until he had corrected the proofs of *Esmond* and these, hindered by a shortage of antique Queen Anne type, took three months to dribble in from the printers. George Smith, with the mixture of hard-headed business sense and lavish generosity that made him a prince of publishers, put the delay to good use by commissioning Samuel Laurence to draw the author he was so proud to have on his list—to 'take off his head', as Thackeray called such transactions. By the time *Esmond* was published, engravings of the splendid result were in wide circulation and Thackeray's face became almost as well known as his name. For the rest of his life strangers astonished him by raising their hats to him in the street, bewildering him with their knowing familiarity.

Smith sent an artist's copy of the portrait to Annie and Minnie in Paris, to console them for the temporary loss of the original, and an engraving to Charlotte Brontë, who hung it at Haworth parsonage, between one of her earlier hero, the Duke of Wellington, and another of herself.

'And so the lion came out of Judah,' she told Smith, having scrutinized every line and feature.

'Hmm,' said Thackeray, 'I never could see the lion.'⁶

But he was delighted with the result and won this most flattering of artists many another commission with his recommendation that he was the only painter in London fit to draw a man with brains in his head.

It was one cheering episode in a particularly dreary time. He was alone in the empty city at the height of the summer, wretched, dreading the coming voyage, increasingly ill, and without even the comfort of the invaluable Samuel James, who had emigrated to Australia to better himself. He missed his daughters, thought constantly of recalling them or going to see them but, since he knew he couldn't stand another parting, did neither.

When he had first planned the American trip, Jane Brookfield had offered to have the girls for as long as they and he wished, another memory that brought him only anguish. Now he was increasingly worried about leaving them for so long under his mother's fraught wing, especially Minnie in whom he saw too much of Isabella's nature for ease of mind. His fears were soon confirmed by Annie, who wrote asking plaintively if he really had to go away, and for his guidance on what they should do with all the religious books their grandmother was pressing on them.

Though he would have liked to have ducked the American tour

himself, Thackeray told Annie firmly that he had to earn the money it would bring, and while he was away she and Minnie must consider themselves as at college and work and work with all their might. His own priorities for their studies were that they should learn to speak French perfectly, since French was a part of politeness, and to play the piano as though they understood it—or at least well enough to send him to sleep after dinner on his return.

On the religious question, he told them to read all they were asked to, and to make up their own minds as every honest man and woman had to. But to balance the evangelistic fervour that had so blighted his youth, he set out for them his own simple, loving faith. It was best, he said, to believe what was good in the Bible, to cling to Christ's '*Love* your enemies', not the wicked old eye for an eye and tooth for a tooth.

'And tell my dearest Mother,' he advised, 'that I of all people have a right to speak to you on religious subjects.'[7]

Mrs Carmichael-Smyth could not agree. She was to have her grandchildren for six months, perhaps a year. She was deeply concerned about the state of their souls. Here was the chance to save them. Having made Annie thoroughly miserable, she toyed with the idea of offering to surrender her guardianship to someone who shared their father's views, and wrote to Thackeray about 'the painful difference that alas! & alas' had come between mother and son, grandmother and grandchildren:

'If the dear children were not with me, I would shut it up & only refer to it in my prayers—but they are here, they are under my teaching & that teaching must be f^{rm} what I believe it to be the "word of GOD"—I must dwell upon every passage that more particularly assures the believer of the promises made to him—As for instance in our reading yesterday we left off at the 36th v. of 10 c of John, & at the 35th v: I said "remember children & write it in y^r hearts & may GOD keep it there—that it is the word of GOD & that 'the Scripture cannot be broken'—it is our Lord himself who speaks" . . . I cannot have them with me, without teaching them, that "all Scripture is given by inspiration f^{rm} GOD, & that as "children they must know the Holy Scriptures, that "are able to make them wise unto salvation"—I would rather take St Paul's authority in this last quotation than anything you or any Man can say—the conflict is a very severe one between the two duties—not f^{rm} a moments doubt in my own mind, but f^{rm} the great pain of implying to them ever that you are wrong—The work will not be mine if they are brought to recognise the truth of GOD'S word—poor Nanny's is a stiff heart of unbelief . . .'[8]

Having offered to make the supreme sacrifice of relinquishing her charge, she convinced herself, however, that there was a 'higher duty' to be fulfilled than abiding by an earthly father's wishes, and it was not until four months later, when Thackeray was three thousand miles away, that she finally posted the letter—with a postscript which must have afforded him some grim amusement:

'. . . you may find some assurance of the children's faith in you when I tell you that they w^d think it a crime to think otherwise than as you have told them—& so firmly am I convinced that *I can* do nothing, that I have ceased for some time to read the Scriptures with them . . . I have begged them to read the Bible daily'.[9]

But even now this tough old fundamentalist would not give up. If she could do nothing herself, there were others who might yet succeed.

'We are to go to M. Monod,' twelve-year-old Minnie innocently informed her father, 'and he is to preach us a sermon every week, and we are to copy it and I daresay I will make a hash of it.'[10]

Thackeray's mother, as he had told her many years before, when she had determined on a point was mighty resolute. She had chosen the most famous Protestant teacher in France, Adolphe Monod, a brilliant Calvinist theologian, whose burning eyes and persuasive voice had his impressionable young audiences weeping with emotion.

'Ah, mes enfants, fuyez, fuyez ce monde!' he beseeched the crinolined rows, the eager young hearts hovering on the threshold of that delightful world he would have had them flee. To Annie he seemed like the St Paul of her own time. She longed to believe, to rise and follow, and his classes, which cost so many tears and provoked so much anguished discussion, remained with her always as one of the most moving experiences of her life.

When her letters, full of aching doubts and a stolid eagerness to reconcile the irreconcilable and disappoint no one, eventually reached him in America, Thackeray wrote to his meddlesome mother that he wished 'that confounded Monod had been at the bottom of the sea,' and accused her of persecuting with tears and maternal pangs just as earlier crusaders had attacked with fire and the sword. He was forty-two, he told her, he had opinions of his own, and chose to act by them. But he knew he couldn't win.

Thackeray had sailed from Liverpool on the *Canada*, Cunard's luxury sail-and-steam ship, at the end of October, and compared with the horrors of his imagination it was an almost comfortable voyage, brightened by the sea-sick remedy of champagne by the pint, and the company of a brace of poets: Britain's Arthur Hugh ('Say not the struggle naught availeth') Clough, a swarthy-faced young man who walked the decks in a wide-awake hat and mustard-coloured inexpressibles; and America's James Russell Lowell, future editor of the *Atlantic Monthly*, a mixed blessing since he came complete with a wife who at first struck Thackeray as an awful, supercilious woman.

Clough, he had met before, during his turbulent visit to Oxford after 'Clevedon in '48', and had immediately felt the most enthusiastic liking and admiration for the man, largely inspired by the way he had sat down in an inn yard and started to teach a child to read from a scrap of *Punch* he'd found lying on the ground.

But he also thought his poetry, though rough, contained the genuine sacred flame of genius, suspected he had been crossed in love, admired his learning, and approved his stand against 'Gothic Xtianity', which had led him courageously to give up his Fellowship and university prospects. It was a catalogue of virtues exactly suited to win Thackeray's marshmallow heart.

Clough returned his regard with a kind of dogged fascination, not quite sure what to make either of the man or his works, and feeling vaguely dissatisfied with his own showing at their meetings.

'Thackeray and I get on very swimmingly, every now and then—he is a good creature . . .' he wrote to the girl he was to marry. 'He's much more into actual life than I am—I always feel that—but one can't be two things at once, you know. He likes me, I think, though we seldom get on much in talk.'[11]

Thackeray mooched around the *Canada* in a vast flat travelling cap, busy absorbing the secrets of navigation, puzzling over the mysteries of latitude and longitude, which haunted him when he climbed into his narrow berth at night, and, in the end, marvelling at the skill that could guide a ship over three thousand miles of pathless ocean, through storm, fog and darkness, as though a rope had been pulling her all the way from Liverpool and her destination had been inevitable from the start.

That the Captain, after ten days at sea, should know to within fifteen minutes where and when to look for the first welcoming light of North America, that he should calmly interrupt his carving at dinner merely to verify that it had been sighted, and then carry on slicing the sirloin, was a miracle of judgement he felt deserved a medal, a royal decoration, and proposed the Order of Britannia to honour such courageous expertise, as the Garter honoured the 'ornamental classes'.

On calm days, safe in the hands of these capable sailors, he ate his dinner, drank his champagne and smoked his cigar 'in the fiddle', with all the good fellows on board. When the wind came, slamming dead into the *Canada*'s bows, and the great rolling Atlantic heaved beneath her, he dived into the privileged private cabin his 'illustrious character' had gained for him, and there, having called for a steward and basin, reclined amid the fetid odours rising from Mrs Carmichael-Smyth's life-belt. Ha! he thought, as Bryan Procter's ballad, *The sea! the sea! the open sea!*, lurched into his mind, it was all very well to write about the delights of the ocean in Upper Harley Street.

Clough wandered down during the storm to cheer his two-day misery, and borrowed one of the copies of *Esmond* that had arrived with split-second timing just as the tender was about to leave the Liverpool quay, but it was not until later, after a long evening of puns, jokes and stories at Lowell's Boston home, where Longfellow, Dana, Edmund Quincy, Estes Howe, Professor Felton of Harvard, and James Fields, gathered to fête the visiting English lecturer, that Clough solved at last the puzzle that had been bothering him.

'Thackeray doesn't sneer,' he wrote then: 'he is really very *sentimental*, though a little coarse too sometimes; but he sees the silliness sentiment runs into and so always tempers it by a little banter or ridicule.'[12]

2.

Thackeray had spent his last few weeks in England lecturing at Manchester and Liverpool, and, in the latter city endured precisely the nightmare he had tried to guard against: a huge hall, the Philharmonic, the most beautiful room he had seen, built for two to three thousand people, with an audience of two hundred shuddering in its vast emptiness.

'It is like dinner for 20, and 3 people to eat it,' he had told Lady Stanley before joining her for a final weekend at Alderley. 'They go away and say unto each other what a good dinner & so forth but I don't think they'll have the courage to come again.'[1]

The audiences had improved, but he was to take another blow to his morale in Liverpool before he left. Leafing through the *New York Herald* in the reading-room of the Athenaeum there, he had found his own visit mentioned in highly uncomplimentary terms, himself described as a Cockney author and literary snob, and the people who were preparing to receive him as old-womanish societies with an unpatriotic zeal for toadying to foreigners while ignoring local talent.

'There might be some excuse for our giving flattering receptions to such writers as Macaulay, Bulwer, Dickens, or even James, of the "solitary horseman" school,' said the *Herald*, 'but as for fêting Thackeray, it is . . . ridiculous . . .'[2]

The *Herald* kept up its battering all the time he was in New York, so ferociously that a neighbouring breakfaster hid her copy under the tablecloth when Thackeray appeared in the hotel dining-room, but it was in the minority. Its rivals seized on him delightedly, and, with a passion for personal detail then unknown in Britain, offered him up to their readers in minutely observed instalments. Every gesture, or lack of gesture, was watched and commented on (if he had suddenly found that all the pockets had vanished from his coat and vest he would unquestionably have postponed his lectures until they appeared again, said the *Times*, having studied the continual plunging of his hands into one or the other of them).

His size, his clothes, his hair and his voice were analysed. His old gambling losses, even ancient John Goldworthy and his plush breeches, were remembered and recorded as an indication of the style he had kept even in adversity. From the flimsiest foundations were drawn the wildest surmises, a reporting technique Thackeray himself pushed to the splendid limits of absurdity—'In religion a Parsee (he was born in Calcutta)'—in a Titmarshian self-portrait of which, since he was still at odds with *Punch*, his old magazine, *Fraser's*, found themselves the grateful beneficiary.[3]

And it was not only the journalists who practised such open scrutiny. A young beauty at a grand Washington dinner-party told him with large-eyed seriousness how much she admired his hands: 'All Englishmen keep their nails well.' And, as she watched those surprisingly small hands during the course of the meal, she congratulated him on his manner of 'conveying his food to his mouth.' All Englishmen, she thought, conveyed their food well to their mouths.

To an English gentleman it was startling, but Thackeray soon discovered that he enjoyed uncomplicated American honesty. Like many a later visitor, he found Americans at home a thousand times more considerable than could have been judged from isolated en-counters in Europe. Before their open-hearted generosity and naturalness, petty British prejudices slunk away in shame, and it was the very qualities that were most sneered at in the old world that appealed to him in the new. The youth, size, and brash vigour of the country thrilled him.

There are 500000 people in this city about w^h we know so little—' he told Minnie from Philadelphia; 'there's one street with shops on each side 6 miles long—there's New York with 700000—Boston, Cincinatti scores more vast places—only beginning too and evidently in their very early youth whereas we are past our prime most likely . . . Everybody prospers. There are scarce any poor. For hundreds of years more there is room and food and work for whoever comes. In travelling in Europe our confounded English pride only fortifies itself, and we feel that we are better than "those foreigners" but it's worth while coming here that we may think small beer of ourselves afterwards. Greater nations than ours ever have been, are born in America and Australia—and Truth will be spoken and Freedom will be practised, and God will be worshipped among them, as they never have been with the antiquarian trammels that bind us in the Old World.'[4]

He never went into a house in New York where there wasn't a great clattering of hammers in the passage, a knocking down of old walls and a building up of new, or where the family wasn't preparing to move. No one was quiet, everyone was thrusting upwards and onwards. A house twenty years old was considered worn out and used up, scaffolding and barricades blocked the streets as buildings were pulled down, altered, added to, replaced. Every chance was open to everyone; everybody was his neighbour's equal. It made him tipsy to walk about the place, and set his brain whirling to think of it.

The Americans, he wrote home, began without a dollar and made fortunes in five years: 'There's rush and activity of life quite astounding, a splendid recklessness about money w^h has in it something admirable too. Dam the money says every man. He's as good as the richest for that day. If he wants champagne he has champagne, Mr. Astor can't do more. You get an equality w^h may shock ever so little at first, but has something hearty and generous in it. I like the citizenship and general freedom. And in the struggles w^h every man with whom you talk is pretty sure to have had, the ups and downs of his life, the trades or professions he has been in—he gets a rough and tumble education w^h gives a certain piquancy to his talk and company.'[5]

The first few times a shopboy failed to call him 'Sir', he winced, but he had little doubt that American values were the right ones.

'There's beautiful affection in this country,' he wrote to Albany Fonblanque, with whom, as with Forster, he had had his differences, 'immense tenderness, romantic personal enthusiasm, and general kindliness and serviceableness and good nature w^h is very pleasant and curious to witness for us folks at home, who are mostly ashamed of our best emotions, and turn on our heel with a laugh sometimes when we are most pleased and touched. If a man falls into a difficulty a score of men are ready to help.'[6]

Had he been younger, he was afraid he might have sneered, simply because it was different, but in maturity he marvelled. Even the glittering and uncomfortable splendour of the rich New Yorkers' homes, furnished like the most splendid gambling houses, and of their womenfolk, lean as greyhounds, frail only in looks, tricked out as splendaciously as French actresses, grew handsome and unexceptional to his accustomed eye.

Like the company of bright young men in England, the youthful blood beating in the pulses of America rejuvenated him. He was fit, eager for new sensations, and not in the least abashed to find that in the land of equals he was a far greater swell than he had ever been at home. For the first time he fully recognized just what his books had done for him when he heard a young bookseller working his way through the carriages of an American train, crying his wares: 'Thackeray's works! Thackeray's works!'

'So, here it is,' he thought. 'After fifteen years, here is the fame they talk about.'[7]

He bought a copy of *A Shabby Genteel Story* from the boy's basket, and felt a tremendous urge to shake the bright-faced young merchant by the hand.

For Dickens, ten years earlier, flags had been flown in the streets and drums beaten. For Thackeray, there was no such public display, but everywhere arms were outstretched in welcome. '. . . they read our books as if we were Fielding,' he said in astonishment, and they remembered them with endearing accuracy. Already, he was regarded as a friend.

'Make yourself at home,' said a great jolly hostess, one of the few fat white women he was to see in the States. 'Law bless you! We know you *all to pieces*.'[8]

Cheap reprints of *Esmond* sprang up everywhere, and the firms advertising them placed its author in noble company: 'Bangs, Brothers and Co. issue, wholesale and retail, 8vo. editions of Addison, Thackeray, Steele, etc.'

A New York hatter, with a flair for self-promotion (during Jenny Lind's American tour he had taken the best box in the house and hung one of his hats in it) offered to compensate him for the lack of regular royalties by 'furnishing his head with all the external ornament it might require.' Even the publishers, still tenaciously fighting an international copyright bill, opened up their safes and disgorged.

'So this is a "pirate's" daughter, is it?' Thackeray asked, when James Harper, in an office surrounded by bookcases crammed with loot, including many of Thackeray's own unpaid-for works, introduced him to his youngest child. But business acumen, if not conscience, was making even Harper less of a buccaneer. To be first off the mark with *Esmond*, he had paid for an early proof copy from England, and he now offered Thackeray $1000 for a similar deal on the book of lectures.

Appletons, who had rushed out a complete edition of his works, including some of the early magazinery he would have preferred to remain forgotten, splashed the new Laurence portrait in their publishing house windows, and handed over a share of past profits as well as new. For the last book in their neat little red-bound series, Thackeray wrote a preface, using it to apologize publicly to Bulwer-Lytton for the youthful jokes he had made at his expense, a peace-offering to which he later drew Bulwer's attention.

'It's a wonderful country and money grows here,' he cried. It would have been worth the trip just to make contact with the publishers, whose future interest might add something like forty per cent to everything he wrote.

In payments for books, and by reading his lectures at a rate approaching £1 a minute, he made nearly £1500 in the first six weeks. Annie, Minnie and Mrs Carmichael-Smyth were told to add bonnets to the dresses he had promised them for Christmas; Eliza, manning rented-out Young Street, received a £5 bonus; and the Kensington beef and coal fund for the poor found itself £10 the richer. The rest he invested in American railway shares, with interest at seven or eight per cent, way above Britain's normal three per cent—and precariously higher, thought cautious Barings of London, than the four per cent American stock they would have recommended.

'I am beginning to think and tremble like a money-saver already,' he told the ladies of Chesham Place. 'The sensation is so new to me!'[9]

He was still in America when the first dividend arrived, and it was the sweetest money he had received since the first few guineas he had earned.

James Fields in Boston, and Willard Felt, of the Mercantile Library Association, New York, the two men who had done most to get him there, organized the early lectures, and the great showman, Phineas T. Barnum, having shown him over his New York museum, offered to stage-manage the rest. But Thackeray preferred to keep control, and the bulk of the profits, in his own hands, aided by Eyre Crowe, whom he had taken with him.

'Crowe is my immensest comfort,' he wrote early in the tour. 'I couldn't live without someone to take care of me, and he is the kindest and most affectionate henchman ever man had.'[10]

On board the *Canada*, the henchman had been even more 'puky' than his chief, and even when well he wasn't the best and 'cutest' secretary a man could find, as Thackeray told him when Crowe had doubted his capacity for the job. But he had other, more valuable qualifications, not least the comfort of long association.

In Thackeray's mind, he was bound up with the happiest years: Paris, and the Crowes' Saturday soirées, when Eyre was a child, and

Thackeray in love; and Coram Street, a few years later, where Crowe as a schoolboy remembered Isabella, red-haired and gentle, delightful at her own fireside. There were very few people he would have the face to dictate his books to, as he did to Crowe, Thackeray told him: 'I don't know such a person at all except, my dear Nanny:—and then consider your powers of silence. These are invaluable.'[11]

This accommodating young man slipped easily into all kinds of society, and if he lacked what Thackeray called 'spryness', he made up for it with a blessed evenness of temper. After months together, living at the closest quarters with scarcely a day apart—sharing even the same sketching pen—Thackeray could still say that Crowe had never once ceased to make puns or be in a good humour: 'We laugh and roar with absurd jokes—we get on à merveille.'[12]

For that, he was prepared to forgive a great deal. On their first train journey, tucking into a good lunch at a wayside station, scatterbrained Crowe failed to hear the departure whistle and, with the luggage tickets in his pocket, roused himself just in time to see the fast train disappearing down the track with Thackeray inside it. A slow, slow train, and many hours later, when he arrived at the Clarendon Hotel in New York, he found 'the chief' in excellent spirits, entertaining the historian and statesman, George Bancroft, the luggage retrieved, and two reporters given the slip.

Horace Greeley, founder of the New York *Tribune* and the *New Yorker*, was another early visitor to the Clarendon, where he coached Thackeray in the finer points of American politics. He also instructed one of his brightest staff writers, Henry James, Sr, to concoct a kindly puff for the *Tribune* to refute the *Herald*'s more frigid blasts. In print, James praised. Privately, he was less appreciative. Thackeray, he told Emerson, couldn't see beyond his eyes, had no ideas, and was merely a sounding-board against which his experiences thumped and resounded. He was the merest boy. Thackeray, had he known, would have agreed with most of it.

On James's nine-year-old son, the future novelist, he made a more alarming impression. Thackeray, the children's friend, struck this one into a paroxysm of awkward shyness with the first words he spoke to him:

'Come here, little boy, and show me your extraordinary jacket!'

Henry had been hovering around his father's study door making his own observations. Suddenly he found himself standing before the enormous, celebrated visitor, a kindly hand on his shoulder, and 'the spectacles of wonder' bent upon his tightly-fitting coat with its long, single row of brass buttons.

'If you were to go to England,' Thackeray told him at last,

amused to find the son of a well-to-do New Yorker in the dress of a London pageboy, 'you would be called "Buttons".'

Though not understanding the implication, the jacket was forever compromised in Henry James's young mind by the awesome confrontation. At a later meeting in Paris, with all five James children, Thackeray did better. Then, it was Henry's seven-year-old sister who drew the scrutiny of the spectacles as she sat beside him in a fashionable array of flounces. Overcome by curiosity, Thackeray for a fleeting second tested the structure beneath the frills.

'Crinoline?' he exclaimed, with a ludicrous expression of horror. 'I was suspecting it! So young and so depraved!'[13]

By that time, Henry was fourteen, and man enough to appreciate the joke.

Even in America, where no profession was considered *infra dig*, and lecturing was positively honoured, Thackeray retained his gentlemanly distaste for self-publicity. Told in Philadelphia that 'Mr Buckinghamm of London' had personally called on all fourteen newspapers in the town, he replied that Mr Buckinghamm might well have done, but he be dimm'd if he'd go hat in hand to any newspaper editor, and was glad to find that they were pleased rather than otherwise by his independence.

Crowe was the one who was sent ahead to beat the drum and set up the booth, and, considering how little either of them knew of the country, did remarkably well, except in Washington, where they arrived in the middle of the season for concerts, parties and banquets, and had to wait until Lent before such serious business as lectures could be considered.

'I wish you could send me out a couple of new stomachs from England,' Thackeray told his daughters, as he was drawn into the social whirl. 'Mine is still very good but it's trials are awful. The wittles I am obliged to eat for your sakes young ladies is prodigious'.[14]

In idleness, he got into trouble, too—over a statue of President Andrew Jackson by a young American of talent but no training, Clark Mills. Local reaction to the monument ranged from blind pride to deepest embarrassment, and Senator Charles Sumner, an amusing man who refused to let chauvinism interfere with his artistic taste, witnessed Thackeray perform one of his noblest acts of discretion in connection with it. They had been on a tour of the Capitol, where the English visitor had impressed the party with his sound and complimentary judgements on the American art displayed there, but Sumner knew that Jackson and his awful horse lay on their homeward path: if Thackeray were to retain his popularity he had somehow to be 'coached' past without incident.

'The conversation hung persistently upon art matters,' Sumner recorded, 'which made it certain that I was to have trouble when we should come in view of that particular excrescence. We turned the dreaded corner at last, when, to my astonishment, Mr. Thackeray held straight past the hideous figure, moving his head neither to the right nor left, and chatting as airily as though we were strolling through an English park. Now I know that the instant we came in sight of poor Jackson's caricature he saw it, realized its accumulated terrors at a glance, and in the charity of his great heart took all pains to avoid having a word said about it. Ah, but he was a man of rare consideration.'[15]

Such restraint could hardly last. Backed into a corner by a Congressman at a party and asked if he did not think Mills' the finest equestrian statue in the world, Thackeray, in the privacy of that corner, felt bound to answer No.

'Well, sir,' said the Congressman, 'but you must remember that Mr. Mills had never seen a statue when he made this!'

As mildly as he could, Thackeray suggested that seeing other statues might do Mr Mills no harm.

Next day, he was soundly thrashed in a Washington paper for the impertinent criticism and offensive arrogance which Englishmen adopted towards men and works of genius in America.[16]

On slavery, he did better. This was the great American issue of the day. Mrs Stowe's *Uncle Tom's Cabin* had been published only a few months before Thackeray's arrival, and within a year three hundred thousand copies had been sold. Its shockwaves were reverberating round the world. The ladies of England, with the beautiful Duchess of Sutherland in the van (and Bulwer-Lytton, 'the Knebworth Apollo', cheering from his chariot) signed an anti-slavery manifesto—or 'womanifesto' as Thackeray called it with distaste, fearing it would do nothing but stir up bad blood between the two countries. One injudicious remark from himself, and he knew he might as well pack up his lectures and go home.

With remarkable prudence, he watched, listened, sifted the evidence, and stayed calm, aided by a hideous daguerreotype of Mrs Stowe (when he later met her and found her to be gentle, honest and 'almost pretty', he was safely back in England), and two growing beliefs: that the black man then was not intellectually equal to the white; and that the Americans' counter-argument was true—the poor in Britain were worse off and more miserable than the American Negro, and Britain should do something about her own shame before meddling in the affairs of another country.

'I don't believe Blacky *is* my man & my brother,' he wrote home to Mrs Carmichael-Smyth, 'though God forbid I should own him or flog him, or part him from his wife & children . . .They are not suffering as you are impassioning yourself for their wrongs as you read Mrs Stowe they are grinning & joking in the sun; roaring with laughter as they stand about the streets in squads . . . but where the two races meet this weaker one must knock under; if it is to improve it must be on its own soil, away from the domineering whites; & who knows whether out of Liberia there mayn't go forth civilizers & improvers of the black race . . .'[17]

As he travelled south, crossing the pretty Rappahanna river where he had placed the Esmond family estates, every plantation owner he met urged him to go off alone and explore his land and slave quarters. He saw the Sunday parades of sleek, well-fed Negroes in their bright clothes and prodigious bonnets, and was served by a black waiter with five gold studs as big as medals in his shirt, two gold chains across his stomach, and a gold ring on his finger. In Charleston he went to a black ball and was dazzled by the white dresses, feathers and tiaras. He visited a Negro village and inspected their rations. And he thought of English labourers with ten children and ten shillings a week.

If it rained, the black servants were kept home and dry—not, it was true, from compassion, but because they were susceptible to colds, and the doctor charged a dollar a visit. Again the English contrast came to mind: 'Fancy Lady Londonderry caring on a winter night whether her *gens* were suffering from cold or not!'[18]

In the warm southern states, amid the laughter and singing, it was Lady Londonderry's great hulking footmen Thackeray pitied, with their padded calves, shameful plush, their hair plastered in bear's grease and flour, and the prospect of a segregated workhouse when their usefulness was over. There was the man and brother he could tremble for, the kith that made him think 'there but for the grace of God . . .'

Only the black children aroused his pity and affection: the 'little elfin bit of a brat' who pinched his elbow when Thackeray failed to notice the bread he was offering at dinner, and who had been known to hit his master in the back to make him attend; and another black imp who spent an entire meal standing with his back against the sideboard, making faces at a slightly older colleague who whisked away the flies with a peacock feather fan. The goodness of their masters to these children was very pleasant to witness, he said, and he wished more of his countrymen could see it.

In the end, he believed it would be the absurd economics of the institution that killed slavery, not the abolitionists. When the white men needed to compete for their jobs, the financial burden would be relinquished readily enough by the owners.

'In a house where four servants would do with us,' he wrote, '(servants whom we can send about their business too, when they get ill and past work, like true philanthopists as we are) there must be a dozen blacks here, and the work is not well done.'

And for that working dozen there were twice as many or more too old, too young, too clumsy for employment, yet who still had to be fed and clothed.

'The rule is kindness, the exception no doubt may be cruelty. The great plenty of this country ensures everyone enough to eat . . . This to be sure leaves the great question untouched that Slavery is wrong. But if you could decree that Abolition tomorrow, by the Lord it would be the most awful curse and ruin to the black wh. Fate ever yet sent him. Of course we feel the cruelty of flogging and enslaving a negro—Of course they feel here the cruelty of starving an English laborer, or of driving an English child to a mine—Brother, Brother we are kin.'[19]

Crowe nearly got him into trouble by producing his sketchbook at a Richmond slave market, from which he was swiftly ejected, but with his own belief that current practice was preferable to any quick alternative, Thackeray managed to tread the delicate tightrope without stirring the wrath of either North or South.

21

Sally Baxter

Out of the frying-pan

In the north, New York, Boston, Philadelphia and Washington were
Thackeray's chief headquarters; in the south Richmond, Charleston
and Savannah. He lectured in halls, assembly rooms and churches,
and was more astonished to find himself performing on the stage of
a regular theatre in Savannah than delivering his lay-sermons from
the pulpit of the Unitarian chapel, Baltimore.

Before leaving England, he had debated long on whether he would
write a book about his experiences, and had decided—almost
definitely—that the answer should be No. Those of previous English
travellers, especially Dickens and Mrs Trollope, had caused anger
and mistrust in the new world, and fed the prejudices of the old;
and, anyway, he felt he had risen above the production of light-
hearted travelogues. A grave old gentleman, the father of young
ladies, shouldn't be comic and grinning too much, he told Annie and
Minnie.

Hedging his bets, he issued a warning to friends to keep his letters,
since he might ask for those back again for publication, but it was
not long before he gave up this idea too.

'I hope you have kept carefully all those "Letters of a traveller in
America" which will form the basis of my future work in 6
volumes . . .' he waggishly asked Albany Fonblanque, in the first
letter he had managed to send him in four months of travelling.
'What could Dickens mean by writing that book of *American Notes*?
No man should write about the country under 5 years of experience,
and as many of previous reading. A visit to the Tombs, to Laura

Bridgman and the Blind Asylum, a description of Broadway—O Lord is that describing America? It's a mole or a pimple on the great Republican body, or a hair of his awful beard and no more. I have hardly seen as much as that; and gave up sight-seeing at once as impossible to a man in my position here. Your room is besieged all day by visitors, you go about from dinner to tea-party and ball, and the people don't talk to you but try to make you talk. "Well Sir, how do you like our country Sir?" that's the formula, and as you are answering this query, the host comes up and says: "Allow me Sir to introduce you to Mr. Jones of Alabama, Sir"—shake hands with Jones of Alabama, query as before; it is not answered when you are presented to Mr. Smith of Tennessee. "We know you very well Sir," says S. of T. "your works are extensively read among us, allow me to present you to my Lady, Sir, who is a great admirer of" etc.— Mrs. Smith of Tennessee then commences: "How do you like our etc. Sir"—and, by Heaven, evening after evening passes off in this way. I know 100 people more every day, and walk the street in terror lest every man and lady I meet should be my acquaintance of the night before.'[1]

Such mild outbursts convinced him that if he published anything, he too would be damned, and financially the American goose was 'much too good a goosey' to be killed off so foolishly. He had also made too many real friends among the hoards of acquaintances to wish to risk giving pain. '. . . if I cut jokes against them may I choke on the instant,' he told Mrs Procter.[2] He would speak out only if he could prove that his name was truly Makepeace; if he could use his knowledge to increase love and understanding between the two countries.

As in England, his new friends spanned a wide social spectrum, from the Brahmins of Boston and members of New York's Upper Ten Thousand, to newspapermen and exiled Irish rebels encountered on trains. A few he had known before in London, like James Fields, who was waiting to greet him on his first night ashore with a prepared joke and just the kind of convivial evening he relished.

In London, Thackeray had closely questioned Fields about American oysters and their reputed great size. Marvellous tales were told of them, none of which he believed. Fields had remembered. As he led Thackeray into the dining-room of the Tremont House Hotel, he apologized for the extreme smallness of the shellfish that would be served to him that night, then sat him down before a dish laden with six of the largest specimens to be found in all the eastern states.

Thackeray, fork upraised, studied the Falstaffian monsters anxiously, then turned to Fields with a look of anguish: 'How shall I do it?'

Fields described the simple process by which the free-born citizens of America normally tackled the job, and Thackeray raised his fork again. Passing over the largest, as too reminiscent of 'the High Priest's servant's ear that Peter cut off', he plunged his weapon into one of its bloated companions, and bowed his head as though saying grace.

All eyes were on him. He opened his mouth, struggled for a moment, then came to rest, gazing at the five remaining over-occupied shells with comic despair.

'How do you feel?' asked Fields.

'Profoundly grateful,' Thackeray gasped, 'and as if I had swallowed a little baby.'[3]

With Fields, Thackeray's exuberance knew few bounds. When the conversation became too serious, he asked leave to enliven it with a comic song, or executed a brief double-shuffle. On hearing that his first course of readings was sold out, he broke into a great shouting and dancing in the street, and when Fields finally prised him away from some sketches he was doodling over in order to get him to the hall on time, he rode there with his legs thrust out of the carriage window in tribute to his magnanimous subscribers.

Sitting in a concert audience with Fields before his own lectures began and before he knew anyone else in the city, Thackeray confounded the little publisher by giving a penetrating analysis of everyone who entered the auditorium. It was a gift he rarely showed off, though sometimes, unconsciously, he was led to speak of men of apparent probity as though he knew of some dark and terrible crime they had committed, in one case a murder, long before those misdemeanours became generally known. In some way he didn't understand, these uncomfortable facts seemed to be actually revealed to him as he watched or talked to people, and on this occasion he left Fields shuddering for many years afterwards whenever he saw one particular victim of this alchemy walking the Boston streets unaware that his respectable façade had been pierced.

Boston reminded Thackeray of Edinburgh or one of England's richer cathedral towns: Tory and donnish, with a decorous, well-read and pleasant society living in comfortable old homes with handsome libraries and cellars full of famous old burgundy and claret. He came to regard it as his 'native place', enjoying its high-powered intellectualism and refusing to be cowed even by George Ticknor, the wealthy magnate and littérateur, who ruled the social scene.

Ticknor, in Trollope's phrase, had an air of wrapping his toga around him as he stepped down among the populace, and was used to a certain deference to his opinions.

One sign of a gentleman was to be good-looking, this great blue-chinned caesar informed Thackeray at a dinner-party, since good blood showed itself in good features.

'A pretty speech,' replied Thackeray, 'for one broken-nosed man to make to another!'

Ticknor's restive subjects passed around the retort delightedly. [4]

Of all the eminent Bostonians, it was Prescott, the half-blind historian of Spain, whom Thackeray found most congenial, and it was in his Beacon Street library that he saw the two crossed swords that were to inspire the main theme of *The Virginians*, the weapons which the grandfathers of the historian and his wife had wielded against each other in the Revolutionary War. Five years later, at the start of his American saga, Thackeray was to mention them and to praise their current owner. Prescott's thanks were equally warm: 'I could not have wished anything better, nor certainly have preferred any other pen to write it, among all the golden pens of history and romance.' [5]

In Philadelphia, he got off to a less auspicious start socially. A long, heavy, all-male dinner with eighty or so guests had been prepared in his honour, and, unlike Dickens or Macaulay, Thackeray was incapable of playing the great roaring literary lion before so many strangers. He disappointed, and he knew it, and it worried him. But a few nights later he restored the faith of a small band of the disappointed over roast oysters and terrapin at Prosser's, a cellar-restaurant to rival his favourite London dives.

There, perching his large frame on one of the curtained benches, he rounded off the evening with a tremendous rendition of *Little Billee*, watched by grinning Negro waiters and Prosser's great fat shining black cook, and was soon so popular that the Philadelphians urged him to become British consul to the city.

If anyone could have persuaded him to apply for the job, it would have been the chief instigator of the scheme, William Bradford Reed, District Attorney of Philadelphia, part-time Professor of American History at the state university, and future American Minister to China. His home, like Dr Brown's in Edinburgh, became Thackeray's 'house of call', a refuge where he was as welcome in the nursery as the drawing-room. But Reed proposed the consular plan while Thackeray was in America. Visions of old friends, old haunts, Europe on his doorstep, the Athenaeum library, rides in the park—his loyal, loving, infuriating, Old Testament mother—rose before him, and he declined.

A year later, however, back in England, when he heard that a new Secretary was to be appointed to the Washington legation, he immediately put his name forward. But he was too late. Lord Clarendon, the Foreign Secretary, told him that the post was already filled, and that anyway it would not be fair to appoint anyone from outside the service. '. . . the first was an excellent reason, not a doubt of it,' Thackeray told Reed.[6]

When Reed later published the letter, postman Trollope's sense of humour deserted him completely, and he issued a stern posthumous reprimand for such levity against professionalism.

Thackeray was very taken with Washington. A pleasant, lively place, he thought, rather like Wiesbaden, with politics and gaiety straggling all over it. He took lodgings over a music shop in Pennsylvania Avenue, where he was looked after by a pipe-smoking Negress who knocked out her pungent dottle in his stove, and from there he sallied forth to enjoy the town, sponsored by the British Minister, John Fiennes Twisleton Crampton, a most hospitable envoy.

He was invited to dine at the White House, and flattered by the attentions of not one President but two: outgoing President Fillmore, and President-Elect Pierce. Washington Irving, almost as old and even more revered than his own Rip Van Winkle, seeing these two leaders of his country arriving in amiable partnership for one of the lectures, cocked his wrinkled little brown-wigged head on one side and put an old English saying to excellent use: 'Two Kings of Brentford smelling at one rose!'

Irving, another artist manqué, who had achieved Thackeray's intermittent dream by becoming both a famous writer and a distinguished public servant, was the most loved and lionized of all American celebrities. Thackeray saw him as the Goldsmith of his time and was charmed by the simplicity of his life, given over to the support of a multiplicity of nieces, and by his fifty years' faithfulness to a long-dead fiancée.

While Thackeray could take off his hat, as he liked to say, to such steadfast loyalty, he was happy to discover that his own heart was still made of a more inflammable composition: in America, he had already found beauty enough to set it smouldering again most satisfactorily.

'There was a young Quakeress at the lecture last night—listening about Fielding,' he wrote. 'Lord Lord how pretty she was! there are hundreds of such everywhere—airy looking little beings with . . . camellia . . . complexions, and lasting not much longer.'[7]

In Boston, Mrs George B. Jones, wife of a local jeweller, became a particular favourite. In Washington he spread his affections more widely. There, he said, he had the run of half a dozen beauties, some of them alarmingly young since American girls were launched into the world at sixteen. He told Annie and Minnie he wouldn't like his own daughters to be as forward and commanding as their trans-Atlantic cousins, but even so found himself very ready to banter with and flatter any number of teenage sirens who came fluttering up to tell him they had read *Vanity Fair* twelve times at least. It was balm to his wounded ego, and nowhere did he find the cure more delightful than in New York.

Since he had been told that it would not do to take 'cold joints' to that pace-setting city, Thackeray had given his first lectures in the heart of Manhattan, and been well rewarded for his prudence. His readings, delivered from a high scaffolding rostrum before the pulpit of Broadway's Church of the Unity, were so popular that he began a second series before finishing the first. More important, he met a family so exactly suited to his tastes and needs that enthusiasm for them coloured his view of their entire country.

They were the Baxters, and he was introduced to them by Lady Ashburton's nephew, Henry Bingham Mildmay, a dapper sprig of the English aristocracy, who was wooing, with only moderate success, the elder daughter, Sarah—or Sally as she was called, to Thackeray's disgust ('fancy Abraham calling Sarah Sally!'). The Baxter ladies were already avid fans and Mildmay, hoping no doubt to improve his own position, insisted that Sally's father accompany him when he went to call on Thackeray at the Clarendon Hotel.

Thackeray took an immediate liking to this modest man, and to his two young sons when he met them, but it was the ladies of the family who captivated him, who kept him calling again and again at their brownstone house on Second Avenue. Young Mildmay, so far from furthering his suit, had landed himself with a rival.

Like Mrs Lambert in *The Virginians*, Mrs Baxter was one great syllabub of human kindness, a pretty woman in her early fifties, who soon knew the full history of Thackeray's battered heart. Her younger daughter, sixteen-year-old Lucy, and Lucy's inseparable cousin, Libby Strong, became favourites in their own right, and because they reminded him of his own daughters. The two absurd birds, Thackeray called them—absuerd buerds, when he was waggishly copying their own pronunciation.

And then there was Sally. At nineteen, a clever, proud, restless beauty, Sally fired into explosive life the volcano beneath his waistcoat that Thackeray had believed to be all but extinct. Here, he thought, looking at her for the first time, laughing, provocative, a red ribbon threaded through her brown hair, here was Beatrix Esmond, just as he had described her.

'I have been actually in love for 3 days with a pretty wild girl of 19 (and was never more delighted in my life than by discovering that I could have this malady over again),' he confided to Mrs Procter. [8]

He mentioned her so often in his letters to Kate Perry and Jane Elliot that they grew tired of her name and angry at his fickleness. In Boston, finding that the Ticknors knew her, he 'ran up her flag', and owned he sailed under it. In Paris, the Major nodded his old head and teasingly told Annie and Minnie that he had had a visit from Miss Sally Baxter while they were out. Thackeray spread the word so wide that several months after his return to Europe, he heard an American voice calling to him from a carriage perched half-way up a Swiss mountain, wanting to know how Miss Baxter did?

He was back at the old business of writing letters and putting them into the fire, of haunting parties and balls, keyed up to receive a glance from a pair of bright young eyes and to return it. Within days of meeting her, Thackeray knew that Sally would be the heroine of his next novel, and when he wrote *The Newcomes* he portrayed her as Ethel, the most delightful of all his fictional womenfolk—Beatrix with a heart and a conscience.

Like Ethel, Sally was worthy of more than the flattery of the foolish young beaux who hovered round her, attracted by her beauty and bewildered by her sarcasm. Thackeray saw her as a brave, noble young creature, full of life and laughter, her beauty heightened by her waywardness and a spirit that yearned for some barely conceived fulfilment. He thought her accent adorable, and the way she used little words much better than wit. Her smile was sometimes too saucy, her treatment of her mother, like Beatrix Esmond's, a shifting pattern of outrage and pretty caresses. She was a great and intelligent beauty in the making, and Thackeray felt a man again when she practised her wiles on him.

For him, she had what he called an *amour de tête*: she flirted with him, sparred with him, and drove him wild by staying up in her room when she knew he was waiting in the library. When she came down, the odds were that they had 'a skirmish'. She confided to him the delights and frustrations of her young life, her scorn of the social marriage market. She drew on his wisdom and humour, and later recognized many of her own remarks in *The Newcomes*. Like Ethel, she toyed with the idea of selling herself to a wealthy *parti* to ease her family's financial problems, but if such a match meant Bingham Mildmay, Thackeray was dead against it.

'No—go and live in a clearing—marry a husband masticatory, expectoratory, dubious of linen, but with a heart below that rumpled garment . . .' he told her; 'help the help, and give a hand to the dinner yourself—yea, it is better than to be a woman of fashion in London, and sit down to a French dinner where no love is.' [9]

She had so much character, resolution and good temper, he urged her, she would be happy making others so, and would accommodate herself to any deficiencies in *savoir vivre* like a young philosopheress.

He clearly saw the folly of his own attachment. In his last series for *Punch* he had written of the absurdity of ancient bucks who still pranced before the young ladies, edging away more suitable competition with their creaking, superannuated elbows, and could imagine only too well what the world would say if the silver-haired satirist himself launched out along that path. But he also understood the benefit of the renewed stirrings of desire. They distanced him from the pain of his break with the Brookfields, shattered the sterile cocoon of self-pity. If, as he said, he felt warmed by the youthful blood coursing through the veins of America, it was largely due to Sally.

The Baxters' brownstone home, the 'dear old friendly Brown House', became the place he liked best to be in all America, a guaranteed haven where he could be sure of a welcome from the oldest and youngest of the ladies, if not always from Miss Sally. On lecture days, sharing their evening meal, the claret pitcher before him, Mrs Baxter's admired brandy-peaches and pickled walnuts close at hand, he would roll out the opening sentences of that night's performance in tones of exaggerated gloom.

On other evenings, when Mrs Baxter had expressly told her children not to ask him to stay should he call, since she hadn't such a dinner as she would care to give him, he would bound in with some small gift he knew they would like, and the winning inquiry that now they would have to ask him to dinner, wouldn't they?—which sent the younger Baxters into insubordinate paroxysms of laughter.

Just as he called Sally 'Beatrix', so Thackeray dubbed her mother 'Lady Castlewood', and, like Esmond, poured out to the one his infatuation for the other. When he finally left New York to return to Boston, he wrote to Mrs Baxter:

'Isn't it all written before in the Chronicle of Esmond the son of Esmond? That weak and elderly gentleman saw a number of faults in a certain bright & beautiful Mistress Beatrix, who nevertheless played the mischief with his heart: and I don't think he was ever more glum than I at this present sitting alone and looking at the bleak and sulky snow coming down on my prospect at the commencement of this happy New Year. Do *all* the victims I wonder write and pour out their griefs to you? Poor Bingham! I feel like him rather, as if I had been just on the point of going down; & escaped only in my clothes, leaving I don't know how much of the most valuable of my heart's luggage behind me—'[10]

To Sally herself, he wrote two letters, and burned them. They were too long, too sentimental and too fond. In the one he finally sent, he told her:

'A pen that's so practised as mine is runs on talking and talking: I fancy the people I speak to are sitting with me; and pour out the sense and nonsense jokes and the contrary, egotisms—whatever comes upper most. And you know what was uppermost yesterday. My heart was longing and yearning after you full of love and gratitude for your welcome of me—but the words grew a little too warm. You wouldn't like me to write letters in that strain You might tell me to write no more: and if you did I should burst out into a misanthropical rage again—Please to let me write on: and make my frank claim to have a little place in Beatrix's heart. I told my children what a place she had got in mine. I would not hide from them or from you those honest generous feelings. When the destined man comes, with a good head and a good heart fit to win such a girl, and love and guide her; then old Mr Thackeray will make his bow and say God bless her . . .'[11]

Thackeray did not fail to inform Jane Brookfield that he had found Beatrix in New York, and basked in her bright eyes. He couldn't live without the tenderness of some woman, he told her, and expected when he was sixty to be marrying a girl of eleven or twelve, innocent, barley-sugar-loving, in a pinafore.

Throughout the lonely months in London, he had approached the Brookfields only rarely and with caution. He had been once to Cadogan Place, and wrote then: 'They are launching out in the dinner-giving way and had 12 people; and we all grinned and laughed a great deal.'[12]

Brookfield was wary, Thackeray uncomfortable, and Jane—Jane was preparing to put all their counters back on 'Go' and start off the same old game all over again. The polite little notes and formal invitations that had marked the beginning of the affair had begun once more to arrive at Young Street, but this time Thackeray had refused to play.

His farewell before going to America, restrained and public at a London party, brought a gentle reproach across the Atlantic from Jane, but Brookfield had made it clear that he wanted nothing more intimate by pointedly turning from Thackeray and asking Kate Perry to accompany them home. Thackeray had bowed to his will. He had made no move to see Jane alone, but the obvious exclusion on the eve of a hazardous voyage and a long parting revived the old bitterness. When the English reviews of *Esmond* eventually reached him in America, he drew a certain satisfaction from imagining how mad 'poor Tomkins' must have been at the critics' preoccupation with the marital aspects of the book, and hoped it would make him treat his wife better in the future.

With the safety of the ocean between them, he again wrote occasionally to Jane, the accustomed long letters, but the fight to keep clear of dangerous sentiment, and the knowledge that she was once more pregnant, lowered over them. There were moments when he thought of her tenderly, picturing her sadly trimming up little caps and long clothes, making her preparations to live as well as she could after the shipwreck. But at other times he found it difficult to forgive her that second child, and knew in his heart that the greatest benefit of the American trip would be to confirm their separation:

'She may go on with her maternal duties without my furious eyes haunting her in her duty,' he wrote to Chesham Place. 'I hope they'll go away for the summer when I come. It is decent that we should not meet much. However much I may love her & bless her and admire her, I can't forgive her for doing her duty. Everybody else may & should applaud her and I do too. But I hope she'll have the courage to go into the country when I come back, & increase her family in seclusion.'[13]

He was still desperately torn in his feeling for her, and as he moved south, away from the flames of Sally Baxter's healing fire, the old wounds and longings throbbed again. As Lady Day approached, he asked Kate Perry to send her a birthday token:

'. . . from one who remembers her all day & all night and loves and blesses as if she were an angel in heaven—Suppose you were to buy a lily with two little lilies on the stem if possible and send it as a salutation and without any name. God bless her. For all the pain and grief to both of us: I would not have *not* had her love for anything in the world. It's apart from desire, or jealousy of any one else, that I think of her and shall always.'[14]

Yet, in the same birthday month, he wrote the most cutting commentary on her return for that love, in a poem called *The Sorrows of Werther*, a biting summary of the story that had left Jane virtually unmoved:

> Werther had a love for Charlotte
>   Such as words could never utter;
> Would you know how first he met her?
>   She was cutting bread-and-butter.
>
> Charlotte was a married lady,
>   And a moral man was Werther,
> And, for all the wealth of Indies,
>   Would do nothing for to hurt her.

So he sighed and pined and ogled,
   And his passion boiled and bubbled.
Till he blew his silly brains out,
   And no more was by it troubled.

Charlotte, having seen his body
   Borne before her on a shutter,
Like a well-conducted person,
   Went on cutting bread-and-butter. [15]

22

The Newcomes

London, Paris, Switzerland and Rome

Thackeray left America with dollars still untapped in the vast bulk of the continent. Tales of exploding Mississippi paddle-steamers and long days of travelling had whittled away his courage for a great sweep inland and northwards to New Orleans and the Middle West. Instead, he retraced his steps up the eastern seaboard from Savannah, and by mid-April was with the Baxters once more, in time to celebrate Lucy's seventeenth birthday, and mark it with a poem in more hopeful vein.

He planned to spend only a week in that seductive city, indulging in being a gentleman instead of a 'pulpit quack', before pushing on to Montreal, Cincinnati, Rochester and Buffalo. Though he could still surprise himself by working up an actorish interest in the readings when they were in progress, he was becoming heartily tired of them, often tempted to set fire to the dog-eared pages and so have done with the business. When they were published, he said, even poor Jack Forster would hardly be able to sneer at them as much as he did himself.

More than a fortnight later, having made one solitary lecturing excursion to Albany, he was still in New York, reading the newspapers in his room at the Clarendon, when he saw that a Cunarder, the *Europa*, was sailing that day for England. He had been away for almost six months and homesickness overcame him. Whirling into action, he told Crowe to get their bags packed while he dashed to Wall Street to take berths.

By eleven, they were speeding down Broadway. As they jumped

into a tender on the East River, the shipping agent shouted 'Hurry up—she's starting!' Almost as they reached the top of the ladder, the *Europa* was steaming briskly ahead, and Thackeray rushed off the most important of his good-byes and thank-yous to send ashore with the pilot.

'No one,' he told the husband of sympathetic Mrs Jones of Boston, 'can be more astonished than myself at finding myself actually under weigh and bound to Europe . . .'[1]

On board he discovered an officer who had sailed with Dickens on his first terrifying Atlantic crossing, and doing a little checking up on his rival, found that even in a hardened sailor's estimation, the *American Notes* description had exaggerated nothing. Thackeray and Crowe were luckier. With favourable winds, often under full canvas, they sped towards Liverpool. As they rounded Cape Clear, they shouted 'Old England!' into the bright morning air—thus knocking yet another stake into sensitive Anglo-Irish relations—and after a mere ten days and fifteen and a half hours at sea found themselves on land again, quaffing turtle soup at the Adelphi Hotel.

The following night, the returned traveller caused a most satisfactory sensation, appearing unheralded at one of Lady Stanley's grand Dover Street balls, full of ecstatic praise for America, his watch still registering New York time.

'I pulled it out last night and showed it to the people at the ball,' he wrote to Mrs Baxter, 'and said There thats the *real* time—They said Isn't this a beautiful ball and says I—Pish this is nothing—Go to New York if you want to see what a ball is . . . as if there could be any balls after New York! . . . My praises of the American women are going all about town, & Lady S says are outrageous.'[2]

Bingham Mildmay's brother, lounging over to talk about America in a pertly condescending manner, so epitomized British arrogance and wooden-headedness for him that Thackeray felt greatly tempted to wring his little neck. Lurching about in his cabin on the *Europa*, and later dressing at Young Street, Thackeray sentimentally kissed the collars Lucy Baxter had mended for him, and felt a mission rising within him whenever he thought of the good friends he had made on the other side of the Atlantic.

'By Jove, how kind you all were to me! How I like people, and want to see 'em again!' he wrote to Reed. 'You are more tender-hearted, romantic, sentimental, than we are. I keep on telling this to our fine people here, and have so belaboured your country with praise in private, that I sometimes think I go too far. I keep back some of the truth: but the great point to try and ding into the ears of the great stupid virtue-proud English public, is that there are folks as good as they in America.'[3]

A few weeks later, Thackeray was to see, confirmed in print, that the love—and the surprise that there should be love—was mutual. George William Curtis, writing in *Putnam's Monthly Magazine*, said:

'The popular Thackeray-theory, before his arrival, was of a severe satirist, who concealed scalpels in his sleeves and carried probes in his waistcoat pockets; a wearer of masks; a scoffer and sneerer, and general infidel of all high aims and noble character. Certainly we are justified in saying that his presence among us quite corrected this idea. We welcomed a friendly, genial man . . . We conceive this to be the chief result of Thackeray's visit, that he convinced us of his intellectual integrity; he showed us how impossible it is for him to see the world, and describe it other than he does. He does not profess cynicism, nor satirize society with malice. There is no man more humble, none more simple.'[4]

Thackeray resisted appeals to lecture on his travels. The crowds he envisaged were tempting, but he planned to go back to that dollar-rich country in the autumn with a new series of readings, and chose the course of discretion. Having rushed away, he could scarcely wait to return. To the three Baxter ladies, his 'friends in the sunset', he wrote in animated rotation, spilling out the egotisms as freely as he did to Kate Perry and her sister, as he had once done to Jane. When he visited his parents and children at Paris, and saw signs of the American invasion, the grand barouches with splendid liveried servants wheeling down the avenues, heard again those well-remembered accents, spoken with a certain 'twang in the nose', he was lost in nostalgia for his 'beloved Republic', and when he saw an American girl with bright brown hair and laughing eyes in one of those brisk equipages, the old passions thrilled again.

'—a great gush of feelings came tumbling out of this bussam at the sight,' he wrote to Sally. 'I wanted to run after the carriage to stop it and speak to her and say "Do you know anything of one S.B. of New York?" The carriage whisked away leaving me alone with my feelings—O ye old ghosts! I declare I saw nothing of the crowded city for a minute or two so complete did the *revenans* hem me in— Nothing is forgotten. We bury 'em but they pop out of their graves now and again and say Here we are Master. Do you think we are dead? No, No, only asleep. We wake up sometimes we come to you we shall come to you when you are ever so old; we shall always be as fresh and mischievous as we are now. We shall say Do you remember S.S.B. do you remember her eyes? Do you think she had 2 dimples in her cheeks and don't you recollect this was the note of her laugh, that used to be quite affected at times but you know the music of it, you poor old rogue?'[5]

But, inevitably, the old world began once more to press in and edge out the new. George Smith and Bradbury and Evans, in rivalry for a new Thackeray novel, pushed up the price so high he succumbed to their persuasion. In gratitude for their early faith in him, he chose Bradbury and Evans's much lower offer, but it was still £3600, more than three times as much as they had given him for *Vanity Fair*. Coining money, he called it.

With Harper's promised payment for early English proofs, and a handsome Tauchnitz edition, he optimistically reckoned he would be able to set aside £3000 for his daughters, as much clear profit as he was likely to make lecturing again in America. And so the second proposed Atlantic crossing was postponed while he met again the spur, stimulus and agonies of the old yellow-covered numbers.

Broody with the new story, he shuttled to and fro across the Channel, uneasy if he stayed too long in Paris, where the Carmichael-Smyths now had the Laurence portrait swaggering on a wall of their small apartment, making him feel more of an out-of-place heavy old swell than ever, unable to carry his daughters back to London until he had found a new governess.

While Mrs Carmichael-Smyth waited in tearful anticipation for the day when she would be called upon to 'yield her place to the stranger,'[6] he set up a two-month hue and cry for another impossible paragon. He had three teeth out ('Miss Sally, I shall never fall in love any more') and lounged and gormandized as though he had 'been born a Marquis'. He was proud to boast that he existed entirely on his literary earnings, but there were times when rich living made him forget that he had to keep writing to do so.

He took on an admirable new manservant, Charles Pearman, a smart young footman from a London club. But a governess he couldn't find, and at the end of June he set off again to scoop up his daughters for a Continental tour, his professed aim being to find a pleasant, quiet place to begin work in.

Three days out, at Baden Baden, 'the prettiest booth of all Vanity Fair,'[7] surrounded by London society *en voyage*, amid the clatter and whir of the *rouge et noir*, he began *The Newcomes*, the first writing he had done for thirteen months, and in the opening pages launched a display of literary pyrotechnics as brilliant as any he had produced in his twenty-year career. Mischievous, laughing at those who called him cynic, cloaking his finer thoughts in wicked irony, he told his readers:

'This, then, is to be a story, may it please you, in which jackdaws will wear peacocks' feathers, and awaken the just ridicule of the peacocks; in which, while every justice is done to the peacocks themselves, the splendour of their plumage, the gorgeousness of their dazzling necks, and the magnificence of their tails, exception will yet be taken to the absurdity of their rickety strut, and the foolish discord of their pert squeaking; in which lions in love will have their claws pared by sly virgins; in which rogues will sometimes triumph, and honest folks, let us hope, come by their own; in which there will be black crape and white favours; in which there will be tears under orange-flower wreaths and jokes in mourning-coaches; in which there will be dinners of herbs with contentment and without, and banquets of stalled oxen where there is care and hatred—ay, and kindness and friendship too, along with the feast. It does not follow that all men are honest because they are poor; and I have known some who were friendly and generous, although they had plenty of money. There are some great landlords who do not grind down their tenants; there are actually bishops who are not hypocrites; there are liberal men even among the Whigs, and the Radicals themselves are not all Aristocrats at heart.'

He was afraid it would be a retreat from the high ground he had occupied in *Esmond*, but then that book, he said still smarting from *The Times*'s slashing review, had been a failure as well as being immoral: he would take pains and write careful books when he had made £10,000 for his young ladies. Even so, he strove with *The Newcomes* as he did with all his works, and when he wasn't writing, read other admired authors with an eye to self-betterment. The deuce was in it, he said, while reading *Don Quixote* and Tacitus, if his own style didn't improve in the process.

Early on, he hit on the idea (borrowed, he suspected, from Bulwer-Lytton) of making Pendennis the narrator of the story, and at once felt the lifting of a great weight from his mind. Under that disguise, he could say many things he would not have dared to venture on in his own person, now that it *was* a person and he knew the public was staring at it.

It was also a relief, after *Esmond*, to be free from the encumbrance of research. All he needed was fresh ink, a good pen, free-flowing paper and his own imagination, an imagination he berated, compared unfavourably with Dickens's, called used up and worked out, yet which produced, in circumstances most authors would have found intolerable, a vast novel that did a great deal more than simply increase his daughters' inheritance.

Many years later, Henry James, of the brass-buttoned jacket and a sparer mode of novel-writing, was to call it 'a great loose baggy monster'.[8] In fact, it was the most closely planned of all Thackeray's serial stories. With an air of astonished pride, he confided to his readers that the whole plot had been 'revealed to him somehow' when he strolled away from his daughters one day and into a wood near Berne. For once, he knew enough of his own story-line to drop clues into the early chapters and gather them up at the end.

But to his readers such literary niceties meant little compared with the rich feast of scenes and characters he offered them every month. In twenty-four numbers he was to present the great world of London with such precision that worldly men's daughters were forbidden to read it. In *Esmond*, he had brought to life a distant age. In *The Newcomes*, he preserved his own for posterity.

The Cave of Harmony and the Haunt, the banker's parlour and the London club, the Inns of Court and the Brighton lodging-house, the studios of young painters and the political hustings, are woven as clearly into his tapestry as the annual pilgrimages of the rich and the jangling dance of the marriage market. He raided his own past for details of the Anglo-Indian colony and the banking disaster—that 'complicated, enormous, outrageous swindle'—that had swept away his patrimony. He drew characters from the life, with both bitterness and love.

'That's my she-devil of a mother-in-law, you know, whom I have the good-luck to possess still,' Thackeray told a group of friends,[9] as he read out the final chapter, the pages that told of the death of the Colonel, a brave man beaten into senile childishness by Mrs Mackenzie, 'the Campaigner', whose venomous self-righteous harangues echo those of Mrs Shawe when Thackeray took the suicidal Isabella to her in Ireland.

The cast he presented was vast and memorable: old Lady Kew, the wicked, worldly grandmother—sister to the Marquis of Steyne, thus stretching the canvas further, to take in *Vanity Fair*—parading her old bones still at all the tribal rituals, clawing on to life by the determination to see her granddaughter married magnificently, if not happily; the Marquis of Farintosh, with his opera girls and toadies, a tantalizing hint of what Thackeray could have done with the type had he not been fettered by Victorian taboos; the young Lord Kew, who had also sown his wild oats, but who remained noble in spirit as well as in *Debrett*; the odious Barnes Newcome, prematurely shrewd, with not an atom of compassion or morality in his shrivelled little heart, the natural winner in all his dealings with that great good foolish innocent, his uncle; the Comte de Florac, an ageing, Gallic Peter Pan, his wife, '*née* Higg of Manchester', and his mother, the truly *grande* and tragic *dame*, beside whom even old Lady Kew did not care to measure herself; Ethel, her young counterpart, the natural-born aristocrat; and poor little Rosey Mackenzie, blighted by her mother's brutal whirlwinds and fortune's nipping frosts.

'So "Clive Newcome" has actually married that pretty simpleton,

"Rosy Mackenzie"—Isn't it abominable? Really, it is very provoking of Thackeray that he will make his heroes and heroines marry the wrong people just as they do in real life,' Mrs Stirling, the actress, complained to a friend while the yellow-covered numbers were engrossing their first audience. [10]

Young Clive, the handsome, humorous, sensitive artist, initiated into many new worlds, receiving their pleasures, their intentional insults and unconscious thrusts, as Thackeray himself had done, was, as Mrs Stirling implied, worthy of a better mate. Tormented by passion for the near-inaccessible, a brave champion of his chosen profession, and of J.J., the humbly born, humble-souled artist of genius, he is a creature rare in Thackeray's works, a hero.

But for Thackeray's first readers, it was Clive's father, the Colonel, the simple soldier, retaining in age the purity and grace of childhood, who formed the magnetic focus of the novel. Shown with all his faults and foolishness, his stubbornness and narrowness of vision, he nevertheless represented the Victorian ideal of manliness, and for that one character his creator was released by many from the charge of cynicism.

At times, the Colonel exasperated Thackeray as much as the models he had 'angelicized' to make him—his stepfather and Charles Carmichael (who, under cousin Mary's influence, had dropped the ordinary-sounding Smyth from his name).

While staying with friends and still trying to keep up with his writing, Thackeray was asked if he had slept well. 'How could I,' he grumbled, 'with Colonel Newcome making a fool of himself as he has done?' [11]

He knew some of his friends, like Mrs Procter, thought the Colonel was rather a twaddler, and at the end of the eighth number packed him off to India for three fictional years, feeling that the story breathed more freely without him. When he brought him back, it was with riches enough to make everyone he loved best perfectly miserable.

Returned from the battlefield, the gallant old warrior was destined for many misfortunes and a deathbed scene which, along with Dickens's disposal of Little Nell, was to become the most famous in Victorian fiction. But whereas most people would now agree with Oscar Wilde, that one needs a heart of stone not to laugh at the death of Little Nell, even in an age when natural death has become the great unmentionable, few remain unmoved by Thackeray's farewell to the Colonel.

So great was contemporary admiration that Thackeray was taken to task for not respecting the character enough himself. Dicky Doyle, who did the illustrations, thus leaving Thackeray free to travel, was disturbed because he appeared to sneer at the Colonel for not being a man about town, and the American poet, artist and clergyman, Christopher P. Cranch, one of the group to whom Thackeray read out the death scene in a room over the Cyder Cellars, was greatly distressed by Thackeray's reaction to a band of artists and journalists, a shirt-sleeved, cheerfully abusive Morgan John O'Connell in the van, who burst in and shattered the mood.

'Well, Thack,' O'Connell greeted him, 'I've read your last number. Don't like it. It's a failure. Not so good as the rest!'[12]

As Thackeray, with matching good humour and freedom of expression, sent the rabble packing, Cranch pondered the duality of his nature: the thoughtful, tender and purely literary, combined with what he could only politely call Bohemian. It disturbed him that Thackeray should be on such good terms with the noisy, jostling intruders, and even more that their interruption should have had no visibly jarring effect on him.

Nathaniel Hawthorne, when told of the scene, was scandalized at Thackeray's 'coolness in respect to his own pathos'. He recalled how *he* had struggled and failed to read the last pages of his *Scarlet Letter* to his wife, and how *his* voice had swelled and heaved, as if he were tossed up and down on an ocean, as it subsided after a storm.

Thackeray, too, had done his share of mourning for the Colonel. He had blubbered as he made him answer 'Adsum' to the last roll-call of life, but more than a month had passed between the writing and the reading. He couldn't go on forever weeping over his own work, and was later to argue, forcibly, that anyway he considered Dickens's Dan'l Peggotty a finer gentleman than his own candidate for the title.

2.

At the beginning of September, Thackeray returned briefly to London. In two months he had piloted his children from Paris to Mannheim, Baden, Basle, Malleray, Neuchâtel, Lausanne, Vevey, Geneva, Bulle, Fribourg, Berne, Thun, Escholzmatt, Lucerne, Zürich, Basle again, Heidelberg, Frankfurt, Cologne, Ostend, and home via Dover. And in that time he had written the first four numbers, despite several bouts of illness, including a 'smart fever' at Frankfurt that had begun alarmingly like the *Pendennis* cholera scare. It was to take him another two months, in comparatively good health and stable circumstances, to finish the fifth.

Switzerland and the Rhine he had found completely conquered by Americans, and not the kind of Americans he would have wished to represent their country: cigar-sucking, expectorating, back-slapping and gesticulating to make up for a total lack of any foreign language.

'If you could have heard Mrs Boggs of the USA,' he wrote to Mrs Baxter's brother, 'speaking through her nose at the Inn at Malleray last night surrounded by the sweetest sights skies landscapes odours of nature: with tinkling cows coming home, with sunset blushing on the white village—buildings, and the beautiful hills veiling themselves in purple shadows—by Jove it was death & discord to hear Mrs Boggs—There was a gentleman of the party who delivered his opinions not nasally but orally.'[1]

He knew it wasn't civil to write a man a letter full of abuse of his own countrymen, but he had to unbosom himself to someone, and would not have done so to his own compatriots even if they hadn't sneered: 'Are *these* the Americans you are always bragging about?'[2]

At Basle, watching a more attractive group at the table d'hôte, he had just told Annie and Minnie how nostalgic they made him feel, when five of them put their knives down their throats. Annie and Minnie giggled at his discomfiture.

'My dear, your great-great-grandmother, one of the finest ladies of the old school I ever saw, always applied cold steel to her vittles,' he told them. 'It's no *crime* to eat with a knife.'[3] But all the same he wished that five at a time wouldn't do it. He wished the men didn't look so awful, he would have liked them to speak a little French, as even the patronizing British had learned to do, and he would especially have liked them not to write in hotel Strangers' Books as one had done:

NAME	COUNTRY	PROFESSION	WHENCE COME	WHITHER GOING
Smith F.	*U.S.A.*	*Clergyman*	*Genêvre*	*Over the whole lot*
Smith T.				

Why didn't they send over some proper Americans? he asked the Baxter family. Nothing could dim his ardour for *them*: 'often . . . about the hour of sunset, my heart, w^h knows that much of geography, flies over to the West, and lands amongst you and holds out its hands, and says God bless you all, and blows its nose to conceal its emotions . . .'[4]

Maintaining still such kindly views, praising extravagantly in the face of all evidence to the contrary, Thackeray, the master of irony, found himself beaten at that mischievous game by blinkered American chauvinism. When the first number of *The Newcomes* appeared in the States, one unfortunate sentence was pounced on and used to prove that he, like all the rest, had taken American gold and returned home to laugh at and revile the American people.

Thinking himself into the mood of George II's smug, jingoistic

England to introduce the first of the Newcomes, he had written of Mr Washington then heading his rebels in America with courage worthy of a better cause.

The outcry was immense. In a letter to *The Times*, who had spread the news of America's wrath in England, Thackeray pointed out that his satire, if satire it were, had been directed not at Americans but at the English of a previous century, who had been instructed ('until they were taught better manners') to call General Washington 'Mr. Washington', and to refer to the Americans as rebels throughout the course of the war, but he was not absolved, and a month later he asked Mrs Baxter:

'Can't we find any plan of healing that absurd "Mr Washington" feud? I feel myself shocked and pained by it as if some dear friend had turned round to abuse me; I who for once in my life kept my own council; who have got to consider yours as my country almost; who have praised the States so outrageously since I came home, & made myself such a violent partizan—How dare people think I could be guilty of such stupid abuse as that they attribute to me? I who love and honor Washington as I love & honor no other man?—"It serves you right"—a man said to me in London—You see what good you have got by praising the States—O it puts me into a rage!'[5]

It was the end of a period of unusual contentment. Despite his illnesses and the lack of a governess, the Swiss tour had been a huge success. The sun had shone—strongly enough to burn the skin off all their noses; the writing had gone well; Charles Pearman, a model servant, had striven with Annie and Minnie, his 'other 2 slaves', to make him comfortable.

'. . . plenty of work play health money good children. What could man ask for more?' he had written to Kate Perry and her sister before the Frankfurt fever: '—only one thing that he can't have. That one thing everybody nankers after no doubt.'[6]

When he first saw the Brookfields after the birth of their second child, a son, he was fooled by Jane's behaviour—that sweet hypocrisy for which he was always praising women in his books—into believing that the clergyman and his lady were truly reconciled. When he began to suspect otherwise, he invented a new commandment for himself: '"Thou shalt not pity thy neighbour's wife". Keep out of his Harem; & it is better for you & him.'[7]

It was a resolution he tried to convey to Brookfield in a reply to yet another invitation to Cadogan Place. 'Now after 2 years asunder,' he wrote, 'when there are no more rages on my part, I pray you to forget savage words, as I do (for I don't remember what I said or wrote only that a great deal of it was furious & unjust)—Forget all this if you can and remember the friend of old days.'[8]

But Brookfield, as miserable with Jane as Thackeray was without her, could not forget. He had begun that year by recording in his diary a conversation with Carlyle:

'Marriage,' Brookfield had said, 'is dipping into a pitcher of snakes for the chance of an eel.'

'Ay,' Carlyle had agreed, picking up the idea with enthusiasm, 'and eels have a faculty by very natural transformation for becoming snakes.'

Brookfield had not argued with him.

At their rare meetings, Thackeray watched him trying, as he thought, to smother his hatred, only to have that insuppressible Jack-in-the-box come rushing out again.

'I fancy I see him clapping down the lid,' he told Kate Perry. 'As for JOB . . . I think I am nearer her, when away than when sitting by her, talking of things we don't feel—with poor Tomkins's restless eye ever & again trying *not* to look at us. I knew the time when she walked: but never went. It mustn't be: it mustn't be: and it's happier that we should love each other in the grave as it were, than that we should meet by sham-chance, & that there should be secrecy or deceit. When you see her preach this to her again & again. Many & many a time a friend of mine whispers me (he is represented in pictures with horns & a tail) My good friend *à quoi bon* all this longing & yearning & disappointment; yonder gnawing grief and daily nightly brooding? a couple of lies & the whole thing might be remedied. Do you suppose other folks are so particular? Behold there are 4 children put their innocent figures between the Devil and me: and the wretched old fiend shirks off with his tail between his hoofs. Go and wipe away her tears, you dear kind sisters of charity.'[9]

There were other tempters too, though, besides the devil: those same tender, sentimental sisters of mercy, reinforced on occasion by Mrs Fanshawe, who lured Thackeray into at least one unexpected meeting with Jane. The ladies of Chesham Place never stopped passing on the tales of wretchedness and yearning, showing the letters from one to the other, keeping alive the love and the grief. At the bottom of one of those shared pages there is a message still, scrawled in Jane's shaking hand beneath Thackeray's neat, slanting script: 'when writing some day will you tell from me this—poor Thackeray when I'm in London, he seems ever here.'[10]

On his return from America, Thackeray told Mrs Baxter that he had been near the '*frying-pan*' again without beginning to fry. It might just have remained true without that constant womanly chorus, or if he could have found in London another girl to match Mrs Baxter's daughter. For several years there had been two other

young beauties who had given zest to his forays into the world—
Lady Stanley's daughter, Blanche, and Virginia, sixth of the seven
remarkable Pattle sisters—but now they too were beyond his reach,
new mistresses of great country estates, preoccupied with the
business of producing heirs.

Blanche, a clever, romantic and imperious blonde, who joined
Sally Baxter in forming the character of Ethel Newcome, had un-
willingly married the seventh Earl of Airlie, leaving Thackeray to
complain to her mother that he would have preferred her to have a
house within dinner-distance of London to a castle in Scotland
however splendid and ancient.

Virginia's beauty he had spotted when she was still a child, and
when she came out he was enraptured by her, in company with a
great many other connoisseurs. His letters to Mrs Brookfield had
been liberally seasoned with teasing rhapsodies on this younger,
divine creature, he astonished Annie and Minnie with the extraordinary vivacity of his conversation whenever he met her, and he
blew up a full-scale literary tempest by putting her into one of his
'Proser' papers for *Punch* as Erminia, a young lady endowed by
nature with almost every perfection.

The poet, Henry Taylor, a most grave and learned gentleman, also
appeared in the piece, under the name of Timotheus, and the story
was told of how he, like every other man of taste, had fallen for the
beautiful Erminia, with such ardour that had not Mrs Timotheus
been an exceedingly sensible person, it would undoubtedly have
caused friction in their marriage.

So proud was Thackeray of his sly digs and luscious praises, that
he read them out at the Elliots, where Henry Taylor was also a
regular visitor, and proposed carrying them round to Erminia
herself. When the article was published, a few months before
Virginia's marriage to Lord Somers's heir, Viscount Eastnor, he was
amazed at the uproar it caused. Mrs Taylor's family, the Spring
Rices, were up in arms, Virginia's eldest sister, Mrs Cameron, the
photographer, cut him, and Lady Ashburton wrote from The
Grange to suggest that he postpone his visit since Henry Taylor was
also in residence and she could see from his manner that it wouldn't
do.

Thackeray, furious, thought himself the innocent victim of petty
social persecution, and it was not until Jane Brookfield persuaded
him to see the article from Mrs Taylor's point of view that he had
become contrite enough to send the Taylors a handsome apology—
and Lady Ashburton a sketch of a donkey let loose in a chicken-run.

Now, in the autumn of 1853, he had no one to inspire such
invigorating folly. Sally was three thousand miles away, Isabella

was lost to him in her own little housekeeping world, and Jane Brookfield, though still apparently accessible, was a solace he was determined to deny himself. Since Jane showed no inclination to use London only when he was absent, it was Thackeray who once more fled from temptation.

There was great pressure on him to winter with his parents in Paris. The Major had suffered a stroke while he was in America, and, at seventy-two, was becoming frail; his mother was fretful; there was still no governess. But after a month or so in lodgings in the Champs Elysées, writing with enormous labour, he knew he had to move on. He was plagued by a restlessness that only constant travel could ease. 'I begin to feel most tranquillity in a railway carriage now; and retirement in an inn,' he told Mrs Baxter.[11]

If he stopped anywhere for long, the great yawning emptiness of his domestic life became intolerable. With a brief flaring of youthful recklessness, he thought of leaping again from the frying-pan into the fire by taking his daughters to join the Baxters at Saratoga Springs, but at last he decided on Rome, where he planned to set part of *The Newcomes*.

3.

On the journey to Marseilles, the young Misses Thackeray lost their shawls. On the voyage to Genoa, Annie, having left her porthole open, woke in the night to find water lashing over her and ran through the ship screaming that they were sinking. After a trip ashore, to buy new shawls, rascally boatmen rowed them part of the way back to the steamer then rested on their oars, demanding more money.

While the ship sent up departure flares, two young fellow passengers reasoned and remonstrated in halting Italian, but it wasn't until Thackeray, rising 6ft 3in in the stern of the rocking boat, shouted in loud and forceful English, 'Damn you, go on!' that they began to move again, amid surly mutterings.

On the road from Civitavecchia to Rome, with an alert out that brigands had been sighted, their post-chaise broke a trace and killed a postilion. They were surrounded by wild-looking shepherds and peasants with pitchforks, and Thackeray clung to the eighty gold louis in his pocket.

At dusk, at last, they reached the Eternal City, and went first to the Hotel Franz, a debt of honour, since the *padrone* had never sent a bill for the two months Thackeray had stayed there at the end of his Cairo to Cornhill voyage, the *Barry Lyndon* days when his pockets were bare of gold louis or any other coin, and his letters of credit were filed, inaccessible, at the post office under the name of 'Mr *Jackeray*'.

On his first afternoon, asleep on a sofa, Thackeray was bitten so fiercely that when a scandalized chambermaid disclaimed all knowledge of fleas, he suggested with heavy irony that he must have been attacked by a scorpion. In Rome, surrounded by the encroaching Pontine Marshes, it was more likely to have been a mosquito, and within days he was in bed with a fever, and what he called an 'attack of the bowowels', being bled and blistered, taking calomel, living on bread and water, and refraining from cigars.

It was an appalling start for an author with a book burning in his brain, publication already begun, unreliable posts, and only two monthly numbers left in hand. And it never really improved. For two months in Rome and seven weeks in Naples—where Annie and Minnie went down in succession with scarlet fever—he was dogged by illness: a regular cycle of fever and spasms, followed by weakness, languor and depression, which he at last admitted was 'the confounded Italian Malaria'.

It was the year he had worked for for so long, the year in which he had at last begun to put money away, and to spend the rest with a clear conscience. He should have been happy, but at least he found himself sumptuous surroundings in which to be miserable.

With the help of Robert Browning, he chose an apartment in the Palazzo Poniatowski, a noble old building on the via della Croce, which also housed, on the ground floor, the premises of 'the two best pastry-cooks in Christendom'[1]—a fitting address for a man who could still, between bouts of sickness, savour the childhood memory of three-cornered puffs and dear old plumcake.

Their quarters were vast, magnificent and expensive, large on living-rooms—a library, a Chinese museum, a dining-room, salons hung with inferior paintings in superb gilded frames, crammed with *objets*, statuettes, wax flowers, and uncomfortable furniture fit for an antique showroom—and short on bedrooms. Thackeray gave his daughters the only one, took the dressing-room for himself, and Charles Pearman slept in a cupboard in the hall.

The windows stood open to the warm December air, white doves cooed and fluttered on the sills, unfamiliar noises of life and bustle, music and plashing fountains rose from the *piazza*, and Annie and Minnie flew from room to room feeling like enchanted princesses. In the end it was his children's enthusiasm and pleasure which made the excursion tolerable, especially Annie's.

At sixteen, she was turning into the greatest blessing of his life, the companion he had so long needed in his own home, an eager helper and worshipper, who understood his ways, laughed at his jokes and consoled him when he was dismal, which, as he told her with a smile that only half masked serious belief, was the wont and duty of women in life. To hear her singing in a neighbouring room, to watch her obstinate determination to be pleased, chased away his wearisome blue devils.

Between them, his daughters made life bearable, but they also presented problems. In a light-hearted grumble, he complained that a man who travelled with two children and no governess inevitably found himself 'pretty much the tall confidential old family servant of the young ladies': he lost his liberty, spent five times as much, and always had to take the worst room.[2] More seriously he worried, as he got up before dawn to work in the peace of the still sleeping house, or struggled through a fit of fever to make up short copy, that his art was dying in the midst of trivial domestic duties; that he could see not one pennyworth of the artist's life he had gone to Rome expressly to look for and put into his book.

'Having to be with ladies is very moral right paternal & so forth,' he wrote to Percival Leigh, who was guiding his numbers through the press in London; 'but, having to dine with my little women at home, I couldn't go to Bohemia. You can't talk about Art & Ragamuffins when you are playing the Papa; and conversing with Mrs Smith about Mrs Jones's evening party.'[3]

For his daughters' sake, he undoubtedly saw a lot of ladies in Rome for whom he had no very great affection—Fanny Kemble, at full emotional pitch, being a prime example.

It was, as Annie overheard Miss Kemble say, a very hard and difficult hour of her life, one in which she needed all her courage to endure her daily portion of suffering. She had divorced her American planter husband, Pierce Butler, after walking his estates, tears streaming from her eyes, her heart wrung with pity for the slaves, feeling in her own independent and commanding nature the tortures of bondage more keenly than it was given to most humans, free or bound, to experience.

Thackeray, though he had found it disagreeable to accept the man's hospitality, had visited Butler when he was in Philadelphia, hoping to carry back news of Fanny's two daughters, but, though he had pointedly asked after them, they had not been produced.

The marriage had been a disaster and to contain the passions that still rent her, Fanny Kemble espoused a self-imposed and seemingly trivial discipline. Every night, whatever her mood, she played a set number of games of Patience. She wore her gowns in strict rotation. If a plain black came to the fore on a festive day, that was the one she appeared in. At Elizabeth Barrett Browning's, on a night when no one but Annie and Minnie was sharing the peaceful fireside, Miss

Kemble arrived to join them robed like an empress in imperial crimson edged with gold.

'How do you suppose I could have lived my life,' she asked, 'if I had not lived by rule, if I had not made laws for myself and kept to them?'[4]

But, despite such preoccupation with her own trials, she was generously attentive to Annie and Minnie, whom she took out driving with her, crying 'Andate al Diavolo!' when the coachman asked for directions, and singing with such abandon as they careered through the streets that Annie blushed with teenaged embarrassment. In Rome, Thackeray 'learned to admire but not to endure' Miss Kemble.

More to his taste was her only slightly less dramatic sister, Adelaide Sartoris, the youngest of the Kemble progeny. Some years earlier, describing her performance at one of the Procters' musical evenings, at which she had magnificently disjointed the nose of a rival *prima donna*, Thackeray had written:

'She was passionate, she was enthusiastic, she was sublime, she was tender—there was one note w^h she kept so long, that I protest I had time to think about my affairs, to have a little nap, and to wake much refreshed, whilst it was going on still—at another time overcome by almost unutterable tenderness she piped so low it's a wonder one could hear her at all—in a word she was mirobolante. the most artless affected good-natured absurd clever creature possible—when she had crushed Gagiotti who stood by the piano hating her and paying her the most profound compliments—she tripped off on my arm to the cab in waiting. I like that absurd kind creature.'[5]

In her gay, fresh, flower-filled Roman salons, Mrs Sartoris gave the best tea-parties and musical evenings of the winter, eclipsing even the Duke of Northumberland, but Thackeray, ill, languid, getting up at seven each day to struggle through his work, claimed to find amusement nowhere.

'I'm going about without a leg, without an eye, without caring for anything, yawning from party to party,' he told Kate Perry. 'I wonder people ask me and think they must find me very disagreeable.'[6]

Elizabeth Browning was inclined to second this opinion. 'Mr. Thackeray . . . complains of dulness—he is disabled from work by the dulness,' she informed her sister. 'He "can't write in the morning without his good dinner and two parties over-night." From such a soil spring the *Vanity Fairs*! He is an amusing man-mountain enough and very courteous to us—but I never should get on with him much, I think—he is not sympathetical to me.'[7]

She dismissed his conversation as 'small-talk by handfuls of glittering dust swept out of salons,'[8] but by the time he left, Thackeray had won her heart by his kindness to her four-year-old son, Penini, and she had won his with her fondness for his daughters.

There was one household, however, in which Thackeray found relief from his own miseries by consoling others with a fresher grief, that of William Wetmore Story, the American lawyer and poet. At the age of twenty-nine, with a wife and two small children, Story had thrown up his legal career and gone to Rome to learn to be a sculptor. That in itself was enough to endear him to Thackeray, who felt sad and ashamed to the end of his life when he thought of the neglect of his own artistic talent, but it was the death of the Storys' baby son which had him calling again and again at their house, comforting the parents and cheering their young daughter, Edith, a victim like himself of the confounded malaria.

Some pictures he had drawn for a party Annie and Minnie had held on Twelfth Night had given him an idea for a children's book and, night after night, chapter by chapter, he carried it round to Edith, braving the tiny guard on her door—Penini Browning, tramping steadfastly up and down with his toy gun to prevent other horrid maladies from entering—to sit on her bed and enchant her.

Hans Christian Andersen and Master Browning's father also honoured her sickroom, but no other visitor could match Thackeray and his nightly fantasy. 'After he had done reading we talked of the people in the story—' wrote Edith, 'they were real people to me and to him.'[9]

Over the next few months, when he was too ill to work on *The Newcomes*, Thackeray polished and expanded the tale, astonished at the ease with which the 'folly' flowed from his pen, turning it into the most famous of all his Christmas books: *The Rose and the Ring, A Fire-side Pantomime for Great and Small Children*, a confection of sheer delight, with its magical effects and unanswerable logic.

'If you ride a fairy horse and wear fairy armour, what on earth is the use of my hitting you?' Thackeray makes King Padella ask the hero, Prince Giglio. But since *padella* is the Italian word for frying-pan, the King has less trouble in subduing a rival monarch, Cavolfiore, and his nobles, the Broccoli, Articiocchi and Spinachi.

The book's most supreme moment is the transformation into a doorknocker, described in painful detail, of the objectionable doorman, Gruffanuff, for unwisely thumbing his nose at the Fairy Blackstick—the brazen man turned into brass for making that 'most odious vulgar sign'. But it is all enchantment, from its illustrations to its rhyming page headings.

Samuel Laurence's study of Thackeray at the time of *Henry Esmond*, a portrait that greatly pleased the sitter and caused Charlotte Brontë to exclaim: 'And so the lion came out of Judah!'

A sketch for the title page of *Rebecca and Rowena*, which Thackeray sent to Jane Brookfield and her husband, the 'W' and 'JB' of the note in the top right-hand corner.

(*Above*) Thackeray in chains – at the foot of Mrs Brookfield's sofa.

(*Left*) Thackeray and the Brookfields as seen by Thackeray, the small, bespectacled lapdog of the picture.

(*Below*) A sophisticated Thackeray doodle, executed at a *Punch* dinner.

Thackeray's daughters, the adoring Annie (*top*) and the uncomfortably perceptive Minnie (*bottom*).

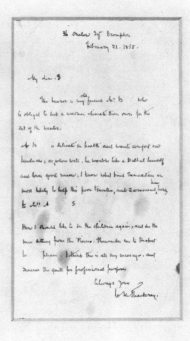

A letter and sketch, presumably addressed to the Sartorises in Rome, recommending to them the sick William Brookfield, long after Thackeray's traumatic parting with the parson and his enchantress of a wife.

The Reverend William Brookfield and his wife in later years, estranged and battered.

Sally Baxter of New York: loving her, Thackeray saw all America through
rose-tinted spectacles.

The burly back-view of Thackeray in his last years, instantly recognizable to
his contemporaries.

Thackeray in his early fifties, shortly before his death.

Thackeray's library and office at 2 Palace Green, Kensington, the mansion he built out of an inkstand.

Meeting of the Duke of Marlborough and Prince Eugene of Savoy behind an oak tree at Ramillies.

Note. You goose, how can you see them unless you go behind the tree?

A Thackeray joke, drawn on *Cornhill* paper.

The author at the end of the story, in his Palace Green library.

If he had to stop writing novels, said Thackeray, he could earn his living by writing the Lord's Prayer or the Creed in miniature on coins. This example, on Garrick Club notepaper, has the whole of the Lord's Prayer squeezed into the space of a threepenny piece.

23

Four Royal Brutes

A return to quackery

Soon after his return from America, Thackeray had bought a new house at 36 Onslow Square, in Kensington's neighbouring borough of Brompton, an area more fashionable than Young Street and slightly closer to town. He was to pay just over £2000 for it, spread over three years, and when he made the journey to Rome left builders pulling down walls and putting in pipes.

Having learned a thing or two about plumbing in the States, he allotted Annie and Minnie not only a floor to themselves, but also a bathroom ('I know where I got the hint of the bath-room,' he told Lucy Baxter), and over the months, discarding the Young Street traps as too decrepit for his smart new quarters, furnished it with choice pieces from London salerooms and Paris dealers, spending so much that he had to bully his publishers into prompt payment in order to meet his instalments on the house itself. He turned it into a small gem—and all the while, restless, ill and lonely, couldn't bear the thought of living there.

He had moaned about Young Street for years, but when the time came to leave, walked out, on a sentimental impulse, several days before the new house was even partially habitable, 'glad, as usual, to get away . . . without a parting.' He had been there for eight years, the years that had seen his rise to fame and fortune, and later, when James Fields asked for a guided tour of all his London homes, Thackeray instructed him, as they stood outside the comfortable, bow-fronted Young Street façade: 'Down on your knees, you rogue, for here "Vanity Fair" was penned! And I will go down with you, for I have a high opinion of that little production myself.'[1]

Even as he was moving into Onslow Square, and crying out 'O the upholsterers, the carpeters, the fenderers the looking glass people . . . O their bills their bills!' he was scheming to take another house at Boulogne for the summer, and to write a series for *Punch* to pay for it. One day's work making fun of the early idiocies of the Crimean War would, he reckoned, pay the rent for a month.

Within five weeks he was back in France with Annie and Minnie, the cook, the maid, Charles Pearman, and Mr Sleap, the amanuensis, waiting to welcome the Major and Mrs Carmichael-Smyth to the Château de Brecquerecque, a many-roomed, melancholy pile on the Paris Road, surrounded by high walls and a dank but pleasant garden, with one milk-jug as the sole item of crockery supplied by his noble landlord.

Dickens was also spending that summer at Boulogne, writing *Hard Times* in a villa brimming over with his seven sons, two daughters, and a constant flow of visitors. After dining there, Thackeray wrote to a young friend: 'We played at forfeits and the game of "buzz" Do you know it? I think even buzz would tire me after a certain number of enjoyments.'[2]

He didn't stay long enough to put it to the test. His family remained at Boulogne for two and a half months, but Thackeray, diluting domestic duty with solitary excursions, was with them for barely four weeks, and those, like his time in Rome, were begloomed by illness.

Every month after leaving Italy he was to have at least two or three days of illness, sometimes spasms, sometimes aguish fever. If the doctor allowed him enough calomel at the start, he could occasionally cure himself in a day, otherwise he had to endure 'the aggravated symptoms vomiting &c . . . 3 days of the business comme a l'ordinaire.'[3] He was bled, had lingering trouble with his bowowels, and his face broke out in blisters, which he treated himself with a poultice ingeniously manufactured from his breakfast toast.

He was only half-way through *The Newcomes* when he had hoped to be finished with it, and his stricture again began to play up, often keeping him out of female society completely. The result was dismal misanthropy and a feeling that he was 'a very venerable old bird' indeed, seventy at least, instead of just turned forty-three.

'I mope about alone, avoid company, sit up stairs in my room, and am sick of being unwell that's the fact,' he told Mrs Procter. 'I have not seen a soul, or feel as if I hadn't: when I do see people and they talk I think about something else—I don't know exactly what . . . Good God how Miss Smith did talk at Brighton! I nearly jumped out of the window. I would but the Cunninghams might have been in the street.'[4]

Yet even in this appalling state, he packed his house with refugees. Eyre Crowe's youngest sister, twenty-three-year-old Amy, having nursed her mother through a last long and painful illness, was at odds with her father over his plans to remarry, and without a home, so Thackeray invited her to Onslow Square, as he did Isabella's brother, Arthur, Arthur's wife, and his 'infernal dog'. But when Mrs Carmichael-Smyth asked Annie and Minnie to squeeze their Paris friend, Laura Colmache, into the bulging household, he finally called a halt—causing a rift between his daughters and their grand-mother, which he then had to heal.

'Suppose they put the question to me some morning, when there are 2 bills and a printer's boy in the passage, and I am thinking of Colonel Newcome, likewise of Arthur Shawe & his wife, and that dog dam that dog that dirties the carpets, plunges about the rooms & howls when separated from his master?' he wrote to Paris: '— Suppose the girls at such a moment say "Papa what shall we do about Laure?—I pull an immense long face, say "the House is full. Confound it let's talk about Laure another time"—They are frightened to ask me, & then their Granny gives them a lecture. The blame is mine & not their's . . .'[5]

He could hear Arthur Shawe talk, splash and snore through the door to his own room, and when he went into the drawing-room, still thinking of the three numbers he was trying to write that month, his grim, sick face so scared everyone that conversation stopped and he was driven out again by the ghastly silence.

Since a further procession of hopeful governesses had failed to produce a likely candidate, he thought of asking Arthur Shawe's wife to stay on when her husband's regiment left for the Crimea, but he knew she would spoil his fireside for him. He liked her, thought her a kind little creature, but there were some people who clammed him up and made him dumb no matter how hard he tried to be genial, and she was one of them.

In the end it was Amy Crowe who solved the vexed problem of a companion for Annie and Minnie, staying with them for eight years. Thackeray called her a 'dear good little Dorit', so cheerful, so sweet-natured and gentle that no one was jealous of her. He made sure she knew he considered it the greatest good fortune that they all needed each other, and more subtly indicated that he had money enough not to count the cost.

As he put the finishing touches to *The Rose and the Ring* for Christmas publication, he was inspired, ill as he was, with a scheme more in keeping with his old madcap days of magazinery: 'A Pack of Nonsense', a set of playing cards with characters similar to those in his Christmas book. He imagined them appearing first in *Punch* and then going on sale at railway stations and the Crystal Palace, new home of the Great Exhibition, but Bradbury and Evans were not enthusiastic, and, having drawn some of the cards, Thackeray abandoned the project.

Despite his difficulty in getting the text written on time, he was also obviously itching for Dicky Doyle to be so late with his illustrations for *The Newcomes* (a close-run thing at times) that he could use it as an excuse to take that job back into his own hands again, too. And, since it was now seven years since he had been called to the Bar, he cultivated his political contacts, lobbied for a magistracy, and at the last moment was thwarted by a change of government and his own hesitation when it came to the point of actually asking for the favour.

He wrote a play, *The Wolves and the Lamb*—'a masterpiece in 2 acts'—which was turned down by two managements. 'Rrrejected!— O torture!' he cried. Later, at a *Punch* dinner, when it was said that William Jerrold's plays had all been damned, Thackeray replied that Jerrold was a damned clever fellow: his own play had never got into a position to be damned or otherwise.

He also took what he called a short charity cruise in the provinces, with a lecture on *Charity and Humour* which he had written originally for one of Mrs Baxter's pet fund-raising schemes, using it again to make money for others rather than himself.

And whatever else he did, ill or well, travelling or fighting to keep ahead with his work, he now had a formidable amount of mail to deal with—five thousand letters a year by his own calculation. He was asked to make speeches, to sit on learned bodies; he was sent 'fugitive poems' by old gentlemen he had met on trains, pleas for help from widows who couldn't spell, tributes of slim published volumes from obscure authors, and much, much worse, manuscripts from unpublished writers who wanted his verdict and a quick route to fame. He also attracted his share of anonymous abuse, the obscene outpourings of sick or jealous minds.

'Nobody knows this work until he is in it,' he said, 'and of course, with all this, old friends hint you are changed, you are forsaking us for great people and so forth . . .'[6]

He found time, however, in the December of 1854, to hear a young relative, John Irvine, give that year's Latin oration at his old school's Founder's Day, and as he sat in the candle-lit chapel, in the shadow of the founder's great tomb, memories of his own childhood torments were immeasurably softened. He scanned the shining rows of bright-faced boys and the black-gowned gentlemen pensioners, the poor brothers of the Charterhouse, coughing feebly in their pews, and having made his own oration at the following dinner, told those around him that he would put it all into his book.

Colonel Newcome was to become a 'Codd', as the pensioners were known, and in the spring, when he was ready to plan the last chapters, Thackeray again returned to Charterhouse to ask headboy Irvine to take him on a tour to refresh his memory.

There was one sticky moment when, looking through the school's Green Book to see how his contemporaries had fared in the world, he found that he had been repaid in kind for his early abuse of the establishment as the 'Slaughterhouse'. Under his own name was written only 'Trin. Coll. Camb.' and 'Sub-editor of the *Globe*'. No *Vanity Fair*, no *Pendennis*, no *Esmond*, and though he had written for the *Globe* in his scrambling freelance days, he protested indignantly at the yawning omissions and that undistinguished, untrue title, sub-editor.

The main purpose of the visit was more propitious. He wanted to see and talk to a 'Codd', and Irvine, making a swift choice between the only two he knew well, rejected 'Larky' Miller, still larky at a very ripe old age, and led the way to blind Captain Light who was looked after by a daughter he rather admired.

'How d'ye do, Miss Light?' said young Irvine proudly. 'I have brought Mr Thackeray, the author, to see you and the Captain.' He then blushed to the roots of his youthful scalp, remembering too late that Thackeray was said not to like being introduced so specifically. [7]

The final description of Colonel Newcome in his pensioner quarters was based on this visit, but when it was published it was thought altogether too rosy by many who had grimmer tales to tell of Charterhouse charity, Dickens, whom Thackeray had been praising lavishly up and down the country in his fund-raising lectures, being one of them. Dickens knew all about Thackeray's generous public tributes, and had thanked him for them, but that didn't stop him doing his duty, as he saw it, in the Charterhouse affair. Not content with a private reprimand, he made sure that his magazine, *Household Words*, printed an article with the aim of knocking 'that destructive bit of sentiment in connexion with the poor brothers slap over as with a rifle-shot.' [8]

Thackeray had written those last pages in Paris, where he had dashed with his daughters in 'a beautiful act of filial duty,' the Major again being seriously ill, and Mrs Carmichael-Smyth distraught. He had chosen his new house at Brompton largely for one room, his own first-floor bedroom-study, with its view over a noble old avenue of trees into Onslow Square gardens, and he had used it so little in the first year of ownership that no more than ten pages of the book had been written there.

Throughout the run of *The Newcomes* he had been mulling over subjects for his next course of lectures, trying to get away from his first choice—Britain's Hanoverian kings, the four Georges. He knew that if he tackled them he would say something impudent, and if he wanted to become a magistrate or any other kind of public servant, it would be wisest to keep a civil tongue in his head. He also knew that simply because it would be better to leave them alone, because he felt no Heaven-sent mission to undertake the job, he was most likely to find himself doing it.

For a while he worked up enthusiasm for another glittering quartet from his favourite century, Chesterfield, Wharton, Walpole and Brummel: 'Men of the World! . . . what fun & satire! what an opportunity for young men to learn about Euroapian manners!' he had written to Mrs Baxter.[9]

It was relatively safe ground, of the type he had been cultivating more assiduously as his growing fame and income elevated him to a sphere from which the social and political panorama could be viewed more objectively. Inevitably, the result was a weakening of his old, always shaky republican principles. With his exceptionally pronounced doubleness of vision, he was the least likely candidate to produce an answer to the great social problem of the day: the division of property and labour—how to improve the lot of the workers, while still leaving the wealth-creators with money enough to invent and expand, a still familiar conundrum.

The remedies put forward by the revolutionaries appeared to him more absurd, detestable and tyrannical than the *status quo*, and since he could see no sign on the horizon of the man of almost God-like wisdom needed to settle it, he took the world as it was and did his best for his own small corner of it, while waiting for the crash to come in Britain as it had in France.

Soon after finishing *Vanity Fair*, he had written to that still fiercely radical lady, his mother, that society seemed to him to be in the last stages of corruption, and he felt there must be a terrible time coming. 'What a good martyr you would make,' he told her, 'and what a fat worldly cowardly one I should be!'[10]

Even then he had felt he was becoming a sadly lukewarm reformer, and while other writers were employed as by instinct in unscrewing the old framework and getting it ready for the smash, he, in *Pendennis* and his articles for *Punch,* had taken only a minor pleasure in his 'own little part in the business and in saying destructive things in a good humoured jolly way.'[11]

With greater knowledge of leading politicians, even this *divertissement* palled, and he was beginning to think of himself as a Whig and a quietist when the Crimean War jolted him out of his complacency. At first the war had seemed a joke, which he had played with through the summer of 1854 in his series of mock-communiqués for *Punch, Important from the Seat of War! Letters from the East by Our Own Bashi-Bozouk*. Then came Balaclava and Inkerman, and the terrible winter with the makeshift British army, commanded and supplied with brutal inefficiency, frozen and starving, impotent before Sevastopol.

For Thackeray, the laughter stopped when Kinglake and Austen Layard, the MP and celebrated excavator of Nineveh, returned with first-hand accounts, an awful budget of stories of incapacity, mutiny and imbecility, and another old friend, William Howard Russell, the pioneer war correspondent, exposed the chaos and humiliation in his dispatches to *The Times*.

The governmental upheavals that Russell's courageous reporting eventually brought about were equally nauseating to him: Lord John Russell, previously admired as a friend and a minister, butchering his cabinet colleagues before the collapse of his coalition with the Peelite Lord Aberdeen, then Lord Palmerston, another esteemed man, calmly stocking and restocking his cabinet from the same small group of preferred peers.

'The Pococurantism of the Whigs is awful', wrote Thackeray after that horrendous winter and the change of government: 'the way they wont & cant see the state of the country: and one Lord turned out fill his place with another Lord. It's an insult to the English honor . . . I can't bear it no longer and am growing horribly Radical.'[12]

Outrage against the aristocracy was so great that Lord Palmerston did try to leaven his cabinet with untitled ministers, for a time dispensing with the services of Lord Stanley (only a second baron) to make way for a newcomer, a move Lady Stanley thought grossly unfair. Britain, she said, had no aristocracy in the foreign sense: 'half the Peerage have no Grandfathers & have become peers because they were men of some sort of eminence.'[13]

Thackeray was in no mood to agree even with this good friend, and when Austen Layard and the industrialist Samuel Morley launched the Administrative Reform Association in the spring of 1855 he immediately became involved with it. He sat on the platform at their first public meeting at Drury Lane theatre that June, and when he was called to Paris by the Major's illness, offered to return to address the next one, at which Dickens was to make his first major political speech. The cost to him would be trifling, he assured the organizers, in an artless display of his own privilege, since he travelled free on the South-Eastern Railway.

He was not recalled, but fired by the reports of Dickens's 'capital speech', set about writing one of his own for later delivery. Dickens's reaction to this call to increase the power of the middle classes was an instinctive thrust to the aristocratic jugular. Thackeray's approach was equally characteristic: an appeal to sweet reason, fortified by historical precedent, and fatally diluted by a sympathetic understanding of the enemy.

'I am disposed to look not quite so angrily as some gentlemen here at the conduct of our governing classes,' he wrote in the draft he hoped he would be able to remember. '. . . If all of us here happened to be Earls or let us say the eldest sons of Earls with a prospect of a seat in yonder begilt and befrescoed hall at Westminster . . . we should be naturally hostile to the proceedings of certain agitators out of doors . . . Why gentlemen if we had hereditary seats in this theatre comfortable wadded stalls in w^h we and our descendants might sit forever and see the opera for nothing we should be peevish I daresay and object to changes of a system w^h worked very well and made us very comfortable . . . there is always this struggle going on between those who have and those who want to have. It is this struggle w^h makes what we call our glorious constitution. The people are always pressing on: the governing classes are always saying no and always yielding in the end . . . There is no call of angry words on our side so much as of constant pressure.'

Nevertheless, he argued for complete Parliamentary reform, not just that of the Civil Service, to which the Association was ostensibly dedicated; for an amended franchise, the adoption of the ballot system of voting, and an end to 'that enormous bullying bribing blundering lying w^h we read of in elections & committees afterwards—that . . . stealthy popping of five pounds into drunken voters hands.'[14]

The Association died before Thackeray had a chance to make his plea in public, but his crusading spirit was roused, and when he finally sat down to write his second set of lectures, he turned not to the safe men of fashion and wordly wit, but to the dangerous Georges. Even his passive, platform participation in Administrative Reform had caused a governing peer to cut him at one of his clubs; now he prepared to put his head more openly on the block, with his bitterly sardonic view of Queen Victoria's grandsires and uncles; to question not only the ability of the aristocracy, but to applaud the demise of 'that strange religion of king-worship', to point out that around ancient royal splendour whole nations had huddled, ruined and enslaved, and to show that in the very centre of royalty itself there were 'horrible stains and meanness, crime and shame'.

He booked an Atlantic passage for mid-October, leaving himself with little more than a month in which to write eight hours of lecturing, and when a few friends at the Garrick asked him to name his night for a farewell dinner, chose the last one, in a craven bid to escape a drawn-out parting with his daughters.

But this cowardly ploy grew into an even greater ordeal. The few friends swelled to sixty, with a hundred more turned away for lack of room. It was a full-scale tribute with a menu containing such delicacies as turtle soup *à la* Hobson Newcome, omelettes *à la* Becky Sharp, and a salmi *à la* Fotheringay, a raft of speeches—one of which he had to struggle through himself—and Dickens, breaking off work on *Little Dorrit* to race up from Folkestone to take the chair.

2.

On returning from his first trip to America, Thackeray had written to Sally Baxter:

'I think when I come back to New York I shan't come and see you any more. It would be the best way depend on it. We have had such a good time Wir haben uns alle so Lieb that we shall never be able to beat it. You won't like me with my hair dyed I know and I have grown so fat it is quite awful.'[1]

But even before his berth was taken he was eagerly making plans to see the Brown House again and, with a hazy grasp of geography, begging the whole Baxter family to meet him at Boston so that they could go holidaying together to Niagara Falls before his serious work began.

When he set foot again on American soil it was to find the Baxters, a score of other welcoming friends, and a vastly increased reputation awaiting him. Only one detail marred his triumphant return, a blow for which he was totally unprepared: Sally Baxter was soon to be married.

It was an event he had claimed he would hear about with a feeling of perfect pleasure. When put to the test, the claim was proved to be false. He tried to convince himself that Sally had 'not improved', that she had been awfully flattered and spoiled, that he didn't envy the young man. But her marriage and his own ill-health shattered the rose-tinted spectacles through which he had first viewed America, and replaced them with a pair of unattractively bilious hue.

The slim alert faces he had once so admired now appeared lean, hard and narrow-eyed; the infectious, pulsing, thrusting energy had become a senseless, restless, sordid greed. The egalitarian dinner parties and balls, so stimulating when Sally's bright eyes had illuminated them, now disgusted him with their vulgarity.

To begin with it seemed that even his lectures might fail. This time he had brought to America an untried product which he himself barely knew. All the old nervousness returned. He spent the first few days in his old rooms at the Clarendon, conning them over and rehearsing them, embarrassed to be overheard by Charles Pearman who, promoted to the rank of temporary clerk, sat in the next room copying out the rest of the pages in a handwriting as clear as print.

By night, he dreamed he was reading them to an audience of three reporters and two small boys; and by day, when he wasn't rehearsing, he lived the all too real nightmare of racing to finish the lecture on George IV in time to deliver it. He even rationed his visits to Second Avenue. They weren't, to be sure, as pleasant as they had been, but Mrs Baxter was as kind as ever, producing for his first Brown House dinner an especially admired jar of brandy-peaches that she had hidden away until he returned.

He never found a replacement for Sally. His embarrassing internal disorders did not fit well with flirtation, and on this trip he took more pleasure in masculine company, particularly that of a newly met young writer, the golden hero of his age among travellers.

'I have fallen in love with Bayard Taylor,' Thackeray wrote to Jane Elliot. 'He was a poor boy almost without shoes 10 years ago, since then he has travelled the whole world over to Europe, Egypt, Nubia, China, Japan, buried a wife whom he married in the last stage of consumption—made 6000£ by his books and lectures . . . and is one of the most interesting men I have ever seen in my life.'[2]

Despite Thackeray's cautious nurturing of his health, and an injunction to Taylor not to feast him at Delmonico's—'it is a sin to spend so much money on the belly'[3]—they both entertained each other at that superior hostelry, Taylor hosting a Sunday breakfast that lasted five glorious hours, and Thackeray a dinner from which he returned to the Clarendon so mellow that he wandered into the suite below his own, a mistake only discovered when, with his boots and several more intimate garments removed he heard a sweet female voice calling out 'Georgy!' from the bedroom.

It was to Taylor, on a future London visit, that he passed on his cherished Weimar trophy, the memorial of youth and romanticism that had hung for over thirty years in his study—Schiller's sword.

During his first month in America, Thackeray was booked to give his series of lectures four times, in and around Manhattan, in halls and churches with every seat already sold. People, as Charles Pearman wrote in his diary, were mad to see the author of *The Newcomes*, hundreds of letters arrived asking for his autograph, and the papers announced his arrival in two colours.

But on the first night he found he had written too much, and in trying to edit as he read, nearly broke down. He felt there was a doubt, almost a defeat. His audience hadn't known what to make of George I and his strumpets. ('Too smutty for the fair sex,' was Charles's comment.)[4]

He knew that some of the newspapers had severely flogged him, though he claimed not to have read them. He was too old a hand for that, he said: 'I . . . have the news from Charles who grins & informs me Tribune not very complimentary to you this morning Sir.' But, as the *Tribune* pointed out, the interest increased as the Georges succeeded each other, and there was promise of 'an abundant harvest of instruction and a richer enjoyment from his dissection of the three remaining brutes.'[5]

Only with George III could he give his audiences the commodity they really wanted—sentiment—and in his hands that great American bogey brought them close to tears. With practice, however, he had them lapping up even George I, and when two and a half thousand people, 'thronged chock up to the ceiling' of a brilliant hall in tranquil little Brooklyn, received that ignoble monarch with rapture, he knew he had won through and it didn't matter what the papers said.

There was nothing like success, he told the ladies of Chesham Place, and he felt fifty per cent better the morning after achieving it.

Though he lectured as many as five nights some weeks, when he slipped in an alms-raising *Charity and Humour*, he didn't miss a performance through ill-health until he got to Boston, but it was a near thing at times. After the terrifying rush to finish his hatchet-job on George IV, he had a cold fit, spent the afternoon in bed, and rose only just in time to go out and 'jaw in rather feeble broken winded accents.' And with the first course of a Press Club dinner, he was struck with a shivering attack and had to be put to bed at the Astor House Hotel, where the dinner was being held. That made four bouts in a month, and on the advice of a New York doctor, he began stowing in the quinine.

He was already counting the days he had been away, loathing the lecturing business more than ever, and longing to bolt, but the rest from writing would, he hoped, prove in the end to be the best of all medicines, and the illnesses, rather than persuade him to quit, gave him the determination to press on: 'They say my lad work during your brief period of strength & popularity. Try and replace some of that patrimony wasted.'[6]

They turned his second American tour into a far more dedicated financial assault than the first. The balance sheet was constantly before his eyes; all success was notched up in dollar signs, and all returns compared with that long-lost inheritance.

'O Ye Gods wont I be glad to come back leaving 500£ a year behind me in this country!' he wrote. 'Then grim death will not look so grim—Then the girls will have something to live upon or to bestow upon the objects of their young affections—then, when the house is paid for, we may live and take things easily—then, when I have written 2 more novels, for w^h I shall get 5000£ apiece—why then, at 50, I shall be as I was at 21.'[7]

He was often to feel ashamed of the amount of time he spent preoccupied with the mean excitement of money-grubbing, yet, when he saw the prospect, still fairly distant, of collecting at last that magic £10,000 for his daughters, he immediately decided that nothing would satisfy him but that they should have not £10,000 between them, but £10,000 apiece.

He socialized less, travelled further, made more raids on the suburbs and villages, and in a more professional manner put the business arrangements almost entirely into the hands of the mass of societies that sent invitations pouring in from all over the country. In New York, the young men of the Mercantile Library Association wrote his business letters for him, fetched him in coaches, marked out his routes, and went darting off to Brooklyn, New Jersey, Troy and Williamsburg to prepare for his arrival, and when he travelled further afield, there was generally an association official waiting to greet him and offer similar aid.

At Baltimore, this proved to be a young merchant, Charles Bradenbaugh—a provincial Warrington, Thackeray called him—remarkably well-read, as soft-hearted as the man he was to look after (they had a fine weep together over Annie's splendid letters), and patently lonely in a society as precisely stratified as any in Europe. Bradenbaugh's kindness and admiration almost frightened him. 'Bon Dieu,' he wrote, 'how I should like to be as good as that friendly soul thinks me to be!'[8]

There were many other happy meetings, too. Longfellow, kindly and pleasant, with pretty children, threw a party for him at his Cambridge home, the house George Washington had occupied when in command outside Boston, and brought in Ole Bull, the 'madcap fiddler', to delight him as much with his talk as his music.

As a Christmas present, the Storys, returned from Rome, gave him another treat: young Edith and her friends acting out *The Rose and the Ring*. While Washington Irving's odd little cottage beside the Hudson, Sunnyside, provided the focus for one of the happiest days of all.

Having gone out to Yonkers, a pretty, bustling village planted over with five hundred brand new little villas, to give his *Charity and Humour* lecture, Thackeray had continued on, riding nine miles beside the river on a balmy December day, and at the end of the journey found Irving, at seventy-two as spritely and whimsical as ever, finishing the second part of his five-volume life of that other Washington, America's first President.

'This is very jolly! How jolly!' Thackeray exclaimed again and again to his delighted Yonkers host, Frederick Swartout Cozzens.

The welcome of old friends everywhere gave him a 'choky sort of feeling of gratitude,' but even so it wasn't long before he was uncomfortably aware of a surge of anti-British feeling in the States, a resentment ostensibly caused by the enlisting of American mercenaries to fight with the British army in the Crimea, and in high government circles he was to hear confident talk of war between the two nations.

His friend of the first visit, the British Minister, Crampton, was at bay in Washington, soon to have diplomatic relations severed and to return to London a very irate envoy. No affable Presidents graced the lectures on the Georges. There were no invitations to dine at the White House. Washington, that jolly American Wiesbaden, now seemed the dullest place on earth, and Thackeray thanked his stars that he had been refused a job with the British legation.

The country was also suffering the worst winter of the century. The crowds still turned out, flocking through the snow, 'peopling the railway cars' to hear him, even on Christmas Eve in a sleepy little village like Greenfield, Massachusetts. At Boston, he had to hire a theatre after hundreds had been turned away from his lecture hall, and at Baltimore at least five hundred 'amiable maniacs' ploughed through a snowstorm so furious that no reasonable mortal would have braved it. But the tales of blizzards, railway lines blocked, and stranded passengers burning coaches to keep themselves warm, made an ominous Greek chorus to his wanderings. If he were snowbound in his infirm condition, he feared he would never get out.

And as if the immediate chill were not enough, James Fields, that firmest of friends, involved him in one of the most intolerable evenings he had ever spent, listening to a talk on the genuine Arctic regions at a meeting of a scientific club, held at the Boston home of one of its most distinguished members.

Fields had reluctantly passed on the invitation, and Thackeray had unwisely accepted it. The worst fears of both were realized when, as Fields was to phrase it, 'a dull, bilious-looking old gentleman rose, and applied his auger with such pertinacity that we were all bored nearly to distraction.'

Fields daren't look at his suffering friend, but sensed what was happening when Thackeray deliberately eased himself out of his prominently placed chair and moved noiselessly into a dimly lit ante-room. Knowing that Fields would now be watching him, he there proceeded to show his manic frustration in a series of pantomime murders. First, he threw an imaginary person—Fields—on to the floor and repeatedly stabbed him with a handy paperknife. Then, as the dull lecture rolled on in the adjoining room, he fired an imaginary revolver several times at an imaginary head. Still the speaker droned on about his interminable icy wastes, and Thackeray, borrowing a small vial from the mantelpiece and a scene from *Hamlet*, poured the imaginary juice of cursed hebenon into the porches of Fields's imaginary ears.

'What *was* the matter with Mr. Thackeray, that night the club met at Mr. —'s house?' a ponderous young member asked Fields many years afterwards.[9]

Though he knew his own audiences would be smaller and less discerning, Thackeray was relieved, at the start of the new year, to move southwards, and when his train did break down and trap him for eight hours in a swamp between Richmond and Charleston, at least he sat out the inconvenience in relative warmth.

He left the north without returning to New York even for Sally Baxter's December wedding. On his previous tour, he had invited himself to the Brown House for Christmas day and made as light of the trip from Boston and back as he would have done a stroll in Kensington Gardens. This time he used his ill-health, the weather and that same journey as an excuse for staying away. He would as soon see one of his own children have a tooth out as see Sally married, he told her father in an only half-humorous letter, and he did not intend quite to forgive her: 'It is the highest compliment that I can pay her.'[10]

He knew it was churlish in the face of the Baxters' many kindnesses. He knew it would hurt them. But he couldn't do it. Instead, he spent the day reading a life of Goethe, the old rogue who at seventy-five had had an unhappy attachment for a schoolgirl.

Six weeks later he found himself sharing a hotel with Sally at Charleston, where the bride, the new Mrs Frank Hampton, was enjoying the winter season with its races and balls before becoming châtelaine of the impressive Hampton estate, Millwood, near Columbia. For Thackeray, they were days both painful and pleasant as he watched her, looking enchanting, bearing her new name and station with great good sense and grace, adorning the court of her father-in-law, Colonel Wade Hampton, a man of great rank and political influence in South Carolina.

Thackeray bestowed on this grand seigneur the highest praise in his repertoire when he likened him to a fine old English gentleman. He thought Sally's husband more like an Englishman than an American, too: a big, broad, honest, handsome, gentlemanlike fellow, who had compassion and courage enough to stay on his plantations and nurse his Negroes through the cholera. He wasn't a 'literairy cove', but he was a far cry from the New York whipper-snappers who had danced around the queen of the revels when Thackeray was there before. Only to Annie and Minnie did he hint that young Hampton was of the same bluff type as their Uncle Charles, the Major's brother, for whose intellect Thackeray did not have the highest regard.

Sally's husband and her middle-aged admirer struck up an alliance in their mutual antipathy towards a local celebrity, the dashing Mrs Henry King, who, having written several novels, not well known outside her own city, treated everyone with aggressive brilliance, and Thackeray with an unwelcome, arch confederacy.

To the Baxters, Thackeray referred to her either as 'the "fast" lady of Charleston', or 'the Individual.' On his first visit, she had told him he was the one man in the world she had wanted to meet, though she knew she wouldn't like him, nor he her. To which Thackeray had replied that he didn't care a fig one way or the other.

On this visit, they had another confrontation at a dinner-party, when the conversation turned on the tribulations of authors.

'You and I, Mr Thackeray,' said the fast lady, leaning boldly across the table, '*being in the same boat*, can understand, can we not?'[11]

A silence fell, a thundercloud descended, and the pleasure of the entertainment was at an end.

For the rest of his life Thackeray kept in his room a Currier lithograph of 'The Belle of the West', a coloured print which reminded him of Sally as he had first known her, and she was to turn to him in the wild, sad rages that were to rack her, and the creeping death by tuberculosis that was all too soon to bring an end to her laughing, noble beauty.

'I shant write to her much—I cant,' Thackeray told her mother when he left Charleston: '—and it's quite best, when people of different sexes are married or unmarried, that those ultra sentimental friendships should be caught and throttled and drowned in cold water.'[12]

It was a resolve he kept better than most, but it left Sally adrift amid alien Philistine splendour crying out to a kindred soul who had learned too well the danger of pitying another man's wife. Thackeray had placed all three Baxter ladies along with Jane

Brookfield and the Elliots as all he cared for outside his own family, but the magic left the Brown House when Sally slipped away from it on her husband's arm, and yet another shutter came down in Thackeray's heart.

Had it not been for reports of snow mountains blocking his route back to the north, Thackeray might well have travelled no further on his second tour than the first. At Savannah, he stayed once more with one of the tremendous breed of cotton merchants, Andrew Low, a wealthy angel of mercy who on his first visit had plucked him out of a bed-bugged hotel and installed him in his own luxurious home, a paradise of peace from which he strolled at night to lecture to languid little audiences of three or four hundred people far too lazy to laugh or applaud. The softening process might again have tipped the balance, but the forecasts from the north were increasingly bleak, and this time he made the great trek inland.

For hundreds of miles, as he travelled by grimy train and riverboat, among dirty passengers spitting, chewing, cursing and cutting their gums with their penknives, the vista was one of endless swamp and pines with only the occasional oak draped in dreary, funereal moss to arrest the eye, a view as mournful, he said, as a tributary of the Styx. And when he stopped, the hotel life was equally unattractive: 'rows all night, gongs banging at all hours to the dirty meals, knives down everybody's throat, dirty bucks straddling over the balconies their dirty boots as high as their heads, the bar-rooms resounding with blasphemies.'[13]

A 'sort of triumphant barbarism' reigned over those steaming regions. He got used to the spitting, but not to the blowing of noses with fingers ('there's one elegant way of operating with one forefinger applied to one nostril w^h I'll show any company of ladies when I get home'[14]), and came to dread the arrival of the inevitable gentleman who conducted him up bad roads, past hideous new buildings, and who described the people he was to read to as 'quite a fine audience whole souled people Sir, the most distinguished of our citizens Sir.'

He was slightly less detached about slavery this time too. The black imps playing in the sunshine still charmed him and ruined him in five cent pieces, but at Charleston he had felt the cold touch of reality when he learned that one of his hosts of the previous visit had sold up his splendid establishment and left that part of the country. He hadn't liked to ask what had happened to the little black bread-server who had pinched his elbow at that man's table, who had been brought up amidst the greatest kindness and luxury. It was all too likely that he too had been sold, along with the bricks and mortar.

Suddenly, there was the kind of personal involvement that made him worry about his own servants. On both trips to America, he remembered the lone sentinels left to guard his London homes and asked friends to go and cheer them, and on this second tour, he was also troubled by Charles Pearman's lonely lot. The capable young ex-footman was the immensest comfort to him, ill or well, and a great champion of the family.

'He . . . seems really to like us,' Thackeray wrote to Annie and Minnie after Charles had delighted him with his partisan comment on a previous night's success: 'I wish the young ladies could have seen that theatre full at New York Sir.'[15]

But unlike Eyre Crowe, who had been invited out with his 'chief', and could amuse himself for hours with his sketching, the young valet was too shy to make friends and, except on departure or arrival days, had little to keep him occupied.

'What do you do in the evening, Charles?' Thackeray asked him.

'I read the paper, Sir, and I lay on my bed,' the young man replied, his eyes filling with tears.[16]

There were two oases on Thackeray's southern route: Mobile, where he found an excellent clean hotel and pleasant company, and romantic New Orleans with its picturesque quays, its old French houses, and the sound of the sweet French tongue. In the latter, he made $1650 in a fortnight, discovered he could eat and drink more with less physical cost than anywhere else in the world, and bought himself a soft, broad-brimmed hat that had Charles grinning and a local man offering to sell him a field-hand. But except for those great cities, the two-month slog was a near-disaster.

Despite the promise of vast sums to be won, the lure which had steeled his determination and deflected him from a longed-for holiday in Havana, he did little more than cover his expenses as he talked his way through Georgia and Alabama, and for miles and weeks found himself in the train of a travelling human circus that did little for his self-esteem.

On his first American tour he had wondered what he was doing in the entertainment business when a shabby man stepped up to him after a Boston lecture and offered to exchange season tickets. His own had shown him to be the owner of the Mammoth Rat. Now, in the south, he often lectured in tin-roofed halls recently vacated by a posse of Wild Men or the Armageddon Lecturer.

'Hullo! Whither is the prophetic Spirit carrying me?' Thackeray wrote in the middle of a particularly seer-like letter home. '. . . There has been a fellow lecturing at my heels and over me in the same towns sometimes, on the battle of Armageddon and how the

US are clearly foretold in the Apocalypse . . . I suppose some of his divine furor has leaked through from his lecture room to my pulpit.'[17]

When he finally braved the perilous paddle steamers of the 'Mrs Sippy', the competition was even more alarming: Colonel Wood's Travelling Museum—a giantess, a bearded lady and her children, a boy of three (The Infant Esau) also with handsome whiskers, and a six-year-old girl who seemed to Thackeray rather pensive about the smooth state of her chin, and a French bird-warbler, all doubtless destined to perform at the same fair as himself.

Even among the normal passengers there were two actors, an Indian chief, a mad woman screaming and calling to people from her stateroom, and a gentleman from the deck with delirium tremens who wandered into the genteel cabin with his coat off. At mealtimes, the giantess, the bearded lady, her most valuable asset judiciously covered with a red handkerchief, and the Infant Esau, all put their knives in their mouths, making Thackeray feel that he had strayed into a den of ogres.

'I tell you it is not a dignified métier, that w^h I pursue,' he sighed to Kate Perry.[18]

It was not a particularly safe one, either. As he had stood on the levee at New Orleans, waiting to board his great white pasteboard castle of a ship, surrounded by farewell gifts of brandy and wine, one of his new, magnificently hospitable cotton merchant friends had whiled away the time with pleasant travellers' tales of the explosive nature of river-boats.

'Look there Sir!' his friend had directed. 'There aft the White Mansion do you see? that post was knocked out by a piece of the boiler of the John Jones w^h burst here Sir—here on this spot where we are standing—and the hands and mangled limbs of the people were scattered and a mule by G— Sir was cut in two in a dray and I saw it lying where you stand now!'[19]

Earlier that same morning Thackeray had read of a ferry catching fire on the Delaware, killing twenty-five, and another on the Red River bursting her boilers, mutilating untold more.

As his own steamer, creaking, groaning and shuddering in every flimsy rib, had struggled against the current, and the deck at night had become a great firework display as the funnel belched out stars that fell sparkling, gleaming and blackening all around, Thackeray had fully expected to meet a similar fate. But at last, having been shivered into several bouts of illness, he was able to report: 'We are over the Mississippi with only 2 fires by the way to égayer the journey. One burned down the cook house another only burned a hole in the roof of the steamer Law bless you it was nothing!'[20]

It had taken eight days, and when he finally landed at St Louis, he found that the great cities of the mid-West which he had planned to plunder were just emerging from the grip of the brutal winter. As the ice broke up, few people had time to spare for lecture-going. If the takings were leaner than he had hoped for, St Louis did, however, provide him with the story he most liked to tell about the trip, the conversation of two Irish waiters, overheard while he was dining at Barnum's Hotel:

'Do you know who that is?' asked the first.
'No,' said the second.
'That is the celebrated Thacker!'
'What's *he* done?'
'Damned if I know!'[21]

By the time he boarded the train again for New York at the beginning of April, Thackeray had many happy days and pleasant encounters to remember, but too many of them had come from the first few weeks of the odyssey, and it was with a sense of profound relief that he accepted an invitation to stay with a jolly bachelor, William Duer Robinson, rather than return to even so good an hotel as the Clarendon.

With Robinson and the two other bachelors who shared his Houston Street house—lawyer Samuel E. Lyon, and J. C. Bancroft Davis, diplomat and American correspondent of the London *Times*—he knew there was every prospect of the kind of civilized evenings, with a drink in his hand and no call to play the lion, that he needed to restore him.

'Then was the time to see Thackeray at his best, because then he was like a boy,' said Lester Wallack, an English actor making his fortune in New York, who was soon to become a fifth at those late-night sessions.

On first meeting him, Thackeray, with his height, his spectacles, his chin in the air, had struck young Wallack as the most pedantic, pompous, supercilious person he had ever met. It was an opinion he quickly changed.

'It did not matter how ridiculous or impossible might be the things I said,' Wallack remembered, 'he would laugh till the tears ran down his face; such an unsophisticated, gentle-hearted creature as he was.'[22]

From that chaste Houston Street sanctuary, which he dubbed 'the Bower of Virtue', Thackeray organized what was to prove a suitably disastrous climax to his 'most prosperous odious tour'.

Heartily tired of the House of Hanover, he was delighted when a young bookseller suggested he read the *Humourists* again at

Philadelphia for an attractive set fee. There was also talk of reviving them in New York. But the Philadelphia audiences were so poor as to mortify Thackeray's friends in that city, and quite obviously raised nothing like the amount he had been promised.

Thackeray himself appeared to take it good-naturedly. 'I don't mind the empty benches,' he told William Reed, 'but I cannot bear to see the sad, pale-faced young man as I come out, who is losing money on my account.'[23]

Nevertheless, a bargain had been struck, and through Reed's agency the promised sum was sent to New York. No acknowledgement, or word of gratitude for the young entrepreneur came from Thackeray, and when Reed saw in the newspapers that he had once more left the country without warning, his good opinion began to falter. The following day, too late for argument, a banker's draft returning a quarter of the fee dropped through Reed's letter-box, together with an emotional farewell.

After the Philadelphia débâcle, the New York scheme for the *Humourists* had been abandoned, and Thackeray, who had planned to stay until June, hadn't even waited for a Cunarder, but had sailed suddenly on the United States Mail Steamer *Baltic*: 'running away from his friends,' said Bayard Taylor, 'for fear of having to say good-bye.'

On 7 May, after a wretchedly uncomfortable voyage, during which he had one of his worst attacks, he arrived back at Liverpool, an eight days' beard covering an unusually brilliant eruption of blisters.

24

Electioneering

A lamb to the slaughter

To announce his return to London this time, Thackeray stormed into a Garrick Club dinner, made a 'Yankee speech', and was in sad need of the 'sober-water' next morning. Physically, he was in a terrible mess. His doctor told him he had trembled at the risk he was taking all the time he had been in the States—and, despite that Yankee speech, he had to admit that he was not nearly so good an American as he had been after his first visit.

Though he had claimed never to read the American notices of his lectures, he knew some of the more wounding phrases by heart, and, as he told Mrs Baxter, that heart though generous was dreadful unforgiving. In most places, he had found two papers that applauded him, and two that attacked with a malignity and ignorance that made him sad as well as angry, especially when he discovered that most of his assailants were not American-born, but Irish or English immigrants.

In New York, his old enemy the *Herald*, having suggested that the chief benefit of his readings would be to enable the young fellows to see lots of pretty girls, who would go to hear the lion roar, not knowing that he was only Snug the Joiner after all, had gone on to assert that no more research or labour had gone into his lectures than into many an article in the *Herald*. That had really rankled.

The *Philadelphia Bulletin* had declared the *Four Georges* against good taste, morality and historical truth, written for a nation of snobs, and containing little but a sort of polished scurrility and mere scandal-mongering. The lecturer would not, they had implied, care to damage his reputation by repeating them at home.

A New Orleans critic, mistaking a reference to Lord Carlisle of the time of George III, for one to Thomas Carlyle, and a kindly mention for ridicule, had soundly whipped him for a vicious attack on a fellow writer.

And in Boston, though he had drawn audiences of over a thousand people, and repeated 'George III' to another of two thousand, there had been those who didn't want to be pleased, and who had criticized severely.

'He was not heavy and instructive enough for Boston,' said Story, 'and only a few dared thoroughly to like the light and genial sketches of manners he gave us in his inimitable way. Oddly enough, *our* people objected to him that he pitched into the Georges and called them names.'[1]

Story himself did little to redress the balance. When a friend grumbled that he could find all the facts and anecdotes Thackeray had used in his own library, Story had laughed and said he was astonished to hear him say so—'for I thought Thack had invented them all.'

Thackeray had tried to remember how he had laid about him in his own young days, and how generally he had taken a good tall mark to hit at, but when, in Savannah, he had heard he was also being attacked at home, and by his old nose-breaking friend, Venables, his wounds and fury had broken out afresh:

'What is this about the Saturday Review?' he had asked Kate Perry. 'After giving V. Harcourt 2/6 to send me the 5 first numbers, and only getting No I, it is too bad they should assault me, and for what? My lecture is rather extra loyal whenever the Queen is mentioned, and the most applauded passage in them I shall have the honour of delivering to night in the Lecture on George II where the speaker says. "In laughing at these old-world follies and ceremonies shall we not acknowledge the change of to day? As the mistress of St James passes me now, I salute the Soverign wise moderate exemplary of life, the good mother, the good wife, the accomplished lady, the enlightened friend of art, the tender sympathizer in her people's glories and sorrows" Whack Whack Whack—I can't say more, can I? and as for George III I leave off with the people just on the crying point. And I never for one minute should think that my brave old Venables would hit me, or if he did that he hadn't good cause for it.'[2]

In his miserable journeying through the South, however, he had dwelt on Venables's charge that his lecture on George IV was grossly unpatriotic, and it had given him just the excuse he needed to let off some of the steam politeness forbade him aiming at his American

tormentors. By Jupiter, he had said, if they started to attack him
when he got home, it would do him good. He had always believed he
could hit harder than any man alive, though he never did. But now
he had some money, he felt a grand sense of independence and a
fight would be just the thing to warm up his sluggish old blood.

By the time he returned to England the lust for combat had died,
but the hurt stayed with him. He didn't think he would ever return to
America, not as a public performer, anyway. He couldn't endure the
degrading ordeal of Press abuse again, he said, the attacks of
scoundrels who had managed to offend and insult the most friendly
stranger that had ever entered the country or quitted it.

The new house in Onslow Square that had seemed so desolate before
he went away looked gay and pretty to him now, full of handsome
things—all paid for too—and if he had to be ill, he couldn't think of
a pleasanter place to suffer in than his own bedroom-study, with its
bed as narrow and Spartan as Colonel Newcome's, and the kind of
view that W. B. Astor couldn't have in New York with all his money.

An American doctor's temporary repairs had seen him through
the voyage home, but now more serious work was obviously
necessary, and he decided to lay up his crazy old hull and see if it
couldn't be made seaworthy again. In a secluded room at the home
of his hydraulics doctor, Henry Thompson, an authority on strictures of the urethra, he had his keel, hulk, pumps and machinery
hauled over and tinkered up—a far more painful operation than
Thackeray's nautical imagery made it sound—and for a while at
least gave up 'the pomps & vanities of this wicked world and all the
sinful lusts of the season'.[3]

He felt sorry for himself as he suffered Thompson's probing
instruments and the recurring attacks of spasms and fever, but even
more so for Annie, who, at just nineteen, should have been enjoying
her first summer as 'out young lady'. He did manage to take her to
two grand balls, but had to leave at one o'clock, just as the fun was
at its best, and suffered an ague attack after both of them.

In America, after paying his heavy expenses and buying lavish
parting gifts from Tiffany's, he had made £3000 clear profit, most
of which he had invested in American railway stock, and on his
return to London, despite his ruffled feelings, took a £1000 share in
the proposed trans-Atlantic telegraph cable.

'I felt glad somehow to contribute to a thread that shall tie our two
countries together—' he wrote to Sally Hampton; 'for though I
don't love America I love Americans with all my heart—and I dare
say you know what family taught me to love them . . . we'll hold
each other by the hand then.'

With so much capital tied up, after two idle months of doctoring he could see the bottom of the stocking again, and though still far from well leapt at Bradbury and Evans's offer of £6000 for a new serial—£300 a number. He liked to say that his invention always began when the money ran out, but this time it failed him, and so did the excitement of travel.

Having escorted his daughters on a short Continental tour, he ended up in Paris in a favourite room at the Hotel Bristol, sitting at the same desk at which, five years earlier, he had written many a longing letter to Jane Brookfield, still with not a single page written to his satisfaction. He had a story in his head which accompanied him on his walks, woke him up at night, prevented him from hearing what was said at the theatre or in company, and yet which was further from his grasp than ever.

'It seems to me as if I had said my say; as if anything I write must be repetition,' he told Kate Perry and her sister, 'and that people will say with justice he has worn himself out, I always told you he would, &c &c. But 6000£ is a great bribe isn't it? Suppose I do wear myself out, & that posterity says so, why shouldn't she? and what for care to appear to future ages (who will be deeply interested in discussing the subject) as other than I really am?'[4]

The parenthesis was ironic: posthumous fame was never important to him, and he couldn't understand why it should interest others. But he did care for his current reputation. 'I can't jump further than I did in the Newcomes, but I want to jump as far,' he said, and so burned several abortive beginnings.[5]

When he returned to London, Whitwell Elwin, a vague, eccentric, Dr Primrose of a parson, new editor of the *Quarterly Review*, in an autumnal walk back to Brompton, urged him to confound his critics by writing a book which contrasted the blessings of a happy family with the vexations and hollowness of fashionable life.

'How can I describe that sort of domestic calm?' asked Thackeray. 'I have never seen it. I have lived all my life in Bohemia.'[6]

Elwin reminded him that in *The Newcomes* he had said that the story of J.J., the modest little painter of genius, had been 'revealed' to him, and asked why he didn't write that.

It was the book he had begun, Thackeray told him, but it had proved altogether too melancholy. He had planned to show J.J. married, then make him fall in love with another man's wife, rescuing him eventually through his attachment to his children. Elwin, as well briefed in the history of Thackeray's heart as his other intimate friends, begged him to choose another subject.

Having worked himself into a mood of almost intolerable despair by delving back into his own wretchedness for J.J.'s story, Thackeray did, at last, give up the project—and, for a time, the whole idea of serial writing. In the old *Humourist* lectures, he had spoken with envy of Addison, who had not begun his serious flow of work until he was thirty-six, when he was full and ripe, who had 'not worked crop after crop from his brain, manuring hastily, subsoiling indifferently, cutting and sowing and cutting again, like other luckless cultivators of letters.'

Thackeray, at forty-five, decided to let his brain lie fallow for a few months more. There was great demand for his readings, and though still far from strong, he set about riding that relatively easy tide. To prove to himself that his American attackers were as wrong as he thought they were, he had already read the lectures to a group of friends at Onslow Square, and triumphantly reported to America afterwards that they had been a huge success.

The terrible Venables had spoken highly of 'George I', and so had Minnie, of whose criticism, he said, he was more afraid than of anyone's. Old Lady Morley had cried over 'George III', and her husband, who had been a member of that King's court, had not been in the least scandalized. He had read the lectures straight from his American manuscript, too.

At Edinburgh, where he had long ago promised to launch this second series, the reception was even more ecstatic, and Thackeray was soon writing: 'How well I am! in what good spirits! the daily occupation and movement agrees with me. Thinking about one's self (& writing novels is that) is not wholesome for too long at a time.'[7]

As his health improved he began to look admiringly in the direction of one Miss Block, who sang ballads very prettily, but that piece of sentiment was knocked on the head when Dr Brown's wife told him that Miss Block was under the care of a 'rubbing doctor', who had ordered her to be massaged for two hours each day with lard.

'I am not in love with Miss Block any more,' Thackeray told his daughters. '. . .don't like the idea of a young lady rubbed with lard—of course she has a female rubber—but still . . .'[8]

Despite his ungallant references to the morals of Mary Queen of Scots, which had three of the formidably hospitable publishing Blackwood brothers forming a good-natured cabal to hiss him, the lectures were so successful that he immediately had to repeat them. By the time he left he calculated that he had drawn three per cent of Edinburgh's entire population, a sum which set him casting greedy eyes on three per cent of London.

In a month he had made £500, merely, as he said, for standing on his legs and reading for sixteen hours out of a written book.

'What is the meaning of all this popularity?' he asked. 'Why, I shall be making another great harvest in England and Scotland if I don't mind—and I must do it if the chances offer, though I don't like it.'[9]

During November and December, constantly dosing himself with calomel to keep the spasms at bay, travelling always with Charles Pearman to look after him, he read night after night at Glasgow, Paisley, Dumfries, Hull, Bradford, Derby, Manchester and Liverpool.

Glasgow produced a tremendous turn-out this time, but his pleasure was soured by the wily organizers of the local Athenaeum. Having booked his series for a set fee of £100, based on the calculation that he would be speaking to no more than six hundred people, they had then booked the City Hall with room for three thousand and pocketed an extra £500 to £600 themselves. Their elaborate thanks at the end of each performance provoked his enduring ire.

For almost seven months he carried on 'killing & eating the Georges' all over the country, filling up the stocking with a speed that astonished him. He began the new year of 1857 at Bath, repeated the whole series four times in London before the middle of February (for a total of nearly £1000), added Brighton to his schedule, and on one Saturday in mid-January read there at two o'clock, returned to London and performed again at the Marylebone Literary and Scientific Institute at eight. He was, he said, like a man playing at roulette and winning, concentrating on nothing but the leap and whirl of the ball and the raking in of the money.

At the end of January, London was placarded with his name, in vast type, announcing the lectures at the Royal Surrey Gardens, more familiarly known as the Surrey Zoological, a vulgar display which exhausted the last vestige of patience in many of his more exalted friends, with whom he was already in disgrace for 'speaking disrespectfully of the Georgyporgies'.

'I writhe at the exclusion . . .' wrote Thackeray. 'The bigwigs and great folks are furious. The halls of splendour are to be shut to me— and having had pretty nearly enough of the halls of splendour I shall be quite resigned to a quiet life outside them.'[10]

By 13 February he was back in the north, travelling from Halifax to Sheffield (where 'poor old Brookfield was born'), and on to Leeds, York, Newcastle, Carlisle, Glasgow again, Kirkaldy, Dundee, Aberdeen, Banff, and Inverness. For late April and May he sold himself to 'a Barnum', Willert Beale, the London impresario and music publisher who had organized the Brighton lectures and been responsible for the Surrey Zoological advertisements. Impressed with the takings, Beale offered £1500 for a month-long whirlwind tour through the Midlands and south-west.

Should the fee be £50 or fifty guineas a lecture? asked Beale, as they shook hands on the deal.

'Guineas,' said Thackeray, 'decidedly guineas.'

It was a decision the impresario chose to forget when he paid for the first five readings.

'What's this, W.B.?' asked Thackeray, studying the cheque. 'Pounds? Our agreement says guineas, and guineas it must be.'

'You are well aware the lectures so far have involved a very heavy loss,' Beale countered, building on the fact that some of these later readings did not draw great audiences.

But Beale was no pale-faced novice, and Thackeray had a pretty shrewd idea of the overall profits. 'That's not my affair,' he told the impresario. 'I am not to know what occult means you have to protect yourself from loss. Guineas, W.B.! Guineas it must be, and nothing less! I must have the shillings.'[11]

George Hodder, an out-of-work newspaper hack who had acted briefly as Thackeray's secretary while he was writing the *Georges*, oversaw this tour, employed by Beale, but travelling with the lecturer. He soon noticed that Thackeray, who had to pay his own expenses, gave less attention to the shillings when he was spending them, and learned to watch with amusement his reaction to new hotel rooms. If these looked out on to trees and flowers, Thackeray, who had proved he could work anywhere, even his own study if he had to, would invariably exclaim: 'This is a nice room. I could *write* here!' It was a remark he had made in deepest Georgia, when he found some temporarily homeless friends living in their slave quarters.

Regarding Thackeray as a man of giant intellect and frightening perception, Hodder often felt he was treading on volcanic ground. He was never to inspire the easy companionship Eyre Crowe had done, and, as a consequence, was occasionally to come up against what he thought of as a constitutional reserve in Thackeray, a certain cold austerity of manner; but he also saw many more endearing facets.

From Leamington, despite his gruelling schedule, Thackeray rushed up to London to add his weight to getting his old sparring partner, Douglas Jerrold, elected to the Reform Club, and when Hodder met up with him again, en route for Norwich, his first sight of him was of a beaming face, thrust out of a still-moving carriage window, calling down the platform: 'We've got the little man in.'

He also learned to admire his fortitude. On the last night at Norwich, Thackeray was scarcely well enough to get to the hall and it was only the audience's welcoming storm of applause that gave him the will to struggle through to the finish. The next morning, when Hodder called at his hotel, he found him still in bed, closely covered with blankets, suffering great pain, and begging not to be looked at since he knew he was a hideous object. He refused all aid, except for just enough money to see him through the attack.

When Hodder later asked if he had had the best medical advice, Thackeray said yes: 'but what is the use of advice if you don't follow it? They tell me not to drink, and I *do* drink. They tell me not to smoke, and I *do* smoke. They tell me not to eat, and I *do* eat. In short, I do everything that I am desired *not* to do, and, therefore, what am I to expect?'[12]

There were times in the simple, God-fearing communities of northern Scotland, which Thackeray reached through the winter snows in old-fashioned coaches, with the post-horn blowing as the horses clattered into remote inn yards, that he felt ashamed of himself and his *Georges*, pained for the honest squires and country gentlemen with noble notions about Church and Crown, who had to sit and listen to a sneering, sceptical Londoner. And other moments when he talked to dedicated parsons and doctors and compared their lives and pay with his own, that he hung his head and thought how lucky he was.

But there were many occasions when he was embarrassed for happier reasons. His great pathetic face crumpled like a baby's from astonished pleasure, when at dinners and before audiences of thousands he heard himself praised and his books spoken of with true understanding by men he admired and whose judgement he respected.

By the time he laid them to rest, his 'late gracious Sovereigns' had made him over £5000, and he had the triumphant satisfaction of knowing that they had been liked more in Britain, where the subject was better known, than in America. In her country, he told Sally Hampton, he knew they had thought he had taken them an inferior article, glass beads as it were for the natives. In Britain only two papers had abused him, and even they didn't say, as the *Herald* had done, that any young man could have sat down in their office and written such lectures in an evening.

When he returned to the Garrick Club the wags told him he should carry on with the eight Henrys, and then the sixteen Gregorys, after which his public would be so exhausted he should wind up with the single John.

'And that,' said Douglas Jerrold, 'a *cheap* one!'[13]

2.

While Thackeray was touring with the *Georges*, a general election was called, and two Edinburgh factions asked him to stand for the city. He was tempted, but he knew that he had little chance of winning. Some of his views would have been acceptable enough—his desire for increased suffrage, the ballot, and fixed Parliamentary terms—but he was monstrously unsound on the Sabbath question. He wanted innocent places of entertainment to be opened to the working man on Sundays, a dangerous view anywhere in Britain, and guaranteed political suicide in Scotland. He also believed that while the State supported any Church establishments it should continue its grants to the Roman Catholic college at Maynooth—another red-hot issue. Edinburgh was still prepared to risk him, but Thackeray declined.

He also said no when the Whigs offered to nominate him for an English borough. His second view of politics and universal suffrage in America, especially in the South, had once again swung him away from radicalism.

'The rabble supremacy turns my gorge,' he had written from the Mississippi. 'The gentlemen stand aloof from public affairs, and count no more than yonder Irish bog trotter who is driving a pig before the window or those two illiterate blaspheming ruffians who were cutting their gums with their penknives in the bar—I couldn't bear to live in a country at this stage of its political existence'.[1]

The experience had 'whiggified' him, but not enough to make him want to join the party, not now that he had some capital behind him. Since he was a man of independent means, he told the Whigs, since he had fifteen thousand subscribers for his books and could draw scores of thousands of people with half-crowns in their hands to hear his lectures, if he went into Parliament, it would be as an independent.

He knew he shouldn't be thinking of politics at all until he had written the new novel and made his £20,000, but his success with the *Georges*, his apparent high standing throughout the length of the land, had bolstered his opinion of his worth and stirred up old ambitions. 'Every man would like to make a mark as a Citizen of his country,' he told William Reed, when he heard of his appointment as American Minister to China, and pictured the frigates saluting him as he entered the Canton river.[2] For his own part, he felt he could now look to something better than beakships, and spent a few pleasant moments considering what title he would choose if the occasion presented itself: Lord Brompton? Or was that too modest?

He knew he wouldn't be happy in politics, they would interfere with his digestion, but with the game there, it seemed fainthearted not to play it. He also mistrusted his motives, thinking uncomfortably of the frontispiece he had drawn for *Pendennis*: his hero pulled one way by innocence, the arts and domesticity, the other by worldly pleasure and greedy ambition.

'"Retire and paint pooty little pictures" says Ease, perhaps Conscience: "Retire and work at literature at history—"' he wrote. '—But that game is very tempting.'[3]

During the months leading up to the March election, he managed to resist, the pull of the angels being augmented by Beale's fifty guineas a lecture. But no sooner was it over than he began casting about for a likely by-election, and in July, when his friend, Charles Neate, was unseated at Oxford, for what Thackeray called a twopennyworth of bribery he had never committed, he stepped in there, as an independent, against Viscount Monck, an attractively uninspired Whig.

Having made his headquarters at the Mitre Hotel, and published his address to the electors of the city, Thackeray wrote jauntily to his daughters:

> My dearest little women, as far as I can see,
> The independent Woters is all along with me,
> But nevertheless I own it, with not a little funk,
> The more respectable classes they go with Wiscount Monck;
> But a fight without a tussle it is not worth a pin,
> And so St. George for England, and may the best man win.[4]

'I hope *not*,' said Lord Monck generously when Thackeray repeated the last phrase to him.

But all too soon events took on an air of *déjà vu*. Thackeray had already described what was to happen to him in *The Newcomes* when the equally innocent Colonel ventured into electioneering. Like his fictional creation, Thackeray also fought in the most gentlemanly manner, refusing to speak an unfriendly or disrespectful word against his opponent, forbidding all bribery and sharp practice amongst his supporters, trusting the other side to play an equally honourable game.

Gritting his teeth, both true and false, he toured the city asking for votes from the small band of registered voters (less than three thousand in that time of limited suffrage), complimenting those who honestly said they were promised to the other side, showing his contempt for anyone who indicated he was open to financial persuasion, loathing some of the shoulders he was forced to rub against.

Had the poll been put off for a single day, he knew he would have kicked one fat auctioneer who familiarly and regularly called him

'Thackeray', and he didn't much care for the humiliation of being told by maids on doorsteps: 'Are you Mr. Neate's friend? Master's h'out, but he said I was to say he would vote for yeou.'[5]

He joked in his speeches about his reputation for breaking down, which had freely been used against him, and said that if he felt strongly enough on any point, he believed he'd got brains enough to express himself. But with the heckling and bustle of the hustings, so different from the ordered lecture room and familiar text, he was led into statements that were gifts to the opposition, and occasionally into complete silence. 'If I could only go into the Mayor's parlour for five minutes, I could write this out quite well,' one of his aides heard him muttering in the shambles.

He had expected his reputation to help him, but that piece of vanity was quickly exploded. He claimed to have met only two voters who recognized his name, and sent an urgent plea for Dickens to join him to explain who he was. He thought there might be as many as six or eight who had heard of him.

Even so, he posed too great a threat for the Whigs' comfort. A senior party man appeared mysteriously in the city, took the temperature, and vanished—along with Lord Monck. Then, as Thackeray remarked ironically in one of his speeches, it was announced that a powerful requisition from the City of Oxford had invited Mr Cardwell to fight the seat in place of the Viscount.

Edward Cardwell, a future Colonial Secretary and brilliant Secretary for War, who had held the constituency for five years before narrowly losing to Neate, was a far more formidable adversary. Thackeray, blindingly honest, publicly admitted that he doubted if he would have stood had he known from the start that he would be opposing a statesman of such talents and ability.

With the advent of Cardwell, the heat was on. A broadside appeared attacking Thackeray's views on the Sabbath, slipping theatres (terrible thought) into the list of entertainments he would have permitted on Sundays. Another used his own kind of humour to telling effect:

CARDWELL is a man of Practice

Cardwell is a man of *Fact.*

Cardwell is a man of Political Renown

Cardwell helped to give the Poor Man Cheap Bread

Cardwell gave the Poor Ballast Heavers a fair day's pay for a fair day's work.

THACKERAY is a man of Promise.

Thackeray is a man of Fiction.

Thackeray is a man of *Novel* Greatness.

Thackeray gave him Vanity Fair.

Thackeray has promised Concert Room Pleasures on the Sabbath Day.[6]

On election day, Thackeray polled 1,005 votes, Cardwell 1,070, and Thackeray conceded defeat in the manner in which he had sought to win. He would retire, he said, to his pen and his desk, leaving the representation of Oxford to a man who understood the business far better than he did.

But for the Sabbath Question, he felt sure he would have won, even against Cardwell, but on that point he vowed he would never truckle or change, not to achieve any promotion or glory. After paying all his election bills, he received £13 change out of £900, and sold his trans-Atlantic telegraph share to raise the money.

'It was,' he said, 'a cowardly robbery of a poor, innocent, rightly-served man. And if I had won—that is the beauty of it—I should have been turned out, my agents, in spite of express promises to me, having done acts which would have ousted me.'[7]

25

The Virginians

Past the time of snivelling grief

The 'bleeding' at Oxford cured Thackeray of his desire for other fields of glory. He knew now that nothing could provide so well for him as his pen and his wagging jaws, and though his Edinburgh friends approached him again at the next sign of an election, he flirted only a little and didn't fall.

His ill-health remained a burden, but it had settled into a pattern he could endure. It couldn't be helped, he said, and one bout finished, the best way was to shake it off and think no more about it until the next time he was down. The chills and fever were now more probably brought on by recurrent kidney infection, a result of his old enemy, the stricture, than by lingering malaria, and he knew that no amount of tinkering could cure that for long.

There was the 'heroic remedy', surgery, which he was told was the only effectual treatment in his case, but Thompson, who would not have hesitated with most people, was afraid to perform the operation on such a well-known public character. Thackeray was equally reluctant. Dr Brown suggested he consult his old teacher, the great Edinburgh surgeon James Syme, another authority on strictures, but to the end of his life Thackeray delayed, with the refrain, one more book then . . .

Instead, he had doctors always about his 'hydraulic engine', and his diaries, some years little *Punch* pocket-books, printed with jokes and Leech's cartoons, became spare, stoical records of sickness and spasms, the time they came on, the time they were relieved, the medicine required, and his languid condition afterwards.

He was so constantly ill, often with such 'atrocious pains of the inner man', that he couldn't believe he would live long, and often did not much care. '. . . where's the pleasure of staying when the feast is over and the flowers withered and the guests gone,' he asked. 'Isn't it better to blow the light out than sit on among the broken meats, and collapsed jellies, and vapid heeltaps? . . . except for the young or very happy I can't say I am sorry for any one who dies.'[1]

The inevitable accompaniment of his physical ills was what he called disordered spirits, but even with these he came to terms. He no longer expected to be completely happy. He sat up in his room, silent, solitary, preoccupied, apparently melancholy, but in fact in a pleasant, bearable, grave, grey frame of mind. He still grumbled, but without rancour. To Mrs Baxter he wrote: 'I trust my dear friend that if you know me for a hundred years to come you will never find me otherwise than good-natured & discontented.'

Affluence played a large part in this new feeling of resignation. The pride in possessions he had shown from Cambridge days, when he had decorated his rooms from ochred woodwork to marbled fireplace, and filled them with choice books and prints, could now be given full rein. He called his invested wealth 'the Good for Nothing Money' and discounted it, but at last he had the security of knowing that whatever happened, if he had to stop work completely, he had his own house and an income from dividends and copyrights of at least £650 a year.

There were still days when finding actual cash presented a problem, moments of crisis when the American railways failed to pay promptly on quarter-day, but then, as he said, he lived a great deal more lavishly than he had ever done before. He gave good dinners, his house was full of pretty things, and his cellar had just been increased by a £100-consignment of eighteen dozen bottles of '48 claret that would not be ready to drink for four years.

Often the lecture money was spent before it was earned. One night's fee was earmarked for Mrs Carmichael-Smyth's 'ivories', another was handed over on the spot to Dr Thompson, who would never send a bill. When the Beale tour was finalized, he promised Amy Crowe £100. His parents and children were told to spare themselves nothing when for two hours' lecturing he could make another £50.

Afraid of becoming idle, he considered deliberately increasing his expenses so that he would be driven to his desk again, and asked his family what they thought of a £3500 mansion and six acres at Southampton. He would christen it 'Georges' and pay for it out of them.

He toyed with the idea of returning to India, where he now had enough friends and relations in high places to ensure a jolly winter for himself and his daughters. Twelve lectures, he calculated, would pay for that.

Soon he had an open carriage, a smart new brougham, and a new cob for himself, on which he found time to ride only once or twice a fortnight when the beast was often too fresh for comfort. For a time he had a coachman (five feet tall and weighing seven stone) who regaled local tradesmen with technicolour tales of how he had to carry his master (six feet three and usually far too well padded) up to bed, drunk every night. When he found a good, honest man to take his place, he hadn't the heart to dismiss him at the end of the season, and Sims the coachman joined his permanent payroll.

If he had time on his hands and money in his pockets, he spent both buying 'pooty things' for Onslow Square. His tall, broad figure, browsing among the antique shops and bookstalls, or strolling through London's clubland, became as familiar as Dr Johnson and his rolling gait had once been in Fleet Street.

Before long, he was adding up his accounts and crying out in horror. In three months, he had spent £800, out of which he claimed only £35 had gone on his own personal expenses. '. . . we are not good managers thats the fact,' he admitted, 'and make less show with 3000 a year than many people with 1800. Why Lady Rodd in her great family Coach doesn't spend as much as I do. But I wonder whether she has any bowels of compassion?'[2]

He put the annual cost of his own benevolence at £500. It flowed out in sums ranging from regular pensions of £5 a month to one-shot payments of a hundred or more. He kept whole families alive for years, like the hapless Corkrans, who abused him for not doing more. He reimbursed Isabella's Mrs Bakewell when her silver was stolen, and then had to listen to her complaining for months about her loss, while inwardly groaning that in effect he was the one who had been robbed.

'Yesterday I only got 5 letters asking me for money,' he told his daughters one December morning. 'One from poor Eyre 5£: one from Mrs Beckwith 5£: and then when I was settling to work comes your Uncle Arthur who informs me that he is about to be arrested for a bill of 235£—w^h I shall end by paying. Isn't it jolly?'[3]

A few years later, bumping into a preoccupied Anthony Trollope on Horse Guards Parade, he learned that another friend was in even greater trouble: William Webb Follett Synge ('Doubleyou Doubleyou', in Thackeray's waggish language), needed £2000 immediately.

He had first met Synge, a young British diplomat, in Washington, had dashed from France to give his American bride the kind of welcome he had received in her country, when Synge first brought her to England, and had whisked her out of miserable lodgings into Young Street, where he had insisted she should be the lady of the house and he the lodger. Their two-year-old son, William Makepeace Thackeray Synge, was his godchild. He had already had a sleepless night puzzling over a preliminary note indicating that financial help was needed, and when Trollope named the sum, Thackeray swore and exploded: 'Do you mean to say that I am to find two thousand pounds?'

Trollope pointed out that he hadn't suggested anything, except that they might discuss the matter.

Suddenly Thackeray's manner changed. With a sheepish smile and a sort of wink from behind his spectacles he whispered, as though ashamed of his meanness: 'I'll go half if anybody will do the rest.'[4]

Trollope himself did the rest, and Synge had his money. It was all done in a friendly but most businesslike manner, with the loan to be repaid over a set period, at five per cent interest, and the details entered into Thackeray's diary with the precision he had once applied to bills of exchange during his early connection with Birchin Lane.

The only person to whom he had a constitutional aversion to giving money was Mary Carmichael. After seventeen years he still owed £450 of the £500 she had lent him, and had never reimbursed her for some of Isabella's early medical bills. Long after he could afford to disgorge in full, he continued to prevaricate. He talked of paying for her eldest son, Chéri, when he went to university. He thought of giving the boy his Suez Canal shares. He did everything but hand over the cash and be done with it.

The two families now lived close to each other at Brompton, but relations between them were not harmonious, and neither, in the main, were they between Mary and her husband. Charles, who still sported the fierce military moustachios Thackeray had borrowed for Colonel Newcome, and spiced his conversation with the boisterous language of the mess, had inherited a large share of Carmichael eccentricity, his particular mania being household economy. If guests stayed too long, he turned out the lights, and if too many scraps accumulated in the kitchen, he gathered them up and threw them over his wife as she lay in bed—yet another Victorian lady who draped well on a sofa and took up the study of her own ill-health.

Of the two, Mary was the more dangerously irrational, consumed with rage at an inscrutable providence which could raise Thackeray, the unexceptional boy, to such spectacular heights, and leave her, the bold and talented beauty, in obscurity. Totting up his financial prospects on his second American tour, Thackeray had written to

Annie: 'When I have got those 20000 I think Aunt Mary will bust with fury.'[5]

Between them, the Carmichaels involved him in rancorous arguments with their friends, and then barred their doors to him when his verdict went against their own. Injudicious letters from Mrs Carmichael-Smyth, and the meddling of that same Mrs Parker whose tale-telling had accelerated Isabella's tragedy, stirred up more trouble. Mary cut Thackeray and Annie in the street, dragging pale, haggard little Chéri away from them. Thackeray put Mary out of bounds to his daughters—'Granny will be off to Aunt Marys at once but not you if you please young ladies'—and so it went on.

When the Carmichaels' marriage was going well, Charles sided with his wife. When they were feuding, he appeared at Onslow Square, apologetic and miserable. Either way, his behaviour was likely to be odd. But if the Carmichaels were uncomfortable neighbours, they did at least serve to point up the harmony within Thackeray's own home, his innocent *ménage à trois*. He could still sigh that a man without a woman was a lonely wretch, and console a widower with a tender reminder of his own tragedy—'Dear fellow, a dead sorrow is better than a living one'[6]—but with Annie and Minnie now old enough to be companionable, he could also say that in place of the one wife whose want had made him so miserable for so long, he had two little ones, not in the least jealous of each other, and was at last most comfortable in his harem.

He had not visited Isabella for many years, but he had constant reports of her, knew that she was well and cheerful, and looked at least ten years younger than her age. The cruellest fate he could imagine for her now was a sudden return to reason. If that happened, she would find the lover of her youth a grey-haired old man, and her babies grown to womanhood.

Jane Brookfield came almost into the same category of living sorrow. Now, when he lingered over his memories of his love for her, it was not, he said, with tears—he was past that time of snivelling grief—but with his usual deadly cheerfulness and funereal good humour.

'Let the young folks step in and play the game of tears & hearts,' he had written to Kate Perry from America. 'We have played our game: and we have lost. And at 45 we smoke our pipes and clear the drawing room for the sports of the young ones . . . We get out of the stormy region of longing passion unfulfilled—we dont love any the less, please God.'[7]

In *The Newcomes*, as in many of the letters he had written to Jane during earlier separations, he had asked: 'If we love still those we lose, can we altogether lose those we love?' His answer was no, and he had constantly in mind some vague heavenly reunion when that love would again be shared. But at one time the news he heard of his dear lady threatened to take even this comfort away from him. She had always been what he called 'one of the Gothic believers', and in one of the letters passed on to him by Kate Perry indicated that under the influence of that other long-term admirer, Aubrey de Vere, she was thinking of becoming a Catholic.

'If she does that, I feel somehow as if she wanted us to be parted in Heaven too, and the idea frightens me,' Thackeray wrote to Chesham Place. 'Going over to Rome is like her taking a second husband. I have got accustomed to the Inspector, but I dont think I could forgive Don Basilio . . . or her at his knees whispering her heart out to him . . . She's a woman quite capable of skipping into a chapel, popping into a confessional before a priest who would hear her, soothe her, absolve her, baptize her and send her home engaged to Catholicism before she knew where she was: and then she would tell her husband: and then it would be bonjour, and away would go Magdalene & Arthur with the Inspector in one cab; and she in another to our Lady of Sorrows and two guineas a week for her board; and good-bye to children, and to friends whom she loves as sister, and to those who have loved her as women are not loved every day—I can see Aubrey de Vere coming in with his sanctified smirk to visit her afterwards and the rest of the shavelings coaxing and squeezing her hand and giving her precious conversation & dainty little penances, and making much of her, and leaving her when the next interesting convert came. Ah my dear Love your children and cleave to them: say your prayers in English . . .'[8]

Jane did not become a Catholic. She became pregnant again. Kate Perry and Jane Elliot, as usual, were first with the intimate news, and in his reply to them Thackeray showed with what bitterness he had received it: 'My dear dear JOB. So her health does not allow her to walk and there's actually a little No 3 in preparation! That pretty well finishes matters. Suppose the way ever so clear. Her children, if they are brave children, would hate a sham father. There's something immodest in the marriage of an elderly woman with children even to a charming lovyer like me . . .'[9]

He had already written in *The Newcomes* that many a man and woman had been incensed and worshipped, and shown no more feeling than was to be expected from idols. In his next book he was to be more scathing, likening calm, siren enchantresses to that cool, sweet, shining pond in which the dog in the fable saw reflected his own image and that of the bone he was carrying, a reflection at which he greedily snapped, thereby losing the juicy morsel he already had in his grasp.

'Oh, absurd cur!' wrote Thackeray. 'He saw the beef-bone in his own mouth reflected in the treacherous pool, which dimpled, I daresay, with ever so many smiles, coolly sucked up the meat, and returned to its usual placidity. Ah! what a heap of wreck lie beneath some of those quiet surfaces! What treasures we have dropped into them! What chased golden dishes, what precious jewels of love, what bones after bones, and sweetest heart's flesh! Do not some *very* faithful and unlucky dogs jump in bodily, when they are swallowed up heads and tails entirely? When some women come to be *dragged*, it is a marvel what will be found in the depths of them.'[10]

He did not, he said, intend to fall in love again. Even socially women had lost some of their charm for him, and more ambitious entanglements were becoming increasingly unlikely. At a *Punch* dinner, where the talk was always free, and Thackeray's freer than most, he discussed his stricture and the hideous umbrella-like instrument he had to use on his 'erectile tissue—erectile disuse it has now fallen into.'[11] At forty-seven, he told Dr Brown, 'Venus may rise from the sea, and I for one should hardly put on my spectacles to have a look.'[12]

Soon after their move to Onslow Square, Annie, stealing into her father's study, had told him how glad she was that he hadn't died during his *Pendennis* illness, or she and Minnie would never have known him so well or learned to love him so much. Thackeray, covered in confusion, mumbled that he agreed with her but didn't believe such sentiments should ever be spoken.

Thackeray! whose sleeves had displayed so many bleeding hearts! Who spoke as emotionally of his daughters as he had done of all the other great passions in his life. He was constantly telling anyone who would listen that his dear fat Nan was the best girl he had ever seen anywhere, and that he was brutally happy she wasn't handsome enough to make an early marriage likely.

When romance did threaten tó disrupt the household he had just begun to enjoy, he was panic-stricken. Mrs Carmichael-Smyth had raised the scare while the girls were staying in Paris, naming a young parson as the object of Annie's affections, a handsome and amusing young man, but with only one lung, no money and expensive habits. The advice with which Thackeray bombarded his daughter was very different from the love-in-a-clearing dream he had once peddled to another young girl in New York.

Who was to finance this folly, he asked, this luxury of a husband, of little darlings, of bills to pay, house to keep etc. etc.? The Revd Mr Creyke, with his beautiful whiskers, couldn't, and it was as much as he himself could do to scrape together enough to keep his two daughters and their mother. 'You must marry a man that can keep you—and you've just pitched precisely on the gentleman that cannot,' he told his dearest Fat.[13]

It was not until he had blasted his way through the subject, demolishing it with a thunderous hammer-rain of blows, that Annie told him, laughing, that it had all been a romantic notion of her grandmother's, she had never been in love at all. To make quite sure he wasn't being humbugged, Thackeray invited the young gentleman to a family dinner, and applied his famous scrutiny to everyone's reactions.

As their friends married, both girls began to 'bewail their Virginity in the mountains', as their father phrased it, but during his lifetime no great romance swept either of them away from him.

Annie returned his love with blind adoration. Minnie's devotion was less reverent. On a country visit, she commented saucily that perhaps her father, that erstwhile chronicler of snobs, was in such excellent spirits because he was surrounded entirely by baronets and admirals, and at Edinburgh made great sport of the awe with which he was regarded in that serious city. Dr Brown, she reported, was delighted with even the most stupid anecdote about his shaving-brushes, treasured a photograph which was quite the most monstrous likeness ever taken, and saw nothing odd in the fact that intelligent people should still like to discuss where they had sat at his lectures.

Thackeray was only just becoming 'familiar' with this bright, iconoclastic, less pliant younger daughter, who could appear so childishly vulnerable, yet who had, in his estimation, the shrewdest head in the family. If either of the girls were away he soon complained that the house was not a home at all and mooched around unsettled until they were together again. He liked listening to their chatter and told his mother that they did all the fun and observation now.

If they wanted anything enough, they were sure to wheedle it out of him. When they pined to hold a 'drum', a large, catch-all evening party, Thackeray resisted for as long as he could, knowing that the many different levels of society they moved in would cause all manner of complications: 'we know great people & small, polite & otherwise,' he explained, 'the otherwise are not a bit comfortable in company of the others but get angry if they are not asked.'[14]

Annie and Minnie won. The house looked pretty, its fireplaces crammed with flowers for the occasion. Those who were invited obviously enjoyed it. Those who were not, convinced the young hostesses it would be wise never to hold a drum again.

Annie had been 'house mistress' since she was eighteen, but

Thackeray summed up her domestic accomplishments with the drawing of a goose. Afraid of doing anything that might not please him, she constantly plied him with questions, which Thackeray as relentlessly tried to dodge. He would, he told her, leave whatever it was to her own excellent judgement. When they reached an impasse, he laughed at her: 'I defy you to get anything out of me.'[15] From the goodness of her heart, she fell into all sorts of scrapes, for which she scourged herself painfully long after Minnie's wiles had extricated her from the muddle.

When he was away lecturing, Thackeray still had to keep half his mind on Onslow Square, reminding his 'loaves' to see that the maid had a fire in her room in cold weather, warning against overworking the brougham horse when their junketings seemed to be getting out of hand, telling them to get the bedroom bell-pulls checked when visitors were coming to stay. When he received a letter from Annie sighing over her passing youth, he began to wonder if another, more serious 'TOMKINS' hadn't appeared on the scene and sent more instructions for his entertainment.

'I shall be very glad to see him', he lied. 'Dont give him the Liverpool Port if you ask him to dinner—that is too good for young fellows—the Balfour wine is excellent, and the Kensington claret mind not the 40 or 60—the young beggar doesn't know about wine yet.'[16]

And when a Mr Carter sent him a brace of geese for Christmas, he could still find time to thank him with some illustrated poems, the first complimenting Carter on reversing the old recipe of stuffing a goose with sage, by the nobler plan of stuffing a sage with goose, and the second reflecting the general excitement the gift had roused in his household:

'Lawk, Miss Anny, Lawk, Miss Minny!' thus cries Gray the cook,
'Two such beautiful geese is come! Only come and Look!
'Lor, how plump and brown they'll be! Lor, how plump and juicy!
Well, of hall things I declare I do love a goosey!

'Two fat geese, how genteel! Only think of this, miss!
Don't they come convenient for the dinner at Chrismiss!
'One shall be for the Servants' 'All, and one for the parlour arter,
And I never shall see a goose again, without thinking of Mr
    Carter.'[17]

Gray, the cook, faithful but affected and tearful, stayed with Thackeray almost to the end of his life. Charles Pearman's tenure of office was briefer. The trip to America had turned his head and made him discontented. 'Mr. Charles Pearman has not resumed his livery on his return to his native countfy,' reported Thackeray, 'but dresses in black and is a much greater man . . . I suspect [he] aspires to be a flunky in a family of superior rank.'[18]

Inspired by the company he kept in the servants' hall next door, home of the sculptor, Baron Marochetti, Charles now found it quite impossible to carry on without the help of a footman, a liveried footman, so, when Annie, Minnie and Amy Crowe ate a simple meal of mutton chops together, they had the pleasure of being waited on by two menservants, who walked round and round them in the greatest state.

At last Charles handed in his notice and departed, leaving a remembrance behind with the plain, thirty-five-year-old, hitherto respectable housemaid, who had been with Thackeray for twelve years. Even from this understanding establishment, poor Eliza had to go, while her master, muttering 'comme à l'ordinaire I know who will have to pay the Doctor,' dug into his pockets to help her.

In place of the 'seductive Charles', he took on a Frenchman, and then a year later another Charles, who turned out to be 'a roguypoguy', under whose régime brandy bottles mysteriously emptied and favourite ties disappeared from drawers.

Secretaries came and went with even more disrupting frequency, presenting as great a problem as governesses had once done. With illness and increasing years, the writing got slower, sometimes with a pause of a quarter of an hour between sentences, and it embarrassed Thackeray to have a stranger sitting in the room when he felt like dictating, waiting with pen poised as he paced in search of the elusive images. But he kept on trying out new recruits, one of whom proved to be deaf and shouted out 'What?' every time he began to spout.

For four years he suffered, intermittently, a wild Irishman, Samuel Langley, who drove him to distraction, was sacked times innumerable, and taken on again largely for his meticulous, almost fanatical proof-reading. He was intolerably talkative, sometimes scarcely sane, and the very opposite of spry.

'Mr. Langley, where is the Cicero? in two volumes quarto. I want a quotation out of it,' Thackeray reported himself as saying. 'Mr. Langley maunders along the room helplessly. He wont find it: I shall: and he will be persuaded that he found it and that I cant possibly get on without him.'[19]

Thackeray could never keep a full set of his own works at hand in that library. George Hodder, when he was working for him, told him how Dickens had all his, neatly bound and ranged in order of publication. 'Yes . . . I know Dickens does,' said Thackeray, 'and so ought I; but fellows borrow them or steal them, and I try to keep them, and can't.'

He was far too grateful to his servants and too sympathetic with their dull lives to expect or demand perfection, or even total honesty. He turned a blind eye to the strangers who haunted his kitchens, the shadowy figures with bulging baskets who flitted into the dusk up his area steps, his retainers' retainers, and said in a *Roundabout Paper* that if you wanted obsequious civility and willing service, you couldn't have truth too:

'Suppose you ask for your newspaper, and Jeames says, "I'm reading it, and jest beg not to be disturbed;" or suppose you ask for a can of water, and he remarks, "You great, big, 'ulking fellar, ain't you big enough to bring it hup yoursulf?" . . . if you made similar proposals or requests to Mr. Jones next door, this is the kind of answer Jones would give you.'[20]

Thackeray himself didn't like to make too many demands. He got a chalk-mark, an irritating little chalk-mark which had been annoying him for weeks, removed from his front door by mentioning it in that same roundabout article, and used his printed homily to make many a point that, more privately, he had tried to instil into his mother, a great sacker of maids and monotonous complainer about their misdeeds.

'. . . pray dont send away Martha,' he had begged her, when she was threatening yet another dismissal. 'Remember how admirably attentive patient and good humoured she has been during your illness how she gave way to Eliza and wasn't jealous of that superior favourite how natural it is for a woman who has to pass night after night alone in that glum kitchen by that one candle to want companionship and amusement from time to time. *We* are no companions to servants, speak condescendingly to them for what we want, can't amuse or talk with them—Let them have their chance of friendship and freedom. their share of light & holyday out of doors. How good my 3 servants have been to us! If I am ill what care they take of me! What a little we pay them back! That word "master" ought to be abolished I think, and have ideas of a small fund to be placed annually to their secret account and given to them when they leave or are sick or I die.'[21]

The Carmichael-Smyths, with their illnesses, their servant troubles, and their residence in Paris, were now the most disturbing factor in Thackeray's domestic life. Within days of his first Scottish tour with the *Four Georges*, when he and his daughters were staying at a friend's country house before travelling north, Charles Pearman had arrived hot-foot on the doorstep with an urgent telegram from the Major. Mrs Carmichael-Smyth was ill; they were needed immediately.

Having crossed at speed to Paris, they had found the Major in a state of great alarm, and Mrs Carmichael-Smyth more frightened than seriously stricken, not at all eager to meet the Maker of whom she was constantly preaching. The homœopathic doctors had come in relays, followed by the 'Regulars', and at last her fever had yielded. Thackeray, feeling guilty, had gone off to keep his commitments, leaving Annie and Minnie, who were to have gone with him on their first grown-up tour, to nurse their grandmother.

There had been too many such scares over the past few years, too much time and energy wasted by 'the Breadwinner' in such dashes across the Channel, and once the girls were installed with Mrs Carmichael-Smyth there were the inevitable tears and battles before he could get them back again. His mother wouldn't take on the companion and extra servant he felt she needed and was prepared to pay for, the Major was still resolute in his refusal to live in England, and they were no longer fit to live alone. He was constantly being emotionally blackmailed, made to feel that he was the one who ought to move.

'My dear old folks keep me in endless perplexity—indeed when didn't they?' he wrote to Jane Elliot in the midst of his lecturing. 'It's small comfort I get out of the anxious loves jealousies glooms despondencies of that poor old mother; to whom we're always going, and who is always miserable at parting from us, or in grief for one cause or another. That most faithful uxorious exacting old gentleman weighs down her life with his dullness—cares for no amusement but his fireside, and to tell stupid articles out of the newspaper, doesn't like much talking or too many candles even in his room—keeps us all mum and dismal . . . that poor old Bird who has paired with my maternal Hen these forty years, and feels that he has no business in our nest at all . . .'[22]

He had begun to fear for his mother's reason. Her nerves had broken down, she was sleepless unless amused, and yet she was allowed no diversions. On the other hand, if the Major were forced to give up his independent command, the chances were that he too would become ill.

'You see what you do when you marry.—what slaves you become—' he told his daughters, selfishly pointing a lesson from his mother's predicament. But then in fairness added: 'Well? and what immense happiness you enjoy I daresay with the right man. These folks' pleasure has no doubt been very greatly increased during 40 years by their living together—the bottom of the cup is rather bitter. So may other dregs be.'[23]

During the summer of the Oxford by-election, the Major was persuaded to set foot once more on British soil, and Thackeray took a house at Brighton for three months for his parents and children, while he stayed mostly in London, bent on doing a great stroke of work on a new novel, *The Virginians*, the story he had first thought of when he wrote the preface to *Henry Esmond* five years before.

The Virginians was to tell of the twin grandsons of that earlier hero, George and Henry Esmond Warrington, who were, in turn, ancestors of the scene-stealing Warrington of *Pendennis*. As Thackeray fought with ill-health, the book rambled, lost direction, stayed rooted in England when he meant to return the plot to America, and never quite reached the promised dramatic climax: the Warrington twins shown in direct combat in the opposing armies of the American War of Independence.

It never reached its hoped-for circulation either. Bradbury and Evans printed twenty thousand copies of the first number and sold only sixteen thousand. 'I tremble for the poor publishers who give me 300£ a number—' wrote Thackeray. 'I don't think they can afford it and shall have the melancholy duty of disgorging.'[24] On his own initiative, the fee was reduced to £250.

'I am constantly unwell now—a fit of spasms—then get well in about 5 days; then 5 days grumbling and thinking of my work; then 14 days work and spasms da capo—' he told the Baxters half-way through: 'and what a horribly stupid story I am writing! Dont tell me. I know better than any of you. No incident, no character no go left in this dreary old expiring carcass—'[25]

For most of the run he was writing intolerably close to every deadline. One month, when he had two bouts of illness, his number appeared without plates, and at the end he failed to get the last chapters finished in time for the traditional double number.

As a summary of the novel as a whole, Thackeray's own description—'devilish stupid, but at the same time most admirable'[26]—was too close to the truth for comfort. But it was still better than most of his rivals could do, and the writing was a joy—pure Saxon, *Harper's* called it.

This time *Harper's Magazine* paid him $100 a month for early proof sheets, and squealed for help when the *New York Tribune* pirated the text. Thackeray mildly pointed out to his own newly reformed buccaneers that, in the absence of international copyright laws, he was powerless to stop such sharp practices, though he would naturally have liked to have been of service to a house which showed itself inclined to act in a kind and friendly manner towards English literary men. *Harper's*, equally impotent, had to be content with a moral victory. When they published the second number, they made several subtle alterations, and watched the *Tribune*, who vowed that they too received the text direct from England, copy every one.

In *The Virginians* a thousand flickering, smoking candles illuminate a card-playing, cheating, gambling, decadent British aristocracy. The second Hanoverian George's monstrous Hanoverian mistress, with her gross, butchered English, holds court in a Tunbridge Wells once more aswarm with sedan-chairs carrying the painted, powdered, privileged and corrupt on their round of frivolous pleasure, while the third Hanoverian George prepares to fight his pure young American colonies.

In fair contrast, Thackeray also portrayed honour and decency at home, mainly through the Lamberts, the kind of loving, domestic family he had told Elwin he didn't know enough about to describe. Inevitably, the sugar content in such a group was high, but he diluted it very palatably by making Lambert *père* a pleasantly waggish gentleman, who, like Thackeray himself, made the most grotesque jokes when he felt most tender-hearted, and in his fond but unsentimental treatment of the Lambert girls, Theo and Hetty, who were, he admitted to Mrs Baxter, very like his own daughters, though he denied it if accused.

Theo, like Annie, was not a particular beauty, her feet were not so miraculously small that they couldn't be seen without a telescope, and she too had a propensity to consider herself a miserable sinner. Hetty was prettier, saucier, and a more complex mixture of selfish sensibility and passionate loyalty.

Of the twins, Harry was the traditional hero: blond, handsome, generous and bone-headed (and there is a delightful scene when the clever, well-read Lambert girls and their father discover this last aspect of the young man's character). George is the sensitive intellectual, an even closer portrait of the dark, contemplative side of Thackeray's nature than his grandfather, Henry Esmond, had been. In writing of him, Thackeray revealed many emotional secrets, from the jealousy of a young boy who fears his widowed mother is to remarry, to the discontent that dogged him even in success.

In an act of creative incest, George Warrington marries Theo, goes through trials of poverty, reaps all the domestic blessings Thackeray would have wished for himself, and, at the end, a baronet, with fat country estates, an intelligent devoted wife and good children, he is still melancholy and unsatisfied—yawning in Eden. Thackeray cut short a confession George Warrington starts to make on his dissatisfaction with his seemingly perfect marriage, but there is enough left to show that the author, in some moods at any rate, had come to believe that if all his desires had been fulfilled, if Jane Brookfield had been his, the reality would never have matched the dream, that even paradise after a certain time would have had a wearisome sameness about it—'only Eve, for ever sweet and tender and figs for breakfast, dinner, supper, from week's end to week's end!'[27]

He overcame one of the chief difficulties that had been worrying him, the finding of new characters, by introducing American ones, especially two sharp young cookies, Harry's shrewish wife and the resolute little beauty, Miss Lyddy Van den Bosch, who becomes mistress of Castlewood Hall. He also triumphantly rounded out the character of Henry Esmond's daughter, Madame Rachel Esmond Warrington, the twins' mother, whose presence, as editor, had hung fussing and censorious over the earlier Esmond chronicle. Aggressive, vain, self-righteous, with a direct line to the Lord, destructive, absurd, unforgettable, she is the perfect proof of a thought Thackeray was to put into words in his next book when he wrote that if anyone should compose a history of the harm done in the world by those who believed themselves to be virtuous, it would prove a curiously edifying work and provide comfort for many a poor oppressed rogue.[28]

He amused himself by briefly reintroducing an old friend from the past, the Chevalier de Barry from *Barry Lyndon*, and in presenting the forebears of Foker of *Pendennis*, and the Floracs of *The Newcomes*, and as always endowed his minor characters with delightfully evocative names, like Sir Lancelot Quintain, a pattern of knighthood and valour. It was the kind of joke he spread widely throughout his works from the old India hand Sir Rice Curry and the toady Tom Tufthunt in *A Shabby Genteel Story*, to Admiral and Mrs Davis Locker and Captain Woolcomb, the dusky mulatto, in *Philip*.

Pendennis had been particularly rich in these absurdities, with Sir Derby Oaks of the turf, Lord Magnus Charters, heir to the Marquis of Runnymede; the Arabian experts, Professor Sandiman and Bedwin Sands, the intolerable country neighbours, the Fogeys of Drummington, the Squares of Dozeley Park, and the Welbores of The Barrow, and Captain Broadfoot of the Dragoons, an 'unlucky' partner on the dance floor. But *Vanity Fair* probably produced the most brilliant, for there, as well as the happily prolific Revd Felix Rabbits, we have the illustrious ruling house of Pumpernickel—his Transparency the Duke and his Transparent family.

In *The Virginians*, Thackeray's most daring *coup* was the bringing back of Beatrix Esmond in old age, the cast-off mistress of at least two royal lovers, one Stuart and one Hanoverian, the widow of both an English bishop and a dubious German baron. Gross and raddled, sitting unrecognizable beneath Kneller's portrait of her in her siren youth, bent still on destructive pleasure, inwardly mourning the one good man who had offered her his life, teaching the wicked ways of the Old World to his Virginian grandson, Beatrix is the supreme creation, greater by far than the real characters Thackeray included in the story—Dr Johnson, David Garrick, the Generals Wolfe and Washington. He researched painstakingly to make those past heroes true to life, but it is the fictional Beatrix Baroness de Bernstein who lives.

Thackeray also worked hard to make *The Virginians* a trans-Atlantic olive branch, becoming at times so conscious of projecting his middle name of Makepeace that it hampered the writing and led to something less than historical truth. Even so, he still didn't escape American wrath, and once more it was George Washington who got him into trouble. That he should portray him at all in a work of fiction, something no American had dared to do, was thought by many to be intolerable. That he should show him as a man—a rather cold and humourless man, though excellently brave and honourable—rather than as a deity, the almighty Father of his Country, was considered by at least one angry letter-writer to *Harper's* to be actually sacrilegious. It was a controversy that raged in the magazine for many months.

Thackeray did, however, find many American champions, and none more ready to take up the quarrel on his behalf than George Curtis, who defended him in print, and told Thackeray himself that he wouldn't think writing was all vanity if he could see the laughter and tears of the group of young and old to whom he read the story each month.

Thackeray's Yonkers host, Frederick Cozzens, also wrote to encourage him. After the first few numbers, he had only one complaint, he said, that Washington had been made to use language unbecoming an officer and a gentleman, whereas the speech of old 'Virginny' had been amazingly pure and polite. Otherwise, he told him:

'Your "Virginians" have surprised and pleased all your intimate friends. We all think your pictures of Virginia life are perfect and wonder how you are able to do it. "Oh!" said Irving to me the other day in that sweet, husky, honeycomb voice, "What a fine book he will make of that!" "Have you read it Mr. Irving?" I asked. "No, I have so much to do, but I know Thackeray. I know what he is capable of doing, a man of great mind, far superior to Dickens. Dickens's prejudices are too limited to make such a book as Thackeray is capable of making of the 'Virginians'.'"[29]

26

A Witch's Broth

The Garrick Club affair

Thackeray and Dickens, Dickens and Thackeray: the comparison between the men and their works sprang instantly to most people's minds when they thought of either, as it did to Washington Irving's. Both men had their personal and literary adherents, who praised the one by damning the other, and during the course of *The Virginians* the two armies burst into vociferous attack in the longest and most distressing of all Thackeray's literary quarrels: the Garrick Club Affair.

Chief ingredient in this witch's broth, as Dickens came to describe the conflict, was a jaunty young rogue called Edmund Yates, son of the actress—'Mrs Yates. Mrs Yates. Mrs Yates! She is so pretty, so fascinating and so ladylike'—who had sent Thackeray into ecstasies at Charterhouse.

By day Yates worked at the Post Office, by night he earned extra money as a playwright and hack journalist. When the Garrick quarrel blew up he was twenty-seven, had had four short-lived farces performed on the London stage, and had achieved his main ambition, that of introducing the gossip column to a respectable journal, by becoming 'The Lounger at the Clubs' in Henry Vizetelly's *Illustrated Times*. He had also just begun editing a new penny paper, *Town Talk*. He was energetic, entertaining, and, in Victorian terms, something of a bounder.

The most distinguished of the clubs at which Yates lounged was the Garrick. He had become a member at an early age, seconded by Andrew 'Foker' Arcadeckne, and elected largely out of admiration for his mother. It was there that he and Thackeray mostly met. Outside, they had little contact, but what there was, on Yates's own account, was cordial. When the birth of his twin sons was announced Thackeray wrote to him (apparently in answer to a request for his autograph) asking if he should condole with or congratulate him on the event.

When they met in the street and walked together past two barrels of oysters, one marked a shilling and the other fifteen pence, Thackeray, pointing to the occupants of the shilling barrel, drawled: '*How* they must hate the others!' [1]

Simple jokes, but agreeable when made by a man at the peak of his profession to an admiring novice, and Yates, whatever he was to say of Thackeray, was always to declare himself a devoted worshipper of his works. It was *Pendennis*, he claimed, which had first inspired him to become a journalist.

Dickens, however, was to prove more congenial to him as a man, and shortly before the Garrick quarrel he joined what Carlyle, with distaste, called Dickens's 'squad', the band of yesmen who did more harm than good with their partisan flattery. Before long he was earning Dickens's eternal gratitude for a manly service (a thoroughly Dickensian phrase) in connection with Dickens's private domestic traumas, which were then speedily becoming a public scandal.

For several years, Dickens had been living at a pitch of nervous tension unusual even for him. His marriage was becoming an intolerable burden, and he described himself as being in an altogether dishevelled state of mind, with miseries of ancient growth threatening to close upon him. Like David Copperfield, he fretted for the one happiness he felt he had missed in life, for the one friend or companion he had never made.

When Douglas Jerrold died, he threw his frenetic, pent-up energies into organizing benefit shows for the widow and children, putting on plays at his home, and then taking them round the provinces with a cast of professional actresses and amateur gentlemen. The applause for his own performances was ecstatic, and in that heady, emotional atmosphere he found his missing friend in the youngest of the actresses, Ellen Ternan. In one of the roles he was playing, Dickens, as an older man, had to fall in love with young Ellen and shower her with jewellery. Off stage, he began to do the same, as Catherine Dickens, a loving, long-suffering but inefficient and uninspiring wife, discovered when a jeweller mistakenly sent a bracelet to Tavistock House instead of Miss Ternan's lodgings.

In the separation negotiations that ensued, Dickens, as eager as ever to appoint seconds, sent in Forster to act for him, while Mark Lemon spoke for Catherine. Another house was found for Mrs

Dickens and her eldest son, Charley, while the rest of the family stayed with their father and Georgina Hogarth, Mrs Dickens's sister, who had long been in control of the household.

After twenty-two years of marriage and the bearing of ten children, Catherine Dickens was dispossessed, and her husband determined that the world should not only accept but approve his rejection of her. The crisis had come just as he was about to embark on a marathon tour of Britain with his first non-charity readings from his novels, a disastrous moment to be involved in scandal. The gossip linking him with Ellen Ternan drove him close to frenzy, and Thackeray, with the most admirable intentions, was to spread that infuriating rumour.

Ever the champion of ladies in distress, Thackeray's sympathies went naturally to Mrs Dickens, whom he was to comfort and try to help through the first months of her Victorian shame, but he was also ready to defend her husband from the worst of the charges circulating about him.

He had only just been told about Ellen Ternan himself when at the Garrick he heard someone spreading the far greater scandal that Dickens had left his wife because of an intrigue with his sister-in-law.

'No such thing,' Thackeray had cried in horror. 'It's with an actress.'[2]

Only the last half of that conversation was relayed to Dickens, and Thackeray swiftly received a note 'authorizing' him to contradict all such slurs, on Dickens's own solemn word and his wife's authority.

To the manager of his readings, Dickens sent a more detailed letter, accusing his wife's mother and youngest sister of spreading the calumny, proclaiming his great attachment and regard for the young lady in question, whose name he wouldn't mention since he honoured it too much, and vowing upon his very soul that there was no more virtuous or spotless a creature. Since Dickens gave the manager discretion to show this letter to anyone he thought it might concern, parts of it inevitably ended up in print, a circumstance which pushed Dickens to the very pinnacle of folly.

In a ferment of exasperation against the prurient tide of gossip, he published a most intimate and ungallant explanation of his separation from his wife and a denial of all other rumours in his magazine, *Household Words*, a document that disgusted even the faithful Forster. Mark Lemon refused to reprint it in *Punch*, and Bradbury and Evans, who published both journals, supported him.

Dickens retaliated by closing down *Household Words*, and forbade his entire family, including Charley, who was engaged to Evans's daughter, to speak to those who had failed to stand by him in his hour of most desperate need. In a moment of utter madness he had thrown the scandal wide throughout the country and alienated many friends who could not stomach this latest unchivalrous conduct towards his wife.

Edmund Yates, however, remained a staunch ally. In the first issue of *Town Talk*, he launched a regular literary gossip column with a glowing account of Dickens and his readings (and mentioned, erroneously, that Thackeray was receiving £200 a number from Bradbury and Evans for *The Virginians*). The following week, on the same day that the extraordinary *Household Words* declaration appeared, he praised both Dickens and his statement in the *Illustrated Times*, and in *Town Talk* printed a brutal pen portrait of Thackeray.

Except for its reasonably fair assessment of his writings, this was a thoroughly vicious attack, beginning with a description of his physical appearance and going on:

'No one meeting him could fail to recognise in him a gentleman; his bearing is cold and uninviting, his style of conversation either openly cynical, or affectedly good natured and benevolent; his *bonhomie* is forced, his wit biting, his pride easily touched—but his appearance is invariably that of the cool, *suave*, well-bred gentleman, who, whatever may be rankling within, suffers no surface display of his emotion.'

His lectures on the *English Humourists*, wrote Yates, were 'attended by all the court and fashion of London. The prices were extravagant, the Lecturer's adulation of birth and position was extravagant, the success was extravagant. No one succeeds better than Mr. Thackeray in cutting his coat according to his cloth: here he flattered the aristocracy, but when he crossed the Atlantic George Washington became the idol of his worship; the "Four Georges" the objects of his bitterest attacks. These last-named Lectures have been dead failures in England, though as literary compositions they are most excellent.'[3]

Town Talk was a cheap, insignificant little paper, and Thackeray, like most other people, would not normally have read it. But when a mutual friend showed him the two copies in which he was mentioned and told him who was responsible, his reaction was prompt and predictable. He wrote to Yates, pointing out that while his writings were public property, and open to any remarks critics thought fit to make, his personality and his private dealings with his publishers were not included in this licence.

'As I understand your phrases,' he told him, 'you impute insincerity to me when I speak good-naturedly in private; assign dishonourable motives to me for sentiments w^h I have delivered in public, and charge me with advancing statements w^h I have never delivered at all.

'Had your remarks been written by a person unknown to me, I should have noticed them no more than other calumnies: but as we have shaken hands more than once, and met hitherto on friendly terms . . . I am obliged to take notice of articles w^h I consider to be, not offensive & unfriendly merely, but slanderous and untrue.

'We meet at a Club where, before you were born I believe, I & other gentlemen have been in the habit of talking, without any idea that our conversation would supply paragraphs for professional vendors of "Literary Talk", and I don't remember that out of that Club I ever exchanged 6 words with you. Allow me to inform you that the talk w^h you may have heard there is not intended for newspaper remark; & to beg, as I have a right to do, that you will refrain from printing comments upon my private conversation; that you will forgo discussions however blundering, on my private affairs; & that you will henceforth please to consider any question of my personal truth & sincerity as quite out of the province of your criticism.'[4]

Yates, his own tender sensibilities stung to the quick by such stern language, took the angry blast to Dickens for advice, and Dickens, already incensed by those who had tried to tell him what should be published and what should not, was very ready to give it. He was later to describe the article as being in bad taste and infinitely better left undone, yet he scrapped Yates's proposed reply, in which Thackeray was reminded of his own early attacks on Bulwer-Lytton, and which might just have had him crying *mea culpa*, and dictated one, which purporting to come from a young unknown to an older man of undisputed position, was as grossly insulting as such a letter could be.

General Post Office,
June 15th, 1858

Sir,

I have to acknowledge the receipt of your letter of this day's date, referring to two articles of which I am the writer.

You will excuse my pointing out to you, that it is absurd to suppose me bound to accept your angry 'understanding' of my 'phrases;' I do not accept it in the least; I altogether reject it.

I cannot characterize your letter in any other terms than those in which you characterized the article which has given you so much offense. If your letter to me were not both 'slanderous and untrue' I should readily have discussed its subject with you, and avowed my earnest and frank desire to set right anything I may have left wrong. Your letter being what it is, I have nothing to add to my present reply.

Edmund Yates.[5]

Thackeray, unwilling to argue further with Yates, but finding it impossible to ignore such an uncompromising riposte, sent copies of the article and correspondence to the Garrick Club committee, asking it to decide whether his complaints were justified.

As Yates himself had heard Thackeray say at one of the club's annual dinners, the Garrick was to him ' "the G.," the little "G", the dearest place in the world'. He had been a member almost from the start, and now that his lecturing was over, it was once again his treasured, companionable. haven, an escape from domestic irritations, a refuge from the tyranny of his desk. His reasons for protecting that sanctuary were not, however, entirely selfish.

To a sympathetic Charles Kingsley, he explained that the Garrick was a great deal more intimate and relaxed than most other clubs, a place where men for over a quarter of a century had been in the habit of talking freely to one another in a small room no more than fifteen feet square. If the penny-a-liner were once allowed to penetrate that sanctum and print his views on the conversation he heard and the people he met there, its comfort and friendliness would be finished.

Dickens was also a member, but despite his reputation for being gregarious and something of a Bohemian, he was not a clubman in the sense that Thackeray was. Dickens liked to hold the stage or sit apart. On his not too frequent visits, he mixed neither with the older, gentlemen members, Thackeray's chief friends, nor the younger, more boisterous players, who, nevertheless, looked upon him as their leader.

He was, however, on the committee, and when he learned of Thackeray's action, one which to his mind showed an amazing lack of discretion, he again helped Yates to write a letter, this time a far more deferential composition, addressed to the club's governing body—the committee on which he, Dickens, sat and through which he would shortly be called upon to give an unbiased opinion.

At Dickens's dictation, Yates submitted the argument that since the offending article had made no reference to the Garrick nor to any conversation held there, the club had no power of jurisdiction in the matter, though, with the very greatest respect, he declared himself ready to bow to the correction of the committee on that point.

When the committee, with Dickens's as the lone dissenting voice, ruled that such issues did come within its province, and ordered

Yates either to make ample apology or resign, since such articles by one member against another were intolerable in a society of gentlemen, Yates, on Dickens's advice, decided not to bow after all, and the debate was thrown open to a general meeting of all members.

By this time the club was in considerable uproar and Dickens, guessing that Thackeray would keep a dignified distance from the proceedings, dissuaded Yates from putting his case to the meeting in person. Instead, he helped to prepare a statement in which Yates offered to make the most grovelling apologies to the club—though none to Thackeray—and, still without revealing his own involvement, was one of the chief speakers on his behalf. But once again Yates lost, by seventy votes to forty-six. His name was struck from the club's register, his subscription was returned to him, and Dickens resigned from a committee which seemed to him to have gone perfectly mad.

'I really never met with such ridiculous assumption and preposterous imbecility in my life before,' he wrote to another of Yates's supporters. 'Like Fox, I should "boil up with indignation" if I had not a vent. But I have. Upon my soul, when I picture them in that back-yard, conceiving that they shake the earth, I fall into fits of laughter.'[6]

For the establishment, Frank Fladgate, the mild, courtly doyen of the club, communicated the news to Thackeray, adding the latest *bon mot*: 'Y's conduct has been very un Y's.'[7]

Dickens, still firm in his opinion that the 'coarse and arrogant' tone of Thackeray's letter made an apology impossible, urged Yates to investigate the legality of the proceedings. The committee also took legal advice, and for four months little appeared to happen, except in the pages of the penny press, where Yates's supporters, like midges, kept nibbling away through the dog-days of summer. Thackeray, who had already sunk to their level once, by referring to Yates in *The Virginians* as 'young Grubstreet, who corresponds with three penny papers and describes the persons and conversation of gentlemen whom he meets at his "clubs,"' allowed himself to be irritated into one more foolish swipe: an explanation, in a later number, of how he preferred not to be joined in chummy literary fellowship with such writers as Tom Garbage, esteemed contributor to the *Kennel Miscellany*.[8]

Both he and Dickens spent most of the lull out of London, Dickens giving his readings, Thackeray on the Continent. They met only once, when Thackeray was standing with Fladgate on the steps of the Reform Club.

'We spoke as if nothing had happened,' Dickens wrote to Yates, '—except that Fladgate's eyebrows went up into the crown of his hat, and he twisted himself into extraordinary forms.'[9]

His humour at the expense of the other side came to an abrupt halt, however, when he returned to town in the autumn and discovered that Yates had engaged the services of Edwin James, Q.C., one of the most flamboyant and successful courtroom performers of his day, a bullying, unsqueamish operator who was to be disbarred three years later for longstanding malpractices, and whom Dickens was to put into *A Tale of Two Cities* as Mr Stryver: 'stout, loud, red, bluff, and free from any drawbacks of delicacy.'

Having given Yates a favourable opinion, Edwin James was pressing for a court case, a star-studded spectacle for which he proposed mustering as many of Thackeray's old victims as could be brought to testify. He also made it clear that he would put Dickens into the witness-box. At this Dickens took fright, and in a letter of appeasement to Thackeray, admitted advising Yates from the start.

Once again, he suggested the old tactic of seconds. If Thackeray nominated a friend, he, Dickens, would act for Yates. If Thackeray should not agree, then he asked that his letter be burned.

Thackeray, sickened and angry, did not agree, and did not burn the letter. He composed a civil but unyielding reply, pointing out that since he had submitted the case to the club he could no longer take part in the dispute personally, and enclosed a copy of a letter to the committee in which he passed on Dickens's offer to mediate, and expressed his own desire for a peaceful termination to the affair.

To the club he did not mention Dickens's confession of his advisory role, but privately, among friends, he was less discreet.

Dickens for his part was furious at having his spurned olive branch made public, and the quarrel once more whirled into rancorous motion. Yates, who had diplomatically held his fire, broke out again in the *Illustrated Times* with a torrent of abuse against the club's titled members, Thackeray's friends and supporters, and followed it with a parody of the *Ballad of the Bouillabaisse* so vicious that six of his colleagues threatened to resign.

Young Charley Dickens, who, despite his father's orders, remained on good terms with Bradbury and Evans, took Yates to task in *Punch*, reminding him that a journalist should also be a gentleman, an action for which his father removed his name from the proposal list at the Garrick.

For legal purposes, Yates had himself ceremoniously ejected from the club, and, at last, issued a writ. The committee pleaded, successfully, that it could not be sued, since the property of the club was vested in its trustees, and against the trustees there was no action possible except a suit in chancery, a lengthy and costly procedure which Yates could not afford.

Outwitted, Yates and Dickens published a pamphlet, *Mr.* *Thackeray, Mr. Yates, and the Garrick Club: The Correspondence and Facts*, ostensibly the work of Yates, but, like his letters, largely or wholly written by Dickens, who, worried by new rumours, incorporated into it specific denials that he had either financed Yates or incited him to write the original article.

The partisanship engendered by the dispute was a long time dying, and Thackeray's victory, such as it was, proved to be a bitter one.

'What pains me most is that Dickens should have been his adviser,' he told Charles Kingsley: 'and next that I should have had to lay a heavy hand on a young man who, I take it, has been cruelly punished by the issue of the affair, and I believe is hardly aware of the nature of his own offence, and doesn't even now understand that a gentleman should resent the monstrous insult w^h he volunteered. Scores of the pennyaline fraternity have written on his side, and a great number of them are agreed that it's the description of *my nose* w^h makes me so furious—Not one of them seems to understand that to be accused of hypocrisy of base motives for public & private conduct & so forth—are the points w^h make me angry—and I look for more press libels immediately showing how I have ruthlessly persecuted an excellent & harmless young man, and how Dickens has exhausted every possible means to make peace—Dickens who dictated Yates's letters to me, who made him submit to the Committee, then call a general meeting, & then go to law.'[10]

Yates never was to understand his wrong. Towards the end of his life, not long after he had served a prison sentence for criminal libel, he painted a pathetic picture of himself at the time of the *Town Talk* article: a young man, toiling away after his day's work at the Post Office, struggling to supply short copy, with a master-printer at his elbow urging him on, and page after page being carried off to the compositors as soon as it was written. For those careless words he had had to endure for thirty years the charge 'He was expelled from the Garrick,' and for thirty years could find no other respectable club willing to accept him. He saw himself as the misused innocent in a personal battle between giants.

The giants themselves saw it differently. Thackeray had torments of conscience over the result, but he never doubted his own motives. *Punch* friends with tougher hides told him he should have treated the article with the contempt it deserved; 'Jacob Omnium' Higgins, in most omnipotent mood, informed him he was utterly in the wrong; but for Thackeray it was a matter of honour. Yates, an acquaintance, had cast a stain on that honour, and if not stopped might well do the same to others. He had felt obliged to take notice of the fact.

Yates's theory that he had persisted in his persecution as a means of striking at a rival, was a gross misjudgement, for Thackeray had no professional jealousy. Throughout his career, he went out of his way to praise Dickens's books whenever he could, so much so that Jane Brookfield once accused him of being generous only because it was the sort of thing he thought he ought to do. But Thackeray, a man of far wider literary tastes than Dickens, who probably could not find much in Thackeray's works to admire, genuinely considered his chief rival to be the greatest 'genius' of the day. On the other hand, he thought that he himself used the English language a great deal better. He was content to leave it at that.

He had no desire to wipe out a rival, no wish to be thought good only because the competition was bad, nor, indeed, did he have any ambition to be universally popular. There were some people by whom he preferred to be disliked. The hostess who ran shrieking to her cook, 'Martin, don't roast the ortolans; Mr. Dickens isn't coming,' when Thackeray arrived for dinner and presented Dickens's apologies, was the kind of admirer he was content to do without—though he remembered the incident, and used it in *Philip*.[11] And there were many others whose praise worried him more than their abuse.

Even in the midst of the Garrick affair, he showed no inclination to snipe at Yates's busy defender by disparaging his works, as he proved late one night in Paris. At the time Thackeray was particularly unwell and so baffled by the logistical problems he had given himself in *The Virginians* that he had just begged a visiting American to write a chapter for him.

The setting was conducive to indiscretion: Father Prout's raffish quarters behind the Palais Royal, with a young Irish profligate sleeping off his troubles under a pile of blankets in one corner, the Irish poet, William Allingham, eager for literary discussion, sitting in another, brandy and water close at hand. Thackeray allowed himself a slight grumble at the unmusical poetry and formidable health of Robert Browning—'what spirits he has . . . He almost blew me out of bed!'—but refused to be drawn on Dickens.

'Any story of Dickens might be improved,' said Allingham, 'by a man of good taste with a pencil in hand, merely scoring out this and that.'

'Young man,' replied Thackeray, in a rich Irish brogue, 'you're threadin' on the tail o' me coat!' And then, in answer to Allingham's puzzled look: 'What you've just said applied very much to your humble servant's things.'[12]

He tried to be fair to Dickens the man, too. For several years, especially after their shared interest in administrative reform, they had rubbed along reasonably well together, and Thackeray had come to consider the meddlesome hangers-on as the cause of most of the trouble between them. But his instinctive gut reaction to Dickens never changed, as is evident from a throw-away sneer to Mrs Procter when he heard how delighted Dickens had been with a working-class audience at a reading of *A Christmas Carol*: 'my soul is full of envy; and I think of coming back and reading Yellowplush in costume at Islington.'[13]

He thought Dickens pandered to the masses, just as Dickens saw him as a toady to the aristocracy, and when 'the Great Moralist' at last admitted his full involvement with Yates, all the old suspicions flooded back, that if he didn't resent Dickens's success, Dickens certainly resented his.

'O for shame, for shame!' wrote Thackeray, after reading that letter of appeasement. 'But what pent up animosities and long cherished hatred doesn't one see in the business! "Theres my rival, Stab him now, Yates—" and the poor young man thrusts out his unlucky paw.'[14]

Around the *Punch* table, the accusations were much the same. When Yates was defended there it was on the grounds that he had only been acting for Dickens, 'Who never spoke well of Thackeray or anybody else.'[15]

But Dickens, too, had believed he was fighting for a principle— the right to publish and not to be damned, the licence for an author to decide for himself what was good taste and what was bad. He certainly felt he had a grievance against Thackeray for the actress remark, and was no doubt irked by his sympathy for Mrs Dickens. He may even have read terrible personal insult into a catalogue of skeletons in closets which Thackeray included in *The Virginians*. In listing the trials and passions of 'Mrs. A', 'Mrs. B' and so on, Thackeray had unfortunately arrived at 'Mrs. D' when he sketched a vignette of a doting wife and a deceiving husband.[16] He had written the piece before he had ever heard of Ellen Ternan, but Dickens was not to know that.

It may be that he said the equivalent of 'Who will rid me of this turbulent priest?' but Yates's gutter-press retaliation was not something Dickens would have normally condoned. At that time of domestic turmoil and public adulation for his readings, however, his judgement was fatally clouded, his belief in his own infallibility immense. He would brook no argument and listen to no advice. Even Forster considered him scarcely sane.

During the few years that remained of Thackeray's life, he and Dickens met rarely and did not speak, until within a month or so of his death, Thackeray could stand it no longer. If he really wanted to end the quarrel, Dickens's daughter, Kate Collins, told him, he must make the first move since her father was too shy and too proud to begin.

'But,' objected Thackeray, 'I too am shy and proud.'

Nevertheless, when he saw Dickens at the Athenaeum a few days later, he ran down the stairs after him and insisted on shaking hands, saying he couldn't bear to be on anything but the old terms with him.

Thackeray rushed home, thrust a beaming face round Annie's door, and told her what he'd done. Kate Collins had to wait longer for the news from her father. During a morning in his company at Gad's Hill, he said not a word of the affair, then tersely at lunch asked her: 'You are very fond of Thackeray aren't you?' When Kate agreed, he told her coldly she need worry no more. They had met and shaken hands.[17]

27

The Cornhill Magazine
Of laurel wreaths and thorns

Thackeray decided that the swellest and most dignified reaction to Yates's and Dickens's pamphlet was to ignore it, and miraculously he kept to that decision. Instead, he threw himself into finishing *The Virginians*, and in the late summer of 1859 was at last able to call together a dinner-party at Greenwich to celebrate its completion. 'Six o'clock sharp,' he had ordered his guests. At seven, still in his morning frock-coat, he bounded into a room full of glum and ·hungry friends, pirouetted on one leg, clapped his ink-stained hands, cried out that the last page had just gone off to the printer's, and led the way to a thoroughly overcooked dinner.

Once the book was done he had promised himself a year's complete rest from all writing, but long before that Greenwich evening he had become involved in another venture, one which was to double rather than ease his work-load. His old ambition to edit a magazine had dimmed at times, but never died, and for several years he had discussed with George Smith the possibility of starting a new publication with himself at the helm.

While he was writing *The Newcomes* he had drawn up plans for a daily sheet of general criticism on literature and life, in the style of Addison and Steele's *Spectator* or *Tatler*. He saw it as being scrupulously frank and just in its comments, living up to the name he wanted to give it—*Fair Play*.

But just as he had been on the point of giving Smith the go-ahead, a careless line in one of the rare articles of his later years had stirred up such a farrago of hurt, resentment and abuse among his old

Punch colleagues, that he had once again held back. The article, commissioned by Whitwell Elwin for the *Quarterly Review*, had been a tribute to the art of John Leech, and Thackeray in a burst of enthusiasm had written: 'Fancy a number of *Punch* without Leech's pictures! What would you give for it?'[1]

The writing fraternity had been outraged. Jerrold had called him a snob and a flunkey; even sane, scholarly Percival Leigh had had to be soothed with an apologetic letter; and Thackeray's appetite for editorship had vanished.

'If in writing once in five years or so a literary criticism intended to be good-natured, I managed to anger a body of old friends, to cause myself pain and regret, to put my foot into a nest of hornets, which sting and have their annoyance too, to lose rest and quiet, hadn't I better give up that game of "Fair Play" which I thought of, stick to my old pursuits, and keep my health and temper?' he had asked Smith.[2]

For four years, Smith had let the matter languish, then, early in 1859, just as the Garrick Club row was drawing to a close, he was inspired with an idea for a far more ambitious project: a monthly magazine, combining the best features of the half-crown quarterlies with a long novel in instalments, all for the same price as those monthly numbers Thackeray and Dickens had been producing for so long—one shilling.

Having assessed Thackeray's capacity for routine business, Smith didn't picture him as editor of such an enterprise, but he did see it as a means of achieving one of his own ambitions: the tempting of Thackeray away from his quixotic allegiance to Bradbury and Evans and into the Smith, Elder, fold for good. Until then, he had managed to capture only *Esmond, The Kickleburys on the Rhine*, the *Humourists* lectures, and *The Rose and the Ring*. Now he saw his chance to scoop the next big novel, and set about securing it in his usual grand style, preparing a contract which offered Thackeray £350 a month for all preliminary rights, both serial and in book form, at home and abroad, and half shares in all cheap reprints.

'I wonder if you will consider it,' he asked, as he handed it over, 'or will at once consign it to your waste-paper basket!'

'I am not going to put such a document as *this* into my waste-paper basket,' Thackeray replied with a slow smile.[3]

He might want to give up novel-writing, he told his friends, but how could he refuse when he was offered such prodigious sums?

He and Smith planned the magazine together, and when no one else with a resounding enough name could be found to take over the editorial chair, Smith changed his mind and decided to offer him that too, with himself standing close behind it to supply the business acumen. They were to have an equal veto on contributions, and Thackeray a further £1000 a year.

In the autumn, they christened the new venture the *Cornhill Magazine*, taking the name from the London street in which Smith presided over his banking, trading and publishing empire. It had, said Thackeray, a sound of jollity and abundance about it, and between them they made sure it lived up to that description.

'We secured the most brilliant contributors from every quarter,' Smith was to claim with justifiable pride. 'Our terms were lavish almost to the point of recklessness.'[4]

George Eliot was to receive the highest fees for fiction (£7000 for *Romola*), and Thackeray the most for short articles: twelve guineas a page for his monthly *Roundabout Papers,* the charming, wandering essays that were to be praised as the best work of his last years, and to give him the greatest pleasure to write.

Before *The Virginians* was finished, he began canvassing the kind of contributor he hoped to tempt, those who would reflect his own *cachet* and make it a man-of-the-world magazine. He determined that it should have no party or sectarian bias, that it should leave alone those subjects on which it was already plain agreement was impossible, and be so impeccably moral that no lady or child would blush at its contents. Like a pastrycook who has gorged on too many cakes and yearns for more savoury fare, he was more interested in fact than fiction, and aimed to throw his pages open to any man or woman who had anything interesting or exciting to tell and could express themselves in a literate manner. He wanted, he said, as much reality as possible.

With his name on the masthead, and Smith's bullion in the hold, the magazine was famous long before it appeared. Anthony Trollope, Post Office surveyor and modestly successful author, heard of it in Ireland, and diffidently offered a series of four short stories. Within a week he received two replies, both ignoring the stories, but asking for a major novel with which to launch the first issue.

One was from Smith, mentioning what Trollope called 'some interesting details as to honorarium'; the other from Thackeray, welcoming him aboard, and praising his previous works: 'There was quite an excitement in my family one evening when Paterfamilias (who goes to sleep on a novel almost always when he tries it after dinner) came up-stairs into the drawing-room wide awake and calling for the second volume of *The Three Clerks*.'[5]

As far as Trollope was concerned there was only one drawback: he was a man of firm principles, who believed that the public should not set eyes on the beginning of one of his books until he had seen the end of it. But even Trollope's resolve proved amenable to Smith's persuasion. The details, as Trollope called them, were £1000, nearly twice the sum he had been promised by Chapman and Hall for a half-finished Irish novel. He clinched the deal on a quick trip to London, began the new story on his return journey across the Irish Sea, and gave it the clerical setting Smith and Thackeray insisted on.

'The details were so interesting that had a couple of archbishops been demanded, I should have produced them,' said Trollope. The result was *Framley Parsonage*, his greatest success in his lifetime—glory he attributed to producing it under Thackeray's banner.[6]

Swamped by editorial duties and often so ill that he could neither read nor write for days at a time, Thackeray had not been able to provide the big fictional attraction himself. Instead he offered a *bonne bouche*, his rejected play, *The Wolves and the Lamb*, turned into a six-part story and rechristened *Lovel the Widower*.

Father Prout was commissioned to write an inaugural ode for the first edition, there was a poem from Mrs Archer Clive, then came the factual pieces Thackeray was so keen on: G. H. Lewes, with the first of his series of studies of animal life; Thornton Leigh Hunt with an article on his father; Sir John Bowring, giving the fruit of nine years' Eastern experience in a description of the Chinese and the 'Outer Barbarians'; extracts from the private journal of one of the officers on board the *Fox*, then newly returned from her search for Sir John Franklin and his lost Arctic expedition—a splendid *coup*; and General Sir John Burgoyne, who had served under Moore and Wellington, warning of the danger of the militant French nation—'armed to the teeth, and ready to do battle for any cause.'

It was, said Milnes, reading an early copy, almost too good for the public it was written for and for the money it had to earn.

When it went on sale on the first day of January 1860, it made publishing history. Despite the fact that a rival, *Macmillan's Magazine*, had managed to beat them to the bookstalls by a couple of months, over 110,000 copies were sold, a record for a British periodical, and it was estimated that it was read by at least half a million people. Thackeray, almost beside himself with joy, dashed to Paris, where he met just the man to share his exuberant mood, James Fields.

'London,' he told Fields, throwing up his long arms, 'is not big enough to contain me now, and I am obliged to add Paris to my residence! Great heavens, where will this tremendous circulation stop! Who knows but that I shall have to add Vienna and Rome to my whereabouts? If the worst comes to the worst, New York, also, may fall into my clutches, and only the Rocky Mountains may be able to stop my progress!'[7]

As they gazed into the glittering jewellers' shops of the Palais Royal, Fields had to restrain him from rushing in and filling his pockets with diamonds and other tempting trifles. 'How can I spend the princely income which Smith allows me for editing the *Cornhill*, unless I begin instantly somewhere?' Thackeray objected.

He took Fields on a gastronomic tour of the city, and whenever he saw a group of Parisians talking excitedly together, dramatically clutched the American by the arm and hissed: 'There, there, you see the news has reached Paris, and perhaps the number has gone up since my last accounts from London.'

His spirits were tremendous. He couldn't sleep, he said, for counting up subscribers.

Thackeray's greatest assets as an editor were the glamour of his name and his wide knowledge of so many strata of society. He knew what people were talking about and wanted to read more of, who were the best writers on such subjects, and how to persuade them to write for him.

Tennyson originally refused Smith's request for a contribution, but speedily obliged Thackeray, sending him *Tithonus* for the second issue, and even Robert Browning, usually adamant in his belief that poetry had no place in magazines, allowed his wife to write for the new editor. *A Musical Instrument* ('What is he doing, the great god Pan') first appeared in the *Cornhill*, and soon Thackeray was deluged with copy from Elizabeth Barrett Browning, a rain of gems which showed up his greatest editorial weaknesses. He was too soft, and too chaotic, especially where the ladies—'the fair'—were concerned.

To say no, he claimed, often cost him a morning's peace and a day's work, and to find the rejected manuscripts took even longer: 'Oh, those hours of madness spent in searching for Louisa's lost lines to her dead Piping Bullfinch, for Nhoj Senoj's mislaid Essay!'[8]

When Mrs Browning sent him *Lord Walter's Wife*, he felt it transgressed the magazine's strict code of morality (only Thackeray himself was allowed to bend that), but how to say so? He put off the task for as long as he could, then approached it with anguished delicacy.

'Has Browning ever had an aching tooth w^h must come out (I don't say Mrs Browning, for women are much more courageous)—' he asked her, 'a tooth w^h must come out and which he has kept for months and months away from the dentist? I have had such a tooth a long time, and have sate down in this chair, and never had the courage to undergo the pull.

'This tooth is an allegory . . . Its your poem that you sent months ago—and who am I to refuse the poems of Elizabeth Browning, and set myself up as a judge over her? I cant tell you how often I have been going to write, and have failed . . . In your poem you know there is an account of unlawful passion felt by a man for a woman—and though you write pure doctrine and real modesty and pure ethics, I am sure our readers would make an outcry . . . To have to say no to my betters is one of the hardest duties I have—but I'm sure we must not publish your verses—and go down on my knees before cutting my victims head off, and say "Madam you know how I respect and regard you, Brownings wife and Peniny's mother: and for what I am going to do I most humbly ask your pardon".'[9]

Mrs Browning generously told him to consider the famous tooth as extracted under chloroform, with no pain to anyone, but stung by his 'kind way of naming her dignities'—those domestic titles of wife and mother—she didn't let him off without an argument, a reversal of the polemics he had once used himself against the very taboos he was now determined to maintain.

Did he consider that paterfamilias, with his oriental traditions and veiled female faces, had dealt successfully with the evils he was objecting to? she asked. Perhaps women, with their quick pure instincts and honest innocent eyes, might do better, simply by looking squarely at the facts and calling them by their proper names.

'I, being vain,' she wrote, '(turn some people out of a room and you dont humble them properly) retort with—"materfamilias!"'[10]

Anthony Trollope was also to offer a story in which a married woman met with temptation, and Thackeray received his reply to the Cornhill's rejection just as he had risen from his sick-bed and was still feeling too weak and cowardly to risk entanglement even in a postal argument.

'I told one of the girls to read it,' he eventually wrote to Trollope. 'I give you her very words—I can't help it if they are not more respectful. She says . . . "He is an old dear and you should write him an affectionate letter."'[11]

It was only after hearing this verdict that Thackeray had had the courage to look at Trollope's great clumping piece of humorous self-vindication himself.

When Adelaide Procter sent him two poems to choose between, he wasted a great deal of time in drawing a donkey poised between two equally enticing bales of hay, and astonished Edwin Landseer by repaying him for the small drawing of a black sheep for one of the Lovel episodes with a carefully chosen decanter—or 'ewer'.

His house and mail-bag were besieged by would-be contributors, offering him the possible, the impossible and the outrageously awful. If he felt they were worth encouraging he took pains to do so. 'The verses are so good that they ought to be better,' he told the spinster authors of one poem. 'Why leave careless and loose rhymes such as those marked? Why not polish the verses more and more and make them as bright as they possibly can be? Indeed they are worth all the trouble, I hope to have them back at an early day . . .'[12]

But all too often they showed no talent at all, and were accompanied by notes from friends he was loath to disoblige, requests to rewrite what he couldn't understand, or explanations that the hopeful author was a poor governess with an invalid mother and younger brothers and sisters to support, an approach guaranteed to wring his heart and empty his pockets. In a *Roundabout Paper*, which he called 'On Thorns in Cushions', he poured out a torrent of such tortures of the editorial chair, and begged his tormentors to bombard the Cornhill offices, not his home.

Surrounded by servants, and with a daughter who was also beginning to write in earnest, Thackeray still remained curiously open to invasion. Many a time Annie wrote in her journals of throwing herself into her father's study with domestic or personal problems and of how it seemed to disturb him. The tax man, the rent collector, a contributor could all suddenly appear before him just as the ideas were beginning to flow. Turgenev called, without any explanation except that he was a foreign admirer of his works. He was asked to dinner. An equally unknown German pianist was allowed to waste his time with a proposal that Thackeray should write two songs, which the musician would then set to music and graciously dedicate to him. The German was given a cigar, which he threw into the fire, saying: 'Ah—we pay duppence for a zigar like zis at Brussels.'[13]

'Damn him,' said Thackeray, when he told of the man's impudence. But still the door-bell rang and the tide of visitors washed over him, and still he was prepared to go to infinite lengths for those who appealed to him by their need, their brains, or their beauty. With regard to the last attraction, Smith's joint say in the magazine's affairs was often to prove invaluable.

'I hope, Smith, you won't exercise your veto upon that,' Thackeray told him one day, as he handed over a contribution.

'Why?' asked Smith. 'Is it in your opinion so very good?'

'No, I can't say it is really good; but it is written by such a pretty woman! She has such lovely eyes and such a sweet voice.'

Reading the article uninfluenced by visions of its author, Smith found no difficulty in turning it down, so Thackeray invited him to dinner, sat him unknowingly beside the beautiful contributor and watched him enjoy his evening.

'What do you say *now* about that article, my young friend?' he asked in a tone of triumph next time they met.

If it were a question of putting the writer, rather than the article, into the *Cornhill*, said Smith, he might well change his mind. [14]

Any venture as successful as the *Cornhill* was bound to have its detractors and petty pin-prickers, and those who could find nothing else to criticize complained that it was absurd to name a magazine after a piece of London, but they were soon silenced when the idea caught on and the *Temple Bar*, the *St James's*, the *Belgravia*, the *St Paul's* and the *Strand* also appeared on the bookstalls.

Only one attack caused any real resentment, and that came from a predictable quarter—Yates. Before the magazine had gone on sale, he had sent Thackeray a poem for it, together with a saucy note expressing his confidence that personal animosity would not be allowed to influence the editor's judgement. It is unlikely that Thackeray himself replied, and five months after the first number was published, Yates produced a nasty little swipe against the magazine in another of his London clubland columns, this time for the *New York Times*.

Already the *Cornhill*, which had gone up like a rocket, was coming down like the stick, he wrote, giving its circulation as forty thousand, less than half the figure it had settled down to. And building on gossip from his fellow Post Office worker, Anthony Trollope, who it seems had never heard of the Garrick Club affair, he described some of the lavish monthly dinners with which Smith entertained his contributors at his home, portraying Smith as totally unread and quoting conversations which made all parties appear foolish. Annie's first published article, *Little Scholars*, also came in for attention. It bore traces, said Yates, of having been touched up by the parental hand.

Thackeray had been so proud when Smith refused his offer to send *Little Scholars* to another magazine that he had scooped James Fields off a London pavement and into his cab just so that he could tell him about it. 'When I read it, I blubbered like a child,' he said, 'it is so good, so simple, and so honest; and my little girl wrote it, every word of it.' [15]

Yates's article was circulated in England through the *Saturday Review*, which used it ostensibly to deplore American scandal-mongering, but largely to work off some of its own grudges against Thackeray and Smith. Trollope, an innocent newcomer to the London literary scene, still at sea on its seething currents, was appalled at the trouble he had caused by his delighted gossip of the magazine's internal affairs.

'I know I have done wrong, and you may say anything you like to me,' he told Smith meekly.[16]

Smith and Thackeray were inclined to ignore both Yates and the *Saturday Review*. Smith had a reasonably tough hide, and Thackeray was learning to smother his howls of pain. Also, as he was to point out, he wasn't the chief target in this instance, and it was wonderful how gallantly one could bear the misfortunes of one's friends. But Smith's wife was so outraged at the insult to her husband that Thackeray was at last persuaded to annihilate his assailants in a *Roundabout Paper*—'On Screens in Dining-Rooms'.

When his lecturing money had first begun to pour in, Thackeray had written 'Dominus providebit'. With the advent of the *Cornhill* he was provided with a great deal more. During his years of editorship the circulation of the magazine averaged 85,000, at a time when *Punch*, for example, could manage only 30,000, and Smith, early on, had brought tears to Thackeray's eyes by doubling his editorial salary. In all, he was receiving around £7000 a year, and shouted 'Cockadoodleoodloodle' as he totted up his accounts.

By comparison, his total earnings for the previous twenty years—£32,000—had been meagre. The lectures had made him £9,500, *The Virginians*, £6000, and *Vanity Fair*, in all its various editions, no more than £2000. As he thought of his new riches, he told his mother that she mustn't say a word against filthy lucre, since he could see the use and comfort of it more and more every day. His expenditure raced to keep abreast of his income and occasionally, even now, shot ahead.

'Well, you know a bank whereon the wild thyme grows,' Smith told him when he needed a loan, and Thackeray diffidently drew on that ready credit by walking every so often into Smith's office with his trouser pockets turned inside out.[17]

Smith would reach for his cheque book and look up inquiringly. Thackeray would mention the sum needed. And the transaction would be complete.

When he died, a note was found in his desk showing how much he had overdrawn: 'I.O. S.E. & Co., 35pp.' Smith, Elder had paid him for thirty-five pages of copy he had not had time to produce.

His agreement with Smith relieved him of all financial worries and the business of dealing with foreign publishers. The only rub was the actual job of editing, and as time went on he funked it. He read less, lost more, and felt his own writing was suffering. After *Lovel the Widower*, his chief contribution was the *Four Georges* lectures, and it was not until the autumn that he began work on the full-length novel Smith had been so eager to win from Bradbury and Evans.

For some time he had toyed with the idea of completing the medieval saga he had begun nineteen years before in Paris, when Isabella was at Esquirol's, and planned to weave into it the ancestors of all the major characters from his later works. It would be a most magnificent performance, he said, and nobody would read it.

In the end he went back even further, to *A Shabby Genteel Story*, taking up the plot again a few years on, and calling it *The Adventures of Philip on His Way Through the World: Shewing who robbed him, who helped him, and who passed him by.*

Once more he poured into it a great deal of his own life: Charterhouse, his early days of law and struggling journalism, his courtship of Isabella, and their first years of married happiness. Mrs Shawe appears at her most vindictively appalling, and Pendennis, mellow and urbane, narrates. All the old wounds are paraded, and in both *The Virginians* and *Philip* there is an incident which shows how fresh they remained. In both books, when the hero is told he can't marry the girl he loves, he hears the raking of a fire in the room above, where the girl sits banished and alone. 'When I hear a fire poked overhead now—twenty years after—the whole thing comes back to me,' he wrote, 'and I suffer over again that infernal agony.'[18]

Of love, Thackeray wrote in *Philip*: 'Some people have the complaint so mildly that they are scarcely ever kept to their beds. Some bear its scars for ever.'[19] Without love, he said, life was just death.

The past came flooding back, but no longer could it bring with it the illusion of youth. Thackeray was ill and feeling far, far older than his years. 'Why didn't they buy me at 30,' he asked, 'not the tired old horse at 50?'[20] He was weary of novel-writing, and told even his readers that he considered it rather absurd for elderly fingers to be still twanging Dan Cupid's toy bow and arrows.

'I can repeat the old things in a pleasant way,' he explained to *Quarterly Review* editor, Elwin, 'but I have nothing fresh to say. I get sick of my task when I am ill, and think, Good heavens! what is all this stuff about?'[21]

He planned *Philip* well and kept to his plot, but the ultimate effect was of an endless *Roundabout Paper*, as his profound, ironical or highly personal asides grew ever more expansive.

'He's clever always, but he goes round and round till I'm dizzy for one, and don't know where I am,' said Elizabeth Browning. 'I think somebody has tied him up to a post, leaving a tether.'[22]

For those who loved Thackeray and cherished every profusely scattered gem, it was a feast. For those who wanted a continuous story, it was maddening, and when *Framley Parsonage* ended, the circulation of the *Cornhill* dropped, even though *Philip* had by then been running for four months.

Thackeray was also finding it more difficult to agree with Smith on other contributions, and at last a more than usually heated disagreement convinced him that it would be better to give up his thorn-cushioned editorial chair, keep a friend, and pay more attention to his writing. It was all done most amicably: Smith included his humorous, jubilant resignation address to readers in the next issue of the magazine, and Thackeray's future *Roundabout Papers* were sprinkled with references to the new editor—'no soft and yielding character like his predecessor.'

When Thackeray had first shaken hands on his agreement with Smith, he told a friend that he had sold himself into slavery for two years. He was to keep his chains for just a few months longer than that, and though they chafed more every day, he won much praise for his editorship. Trollope, not the easiest man to get along with even when he adored and admired someone as much as he did Thackeray, called him 'the kindest of guides, the gentlest of rulers, and, as a fellow-workman, liberal, unselfish, considerate, beyond compare.'[23]

His tact and understanding were there for all—the great guns and the beginners. John Hollingshead, a former commercial traveller and cloth merchant, brash and cocky at his first interview, volunteered the defiant information that he used short words because he wasn't always sure he understood long ones and there might also be some difficulty about spelling them, but Thackeray, liking what he had already written, put his behaviour down to nerves and won Hollingshead's regard with his gentleness and charity.

Young Frederick Walker, who was discovered by Smith to illustrate *Philip* when Thackeray found he couldn't cope, was even more nervous, so paralysed by shyness that he was virtually speechless when Smith escorted him to Onslow Square to prove his capabilities for the job. After a painful few minutes, Thackeray stood up and said: 'I am going to shave, would you mind drawing my back?'

It was, as Smith wrote later, an idea as ingenious as it was kind. Had Walker been asked to draw Thackeray's face he would scarcely have been able to hold a pencil.

For a time twenty-one-year-old Walker copied Thackeray's designs on to wood blocks for the printers, then, finding his tongue to surprising purpose, told Smith he wasn't going to do the work any more. It offended his artistic self-respect, he said. It wasn't original work. His friends told him he should do original work. Any fool who could draw at all could copy other people's designs. Thackeray gradually gave him his head, and by the time Walker died, only fourteen years later, he was one of the most famous artists of his day, with an illustration for *Philip* among the best remembered of his works.

Bringing on such men, was for Thackeray, one of the few pleasures of editorship.

28

Finis

. . . like the hero at the end of a story

FINIS

Throughout the *Cornhill* years Thackeray had been grappling with another project: the building of a house. And within days of casting off his chains, he moved into it: No. 2, Palace Green, Kensington, the pride of his last years. It stood at the foot of a leafy avenue that was to become known as 'Millionaires' Row', facing a peaceful old green, ancient elms and the sprawling roofs and chimneys of Christopher Wren's Kensington Palace, home of the kings and queens of Thackeray's favourite century.

He had bought the land and a dilapidated old mansion two years earlier, reluctantly pulled down the original building when it was found too unsafe to renovate, and built himself a monument to achievement. In bright red brick, designed on lavish lines in the style of Queen Anne's reign, its cost rose from an estimated £4000 to £6000 and then went higher still—'all made out of the inkstand'. He was particularly proud that most of it had come out of current income, though there had been times when Smith was warned 'My vampire wants blood' and knew that the trouser pockets would shortly be turned inside out again.

His relatives were outraged at such prodigal expenditure. His friends calculated the rentable value of the house, and murmured at his presumption. Charles Carmichael, who had never made a joke in his life, told him to call it Vanity Fair. It was the only subject, except for her bad timekeeping, on which Annie and her father ever seriously quarrelled. She couldn't bear to see him ill and struggling to work in order to build something which to her seemed so unnecessary, and she said so, not only to him but to friends.

'If anybody knew how I hate the sight of a "new book by Mr. Thackeray," I think they wd be kind enough not to buy a single copy,' she told a visiting American. 'I'm sure "writing-books-&-going-out-to-dinner-to-shake-them-off" is the real name of his illness.'[1]

When it was finished, she wanted him to let it and retire quietly to the country, to give up at fifty, to sneak back into the little, scrimping world he had spent thirty years labouring to escape. She couldn't understand that for him Palace Green was not just a house, but a symbol: a proclamation that he had worked his way back from all manner of disaster, and won.

While 'the Palazzo' was a-building, Thackeray dragged his friends around it, excited as a child; when it was finished but still unfurnished, he staged an elaborate housewarming: two performances of *The Wolves and the Lamb*, the playbill headed with a typical pun—'W. Empty House Theatricals'. Minnie acted, Amy Crowe was property mistress, Gray cooked for the suppers that followed, Annie was hostess, and Thackeray, in a non-speaking role, appeared in clerical costume to bless the audience in old-fashioned pantomime style.

Great fires were lit in all the rooms, the house came alive with colour and laughter, and even Annie now caught its magic. 'I suppose this is the *summit*,' she thought as she stood beside her father to say good-bye to their guests. 'I shall never feel so jubilant so grand so wildly important & happy again.'[2] It was, she wrote in her diary, a feeling like fate knocking at the door.

Thackeray lavished as much attention on furnishing the house as he had on building it. Everything was in keeping with the period of its design, everything was in exquisite, uncluttered taste. He bought beautiful old glass and china, some of which later went to museums, and moved the pieces around, searching for the perfect place to display them, which sometimes proved to be in another house altogether. Annie, walking towards Palace Green one morning, met her father coming in the opposite direction, carefully balancing a pair of blue Dutch pots. He had thought of exactly the position to show them off: the dining-room mantelpiece of Leech's new home down the road.

In the summer, he wrote the last lines of *Philip* as he sat in his lofty, book-lined study, its windows open on to his own gardens and the view over green and palace which never ceased to enchant him, and wrote to his mother:

'Think of the beginning of the story of the little Sister in the Shabby Genteel Story twenty years ago and the wife crazy and the

Publisher refusing me 15£ who owes me £13.10 and the Times to which I apply for a little more than 5 guineas for a week's work, refusing to give me more and all that money difficulty ended, God be praised, and an old gentleman sitting in a fine house like the hero at the end of a story!'[3]

Thackeray was to enjoy the elegant luxury of Palace Green for less than two years, but it was never the folly his relatives and friends tried to make him believe. When he died it brought a handsome profit, and it gave immense comfort to his last months. In its calm rooms, he came to terms both with life and death.

Politically, he had become a conservative, preferring the established order, however imperfect, to all known alternatives, able to smile at his own perfidy. Once he had been considered a dangerous man, he wrote in *Philip*:

'Now, I am ready to say that Nero was a monarch with many elegant accomplishments, and considerable natural amiability of disposition. I praise and admire success wherever I meet it. I make allowance for faults and shortcomings, especially in my superiors; and feel that, did we know all, we should judge them very differently. People don't believe me, perhaps, quite so much as formerly. But I don't offend: I trust I don't offend.'[4]

From death he expected neither glory nor retribution, and sought no comfort or revelation from man-made religion. With his heart he believed in an all-loving, all-encompassing God, and was content not to trouble his head with finding reasons to support so incomprehensible a faith. 'What numbers of gates to heaven have *we* built?' he had once written to Mrs Baxter, 'and suppose after all there are no walls?'[5]

In the next world he expected to be not one whit better off than he was in his new house, with its cellar full of choice vintages, with good daughters, and an abundance of friends.

After he had finished pounding the country with his *Four Georges*, Lady Stanley had rehabilitated him in society by gathering in her London drawing-room an audience of those who had previously condemned him only on hearsay, albeit choosing 'George III', the least offensive lecture, for the experiment. Before this noble and prejudiced assembly, Thackeray, looking like a colossal infant, smooth, white and seemingly unperturbed, had read his piece in an easy, conversational tone, watched in amazement by his own personal guest, the American historian, John Lothrop Motley.

Had he exposed democracy or Southern chivalry in the same way before a gathering of the free and enlightened in America, said Motley, he would have been tarred and feathered on the spot, but so far as he could see, Lady Stanley's guests had been quite as unconcerned as the lecturer, laughing heartily and with not so much as a wince as he had pointed up the foibles and absurdities of that not too distant reign.

Thackeray had wanted to retain his entrée to the great world not only for himself, but for Annie and Minnie too. Their own rank in life, he had told his doubtful mother, was no better, no cheaper, and certainly not so amusing. But Annie and Minnie were less ambitious, and as marriageable young ladies with neither lineage nor great fortune to recommend them, less welcome than their famous father. Thackeray, a little hurt but no longer so eager himself for the full whirl of the London season, adapted philosophically.

'I have well nigh broken with the world the grand world and only go to the people who make my daughters welcome,' he wrote. 'The fine ladies won't: or is it that the girls are haughty, and very difficult to please? They won't submit to be patronized by the grandees at all, that's the fact: and I think I rather like them for being rebellious and independent—more so than their Papa, who is older and more worldly.'[6]

On his own account, however, he still enjoyed his links with the leading men in the most powerful country, and took his place among them on the ritual occasions that marked the social year. He sat at the top table at great banquets, he was cheered more than anyone except the Prince of Wales at a Harrow Speech Day, and was a guest at the Prince's Windsor wedding.

He breakfasted with Gladstone, dined with Lord Palmerston, and when one of the great men let him down, appeared at the *Punch* table in excellent humour, with a terrible pun, and the kind of fond insult that was current coin there: he had thrown over a hostess to dine with Lord John Russell, he told them; Lord John had then thrown over him, and since it had come to *pis aller*, he would eat his peas with them.[7]

A few weeks earlier, when the talk at *Punch* had focused on the sad case of a lady who had had her bladder taken out and sewn up, he had improvised: 'There was a poor lady grown sadder By having disease of the B[ladder]: They put her to bed And sewed it with thread. And then the Chirurgeon had her!—only fancy the brutal Chirurgeon taking a mean advantage of her helplessness.'[8]

He still finished many an evening at Evans's supper rooms where he was permitted the exceptional licence of calling Mr Green, the proprietor, Paddy, and was in turn addressed as 'dear boy', and where he listened for hours in rapt silence to the choristers, who wore surplices by day to sing in Westminster Cathedral, and evening dress at night to entertain with glees, madrigals and ballads amid the devilled kidneys, Welsh rabbits, mutton chops, brandy, beer and tobacco of Mr Green's establishment.

Occasionally, he would revel there, or in some other melodious cellar, till the early hours of the morning, and then offend his fellow roisterers later in the day when, involved once more with the business of life, he passed them by with a small, unsociable wave or two fingers touched to the brim of his hat.

'Who would think that we were up till four o'clock this morning together, and that he sang his "Reverend Dr. Luther", and was the liveliest of us?' asked a furious young Bohemian, stamping the pavement with rage, as Thackeray passed solemnly by on his horse, ignoring an outstretched hand and offering no audible greeting.[9]

The unyielding cast of his pale, set face was taken as a personal insult, but the appearance he presented to the world was often at odds with the feelings of the inner man, as Thackeray himself discovered. Many years before in a crowded Paris salon, where, as usual, he had stood head and shoulders above most people present, he had seen one other face, suspended at the same altitude, staring back at him, melancholy and blank. It had been some time before he had recognized it as his own reflection in a mirror.

He could offend too when suddenly attacked by pain, as he offended Trollope at their first meeting. George Smith, at the *Cornhill*'s inaugural dinner, knowing of Trollope's vast admiration for the author of *Esmond*, introduced him with a considerable flourish, but Thackeray, wrenched by a sharp spasm, managed only a curt 'How do?' before turning immediately on his heel. Trollope, well known for his quick temper, made a wrathful vow never to speak to him again, but he was let into the secret of Thackeray's internal troubles.

Even when well, Thackeray could puncture pomposity with a cold stare or a drawled sarcasm. Lord Ashburton said he was 'as tender as a woman but as cruel as Robespierre', a description which intrigued its subject. 'I wonder whether it's true?' Thackeray asked when he was told—as, of course, he was.[10] He rarely intended to give pain, but as Trollope pointed out, if he saw a foible he trod on it and tried to stamp it out.

He was called a snob, aloof and a heartless cynic by those who didn't know him well, or those he mistrusted. FitzGerald, from his self-imposed exile, was always asking now: 'Is Thackeray spoiled? I am told he is.' On the few occasions when he went to see for himself, he discovered, as of old, that the wonder was that Thackeray could still abound with such simple, childish, loving fun. An evening with FitzGerald and James Spedding, that other strange, introverted, melancholy friend from the past, did her father more good, said Annie, than a dozen bottles of black dose alias poison.

There were several other old comrades who stayed away in the last years, especially if they were also friendly with Dickens and Forster, a neat parcelling of loyalties Thackeray found hard to understand. 'Ah if I dared but put all those fellows into a book!' he wrote. 'And suppose they put me into another—giving their view of your humble servant? Those books would be queer reading.'[11]

After the Garrick Club quarrel ranks were drawn so closely that when the guileless little clergyman and editor, Whitwell Elwin, the most endearingly enthusiastic of all Thackeray's admirers, left his Booton rectory to stay with Forster in London, he often found it impossible to see Thackeray at all, a circumstance Thackeray deplored in a typically forgiving and absurd letter, written on the back of his prospectus for the *Cornhill Magazine*:

'In happier times the owner of the umble name signed to this prospectus used occasionally to have an honoured visit and remembrance from the Reverend Doubleyou E.

'That divine has however made *ascertained visits to London*, where he has been locked up without being allowed to communicate with acquaintances of ahappier ayears. Flere tacere is my motto: has this pockethandkercher (the writer uses it) been so utterly wrung with grief that it can't mop up a pint or two of hagony more? O Elwin O rector of Boo-ooo-oo-hoo-hooton! . . .'[12]

It worried him that he had too many friends and too little time to do them all justice, but he did the best he could. Visiting Americans found a ready welcome and return for their own hospitality, and though he never saw the Baxters again he kept constantly in touch by letter. When he dined at the Garrick with William Howard Russell, just before Russell left to report the American Civil War, he cut off a lock of his hair, placed it in an envelope on which he wrote 'Be kind to the bearer of this,' and told Russell to present it at Second Avenue.

He pressed the Baxters to accept money, which he couldn't at that moment afford, when he heard that the family was suspected of sympathy for the South and feared their livelihood might suffer, and endured with them the agony of divided loyalty.

With Sally, he had continued to be cautious. She had sent him 'such a damp' letter just before the birth of her first child that he delayed his reply until after the event, and answered her later cries of distress mostly in family letters to her parents.

She wrote to him as though she were stricken with some mortal malady and said she was a wreck, Thackeray told Mrs Baxter, but remembering the old dramatic flights that had drawn him to the Brown House not knowing whether he would be smiled upon or scorned, he seems not to have realized how ill she really was.

'There Miss Sally—' he told her, 'you howl on your sea-shore and I will roar from mine. Come let us placidly take leave of our friends . . . go each to the top of a rock, and jump over and end our troubleoubleoubles in the midst of the sad sea waves' bubble-ubblubbles . . . My dear it is all liver.'[13]

Even so, he didn't care to think too much of the four children she bore to her great honest Philistine of a husband, and took the old print, 'The Belle of the West', with him when he moved to Palace Green.

The Civil War was to bring him many sorrows and mercenary annoyances. One Christmas was irretrievably shadowed by the news that Andrew Low, his splendid Savannah host, was a Confederate prisoner, with his life at risk. His American railway stock paid no dividends, and stung by a spiteful article against British investors in that old irritant, the *New York Herald*, he sold his American shares at a loss—all that hard, ignominiously won money—and wrote an angry *Roundabout Paper* on the subject, which he was later to regret. But it was the plight of the Baxters which tore his heart.

Sally, still only in her late twenties, dying swiftly now of tuberculosis, was alone at Charleston, her husband having ridden off with his brother's brigade to fight the North, where all those she truly loved still lived. Her father and Lucy tried to get through the Confederate lines to be with her, but were turned back. She knew, as she wasted away, suffering one haemorrhage after another, that they would not hear for months whether she were alive or dead.

To Thackeray, she wrote a brave, moving account of her country's troubles, of kinsman fighting kinsman, over ground in which their ancestors, intermarried from North and South, had long lain buried in peace. As a military band, celebrating a Southern victory, played Strauss waltzes beneath her window, she thought back to her days of ballroom belledom and of Thackeray, watching her over his spectacles, half cynical, half pitying. She told him of the fate of the New York dandies who had hung about her then. Some who had married Southern brides were returning with sword and gun. Others were already dead.

A few months later Sally herself died on the Southern plantation that had never felt like home, and Thackeray, lying awake in the grey dawn of a Christmas morning, not long after hearing the news, stared out at the Kensington Palace elms and thought of her.

'I know there is no consolation,' he wrote to the Baxters later that day. 'I lost a child myself once, that's enough to say that I understand your grief. That journey of Lucy and her father is the saddest thing I have read of for many a long day. I look at Sarah's face in the photograph book and then at a print w[h] I have had for many years because it was like her when I first saw her . . . What a bright creature! What a laugh, a life, a happiness! And it is all gone; and you dear people sit bewailing your darling . . . How well I remember that first look of her, with the red ribbon in her hair! and next is that sad matron, and next your letter. What a warm welcome, what a kindly fireside, what kind faces round it—and hers the brightest of all! . . . I have been thinking . . . of that hospitable table in your dining room, and the Spirits moving about; and looking up wistfully in this big lone room, lest a form should make itself visible.'[14]

Henry Adams, son of the American Minister to London, who had also known Sally, met Thackeray not long afterwards at the home of Sir Henry Holland. Thackeray was pulling on his coat downstairs, laughing because, in his usual blind way, he had stumbled into the wrong house and not discovered his mistake until he found himself shaking hands with the wrong host. Then, as he saw Adams, his tone suddenly changed, and speaking of Sally his voice trembled and his eyes filled with tears.

2.

Above his bed, during his last years, Thackeray kept a copy of Dürer's 'St George and the Dragon', a gift from his Onslow Square neighbour, Marochetti. It was a reminder, he said, of his own two dragons, indolence and luxury, especially the luxury of rich food, though he didn't expect to overcome them. Towards the end, he admitted to drinking brandy and soda before breakfast to give himself an appetite, and told tea-party hostesses that whisky suited him better than tea.

In both wine and food he was a recognized connoisseur, a gourmet rather than a gourmand, a man who could enjoy a good meal and a good bottle by himself just as well as in company. A barrister, intrigued by seeing him several times walking purposefully along Holborn against the evening tide of lawyers, turned one night and followed him, tracking him to a coffee-house, where he settled down apparently to dine alone.

When later confronted with this piece of intelligence, Thackeray smiled in delighted remembrance. 'Ah,' he said, 'that was when I was drinking the last of that wonderful bin of port. It *was* rare wine. There were only two dozen bottles and a few bottles over, when I came upon the remains of that bin, and I forthwith bargained with mine host to keep them for me. I drank every bottle and every drop of that remainder by myself. I shared never a bottle with living man; and so long as the wine lasted, I slipped off to the Gray's Inn coffee-house with all possible secrecy short of disguise, whenever I thought a dinner and a bottle by myself would do me good.'[1]

Thackeray had written 'I live in the world & can't help myself, and have an awful but deserved reputation for worldliness,'[2] yet there was no sight nor sound that moved him so much as Charity Children's Day at St Paul's Cathedral, when five thousand well-scrubbed waifs with cheeks like nosegays and sweet, fresh voices, gathered to sing ancient hymns of praise. He never missed it if he could help it, and told Motley it was better than the Declaration of Independence.

Never noticeably an animal-lover in his early life, in his last years he was surrounded by cats, dogs and an unsociable, waddling parrot, none of them properly housetrained. A favourite Italian greyhound was constantly 'mistaking the nature of his apartment', and Gumbo, one of a pair of puppies named after the black servants in *The Virginians*, ate everything from books to sewing needles before he was given away to one of the young Synges.

When Thackeray later visited Gumbo's new residence, the dog, inspecting the pavement outside the house, spotted his carriage driving up the road, made a magnificent running leap through the window, landed on Thackeray's knees, knocked off his spectacles, and licked his face in ecstasy. That the enthusiasm was mutual is clear from Thackeray's portrait of Brownie in *Philip*, the little Skye terrier who stays loyal to the hero even after he is discovered to be penniless.

During the Palace Green years there were several other changes to the household. A pretty new maid turned out to be literary and quoted from the *Cornhill*. The butler was a faithful, reckless youth who fell about the establishment breaking china. Gray, the cook, finally left, and so did Amy Crowe. After living for eight years as one of the family, she married one of Thackeray's favourite young cousins and protégés, Edward Thackeray, V.C., son of the Reverend Francis, whose handling of his nephew's patrimony had been so disastrous. She was married from Palace Green, and Thackeray was so distraught at losing her that after the wedding breakfast he rushed off to Millais's studio and spent most of the afternoon in tears.

Gentle little Amy's place was taken by a far less restful character—Mrs Carmichael-Smyth.

Late in 1859, the Major, having at last relented and agreed to live in London, Thackeray had taken a house for his parents at Brompton Crescent. He supported them, called in on them each day as he walked into town, the granddaughters for whom Mrs Carmichael-Smyth had pined were close at hand, but still that difficult lady was not content.

'. . . my mother gets very rebellious and wants to go back,' wrote Thackeray. 'There's a little clique of old ladies there who are very fond of her and with whom she is a much more important personage than she is in this great city. If anything happens to the Major she will go to Paris and give us the slip and grumble when she is there and presently come back.'[3]

Two years later, his prophecy came true. The Major, aged eighty-one, died on a visit to his native Scotland, and Thackeray, travelling north to bury him in an Ayr churchyard, placed on his gravestone the words with which he had said farewell to Colonel Newcome: '*Adsum*—And lo, he whose heart was as that of a little child, had answered to his name, and stood in the presence of The Master.'

For a time, Mrs Carmichael-Smyth wandered about happy nowhere, then at last settled at Palace Green, with her lack of humour and abundance of grim religious views. Thackeray, watching her effect on Annie and Minnie, thought of writing into his will his express wish that his mother and children should not live together after his death.

In one of his last *Roundabout Papers*, Thackeray quoted Byron's lines, 'So for a good old-gentlemanly vice, I think I must take up with avarice', and pronounced saving to be a useful and not unbecoming occupation for a man's declining years. It was a theme on which he gave little lectures to those who had been even more profligate than himself, when he was about to ignore it by coming to their aid.

'I was very angry because he said I had been a reckless old goose—' said an artist, after Thackeray had visited his chilly garret; 'and then a £100 falls out of my writing-book . . . I never saw him do it . . .'[4]

He learned to draw the line at monuments to the dead, telling the ladies who wished to commemorate the author of 'The boy stood on the burning deck': 'I am known as a willing horse, and have such a number of live people on my back that I fear I must not let poor M[rs] Hemans's statue get up and ride.'[5]

But avarice, becoming or not, was beyond him, and a year after finishing *Philip* he needed to make money again to cover his expenses. For many years he had promised himself that in his comfortable old age, when his imagination had been milked dry, he would turn serious historian, pottering pleasantly over old volumes and dusty manuscripts. By the time he moved to Palace Green this ambition had taken more definite shape. In that splendid reproduction of a Queen Anne mansion, with the palace the queen had lived in before its windows, he planned to take up the chronicle of England where Macaulay had had to leave off, and write the history of her reign. But the cost of building his house and of selling his American investments made him once more put off the scholarly dream and sign up with Smith for another serial novel.

Before long he was walking around again his pockets bulging with the latest chapter, groaning with the effort of his labour, complaining of the difficulty of disposing of this character or that, prophesying failure, or reading out nuggets that showed he might yet succeed. He called the new story *Denis Duval*, determined that it should have none of his old faults, pulled himself up sharply as soon as he began to wander and philosophize, and planned to pack it with as much excitement as a Dumas adventure.

There was only one problem. For the early chapters, he needed to know something about sailing and the sea, as he explained in a letter to Albany Fonblanque, written in the character of his young hero:

'I am a little boy born in the year 1763 at Winchelsea where my parents lived, having been expelled from France after the Revocation Edict of Nantes, which I suspect brought the Fonblanques to England too.

'My grandfather was Precentor and Elder of the French Church at Winchelsea, a perruquier by trade, but a good deal engaged in smuggling. I went upon various smuggling expeditions . . .

> 'I learned to scuttle a marling spike
> reef a lee-scupper
> Keelhawl a bowsprit

as well as the best of 'em . . . but as I don't know the difference between a marling spike and a binnacle, I must get information from somebody as does. And who knows better than you?'[6]

He kept volumes of his favourite, worldly essayists, Montaigne and Howell, beside his bed to 'prattle' him to sleep again when he woke in the night, but even so he was often downstairs at four o'clock, long before the household was astir, and ready with news of Duval's latest escapades by the time Annie and Minnie appeared.

'The Countess is growing very mad,' he told them one morning, with a tragic face. 'St. Sebastian has just appeared to her stuck all over with arrows looking like a *fricandeau*.'[7]

For the first time, he was putting Isabella's insanity into a story and showing his mad countess trying to abandon a daughter by the seashore. Again a simile he had already used in *Esmond* and *The Virginians* came into his mind, that of looking back on life as a huntsman looks at the leaps he has taken in the heat of the chase, marvelling at his survival.

*

Annie was also hard at work. When she was young, Thackeray had told her to stop trying to write books herself and to read other people's, but once she had shown she had talent, he gave her nothing but proud encouragement.

'Cornhill with "Out of the World" . . .' she wrote in her journal of one of her pieces. 'One evening Papa said "I am reading something I like very much. It is like George Sands writing—I said Oh Papa.'[8]

Soon she graduated from short factual pieces to a novel of her own, *The Story of Elizabeth*, which she handed diffidently to George Smith as he was about to leave the house one morning. Smith, having accepted it for the *Cornhill*, sent a copy of the proofs to Thackeray, but he never managed to read it all, and when Fanny Kemble tried to persuade him he would enjoy it, he told her: 'It would *tear my guts out!*'[9]

His mother was the same, she said she couldn't read his books, he told the gentlemen of *Punch*, and added quickly 'as many people do,' before a great facetious chorus could say it for him. But he proudly passed on the news that Smith, Elder were in raptures over it, and read enough to praise her style. She had, he said, all his better parts and none of his worse. 'Minerva from the brain of Jupiter,' replied a *Punch* friend obligingly.[10]

When *The Story of Elizabeth* appeared in book form, however, it was seized on as a bludgeon with which to beat him. The *Athenaeum*, edited by Hepworth Dixon, a virulent anti-Thackeray man, published an old-fashioned slashing review reeking with pseudo-judicious spite, implying that Annie would have been a nicer person and a better writer had she had a different father. Her plot's similarity to *Esmond*—a mother and daughter in love with the same man—was also treated by scathing innuendo.

Thackeray blamed Hepworth Dixon and his right-hand man, John Cordy Jeaffreson, for the attack, and he soon had a chance to indicate, equally obliquely, what he thought of them. The two men were members, like himself, of a small dining group, Our Club, and the review appeared on the same day that Thackeray was due to address the club's annual Shakespeare dinner. He used his speech to censure the malicious detractors, who, in every age, had sought to deny talent. Who remembered now the miserable rivals who had maligned Shakespeare? he asked. Only a very few could give their names, and they did so with contempt.

He left the dinner early and later that evening described Jeaffreson as a man who, in order to give him pain, had slapped his daughter's face. At the time Jeaffreson appears to have done nothing to refute the charge, though much later he denied writing the criticism.

Following the death of Douglas Jerrold, the founder of Our Club, Thackeray had become its guiding spirit, but after the Shakespeare dinner he went to no more of its meetings. The club's secretary, a small, badly crippled hunchback with a dog-like admiration for men of letters, and especially for Thackeray who defended him when the banter became too rough, took soundings among the members and told him that if he returned, steps would be taken to make Hepworth Dixon resign. Thackeray refused. He had already driven one man from a club, he said, and had no desire to repeat the exercise.

There the matter would have ended had not Dixon, later in the year, formed a much publicized national committee to celebrate Shakespeare's tercentenary, and made sure of having his own way with it by appointing Jeaffreson and other *Athenaeum* henchmen to its official posts. Invitations, signed by Dixon, were sent to various dignitaries asking them to become vice-presidents: Bulwer-Lytton, Dickens, Tennyson and Thackeray being chosen to represent literature. Thackeray did not reply. Nor did he acknowledge a further invitation signed by Jeaffreson, and when Henry Vizetelly, who, like most of literary London, knew the reasons for his silence, tried to get him elected out of hand at a committee meeting, he found himself outnumbered by *Athenaeum* men who sanctimoniously agreed that the committee should not demean itself by making a third approach.

Vizetelly threw the issue open to the public by writing a blow-by-blow account of the shoddy manoeuvres of Dixon and his 'contemptible clique' which he published in his own magazine, the *Illustrated Times*, in 'The Lounger at the Clubs' column—thus adding a further act to the wretched farce, for Yates, horrified that his chums might think he had written the exposé, which was picked up and widely circulated by other papers, publicly announced his resignation from the magazine.

Thackeray maintained complete silence throughout, but he kept and annotated all the newspaper cuttings, and inwardly writhed. It was a squalid, spiteful incident which darkened the last weeks of his life and became a major scandal when he died in the midst of it. The committee had planned to raise £30,000 for a monument to Shakespeare. In the end it planted a small sapling on Primrose Hill, which showed little inclination to flourish.

Thackeray's last year was almost a model of planned leave-taking. His health had seemed better and he joined Annie and Minnie in several excursions to see old friends, including Richard Monckton Milnes, now Lord Houghton, at Fryston, the great Yorkshire mansion that had first brought him comfort over twenty years earlier when he had escaped from nursing Isabella alone in Paris. While he was there, an April gale brought down a great tree, the pride of the woods, and as the house-party went out to inspect the fallen giant, Milnes heard Thackeray murmuring to himself, 'An omen! an omen!'[11]

From there, they had gone on to Hampsthwaite and for the first time seen the land from which had sprung the race of Thackeray. In the summer there had been trips to Greenwich and a return to the Continent, where Thackeray had once again enjoyed the theatres and old haunts of Paris.

As the year died and December came, the last weeks of his life followed the same nostalgic pattern, as, between bouts of illness, he retraced many a once well-trodden path. At Charterhouse Founder's Day, he sat beside Leech and proposed one of the toasts. On a golden winter Sunday, he went to hear the evening hymns sung in the Temple church, close to his old law student chambers, and afterwards, with the joyous notes of the anthem—'Rejoice and again I say unto you rejoice'—still ringing in his ears, climbed a familiar crooked staircase with Annie and Minnie to take tea in a young friend's rooms, the kind of low-raftered, smoke-wreathed, mutton-chop bachelor quarters he had made famous in *Pendennis* and *Philip*.

He dined with Dr John Merriman, a Young Street neighbour and friend, and as his host strolled back with him late at night to Palace Green, paused outside the old house at No. 13. Thinking back over his career, he told Merriman that of all his ballads *The Cane-Bottomed Chair* was his favourite, and that he thought *Vanity Fair* the best of his novels.

He appeared for the last time at the *Punch* table, where he pretended to urge one old friend to throw an excessively merry party, so that they might all feel young again, and a few days later dined at the Garrick looking fit and buoyant with fun.

He talked cheerfully to Dickens at the Athenaeum, describing the cold shivering fit that had left him still weak after three days in bed, and laughingly outlined a new remedy he thought he might try. He thrust the latest pages of *Denis Duval* into the hands of another old friend and told him that when it was finished he would subject himself to the skill of a clever surgeon and be no more an invalid.

But there was not time enough left either to finish the book or to cure the stricture, and at home with his family he took off his jester's mask and waited for the end. He had felt for a long time that he was about to die and told Annie that he didn't care, except for leaving her and Minnie. He talked to them of the past, of Isabella and Jane Brookfield, still his ideal of womanhood, and when Annie asked which of his men friends he had loved the best, said why, dear old Fitz, to be sure—and Brookfield—they would all be merry in hell together.

On the morning of Wednesday, 23 December, when Annie went into her father's room, she found him lying still and large-eyed in bed, obviously in pain. He held her hand and told her: 'It can't be helped, darling. I didn't take enough medicine last night. I have taken some more. I shall be better presently.'[12]

As the day wore on, it seemed that the medicine had worked its usual cure. In the afternoon he sat reading for a while in Kensington Gardens, and when his family retired for the night, they did so with easy minds. But as Thackeray himself prepared for bed, the spasms and retching began again. His man begged to be allowed to sit up with him, but Thackeray refused. His mother heard him moving about during the night, but it was not unusual enough to cause concern. The next morning, he was found dead, his arms thrown back above his head, his face rigid as though he had suffered terrible pain. He was fifty-two. His body, which, in his middle years had weighed over fifteen stone, was gaunt and wasted by the years of ill-health.

Dr Merriman diagnosed the chief cause of death as cerebral effusion—the bursting of a blood vessel in the brain, most probably caused by a violent attack of vomiting.

On 30 December 1863, he was buried at Kensal Green cemetery, close to the place where his daughter, Jane, had rested for over twenty years. His great contemporaries in literature and art stood round his simple grave in clear, crisp, winter sunshine. Faces instantly recognizable to the knots of newspaper reporters, merged with those of black-bearded Bohemians and the readers who had known him only through his writing. It was estimated that as many as two thousand mourners made their way to that shabby London suburb to pay their last respects.

Dickens was there with his son-in-law, Charles Collins, brother of Wilkie, one of the greatest friends of Thackeray's last years. Beside them stood Brookfield, and even Yates was said to have made one of the throng. There were some complaints that the swells were noticeably absent, but at that time of the year the swells were not in town.

When his *Punch* colleagues had first learned of his death at a Christmas party, they had stood stunned and silent, until one of them had said: 'I'll tell you what we'll do. We'll sing the dear old boy's "Mahogany Tree;" he'd like it.'[13]

The man who, in Trollope's splendid phrase, 'kept his heartstrings in a crystal case,'[14] would also have liked *Punch*'s contribution to the great flood of published tributes that flowed on well into the new year—Tom Taylor's loving answer to his critics:

> He was a cynic: By his life all wrought
>   Of generous acts, mild words, and gentle ways:
> His heart wide open to all kindly thought,
>   His hand so quick to give, his tongue to praise . . .
>
> And if his acts, affections, works, and ways
>   Stamp not upon the man the cynic's sneer,
> From life to death, oh, public, turn your gaze—
>   The last scene of a cynical career!
>
> Those uninvited crowds, this hush that lies,
>   Unbroken, till the solemn words of prayer
> From many hundred reverent voices rise
>   Into the sunny stillness of the air.
>
> These tears, in eyes but little used to tears,
>   Those sobs from manly lips, hard set and grim,
> Of friends, to whom his life lay bare for years,
>   Of strangers, who but knew his books, not him.

Postscript

As Thackeray had feared, Mrs Carmichael-Smyth proved a terrible burden to his daughters after his death, demanding all their sympathy and attention when they themselves were at the brink of emotional collapse, imposing on them once again her religious views, and so denying those of their father. She made them feel guilty, complained of them to friends, and dragged them to Brittany, where the three distraught women, knowing no one, having no escape from each other's company, came close to madness. Annie was twenty-six, Minnie twenty-three. Thackeray had been the absolute focus of their lives, and now he was there no more.

In the autumn of 1864, they at last settled with a quieter, more tolerant grandmother, in a new, small house at Onslow Gardens, close to Onslow Square, where, within a few weeks, Mrs Carmichael-Smyth also died. On the first anniversary of her son's death, she was buried next to him at Kensal Green.

Three years later, Minnie married Leslie Stephen, younger brother of one of Thackeray's friends and *Cornhill* contributors. She had one daughter and died suddenly at the age of thirty-five. Stephen later became editor of the *Cornhill* and of George Smith's most splendid legacy, the *Dictionary of National Biography*. A few years after Minnie's death, he married again—a daughter of one of the beautiful Pattle sisters—and fathered Virginia Woolf.

Annie, who continued to write and became a literary figure herself, didn't marry until 1877, when she accepted Richmond Thackeray Willoughby Ritchie, grandson of Thackeray's laughing

Aunt Ritchie; he had first proposed to her when he was at Eton, and married her when he was twenty-three and she was forty. They had a son and a daughter. Ritchie became Secretary of State for India, was knighted in 1907, and died in 1912, seven years before Annie, who lived to the age of eighty-two.

Isabella survived for thirty years after Thackeray's death, maintaining the same placid, retired life, visited by Annie, playing gay dance music on the piano, with flying little white hands, for the grandchildren she did not recognize as her own, and wearing to the last the ominous opal mourning ring her husband had bought for their engagement.

Thackeray had provided well for them all, better than he had calculated a year before his death, when he set down his assets at £18,000. When he died, he still owned the house at 36 Onslow Square, then valued at around £2,600. The Palace Green mansion was sold for £10,000, and his furniture, books and wines fetched another £3000 at auction. His copyrights, which he had thought might sell for £4000, were bought for £10,000 by George Smith. However, as he had been in the process of changing his will, the legal ramifications caused by Isabella's incapacity were a gift to the lawyers, and it was many years before the courts agreed that the estate should be divided equally between Thackeray's widow and his daughters.

While reading the memoir of a friend, Thackeray had once told Annie: '*Mind this* there is to be nothing of the sort published about me when my time comes.'[1] It is thought he may only have meant he wanted no sickly Victorian eulogy, but Annie took it to be a total ban and remembered his words as a sacred commandment. For many years she wrote nothing about him herself, and tried to dissuade others from doing so, a situation which discouraged friends and left the field free for the guessers and detractors. Only in 1898 did she begin to set the record straight by writing long biographical introductions to Smith's reprints of his books, expanding them again for the collected edition brought out to mark the centenary of his birth in 1911.

The Baxters, who would have welcomed an addition to their income, put aside plans for publishing his letters to them, when Annie told them what her father had said, and it was not until 1904, long after Annie herself had broken the embargo, that Lucy edited them for sale in America and England.

Mrs Brookfield was not so co-operative when she became pressed for money. All through Thackeray's last years, when he had stayed away from the Brookfield household, 'for fear of bringing down a scolding on the poor woman,'[2] Annie had remained a constant visitor, and when Thackeray died, Jane was quick to comfort her. 'She has taken us under her kind wing,' Annie wrote in the autumn after his death, 'she is coming to live close by only to be near us. All this terrible year she has been so good to us all three that I do not know how we could have dragged through without her.'[3]

The Brookfields now lived a life of civilized estrangement. In 1861, Brookfield had finally accepted a country living, that of Somerby-cum-Humby in Lincolnshire, though he remained a schools inspector for several years and regularly preached in London. Jane did not grace the Somerby rectory, and neither for long at a time did her husband. In 1862, he was appointed a chaplain to Queen Victoria, and seven years later, through the influence of Lord Lyttelton, was made Honorary Canon of Ealdland, with a stall in St Paul's Cathedral.

His letter of thanks to his old pupil was typically irreverent: 'One good at least it will do—it will put an end to the racking sleepless nights of perplexity through which I have debated within myself whether a Royal Chaplain or a Canon goes in to dinner first.'[4]

Jane wrote several not very good novels, the first and best of which was published the year after Thackeray's death. Her husband died, ten years later, at the age of sixty-five, and she lived on for another twenty-two years, scraping by on an inadequate income. 'Had she been inclined to change her state and move in a higher and more exclusive sphere,' wrote her younger son, 'she had several opportunities for re-marrying, but her love for her children made her consider them, and she concluded to devote the rest of her life to them.'[5]

By the time she was widowed, her youngest child was seventeen, and her eldest, twenty-four-year-old Magdalene, had already married William Ritchie, elder brother of Annie's future husband. (The daughter of this Ritchie-Brookfield match was further to link the families by marrying Charles Thackeray, son of Edward Thackeray, V.C., by his second wife.) Arthur, the elder son, joined the army, became a colonel, and when he wrote his autobiography called it *Annals of a Chequered Life*. Charles, the youngest did what many had thought his father should have done: he became an actor.

By 1887, when Jane was sixty-six and her sons in their early thirties, they were all in such need of money that she published a selection of Thackeray's letters to herself and to Kate Perry, first in *Scribner's Magazine*, in New York, and then in book form in America and England. Annie, who by that time had held to her father's wish for twenty-four years, did not approve, and neither did George Smith, whose Thackeray copyrights specifically covered his correspondence as well as his books.

A comparison between Jane's edited letters and the originals makes interesting reading. Not only did she excise passages which might offend others, but she made more subtle changes to bear out her demure submission that most of the letters had been written 'to my husband, the late Rev'd W. H. Brookfield, and myself.' In this cause, 'My dear friend' became 'My dear friends', and Thackeray's more steamy pleas and indiscretions were deleted. She ironed out his sillier jokes and comical spelling, transcribed inaccurately and dated wrongly. Even so, she left plenty to show that his love for her had been something far beyond the normal run of friendship.

She sold the originals soon after they were published, and went on selling batches of his letters for the rest of her life. Three days before she died, she wrote to the bookseller who disposed of them for her, asking him to find another buyer. For the most part they were letters in which Thackeray had made her a gift of every fleeting thought that had entered his brain, and offered her the freehold of his great, idiotic, loving heart. But Jane and her sons needed money. She sold the most valuable thing she had.

In old age, she liked to tell of the last time she had seen 'dear Thackeray'. He had appeared, standing beside the horse of her hansom cab in Piccadilly, looked up at her smiling radiantly for a while, and then as swiftly vanished. When she returned home soon afterwards, she found Annie's note telling her that he had died the previous night. As a widow, she lived surrounded by portraits—Brookfield, Thackeray, Carlyle, Hallam, Adelaide Sartoris. 'A museum of the beloved dead,' she said when they were recognized.[6]

She and Kate Perry outlived them all, clinging to each other and their memories.

A bust of Thackeray, made shortly after his death by his friend and neighbour, Baron Marochetti, stands in Westminster Abbey. His own monument to a life he continually called idle, the house at Palace Green, is now the Israeli Embassy, handsome still, but sadly shuttered and fortified with security devices. The book he ultimately thought of as his greatest work, *Vanity Fair*, received a curious trans-Atlantic, twentieth-century accolade: as *Becky Sharp*, it became the first ever all-talking, Technicolor motion picture.

SOURCE NOTES

The owners of manuscript material referred to in these notes are indicated in brackets after each reference. More information about them is given in my list of acknowledgements.

Where the same published work appears several times in a chapter, I have given the full details only once, and where works are mentioned frequently throughout the notes, I have identified them simply by author or abbreviated title. The key to these is given below:

Biographical Introductions. Introductions written by Lady Ritchie (Annie Thackeray) to *The Works of William Makepeace Thackeray*, 13 vols, London, 1898–9

Chapters. Anne Thackeray Ritchie, *Chapters from Some Memoirs*, London, 1894

Collection of Letters. A Collection of Letters of W. M. Thackeray, 1847–1855, edited by Mrs Brookfield, London, 1887

Fields. *Yesterdays with Authors*, James T. Fields, London, 1872

Hodder. *Memories of My Time*, George Hodder, London, 1870

Letters I, II, etc. *The Letters and Private Papers of W. M. Thackeray*, edited by Gordon N. Ray, 4 vols, Oxford, 1945–6

Merivale and Marzials. *Life of W. M. Thackeray*, Herman Merivale and Frank T. Marzials, London, 1891

Milnes. Life, Letters and Friendships of Richard Monckton Milnes, 2 vols, T. Wemyss Reid, London, 1890

Brookfield. *Mrs Brookfield and Her Circle*, Charles and Frances Brookfield, 2 vols, London, 1905

RP. Thackeray's *Roundabout Papers*

Trollope. *Thackeray*, Anthony Trollope, London, 1912

TS Silver diary. Typescript of Henry Silver's diary of *Punch* table talk

Works. The Oxford Thackeray, edited by George Saintsbury, 17 vols, 1908

1

THE PEDIGREE
pp. 1–14

[1] Edmund Yates, *Town Talk*, 12 June 1858; *Some Experiences of a Barrister's Life*, William Ballantine, London, 1882, I, 135

[2] Milnes, II, 113; *The Correspondence of Thomas Carlyle and Ralph Waldo Emerson*, London, 1883, II, 229–230

[3] For Anne Becher's romance see *Letters I*, cxii–cxiv

[4] *Thackeray: The Uses of Adversity*, Gordon N. Ray, Oxford, 1955, 430

[5] 'On Letts's Diary', *RP*

[6] 'George III', *Four Georges*

[7] *Letters II*, 609

[8] *Biographical Introductions*, VIII, xvi

[9] *Letters I*, 1–2

[10] 'On Letts's Diary'; *Letters II*, 669

[11] *Letters I*, 5

[12] 'On a Peal of Bells', *RP*

[13] *Letters I*, 8–9

[14] 'On Two Children in Black', *RP*

[15] *Biographical Introductions*, VIII, xviii

[16] 'On a Peal of Bells'

2

CHARTERHOUSE
pp. 15–29

[1] *Letters II*, 501

[2] *Some Few Thackerayana*, D.D., *National Review*, XIII, 1889, 794–803

[3] 'Thorns in the Cushion', *RP*

[4] 'De Juventute', *RP*

[5] *A Memorial of Thackeray's Schooldays*, J. F. Boyes, *Cornhill*, XI, 1865, 118–127

[6] *Letters II*, 64, 256

[7] 'On a Peal of Bells', *RP*

[8] the same

[9] 'De Juventute'

[10] the same

[11] *Recollections of Thackeray*, Richard Bedingfield, *Cassell's Magazine*, II, 1870, 296, 108

[12] *Cornhill*, XI, 125

[13] *Letters I*, 23

[14] TS Silver diary, 8 January 1862

[15] the same, 21 October 1858

[16] *Letters I*, 22–24

[17] *Reminiscences Chiefly of Oriel College and the Oxford Movement*, Thomas Mozley, London, 1882, I, 63–64

[18] *Letters I*, 25

[19] the same, 59

2.

[1] Merivale and Marzials, 57–58

[2] *Pendennis*, chapter three

[3] *Letters III*, 246

[4] *Miss Williamson's Divagations*, Anne Thackeray Ritchie, London, 1882, 150

[5] *Letters III*, 13

3

CAMBRIDGE
pp. 30–43

[1] *Letters I*, 31

[2] the same, 35

[3] the same, 37–65

[4] the same, 39–40

[5] the same, 52

[6] the same, 44

[7] the same, 65

[8] the same, 28

[9] the same, 45

[10] the same, 38, 78, 33

[11] 'On University Snobs', *Book of Snobs*

[12] *Letters I*, 56
[13] *Works*, I, 2-3
[14] *Letters I*, 76
[15] Merivale and Marzials, 61

2.

[1] *Letters I*, 99
[2] the same, 91, 92
[3] the same, 91, 85-86
[4] the same, 93
[5] the same, 90-91

[6] the same, 98
[7] Merivale and Marzials, 61
[8] *Letters and Literary Remains of Edward FitzGerald*, ed. W. Aldis Wright, 7 vols, London, 1902, I, 91
[9] *Letters I*, 107
[10] Merivale and Marzials, 60
[11] *Shrove Tuesday in Paris, Works*, III, 499-507
[12] *Letters II*, 542, 541
[13] 'Ogres', *RP*
[14] Merivale and Marzials, 236

4

WEIMAR
pp. 44-52

[1] *Letters I*, 112
[2] the same, 115
[3] the same, 127
[4] the same, 125-126
[5] the same, 133
[6] the same, 146
[7] *Goethe's Last Days, Fortnightly Review*, LIV, 1890, 338-339
[8] *Letters I*, 147
[9] the same

[10] *Life of Goethe*, G. H. Lewes, London, 1855, 562
[11] *Letters I*, 130
[12] *Milnes*, II, 481
[13] the same; *Letters I*, 136, 148
[14] Lewes' *Life of Goethe*, 561
[15] *Letters I*, 135-136
[16] the same, 143
[17] the same, 144

5

JOURNALISM *V.* THE LAW
pp. 53-67

[1] *Letters I*, 182
[2] the same, 161
[3] the same, 167
[4] the same, 151
[5] the same, 187
[6] the same, 190
[7] the same, 160
[8] *About Two Great Novelists, Temple Bar*, LXXXIII, 1888, 193
[9] Fields, 28
[10] *Letters I*, 195
[11] 'On a Pear Tree', *RP*

2.

[1] *Letters I*, 156
[2] the same, 208
[3] the same, 271
[4] *Mr Thackeray's Writings in 'The National Standard,' and 'The Constitutional'*, ed. W. T. Spencer, London, 1899, 3-4
[5] *Letters I*, 264
[6] *Some Literary Recollections*, James Payn, London, 1884, 164-165
[7] *Lovel the Widower*, chapter one

6

ISABELLA SHAWE
pp. 68-88

[1] 'On the French School of Painting', *Paris Sketch Book*

[2] *Letters I*, 273
[3] the same, 277

[4] the same, 279–280
[5] the same, 290
[6] the same, 291

2.

[1] *Letters I*, 267
[2] *Memoirs of the Life & Correspondence of Henry Reeve*, J. K. Laughton, 2 vols, London, 1891, I, 59
[3] *Letters I*, 295–296
[4] the same, 319
[5] For details of Lieutenant-Colonel Shawe's life and an impressively documented argument for believing him to be WMT's model for Major Pendennis, see Gordon N. Ray's *Buried Life*, London, 1952, chapter five
[6] *Letters I*, 310

[7] *Memoirs and Experiences of Moncure Daniel Conway*, 2 vols, London, 1904, II, 5–6
[8] *Letters I*, 310
[9] the same, 309
[10] the same, 312
[11] the same, 319
[12] the same, 316
[13] the same, 318
[14] the same, 319
[15] the same, clxv

3.

[1] *Thackeray: The Age of Wisdom*, Gordon N. Ray, Oxford, 1958, 187
[2] *Letters I*, 322
[3] the same, 320
[4] the same, 324–325
[5] the same, 341–342

7

MAGAZINERY
pp. 89–104

[1] 24 February 1838
[2] *Letters of Thomas Carlyle to his Youngest Sister*, ed. C. T. Copeland, London, 1899, 86
[3] *Letters I*, 351–352
[4] the same, 395
[5] *Corsair*, July and August 1839
[6] *Nathanial Parker Willis*, Henry A. Beers, Boston, 1885, 254
[7] *Letters II*, 214–215
[8] *Letters I*, 458

2.

[1] *Letters I*, 382
[2] *Jerome Paturot*, *Fraser's*, September 1843
[3] *Letters I*, 388
[4] *The Times*, 8 October 1863; TS Silver diary, 28 October 1863
[5] *Letters II*, 252–253
[6] *Letters I*, 353–354
[7] the same, 366–367
[8] the same, 406

8

PUBLIC TRIUMPH, PRIVATE GRIEF
pp. 105–120

[1] TS Silver diary, 2 March 1859
[2] *Letters I*, 438–439
[3] the same, 443
[4] the same, 459
[5] *On Going to See a Man Hanged*, August 1840
[6] *Letters I*, 454–455
[7] *Life of Sir William Howard Russell*, J. B. Atkins, 2 vols, London, 1911, I, 375

2.

[1] *Letters I*, 461–462
[2] the same, 464
[3] the same, 483–484

[4] the same, 476
[5] the same, 482
[6] *Biographical Introductions*, IV, xxix-xxx

9

THE RESTLESS YEARS
pp. 121–134

[1] *Letters II*, 3
[2] *A Consideration of Thackeray*, George Saintsbury, Oxford, 1931, 111
[3] *Letters II*, 7
[4] *Shrove Tuesday at Paris*, 5 July 1841
[5] *Letters II*, 11
[6] the same, 15
[7] the same, 30–32
[8] the same, 36
[9] *Chapters*, 20

2.

[1] *Letters II*, 60

[2] Major Dwyer's recollections appear as 'Reminiscences of Lever and Thackeray, by Major D—', an appendix to the first two-volume edition of *The Life of Charles Lever*, by W. J. FitzPatrick, London, 1879. They were later incorporated into the text of FitzPatrick's one-volume Lever biography (London 1896), together with additional information about the two authors
[3] *Mr. Yellowplush's Ajew*
[4] *Letters II*, 831–839

10

A BACHELOR OLD AND GREY
pp. 135–150

[1] *Letters II*, 172
[2] the same, 54
[3] *Memories of London in The Forties*, David Masson, London, 1908, 245–248. In Masson's account of this incident, Fraser is named as editor of *Fraser's Magazine*, but a reference to the plagiarism in one of WMT's letters (*Letters II*, 130–131) places it in November 1843, when Nickisson was in charge.
[4] *Letters II*, 110
[5] Merivale and Marzials, 47
[6] *Milnes*, I, 187
[7] *Letters and Literary Remains of Edward FitzGerald*, ed. W. Aldis Wright, 7 vols, London, 1902, I, 222–223
[8] *Greenwich-Whitebait*, July 1844
[9] *A Victorian Canvas*, selections

from Frith's autobiography, ed. Nevile Wallis, London, 1957, 58–59
[10] *Alfred Lord Tennyson; A Memoir*, by his son, 2 vols, London, 1897, I, 266
[11] *Letters IV*, 360
[12] Brookfield, I, 123
[13] the same, 172, 167
[14] TS Silver diary, 10 February 1859

2.

[1] See *Conversations with Carlyle*, Charles Gavin Duffy, 76–77; *Tait's Edinburgh Magazine*, March 1846; *Titmarsh v. Tait, Punch*, 14 March 1846; *Letters II*, 227
[2] *Letters II*, 156
[3] MS letter, 6 December 1844 (*Punch*)

11

PUNCH
pp. 151–160

[1] MS letter 29 May 1846 (Houghton Papers 25³⁰, Trinity College, Cambridge)
[2] *Letters II*, 236–237
[3] the same, 259
[4] the same, 199
[5] G. K. Chesterton's Introduction to the 1911 edition of *The Book of Snobs*, ix
[6] the same
[7] *The Critic*, 17 January 1855, 34–35
[8] *History of Punch*, M. H. Spielmann, London, 1895, 74
[9] *Letters II*, 281–282
[10] *A Box of Novels, Fraser's*, February 1844

2.

[1] *Letters II*, 297, 336
[2] MS letters 20 December 1846 and January 1847 (Hertfordshire Record Office, Lytton Bundle 79)
[3] *Roland Cashel*, chapter twenty-two
[4] *Letters II*, 455–456
[5] *Pendennis*, chapter forty-one
[6] 'Dessein's', *RP*

12

YOUNG STREET
pp. 161–171

[1] *Letters II*, 231
[2] the same, 240–241
[3] the same, 242–243
[4] the same, 233
[5] *Biographical Introductions*, I, xxvii
[6] *Chapters*, 134–136
[7] the same, 81–82
[8] the same, 55
[9] *Records of Tennyson, Ruskin and Browning*, Anne Thackeray Ritchie, London, 1892, 39

2.

[1] *Letters II*, 286
[2] the same, and 288

[3] the same, 382
[4] the same, 335
[5] the same, 265
[6] *Biographical Introductions*, XIII, xvi
[7] *Celebrities and I*, Henriette Corkran, London, 1902, 18–24; *A Little Girl's Recollections of Elizabeth Barrett Browning, William Makepeace Thackeray, and the late Emperor Napoleon, Temple Bar*, December 1894, 553–555
[8] *Letters II*, 255–256

13

VANITY FAIR
pp. 172–187

[1] *Brief Memoir of the Late Mr. Thackeray*, James Hannay, Edinburgh, 1864, 20–21
[2] *Vanity Fair*, chapter sixty-four
[3] Hodder, 277
[4] *A Selection of the Correspondence of Abraham Hayward from 1834–1884*, ed. Henry E. Carlisle, 2 vols, London, 1886, I, 106
[5] *The Ladies of Alderley*, ed. Nancy Mitford, London, 1939, 236, 280. Lady Stanley was not a dowager when she wrote this, but to lessen confusion, since her daughter-in-law features as Lady Stanley in future chapters, I have taken the

considerable liberty of widowing her a few years early

[6] *Pendennis*, chapter thirty-six
[7] *Letters II*, 364–365
[8] the same, 421
[9] the same, 334
[10] *Things I have Seen and People I Have Known*, G. A. Sala, 2 vols, London, 1894, I, 43
[11] *Letters III*, 24
[12] *Chronicles of Holland House, 1820-1900*, the Earl of Ilchester, London, 1937, 365
[13] *Letters II*, 360
[14] the same, 308–309

[15] the same, 300
[16] the same, 297–298

2.

[1] *Brief Memoir*, 4
[2] *Reminiscences of Thackeray*, Major F. J. Goldsmith, *Athenaeum*, 11 April 1891, 474–475
[3] *Letters III*, 451
[4] *Letters II*, 401
[5] the same, 429
[6] Merivale and Marzials, 240
[7] *Letters II*, 375–377

14

MR AND MRS BROOKFIELD
pp. 188-204

[1] Brookfield, I, 49
[2] the same, I, 13
[3] the same, I, 24–25
[4] the same, II, 536
[5] the same, I, 44
[6] the same, I, 49
[7] the same, I, 105
[8] the same, I, 60
[9] the same, I, 80

[3] Brookfield, II, 454
[4] the same, I, 130

3.

[1] MS letter 23 October 1847 (Downside)
[2] MS letter 16 February 1847 (Downside)
[3] MS letter 24 October 1847 (Downside)
[4] Brookfield, I, 227
[5] MS letter 18 November 1847 (Downside)
[6] Brookfield, II, 265

2.

[1] *Letters II*, 245–246
[2] MS letter dated 'Janvier 17th M.D.III.IV.VIII' (Downside)

15

LIAISON DANGEREUSE
pp. 205-227

[1] MS letter 20 September 1848 (Downside)
[2] Brookfield, II, 345–346
[3] *Letters II*, 646
[4] the same, 380
[5] Brookfield, I, 247–248
[6] *Letters II*, 439
[7] MS letter 8 August 1848 (Downside)
[8] MS letter 10 August 1848 (Downside)
[9] MS letters 13 October 1848 and 17

January 1849 (Downside)
[10] MS letter from Mrs Brookfield to her husband, 21 September 1848 (Downside)
[11] *Letters II*, 463–464
[12] Undated MS letter (Rosenbach)
[13] the same, and another dated 'Monday night' (Rosenbach)
[14] From notebook containing WMT's diary for March 1848 (British Library)
[15] MS letter 21 December 1848

(Downside)
[16] MS letter 23 December 1848 (Downside)
[17] *Collection of Letters*, 180
[18] Fragment of MS letter from WMT to Mrs Brookfield (Rosenbach)
[19] MS letter to Kate Perry (Rosenbach)

side). For Mrs Brookfield's 'chill' letter see *Mrs Brookfield and Her Circle*, II, 280–281
[8] MS letter 3 May 1849 (Downside)
[9] 'On Love, Marriage, Men, and Women', part I
[10] MS letter 19 August 1850 (Downside)
[11] 'Some More Words about the Ladies'; *Letters II*, 543
[12] *Thackeray's Works, Edinburgh Review*, 1854, XCIX, 230
[13] MS letter June 1850 (Downside)
[14] *Vanity Fair*, chapter eleven
[15] MS letter dated '29 June. Friday' (Rosenbach)
[16] *Letters II*, 566
[17] the same, 581
[18] the same, 532 (cf. *The Newcomes*, chapter seventy)
[19] *The Literary Life and Correspondence of the Countess of Blessington*, R. R. Madden, London, 1855, I, 176
[20] 'Small Beer Chronicle', *RP*
[21] *Letters II*, 592
[22] *Letters III*, 13
[23] MS letter to Mrs Brookfield, dated 'Sunday 8–12 o'clock' (Rosenbach)
[24] Brookfield, II, 299

2.

[1] MS letter to Kate Perry, February 1855 (Rosenbach). The phrase also appears in WMT's poem *The End of the Play*, which was first published as the 'Epilogue' to *Dr Birch and his Young Friends*
[2] MS letter 2 January 1849 (Downside)
[3] MS letter 19 January 1849 (Downside)
[4] Undated MS letter (Downside)
[5] MS letter dated 'Tuesday Evening' (Downside)
[6] MS letter to Mrs Brookfield, dated 'Ship. Dover. Just before going away', postmarked 1 February 1849 (Rosenbach)
[7] MS letter 28 April 1849 (Downside)

16
PENDENNIS
pp. 228–241

[1] *Rebecca and Rowena*, chapter one
[2] *Thackeray's Letters to An American Family*, ed. Lucy W. Baxter, New York, 1904, 5–6
[3] 'De Finibus', *RP*
[4] *Pall Mall Magazine*, XVIII, 327
[5] the same, 327–328
[6] 18 December 1850
[7] *Collection of Letters*, 48
[8] 8 April 1850
[9] *Pendennis*, chapter thirty-four
[10] 5 January 1850
[11] *Letters II*, 629–635
[12] the same, 636
[13] 'De Finibus'
[14] Brookfield, II, 441
[15] the same

2.

[1] *Letters II*, 661–662
[2] the same, 662
[3] the same, 686; *Pendennis*, chapter forty-four
[4] MS letters, dated 'Hotel Bristol, Place Vendome, Thursday. March 5', and 'Tuesday' (Rosenbach)
[5] *Letters II*, 650
[6] MS letter 9 March 1850 (Downside)
[7] the same
[8] *Letters II*, 665
[9] MS letter 31 July 1850 (Downside)
[10] MS letter 19 Aug. 1850 (Downside)
[11] MS letter dated 'From the old Shop. 21' (Rosenbach)
[12] the same
[13] *Letters II*, 710

17
THE LECTURER
pp. 242–263

1. Trollope, 19, 123
2. 'De Finibus', *RP*
3. MS letter from The Grange, October 1850 (Rosenbach)
4. *Letters II*, 691
5. the same, 748
6. the same, 759
7. Fields, 18–19
8. *Chapters*, 169–170
9. *Letters II*, 773–774
10. *Records of Later Life*, Frances Anne Kemble, 3 vols, London, 1882, III, 360–362
11. *Fortnightly Review*, November 1884, XXXVI, 605
12. MS Journal, 22 May and 12 June 1851 (Trinity College, Cambridge)
13. *Pall Mall Magazine*, XVIII, 329
14. *Charlotte Brontë and Her Circle*, Clement K. Shorter, London, 1896, 424
15. *George Smith, A Memoir*, ed. Sidney Lee, London, 1902, 99–100
16. *Villette*, chapter twenty-seven

2.

1. *Charlotte Brontë and Her Circle*, 413
2. the same, 406
3. the same, 411–412
4. *Letters II*, 441
5. *Letters and Journals of Lady Eastlake*, ed. Charles Eastlake Smith, London, 1896, I, 221
6. the same
7. *Charlotte Brontë and Her Circle*, 197
8. *Letters II*, 697–698
9. *Bookman* (U.S.), December 1925, LXII, 454–455
10. 'On a Hundred Years Hence', *RP*
11. *Buried Life*, Gordon N. Ray, London, 1952, 54
12. *The House of Smith Elder*, Leonard Huxley, London, 1923, 66–68
13. *Charlotte Brontë and Her Circle*, 423–424
14. the same, 416
15. the same, 270
16. *George Smith, A Memoir*, 100
17. *The Brontës: Their Lives, Friendships and Correspondence*, T. J. Wise and J. A. Symington, 4 vols, Oxford, 1922, III, 117–118
18. Brookfield, II, 355–356
19. *Life of Charlotte Brontë*, Mrs Gaskell, London, 1857, II, 243
20. *Charlotte Brontë and Her Circle*, 418
21. *Letters III*, 233
22. the same, 231; *Villette*, chapter twenty-nine
23. *Letters III*, 13

18
HOME AND ABROAD
pp. 264–278

1. *Chapters*, 105
2. *Letters II*, 692
3. the same, 788–789
4. MS letter dated 'Nov. 25. 1850' (Cullum Q1⁷, Trinity College, Cambridge)
5. *Letters II*, 796
6. the same, 794
7. the same, 780
8. *Chapters*, 110–112
9. the same, 117–118 (Lady Ritchie discreetly refers to Frau von Seckendorf as 'Amalia von Z')

2.

1. *Letters II*, 798–799
2. MS letter dated 'written without date, but about 13 Sepʳ' (Rosenbach)
3. Fragment of MS letter (Rosenbach)
4. *Esmond*, Book III, chapter seven,

and Book II, chapter fifteen
5 Fragment of MS letter (Rosenbach)
6 the same
7 MS letter to Kate Perry and Jane Elliot, dated 'Chatsworth if you please Friday' (Rosenbach)
8 the same
9 Undated MS letter to Kate Perry and Jane Elliot (Rosenbach)
10 the same
11 MS note to Kate Perry and Jane

Elliot written on reverse of unsent 13 September letter to Mrs Brookfield (Rosenbach)
12 Brookfield, II, 365
13 Undated MS letter (Rosenbach)
14 *Letters III*, 390–391
15 Brookfield, II, 376
16 *Letters II*, 814
17 the same, 811–812
18 the same, 813
19 the same

19
ESMOND
pp. 279–292

1 Note written on unsent letter to Mrs Brookfield, dated 'written without date but about 13 Sep' (Rosenbach)
2 *Jane Welsh Carlyle's Letters to Her Family*, ed. Leonard Huxley, London, 1924, 234
3 *Philip,* chapter twenty-nine
4 *Esmond*, Book I, chapter eleven
5 MS letter to Kate Perry dated 'Maison Valin, Champs Élysées, Paris, Thursday' (Rosenbach)
6 *Esmond*, Book II, chapter one
7 *The Newcomes*, chapter twenty
8 *Letters III*, 13
9 *Dr John Brown*, John Taylor Brown, London, 1903, 96–97
10 January 1855, LXXVII, 92
11 *Esmond*, first edition, 1852, II, 307–309. An unexplained reference to 'the treachery of Tom Boxer' is all that remains of the jibe in editions published after 1858, when WMT revised the book
12 *Letters III*, 74
13 Fields, 17

2.

1 *Letters II*, 646
2 the same, 648
3 the same, 672
4 *Chapters*, 84
5 the same, 85–86
6 *Letters II*, 801
7 *Letters of Dr John Brown*, by his son and D. W. Forrest, London, 1907, 110
8 *Recollections of Dr John Brown*, Alexander Peddie, London, 1893, 51
9 *Letters II*, 811
10 the same, 628
11 the same, 824
12 *Letters III*, 39
13 the same, 31–32
14 the same, 97
15 Hodder, 283; *Some XVIII Century Men of Letters*, Whitwell Elwin, London, 1902, I, 181
16 *The Times*, 18 November 1851. A letter from Dr Plumptre denying most of the conversation appeared on 21 November

20
AMERICA
pp. 293–308

1 *Letters III*, 219
2 the same, 52
3 the same, 55
4 the same, 114
5 the same, 29

6 *House of Smith Elder*, Leonard Huxley, 63; Mrs Gaskell's *Life of Charlotte Brontë*, London, 1857, II, 284–285
7 *Letters III*, 82

8 the same, 85–86
9 the same, 86–87
10 the same, 153
11 *Correspondence of Arthur Hugh Clough*, ed. F. Mulhauser, Oxford, 1957, II, 327, 361
12 the same, 361

2.

1 *Letters III*, 87
2 18 September 1852
3 *Mr. Thackeray in the United States*, January 1853
4 *Letters III*, 174–175
5 the same, 227
6 the same
7 the same, 155; *With Thackeray in America*, Eyre Crowe, London, 1893, 34–35

8 *Letters III*, 242
9 the same, 132
10 MS letter to Mrs Brookfield, 21–23 January 1853 (Rosenbach)
11 *Letters III*, 79–80
12 the same, 213, 256
13 *Henry James, Autobiography*, ed. F. W. Dupee, London, 1956, 52
14 *Letters III*, 190
15 *Anecdote Biographies of Thackeray and Dickens*, R. H. Stoddard, New York, 1875, xiv
16 'Small Beer Chronicle', *RP*. The statue still stands in Lafayette Square
17 *Letters III*, 187, 199
18 the same, 248
19 the same, 229

21

SALLY BAXTER
pp. 309–319

1 *Letters III*, 225–226
2 the same, 154
3 Fields, 20–21
4 *New Letters of James Russell Lowell*, ed. M. A. DeWolfe Howe, London, 1932, 42. Trollope gives a later version of the incident in his *Thackeray*, 61
5 *Biographical Introductions*, X, xxxiv
6 *Letters III*, 401
7 MS letter to Mrs Brookfield, 21–23 January 1853 (Rosenbach)

8 *Letters III*, 149
9 the same, 297
10 the same, 164–165
11 the same, 151
12 the same, 68
13 MS letter to Kate Perry, 7–14 February 1853 (Rosenbach)
14 MS letter to Kate Perry and Jane Elliot, 3 March 1853 (Rosenbach)
15 First published in *The Southern Literary Messenger,* of Richmond, Virginia, November 1853

22

THE NEWCOMES
pp. 320–336

1 *Letters III*, 259
2 the same, 261, 263
3 the same, 293
4 *Thackeray in America*, June 1853
5 *Letters III*, 283–284
6 the same, 271
7 *The Newcomes*, chapter thirty
8 Preface to *The Tragic Muse*, 1890
9 *Letters of James Russell Lowell*, ed. C. E. Norton, 2 vols, New York, 1894, I, 238–239
10 *The Stage Life of Mrs Stirling*, Percy Allen, London, 1922, 159
11 *Biographical Introductions*, VIII, xxxvi
12 *Letters of James Russell Lowell*, I, 238–239

2.

[1] *Letters III*, 295
[2] the same
[3] the same, 289–290, 293
[4] the same, 296
[5] the same, 331–332
[6] MS letter 28–31 July 1853 (Rosenbach)
[7] *Letters III*, 306
[8] MS letter 24 September 1853 (Rosenbach)
[9] MS letter, dated 'Maison Valin. Champs Élysées Paris. Thursday' (Rosenbach)
[10] MS letter 2 December 1856 (Rosenbach)
[11] *Letters III*, 313

3.

[1] Preface to *Rose and the Ring*
[2] *Letters III*, 328, 351
[3] the same, 350
[4] *Chapters*, 197–199
[5] *Letters II*, 559–560
[6] MS letter 16 February 1854 (Rosenbach)
[7] *Elizabeth Barrett Browning: Letters to Her Sister, 1846–1859*, ed. Leonard Huxley, London, 1929, 196
[8] *Letters of Elizabeth Barrett Browning*, ed. Frederick G. Kenyon, 2 vols, London, 1897, 154
[9] *Thackeray My Childhood's Friend*, Marchesa Peruzzi di Medici (Edith Story), *Cornhill*, August, 1911, NS XXXI, 178–179

23

FOUR ROYAL BRUTES
pp. 337–356

[1] Fields, 27
[2] *Letters III*, 380
[3] the same, 396
[4] the same, 392
[5] the same, 397–398
[6] Merivale and Marzials, 151
[7] *A Study for Colonel Newcome*, John W. Irvine, *Nineteenth Century*, 1893, XXXIV, 588–594
[8] *Letters of Charles Dickens*, ed. Walter Dexter, 3 vols, London, 1938, II, 693
[9] *Letters III*, 358
[10] *Letters II*, 409
[11] the same, 761
[12] *Letters III*, 429
[13] *The Stanleys of Alderley*, ed. Nancy Mitford, London, 1968, 112
[14] WMT's draft speech is partially printed in *Letters III*, 678–684, and *Thackeray: The Age of Wisdom*, Gordon N. Ray, Oxford, 1958, 252–253

2.

[1] *Letters III*, 315–316
[2] the same, 530
[3] the same, 489

[4] *Thackeray. A Personality*, Malcolm Elwin, London, 1932, 312
[5] 2 November 1855
[6] *Letters III*, 505
[7] the same, 528
[8] the same, 547
[9] Fields, 32–33
[10] *Letters III*, 521
[11] *Thackeray's Letters to an American Family*, ed. Lucy W. Baxter, New York, 1904, 13–14
[12] *Letters III*, 604
[13] the same, 587
[14] the same, 589
[15] the same, 514
[16] the same, 558
[17] the same, 588–589
[18] MS letter 14–16 February 1856 (Rosenbach)
[19] *Letters III*, 591
[20] the same, 595
[21] *Critical Essays and Literary Notes*, Bayard Taylor, New York, 1880, 149–150
[22] *Memories of Fifty Years*, Lester Wallack, New York, 1889, 164
[23] *Haud Immemor—Thackeray in America, Blackwood's*, June 1872, CXI, 686

24

ELECTIONEERING
pp. 357–368

1 *William Wetmore Story and his Friends*, Henry James, 2 vols, Boston, 1903, I, 301
2 MS letter 14–16 February 1856 (Rosenbach)
3 *Letters III*, 612
4 the same, 616–617
5 *Some XVIII Century Men of Letters*, Whitwell Elwin, 2 vols, London, 1902, I, 156
6 the same
7 *Letters III*, 633
8 the same
9 the same, 630
10 *Letters IV*, 17, 13
11 Hodder, 271, 290; *The Light of Other Days*, Thomas Willert Beale, London, 1890, 262
12 Hodder, 306

2.

1 *Letters III*, 592–593
2 *Letters IV*, 45
3 the same, 7
4 the same, 49
5 *Thackeray and His Daughter*, ed. Hester Thackeray Ritchie, London, 1924, 113–114
6 *Thackeray: The Age of Wisdom*, Gordon N. Ray, Oxford, 1958, 270
7 *Letters IV*, 64

25

THE VIRGINIANS
pp. 369–384

1 *Letters III*, 639
2 *Letters IV*, 76
3 the same, 121
4 Trollope, 60
5 *Letters III*, 573
6 Merivale and Marzials, 30
7 MS letter 14–16 February 1856 (Rosenbach)
8 MS letter from Ship Hotel, Dover, September 1854 (Rosenbach)
9 MS letter 6 December 1856 (Rosenbach)
10 *The Virginians*, chapter eighteen
11 TS Silver diary, 1 April 1863
12 *Letters IV*, 115
13 *Letters III*, 524
14 *Letters IV*, 80–81
15 Lady Ritchie's MS Reminiscences (Gordon N. Ray)
16 *Letters IV*, 33
17 *Letters III*, 657
18 the same, 613, 609
19 *Letters IV*, 272
20 'On a Chalk-Mark on the Door', *RP*
21 *Letters IV*, 5
22 MS letter 6 December 1856 (Rosenbach)
23 *Letters IV*, 28
24 the same, 56
25 the same, 108–109
26 *Correspondence of John Lothrop Motley*, ed. G. W. Curtis, 2 vols, London, 1889, I, 335
27 *The Virginians*, chapter eighty-five
28 *Philip*, chapter eight
29 *Letters IV*, 73–74

26

A WITCH'S BROTH
pp. 385–396

1 *Edmund Yates: His Recollections and Experiences*, 2 vols, London, 1884, I, 280
2 *Letters IV*, 86
3 12 June 1858 (printed in facsimile, *Letters IV*, between pp 90–91)
4 *Letters IV*, 89–90
5 the same, 91–92

[6] *Letters of Charles Dickens*, ed. Walter Dexter, 3 vols, London, 1938, III, 33

[7] *Letters IV*, 107

[8] *The Virginians*, chapters thirty-five and forty-three

[9] *Letters of Charles Dickens*, ed. Dexter, III, 41

[10] *Letters IV*, 133–135

[11] *Life of Sir William Howard Russell*, John Black Atkins, 2 vols, London, 1911, I, 113–114; *Philip*,

chapter sixteen

[12] *William Allingham: A Diary*, ed. H. Allingham and D. Radford, London, 1907, 76–78

[13] *Letters III*, 341

[14] MS letter to John Blackwood, 12–15 December 1858 (Pierpont Morgan Library)

[15] TS Silver diary, 29 October 1862

[16] *The Virginians*, chapter twenty-six

[17] Information supplied by Mrs Norman-Butler

27

THE CORNHILL MAGAZINE
pp. 397–408

[1] *Pictures of Life and Character*, December 1854

[2] *Letters III*, 417

[3] *George Smith: A Memoir*, ed. Sidney Lee, London, 1902, 106–107

[4] the same, 108

[5] *Letters IV*, 159

[6] Trollope, 51–52

[7] Fields, 30–31

[8] *Letters IV*, 260

[9] the same, 226–227

[10] the same, 228–229

[11] the same, 208. Trollope's offending story was *Mrs General Talboys*

[12] *Letters IV*, 225

[13] TS Silver diary, 10 February 1859

[14] *House of Smith Elder*, Leonard Huxley, London, 1923, 109

[15] Fields, 32

[16] *George Smith: A Memoir*, 121

[17] *House of Smith Elder*, 72

[18] *Philip*, chapter twenty-five

[19] the same, chapter fourteen

[20] *Letters IV*, 136

[21] *Some XVIII Century Men of Letters*, Whitwell Elwin, 2 vols, London, 1902, I, 245

[22] *Letters of Elizabeth Barrett Browning*, ed. Frederick G. Kenyon, 2 vols, London, 1897, II, 391

[23] *W. M. Thackeray*, *Cornhill*, February 1864, 134

28

FINIS
pp. 409–424

[1] *Retrospections of an Active Life*, John Bigelow, 5 vols, New York, 1909, I, 279

[2] Lady Ritchie's MS Journal, 8 February 1862 (Mrs Norman-Butler)

[3] *Letters IV*, 271

[4] *Philip*, chapter five

[5] *Letters III*, 604

[6] *Letters IV*, 235–236

[7] TS Silver diary, 3 July 1862

[8] the same, 12 March 1862

[9] *Best of All Good Company*, W. Blanchard Jerrold, London, 1871, 164

[10] *Letters III*, 608

[11] *Letters IV*, 238

[12] the same, 163

[13] the same, 109

[14] the same, 278–279

2.

[1] *Book of Recollections*, John Cordy Jeaffreson, 2 vols, London, 1894, I, 288
[2] *Letters III*, 19
[3] *Letters IV*, 237
[4] *Collection of Letters*, 181
[5] *Letters IV*, 330
[6] the same, 293–294
[7] *Some Family Letters of W. M. Thackeray*, Blanche Warre Cornish, Boston and New York, 1911, 72
[8] MS Journal, 29 August 1863 (Mrs Norman-Butler)
[9] *Records of Later Life*, Frances Anne Kemble, 3 vols, London, 1882, III, 362–363
[10] TS Silver diary, 26 November 1862
[11] *Milnes*, I, 427
[12] Lady Ritchie's MS Reminiscences (Gordon N. Ray)
[13] *History of Punch*, M. H. Spielmann, London, 1895, 86–87
[14] *W. M. Thackeray, Cornhill*, February 1864

POSTSCRIPT

[1] *Letters IV*, 301
[2] *Letters III*, 388
[3] *Letters IV*, 304
[4] Brookfield, II, 524
[5] the same, 537
[6] *Celebrities and I*, Henriette Corkran, London, 1902, 112–113

INDEX